COLONIAL
LATIN AMERICA

COLONIAL LATIN AMERICA

SEVENTH EDITION

Mark A. Burkholder
University of Missouri–St. Louis

Lyman L. Johnson
University of North Carolina at Charlotte

New York   Oxford
OXFORD UNIVERSITY PRESS
2010

Oxford University Press, Inc., publishes works that further Oxford University's
objective of excellence in research, scholarship, and education.

Oxford   New York
Auckland   Cape Town   Dar es Salaam   Hong Kong   Karachi
Kuala Lumpur   Madrid   Melbourne   Mexico City   Nairobi
New Delhi   Shanghai   Taipei   Toronto

With offices in
Argentina   Austria   Brazil   Chile   Czech Republic   France   Greece
Guatemala   Hungary   Italy   Japan   Poland   Portugal   Singapore
South Korea   Switzerland   Thailand   Turkey   Ukraine   Vietnam

Copyright © 2010, 2008, 2006, 2001, 1998, 1994, 1990 by Oxford University Press, Inc.

Published by Oxford University Press, Inc.
198 Madison Avenue, New York, New York 10016
http://www.oup.com

Oxford is a registered trademark of Oxford University Press

Library of Congress Cataloging-in-Publication Data

ISBN: 978-0-19-538605-9

Printing number: 9 8 7 6 5 4 3 2

Printed in the United States of America
on acid-free paper

For
Our Wives,
Carol Burkholder and Sue Johnson

CONTENTS

Contents

MAPS

PREFACE

Since the first edition of *Colonial Latin America* in 1990, numerous scholars have published valuable works on the colonial and early national periods. From them, we have drawn new material included in the seventh edition. Our debt to our colleagues' recent books can be found in the revised suggestions for further reading at the end of each chapter.

We want to call students' attention to the valuable five-volume reference work *Encyclopedia of Latin American History and Culture* edited by Barbara A. Tenenbaum and to an important volume of bibliographical essays, *The Cambridge History of Latin America*, vol. XI, *Bibliographical Essays*, edited by Leslie Bethell. The periodicals listed in "A Note on Periodical Literature" after Chapter 12 continue to enrich the study of colonial Latin America. We strongly recommend that student readers use these wonderful resources when they begin their research.

We remain grateful for the assistance of Dauril Alden, Kenneth J. Andrien, Jacques A. Barbier, Kristen Burkholder, Asunción A. Lavrin, William S. Maltby, and James S. Saeger. We also thank colleagues who have used the book in classes and offered suggestions for improvement. Special appreciation goes to Linda Arnold, Susan Deeds, Jay Kinsbruner, Herbert S. Klein, Karen Powers, Marianne Samayoa, Susan Schroeder, Joseph B. Solodow, and Richard J. Walter for careful critical readings and helpful suggestions.

We rewrote and reorganized our treatment of the imperial crisis and independence era for the seventh edition. Our central purpose was to recognize and integrate the major new scholarship published in the last decade. The result is that the single, long chapter of the earlier editions has been replaced by three shorter chapters that emphasize the importance of the Spanish *cortes* and the Constitution of 1812 to the political transformation of Spain's American colonies. Our treatment of events in the colonies is now more topical and less focused on regional events and leaders. We also added a new discussion of the Haitian revolution and its regional significance and expanded our discussion of the African influence on early colonial development. Finally, we have updated our Suggested Readings to include recent scholarship.

As we have revised this book for new editions, we have relied heavily on colleagues who have specialized knowledge of the topics we are revising. We thank Grant D. Jones and William M. Ringle for their help as we expanded coverage of the Maya. Martha Few, Bianca Premo, and Susan Socolow provided very helpful advice on gender and family history. Kathryn Burns suggested that we add material on Atlantic Africa, and Karen Flint, Adell Patton, Jr., and especially Lisa Lindsay guided us in developing this material. We are also very grateful to Camilla Townsend for improving our understanding of Mesoamerica and the era of conquest and to Philip P. Boucher for his suggestions about the French and Dutch in the Americas.

Christon I. Archer and Jaime E. Rodríguez O. encouraged our decision to revise Chapter 10, "Crisis and Collapse." We are extremely grateful that they made us rethink the process of revolution and independence and want to emphasize that we alone are responsible for the results as they appear in Chapters 10, 11, and 12.

Prior to this revision, Oxford University Press obtained new readers' reports from five anonymous readers. Whoever you are, we appreciate your constructive comments.

We also thank our many colleagues and their students who have read *Colonial Latin America* and solicit their comments and suggestions for further improvements.

Finally, we want to thank again Sue Johnson and Carol Burkholder for their continued support. We again gratefully dedicate this revision to them.

St. Louis, Missouri   M.A.B.
Charlotte, North Carolina   L.L.J.

Map 1 Topographical Map of Latin America.

ONE

AMERICA, IBERIA, AND AFRICA BEFORE THE CONQUEST

Chronology

c. 100 B.C.–750 A.D.	Emergence and prominence of Teotihuacan in Mesoamerica
250–900	Maya Classic period
718–1492	Christian Reconquest of Iberia from Muslims
c. 900–1540	Maya Postclassic period
c. 1325	Mexica begin to build Tenochtitlan
1415	Portuguese capture Ceuta
1426–1521	Triple Alliance and Aztec Empire
c. 1438–1533	Inca Empire
1469	Marriage of Ferdinand of Aragon and Isabel of Castile
1492	Columbus's first voyage; fall of Granada; Expulsion of Jews from "Spain"; first Castilian grammar published
1493	Papal donation; Columbus's second voyage (1493–96); "Columbian Exchange" begins with Spanish introduction of sugarcane, horses, cattle, pigs, sheep, goats, chickens, wheat, olive trees, and grapevines into Caribbean islands
1494	Treaty of Tordesillas
1500	Pedro Alvarez de Cabral lands on Brazilian coast
1502	Nicolás de Ovando takes about 2,500 settlers to Española, including Las Casas; Moctezuma II elected *tlatoani* of Mexica
1510–11	Diego de Velázquez conquers Cuba
1512	Laws of Burgos
1513	Blasco Núñez de Balboa crosses isthmus of Panama to Pacific

Amerindian Civilizations on the Eve of European Conquest

The Western Hemisphere's history begins with the arrival of its first inhabitants. Most scholars agree that the hemisphere was settled in a series of migrations across the Bering Strait from Asia. There is less consensus about when these migrations took place. Hunting populations expanded rapidly along the West Coast of the hemisphere after 14,000 B.C. Some evidence suggests, however, that human populations may have been present in South America as early as 35,000 B.C. If this is verified by additional research, then some humans probably reached the hemisphere using small boats.

Regardless of the date of first arrivals, it took millennia to occupy the hemisphere. Societies in Mexico, Central America, and the Andean region had initiated the development of agriculture and complex political forms before 5000 B.C. On the other hand, the Caribbean Basin and the plains of southern South America were inhabited less than two thousand years before Columbus' arrival. The hemisphere's indigenous population at the

The main temple at Chichen Itza, near the modern city of Mérida, Mexico. Chichen Itza was the major Postclassic era Maya city.

moment of contact in 1492 was probably between thirty-five and fifty-five million.

Although the Aztecs and Incas are the civilizations best known during the age of conquest, the inhabitants of these empires constituted only a minority of the total Amerindian population and resided in geographic areas that together comprised only a small portion of Latin America's landscape. Aymara, Caribs, Chichimecas, Ge, Guaraní, Mapuche, Maya, Muisca, Otomí, Pueblo, Quibaya, Taino, Tepaneca, Tupí, and Zapotec joined a host of other peoples and linguistic groups that inhabited the Americas; together they formed a human mosaic whose diverse characteristics greatly influenced the ways in which colonial Latin America developed.

By 1500 over 350 major tribal groups, 15 distinct cultural centers, and more than 160 linguistic stocks could be found in Latin America. Despite the variety suggested by these numbers, there were, essentially, three forms or levels of Indian culture. One was a largely nomadic group that relied on hunting, fishing, and gathering for subsistence; its members had changed little from the people who first made stone points in the New World in about 10,000 B.C. A second group was sedentary or semi-sedentary and depended primarily on agriculture for subsistence. Having developed technologies different from those of the nomadic peoples, its

Inca ruins, Machu Picchu, Peru.

members benefited from the domestication of plants that had taken place after about 5000 B.C. The third group featured dense, sedentary populations, surplus agricultural production, greater specialization of labor and social differentiation, and large-scale public construction projects. These complex civilizations were located only in Mesoamerica and western South America. The civilizations of Teotihuacan, Monte Albán, Tiahuanaco, Chimu, and several Maya cultures were among its most important early examples.

Mesoamerica is the term employed to define a culturally unified geographic area that includes central and southern Mexico and most of Central America north of the isthmus of Panama. Marked by great diversity of landscape and climate, Mesoamerica was the cradle of a series of advanced urbanized civilizations based on sedentary agriculture. Never more than a fraction of this large region was ever united politically. Instead, its inhabitants shared a cultural tradition which flourished most spectacularly in the hot country of the Gulf of Mexico coast with the Olmec civilization between 1200 and 400 B.C. While linguistic diversity and regional variations persisted, common cultural elements can be traced from this origin. They include polytheistic religions in which the deities had dual (male/female) natures, rulers who exercised both secular and religious roles, the use of warfare for obtaining sacrificial victims, and a belief that bloodletting was necessary for a society's survival and prosperity. The use of ritual as well as solar calendars, the construction of monumental architecture including pyramids, the employment of a numerical system that used twenty as its base, emphasis on a jaguar deity, and the ubiquity of ball courts in which a game using a solid rubber ball was played were additional characteristics of complex Mesoamerican societies. Long-distance trade involving both subsistence goods and artisanal products using obsidian, jade, shell, and feathers, among other items, facilitated cultural exchange in the absence of political integration. This rich cultural tradition influenced all later Mesoamerican civilizations, including the Maya and the Aztecs.

Following the decline of the Olmecs, the city of Teotihuacan (100 B.C. to 750 A.D.) exercised enormous influence in the development and spread of Mesoamerican culture. Located about thirty miles northeast of modern Mexico City, Teotihuacan was the center of a commercial system that extended to the Gulf coast and into Central America. At its height its urban population reached 150,000, making it one of the world's largest cities at that time. One of the most important temples at Teotihuacan was devoted to the cult of the god Quetzalcoatl, or Feathered Serpent. Commonly represented as a snake covered with feathers, Quetzalcoatl was associated with fertility, the wind, and creation. Following Teotihuacan's decline in the eighth century, the Toltecs dominated central Mexico from their capital at Tula.

Although not clearly tied to Teotihuacan's decline in the eighth century, the Toltecs came to dominate central Mexico from their capital of

Tula by the tenth century. The Toltecs used military power to extend their influence and manage complex tribute and trade relationships with dependencies. Tula was both an administrative and a religious center. It was constructed on a grand scale with colonnaded patios, raised platforms, and numerous temples. Many of the buildings were decorated with scenes suggesting warfare and human sacrifice.

In the Andean region, geographic conditions were even more demanding than in Mesoamerica. The development of complex civilizations after 1000 B.C. depended on the earlier evolution of social and economic strategies in response to changing environmental, demographic, and social conditions. Along the arid coastal plain and in the high valleys of the Andes, collective labor obligations made possible both intensive agriculture and long-distance trade. Irrigation projects, the draining of wetlands, large-scale terracing, and road construction all depended on collective labor obligations, called *mit'a* by the native population and later *mita* by the Spanish. The exchange of goods produced in the region's ecological niches (lowland maize, highland llama wool, and coca from the upper Amazon region, for example) enriched these societies and made possible the rise of cities and the growth of powerful states.

The chronology of state development and urbanization within the Andean region was generally similar to that in Mesoamerica. However, there was greater variation in cultural practices because of the unique environmental challenges posed by the arid coastal plain and high altitudes

Representations of Quetzalcoatl, the feathered serpent, at Teotihuacan. Teotihuacan was the largest of the Classic era cities in Mexico. In the background is the Temple of the Moon.

of the mountainous regions. Chavín was one of the most important early Andean civilizations. It dominated a populous region that included substantial portions of both the highlands and coastal plain of Peru between 900 and 250 B.C. Located at 10,300 feet in the eastern range of the Andes north of present-day Lima, its capital, Chavín de Huantar, was a commercial center that built upon a long tradition of urban development and monumental architecture initiated earlier on the Peruvian coast. The expansion of Chavín's power was probably related to the introduction of llamas from the highlands to the coastal lowlands. Llamas dramatically reduced the need for human carriers in trade since one driver could control as many as thirty animals, each carrying up to 70 pounds. Chavín exhibited all of the distinguishing characteristics found in later Andean civilizations. Its architecture featured large complexes of multilevel platforms topped by small residences for the elite and buildings used for ritual purposes. As in the urban centers of Mesoamerica, society was stratified from the ruler down. Fine textile production, gold jewelry, and polytheistic religion also characterized the Chavín civilization until its collapse. By the time that increased warfare disrupted long-distance trade and brought about the demise of Chavín, its material culture, statecraft, architecture, and urban planning had spread throughout the Andean region. The Moche, who dominated the north coastal region of Peru from 200 to 700 A.D., were heirs to many of Chavín's contributions.

In the highlands, two powerful civilizations, Tiahuanaco and Huari, developed after 500 A.D. Tiahuanaco's expansion near Lake Titicaca in modern Bolivia rested on both enormous drainage projects that created raised fields and permitted intensive cultivation and the control of large herds of llamas. At the height of its power, Tiahuanaco was the center of a large trade network that stretched to Chile in the south. Packtrains of llamas connected the capital to dependent towns that organized the exchange of goods produced throughout the Andean region. Large buildings constructed of cut stone dominated the urban center of Tiahuanaco. A hereditary elite able to control a substantial labor force ruled this highly stratified society. Huari, located near present-day Ayacucho, may have begun as a dependency of Tiahuanaco, but it soon established an independent identity and expanded through warfare into the northern highlands as well as the coastal area once controlled by the Moche. The construction of roads as part of Huari's strategy for military control and communication was a legacy bequeathed to the Incas who, like the Aztecs in central Mexico, held political dominance in the populous areas of the Andean region when Europeans first arrived.

The Maya

Building in part upon the rich legacy of the Olmec culture, the Maya developed an impressive civilization in present-day Guatemala, Honduras, Belize, southern Mexico, and Yucatan. Although sharing many cultural similarities, the Maya were separated by linguistic differences and organized into numerous city-states. Because no Maya center was ever powerful enough to impose a unified political structure, the long period from around 200 A.D. to the arrival of the Spaniards was characterized by the struggle of rival kingdoms for regional domination.

Given the difficulties imposed by fragile soils, dense forest, and a tropical climate characterized by periods of drought and heavy rains, Maya cultural and architectural achievements were remarkable. The development of effective agricultural technologies increased productivity and led to population growth and urbanization. During the Classic era (250–900 A.D.), the largest Maya cities had populations in excess of fifty thousand.

From earliest times, Maya agriculturalists used slash-and-burn or "swidden" cultivation where small trees and brush were cut down and then burned. Although this form of cultivation produced high yields in initial years, it quickly used up the soil's nutrients. Falling yields forced farmers to move to new fields and begin the cycle again. The high urban population levels of the Classic period, therefore, required more intensive agriculture as well. Wherever possible, local rulers organized their lineages or clans in large-scale projects to drain swamps and low-lying river banks to create elevated fields near urban centers. The construction of trenches to drain surplus water yielded rich soils that the workers then heaped up to create wetland fields. In areas with long dry seasons, the Maya constructed irrigation canals and reservoirs. Terraces built on mountainsides caught rainwater runoff and permitted additional cultivation. Household gardens further augmented food supplies with condiments and fruits that supplemented the dietary staples of maize (corn), beans, and squash. The Maya also managed nearby forests to promote the growth of useful trees and shrubs as well as the conservation of deer and other animals that provided dietary protein.

In the late Preclassic period, the increased agricultural production that followed these innovations helped make possible the development of large cities like El Mirador. During the Classic period, Maya city-states proliferated in an era of dramatic urbanization. One of the largest of the Classic period cities was Tikal in modern Guatemala which had a population of more than 50,000 and controlled a network of dependent cities and towns. Smaller city-states had fewer than 20,000 inhabitants. Each independent city served as the religious and political center for the subordinated agricultural population dispersed among the *milpas* (or maize fields) of the countryside.

Classic era cities had dense central precincts visually dominated by monumental architecture. Large cities boasted numerous high pyramids topped by enclosed sanctuaries, ceremonial platforms, and elaborately decorated elite palaces built on elevated platforms or on constructed mounds. Pyramids also served as burial locations for rulers and other elite members. The largest and most impressive buildings were located around open plazas that provided the ceremonial center for public life. Even small towns had at least one such plaza dominated by one or more pyramids and elite residences.

Impressive public rituals held in Maya cities attracted both full-time urban residents and the rural population from the surrounding countryside. While the smaller dependent communities provided an elaborate ritual life, the capital of every Maya city-state sustained a dense schedule of impressive ceremonies led by its royal family and powerful nobles. These ritual performances were carefully staged on elevated platforms and pyramids that drew the viewers' attention heavenward. The combination of richly decorated architecture, complex ritual, and splendid costumes served to awe the masses and legitimize the authority of ruler and nobility. Because there were no clear boundaries between political and religious functions, divination, sacrifice, astronomy, and hieroglyphic writing were the domain of rulers, their consorts, and other members of the hereditary elite. Some scholars have asserted that later during the Postclassic period (900–1540 A.D.) the functions of rulers and priests were more clearly divided and a separate class of clergy appeared.

Scenes of ritual life depicted on ceramics and wall paintings clearly indicate the Maya's love of decoration. Sculpture and stucco decorations painted in fine designs and bright colors covered nearly all public buildings. Religious allegories, the genealogies of rulers, and important historical events were familiar motifs. Artisans also erected beautifully carved altars and stone monoliths (stelae) near major temples. Throughout their pre-Columbian existence, the Maya constructed this rich architectural and artistic legacy with the limited technology present in Mesoamerica. The Maya did not develop metallurgy until late in the Classic era and used it only to produce jewelry and decorations for the elite. In the Postclassic period the Maya initiated the use of copper axes in agriculture. Artisans and their numerous male and female assistants cut and fitted the stones used for palaces, pyramids, and housing aided only by levers and stone tools. Each new wave of urban construction represented the mobilization and organization of thousands of laborers by the elite. Thus the urban building boom of the Classic period reflected the growing ability of rulers to appropriate the labor of their subjects more than the application of new or improved technologies.

The ancient Maya traced their ancestry through both male and female lines, but family lineage was patrilineal. Maya families were large and multiple generations commonly lived in a single residence or compound. In each generation a single male, usually the eldest, held authority within the family. Related families were, in turn, organized in hierarchical lineages or clans with one family and its male head granted preeminence.

By the Classic period, Maya society was rigidly hierarchical. Hereditary lords and a middling group of skilled artisans and scribes were separated by a deep social chasm from the farmers of the countryside. To justify their elevated position, the elite claimed to be the patrilineal descendants of the original warlords that had initiated the development of urban life. Most commonly, kings were selected by primogeniture from the ruling family; on at least two occasions during the Classic period, however, women ruled Maya city-states. Other elite families provided men who led military units in battle, administered dependent towns, collected taxes, and supervised market activities. Although literacy was very limited, writing was important to religious and political life. As a result, scribes held an elevated position in Maya society and some may have come from noble families.

In the Classic period and earlier, rulers and other members of the elite assisted by shamans (diviners and curers who communicated with the spirit world) served both priestly and political functions. They decorated their bodies with paint and tattoos and wore elaborate costumes of textiles, animal skins, and feathers to project secular power and divine sanction. Kings communicated directly with the supernatural residents of the other worlds and with deified royal ancestors through bloodletting rituals and hallucinogenic trances. Scenes of rulers and their consorts drawing blood from tongues, lips, ears, and even genitals survive on frescos and painted pottery. For the Maya, blood sacrifice was essential to the very survival of the world. The blood of the most exalted members of the society was, therefore, the greatest gift to the gods.

In the Postclassic period, the boundary between political and religious authority remained blurred, although there is some evidence that a priestly class distinguishable from the political elite had come into existence. Priests like other members of the elite inherited their exalted status and were not celibate. They provided divinations and prophecies, often induced by hallucinogens, and kept the genealogies of the lineages. They and the rulers directed the human sacrifices required by the gods. Finally, priests provided the society's intellectual class and were, therefore, responsible for conserving the skills of reading and writing, for pursuing astronomical knowledge, and for maintaining the Maya calendars.

Although some merchants and artisans may have been related to the ruling lineages, these two occupations occupied an intermediate status between the lords and commoners. From the Preclassic period, the Maya maintained complex trade relationships over long distances. Both basic subsistence goods and luxury items were available in markets scheduled to meet on set days in the Maya calendar. Each kingdom, indeed each village and household, used these markets to acquire products not produced locally. As a result, a great deal of specialization was present by the Classic period. Maya exchanged jade, cacao (chocolate beans used both to produce a beverage consumed by the elite and as money), cotton textiles, ceramics, salt, feathers, and foods, especially game and honey taken from the forest. Merchants could acquire significant wealth and the wealthiest lived in large multiple-family compounds. Some scholars believe that by the Postclassic period rulers forced merchants to pay tribute and prohibited them from dressing in the garments of the nobility.

A specialized class of urban craftsmen produced the beautiful jewelry, ceramics, murals, and architecture of the Maya. Their skills were essential for the creation and maintenance of both public buildings and ritual life and, as a result, they enjoyed a higher status than rural commoners. Although the evidence is ambiguous, certain families who trained children to follow their parents' careers probably monopolized the craft skills. Some crafts may also have had a regional basis with weavers concentrated in cotton-growing areas and the craftsmen who fashioned tools and weapons from obsidian (volcanic glass) located near the source of their raw materials. Most clearly, the largest and wealthiest cities had the largest concentration of accomplished craftsmen.

The vast majority of the Maya were born into lower status families and devoted their lives to agriculture. These commoners inherited their land rights through their lineage. Members of lineages were obligated to help family members in shared agricultural tasks as well as to provide labor and tribute to the elite. Female commoners played a central role in the household economy, maintaining essential garden plots, weaving, and managing family life. By the end of the Classic period a large group of commoners labored on the private estates of the nobility. Below this group were the slaves. Slaves were commoners taken captive in war or criminals; once enslaved, the status could become hereditary unless the slave were ransomed by his family.

Warfare was central to Maya life and infused with religious meaning and elaborate ritual. Battle scenes and the depiction of the torture and sacrifice of captives were frequent decorative themes. Since military movements were easier and little agricultural labor was required, the hot and dry spring season was the season of armed conflict. Typically, Maya military forces fought to secure captives rather than territory, although during the Classic period Tikal and other powerful kingdoms initiated wars of conquest against their neighbors.

Days of fasting, a sacred ritual to enlist the support of the gods, and rites of purification led by the king and high-ranking nobles preceded battle. A king and his nobles donned elaborate war regalia and carefully painted their faces in preparation. Armies also included large numbers of commoners, but these levies had little formal training and employed inferior weapons. Typically, the victorious side ritually sacrificed elite captives. Surviving murals and ceramic paintings show kings and other nobles stripped of their rich garments and compelled to kneel at the feet of their rivals or forced to endure torture. Most wars, however, were inconclusive and seldom was a ruling lineage overturned or territory lost as the result of battlefield defeat.

Building on the Olmec legacy, the Maya made important contributions to the development of the Mesoamerican calendar. They also developed both mathematics and writing. The complexity of their calendric system reflected the Maya concern with time and the cosmos. Each day was identified by three separate dating systems. As was true throughout Mesoamerica, two calendars tracked the ritual cycle (260 days divided into 13 months of 20 days) and a solar calendar (365 days divided into 18 months of 20 days with 5 unfavorable days at the end of the year). The Maya believed the concurrence of these two calendars every fifty-two years to be especially ominous. Uniquely among Mesoamerican peoples, the Maya also maintained a continuous "long count" calendar that began at creation, an event they dated at 3114 B.C. These accurate calendric systems and the astronomical observations upon which they were based depended on Maya contributions to mathematics and writing. Their system of mathematics included the concepts of the zero and place value, but had limited notational signs.

The Maya were almost unique among pre-Columbian cultures in the Americas in producing a written literature that has survived to the modern era. Employing a form of hieroglyphic inscription that signified whole words or concepts as well as phonetic cues or syllables, Maya scribes most commonly wrote about public life, religious belief, and the genealogies and biographies of rulers and their ancestors. Only four of these books of bark paper or deerskin still exist. However, other elements of the Maya literary and historical legacy remain inscribed on ceramics, jade, shell, bone, stone columns, and monumental buildings of the urban centers.

The destruction or abandonment of many major urban centers between 800 and 900 A.D. brought the Maya Classic period to a close. There were probably several interrelated causes for this catastrophe, but no scholarly consensus exists. The destruction in about 750 A.D. of Teotihuacan, the important central Mexican commercial center tied to the Maya region, disrupted long-distance trade and thus might have undermined the legitimacy of Maya rulers. More likely, growing population pressure, especially among the elite, led to environmental degradation and falling agricultural productivity. This environmental crisis, in turn, might have led to social unrest and increased levels of warfare as desperate elites sought to increase the tributes of agriculturalists or to acquire additional agricultural land through conquest. Some scholars have suggested that climatic change contributed to the collapse, but evidence supporting this theory is slight. Regardless of the disputed causes, there is agreement that by 900 A.D. the Maya had begun to enter a new era, the Postclassic.

Archaeological evidence suggests that during the Postclassic period central Mexican cultural influence increased among the Maya of Yucatan. Centuries later, Maya informants told Spanish priests that their ancestors had been conquered by the Toltecs of central Mexico led by Topiltzin. According to this legend, Topiltzin had been forced into exile by a warrior faction associated with the god Tezcatlipoca. Defeated by the powerful magic of his adversary, Topiltzin, called Kukulcan by the Maya, and his followers migrated to the east, defeating the Maya of the Yucatan and establishing a new capital at Chichen Itza.

In addition to this local legend, there is also archaeological evidence of Toltec influence at Chichen Itza. The Temple of Warriors, a stepped platform surmounted by columns, is similar to an important temple at the Toltec capital of Tula. A characteristic Toltec figure, the *chacmool*, is located at the top of the temple stairs. This sculpture of a reclining figure holding a bowl on his stomach, perhaps to receive sacrifices, has been found at only one Classic era Maya site. Bas-relief carvings of jaguars, vultures holding human hearts, and the rain god Tlaloc at Chichen Itza imitate closely figures at Tula. A *tzompantli*, a low platform decorated with carvings of human heads, and a round temple, called the *Caracol*, are two additional buildings that demonstrated strong Toltec influence. Chichen Itza had twenty-four ball courts, but the largest was much larger than earlier Maya courts and was constructed in imitation of the northern Mexican style. There is some evidence that levels of human sacrifice at Chichen Itza took on a Toltec character as well, with the number of sacrifices increasing dramatically in comparison with Classic Maya practice.

Recent archaeology has undermined the legend of a Toltec conquest. Many influential scholars now believe that changes in Maya iconography and architecture previously accepted as evidence of a Toltec domination of Chichen Itza were probably introduced by the Putun Maya from the Tabasco region on the Gulf of Mexico coast. The Putun Maya were culturally and linguistically distinct from the Maya of Yucatan. They lived on the distant periphery of the Classic era Maya civilization and had developed strong trade and political connections with central Mexico. According to this theory, the Putun Maya first established themselves on the coast and then built a capital at Chichen Itza as their power grew.

Because of their ties to central Mexico, the Putun Maya acted as cultural intermediaries, spreading elements of Toltec cultural practice as they expanded their influence in Yucatan. Some scholars believe that the presence of a small number of Toltec mercenaries at Chichen Itza also contributed to the transmission of central Mexican cultural characteristics. During the city's ascendancy Chichen Itza was larger and better constructed than the earlier Toltec capital of Tula. It was governed by a council or, perhaps, a multiple kingship form of government. The city's rulers exercised economic and political influence over a wide area, imposing tribute requirements on weaker neighbors by military expansion. Although the reasons are not yet clear, it is known that Chichen Itza experienced significant population loss after 1100 A.D. and was conquered militarily around 1221 A.D. Following this catastrophe, the city retained a small population and may have remained a religious pilgrimage site.

By the end of the thirteenth century, the Itza exercised political and economic authority across much of Yucatan. The origin of the Itzas is unclear. As their name suggests, they claimed to be the people of Chichen Itza. The Itza elite claimed descent from the Toltecs and were linguistically distinct from the region's original population. But few scholars accept this Mexican origin. It seems more likely that they were related in some way to the Putun Maya from near Vera Cruz. The Itza are also believed to have founded the city of Mayapan which imitated Chichen Itza's use of military might to impose tribute requirements on neighboring groups.

The Itza eventually established dominion over most of the Yucatan peninsula, but many Maya groups remained independent. At its peak, Mayapan had a population of approximately 15,000. The size of the city's population and the quality of its construction were far inferior to that of either the major Classic centers, like Tikal, or Postclassic Chichen Itza. Unlike the major Classic period cities which had served as centers for agricultural and craft production and as markets, Mayapan served as the capital of a regional confederation that compelled defeated peoples to pay tribute. This oppressive economic system probably provoked the warfare and rebellion that led to the end of Itza domination and the destruction of Mayapan about 1450 A.D. The Itza persisted, despite these reversals, continuing an independent existence in the Peten region of Guatemala until defeated by a Spanish military force in 1697.

From the fall of Mayapan until the arrival of the Spanish in the sixteenth century, the Maya returned to the pattern of dispersed political authority. During this final period, towns of modest size, some with no more than 500 inhabitants, exercised control over a more dispersed and more rural population than had been the case in earlier eras. The cycles of expansion and collapse experienced by Chichen Itza imitated in many ways the rise and fall of important Maya centers during the Classic period. Although no powerful central authority existed in Maya regions when the Spanish arrived, Maya peoples retained their vitality and sustained essential elements of the cultural legacy inherited from their ancestors.

The Aztec

When the Spaniards reached central Mexico in 1519, the state created by the Mexica and their Nahuatl-speaking allies—now commonly referred to jointly as the Aztec—was at the height of its power. Only the swiftness of their defeat exceeded the rapidity with which the Aztec had risen to prominence. For the century before the arrival of Cortés, they were unquestionably the most powerful political force in Mesoamerica.

Among the numerous nomadic and warlike peoples who pushed south toward central Mexico in the wake of the Toltec state's collapse were the Mexica, one of many aggressive invading bands from the north that contemporary Nahuatl-speakers referred to as Chichimec. Ultimately the most powerful, the Mexica adopted elements of the political and social forms they found among the advanced urbanized agriculturalists. After 1246 this emerging Chichimec elite forged a dynastic link with the surviving Toltec aristocracy of Culhuacan. This infusion of the northern invaders invigorated the culture of central Mexico and eventually led to a new period of political dynamism. The civilization that resulted from this cultural exchange, however, was more militaristic and violent than that of its predecessors.

The Mexica became important participants in the conflicts of the Valley of Mexico while the city of Atzcapotzalco was the dominant political power. Valued for their military prowess and despised for their cultural backwardness, Mexica warriors served as mercenaries. They initially received permission to settle in Chapultepec, now a beautiful park in Mexico City, but jealous and fearful neighbors drove them out. With the acquiescence of their Tepanec overlords in Atzcapotzalco, the Mexica then moved to a small island in the middle of Lake Texcoco where they could more easily defend themselves from attack. Here in 1325 or soon afterward they began to build their capital of Tenochtitlan. Despite their improved reputation, they continued for nearly a century as part-time warriors and tributaries of Atzcapotzalco.

By 1376 the Aztec were politically, socially, and economically organized like their neighbors as *altepetl*, complex regional ethnic states, each with a hereditary ruler, market, and temple dedicated to a patron deity. *Altepetl* were, in turn, typically made up of four or more *calpulli*, which also had their own subrulers, deities, and temples. These subdivisions originally may have been kinship based, but by the fourteenth century they functioned primarily to distribute land among their members and to collect and distribute tribute. The ethnic group called the Mexica had only two *altepetls*—the dominant Tenochca and the less powerful Tlatelolca.

The Mexica's first king (*tlatoani*), Acamapichtli, claimed descent from the Toltec dynasty of Tula. After a period of consolidation, the new state undertook an ambitious and successful campaign of military expansion. Under Itzcoatl, the ruler from 1426 to 1440, the Mexica allied with two other city-states, Texcoco and Tlacopan, located on the shores of Lake Texcoco. In a surprise attack the Triple Alliance conquered the city of Atzcapotzalco in 1428 and consolidated control over much of the valley. During the rule of Moctezuma I (Motecuhzoma in Nahuatl) from 1440 to 1468, the Mexica gained ascendancy over their two allies, pushed outward from the valley, and established control over much of central Mexico. Following an interlude of weaker, less effective rulers, serious expansion resumed during the reign of Ahuitzotl from 1486 to 1502, and Aztec armies conquered parts of Oaxaca, Guatemala, and the Gulf coast. By the early sixteenth century, few pockets of unconquered peoples, principally the Tarascans of Michoacán and the Tlaxcalans of Puebla, remained in central Mexico.

When Moctezuma II took the throne in 1502 he inherited a society that in less than a century had risen from obscurity to political hegemony over a vast region. Tenochtitlan had a population of several hundred thousand persons, many of them immigrants, and the whole Valley of Mexico was home to perhaps 1.5 million. Social transformation accompanied this rapid expansion of political control and demographic growth. Before installing their first *tlatoani*, Mexica society had a relatively egalitarian structure based within the *calpulli*. *Calpulli* leaders, in addition to land administration and tribute responsibilities, supervised the instruction of the young, organized religious rituals, and provided military forces when called upon. Mexica *calpultin* (pl.) resident in Tenochtitlan were primarily associated with artisan production rather than agriculture. The *calpulli's* ability to redistribute land held jointly by its members was more important to rural and semirural areas than to urban centers. There also were noteworthy differences in wealth, prestige, and power within and among *calpulli*. The *calpulli's* leader, however—most typically elected from the same family—handled the local judicial and administrative affairs with the advice of a council of elders.

After the Triple Alliance conquered Atzcapotzalco—the critical event in the evolution of the Mexica and the Aztec empires—Itzcoatl removed the right of selecting future rulers from the *calpulli* and *altepetl* councils and gave it to his closest advisers, the newly established "Council of Four" from which his successors would be selected. The power and independence of the ruler continued to expand as triumphant armies added land and trib-ute to the royal coffers. In the late fifteenth century the ruler also served as high priest: Moctezuma II took the final step by associating his person with Huitzilopochtli, the Mexica's most important deity.

Among the Aztec in general was a hereditary class of nobles called the *pipiltin*, who received a share of the lands and tribute from the conquered areas, the amount apparently related to their administrative position and rank. They staffed the highest military positions, the civil bureaucracy, and the priesthood. Their sons went to schools to prepare them for careers of service to the state. Noblemen had one principal wife and numerous concubines. This polygyny resulted in a disproportionate growth in the number of nobles and helped promote military expansion and political alliances through intermarriage.

Except for those in Tenochtitlan itself, the *macehualtin*—commoners who owned land or who lived in urban *calpulli*—benefited comparatively little from conquest. Instead, as the backbone of the agricultural labor force, they remained subject to work demands by the state and the nobility as well as to military service. Moreover, the advent of a powerful hereditary nobility reduced the commoners' ability to influence political decisions. Although a few *macehualtin* advanced in society by means of success on the battlefield, service in the priesthood, or through marriage, the potential for upward social mobility was much diminished after the initial period of imperial expansion.

At the base of Aztec society were the vanquished commoners and slaves. *Mayeques* were commoners whose *calpulli* had lost their lands in war and thus had to work for their conquerors. They formed perhaps as many as one-third of the population in some places by the early sixteenth century, whereas slaves were only a small handful except in wealthy urban centers like Tenochtitlan, where the Mexica often received them as tribute. In addition, judges punished certain criminal acts by enslaving the offender; prisoners of war could be enslaved. And adults in periods of great hardship voluntarily gave up their freedom to ensure themselves food, housing, and clothes. But even though slaves were regarded as property, their children did not inherit this status.

Tenochtitlan became a city of specialists that included numerous crafts-men—goldsmiths, jewelers, and featherworkers—who ranked above other *macehualtin*. Adjoining the city was Tlatelolco, home to a specialized group of merchants, the *pochteca*. Rich and powerful, they tried unsuccessfully to wrest control from the ruler Axayacatl in 1473, thereby losing many of their privileges until Moctezuma II restored all except their exemption from tribute. The *pochteca* handled long-distance trade, even with areas outside Aztec control. Not only did they play an important economic role, but they also provided information to the emperor about unconquered peoples and restive subjects. Despite their aid to and benefits from Aztec expansion, the *pochteca* were excluded from high-ranking administrative and political positions.

Mexica women were excluded from nearly all high public offices and power, although they fulfilled a variety of roles in a society that differentiated clearly between men's and women's activities. At least one public office in each *altepetl*, however, was reserved for a woman who organized and regulated women's activities. Except for a few priestesses, Mexica women typically married men approved if not selected by their parents. Marriage was a social bond that marked reaching full adulthood, but it could also serve a political purpose as the Aztec used the institution to cement political alliances. Once married, Mexica women's household responsibilities included preparation of maize for tortillas, tamales, and gruel and cooking, cleaning, child care, spinning and weaving cloth, and embroidery. They also offered prayers within the household, a reminder that their household duties were important and even sacred. Outside the house they taught, served as priestesses in the temples, sold fine chocolate, herbs, feathers, and other goods, delivered babies, served as curers and physicians, worked as professional weavers and embroiderers, and held supervisory positions in the markets. Prevented from participating in the long-distance commercial expeditions of the *pochteca*, women often controlled warehoused goods and determined the supplies and prices of goods in the markets of Tenochti-tlan. While status as a noblewoman or commoner affected the extent of their participation in these activities— noblewomen relying on servants for many tasks but participating actively in child rearing, weaving, and caring for household shrines—nearly all women contributed to a family's economic well-being. Their significant contributions in enabling their households to meet labor, tribute, and religious obligations help to explain the attraction of polygyny to Mexica men. When husbands were on military campaigns, moreover, wives bore full responsibility for ensuring the continued well-being of their households. Given their economic activities, it was fitting that they owned any property they brought to a marriage and could inherit property and pass it on to their heirs.

The gap between the hereditary aristocracy and the commoners grew during the fifteenth century. The dominant *pipiltin* subjected the rest of society to an increasingly harsh regime. A purportedly growing problem with drunkenness may have been one result of commoners' inability to adjust to the new social and economic realities. At the same time, many nobles lost power relative to that of the ruler and his court.

The economy of Mesoamerica as a whole rested on agriculture with most of the people engaged in the cultivation and harvest of maize, beans, squash, chilies, and a variety of garden vegetables. Because the political and population center of the Aztec state, Tenochtitlan, was located on an island and thus controlled very limited agricultural land, tribute and trade necessarily became the basis of their economy. As the empire expanded, the Aztec forced defeated peoples to send tribute to Tenochtitlan. Because there were no domesticated beasts of burden in Mesoamerica, food could not be sent efficiently over long distances. Valuable goods like cotton cloth, animal skins, brightly colored feathers, jade, precious metals, obsidian, and dyes flowed into the city in an expanding volume of tribute as Aztec armies pushed the empire's borders outward. The *pochteca* supplemented the flow of tribute goods through their trade with subordinated as well as independent states. However, they were prohibited from trading in tribute items. Access to these valuable commodities and scarce raw materials gave Tenochtitlan's craftsmen an important advantage over competing craftsmen in other central Mexican polities. The city's island location provided another competitive advantage as well, for it allowed Tenochtitlan's merchants to distribute many of their goods by canoe to the densely settled communities that lined the shores of the huge lake. By the end of the fifteenth century, Tenochtitlan dominated a regional commercial system in which its merchants exchanged manufactured goods for the foods and specialized products of its neighbors.

The biggest market in central Mexico, in Tlatelolco, daily served tens of thousands of buyers and sellers. The stalls were in neat rows, with foodstuffs dominating the market. Jewelry, feathers, and precious stones were in one row, slaves in another, and cooking utensils and building materials in still another. There was no monetary system, but cacao beans used in a chocolate beverage and cotton cloth were often used to equalize the value of bartered goods.

Religious rituals overseen by a large and powerful priesthood ruled public life in Tenochtitlan. Mexica cosmology was sophisticated and complex. Polytheistic and highly ritualized, the deities included Quetzalcoatl, the culture god associated with Teotihuacan; Tezcatlipoca, the war god of the Toltecs; Tlaloc, the ancient Mesoamerican rain god; and Tonatiuh, the warrior sun. The center of Aztec religious life, however, was the cult of Huitzilopochtli, a demanding tribal god that the Mexica had worshiped before making the long journey south to the Valley of Mexico. As the Mexicas grew in might and wealth after 1428, the cult of Huitzilopochtli expanded as well. Soon the most important god of the pantheon, Huitzilopochtli absorbed qualities previously associated with other deities and continually required human sacrifices. Most importantly, the Mexica used this demanding god to justify their military expansion and the creation of a tribute empire. The imposition of this bloody cult accompanied each new conquest.

The Mexica believed that only the sacrifice of human hearts could provide the magical substance necessary for the sun to rise and the peoples of the world to survive. Although human sacrifice had been common in Mesoamerica for centuries, if not millennia, the Aztec practiced it on an unprecedented scale. Continued warfare and the provision of sacrificial victims to Huitzilopochtli to sustain the sun became sacred duties, and as the Mexica's power grew, bloody public sacrifices to other gods, such as the fertility deity Xipe Totec, were added to their religious practice. The Mexica's special mission justified and required conquest and tribute. This belief sustained continued commitment from noble and commoner warriors alike. Capturing enemies in battle brought tangible rewards, whereas perishing in battle or on an enemy's sacrificial stone secured an afterlife of luxury and pleasure.

War captives, criminals, slaves, and persons supplied by subject peoples as tribute fell victim to the obsidian sacrificial blade atop the great pyramids. After a victory ceremony, warriors often provided a ritual feast for friends and relatives, in which a small portion of the sacrificed captives' flesh was served as a paté. But by the mid-fifteenth century Aztec military expansion had slowed and, with it, the supply of sacrificial victims. To solve this shortfall, the Aztec fought "Flower Wars" with their neighbors. Flower Wars were limited conflicts infused with ritual meaning that had occurred as early as the fourteenth century. After taking their prisoners to Tenochtitlan, the Mexica brought in aristocrats from Tlaxcala and other rival states to witness the sacrifices, which might include their own people. Seated in flower-covered boxes, the guests learned a political lesson that transcended the ceremony's religious content: Rebellion, deviance, and opposition to the Aztec state were extremely dangerous. Indeed, in 1487 the Mexica dedicated the new temple of Huitzilopochtli in Tenochtitlan by sacrificing more than twenty thousand persons.

Although conquered *calpulli* and *altepetl* continued to worship their own deities, they were forced to accommodate the cult of Huitzilopochtli within their religious life. Some scholars suggest that images of important deities were taken to Tenochtitlan, where they were kept in a pantheon of captive deities. In short, the Aztec exploited their conquered peoples, giving—commoners at least—little in return. Not surprisingly, such exploitation fostered considerable hostility toward the Aztec in much of central Mexico.

The Aztec united their conquered territories through taxation and tribute rather than strong cultural or political institutions. Resident tribute collectors were the sinews of the empire and received tribute payments every eighty days. Often, this tribute was in addition to what the commoners already paid their local rulers. Behind the tax collectors stood the army, the ultimate weapon to enforce the payment of taxes and to suppress dissension within the empire. The ruling families in conquered areas well knew that Aztec favor was indispensable to their survival, and in addition, cooperation brought them economic benefits and support for their continued rule. Although their children often married Aztec nobles—thus undermining traditional autonomy—these alliances strengthened family prestige.

While recognizing the human cost of their empire, one must also appreciate that the Aztec did accomplish much. They built magnificent temples, created a generally effective army, and developed an elaborate ideology that tied together warfare, human sacrifice, and religion. They also produced an elaborate cosmology and ritual practice that explained the workings of nature and satisfied spiritual needs. Intellectual life was closely associated with religion and, therefore, the arts of music, dance, and writing had a sacred dimension. The construction and provisioning of Tenochtitlan, the development of extended commercial routes and large-scale markets, the creation of an effective educational and propaganda system, and the spread of Nahuatl as a common tongue throughout the region also were noteworthy achievements.

The Inca

The Inca created the largest indigenous empire in the Americas and developed the most sophisticated political and administrative structure found among native peoples. In the thirteenth century the Inca were one of many competing military powers in the southern highlands of Peru. Then, in less than a century, they extended their empire, Tawantinsuyu, or "land of the four parts," from the Valley of Cuzco on to the northern border of what is now Ecuador and to the Maule River in Chile. The ruler Pachacuti (1438–71) was the prime architect of this territorial expansion and the Inca administrative structure. He first conquered the highland regions near Cuzco and, with his son and successor Topa Inca, pushed the empire's borders into the highlands of northern Peru. Topa Inca (1471–93) later conquered Chimor and extended Inca control over the vast coastal plain and the southern highlands. Huayna Capac (1493–1525) then made the final additions to the empire in successful campaigns against the peoples of present-day Ecuador.

From the beginning, Inca power was rooted in the efficient organization and administration of their resources. Indeed, their conquest and later control of distant regions depended more on their ability to organize and supply large fighting forces than on new military technology or tactical innovations. Relying on nobles for officers, the Inca used conscripted peasants for the bulk of the army, but they also employed mercenaries. After conquering a region, they conscripted its male population and advanced farther into historically hostile adjacent regions, promising the new subjects an opportunity to even old scores and gain the spoils of victory. Unlike the Aztec, Inca armies were not interested in taking prisoners, and thus death in battle was more common. But the Inca's frequent successes were a powerful lure in enlisting defeated peoples for participation in future conquests.

An excellent road system in the Andes and along the coast, the maintenance of a network of runners for communication over long distances, and a system of state-organized warehouses of clothing, food, and weapons facilitated Inca military readiness and political control. The empire had over twenty-five thousand kilometers of road, much of it predating the Inca. Relay

runners could carry messages from Lima to Cuzco in three days and from
the capital to Quito in less than a week. In the absence of writing, they carried *khipus* (*quipus*), multicolored, knotted strings that served as memory aids.

The omnipresent llamas gave the Inca both draft animals and a mobile
meat supply. In addition, every district of the empire reserved some portion of its production—maize, potatoes, wool, cotton, or other goods—for
hard times and also for the Inca army and bureaucracy.

The Inca were superb organizers rather than great innovators; unlike
the Mexica, they sought to centralize their empire around its capital in
Cuzco. They divided it territorially into four major regions, eighty
provinces, and more than twice that many districts, each with a number of
kin groups that controlled land and other resources. At each level were
officials who reported to superiors, the entire pyramidal system culminating
in the Sapa Inca, or ruler. Such a system of communication also functioned
as a chain of command emanating from the ruler. Close relatives of the
Sapa Inca administered the four quarters, and other Inca nobles, the eighty
provinces. Local and regional chieftains, or *kurakas*, headed the smaller
units and formed the local political bases. The Inca generally used the
existing political structures and established elite groups at the local level.
Even when rebellion or insubordination forced changes in the administration, the Inca preferred to appoint officials drawn from the families of
the deposed rulers.

The imperial social structure largely reflected pre-Inca social organization under a growing and more demanding hereditary nobility related to
the Inca rulers. The basic social unit above the family was, again, the *ayllu*,
a kin group that had a common ancestry and a hereditary chieftain or
kuraka advised by village elders. *Ayllu* members worked on the same property, helped one another in a system of mutual obligation, and labored
for their leaders, who provided reciprocal benefits in accord with long-
standing Andean tradition. Individuals unattached to *ayllus* were known as
yanacona and were employed by the Inca rulers to maintain themselves,
favored nobles, deities, and the cult of royal mummies.

Ancestor worship and *huacas*—sacred items or places—were central to
Andean life long before the Inca appeared. Each *ayllu* had its own deities
and shrines supported by land farmed to provide sacrifices to them. On
matters of import, the villagers consulted prominent ancestors—rulers, the
founders of *ayllus*, and *kurakas*—whose mummies were carefully preserved
in necropoli and brought out during ritual celebrations. The demands of
ancestor and *huaca* worship were originally modest—periodic gifts of food,
beverage, and textiles—and the preimperial *ayllus* had little difficulty in
meeting them. But then Pachacuti introduced royal ancestor worship on
a scale that had far-reaching consequences for the empire.

When a Sapa Inca died, his chosen heir, a son born to his principal wife,
inherited the office and responsibilities of the ruler but not his father's
wealth. The deceased Sapa Inca's other male descendants, the *panaca*,
received his physical possessions as a trust to maintain his mummy and

cult. This living court treated the dead ruler as though he were alive, a holy object tangibly linked to the Inca pantheon. Because the *panaca* continued to hold the Sapa Inca's personal possessions after his death, the share of the state's wealth devoted to the royal mummy cults increased. Consequently, new Inca rulers sought to secure their individual honor and reputation by expanding the empire's borders through conquest and thereby increasing revenues. This in turn created a well-endowed *panaca* which would continue to influence political life. The royal mummy cults and the system that sustained them, therefore, contributed in some way to the territorial expansion of the Inca. However, Inca military expansion had political and economic, as well as religious and cultural origins.

Religion was central to the Inca's life. In its upper pantheon was a sky god of innumerable distinct aspects that Spanish chroniclers mistakenly considered to be independent deities. The three principal manifestations of this sky god were Viracocha, a creator god of ancient origin; Illapa, the god of thunder and weather; and Inti, the sun god. Because the Inca rulers claimed descent from one manifestation of Inti, he held the central place in the state's ancestor cult, providing the rulers with links to divinity and the Inca people with a sense of identity and, ultimately, confidence in a mission of expansion. The Inca transported the idols of their conquered peoples to Cuzco where they were kept in the sun temple. In return, they spread Inti's cult as part of their conquest, constructing temples to him throughout the empire. Compared with that of central Mexico, the Inca's priesthood was modest in size. Human sacrifice, moreover, was rare and designed to win the deities' goodwill rather than to maintain the universe. Instead, animals, food, fine textiles, and beverages were the usual sacrifices.

In most of their conquered lands, the Inca maintained the existing productive practices. The peoples of the Andes had long valued collective labor to farm, mine, weave, build, and maintain essential services; reciprocal rights and obligations and custom largely defined the nature of an individual's labor. Before the Inca arrived, the region's inhabitants had developed complex administrative and territorial structures to organize labor for irrigation and cultivation and to provide for the exchange of specialized goods across ecologically distinct zones. Called by some the "archipelago" pattern, the hamlet kinship groups, *ayllus*, placed settlers in distinct ecological zones so as to ensure their access to a range of products—maize, potatoes, cotton, llamas, and coca, among others. The expansion of the imperial bureaucracy, the requirements of the army, and the maintenance of the royal ancestor cults, however, meant that the state had to control any surplus production.

The Inca levied a rotational labor tax, the *mita*, on *ayllus* to secure workers for agricultural lands held by the state and its religious cults, as well as to engage them in the construction of roads, bridges, fortresses, temples, palaces, terraces, and irrigation projects. Terracing and irrigation brought previously uncultivated and, at times, marginal lands into production, usually to grow maize. Expanding on an earlier Andean practice, the Incas

sent groups of colonists from their homes to produce ecologically specialized products in conquered regions. These *mitmaq* also helped secure subject territories militarily.

The state stored the goods produced by labor taxation and specialized
craftsmen in numerous regional warehouses. Administrators distributed
these goods to state employees, to *mita* laborers as payment for their service, and to other persons as the need arose. Shared labor and economic
redistribution existed in the Andes long before the rise of the Inca state;
the Inca's innovation was to organize the resources over a much larger area
and thus mitigate the effects of drought and other natural disasters. There
was no form of money in the central Andean highlands, and private trading was limited to Peru's north and central coasts and Ecuador's highlands.

Inca advances in economic and political organization eroded local
autonomy and social equality in the Andes; in fact, the imperial elite and
the expanding state bureaucracy became almost completely cut off from
the masses of agricultural workers and craftsmen. At the same time, the
kurakas were increasingly separated from the Indian masses.

Inca cultural achievements were based upon those of earlier Andean civilizations. Their monumental architecture featured superb stone masonry,
but the absence of arches and vaulting gave the buildings a squat appearance. Exquisite Inca textiles, ceramics, and silver and gold work also continued older traditions. Astronomical observation was a central concern of
the priestly class, as in Mesoamerica. The Inca may have had three separate
calendars recorded on *khipus*. But elements of both the Inca calendar and
astronomical observations were lost after the conquest. Likewise, the
Mesoamerican glyphs and pictographs were clearly superior to the Inca's
khipus for non-oral communication. In comparison with Mesoamerica, Inca
achievement was most evident in political organization and the expansion
of agricultural productivity through terracing and irrigation. In addition,
the Inca contributed more to the peoples they defeated than did the
Mexica. Increased agricultural production in parts of the highlands; the
introduction of llamas, mainly in northern Peru; and the economic benefits of peace throughout the empire were among the Inca's most important contributions. Moreover, they attempted to centralize their empire
through political organization, the use of religion and ideology, the adoption of the Quechua language, and the resettlement of peoples.

The complexity of the Inca and Aztec empires and their cultural
attainments were unparalleled in the Americas in 1500. Yet these high
cultures shared a number of characteristics with the area's other indigenous peoples: All New World societies lacked iron and hard metal tools,
with the exception of a small amount of bronze used by the Inca. Aside
from llamas and their relatives in the Andes, there were no large domestic animals available for transport, food, or clothing. Humans transported
goods without the benefit of wheeled vehicles. And religion and belief in
the supernatural were widespread. Despite these commonalities, however,
these various New World societies were marked more by their diversity of

Map 2 Major Amerindian Cultures.

cultural, economic, and political achievements, a fact that profoundly affected the course of Iberian conquest and settlement.

The Iberian World in the Late Fifteenth Century

The Iberian peninsula, where the conquistadors and settlers of the New World came from, is but a fraction of the size of the future Spanish and Portuguese empires in the Americas. Long a part of the Roman world, Iberia endured centuries of political dislocation following the Germanic invasions that began in the fifth century. The repeated failure to resolve the problem of monarchical succession and bitter conflicts among Christian sects rendered the Visigothic kingdom incapable of withstanding the Muslim invasion launched from North Africa in 711. Divided by differing regional, political, cultural, and linguistic identities, the Iberians carried to the New World attitudes formed during the Reconquest, nearly eight centuries of intermittent conflict with the Islamic civilizations that had dominated the peninsula. The Iberians' own social, cultural, and geographic diversity enabled the conquistadors to perceive, and to manipulate to their own benefit, a similar diversity in the loose collection of cultures that they encountered in Mesoamerica and the Andes.

With the exception of the Pyrenees Mountains that form its northern boundary with France, Iberia is surrounded by water. The Mediterranean Sea on the east and south extends to the Straits of Gibraltar, the narrow expanse that separates the peninsula's southern tip from Africa by ten miles. The Atlantic Ocean and the Cantabrian Sea encircle the remainder of the peninsula. Just over 225,000 square miles in area, Iberia is slightly smaller than the states of Arizona and New Mexico combined. Its landscape is dominated by mountains whose mean altitude is higher than that in any western European country except Switzerland. Although flatlands can be found, mainly on the Portuguese coast, range after range breaks Iberia's terrain into a patchwork of distinct regions. Coupled with few navigable rivers, the mountains make transportation and communication difficult and obstruct political and economic integration. Although its northern and northwestern parts receive substantial rainfall, much of Iberia is dry. A Spanish proverb summarizes the weather of the great central tableland as "nine months of winter and three months of hell."

The Reconquest

The Reconquest created a cultural legacy that the conquistadors and settlers carried to the New World. Although Christians and Muslims struggled intermittently to control Iberia, from about 718 to 1492, the most active years were between about 850 and 1250. During this time, Christian knights and settlers pushed south from their initial redoubt in the mountains of northern Spain. Although the Reconquest is often labeled a crusade, its religious zeal only complemented the more mundane and important objectives of securing additional grazing and agricultural land. Military action was most frequently a raid for booty, including slaves. But slowly and sporadically the Christians pushed the frontier south.

In 1147 Lisbon was recovered, and in 1179 the pope recognized Alfonso I of the House of Burgundy as the first monarch of the independent kingdom of Portugal. By the mid-thirteenth century the Portuguese had taken the southern coastal region known as the Algarve and expelled the Muslims from their territory. A change of dynasty in 1384 brought the House of Aviz to the throne, and during an almost fifty-year reign, the first monarch, John I, consolidated his position and set the stage for the creation of Portugal's overseas empire.

The Castilian seizure of Seville in 1248 reduced Islamic domination to the kingdom of Granada. Although subsequent Christian princes occasionally engaged the Muslims in battle, the final phase of the Reconquest did not begin until 1482. In that year Isabel and Ferdinand responded to a Muslim attack on a Christian town and launched a war that lasted until the city of Granada surrendered on January 2, 1492.

Royal families, valorous warriors, a militant Church, and military orders founded to spearhead the Christian advance reaped the initial rewards of land, booty, and tribute. Military prowess brought lordship over subject peoples and immediate economic gain; thus serving a king in arms became the Iberian Christians' preferred route to wealth and honor. As the Reconquest progressed, Christian settlers entered the conquered frontier regions, often locating in former Muslim cities and villages. But with the consolidation of territorial gains, the pressure of a growing population for additional land renewed the cycle of military conflict.

The final triumph over the Muslims in Granada reinforced the booty mentality that the Iberian Christians had developed during the long Reconquest. Victorious Christians enslaved fifteen thousand Muslim inhabitants of Málaga alone. Nobles who had contributed to victory gained jurisdiction over areas with large Muslim populations. Commoners received land and in some cases ennoblement for their valor, through royal grants that again confirmed the importance of military service for social advancement. Conveniently, the Christians saw their triumph as evidence that their God actively supported their cause, a belief that they carried into battle against the native civilizations of the Americas.

Iberia in the Age of Ferdinand and Isabel

In the mid-fifteenth century five independent kingdoms occupied Iberia. Portugal, whose boundaries approximated those of the modern country, had a population of perhaps 1 million persons in the late fifteenth century. Thus, it was only slightly less populous than the Crown of Aragon, which held sway in the northeast and maintained long-standing territorial and commercial interests in the Mediterranean, including ties to Italy, Byzantium, and the east. Granada, the remaining Muslim stronghold located in the southeast, had some 500,000 persons; Navarre, a small kingdom in the western Pyrenees, had fewer than 200,000. At the center of the peninsula lay Castile, whose area was more than triple that of either Portugal or Aragon and whose population of perhaps 4.5 million persons was roughly four times as large. This geographic and demographic dominance increased even more when Castile conquered Granada in 1492 and annexed Navarre in 1512.

The most significant domestic event in Iberian history between the mid-fifteenth century and the fall of Granada was the marriage in 1469 of Isabel of Castile and Ferdinand of Aragon. In 1468 Isabel had been reluctantly recognized by her half-brother Henry IV as the heir to Castile; such was the price of peace in his realm. Henry's reluctance can be traced to his wife's daughter Juana. Juana is also known to historians as La Beltraneja, after Beltrán de la Cueva, who was the queen's lover and—according to Isabel's supporters—Juana's father. Although the charge was probably baseless, Henry, a weak monarch, was cursed with the epithet "The Impotent," and Isabel made the most of her opportunity. Aided by a forged papal bull permitting her to marry a close relative, she wed Ferdinand, heir to the throne of Aragon. Isabel was clearly a woman of strong will, who had already rejected marriage to the widowed King Alfonso of Portugal and the French suitor Charles of Valois. Ferdinand of Aragon was the energetic and ambitious son of John II, who saw in Castile the resources necessary to combat French designs on his kingdom's border.

After Henry IV died in December 1474, Isabel declared herself the queen of Castile. In response, Juana claimed the throne in May 1475 with military support from Portugal and an anti-Aragonese faction at the court of Castile. The ensuing civil war ended in Isabel's victory in 1479. When his father died in the same year, Ferdinand became the king of Aragon, and the "union of the crowns" and a "double monarchy" became reality. For the following quarter-century, the "Catholic Kings"—as the couple were later dubbed by Pope Alexander VI—jointly ruled the largest and wealthiest area of Iberia.

The name Spain is often used to describe the realms of Isabel and Ferdinand, but the term erroneously implies a nonexistent unity. Both Castile and Aragon maintained separate economies, political institutions, monetary systems, customs barriers, and lifestyles. Even though the two monarchs worked together so closely that a chronicler recorded, for example, "the king and queen, on such and such a day, gave birth to a daughter," they never, as did their counterparts elsewhere in Europe, sought political unification of their kingdoms. Although their grandson Charles I (later Charles V of the Holy Roman Empire) inherited both crowns, the creation of a single Spanish polity awaited the abolition of the traditional rights (*fueros*) of the Crown of Aragon in the early eighteenth century.

Earlier, during the unhappy reign of Henry IV (1454–74), the most powerful noble families of Castile exerted a political influence that rivaled the Crown's. Henry accordingly attempted to strengthen his power in ways that anticipated actions by the Catholic Kings; he employed *corregidores*, royal agents assigned to major towns, to provide justice and secure compliance with the Crown's will. He also reorganized the Holy Brotherhood (Hermandad), a league of law officers hired by municipalities, and increased the appointment of university-educated officials. Henry's open-handed grants of land, jurisdictional rights, offices, and incomes in an effort to buy the loyalty of high aristocrats ultimately failed, however, and consequently Isabel inherited serious financial and political problems.

Isabel's victory over La Beltraneja enabled her to consolidate and extend her royal authority within Castile. Substantial military and political support from many powerful families during the civil war emphasized their importance as allies and the threat they posed if discontented. Consequently the queen moved carefully to maintain their continued support. By confirming most of Henry's grants to them, she ensured the nobility's economic and social preeminence, but at the same time, she worked to curb their political strength.

The queen used a further reorganized Hermandad to end the anarchy plaguing Castile and bring peace to the countryside. Its agents captured malefactors and meted out justice. The imposition of royal justice restored order in rural areas, and the destruction of castles held by nobles who had sided with La Beltraneja was further evidence of the queen's intention to rule as well as reign. In 1480 the Catholic Kings resolved to increase the number of *corregidores* and to send them into all the major cities. As Henry IV had, they turned to men with a university education to staff many of the royal offices. Both Ferdinand and Isabel turned their personal attention to administering justice—the essence of kingship—and enlarging the judicial system to make

At the time of Spain's conquests in the Americas, blacks, like this drummer in the court of Emperor Charles V, were already a highly visible part of Spanish society.

it more accessible and effective. In addition, they reorganized the Council of Castile. The queen appointed to this supreme advisory, judicial, and administrative body university-educated jurists who were lower-ranking aristocrats or commoners rather than more illustrious nobles. Taken together, the monarchs' actions strengthened the Crown of Castile's authority and increased its ability to implement diplomatic, economic, fiscal, and religious policies.

The Portuguese monarchy in the late fifteenth century was heir to a tradition of strong centralized rule occasionally disrupted by high-ranking nobles eager to enhance their wealth and power. The unprecedented revenue resulting from the Crown's monopoly over trade with newly discovered lands, however, enabled John II (1481–95) to reassert the royal authority lost by his predecessor. John expanded the judicial system and increased the number of provincial administrators (*corregidores*). In addition, he executed for treason the duke of Braganza, the richest and most influential noble in the realm, and enlarged the royal patrimony in the process. Centralization was again ascendant, although, as in Castile, the aristocracy retained social and economic dominance.

Society

Society in Castile and Portugal shared many characteristics: Each kingdom recognized three estates—clergy, nobility, and commoners—and a number of corporate bodies with special legal privileges. Birth and family normally determined an individual's place in the social hierarchy. Ties created through godparentage and client-patron relationships also were important to both societies. Each kingdom contained Jews, Muslims, Italians and other foreigners, and black slaves, and neither had many professionals or merchants.

At the top of the Castilian and Portuguese social hierarchies were a few great families that bore titles of duke, marquis, or count. In Castile the greatest nobles controlled half of the kingdom's land, and in Portugal a similar group of about fifteen families also held noble titles, extensive lands, and economic power. Other titled nobles, often indistinguishable from the first in resources, formed a second tier of Castile's hierarchy. In Portugal some two thousand nontitled nobles received land grants and incomes from the monarchy and constituted an upper-middle nobility. Together these groups were at the apex of their respective social orders. From 1505 onward, high-ranking Castilian nobles could create entailed estates, or *mayorazgos*, which enabled the preservation of property in perpetuity and formed the basis for consolidating still larger estates through marriage.

The remainder of the nobility were knights known as *caballeros* (*cavaleiros*) or gentlemen, *hidalgos* (*fidalgos*). In Castile they used the prefix *don* and proudly displayed coats of arms. Their status exempted them from direct taxation and provided additional privileges denied to commoners. The *hidalgos'* economic resources varied considerably: The wealthiest in Castile were indistinguishable from the poorer titled nobles, whereas the poorer *hidalgos* possessed less than did well-to-do commoners. Commoners coveted nobility for both its social cachet and its privileges. Recognizing their desire for noble rank, Castilian monarchs gave and, from the 1520s, sold to them patents of nobility. Thus in both Castile and Portugal a trickle of new families continuously entered the most privileged class in society.

Commoners accounted for over 90 percent of the Iberian population. Most engaged in agricultural or pastoral activities. Although many owned land, frequently it was just a garden plot. Most commoners worked a noble's land for remuneration that at best provided subsistence. A few commoners held professional positions, serving in the clergy, practicing law, or engaging in commerce. Not a bourgeoisie or true middle class, their highest ambition was ennoblement. Though few succeeded, some of the wealthiest did make the transition. Below them were artisans, themselves divided into guilds ranked by prestige, with silversmiths the most honored and cobblers the least.

Although few in number, successful foreign merchants and their descendants formed colonies in Iberia's commercial centers. For example, Genoa's commercial families had their largest Spanish colony in Seville. Their compatriots and other Italian merchants also resided in Lisbon and other Portuguese ports, from which they controlled the kingdom's long-distance trade. Although Iberian merchants were active in Burgos, Medina del Campo, Barcelona, Lisbon, Oporto, and other trading centers, the noble values of the Reconquest—valor and virture, land, warfare, and religion—stigmatized trade as demeaning for aristocrats. It required the overseas expansion of the fifteenth and sixteenth centuries to modify this attitude.

Slaves constituted a small segment of society, though slavery had long been known in Iberia, as captives taken in the Reconquest fighting frequently were enslaved. But when Portuguese traders began importing slaves from Africa in 1441, they transformed the nature of slavery on the peninsula. By 1492 more than 35,000 black slaves had reached Portugal. Although some remained in servitude there, many were reexported. By the late fifteenth century, both Seville and Valencia in Spain had large slave populations and active slave markets. Most slaves worked as domestic servants or as unskilled laborers, and the association of dark skin with slavery had become firmly established before the settlement of the New World.

Although by the time of the Reconquest Iberia contained Christians, Muslims, and Jews, religious tolerance had disappeared by the early sixteenth century. Isabel and Ferdinand followed up the victory over the Muslim minority in 1492 by giving the Jews four months either to convert to Christianity or emigrate. Perhaps 80,000 of the 200,000 Jews in Castile and Aragon fled rather than give up their faith. But they took with them knowledge and skills that the kingdoms could ill afford to lose, although the remaining *conversos* continued in their occupations as tax collectors, financiers, physicians, and the like. Spain's loss was Portugal's gain, as John II allowed the exiled Jews to enter his kingdom and remain for some months in return for monetary payments. After the prescribed period ended, the wealthiest Jews purchased permits allowing permanent residence. In 1497, however, John's successor Manuel I (1495–1521) ordered the conversion or expulsion of all Jews in Portugal. Some accepted baptism and remained, but others returned to Spain or emigrated to Holland and other countries. Those who remained in the peninsula joined the *converso* or New Christian minorities.

As the final blow in creating religious homogeneity, Isabel and Ferdinand in 1502 ordered the expulsion or conversion of the remaining Muslims in Castile. Approximately 200,000 had already emigrated after the fall of Granada. But because the terms of the 1502 measure made exile tantamount to the confiscation of their property, nearly all of the remaining Muslims accepted baptism. In Portugal Manuel I had ordered the small number of free Muslims to leave in 1497, thus establishing a single religion for his realm as well.

The expulsions imposed a superficial religious homogeneity, but the new converts still suffered discrimination because of their religious background

Map 3   The Iberian Peninsula in the Mid-Fifteenth Century.

and ancestry. "Old Christians" had viewed the *conversos* with suspicion for many years. Systematic discrimination against the "New Christians" in some jobs and in universities then began in mid-fifteenth-century Castile and continued for centuries. The sudden increase in the number of *conversos* in Portugal also created social and religious tensions that resulted in riots, pogroms, and an official discrimination policy forbidding New Christians to hold public offices, receive honors, or marry nobles.

Suspicion that the *conversos* were secretly practicing their former religion led Isabel in the 1470s and the Portuguese in 1547 to establish tribunals of the Inquisition to investigate the genuineness of the *conversos'* Christianity. Indeed, the Spanish Inquisition proved so effective in prosecuting Judaizers that by 1500 it had largely met its initial goal of eliminating them.

Noble or commoner, wealthy or poor, Iberians preferred to reside in cities, towns, and villages rather than in widely scattered dwellings in the countryside. As the Christians moved south during the Reconquest, the monarchs chartered towns and granted privileges to entice occupation and settlement. Town councils were routinely established and aldermen and officials selected. Within Castile seventeen towns (eighteen after Granada was conquered) were represented in the *cortes*, or parliament.

Cities, towns, and villages housed clerics, local officials, merchants, and artisans. Even nobles with rich estates normally spent much of the year in town houses. For the majority of the population—*labradores* who worked the small properties they owned or rented and wage-earning day laborers who worked in agriculture or pastoral activities—towns and villages were home. Most walked to fields in the adjoining countryside each workday and spent few nights away from home.

The settlement pattern of clustered residences fostered pride in the local region, the town, and adjacent rural lands that fell within its jurisdiction. Kinship ties supplemented by bonds created through godparentage resulted in tight extended family groups that were the primary social units, with political and economic overtones. Individuals tended to maintain a strong allegiance to their native region as well as to their families. Local residents regarded outsiders with suspicion; it required years of residence and the development of social and economic ties for an outsider to enter the local society.

Economy

In the late fifteenth century only Seville, Granada, Toledo, and Lisbon had populations in excess of thirty thousand persons. Thus numerous smaller communities provided many of the cultural activities and social and economic opportunities without which Iberians considered civilization nonexistent and living conditions intolerable. Urban centers were the locus of local economic exchange and social contact.

Agricultural and pastoral activities were the foundation of the Iberian economies. Although the yield was low, grain production on the Castilian plateau was ample enough in good years to permit exporting a surplus to the poorer regions of Galicia, Asturias, and Vizcaya to the west and north. In lean years, however, even Castile had to import grain from abroad, and beginning in 1502 the Crown started to fix the maximum price of grain. Portugal was chronically short of wheat and other cereals, and by 1500 imports of grain were commonplace. In contrast, Andalusia exported grain, first to Aragon and later to the New World. Olive orchards and vineyards completed the traditional triad of Mediterranean agriculture in Spain. In Portugal, wine, fruit, cork, olive oil, salt, and fish were the major products.

High-quality wool from merino sheep dominated Castile's exports in the mid-fifteenth century and continued to do so for many years. Vast numbers of sheep held by members of the *mesta*, or sheep owner's guild, migrated annually from summer pastures in Aragon to winter forage in Andalusia and Extremadura. Great aristocrats, monasteries, and small private owners sent their sheep on the great walks that traversed Castile, but even more sheep stayed home. Although restrictions prohibited owners from letting their sheep wander through planted lands, the immense size of the flocks necessarily reduced the amount of land available for agriculture. The pattern of exporting raw materials (wool) and importing finished goods (textiles) was firmly established before Henry IV's reign. Castile lacked a solid industrial base on the eve of empire and failed to develop one in the next three centuries.

Engaging in substantial foreign trade joined northern Castilians with merchants of Barcelona, Seville, and Lisbon in an international mercantile system. The Portuguese, long involved in international trade, in the second half of the fifteenth century were exporting slaves, gold, ivory, and sugar brought from Africa and the Madeira Islands as well as salt and other domestic products in exchange for finished goods. With important bases in Seville and Lisbon, Genoese financiers and merchants comprised an influential foreign presence in Iberian commercial circles.

The Castilian Crown employed a plethora of taxes and tariffs, but the principal source of revenue during the reign of Ferdinand and Isabel was the *alcabala*, a sales tax frequently farmed out to city councils for collection. Although the amount of regular revenue increased more than tenfold during their reign, it was never enough to support the court, the army, and Ferdinand's foreign ventures. Consequently the Crown resorted to borrowing, a recourse that ultimately had disastrous results for the succeeding Habsburg monarchs. The revenue of the Portuguese Crown also rose in the late fifteenth century, but similarly its expenses repeatedly exceeded its normal tax income.

The Iberian world of the late fifteenth century remained fragmented politically but had become substantially stronger through the union of the crowns of Castile and Aragon and the conquest of Granada. In addition, the forced conversion or exile of non-Christians, the Inquisition's activities against suspected heretics, and the imposition of royal justice had brought a unity to Castile that rivaled that achieved earlier in Portugal. The centralization of royal authority had increased in both kingdoms. The Iberian population was expanding as it continued to recover from the ravages of the fourteenth-century Black Death. The African trade and early exploitation of the Atlantic islands was benefiting Portugal. And with technological advances in sailing vessels and sailors' increased confidence in their ability to undertake lengthy voyages, the way was opened for the great era of exploration.

Atlantic Africa in the Fifteenth Century

First Contacts with Europe

Western Europe and West Africa were situated at the far western boundary of the rich medieval trade routes that distributed the products of the Eastern Hemisphere. As these commercial links increased in importance at the beginning of the fifteenth century, the economic power of the Islamic Middle East grew relative to both regions. By the mid-sixteenth century, Portugal's direct entry into both African and Asian trades and Spanish and Portuguese exploration, conquest, and settlement in the Western Hemisphere had transformed these global economic and commercial arrangements. In contrast to the direct colonial rule and substantial European immigration imposed by the Iberians on their American colonies, however, most peoples of Africa remained outside of direct European domination into the nineteenth century.

The Portuguese capture of Ceuta across the Strait of Gibraltar in 1415 opened the era of exploration, trade, conquest, and settlement for the Iberian kingdoms. The arrival of the Portuguese on the Atlantic coast of sub-Saharan Africa in the fifteenth century, and the later appearance of other Europeans, initiated what would ultimately become broad changes in the region. Prince Henry, the energetic, ambitious, and wealthy younger son of John I of Portugal (1385–1433), promoted the exploration of the West African coast—earning from later generations but not contemporaries the nickname "the Navigator," despite his personally having sailed no farther than Morocco. Progress accelerated after 1434 when an expedition finally rounded Africa's fearsome Cape Bojador on the coast of the modern territory of Western Sahara.

By the late fifteenth century, Portuguese ships had coasted Atlantic Africa and with the permission of native rulers established a small number of fortified trading posts. These vulnerable commercial outposts would remain the most common form of European presence for more than three centuries. These fortress warehouses were erected at São Jorge da Mina (Elmina) in 1482 and at other coastal sites, and Portuguese reliance on them reflected several realities. First, with the important exception of the Atlantic islands, the Portuguese generally sought quick profits from trade, avoiding the more expensive and difficult alternative of colonization and the direct control of economic resources in the African interior. Second, while larger and faster vessels armed with cannons gave the Portuguese a clear military advantage in coastal waters and estuaries, native peoples along the West African coast had considerable experience with iron and steel weapons as well as the use of cavalry in combat and were formidable military opponents. As West African states gained firearms through trade, the ability of the Portuguese and other Europeans to impose their will was further reduced. Consequently, the Portuguese could control the sea, but African kingdoms controlled the land, and native merchants, as a result, largely determined the terms of trade.

And finally, the effects of deadly local diseases, notably malaria, yellow fever, and gastrointestinal maladies, retarded any ambitions of the Portuguese or other Europeans to penetrate permanently the interior of Africa. Contemporary accounts suggest that disease killed approximately half of new European arrivals to the West African tropics within a year and another quarter within the second year. A voyage in 1588 to what the English merchants called the "great city of Benin" to purchase pepper and ivory ended in near disaster when a local fever attacked the ship's crew. In little more than a week, the fever took the lives of the captain, mate, and so many crew members that the survivors could barely pull up the anchor.

When Bartholomeu Dias rounded the Cape of Good Hope in 1488, a sea route to India and its spices was open at last. The lure of direct maritime trade with Asia reduced even more the willingness of the Portuguese court to allocate significant resources to controlling the West African coast. They therefore sought to find profits within existing markets and trade routes. The richest gold mines were distant from the coast, and West African gold had long been one of the most important products traded north across the Sahara Desert. Portuguese merchants soon gained access to this profitable commodity through coastal intermediaries. They also began to trade European goods for slaves, purchasing and exporting about 2,200 slaves annually from all of Africa between 1480 and 1499. The Atlantic slave trade eventually came to dominate relations between Africa and Europe. For at least a hundred years after first contacts, however, the Portuguese and other important European coastal traders bought and sold relatively small numbers of slaves. In this era, European merchants purchased a range of African goods including cloth, salt, gold, iron, and copper. They also paid local taxes and generally accepted restrictions imposed by African rulers.

West Africa and West Central Africa, vast regions extending from the Senegal River to the southern reaches of Angola, were home to hundreds if not thousands of ethnic groups often separated by language and other cultural differences. Here, numerous rulers of states of varied size competed for power and wealth. A large number of languages and even more dialects formed three principal linguistic zones: Upper Guinea, Lower Guinea, and West Central Africa. As in contemporary Iberia, the local and regional identities—for example, Bambara, Hausa, Jolof, Mandingo, and other ethnicities—dominated. Few fifteenth-century

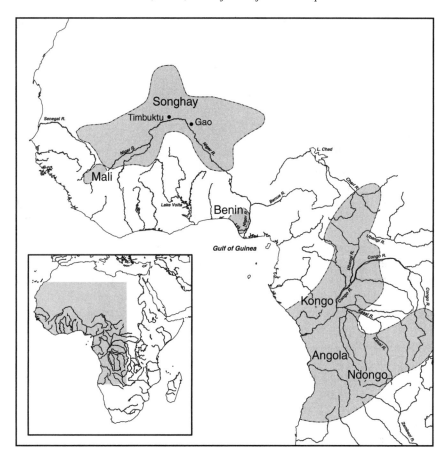

Map 4   West and West Central Africa in the Early Sixteenth Century.

Iberians described themselves as "Europeans" and, similarly, the subjects of West African or West Central African polities were very unlikely to consider themselves "Africans."

West Africa

Throughout the fourteenth century, the empire of Mali was the preeminent power in the interior of West Africa. Mande speakers dominated this empire centered in the lower Gambia and Senegal River areas. The royal court and most merchants were Muslims, but much of the countryside remained outside this faith. The empire's wealth was displayed spectacularly in ruler Mansa Musa's pilgrimage to Mecca. Along his route, which passed through Cairo and other powerful Muslim cities, he distributed so much gold that he drove down the price of this precious metal for years.

Ibn Battuta, who visited Mali from North Africa, provided a favorable if somewhat biased account in the 1350s:

> The negroes possess some admirable qualities. They are seldom unjust, and have greater abhorrence of injustice than any other people. Their sultan (the Mansa) shows no mercy to anyone guilty of the least act of it. There is complete security in the country. Neither travellor [*sic*] nor inhabitant in it has anything to fear from robbers or men of violence.[1]

Despite this wealth, Mali declined and eventually fell to the expanding Songhay empire by the middle of the fifteenth century.

Songhay's capital was Gao, but it also controlled the ancient center of learning at Timbuktu. During the reigns of Sunni Ali (d. 1492) and Askiya Muhammad (d. 1538), Songhay conquered the weakened Mali empire and revived the rich trade routes across the Sahara Desert. As in Mali, the Songhay rulers in this period of rapid expansion needed to fuse the interests of a largely Muslim merchant class, crucial to the court, and a vast rural population tied to the kings in older royal rites and traditional religious practices. The political structures of Songhay were more centralized than those of Mali, with most conquered rulers replaced by royal appointees. Renowned for its learning and crafts and the success of its merchants, the Songhay empire had been created militarily, and Askiya Muhammad, its most ambitious conqueror, gained the throne as a usurper whose power rested on the loyalty of the army.

Although gold remained a crucial trade item, Songhay's currency was salt or cowries, mollusk shells used as currency. In addition to gold, the empire's most important trade items were cloth, food, kola nuts, and slaves. Successful military campaigns enlarged the slave population, and these slaves allowed the empire to increase agricultural production. Visitors were impressed by the intellectual life of the capital Gao and Timbuktu, a manufacturing and commercial center that became the major center of Islamic scholarship in the region. One visitor commented on the city's commercial importance: "Here are many shops of craftsmen, especially those who weave linen and cotton cloth. To this place [Berber] merchants bring cloth from Europe. . . . The inhabitants are exceedingly rich." Another noted, "In Timbuktu there are numerous judges, doctors and clerics, all receiving good salaries from the king. . . . There is a big demand for books in manuscript, imported from Barbary. More profit is made from the book trade than from any [other] line of business."[2]

In the late fifteenth century, numerous small states divided the West African coast. Among them was the kingdom of Benin, located inland from the Niger River Delta. King (Oba) Ewuare established Benin's commercial and political power in the mid-fifteenth century. This expansion of Benin's political and economic influence reduced the authority of other rulers and chiefs. Benin City, the capital, was large and prosperous, as early European visitors universally testified. Women in Benin produced beautiful cotton cloth, and the kingdom's metal goods traded throughout West Africa. Its

At the time of the first European voyages to West Africa, the Kingdom of Benin was ruled by a dynasty of divine kings known as Obas. The king's palace was decorated with numerous brass plaques depicting court life and historical events. This plaque portrays the king in the center, supported by two noblemen. The king's regalia, including coral beads, rich cloth, and brass pendants, demonstrate his wealth and power.

merchants also controlled the regional trade in ivory and pepper. Even after the establishment of the Atlantic slave trade, cloth remained Benin's most important export.

Following first contacts with the Portuguese, the Oba sent an emissary to Portugal to learn about these strangers. This ambassador returned with rich gifts, some Christian missionaries, and a new group of Portuguese merchants. The Oba certainly recognized that European firearms could prove useful in his wars and perhaps thought the missionaries might also strengthen his power. By 1570 trade continued, but Christian missionaries had failed to convert the Oba and his court. Political and economic disruptions arising from the growing European presence on the coast and, more importantly, the pressures of the expanding Atlantic slave trade during the eighteenth century would contribute to the eventual decline of Benin.

West Central Africa

To the southeast, the kingdom of Kongo with its capital of Mbanza Kongo dominated a broad region that included numerous linguistically related Bantu ethnic groups. Kongo was a great regional power that faced few local threats to its political ambitions when the Portuguese appeared in 1483. Kongo's ruler, the manikongo, controlled numerous tributary states and direct dependencies through a bureaucracy made up mostly of kinsmen. At the end of the fifteenth century, the kingdom's population of nearly 2.5 million lived in towns whose officials and merchants administered regional political life, collected taxes, and organized commerce. Its economy relied on an important metallurgical sector as well as on highly productive agriculture. The elites perceived the political benefits that relations with the Portuguese might bring. These included desired trade goods, prestige, and enhanced spiritual power. As in Benin, Kongo had a coherent, non-Islamic religious tradition. Nonetheless, contact with the Portuguese led the manikongo and his court to explore Christianity. Experimentation culminated in 1491 with the baptism of the royal heir, Nzinga Mbemba. As Afonso I, he became the manikongo in 1507 and ruled as a Christian until the 1540s. With the encouragement of the manikongo and his court, Portuguese missionaries pursued conversion across the kingdom and sent many sons of important families to Portugal for instruction in the faith. Many came back fluent in Portuguese as well. Despite this success in inserting Christianity into an African kingdom, Christianity never completely replaced native religious traditions in Kongo. Instead, the two religious practices melded to produce a unique local Christianity. The need for Portuguese allies is an important explanation for the Kongo elites' willingness to sanction the sale of slaves. Nonetheless, as the Portuguese presence grew and Christianity spread, the Kongo royal court began to lose power relative both to the increasingly aggressive and confident Portuguese and to the kingdom's distant tributaries that now saw the chance to assert their own power.

Central to Kongo's decline was the growing importance of the region's slave trade that connected the kingdom to the Portuguese colony of Brazil with its rapidly expanding sugar sector. Although the Kongo royal court's interests initially benefited by using some Portuguese auxiliaries in military campaigns, the predictable result was a dramatic increase in the volume of the slave trade. Warfare became a continuous part of the region's political life as armies made up of Portuguese soldiers and much more numerous native allies campaigned relentlessly. Each campaign and every victory added to the volume of the slave trade, for Kongo's elite required war captives to exchange with the Portuguese for the goods and missionaries which helped support their political power. By the early sixteenth century, Kongo kings had begun to complain of the destructiveness of the slave trade to the Portuguese authorities, even appealing directly to the pope on numerous occasions. But it was too late. The authority of the manikongo and the power of the capital declined while the slave trade roiled the interior and provoked constant warfare. By the end of the sixteenth century, no African state had been more affected by the arrival of Europeans than the Kongo, and nowhere else in Africa had the slave trade become more important.

In these regions of intense contact with Europeans, especially the Portuguese, African peoples incorporated elements of European culture, technology and belief. Scholars refer to these regions as Atlantic Creole cultures. In the Kongo, for example, evangelization by Portuguese priests and African converts spread Christian belief and practice to areas outside direct control by colonial administrators. The Portuguese recruited large numbers of native military allies that, in turn, adapted European tactics, weapons and hierarchies. At the same time the Kongo elite as well as rulers of other African allies of the Portuguese sought access to language, religious instruction, and material goods as ways of strengthening their authority and status.

The Kongo and Angola, areas where Portuguese presence was most intense, were centers of Atlantic Creole culture, but the Ndongo and Matamba, more distant from Portuguese settlement, participated in these cultural exchanges as well. This meant that a large number of slaves carried to the New World had experience with important elements of European culture, including Christian belief, language, aesthetics and material culture, before entering the colonial orbit. Once in the colonies, these prior experiences and adaptations facilitated the rapid development of a slave community.

Slavery was well established in most of Atlantic Africa centuries before Portugal's seizure of Ceuta. Wealth rested heavily on the possession of slaves across the large empires of West Africa as well as in Benin and other kingdoms. Most slaves were taken in wars and came from distinct ethnic groups with their own religious traditions. Rulers and other slave owners used this human property as administrators, soldiers, concubines, domestic labor, field labor, miners, artisans, and in a host of other occupations. Slave owners in sub-Saharan Africa also employed their chattel in a variety of occupations. Slave laborers, for example, produced agricultural products including millet, cotton, wheat, and rice. In the western Sudan, slaves labored in gold mines and, in some desert sites, worked in saltworks. Slave owners used, sold, or traded the products of slave labor, and rulers taxed people rather than land, which was held collectively rather than as private property. In the fifteenth century, war, raiding, and kidnapping in sub-Saharan regions enabled slavers to send annually an estimated four to five thousand victims to Islamic regions of North Africa and the Middle East via routes along the East African coast and the Red Sea, and especially across the Sahara Desert.

The Slave Trade

The Atlantic slave trade expanded during the initial century of contacts between Africans and Europeans and would continue to do so for more than three hundred years. When Portuguese mariners and merchants reached West Africa, they had initially focused on the gold trade, for the scarce, precious metal was the basis for Europe's monetary system and crucial to the growth of markets and long-distance commercial operations. Salt, pepper, ivory, and cloth also proved profitable. Building upon an existing slave trade brought additional profits.

A low ratio of people to land in much of West Africa made control over labor a key to wealth. Coupled with extensive political fragmentation that resulted in ample potential slaves located within traveling distance, this low ratio goes far to explain the development of slavery in sub-Saharan Africa. Slaves were a part of both Mali and Songhay trade and had become important to the West African regional economy as well by the time the Portuguese arrived. Backed by private investors, Portuguese merchants moved slowly down the Atlantic coast of Africa with trading goods that included textiles; copper and brass wristlets and basins; horses, saddles, bridles, and other tack; iron bars; and cowries. As the fifteenth century progressed, the importance of slaves in this trade increased. By the 1450s, fifteen slaves were traded for one horse, suggesting the expected value of slave labor. Central to this slow expansion was the use of slaves in the labor force of southern Iberia and increasingly in the sugar plantations of the Azores and São Tomé. The rapid expansion of sugar agriculture in Brazil would usher in a new era in the slave trade.

The slave trade with the Portuguese, and later with other Europeans, was initially constrained along the West African coast by the decisions of local political authorities. Slavery had an important place in the Islamic world, but rulers' restrictions on who could be enslaved limited the scale of the trade. The result was that slaves flowed only slowly from the states of the interior to the coast and the Atlantic trade. Similarly, Benin controlled the growth in slave exports, even prohibiting the export of male slaves for centuries. Nevertheless, Benin utilized slaves in its own economy and allowed Europeans to import slaves into the kingdom from other African regions as an ongoing part of their trade. Although local rulers were eventually unable to control the mounting flow of slaves crossing the Atlantic, there is no doubt that the Portuguese lacked the military power to overcome their objections during the century that followed first contacts.

Despite the pervasiveness of slavery across the region and despite slavery's economic and cultural importance prior to the arrival of the Portuguese, the historic place of slavery in Africa was essentially different from the form of slavery later developed by Europeans in their American colonies. First and foremost, the Atlantic slave trade extracted a volume of slaves never previously witnessed in Africa. As this trade matured, numbers spiraled upward until reaching their peak in the eighteenth century. Second, the distance that the trade carried its victims also necessarily altered the meaning of slavery, tearing families, ethnicities, and even polities apart by forcefully removing men and women from their native regions, cultures, languages, and religions and relocating them to the distant Americas. Finally, the Atlantic slave trade worsened the status of slaves relative to African customs, reducing legal protections and increasing the power of owners over their slaves.

Atlantic Africa and the Americas had many similarities in the fifteenth century including numerous ethnic states, kingship, frequent wars, hierarchical social structures with strong kinship bonds, multiple religions with prominent priesthoods, indigenous slavery, a variety of languages and dialects, and sedentary agriculture. However, the consequences of contacts with Europe in the fifteenth and sixteenth centuries would be very different. Following the defeat of the Aztec and Inca, the Spaniards established direct rule in the Americas. Other than in the kingdom of Kongo, the Portuguese and other Europeans were unable to establish direct control over African peoples and depended upon the goodwill of local rulers to engage in trade until the nineteenth century. African political and military resources and the prevalence of malaria, yellow fever, and gastrointestinal ailments also slowed the advance of Europeans. With the passage of time, however, the balance of power shifted to Europeans, as measured in the growing volume of the slave trade. As a result of this cruel trade, Africa made important demographic and cultural contributions to colonial Latin America.

First Encounters in the New World

First Encounters

Within this seafaring environment, an obscure Genoese seaman named Christopher Columbus appeared in Lisbon in 1476. Having already sailed in the Mediterranean and possibly to Iceland, he now joined the mariners most advanced in long-distance travel. He sailed with the Portuguese, married the daughter of one of Prince Henry's sea captains, and for a time lived in the Madeiras. A stubborn, brave man, Columbus believed that God had selected him to spread Christianity throughout the unconverted world and assumed that glory and wealth would crown his success. Unable to admit his own faults, he was loath to recognize his subordinates' virtues. Thus despite being a capable seaman, Columbus would prove hopelessly unsuited for administrative responsibilities.

Portugal, England, and France rejected Columbus's appeals to support his scheme to reach the Indies by sailing west. His failure lay in both his demand for substantial personal rewards and an accurate scholarly appreciation that he was grossly underestimating the distance to Asia. Bartholomeu Dias's voyage further reduced Portugal's interest in the project.

Then Columbus's luck changed. Euphoric after defeating the Muslims and securing Granada, Isabel and Ferdinand agreed to support his enterprise, in the hope of great gains for God and Castile. Striking a bargain with the mariner, the monarchs granted him a patent of nobility, the offices of admiral of the ocean sea and viceroy and governor of the lands found, and a tenth of the gold, silver, spices, and other valuables obtained, in the event he was successful.

With three ships and fewer than ninety men, Columbus sailed first to the Canary Islands, confirmed as a Castilian possession in the Treaty of Alcaçovas but still not fully conquered or settled. He set forth again in early September with a year's provisions. After sailing more than three thousand nautical miles, the gamble paid off when on October 12, 1492, Columbus and his men sighted an island in the chain later named the Bahamas.

Further exploration revealed Española and Cuba, the two largest islands in the Greater Antilles. On Española Columbus found the gold he sought and a docile Arawak population. He lavished praise on the natives— "affectionate people and without covetousness. . . . [They] are always smiling"[3]—whom he dubbed "Indians" as a result of believing that he had reached Asia. The Arawaks, also called the Taino, had a peaceful, sedentary, stratified society. They cultivated yucca, sweet potatoes, maize, beans, squash, and other plants and harvested fish, turtles, fowl, and other wildlife. Initially the Arawaks shared their food with the Spaniards and, under their leaders' direction, provided voluntary labor as well. This proved especially valuable when the *Santa María* struck a reef and the dismantled wreck was used to build a fort at Navidad. Thirty-nine sailors remained there while the *Niña* and the *Pinta* returned to Spain in early 1493.

Columbus obtained enough gold through barter on Española to ensure a warm reception when he met Isabel in Barcelona in 1493. Although certain he had reached Asia as intended, Columbus found his sovereigns dubious but anxious for dominion over whatever land he had reached. Following medieval custom and a more recent Portuguese precedent, they asked Pope Alexander VI, a protégé of Ferdinand, for title to the newly discovered territory in return for undertaking the Christianization of its inhabitants. The pope acceded and in a bull dated May 3, 1493, designated the lands as "islands and firm land" located in "the western parts of the Ocean Sea, toward the Indies," an identification that neither confirmed nor denied that the lands were Asiatic. A later bull gave Castile title to the lands west of a north-south demarcation line one hundred leagues west of Cape Verde and the Azores.

This papal donation limited Portugal's ambitions, thus causing John II to react strongly. Faced with the threat of war, in 1494 Castile signed the Treaty of Tordesillas. Under its terms Portugal received all lands east of a line of demarcation 370 leagues west of the Cape Verde Islands. Lands west of the line would belong to Castile, thus giving Portugal title to a portion of the as-yet-undiscovered Brazil.

Columbus's voyage inaugurated a burst of exploration that quickly enlarged Europe's geographic knowledge of the New World and the winds and currents most favorable for sailing to and from it. The intrepid admiral led three more voyages, the last ending in 1504. During these same years, a Portuguese expedition headed by Vasco da Gama reached India by sea. In 1500 Pedro Alvares Cabral followed da Gama's instructions for reaching India by sailing far southwest of Africa to catch the best winds for rounding the Cape of Good Hope. Voyaging farther west than planned, he accidentally made contact with the Brazilian coast. This unexpected development proved the wisdom of John II's insistence on revising the papal donation, although for decades the economic benefits of the Brazilian landfall were modest. In 1501 a small fleet that included the Florentine Amerigo Vespucci sailed along the southern coast of Brazil. Numerous coasting expeditions also proceeded north and south from the Caribbean, but the hoped-for strait across the landmass proved elusive. By the mid-1520s ships had coasted from Nova Scotia in the north to Tierra del Fuego in the south. Added to Magellan's voyage, the explorations provided a view of the world's geography that differed greatly from that of a century earlier. In addition, better knowledge of winds and currents reduced the normal travel time necessary to sail to and from the Old and the New Worlds.

Early Settlements

During the same years that exploration illuminated much of the New World's geography, the first confrontations between Spaniards and Indians took place on Española and the other islands of the Greater Antilles. The quarter-century of experience on the islands revealed problems that recurred over and over when the mainlands were conquered and settled. The different realities of the New World forced the modification of Castilian institutions. Accordingly, the years between 1492 and 1519 were a period of experimentation and capital accumulation that prepared the immigrants for the advance to the mainland.

Columbus reached the Caribbean islands expecting to trade with the inhabitants and to establish factories, or fortified trading stations. This focus on commerce rather than colonization was characteristic of the earlier Genoese and Portuguese expansion in Africa and the Atlantic islands. The Castilian tradition of colonization and settlement used in the Reconquest, however, quickly came to the fore. In late 1493 Columbus returned to Española with fifteen hundred men who included seamen, officials, and the first clerics to venture to the New World. The second voyage was organized to establish a permanent settlement, and so the men brought animals, seed, tools, and trading goods, but no European women.

Most of the early immigrants to the islands were from Andalusia. Soon, however, men from Extremadura and the remainder of Castile joined them. Although their backgrounds varied, commoners predominated, and high-ranking noblemen were conspicuously missing. As a group the immigrants had left Spain in the hope of bettering their lot. Though some sought adventure and glory, most pursued the more mundane objective of wealth. Gold or other riches would open the way to social ascent and the trappings that signified the good life as Castilians viewed it: a large residence, horses, retainers and servants, a Spanish wife, and always the ability to offer hospitality to relatives and friends. To fulfill this dream the settlers asserted control over native labor.

Spaniards who went to the New World expected the natives to work for them. Upon his return to Navidad in 1493, Columbus found that the excesses of the men left behind had resulted in the destruction of their small settlement. The men had physically abused the natives and seized their women; revenge had followed. This incident strained future relations between the Spaniards and the Arawaks, although Columbus did distinguish between "good" or friendly Indians and those that were hostile. But the Spaniards' pillage of foodstuffs during a famine in 1494 and repeated acts of violence eventually drove the natives into a hopeless rebellion. The victors subsequently began punitive expeditions, enslaving the natives and demanding tribute payments from the remaining population.

Columbus had organized his expeditions as a monopoly company. He promised salaries but in fact paid his men irregularly. Dissatisfied with their lot, perhaps half of the settlers on Española joined Francisco Roldán in a revolt against the authority of the Columbus family. When the admiral returned to the island on his third voyage in 1498, he found his brother Bartolomé's authority challenged. To establish peace, Columbus recognized the grants of Indians that his rivals had made to individual Spaniards.

These allocations, or *repartimientos,* assigned a chieftain and his people to an *encomendero,* as the recipient was known, to work whatever mines and properties he held. Because they guaranteed access to needed labor and gave the recipient high status, *repartimientos* were coveted by the early Spanish settlers. With modification this basic institution for organizing labor followed the conquistadors to the American mainlands as *encomienda,* a term long associated with nobility and conquest and its rewards in Spain. It persisted as a major labor institution for decades in some regions and for centuries in others.

Both the *repartimiento* laborers and the enslaved Indians separated from their communities were forced to toil in the fields as well as in placer gold mines. Both forms of work produced hardships. The available gold was limited in quantity, and quickly the streams played out. Accustomed to producing only enough foodstuffs for their own subsistence, the natives proved unwilling or incapable of growing enough to feed the Spaniards as well. Food shortages, malnutrition, and death resulted. The Spaniards' disillusionment was so great that when Columbus offered them the chance to return to Iberia in 1498, three hundred did so, each with an Indian slave.

Subjected to new, harsh working conditions and at times enslavement, abused by the Spaniards, their society disrupted, their diet altered, and the prospect for improvement nil, the native population of perhaps one million in 1492 quickly began to decline, and by the mid-sixteenth century the Arawaks of Española had virtually disappeared.

This disastrous depopulation occurred for a variety of reasons. Spanish rule had turned the idyllic paradise that Columbus had described into a living hell for the natives. Nearly everything the Spaniards did created havoc on the indigenous population, but the demands they placed on the food supply and the conditions under which they made the natives live and labor were the main causes of the decline. The Laws of Burgos (1512) and other legislation to improve the natives' working conditions and to halt the decline failed. Disease, perhaps swine flu, accompanied Columbus in 1493, although smallpox apparently did not arrive until 1518, by which time there were fewer than thirty thousand natives still alive.

The Dominicans in particular protested the Spaniards' abuse of the indigenous population, and in 1511 Father Antonio Montesinos condemned the Spaniards for their abominable callousness and exploitation of the Indians. "Tell me," he queried in the famous sermon, "by what right or justice do you hold these Indians in such cruel and horrible slavery? By what right do you wage such detestable wars on these people who lived idly and peacefully in their own lands, where you have consumed infinite numbers of them with unheard-of murders and desolations?"[4] Later, Bartolomé de las Casas (1474–1566), a former *encomendero* who had witnessed the devastation of the Caribbean islands, angrily excoriated, in an endless stream of publications, his compatriots' abuse of the natives and pushed the Crown toward reform.

Critics of the Spaniards' treatment of the Indians posed the fundamental question of Spain's right to conquer and rule in the New World. The response, duly furnished by learned scholars convened by King Ferdinand, was that the papacy could, as it had done in the bulls of 1493, confer dominion over the pagans to their Christian rulers who then would have the responsibility to convert them. If they refused Christianity and allegiance to the Castilian Crown, the Spaniards could declare a "just war" on them. After 1512 Spaniards were required to read the *requerimiento* to natives before battle. The document stated: "We protest that the deaths and losses which shall accrue from this are your fault, and not that of their highnesses, or ours, or of these soldiers who came with us."

Although the Spaniards' devastation of the native cultures of Española and other islands is beyond dispute, equally apparent was the rapid appearance of Spanish institutions in the Caribbean. In August 1496 construction began on the city of Santo Domingo. Rebuilt in 1502 after a destructive hurricane, it quickly became the first true city in Spanish America. Modeled after Santa Fe, where Isabel and Ferdinand had based their troops during the siege of Granada, Santo Domingo was built on a gridiron pattern that would be the standard form for future Spanish cities in the Americas.

Spanish society in Española centered increasingly in Santo Domingo. Although the urban focus was prevalent in Spain, it became even more pronounced in the colonies. A city provided both stability for the Spaniards' lives and social relations and the amenities of civilization that the settlers tried to reproduce wherever they went. In addition, a municipality enjoyed the important right of communicating directly with the monarch. As the center of government, Santo Domingo housed the governor of the island and, after 1511, the first high court, or *audiencia*, in the Indies. A city council, or *cabildo* (sometimes called an *ayuntamiento*), made up of local citizens (*vecinos*) appeared immediately. A cathedral was constructed in the city, and a university, the first in the Americas, was founded by 1540. As Spaniards moved to other islands in the Caribbean and then to the mainland beyond, they immediately founded municipalities. Without exaggeration one can consider the municipality, and especially its largest variation, the city, as the base for Spanish life and rule in the Indies.

The Imposition of Royal Authority

Unrest and discontent among the settlers was revealed vividly in the Roldán revolt and Columbus's failure to prevent the mistreatment of the natives or to deliver the riches he had promised. After having had these complaints investigated, Isabel and Ferdinand relieved the admiral of his administrative responsibilities on Española. They also licensed expeditions to explore and trade in the Indies, and in August 1500 a royal governor, Francisco de Bobadilla, arrived on the island to find yet another revolt. Sent to replace Columbus, who was still in Española, the new governor acted immediately. Soon he had the admiral bound in chains and on his way to Castile in disgrace. The Crown had begun to assert its authority in the New World and to regain the prerogatives bartered away in the 1492 agreement with Columbus.

Under Bobadilla's rule, gold production increased, and the several hundred Spaniards who still remained on Española enjoyed greater prosperity. Neither the settlers nor the natives revolted, although the expanded mining brought greater disruption to Indian society and probably accelerated the population decline. A drop in royal income from the mines, because Bobadilla allowed the settlers a generous share of the gold, spurred the Crown to replace him in 1502 with Nicolás de Ovando, an experienced administrator from Extremadura.

Ovando left Spain with an expedition of 2,500 persons, including many from his native province, which henceforth became an important source of conquistadors and colonists. The largest group yet to depart for the Indies, it included a broader cross section of Castilian society than had earlier expeditions, and even some families. The availability of free native labor, antipathy toward agricultural labor, and the possibility of rapid enrichment combined to lure most new arrivals to the gold fields instead of settling into the more stable and sedentary existence the Crown had wanted.

Within two years of his arrival, Ovando extended Spanish authority throughout Española. He took the *residencia* of Bobadilla, introducing to the Indies this Castilian check on officials' conduct. Charged by the Crown to promote the natives' conversion and good treatment, he relied on the *encomienda* to fulfill this end. The *encomenderos* paid far more attention to the Indians' obligation to work, however, than to their own responsibility to instruct or take care of them. With all natives now encompassed by the institution, the level of exploitation rose and the population decreased as countless labor gangs were sent to the gold mines. Ovando established fifteen Spanish towns on the island and implemented a policy restricting Spaniards to their own municipalities and segregating them from the Indians, whose own villages were at times combined as their populations fell. This policy of "two republics" or separate existences for Spaniards and Indians followed the colonists throughout the New World but was never fully successful, as the populations were forced to become socially and economically dependent on each other.

The Ovando years from 1502 to 1509 brought prosperity to a rapidly growing number of Spaniards. No longer did the settlers face crises of subsistence. Livestock had arrived with Columbus in the 1490s and multiplied in the following decade. Grazing pigs, cattle, and horses disrupted Indian agriculture and thus hastened the demise of the native population, which in turn opened more land to unchallenged grazing. Gold mining facilitated by forced Indian labor brought fortunes to some Spaniards. Others grew rich from trade as the growing number of colonists imported more goods from Spain. In 1508 forty-five ships were involved in the transatlantic trade. Successful entrepreneurs, for example, the merchants Diego de Nicuesa and Rodrigo de Bastidas, accumulated capital that was used to expand Tierra Firme, the continental southern rim of the Caribbean.

Beyond Española

The pressures and incentives to move beyond Española were several. By 1509 little gold remained on the island, and the colonists were anxious to find precious metals elsewhere. The larger Spanish population of perhaps eight thousand to ten thousand, moreover, meant a greater demand for native labor at a time when the supply was rapidly disappearing. In 1503 the Crown permitted natives to be enslaved only if they had engaged in cannibalism. This restriction was frequently ignored, however, and settlers turned to other islands and the mainland as sources for Indian slaves during Ovando's tenure. The conquest of Puerto Rico began in 1508, and the enslavement of its inhabitants followed. The islands known since the seventeenth century as the Bahamas fell next to the demand for labor, and by 1513 they were depopulated. Cuba followed suit in 1511 after a successful invasion led by its governor-to-be Diego Velázquez de Cuéllar, an experienced old hand who had sailed with Columbus in 1493. The island had some gold, and the Spaniards again employed *encomienda* labor to mine it. The consequence for the Indians imitated the experience on Española. Within a decade, few remained. European livestock—pigs, cattle, and some horses—took their place.

In 1500 the exploration of Tierra Firme began. These early expeditions were generally disastrous for the Spaniards. Mortality was high, and survival rather than gold, pearls, or slaves often became the adventurers' principal concern. By the end of 1510 the Indian town of Darién in Panama became the base of operation in Tierra Firme for the few Spaniards who had survived. Blasco Núñez de Balboa, an Extremaduran who had reached the Indies in 1500, emphasized control over his men and cordial relations with the natives. Unlike many of his contemporaries, he realized that good treatment rather than enslavement, *encomienda*, or demands for excessive tribute from the natives would serve himself and his men better in the long run. But Balboa, despite claiming the Pacific Ocean for Castile in 1513, lost out to more rapacious men.

Pedro Arias de Avila (Pedrarias) arrived from Spain in 1514 as governor of Castilla del Oro, as Tierra Firme was then known, with an expedition of at least 1,500 men. He settled at Darién where illness and famine immediately struck. One contemporary reported that within months two-thirds of the newcomers had died. Under Pedrarias's misrule, greed and cruelty prevailed. Balboa's policy of peace with the Indians was shattered, and he himself was executed in 1519 on trumped-up charges.

In their search for easily extracted wealth by 1519, the Spaniards had devastated the Caribbean and much of Tierra Firme. The native population had been annihilated in some places and barely clung to a precarious existence in others. Despite the destructiveness of this early phase, the outline of colonial economic and political relations was in place. Trade lines to Seville were firmly established. Indian labor was organized in the *encomienda*, and European crops and livestock had been introduced. The appointment of Crown officials and the development of religious institutions restricted the authority of discoverers and early settlers. Experienced Indian fighters were numerous. Cuba, itself the result of a conquest based in Santo Domingo, was ready to serve as the base for a major advance to the North American mainland. The town of Panama would similarly serve as the initial base for expeditions to western South America. The island phase was over; the great age of conquest was at hand.

Notes

1. Quoted in Kevin Shillington, *History of Africa*, 2nd ed. (New York: Palgrave Macmillan, 1995), p. 98, from E. W. Bovill, *The Golden Trade of the Moors*, 2nd ed. (Oxford: Oxford University Press, 1968), p. 95.

2. Shillington, *History of Africa*, p. 103; Basil Davidson, *The Lost Cities of Africa* (Boston: Little, Brown, 1970), p. 93.

3. Quoted in Carl Ortwin Sauer, *The Early Spanish Main* (Berkeley and Los Angeles: University of California Press, 1966), p. 32.

4. Quoted in Charles Gibson (ed.), *The Spanish Tradition in America* (New York: Harper & Row, 1968), p. 60.

Suggested for Further Reading

Adams, Richard E. W. & Murdo J. MacLeod, editors. *Cambridge History of the Native Peoples of the Americas*. Volume 2, Parts 1 and 2: *Mesoamerica*. Cambridge, England: Cambridge University Press, 2000.

Andrews, George Reid. *Afro-Latin America, 1800–2000*. New York: Oxford University Press, 2004.

Boxer, Charles R. *The Portuguese Seaborne Empire, 1415–1825*. New York: Knopf, 1969.

Carrasco, David, editor. *The Oxford Encyclopedia of Mesoamerican Cultures: The Civilizations of Mexico and Central America*. New York: Oxford University Press, 2001.

Clendinnen, Inga. *Aztecs: An Interpretation*. Cambridge, England: Cambridge University Press, 1991.

Cobo, Bernabé. *History of the Inca Empire*. Translated and edited by Roland Hamilton. Austin: University of Texas Press, 1979.

Coe, Michael D. *The Maya*. 7th edition. New York: Thames & Hudson, 2005.

Coe, Michael D., and Rex Koontz. *Mexico: From the Olmecs to the Aztecs*. 6th edition. New York: Thames & Hudson, 2008.

Davidson, Miles H. *Columbus Then and Now: A Life Reexamined*. Norman: University of Oklahoma Press, 1997.

Deagan, Kathleen, and José María Cruxent. *Columbus's Outpost Among the Tainos: Spain and America at La Isabela, 1493–1498*. New Haven and London: Yale University Press, 2002.

Dixon, E. James. *Quest for the Origins of the First Americans*. Albuquerque: University of New Mexico Press, 1993.

Elliott, J. H. *Empires of the Atlantic World: Britain and Spain in America 1492–1830*. New Haven and London: Yale University Press, 2006.

Elliott, J. H. *Imperial Spain, 1469–1716*. New York: New American Library, 1964.

Eltis, David. *The Rise of African Slavery in the Americas*. Cambridge, England, and New York: Cambridge University Press, 2000.

Florescano, Enrique. *The Myth of Quetzalcoatl*. Translated by Lysa Hochroth. Baltimore: Johns Hopkins University Press, 1999.

Hassig, Ross. *Time, History, and Belief in Aztec and Colonial Mexico*. Austin: University of Texas Press, 2001.

Henige, David P. *In Search of Columbus: The Sources for the First Voyage.* Tucson: University of Arizona Press, 1991.

Heywood, Linda M. and John K. Thornton. *Central Africans, Atlantic Creoles, and the Foundation of the Americas, 1585–1600.* Cambridge, England: Cambridge University Press, 2007.

Kamen, Henry. *Empire: How Spain Became a World Power, 1492–1763.* New York: Harper Collins, 2003.

Kamen, Henry. *Spain, 1469–1714: A Society of Conflict.* 3rd edition. London: Longman Group, 2005.

Kubler, George. *The Art and Architecture of Ancient America: The Mexican, Maya, and Andean Peoples.* 3rd edition. New Haven and London: Yale University Press, 1992.

Law, Robin. *The Slave Coast of West Africa 1550–1750: The Impact of the Atlantic Slave Trade on an African Society.* New York: Oxford University Press, 1991.

Liss, Peggy K. *Isabel the Queen: Life and Times.* New York: Oxford University Press, 1992.

Lovejoy, Paul E. *Slavery, Commerce and Production in the Sokoto Caliphate of West Africa.* Lawrenceville, New Jersey: Africa World Press, 2005.

Lovejoy, Paul E. *Transformations in Slavery: A History of Slavery in Africa.* Cambridge, England: Cambridge University Press, 2000.

Lynch, John. *Spain 1516–1598: From Nation State to World Empire.* Oxford, England: Basil Blackwell, 1991.

Maltby, William S. *The Rise and Fall of the Spanish Empire.* New York: Palgrave Macmillan, 2009.

Northrup, David. *Africa's Discovery of Europe, 1450–1850.* New York: Oxford University Press, 2002.

Phillips, Carla Rahn, and William D. Phillips, Jr. *Spain's Golden Fleece: Wool Production and the Wool Trade from the Middle Ages to the Nineteenth Century.* Baltimore: Johns Hopkins University Press, 1997.

Phillips, William D., Jr., and Carla Rahn Phillips. *The Worlds of Christopher Columbus.* Cambridge, England: Cambridge University Press, 1992.

Ramírez, Susan Elizabeth. *To Feed and Be Fed: The Cosmological Bases of Authority and Identity in the Andes.* Stanford: Stanford University Press, 2005.

Rostworowski de Diez Canseco, Maria. *History of the Inca Realm.* Translated by Harry B. Iceland. Cambridge, England: Cambridge University Press, 1999.

Ryder, A. F. C. *Benin and the Europeans, 1485–1897.* New York: Humanities Press, 1969.

Schele, Linda, and David Freidel. *A Forest of Kings: The Untold Story of the Ancient Maya.* New York: William Morrow and Company, 1990.

Sharer, Robert J. *The Ancient Maya.* 7th edition. New York: Thames & Hudson, 2005.

Shillington, Kevin. *History of Africa*, 2nd revised edition. Oxford: Macmillan, 2005.

Smith, Michael E. *The Aztecs.* 2nd edition. Malden, Mass.: Blackwell Publishers, 2003.

Smith, Michael E. *Aztec City-State Capitals.* Gainesville, Fla.: University Press of Florida, 2008.

Solomon, Frank, and Stuart B. Schwartz, editors. *Cambridge History of the Native Peoples of the Americas.* Volume 3, Parts 1 and 2: *South America.* Cambridge, England: Cambridge University Press, 2000.

Sweet, James H. *Recreating Africa: Culture, Kinship, and Religion in the African-Portuguese World, 1441–1770.* Chapel Hill and London: University of North Carolina Press, 2003.

Thornton, John. *Africa and Africans in the Making of the Atlantic World, 1400–1800.* 2nd edition. Cambridge, England, and New York: Cambridge University Press, 1998.

Trigger, Bruce G., editor. *The Cambridge History of the Native Peoples of the Americas.* Cambridge, England: Cambridge University Press, 1996.

Vassberg, David E. *The Village and the Outside World in Golden Age Castile: Mobility and Migration in Everyday Rural Life.* Cambridge, England, and New York: Cambridge University Press, 1996.

TWO

THE AGE OF CONQUEST

Chronology

1519	Fernando Cortés initiates conquest of Aztec Empire; creation of town of Vera Cruz
1520	Smallpox reaches New Spain—first epidemic
1521	Fall of Tenochtitlan; establishment of Mexico City
1524	Creation of Council of the Indies; arrival of twelve Franciscans initiates "spiritual conquest" in New Spain
c. 1527	Smallpox enters Peru
1527–32	Civil war between Atahualpa and Huascar in Peru
1529	Nuño Beltrán de Guzmán initiates brutal conquest of New Galicia
1530	Francisco Pizarro begins conquest of Incas
1532	Capture of Atahualpa at Cajamarca
1533	Execution of Atahualpa; capture of Cuzco
1534	Quito founded
1536	Manco Inca leads rebellion in Peru; Jiménez de Quesada to Bogotá
1537	Pope Paul III declares Indians to be "truly men" and capable of Christianization; Asunción, Paraguay, founded
1538	Battle of Las Salinas and execution of Diego de Almagro
1540	Assassination of Francisco Pizarro; Santiago, Chile, founded by Pedro de Valdivia
1541–42	Mixtón War in New Galicia
1542	New Laws issued
1550	"Debate" between Bartolomé de Las Casas and Juan Ginés de Sepúlveda in Valladolid over conquest and forced conversion of natives
1552	Publication of *Destruction of the Indies* by Las Casas
1570s	Spanish settlement of Philippine Islands
1580	Buenos Aires refounded; Brazil emerges as leading sugar producer in the world

The Conquest of Mexico

The conquest of Mexico gave substance to the Spaniards' dreams of finding great wealth in the New World and initiated a frenzy of later expeditions anxious to emulate this remarkable success. For the daring and imaginative

Fernando Cortés, the conquest brought riches, a title of nobility, and fame, and the Castilian Crown secured new lands, vassals, and revenue. For the native population, in contrast, the conquest ushered in epidemic diseases, depopulation, and centuries of subservience to foreign masters.

Organizing the Expedition

Bored by the study of law and fortunate to have escaped death at the hands of a jealous husband, Cortés chose to leave Spain and seek his fortune in the New World. Reaching Española in 1504 at the age of nineteen, the young Extremaduran benefited from personal connections and received an *encomienda.* He impressed Diego Velázquez and served as his clerk during the expedition to conquer and settle Cuba. Rewarded for his bravery and service with a second *encomienda,* Cortés devoted himself to trade and exploitation of his Indians once the island was pacified. News from the west, however, disrupted this placid existence.

The remnants of a coasting and trading expedition that had reached Yucatan in 1517 returned to Cuba with word of a wealthy and populous Indian civilization different from the indigenous cultures of the Caribbean. Governor Velázquez immediately placed a larger and better-equipped force under the command of his cousin Juan de Grijalva and ordered it back to the land of the Maya. Although the expedition suffered some military losses as the four ships and two hundred men made landings along the Gulf coast to Tabasco, it managed to trade for enough gold to demonstrate the region's richness. At the same time, an emissary of Moctezuma made contact with the expedition. Long before Grijalva returned to Cuba, the Aztec elite was studying drawings of these strange men and their great ships. In the following months Moctezuma consulted with the priests and soothsayers of Tenochtitlan to determine whether the long-awaited return of the deity Quetzalcoatl was imminent.

Discouraged by his cousin's lack of audacity, Velázquez appointed Cortés, his former secretary, to lead a third expedition. Cortés at once demonstrated his energy and leadership. Aided by the well-known stories of the earlier expeditions and his own personal magnetism, he attracted more than five hundred men, one of whom, Bernal Díaz del Castillo, later wrote a richly detailed and beautifully told history of the conquest. As the date of departure approached, Velázquez correctly sensed that Cortés was too ambitious and headstrong to remain loyal. Warned that the governor wanted to remove him from command, Cortés cut short his preparations and set sail on February 18, 1519, with over five hundred men, eleven ships, sixteen horses, and some artillery.

First Contacts

Within weeks of landfall, Cortés had the good fortune to secure two translators. Jerónimo Aguilar, the victim of a 1511 shipwreck, had learned Maya during his unplanned residence in Yucatan. An Indian woman, Malintzin, who spoke both Maya and Nahuatl was offered to the Spaniards as a gift. Later known as Doña Marina, she became Cortés's mistress and bore him a son. Translating in tandem with Aguilar, she provided Cortés with a tremendous political advantage over the Aztec emissaries forced to rely on the Spaniards' translators. In addition, she gave Cortés crucial information about the Aztec state and intentions, in some cases saving the Spaniards from military disaster.

In battles along the coast of Yucatan and again on his march into the interior, Cortés used his military assets with devastating effect. The natives of Mesoamerica fought in massed ranks with slings, spears, two-handed swords edged with obsidian, and bows and arrows. But the mounted Spaniards could quickly flank these native formations or charge directly and break them up. Even when unfavorable terrain limited the cavalry's mobility, the firepower of artillery, steel swords, and armor gave the invaders an advantage. With each victory, moreover, Cortés incorporated into his force the defeated warriors of the Aztec subject states. By the

Fernando Cortés, the conqueror of Mexico.

final stage of his campaign, Indian auxiliaries vastly outnumbered the Spanish conquistadors and contributed immeasurably to Cortés's success.

The Spaniards also had the great advantage of realizing the political consequences of their arrival. Cortés and many of his men had participated in earlier conquests in the Caribbean, an experience that gave them the confidence to compromise and temporize with native leaders until the opportunity arose to impose their will. In addition, the Spaniards believed they were inherently superior to the natives and that their Christian God would lead them to victory. The Indian leaders, not perceiving the general threat to their indigenous culture, decided either to resist or ally themselves with the invaders in response to traditional, local concerns.

Beginning in the 1560s, first Spanish and then native sources claimed that Moctezuma had failed to use all available military power because he had identified the Spaniards' arrival with a returning god. According to one of these authors, when the Aztec ruler met Cortés he affirmed, "We have always held that those who descended from him would come and conquer this land and take us as his vassals . . . we believe and are certain that he [the king of Spain] is our natural lord."[1] The absence of direct contemporary confirmation of this famous speech, however, has led some historians to question its validity.

Two incidents shortly after the Spaniards reached the Gulf coast illustrate Cortés's political skill. Because he had left Cuba in rebellion against Velázquez, Cortés needed to legitimize his command and neutralize the disgruntled men still loyal to the governor. He solved this problem by founding a city, Villa Rica de la Vera Cruz (today Vera Cruz), whose newly elected town council then selected him its chief military and judicial officer. Having legitimized his independence from Velázquez's authority, Cortés further solidified his power by ordering his small fleet destroyed. Cut off from Cuba and facing Cortés's newly created local authority, Velázquez's supporters accepted their defeat and joined the march inland.

Native Allies

Upon reaching Cempoala, the Spaniards were greeted by a friendly and generous *cacique* who provided them with firsthand information about Tenochtitlan. Cortés thereupon began to realize the antipathy that subject peoples felt toward the Aztec and resolved to turn some of these satellites into allies. When the Aztec tribute collectors arrived, Cortés convinced the Cempoalans to arrest them. Terrified by the possible repercussions of this treason but reassured by demonstrated Spanish military strength, the Cempoalans complied. Cortés had gained his first native ally. Yet he sought also to avoid a direct confrontation with the Aztec. Playing a subtle strategy, he released the prisoners and sent them to Moctezuma with protestations of friendship.

Joined by their new ally, the Spaniards continued to march toward the Valley of Mexico via the territory of the fiercely independent Tlaxcalans. Seeing the Cempoalans, the Tlaxcalans presumed that the Spaniards were also allies of the hated rulers of Tenochtitlan and fought them ferociously. For the first time the Spaniards lost valuable horses, of which they had brought only sixteen, and suffered numerous casualties. As related by Bernal Díaz, the major battle was reminiscent of a medieval romance:

> We were four hundred, of whom many were sick and wounded, and we stood in the middle of a plain six miles long, and perhaps as broad, swarming with Indian warriors. Moreover we knew that they had come determined to leave none of us alive except those who were to be sacrificed to their idols. When they began to charge the stones sped like hail from their slings, and their barbed and fire-hardened darts fell like corn on the threshing-floor, each one capable of piercing any armour or penetrating the unprotected vitals. Their swordsmen and spearmen pressed us hard, and closed with us bravely, shouting and yelling as they came.[2]

The intense pressure almost broke the Spanish formation, but in the end Spanish weapons forced the Tlaxcalans to retire. After further days of fierce fighting, the Tlaxcalans at last sought peace and swore fealty to Charles I. Their loyalty to Spain and military assistance to Cortés proved as impressive as their initial resistance.

Entering the Tlaxcalan capital Cortés saw for the first time the urban development of the Mesoamerican heartland:

> This city is so big and so remarkable [as to be] . . . almost unbelievable, for the city is much larger than Granada and very much stronger, with as good buildings and many more people than Granada had when it was taken, and very much better supplied with the produce of the land, namely, bread, fowl and game and fresh-water fish and vegetables and other things they eat which are very good. There is in this city a market where each and every day upward of thirty thousand people come to buy and sell, without counting the other trade which goes on elsewhere in the city.[3]

Both the indigenous tribute system and the urban-based political order suited perfectly the needs and resources of the conquistadors. A small number of Spaniards could control an enormous area and draw off huge amounts of wealth by usurping the traditional prerogatives of the native urban elite and rulers. Because Spanish colonial development would take on this urban character, it was fitting that the military campaigns for control of Tenochtitlan, the region's preeminent urban center, dominated the remainder of the conquest.

Moctezuma's agents arrived soon after Tlaxcala's submission and attempted to convince Cortés that the Tlaxcalans would betray him. Now appreciating how serious the Spanish threat was, they presented Moctezuma's offer to become a tributary of Charles I in return for Cortés's abandoning his march. Cortés cleverly played off these traditional rivals.

He replied politely to Moctezuma's offer but informed the ambassadors that he would greet their lord in Tenochtitlan. As the Spaniards marched toward the Mexica capital, they were reinforced by thousands of Tlaxcalan warriors.

En route to Tenochtitlan, the Spaniards entered Cholula, an Aztec tributary. When informed of a rumored surprise attack, the Spaniards and their native allies responded by massacring some six thousand residents. Convinced by this action that the invaders and their allies were militarily invincible, Moctezuma henceforth made only halfhearted efforts to dissuade them from reaching the capital.

The Aztec Capital

Cortés led his force across the volcanic mountain chain that forms the southeastern boundary of the Valley of Mexico and stood looking down on the splendid complex of cities, lakes, and canals that served as the metropolis of Mesoamerican civilization. Bernal Díaz wrote years later:

> And when we saw all those cities and villages built in the water, and other great towns on dry land, and that straight and level causeway leading to Mexico, we were astounded. These great towns and *cues* [temples], and buildings rising from the water, all made of stone, seemed like an enchanted vision from the tale of Amadis. Indeed some of our soldiers asked whether it was all not a dream. . . .It was all so wonderful that I do not know how to describe this first glimpse of things never heard of, seen or dreamed of before.[4]

For the first time Cortés and his followers fully appreciated their momentous undertaking.

Members of the royal court and finally Moctezuma himself met the Spaniards as they crossed the broad causeway into the capital. After an exchange of ritual gifts in which the ruler stirred the invader's cupidity by providing items of gold, the gifts he knew the Spaniards valued most, he personally led Cortés and his men to quarters in the palace of his father, Axayacatl.

The splendors of Moctezuma's court with its elaborate rituals and opulence impressed the Spaniards. Yet their precarious position in the heart of the Aztec capital was frightening. In a characteristically audacious move, Cortés sought to strengthen his position by forcing Moctezuma under the threat of death to move to rooms in Axayacatl's palace.

The seizure of their ruler provoked a deep crisis among the highest levels of Aztec society. Moctezuma's failure to resist the invaders militarily had already angered many of his closest advisers and kinsmen. Once the undisputed ruler of Mesoamerica's greatest empire, the hostage was now merely a pawn of the foreigners. But despite public signs of submission, Cortés could not be certain that the traditional political discipline of this authoritarian and hierarchical state would hold firm. Popular resistance might still erupt.

From his first contacts with urban centers of coastal Mesoamerica, Cortés encouraged proselytization among the Indian population and sought to demonstrate the impotence and futility of the native religious beliefs. Repeatedly he overrode the advice of Spanish clerics to proceed slowly in order to avoid inflaming religious passions among the natives. Military victory whetted his efforts to promote Christianity, and the subsequent assaults on indigenous beliefs were often unrestrained. Exuberant Spaniards drove native priests from temple precincts and threw down and defaced religious ornaments. After cleaning the temples of the stains and stench left from human sacrifices and whitewashing their interiors, the Spaniards replaced the stone image of Huitzilopochtli or another native god with a cross and the image of the Virgin Mary. The political significance of symbols of the conquerors' religion replacing those of the Mesoamerican gods was apparent to both the invaders and the vanquished.

Threats to Cortés

News that a large Spanish expedition loyal to the governor of Cuba had arrived on the Gulf coast complicated Cortés's plans. Yet with his usual determination he turned the threat to his advantage. Leaving a garrison in Tenochtitlan under Pedro de Alvarado, Cortés marched rapidly to the coast and in a night attack smashed the larger force of Pánfilo de Narváez. Then, by treating the defeated men generously and promising great riches, he succeeded in winning most of them to his side. Quickly beginning the trek back to Tenochtitlan, the enlarged force soon received the distressing news that the Aztec had attacked the Spanish garrison.

During a major religious celebration, Alvarado ordered his troops to attack the unarmed crowd gathered in Tenochtitlan's central square. The assault cost many Aztec nobles their lives, enraged the city's populace, and provoked a massive popular uprising. Alvarado later claimed that the natives had planned to use the celebration as cover for an attack on the weakened garrison, but his attack, like the massacre that Cortés had ordered at Cholula, remains one of the most controversial events of the conquest.

The Aztec made no effort to hinder the Spaniards' reentry into the capital, thus trapping them where their horses and weapons were less effective. Cortés and his reinforced column soon felt the full brunt of Aztec rage. Although the Spaniards' harquebuses and small cannon claimed many victims, the Aztec nearly succeeded in forcing the palace walls defended by the Spanish. Finally the Spaniards led Moctezuma onto the walls, hoping his people would end the attack at the sight of their once-mighty ruler. However, the storm of stones, spears, and arrows continued unabated. According to the most widely accepted account, a stone struck Moctezuma on the head and led to his death three days later.

Convinced that his defeat was imminent, Cortés decided to flee under cover of darkness. His men made careful preparations to avoid detection, covering the horses' hooves with cloth and constructing portable bridges to span gaps cut in the causeway. Finally, they divided the loot they had collected from Moctezuma and others since reaching Mexico. Many of the most recent arrivals loaded themselves down with gold and silver, sacrificing physical mobility in flight for the promise of social mobility later. For hundreds their greed proved a deadly mistake.

Despite the Spaniards' efforts to escape undetected, the Aztec attacked them from all sides before they had cleared the first causeway gap. All pretense of discipline and military order collapsed under the onslaught. Cortés lost more than four hundred Spaniards, four thousand native allies, and many horses before the fleeing Spanish force reached the mainland. June 30–July 1, 1520, truly had been La Noche Triste (the sorrowful night) for the Spaniards. Confident of total victory, Aztec warriors boasted to the hard-pressed Spaniards that they would soon sacrifice them. The Spaniards could, in fact, look back across the causeway and see their captured compatriots being marched up the steps of Huitzilopochtli's temple for sacrifice by the waiting priests. Bernal Díaz later related that before Cortés reached sanctuary in Tlaxcala following this defeat, over half the Spaniards in Mexico had been killed.

Yet even this terrible defeat proved to be only a temporary setback for Cortés. The Tlaxcalans remained allies and provided a safe haven while he rested and resupplied his forces. Native armies recruited from Tlaxcala and other allied Indian states joined the Spaniards for a final assault on the hated Aztec capital. After La Noche Triste, Cortés realized that he must turn Tenochtitlan's island location to his advantage. He ordered a fleet constructed that would allow him to cut off the capital from its mainland supplies of food and water. Thirteen small brigantines were built and then disassembled. Once the Spaniards and their allies reached the shore of Lake Texcoco, they quickly reassembled and launched these small vessels armed with three-quarters of their valuable artillery.

Final Conquest

Cortés divided his force into three columns and began to move up the broad causeways that linked the capital to the mainland. His brigantines immediately proved their value by defeating a large force of Aztec warriors in canoes. Despite the heroic resistance of the city's garrison and the stoic suffering of a population denied adequate food and water by the blockade, the Spaniards slowly pushed toward the city center. At first they found it difficult to consolidate their gains, for each night the defenders retook the buildings that the Spaniards had occupied during the day. Accordingly, Cortés ordered his Indian auxiliaries to pull down the city's buildings to prevent their reoccupation.

The Spaniards also had an unexpected and valuable ally. Smallpox was introduced by one of Narváez's soldiers who had joined Cortés. Previously unknown to the Mesoamerican population, smallpox devastated it. In the confined space of the besieged city, the disease killed many of the people, already weakened by starvation. According to the Indian account of the conquest: "We were covered with agonizing sores from head to foot. The illness was so dreadful that no one could walk or move."[5] Probably many more Indians died in the epidemic than from wounds received in battle. Moctezuma's successor, Cuitlahuac, was among the first victims. Following his death, authority passed to his eighteen-year-old brother Cuauhtemoc. Because the Spaniards suffered no apparent effects from the disease, the epidemic served to confirm the most pessimistic assessments of Spanish invincibility and the impotence of native gods.

Finally, on August 21, 1521, the Spaniards breached the capital's last defenses, and the remaining warriors surrendered. Cuauhtemoc attempted to flee by canoe, but a brigantine captured him. Tenochtitlan, one of the grandest achievements of the Mesoamerican world, was little more than a pile of rubble. Bernal Díaz remembered that "we found the houses full of corpses, and some poor Mexicans still in them who could not move away. . . . The city looked as if it had been ploughed up. The roots of any edible greenery had been dug out, boiled and eaten, and they had even cooked the bark of some of the trees."[6]

Although Cortés emerged victorious, the spoils were far less than anticipated. During the debacle of La Noche Triste the Spaniards had lost much of the treasure accumulated since their arrival in Mexico. Although valuable booty was found in Tenochtitlan's ruins, few of the Spaniards received the immediate gold, silver, and rich *encomiendas* they had expected. Their disappointment produced some ugly confrontations among the victors, and Cortés was able to quiet his followers only with difficulty. In order to still these passions and provide a controlled outlet for his men's destructive energies, he encouraged and helped finance new expeditions to the south and west.

The execution of Cuauhtemoc in 1525 ended the line of Mexica rulers. Although the Spaniards continued to recognize the "natural rulers" of Mexico in the short term and the Tlaxcalans and other allies maintained some autonomy, the conquistadors and more recent arrivals from Spain and from the older colonies of the Caribbean soon became the indisputable lords of the land. Many of these men took Indian mistresses, and a few married Indian women. Doña Marina, Cortés's mistress, for example, became a respected member of early colonial society and married one of his followers. The *mestizo* children that resulted from the longer-lived unions often identified with the culture and religion of their fathers and became an important bulwark of Spanish rule during the later Indian rebellions. By the 1550s, Spanish authority was firmly established in the densely populated regions of New Spain, as the conquered territory was known.

The Conquest of Peru

The fall of the Inca Empire climaxed the initial era of Spanish expansion in the Americas. Later expeditions continued to pursue rumored

El Dorados, and Spaniards and their *mestizo* offspring settled vast new regions. Yet the participants, their financial backers, and the Castillan Crown considered each of these new achievements, often won at an exorbitant human cost, a failure when compared with Francisco Pizarro's spectacular success in Peru.

Early Expeditions

The illegitimate and poorly educated son of a modest Extremaduran noble, Pizarro emigrated to the New World as a young man. After a brief and unexceptional stay in Española, he joined an expedition to the isthmus of Panama. There he participated in Indian wars and slave raids. As an *encomendero* and one of the founders of the city of Panama, Pizarro was by his mid-life a fairly prosperous citizen of a small and obscure city on Spain's expanding American frontier.

In 1522 Captain Pascual de Andagoya sailed in an exploratory expedition south from Panama, hugging the Pacific coast and fighting the head winds. The voyage produced only rumors of a rich and powerful kingdom to the south but spurred interest among some colonists in pursuing them. Governor Pedrarias agreed to let Pizarro and two partners, Diego de Almagro and the priest Hernando de Luque, explore the region. Luque, probably as an agent for wealthier and more prominent men, provided the necessary capital. Pizarro led a small expedition south in 1524 but soon returned to Panama after hardship, famine, and battles with hostile Indians yielded no tangible gain.

A second effort began even more disastrously, and Pizarro was forced to seek shelter on the island of Gallo while Almagro returned to Panama. Refusing a later opportunity to turn back, Pizarro and thirteen men remained. When Almagro appeared with reinforcements and supplies seven months later, the expedition's fortune improved. One of its ships captured a large oceangoing raft laden with gold and silver jewelry, finely woven textiles, and precious stones. Their greed aroused by this irrefutable proof that the rumored civilization existed, the adventurers pushed further south and discovered Tumbez, a northern outpost of the Inca Empire.

Despite this evidence of a rich civilization, Pizarro and Almagro failed to interest the new governor of Panama in supporting further exploration. After borrowing more capital, the partners sent Pizarro to Spain to seek a royal license for their next venture. There he secured a contract (*capitulación*) naming him governor of Peru, and the thirteen men who had persevered with him on the island of Gallo were ennobled. Significantly, Almagro received only the minor title of governor of Tumbez. Before returning to Panama, Pizarro stopped in his birthplace, Trujillo, where he recruited four brothers and a cousin, other kinsmen, and neighbors for his expedition.

The unequal rewards spelled out in the royal contract strained Pizarro's relations with Almagro. Finally, however, the partners resolved their differences and in late December 1530, Pizarro set sail from Panama with fewer than two hundred men. Almagro agreed to follow this vanguard with reinforcements and supplies. After advancing slowly down the coast, Pizarro reached Tumbez. Here evidence of destruction and depopulation revealed that the Inca were engaged in civil war. Joined by a small force led by Hernando de Soto, the expedition proceeded about a hundred miles to the south. There Pizarro founded the city of San Miguel de Piura and awarded *encomiendas* to the Spaniards he would leave behind as a garrison to protect communication with Panama.

Although Pizarro and his lieutenants did not immediately realize it, they were challenging the Inca at a particularly propitious moment. In the late 1520s an epidemic had swept through the northern reaches of the empire. Identified as smallpox by some scholars and the less well-known bartonellosis, a disease of similar symptoms, by others, the epidemic claimed countless victims, including the extremely vigorous and effective Huayna Capac, the Sapa Inca, and his heir apparent. As in Mexico, disease proved to be a powerful ally to the Spaniards.

The deaths of Huayna Capac and his heir provoked a deep political crisis among the Inca. As he pushed the empire's frontier northward into modern Colombia in a long and bitter conflict, Huayna Capac had depended increasingly on professional troops and military advisers rather than the traditional Inca bureaucracy. As a result, the capital, Cuzco, had lost both prestige and power. Thus when news of the Sapa Inca's death reached Cuzco, the court elite immediately confirmed his son Huascar as successor. In Quito another son, Atahualpa, controlled the professional army and retained political control over the newly conquered regions of Ecuador and southern Colombia. A strained peace between the brothers held for nearly two years before Atahualpa rebelled. Disputed successions were not unusual among the Inca, and nearly every Sapa Inca had had to prove his authority militarily. The appearance of Pizarro's tiny expedition, however, transformed this internecine struggle and threatened the survival of the Inca state.

Huascar seized the initial advantage and briefly made Atahualpa his prisoner. However, the large, well-disciplined, and experienced armies that Atahualpa had inherited from his father soon overwhelmed the untried levies organized from Cuzco. His troops took the Inca capital, captured Huascar, and launched a brutal campaign against members of the royal family and nobility who had supported him. Recruited largely from the empire's northern frontier, the victors acted like an occupying army, singling out for particularly harsh treatment the Cañari ethnic group that had provided much of Huascar's experienced military support.

Pizarro's route south brought him close to a large military force escorting Atahualpa to Cuzco. Informed of the Spanish landing earlier, the Inca had sent a trusted adviser into the invader's camp to collect intelligence. Unfortunately for Atahualpa, his ambassador dismissed the Spaniards as an insignificant fighting force and arrogantly claimed that he could take them prisoner with a few hundred men. Pizarro, on the other hand, received remarkably good information about the Inca. He not only knew about the civil war but also managed to communicate with both camps through Indian youths he had captured on an earlier expedition and who now served him as interpreters and spies.

Cajamarca

As the Spanish and Inca forces approached the valley of Cajamarca, Pizarro sent a detachment of cavalry under Hernando de Soto's command to invite Atahualpa to meet. The Sapa Inca at last agreed, and that night Pizarro and his captains met to discuss how they would apply the well-tried model of capturing the enemy leader. With a victorious Inca army at least forty thousand strong camped across the valley, their situation was precarious.

Having determined to seize Atahualpa when he entered Cajamarca, the Spaniards carefully placed men to strike swiftly. Not suspecting his fate, Atahualpa left most of his armed soldiers on the plain in front of Cajamarca and entered the city's central plaza accompanied by five thousand to six thousand lightly armed retainers and servants.

At a prearranged signal, the Spaniards, who had been hidden from view, fired harquebuses and two cannons into the crowded square. Their cavalry then charged into the massed, defenseless Indian formations, cutting down men by the score. The terrified natives attempted to flee but found the city's adobe walls blocked their way. Many were crushed to death as they struggled to escape. As the walls collapsed and the terrified survivors fled onto the plain, the waiting troops panicked as well, and the Spanish cavalry, in pursuit, sealed this initial victory. In the square, Pizarro and his companions reached Atahualpa and took him captive.

The results of this day, November 16, 1532, were remarkable even to the participants. Although not a single Spaniard was killed, and only a few suffered superficial wounds, probably at least fifteen hundred Indians, and by some accounts many more, perished and thousands more were wounded. Surrounded by his victorious army and misinformed about Spanish weapons, the Sapa Inca had underestimated the invaders' fighting potential and stumbled into a well-sprung trap. Without pikes or other means to stop the charging horses, the Inca foot soldiers were nearly defenseless. Their long-distance weapons—stones, arrows, and light spears—had little effect against the Europeans' armor.

The capture of Atahualpa and the unexpected military disaster paralyzed a state already shaken by the recent civil war. Without orders from their monarch, Atahualpa's generals hesitated to act, as they feared that a direct attack would cost his life. The defeated supporters of Huascar, on the other hand, now perceived the Spaniards as allies against the hated usurper Atahualpa.

Housed in the building in which Pizarro resided, Atahualpa shared his meals with the Spanish leaders and tried to determine their plans. Again the Spaniards proved more astute. Pizarro guessed correctly that he could compel Atahualpa to serve Spanish interests. Atahualpa, having observed the plundering of Cajamarca and his abandoned military camp, mistakenly believed that the invaders would leave Peru after seizing whatever treasure they could find. This erroneous belief prompted his boastful offer to ransom himself by filling a large room with gold and another twice over with silver. Pizarro quickly accepted and promised to free the Sapa Inca and establish him in his former capital of Quito once the terms were fulfilled. Atahualpa then sent agents throughout the empire to collect and transport gold and silver to Cajamarca.

In retrospect it is clear that in a futile effort to protect himself, Atahualpa squandered any opportunity to save the Andean peoples from Spanish domination. For despite the events at Cajamarca, his generals still commanded several undefeated armies, whereas the Spaniards were isolated geographically and months away from reinforcements and supplies. But Atahualpa, an absolute monarch even while a prisoner, used his authority to organize the collection and delivery of his ransom rather than to order an attack on his captors.

Atahualpa's rule, however, was recent and fragile, the result of his crushing military defeat of Huascar. Once Pizarro discovered that one of the Sapa Inca's generals held Huascar captive, he ordered his prisoner to deliver his brother safely to the Spanish camp. Instead, Atahualpa, who still thought Huascar and his supporters were the primary threat to his authority, ordered his brother's execution. This political murder was not, however, an isolated incident but only the latest royal murder that Atahualpa had ordered.

Hoping to gain his freedom, Atahualpa encouraged Pizarro to send some Spaniards to help organize the collection and delivery of his ransom. He identified temples at Cuzco and the ancient pre-Inca temple of Pachacamac as particularly valuable. By targeting certain southern shrines located in areas that had supported Huascar, Atahualpa sought further retribution for political disloyalty; the recent civil war still colored his actions. Pizarro duly dispatched small groups of Spaniards to various parts of the empire, and gold and silver flowed back to Cajamarca.

Although the specified amount was not collected, Atahualpa's ransom was indeed worthy of a great king. The Spaniards melted down 11 tons of worked gold to produce 13,420 pounds of 22-carat gold and obtained another 26,000 pounds of pure silver. Each infantryman present at Cajamarca received as his share the incredible sum of 45 pounds of gold and 90 pounds of silver. As was common in all Spanish expeditions, a cavalryman received double the foot soldier's share and the captains even more. Francisco Pizarro received 630 pounds of gold and 1,260 pounds of silver, seven times the share of a cavalryman. Shortly after the ransom's division, Diego de Almagro arrived with 150 reinforcements. The miniscule shares he and his men got from the spoils fueled deep resentment and gave rise to lasting factionalism.

With the ransom distributed, the Spaniards had no reason to remain in Cajamarca. Cuzco beckoned with its great wealth and large population. But

Atahualpa posed a problem. Almagro and the most recent arrivals wanted him executed as a traitor. They traced to him rumors of massing Inca armies, and some local Inca officials appeared to corroborate their ruler's guilt and thus to feed the Spaniards' fear of attack. Pizarro at first hesitated to execute a reigning monarch but then yielded to the pressure. There was neither a trial nor an opportunity for a defense. Provoked largely by fear and greed, Pizarro and his captains simply sentenced the Sapa Inca to death by burning in July 1533. But because the priest Valverde had convinced Atahualpa to accept Christian baptism, he was executed by garroting.

Consolidation of Spanish Power

Despite executing Atahualpa, Pizarro realized the usefulness of his office and quickly appointed a compliant successor, Tupac Huallpa. When this willing puppet died on the march to Cuzco, his brother Manco Inca replaced him. In addition to these political actions, the march to Cuzco produced the conquest's first large-scale pitched battles. Spanish mounted units of fewer than one hundred men defeated the same army that had easily crushed the forces of Huascar and taken Cuzco. In this conflict, Pizarro, like Cortés, had the support of indigenous allies. The Cañari and other ethnic groups that supported Huascar in the civil war seized the opportunity to take revenge on Atahualpa's generals. By the time Pizarro reached the Inca capital, Atahualpa's military leadership was demoralized. Unable to withstand the onslaught, the remnants of the Sapa Inca's once-proud army fled north toward Quito.

Cuzco yielded an even greater treasure than Atahualpa's ransom. In its division Almagro and his men received a substantial share, but the greater number of participants reduced the reward of each. Consequently some bitterness remained between the Almagro and Pizarro factions. In order to defuse tensions, it was decided to mount a new expedition to probe the southern frontier of the Inca realm. Pizarro supplied much of the necessary capital and placed Almagro in command. Manco Inca organized a large force of Indian auxiliaries. Shortly after Almagro departed, Francisco Pizarro also left Cuzco. Correctly believing that the highland city was too distant from other Spanish colonial centers and would remain politically and militarily isolated and vulnerable, he founded a new capital near the coast on January 5, 1535. Named Ciudad de los Reyes because it was founded on Epiphany Day, by the latter part of the century it was known as Lima, a corruption of its native name.

The extraordinary riches that the Spaniards seized in Peru immediately lured their compatriots away from more-established colonies. One of the most famous adventurers thus attracted was the veteran captain Pedro de Alvarado. Not satisfied with the wealth he had already won in Mexico and the results of his conquest of Guatemala, he led a force south to conquer the northern reaches of the Inca Empire. News of this alarming threat to the interests of the Pizarro-Almagro partnership reached their lieutenant Sebastián de Benalcázar, who quickly organized a mixed force of Spaniards and Indians loyal to Huascar and marched on Quito. While Alvarado struggled through the coastal jungles, Benalcázar moved directly into the Andes and engaged the largest of Atahualpa's remaining armies. Once again the Spaniards and their Indian allies demonstrated battlefield superiority. The defeated Inca army burned and abandoned Quito, but Rumiñavi, the leader of the resistance, was finally captured and then burned alive. Alvarado, having reached the highland after Benalcázar's destruction of Inca military power, accepted a bribe of 100,000 gold pesos to return to Guatemala. Many of his followers, however, remained in Peru.

Inca Rebellion

In Cuzco Manco Inca ruled only a shadow kingdom. Both Almagro and Francisco Pizarro had treated him with great courtesy and had sought to protect the useful fiction of his independent authority. But even though Manco enjoyed immense prestige among the indigenous population, the lowliest Spaniard considered himself the Sapa Inca's superior. Spanish exactions and mistreatment finally pushed these defeated peoples too far; the factions of the civil war were ready to unite and rebel under Manco's leadership. Although the Sapa Inca's first effort to flee miscarried, he eventually escaped Cuzco and joined his troops. In early 1536, supported by an army of perhaps 100,000, Manco began to besiege Cuzco while subordinate commanders moved to attack other Spanish settlements.

During the three years since the Spanish surprise attack at Cajamarca, Inca commanders had learned how to neutralize some of the invaders' military advantages. By waiting patiently until the Spaniards were deployed in steep terrain where their horses could not charge, the Inca could maintain their positions and crush them under a rain of rocks, arrows, and spears. Using this approach, Inca troops annihilated large expeditions sent from Lima to relieve the siege at Cuzco. Indeed, the number of Spanish casualties exceeded the number of Spaniards who had been present with Pizarro at Cajamarca.

Despite winning several battles, however, Manco's troops failed to dislodge the Spaniards from Peru. The inability of a native army of more than sixty thousand to force fewer than two hundred Spaniards to surrender in Cuzco demonstrated definitively the permanence of Pizarro's victory. An attack on Lima by the Inca army that had defeated the relief columns ended in the near massacre of some of Manco's finest troops by a Spanish force led by Francisco Pizarro himself. As his main force melted away for the planting season, Manco lifted the siege and retreated toward Vilcabamba where an independent Inca kingdom was maintained until 1572. Frustrated by Manco's continued resistance, Pizarro took revenge on the Sapa Inca's wife Cura Ocllo. She was stripped, beaten, and shot to death by arrows, and later the Spaniards floated her body down the Yucay River so that Manco's forces would find it.

Civil War

Internal divisions prevented the victorious Spaniards from immediately following up their advantage. During the last stage of the siege of Cuzco in 1537, the disillusioned survivors of Almagro's expedition returned from Chile. After a long and difficult march, they had little to show for their hardships. Almost all of the Indian porters and scores of Spaniards had died during the difficult Andean crossings. Back in Cuzco Almagro sought to assert his claim to govern this important city. Having just defeated Manco's warriors, however, the Pizarro family was in no mood to compromise with an ally turned rival.

When negotiations failed to end this impasse, Almagro used his superior force to enter Cuzco and arrest Francisco's brothers Gonzalo and Hernando. Although his closest advisers urged him to execute these dangerous prisoners, Almagro instead attempted to force Francisco Pizarro to accept the loss of the old Inca capital. Gonzalo's escape substantially weakened Almagro's position, but Francisco agreed nonetheless to the rebel's demand to govern Cuzco and secured Hernando's freedom. But the peace was short lived. Within days the Pizarros declared the agreement null and void, and both sides began preparing for war. When the contending armies finally met on the plain of Las Salinas near Cuzco in 1538, Pizarro's forces defeated Almagro's army and captured the old conquistador. Hernando Pizarro ordered the execution of his brother's former partner but, upon returning to Spain months later, was imprisoned for his action.

The execution of Almagro appeared to end the long rivalry between his faction and that of the Pizarros. Yet peace proved an illusion. Almagro's young *mestizo* son, also named Diego de Almagro, inherited the leadership of his father's supporters and rejected Francisco Pizarro's efforts to mollify him. The faction's continued frustration ultimately erupted in violence. In 1541 a group of twenty heavily armed supporters of young Almagro stormed Pizarro's palace, assassinated him, and then forced the terrified city council to appoint the young Almagro as the new governor of Peru.

The Almagro faction's rebellion was doomed from the outset. Upon hearing of the civil war, Charles I sent Cristóbal Vaca de Castro to be governor of Peru, with the mission to end the political chaos. Reaching the colony soon after Pizarro's assassination, Vaca de Castro quickly organized the Pizarro loyalists and in September 1542 defeated the young Almagro's forces. Although the unfortunate youth may have been only a figurehead for the unhappy partisans of his father, he paid with his life for Pizarro's murder.

Vaca de Castro and the supporters of the Pizarros had little time to savor their triumph, however. In November 1542, Charles I issued the famous New Laws in an effort to improve conditions for the Indians and to prevent the *encomenderos* from becoming a true nobility. The New Laws threatened *encomenderos* throughout the Indies, for, among other things, they ordered that their *encomiendas* revert to the Crown after their death. For the *encomenderos* in Peru, one provision was even more ominous, stating that "Indians are to be taken away from the persons responsible for the disturbances between Pizarro and Almagro." As the chronicler Agustín de Zárate later noted, "It is clear that no one in Peru could retain his Indians."[7]

Brought to Peru by the colony's first viceroy, Blasco Núñez Vela, the New Laws and the ill-advised efforts to enforce them played into the hands of the ambitious Gonzalo Pizarro. In the 1540s the *encomienda* provided the economic base for the social and political power of the conquistadors and first settlers. Men who had survived the Indian wars and civil conflicts of Peru's early years would not voluntarily surrender their hard-won financial welfare and place at the apex of the social order. Núñez Vela's intemperate actions and ill-conceived efforts to enforce the New Laws finally convinced the colonial elite that revolt might be necessary to preserve their power. Slowly, an armed opposition to the viceroy began to form around Gonzalo Pizarro. The climax was reached when Núñez Vela stabbed to death a royal official whom he suspected of disloyalty in the viceregal palace.

The *audiencia*, or high court of Lima, already opposed to the viceroy, arrested Núñez Vela in 1544, but he escaped and tried to organize an army in Quito the following year. The forces of Gonzalo Pizarro quickly hunted him down and killed him. Following the ex-viceroy's death in 1546, Gonzalo Pizarro became the effective ruler of Peru. Rejecting advice to declare the colony independent from Spain, he unleashed a reign of terror against Spaniards suspected of disloyalty to him. During his brief rule he executed 340, many more than had died during the conquest.

Gonzalo Pizarro's brutality and the patent illegality of his authority worked to produce an armed opposition. When a new representative of royal authority, the priest Pedro de la Gasca, arrived, Gonzalo's military support melted away. By the time royalist forces cornered his army on the plain in front of Cuzco in 1549, there was no longer a will to fight. Without a test of strength, his men simply crossed the plain to join the royalists and accept pardons. Gonzalo Pizarro was tried for treason and beheaded.

Pedro de la Gasca thus succeeded politically where the violent men of the conquest had failed. Although there continued to be brief challenges to royal authority in the 1550s, he ended an era of civil war that had repeatedly endangered Spanish control of Peru. Soon the colony moved dramatically away from the direct expropriation of Indian wealth and production through the *encomienda* and pushed forward to an economy based heavily on mining. The discovery of silver at Potosí in 1545 and mercury at Huancavelica in 1563 made possible by the 1570s the creation of a mining industry that long dominated the Peruvian economy.

The much-diminished Inca kingdom in Vilcabamba that Manco Inca had established after his flight from Cuzco survived his murder and the rule of two successors. Viceroy Francisco de Toledo, however, finally overwhelmed

BVENGOBIERNO
LAPRECIODETOPAA
maco ynga
tona el capi
ynfante Rey
tan martin
lo Ueuapreso consuco
garua yeo yo
ca —

In 1572 Tupac Amaru, the last leader of the independent Inca kingdom of Vilcabamba, was captured, taken to Cuzco, and executed.

the last Sapa Inca, Tupac Amaru, by military force in 1572. After a trial, the royal prisoner was executed in the central square of the ancient Inca capital. His death ended the saga begun forty years earlier at Cajamarca.

With the conquest of the Inca, the Spaniards gained dominion over a populous and wealthy region extending from Colombia to Chile. The ransom of Atahualpa and the riches subsequently seized in Cuzco far exceeded the precious metals that Cortés and his men had secured in Mexico. The number of immediate beneficiaries in both conquests, however, soon paled in comparison with the thousands of Spaniards who arrived in their wake. Eager to emulate the early conquistadors, these later arrivals joined expeditions that in a few years had combed much of the Western Hemisphere in a vain search for other wealthy native civilizations.

The Ebbtide of Conquest

The Spanish and Portuguese exploration and occupation of Latin America followed no coherent plan devised in Europe. Rather, individual ambition, the desire for personal wealth, and family fame and fortune propelled this unprecedented territorial expansion. Frequently leaders organized expeditions and determined objectives in response to rumors of riches or minimal prior contact with a native culture. The funds, people, and leadership expended in new explorations dangerously reduced the scarce human and material resources of existing settlements. Indian societies were the primary victims of these expeditions. They suffered attacks, often for no other reason than they were along the route of march, and depletion of their populations by death and slavery. In most cases, the indigenous peoples fought to defend their territories. When further resistance proved impossible, many natives fled their traditional lands to escape further depredations.

A handful of large, well-funded expeditions sailed directly from Spain, but small groups of lightly armed Europeans organized in the New World explored most of the Indies and conquered its indigenous populations. Cortés's military force, one of the largest and best armed, numbered fewer than two thousand Spaniards when Tenochtitlan fell. Because most expeditions had few men and limited resources, their success, even survival, often depended on individual leaders' ability and determination. The conquistadors cannot be reduced to a type, but clearly endurance, physical courage, audacity, and cunning, rather than high birth or formal military training, were among the important characteristics of the leaders of this era. Only prior experience in campaigns against the Indians consistently paid dividends.

In addition to the challenges posed by geography and climate and the nearly constant threats of hunger, thirst, and illness, the conquistadors confronted vast populations often understandably hostile at the invasion of their lands. Their weakness and vulnerability in an environment of nearly constant danger increased the likelihood that both the Spanish and Portuguese would seize on exemplary violence as a useful political tool for subordinating native peoples.

Central America

After the destruction of Tenochtitlan, Cortés organized new expeditions under the command of his most trusted lieutenants. They were to subjugate former tributaries of the Aztec confederation and to follow up reports of rich civilizations that remained independent. Cortés himself led a small expedition to impose Spanish rule on Pánuco, located on the coast of the Gulf of Mexico. The arrival of an undisciplined military force sent by the governor of Jamaica, however, soon undid Cortés's pacification of this region. The newcomers' greed and cruelty provoked a violent Indian uprising. The seasoned veteran leaders Pedro de Alvarado and Gonzalo de

Sandoval subdued the new arrivals and then mercilessly crushed the Indian rebellion. The two groups of rebels received strikingly different treatment. Alvarado and Sandoval forgave the Spanish intruders who had caused the uprising but burned to death four hundred captured Indians.

Looking toward southern Mexico, Cortés ordered Cristóbal de Olid to sail to the coast of modern Honduras to follow up rumors of rich kingdoms. Once on his own, Olid imitated Cortés's earlier action at Vera Cruz and declared himself governor. When news of this mutiny reached Cortés, he organized a punitive expedition and left for Central America in 1524.

To prevent an uprising in Mexico during his absence, Cortés took the defeated Aztec ruler Cuauhtemoc and some of his retainers along as hostages. As he struggled with nearly impassable terrain, Cortés also faced a near mutiny by followers who were dissatisfied with their share of the booty taken in Tenochtitlan. Before the expedition, similar complaints had led Cortés to order Cuauhtemoc's torture, but little treasure had been recovered. Many Spaniards continued to believe that Cuauhtemoc knew where more treasure was hidden, while others complained that Cortés treated the Aztec monarch better than he did them. In the midst of this resentment, a native nobleman informed Cortés that Cuauhtemoc had planned an insurrection. Making little effort to determine the truth, Cortés ordered the execution of Cuauhtemoc. Remembered largely for this cruelty, Cortés's failed expedition established neither Spanish authority nor permanent settlements. It did, however, initiate the conquest of Central America.

With the blessing of Cortés, Alvarado undertook a separate expedition to Central America, which proved more successful than his mentor's. In hard fighting, Alvarado's men defeated the Quiche of Guatemala. Although materially poorer and militarily weaker than the Aztec, the Quiche were formidable foes. With a population of forty thousand, their capital of Utatlan impressed the veterans of the Aztec campaign. Built from cut stone and well fortified, the city nonetheless proved unable to resist a determined Spanish attack. In Central America, as in the Valley of Mexico, the conquistadors exploited bitter tribal rivalries that divided the indigenous peoples. The Quiche's traditional enemies, the Cakchiquel, remained on the sidelines watching Alvarado destroy the rival capital. Their turn came next.

The guerrilla tactics and determined resistance of the Cakchiquel so angered Alvarado that he ordered the captured chiefs burned to death, an action he eventually had to defend in a Spanish court. As the resistance crumbled, the Spanish branded and sold as slaves thousands of captured Quiche and Cakchiquel. The king's treasury received the yield from one-fifth of all slaves sold. This merciless exploitation provoked Indian uprisings in 1524 and 1526 that the Spaniards crushed cruelly and ended by taking a new harvest of slaves.

The Maya of Yucatan resisted Spanish domination for more than a decade. Because the Maya were not organized in a unified political state, they proved more resistant to Spanish conquest. In Yucatan the Spaniards faced the difficult task of imposing centralized government on a divided and contentious people. Francisco de Montejo undertook their conquest in 1527, but as late as 1535 the Spaniards found themselves able to control little more than the ground on which they stood. The effectiveness of Maya hit-and-run tactics slowed, but could not stop, the imposition of Spanish authority. They established effective political control only in 1545 and did not defeat the last independent Maya group until 1697.

The Northern Frontier

Throughout the Americas, indigenous peoples with decentralized political structures and little agriculture or urbanization resisted Spanish domination more effectively than did the complex and disciplined Aztec and Inca states. Much of this success came from employing guerrilla tactics that dispersed Spanish resources and neutralized the advantages of superior armaments. On the northern frontier of New Spain such tactics made pacification difficult. Cortés's enemy, Nuño de Guzmán, president of the first Audiencia of Mexico, carved out between 1529 and 1536 a new province, Nueva Galicia, north and west of Mexico City. With its center at Guadalajara, the region was initially renowned for the fierce resistance of its Chichimeca inhabitants.

Spanish interest in Nueva Galicia increased dramatically when Indians showed a small group of missionaries and soldiers a rich silver deposit in 1546. Within four years, thirty-four mines were operating. The Chichimeca, however, struggled desperately to hold back this flow of Europeans, just as their ancestors had resisted the Toltecs and Aztecs. It took a combination of mission settlements peopled by pacified Indians from the south, frontier forts (*presidios*), and an extensive system of bribes paid to the unpacified Chichimeca finally to establish peace in the 1590s.

Exploration of the far northern frontier began in 1540. The reports of Alvar Núñez Cabeza de Vaca, who with four other men had survived an incredible eight-year odyssey walking from the Gulf coast of Texas to Mexico, seemed to confirm Indian tales of great civilizations located in the north. Viceroy Antonio de Mendoza selected his well-born favorite, Francisco Vásquez de Coronado, to lead more than two hundred horsemen, sixty infantry, and over a thousand Indian warriors to the far north. Passing through Arizona, New Mexico, Texas, Oklahoma, and Kansas, Coronado failed to fulfill the expectations that had launched the expedition. Nonetheless, his effort initiated the systematic exploration of the American Southwest and brought the settled agriculturalists of the region, primarily Pueblo peoples, into the Spanish orbit.

Chile and the Pampean Region

The vast, sparsely settled Pampean region contained a variety of indigenous peoples dispersed in small groups. These cultures were based on hunting and some agriculture and lacked significant cities, a complex political organization, and a social hierarchy. This physical dispersal and the absence of an integrated political system proved to be assets when the Spaniards invaded.

To reward Pedro de Valdivia for his service in the crucial battle of Las Salinas, Pizarro gave him a license to pacify Chile. The stories told by participants of Almagro's earlier unsuccessful expedition, however, hindered efforts to recruit men and raise capital to purchase equipment. Borrowing heavily, Valdivia assembled a force less than half the size of its predecessor. Leaving Peru in early 1540, the Spanish reached Chile via the less arduous coastal route.

Shortly after his arrival, Valdivia founded Santiago, but the hostility of the indigenous population placed in doubt the settlement's very survival. An Indian attack while Valdivia was away nearly overwhelmed the settlers. Only the heroic, though brutal, actions of a priest and Inés Suárez, Valdivia's mistress, prevented their annihilation: Following the common practice of terrorizing the natives through violence, they ordered seven hostage *caciques* executed and their severed heads thrown among the attackers.

The discovery of gold in 1552 attracted a new wave of Spanish settlers to Chile, and within a year Chile had hosted more than a thousand colonists dispersed in a series of towns founded along the southern frontier. Fertile soil and a temperate climate contributed to the rapid expansion of agriculture and ranching in the region.

Yet this period of expansion masked Chile's continued military vulnerability. Harsh exploitation by *encomenderos* and the common receipt of brutal punishments embittered the pacified population of the central valley. In the south a large unconquered population with an increasingly effective military capacity still exercised control. In an attempt to secure the small frontier forts, Valdivia put together a force of veteran Indian fighters. The speed, maneuverability, and bulk of mounted Spaniards broke every Indian formation and reduced native heroism to futility.

Everywhere in the Indies the natives adapted—though seldom quickly enough—to the horse and to Spanish weapons. The Aztec dug pits to trap mounted Spaniards. Manco Inca learned to ride and use Spanish weapons. In Chile a former groom in Valdivia's stables, Lautaro, developed a devastatingly successful tactic to use against his former master. By dividing the Mapuche forces into separate units that would attack and then fall back and regroup while others moved forward, he was able to tire the horses and reduce the Spaniards' maneuverability. Brilliantly employing his strategy, Lautaro handed Valdivia his first defeat in 1553, capturing and executing the governor. Not until four years later did an army sent from Peru finally pacify Chile as far south as the border that Valdivia had established in 1552.

Spanish exploration of the Río de la Plata region began with Juan de Solís in 1516. Ten years later Sebastian Cabot began a remarkable investigation of the estuary and inland river system. As a result of trading for a small amount of silver, or *plata*, that was probably Peruvian in origin, he gave the river the inappropriate name of Río de la Plata. After three years and the loss of nearly half of his men, Cabot returned to Spain. For nearly a decade, no effort was made to follow up his voyage.

Fearful of the growing Portuguese presence along the Brazilian coast, the Spanish Crown organized, but did not invest in, one of the largest military forces ever sent directly from the Old World. Pedro de Mendoza arrived in the estuary with ten ships and more than a thousand men. He established a settlement on the low flat south bank of the river in 1536 and was at first welcomed by the Indians of the region. Violence broke out, however, when Spanish demands for food and labor outstripped the natives' hospitality. In the resulting struggle, the fortified mud-and-straw village of Buenos Aires barely escaped destruction. In 1537 Mendoza loaded most of the survivors on ships and sailed for Spain but died before arriving.

Buenos Aires and its few settlers remained under the command of the energetic Juan de Ayolas. After securing the town's immediate safety, Ayolas explored the interior. In 1537, he founded Asunción, Paraguay, near a large population of sedentary agriculturalists, the Guaraní. The native culture permitted the Spaniards to develop an *encomienda*-based economy not unlike those found in Oaxaca, Central America, and central Mexico. Reinforced by refugees from Buenos Aires, Paraguay became a permanent Spanish colony.

During this same period, Spaniards from Peru and Chile entered western Argentina, competing for political preeminence with one another and with the settlers from Asunción. In 1553 the Peruvians founded Santiago del Estero, the oldest permanent settlement in Argentina, and in 1580 Juan de Garay refounded Buenos Aires with settlers from Asunción. This second settlement of Buenos Aires overwhelmingly depended on creoles, the offspring of Spanish couples, and *mestizos*, the children of Spanish and Indian unions. It represented both the culmination of the Spanish colonization effort in South America and the effective coming of age of the native-born Hispanic population.

Northern South America

Early coastal reconnaissance and exploration of the northern South American mainland largely occurred as a result of the Spanish slave raids. As late as 1530 only a handful of permanent settlements existed between the mouth of the Orinoco River and the isthmus of Panama. This comparative isolation ended when Diego de Ordas, one of Cortés's captains, used his influence at court to gain a license in 1530 to explore the Orinoco basin. Like many of his contemporaries, Ordas believed that gold "grew" better near the equator. With more than six hundred Spaniards, he sailed up the Orinoco only to have to endure nearly constant battle and incredible privation. His force broken, the unfortunate Ordas gave up. He died while returning to Spain.

The level of activity altered dramatically after Charles I granted the administration of Venezuela to the German banking house of Welser. The king made this unique arrangement in exchange for the Welser's considerable financial support during his successful campaign to become Holy Roman

Emperor. Governor Ambrosius Dalfinger and Nicolaus Federmann led the first expeditions, which were largely filled with Spanish recruits. Both failed to find advanced civilizations, despite overcoming great hardships. As Dalfinger's expedition moved along the eastern flank of the mountains, the invaders found beautifully finished gold ornaments that the forest Indians indicated had come from the Muiscas or Chibchas. Most of the gold that Dalfinger had collected disappeared when the men escorting it to the coast became lost and perished. Dalfinger himself died as a result of being wounded by a poisoned arrow.

The end for the Muisca, the last high civilization conquered by the Spanish, came quickly once the Andes was penetrated. Ultimately, three separate expeditions entered their territory, but the glory and most of the treasure fell into the hands of the lawyer Gonzalo Jiménez de Quesada. Selected to lead the expedition by the governor of Santa Marta on the Colombian coast, Quesada began with more than 500 Spaniards. But by the time he reached the Muisca realm, only 170 men were left, nearly the same number as were present with Pizarro at Cajamarca.

Approximately one million Muisca were organized in an integrated and well-ordered village system located in rich mountain valleys near the present city of Bogotá. Although sharing the same basic culture and technology, two large political confederations headed by rival rulers, the *zipa* of Bogotá and the *zaque* of Tunja, had evolved.

The Muisca enjoyed material prosperity and relative peace but were politically and technologically less advanced than were the Aztec and Inca. They had no large cities, and even the nobles' palaces were built of decorated wood rather than cut stone. Their textiles had painted rather than woven or embroidered designs, and their tools and weapons were made of stone or wood. Unlike the forest and plains Indians to the east, the Muisca did not use poisons and rarely used bows and arrows.

The Muisca cultivated potatoes, quinoa, sweet potatoes, tomatoes, squash, beans, and a great variety of fruits. Along with salt, cotton, emeralds, and metals, they traded these agricultural products through a well-developed market system. Their most famous product, beautiful gold work, depended on this market system to secure a flow of gold ore from neighboring regions.

In March 1537, when Quesada's men looked out on the broad valleys and prosperous villages of the Muisca domain, they recognized immediately that the terrain was ideal for cavalry. The Muisca, however, struck first. They began their futile struggle with a surprise attack against Quesada's rear guard. The Muisca's initial advantage faded quickly, however, as the Spanish cavalry rapidly advanced over the flat ground and turned the contest into a bloody rout. Although the conquest took a year to complete, the outcome was never in doubt.

The elusiveness of the *zipa*—more than the military competence of his armies—delayed the defeat. Quesada's men, however, moved quickly to capture the other Muisca leader. The *zaque*'s palace yielded 135,500 pesos of fine gold, 14,000 pesos of base gold, and 280 emeralds. Under torture Muisca leaders led the Spaniards to tombs that provided additional booty.

When the *zipa*'s hideout was finally discovered, Quesada launched a successful night attack. Once victorious, he selected a new ruler who foolishly offered to duplicate Atahualpa's ransom to escape further torment. His failure to deliver the promised treasure, however, caused the Spaniards to burn off his feet. The *zipa* died in great agony, but without providing additional booty. Quesada ordered the division of all spoils in June 1538. The governor of Santa Marta received ten shares, Quesada nine, the other captains four, each cavalryman two, and each soldier one. Each share was calculated at 510 pesos of fine gold, 57 pesos of base gold, and 5 emeralds.

Two other expeditions arrived in the Muisca region as Quesada brought his military campaign to a close. Benalcázar, Pizarro's lieutenant who had conquered Quito, was attempting to carve out an independent territory to the north of Peru. The Welser Captain Federmann arrived after having found a pass though the Andes. Avoiding a military confrontation, the three leaders agreed to sail to Spain to allow the Crown to determine the merits of their competing claims for the governorship of New Granada. All were disappointed when Charles V named another man.

El Dorado

Rumors of a wealthy Indian civilization located in the interior of northern South America fueled a last wave of exploration. These tales commonly featured a native prince who covered himself in gold dust, El Dorado. Separate efforts to find this astonishing ruler were undertaken in 1541 by Gonzalo Pizarro; Hernán Pérez de Quesada, the brother of the conqueror of the Muisca; and Philip von Hutten, the last of the Welser explorers. The indomitable Benalcázar pursued this same mirage in 1543. The most important result of this succession of failed expeditions was the navigation of the length of the Amazon by Francisco de Orellana, one of Gonzalo Pizarro's captains.

The remarkable and terrifying story of Lope de Aguirre brings to an end the violent exploration and conquest of this region. In 1559 the nobleman Pedro de Ursúa received a royal license to undertake a new search for the elusive El Dorado. A year later 370 Spaniards and thousands of highland Indians began to march to the east. Ursúa proved to be an inept and ineffective leader more interested in the charms of his mistress than in managing an expedition. As losses to disease and hostile action by forest Indians mounted, mutinous soldiers murdered Ursúa and named the Spanish nobleman Fernando de Guzmán their leader. The real power, however, rested with an embittered commoner, Lope de Aguirre, who, along with his supporters, believed they had not received fair treatment in Peru.

Aguirre forced his puppet Guzmán to proclaim himself in rebellion against royal authority and to assume the title lord and prince of Peru, the Main, and Chile. Aguirre planned to sail the length of the Amazon and then seize Panama as a base for attacking Peru. He soon tired of Guzmán and had him and Ursúa's mistress butchered; indeed, before reaching the

Brazilian coast, this dangerous psychopath had executed all the *hidalgos* in the expedition. The 170 Indian porters who survived the voyage down the Amazon were abandoned to their fate on the banks of the river. On reaching the coast of Venezuela, Aguirre seized the island of Margarita and ordered the governor executed.

Although Aguirre's arrival threw the colonial authorities into a panic, he had only a small force left. Desertions sealed his fate. In a final act of rebellion against conventional moral and legal constraints, Aguirre murdered his own daughter, Elvira, rather than have her captured by royal officers. Outraged by this awful act, Aguirre's own men then killed him. His body was quartered, and pieces of it were displayed in marketplaces throughout the colony.

Brazil

The Portuguese occupation of Brazil shared many characteristics with the Spanish experience in the Río de la Plata region. Brazil had no wealthy, urbanized native societies, and the early exploration and settlement of this vast colony lacked the great drama of Cortés's conquest of the Aztec or Pizarro's triumph in Peru. There were approximately 2.4 million Indians divided among a large number of nonsedentary and semisedentary cultures. Along the coast where the first contacts were made, the Portuguese encountered many large settlements. Language differences and a tradition of armed conflict often permitted the Portuguese, and later the French, to establish alliances and gain a foothold.

Following Cabral's landing in 1500, initial contacts between Indians and Europeans were generally peaceful. At the time, Portugal was using its limited resources for the exploitation of the Far East whose spices and silks found eager buyers in Europe. The Brazilian product that found the largest market was a red dyewood, brazilwood, although tropical birds, animals, and some Indian captives were also sold in Europe. Portuguese and soon French ships anchored along the coast and traded iron tools, weapons, and other European goods to the Indians, who cut and transported the heavy logs. Initially Indians eagerly cut and hauled the brazilwood to the waiting ships. But competition between the Portuguese and French for dyewood placed unacceptable pressure on the Indians and undermined the early barter economy. The attractiveness of European trade goods was limited, and the Indians resisted labor demands that would fundamentally alter their culture. As a result, the Portuguese turned to forced labor to break this cultural constraint on the profitable harvesting of brazilwood.

The creation of more permanent settlements and the introduction of sugar cultivation led to a rapid expansion of Indian slavery. Sugar was produced in Pernambuco in 1526 and was introduced successfully in São Vicente and Espirito Santo in the 1530s. Nearly constant war among the indigenous peoples provided the invaders with a ready opportunity to organize the supply of slaves. With the exception of a few captives kept for sacrifice and cannibalism, native warriors had slain their enemies on the battlefield. Now the labor needs of expanding European agriculture transformed these practices by turning the captives into a commodity. The advent of new weapons and a new objective, procuring captives for market exchange, promoted an increase in native violence.

Divided by ancient rivalries and vendettas, the Indians were incapable of uniting to resist European settlement. The integration into the native elite of Tupí-speaking Portuguese who married Indian women in indigenous rites or lived with them in concubinage further reduced the potential for native resistance. These Portuguese males often gained leadership positions in indigenous affairs. Their *mameluco* children, especially in Bahia and São Paulo, later created a political and cultural bridge between a temporarily independent Indian culture and its future subordination in the context of a colonial society.

By the time that some indigenous groups tried to overthrow the encroaching colonial order in the 1550s, the European population, reinforced by *mameluco* kinsmen and a Crown finally willing to commit resources to Brazil, proved too strong. The Indians had their victories, including killing the colony's first bishop and nearly destroying the Portuguese settlements of Ilhéus, Espirito Santo, and Salvador, but the action of Governor-General Mem de Sá (1558–72) turned the tide. Horses, firearms, and metal weapons and armor provided an advantage that no amount of native heroism or military competence could overcome. Eventually the Tupinamba, the Caete, and the Tupinkin were defeated by the Portuguese, and by the end of the sixteenth century nearly all of the coast between Rio Grande and São Vicente was pacified. Although the French established in 1555 a colony known as France Antarctique near present Rio de Janeiro, Governor-General Mem de Sá captured their island fortress in 1560. By the early 1570s, the Portuguese had eliminated resistance by French settlers and their Tupinamba allies on the nearby coast.

By the late sixteenth century, explorers reached what became the effective territorial limits of Spain's and Portugal's American empires. The conquerors had defeated militarily or subordinated in the new colonial order nearly all the native peoples they had encountered. They had accomplished this enormous undertaking, moreover, with few resources and little government control. As each region fell to conquest and settlement, the Iberian crowns turned to the task of imposing order and elaborating the institutions of government, Church, and economy.

Black Participation in the Age of Conquest

Many black slaves and nearly all free blacks that participated in the conquests and early settlement of Spanish America had been born in or had lived many years in Spain. Most were men. Whether slave or free, the majority spoke Spanish, were baptized Christians, and generally operated within the culture and technology of Europe. Spanish settlers and royal officials in the New World soon requested special licenses to introduce slaves directly from Africa. The Spanish Crown's positive response led to a rising tide of imports. In contrast, Portugal was deeply involved in Africa and in the slave trade prior to the exploration and settlement of Brazil. As a result, African-born slaves defined the black presence in Brazil from the colony's earliest years. Nevertheless, some of the free blacks and slaves that arrived in Brazil in the early years were acculturated residents of Portugal. Although racially distinct and retaining some elements of African cultural practice, these free blacks and slaves joined Spanish and Portuguese settlers in imposing Europe's political domination and culture over defeated indigenous peoples.

The participation of black free men and slaves in Spanish military expeditions in the sixteenth century was so common that many contemporaries took no note of their presence. For example, a free black man served as second in command of Pizarro's artillery at Cajamarca, eventually gaining the rank of captain. The vast majority of black participants were slaves who accompanied their masters as military auxiliaries. They were visible in nearly all the campaigns of the Caribbean Basin and were especially important in the conquests of Puerto Rico in 1508 and Cuba in 1511. Because of the importance of these auxiliaries, conquistadors who were accompanied by slaves commonly claimed extra shares of an expedition's spoils. The wealth gained in the conquest of Mexico allowed some conquistadors to purchase large numbers of black servants, and as a result more blacks were present in succeeding expeditions. For example, Pedro de Alvarado served first as Cortés's lieutenant in the conquest of the Aztecs and then led expeditions to Central America and Peru that included large numbers of slaves. An important presence in Panama by the 1520s, black slaves were part of the expeditions of Pizarro and Almagro that led eventually to the destruction of the Inca Empire. Pizarro was so aware of the importance of black manpower and skill that he secured permission to import fifty slaves to Peru as part of his preconquest agreement with the Spanish king. By the end of the 1540s thousands of African slaves resided in the Andean region.

Many black slaves were able to gain their freedom through participation in the conquests. Eager commanders struggling to find manpower for their expeditions rarely asked black men for proof of their legal status. As a result, scores of slaves escaped bondage by fleeing their masters and locating to new regions; a smaller number joined indigenous communities as runaways. Most commonly, male slaves gained their freedom through their actions on the battlefield. Juan Garrido fought alongside Cortés in Mexico. He had arrived in the Caribbean region in 1502 or 1503 as a slave. Garrido later claimed to have participated in the conquests of Puerto Rico and Cuba before going to Mexico with Cortés. Toward the end of his life he wrote to the king asking for recognition and rewards for his actions: "I served Your Majesty in the conquest and pacification of this New Spain, from the time the Marqués del Valle [Cortés] entered it; and in his company I was present at all the invasions and conquests and pacifications which were carried out . . . all of which I did at my own expense" and without receiving either pay or even a modest assignment of Indians in return. He then claimed to have been "the first to have the inspiration to sow [wheat] here in New Spain."[8]

Many of the most notable and influential of these black conquistadors fought in frontier regions where nearly constant warfare provided numerous opportunities to be singled out for rewards. Juan Valiente was a prominent member of Diego de Almagro's ill-fated Chilean expedition, a force that had included many blacks. Later returning to Chile with the conquistador Pedro de Valdivia, Valiente's heroism won him a substantial estate and one of the five *encomiendas* granted to blacks from Valdivia's force. A runaway slave from Mexico, Valiente—like many of his Spanish contemporaries—had overcome the liability of his bondage and achieved a better life in the Indies. Juan Beltrán, the son of a black man and an Indian woman, also became a stalwart defender of Chile's southern frontier and rose to garrison commander and *encomendero*.

Indians recognized the strong association of blacks with Spanish power, sometimes characterizing them as "black white men." With the establishment of Spanish and Portuguese colonial administration and, especially, with the development of the African slave trade, black judicial and social inferiority was institutionalized. The social fluidity of the conquest era gave way to a colonial social order that presumed black inferiority. Nevertheless, some Spanish and Portuguese owners used their black slaves to super-vise the labor and collection of tribute from free Indian populations. Other blacks trained as artisans and directed Indian draft labor for large-scale public and religious construction projects. Some helped introduce European argiculture, especially the highly specialized production of sugar and wine.

Conundrums and the Columbian Exchange

The exploration, conquest, and settlement of the New World produced numerous problems for intellectuals to ponder as well as exchanges between the conquering and vanquished cultures. The addition of the Western Hemisphere to the Old World's geographic knowledge necessitated the redrawing of world maps. The Iberians' right to conquest, the nature of the Amerindians and the treatment they should receive, and the best means to convert the natives to Christianity were topics debated by Spanish jurists and theologians in particular. On a more prosaic level, plants, animals, and diseases crossed the Atlantic both to and from the Americas and initiated a blending of cultures that continues today.

Cosmography showed the first and most noticeable changes resulting from the exploration of the Americas. Whereas Columbus died convinced he had reached Asia, other early explorers presented evidence that the land reached was a "new world," a territory unknown to the ancients and separate from the "Island of Earth"—the landmass comprising Europe, Asia, Africa, and adjacent islands—that fifteenth-century thinkers considered the only place in the universe where humans could live. The Florentine navigator Amerigo Vespucci's *Mundus Novus* (1503) was the first published description of a major landmass absent from Ptolemy's geography, although the author mistakenly related it to Asia. Cartographers soon had to come to grips with these newly discovered lands. The first map incorporating the Western Hemisphere appeared in Florence in 1506. The publication in the following year of a map by Martin Waldseemüller provided a better representation, showing the continent as an independent entity labeled "America" in honor of Vespucci. After the first circumnavigation of the globe, in the late 1520s mapmakers were able to start doing some justice to the Pacific Ocean and the west coast of the Americas. Gerardus Mercator's map in 1569 ended dependence on the ancients, notably Ptolemy, and opened a new era for cartography. Better detail, of both of the coasts and the interiors of the continents, followed the later coasting expeditions and exploration. Already by 1569, however, voyages to the Americas from Europe were routine, and considerable attention had been given to their inhabitants.

Even as exploration revealed a separate hemisphere unattached to the previously known world, questions about the nature of its inhabitants began to attract attention. The first reports made clear that the natives behaved very differently from the Europeans. Their nudity, for example, immediately caught the Iberians' attention. Columbus related in a letter published more than twenty times by 1500 that with rare exceptions the people of the islands went about unclad. The chronicler of Cabral's landfall in Brazil was particularly enchanted by the women there, "just as naked [as the men and] . . . not displeasing to the eye."[9] Equally impressive to Iberian males was the natives' generosity and less inhibited sexuality; they especially appreciated hospitality that at times included an attractive woman as well as food and lodging.

There were other customs that the explorers found astonishing and even revolting. The Brazilian women's practice of bathing frequently astounded men who rarely washed. Worse in the Iberians' perception was the cannibalism they noted in Brazil, some Caribbean islands, and on the Spanish Main. The human sacrifices and cannibalism later witnessed in central Mexico simply confirmed for them their belief in the Amerindians' inferiority. For some observers, certain aspects of indigenous culture raised doubts about their humanity; a slightly more generous interpretation elevated them to the category of "natural slaves"; yet some contemporaries considered them simple, beautiful, innocent people living according to their instincts. Were the natives truly part of humanity? Did they possess souls and thus the potential for conversion to Christianity? Was conquest just? The answers to these questions largely underlay the Spanish Crown's effort to protect the Amerindians and the clergy's efforts to convert them.

The papal donation of 1493 gave the Crown of Castile both title to the Indies and the initial justification for war against the natives, but other arguments soon supplemented it as reasons for the Spaniards' actions. According to one school of medieval thought, a Christian ruler serving the pope could legitimately declare war on infidels who refused to acknowledge papal authority. Spanish critics of this far-reaching claim denied that such a refusal was adequate to justify war and the seizure of the natives' property. The Dominican Francisco de Vitoria, one of the founders of international law, outlined in the 1530s other reasons justifying Spanish conquest and rule. Although Vitoria opposed war for war's sake, he considered it just if the natives sought to prevent the Spaniards from living among them in peace, opposed the preaching of the gospel, or tried to return converts to idolatry. In addition, the Spaniards could intervene to save innocent people from cannibalism or other "unjust death" or to aid native friends and allies. The eminent humanist and translator of Aristotle, Dr. Juan Ginés de Sepúlveda, was more direct. Employing Aristotle's theory of natural slavery, Sepúlveda argued that the natives' natural inferiority, idolatries, and other sins justified war to civilize them. That is, the barbarity that constituted the natives' very nature vindicated their conquest and even enslavement. Moreover, war would facilitate their conversion to Christianity. By the mid-sixteenth century, these and other related arguments effectively supplemented and even supplanted reliance on the papal donation as a justification for Spanish conquest and rule in the Indies.

In 1537 Pope Paul III stated the Church's official position on the natives' nature. His bull *Sublimis Deus* declared the Indians "truly men" and thus capable of Christianization. More importantly, the bull confirmed the Indians' right to possess property and prohibited their enslavement and the seizure of their property. But this pronouncement failed to terminate Indian slavery in either Spanish America or Brazil.

A broader debate took place in Spain over the conquest and forced conversion of the natives. The principal protagonists were Sepúlveda and the Dominican Bartolomé de las Casas. A former conquistador and *encomendero*, Las Casas's earlier denunciations of the Spanish mistreatment of Indians had influenced the Crown's decision to promulgate the New Laws of 1542. A vehement opponent of conquest and forced conversion, he maintained that the natives had sufficient "capacity" to become Christianized peacefully and live like Spaniards. Sepúlveda, on the other hand, relied on the papal donation and Aristotle's doctrine of natural slavery to justify both Spain's conquest and the use of forceful conversion. The consequence, he argued, was to end barbarous customs such as idolatry, cannibalism, and human sacrifice.

In 1550 Charles I entered the controversy. He convened a panel of theologians and jurists in Valladolid to resolve the debate and ordered an end to conquest until the issue was settled. To the dismay of the combatants, no resolution followed, although Philip II's subsequent ordinance of 1573 using "pacification" rather than "conquest" in outlining the Spanish settlement of the Philippine Islands demonstrated how seriously he considered the questions raised. This well-intentioned distinction would have been more effective if the age of the greatest conquests had not already ended.

The most important long-term consequence of the controversy was the use that Spain's enemies made of some of its assertions. The English and Dutch in particular gleefully seized upon Las Casas's allegations of the conquistadors' cruelty. Adding to the anti-Spanish sentiment that had developed earlier in Italy, foreign publicists elaborated the so-called Black Legend focusing on allegedly unusual and unique Spanish cruelty. So effective was this propaganda campaign that a continuous thread of anti-Hispanic prejudice can be traced to the present day in the English-speaking world. In contrast, there was no similar Black Legend about the Portuguese. The reasons were not that they were less cruel than the Spaniards but, rather, that the Portuguese were not involved in the Revolt of the Netherlands, that there was no equivalent Portuguese conflict with the English, and that there was no Portuguese counterpart to Las Casas whose writing the Protestant propagandists could cite.

The Diffusion of Plants and Animals

The New World provided the Old with more mundane items than topics for theological and juridical discourse and royal soul-searching. In their long-term impact, these items certainly affected far more people. Maize, potatoes, sweet potatoes, beans, and manioc or cassava were the five New World plants that had the greatest influence on diet elsewhere. Squashes, peanuts, tomatoes, a variety of peppers, avocados, cacao, cherimoyas, and scores of other plants have further enriched tables in many parts of the world. Tobacco, too, became internationally popular.

Maize was present throughout much of the Americas when the Iberians arrived. Returning travelers soon carried it to Spain, and its presence in Castile was noted in 1530. Used as a food for animals, maize cultivation generally expanded after that date, and by the late eighteenth century it was a common crop in northern Spain and the provinces of Granada and Valencia. The Portuguese began to grow maize by 1525, and the area devoted to its planting increased substantially in the following years. Only late in the seventeenth century, however, did maize become an important staple on other European tables.

Returning Spaniards introduced potatoes not long after the conquest of Peru. By the mid-1570s a hospital in Seville was feeding patients potatoes. It was well after that date, however, before potatoes became an important part of Europeans' daily fare. Peasants and laborers were the primary consumers of this easily grown tuber. The Irish became heavily dependent on potatoes for sustenance before 1700, and many workers of eighteenth-century Europe found the inexpensive starch a valuable addition to their diet.

No other American plants matched maize and potatoes for their importance in the European diet, but a number of others found their way to Old World tables. Lima, butter, kidney, navy, string, and innumerable other varieties of beans were grown in the New World. These protein-rich forms of "poor man's meat" soon spread to the remainder of the known world. Their frequent cultivation in private gardens rather than fields prevents quantifying their importance, but they are a common addition to meals in many places. Manioc, the staple food crop of Brazil, is now an important crop in the tropics, although rarely found in North America or Europe except as the dessert tapioca. Sweet potatoes and yams are now important secondary crops in many areas of the world but have not impressed many European diners.

Amerindians ate wild game, fowl, and fish but had few and modest sources of domesticated animal protein to share with their invaders. Turkeys found some favor with European palates, and Muscovy ducks were imported for raising in the Old World as well. Guinea pigs, raised by the Inca for food, entered Europe in the sixteenth century but did not become popular there. Some evidence suggests that coastal populations of South America had acquired chickens as a result of contacts with Polynesia before the arrival of Europeans, but, of course, Europe had its own varieties as well.

The Old World provided a wider range of plants and animals than the New did, which transformed the use of extensive regions of Latin America and affected diets and economies as well. Beginning with Columbus's second voyage in 1493, Spaniards began to import plants and animals that would enable them to maintain the customary Andalusian diet. Wheat, olive oil, wine, domestic meat, and cheese were essential foodstuffs without which they could not have the "good life" they sought in the Indies. The early settlers also imported familiar vegetables and fruits to complement their dietary staples. The Caribbean islands were not well suited for many plants the settlers introduced. For example, the sources of Mediterranean sustenance—wheat, olive trees, and grapevines—did not prosper. On the other hand, garden vegetables such as cabbage, radishes, and lettuce did well. Melons and a variety of other fruits also flourished. Sugarcane, introduced by Columbus in 1493, immediately took hold and became a staple of Española's economy for much of the sixteenth century. In the appropriate soil and climate, sugarcane could be grown from the Gulf of Mexico to Argentina. Brazil, in particular, began producing sugar soon after its first settlers arrived, and by 1580 it was the leading producer in the world. Bananas also prospered in the Antilles. Introduced in 1516, they quickly spread to the other Caribbean islands and Tierra Firme.

Compared with the mixed results of early horticulture in the Antilles, the initial efforts at raising livestock were spectacular. Horses, cattle, pigs, sheep, goats, and chickens reached Española in 1493. Indigenous population losses due to mistreatment, the disruption of native agriculture, and disease opened space for imported livestock. Pigs and cattle thrived; their encroachment on native agriculture, however, further exacerbated the drop in native population. As the Spaniards advanced from one island to another, they routinely took with them domestic animals, whose continued expansion in number diminished the effects of decreases in native agricultural products. The Spaniards' ability to travel with a mobile food supply, most notably swine, facilitated their subsequent exploration and conquest beyond the Caribbean.

Whereas Iberians purposely transported domesticated livestock to the colonies, rodents traveled there without invitation. Rats and mice multiplied in such numbers that Peru endured three plagues of them by 1572. Buenos Aires suffered so greatly from rats that the colonists appealed to Saints Simon and Jude for relief.

The American mainlands, unlike the Antilles, provided the proper conditions for the full development of European crops and animals. Although they introduced many European plants, the Spanish colonists were especially anxious to grow wheat, grapes, and olives. Central Mexico by the mid-1530s produced enough wheat that exporters were sending it to the Caribbean islands and Tierra Firme. A decade later, agriculturists in parts of highland Peru also were producing substantial quantities of wheat. Indeed, the Spaniards planted wheat wherever they settled if the climate and topography were right. Growing grapes for good wine was more difficult, however. The first success was recorded in Peru, although one suspects that the 1551 vintage was best remembered for being pressed at all. The region around Arequipa was soon producing wine for resale in a number of markets in the viceroyalty. Tucumán and other parts of the Río de la Plata also supplied eager drinkers with the fruit of the vine. Chile, too, developed major vineyards. In contrast with wheat and grapes, success with olive trees came more slowly. An early settler in Lima, Antonio de Rivera, planted the first seedlings in 1560. Despite his efforts to guard them with slaves and dogs, a plant was stolen and whisked to Chile. Over time a substantial olive oil industry developed in a number of valleys along the Pacific coast of South America.

Most colonists in Brazil relied on manioc made into a flour for a staple food and consumed far less wheat than did their counterparts in Spanish America. The wealthy imported wheat, olive oil, cod, and wine from Portugal. Wheat grown in São Paulo and later in Rio Grande do Sul was for local consumption. The importance of sugar for exportation in Bahia and Pernambuco meant that planters there invariably devoted the best lands to sugarcane. Some colonists also grew tobacco and, for a time, ginger for export. Vegetables and manioc were grown on less fertile land.

Weeds also accompanied Europeans to the Americas. Thistles and nettles were but two weeds that Iberians almost certainly introduced unintentionally. In the pampas of the future Argentina, the Mediterranean giant thistle reached the height of a mounted horseman. In Peru turnips and mint plagued cultivated fields and one author complained that spinach flourished to heights taller than the colonists. Clover proved an intractable competitor against crops in the Andes. Taking root quickly in soil disturbed by travel, construction, and mining, the weeds often fed the livestock Iberians also brought with them.

Although the plants the Iberians brought from the Peninsula and the Atlantic islands considerably changed the New World's arable landscape, the introduction of domesticated animals altered it even more. Pigs were the most important source of meat for the conquistadors, but their significance declined with more settled conditions and the expansion of cattle and sheep herds. Cattle and sheep provided not only meat but also other products—hides, tallow, and wool—for domestic markets. Hides also were exported from New Spain and later from Venezuela, the Río de la Plata, and Brazil. The fleet of 1587 carried nearly 100,000 hides to Seville, most of them from New Spain. Oxen in Brazil were indispensable in many phases of the production of sugar, and their number increased rapidly. Planters used them in hauling firewood, planting fields, and grinding cane. Horses also expanded in number after the Iberians settled in New Spain, in the highland pasture areas of Peru and Ecuador, and in Brazil. Chile and especially the Río de la Plata became sources of quality mounts too. With horses and cattle, a distinctive social type emerged in several frontier regions. Called *gauchos* in the Río de la Plata, *llaneros* on the plains of Venezuela, and *vaqueiros* in the *sertão* of Brazil, these cowboys of mixed ancestry played an important role in pushing back the frontier and providing cattle and their by-products to urban centers and for exportation.

The introduction of European plants and animals enabled the Iberians to emulate and in some ways to surpass the living standards of their peers on the peninsula. Meat became plentiful quickly, and the quality of the colonists' diets was well above that of most Iberians. The consequences of Old World flora and fauna, on the other hand, were quite different for the Indians.

Beginning with their settlement in the Caribbean, the Spaniards required the natives to grow and provide as tribute these new European foodstuffs. Forced to grow new plants with new methods, the natives complied reluctantly. They did not have to eat the new foods, however, and few incorporated wheat or other European crops into their diet. The native response to imported animals, in contrast, was markedly more favorable.

Indians quickly integrated small domestic animals into their lives. Dogs, cats, chickens, and pigs did not require the living space of cattle or sheep. Consequently, many natives kept the smaller animals, but relatively few in densely settled regions maintained herds of cattle or sheep. Indeed, the Spaniards' herds caused the natives no end of trouble as they trod through fields and villages, destroying crops. On the frontiers the story was different. In the interior of Brazil the Indians found it difficult to refrain from hunting cattle as large and easy prey. Natives in the frontier regions of New Spain and Chile, on the other hand, herded the larger domestic animals with the aid of horses. Horsemanship became prized in a number of frontier cultures, and the Mapuche of Chile and Guaicurú of Brazil and the Chaco, for example, expertly rode horses in battle against other natives and the Iberians.

Disease

Diseases joined plants and animals in the passage back and forth across the Atlantic. The Indians' millennia of isolation had prevented them from developing immunities against a series of devastating diseases imported from Europe and Africa. Smallpox reached Española by the fall of 1518 and was carried to New Spain in 1520. The disease then moved through Central America and, no later than 1527, entered Peru. Wherever it passed, the epidemic facilitated the Spanish conquest, as it left an astronomical death toll in its wake. Frequently villages lost half or more of their population; cases of villages losing 90 percent were even reported. Measles struck Mexico and Peru in 1530–31. An epidemic that was probably typhus arrived fifteen years later. A virulent form of influenza followed, after killing perhaps 20 percent of the population in parts of Europe. Yellow fever and malaria came from Africa in the mid-seventeenth century. These and other diseases, which included diphtheria and possibly bubonic plague, further afflicted an already weakened population. By the mid-seventeenth century, the native population of Spanish America was a small fraction—probably less than 10 percent and perhaps not even 5 percent—of its size in 1500.

The timing was different, but the pattern of destruction in Brazil was similar. The first wave of epidemics struck near Salvador in 1562 and a broader area the following year. Probably a variety of hemorrhagic dysentery was the biggest killer. As a contemporary described its painful course, "the disease began with serious pains inside the intestines which made the liver and the lungs rot. It then turned into pox that were so rotten and poisonous that the flesh fell off them in pieces full of evil-smelling beasties."[10] Perhaps one-third to one-half of the native population perished in this initial onslaught. Another wave of diseases, including smallpox and measles, killed thousands in northeastern Brazil in the 1620s. By 1800 the native population of Brazil was probably no more than a quarter of its size in 1500.

It was once believed that syphilis had an American origin, showing that while the consequences of new diseases were far more calamitous in the New World than in the Old, diseases were communicated in both directions. Sources suggest that some of the men with Columbus on his first voyage returned to Barcelona with symptoms of venereal disease. There was certainly a subsequent major outbreak among Spanish soldiers serving in Italy. The disease then spread through Italian and French military forces in 1495. However, we now know that syphilis was present in Europe long before the first voyage of Columbus. The virulence of the outbreak at the end of the fifteenth century, though, does suggest that a different version of the disease was encountered after 1492.

Whatever the qualms raised about the justice and legitimacy of the Iberian presence in the Western Hemisphere, it was clear in the Caribbean from the time of Ovando and in Brazil from the 1530s that the invaders were going to stay. To the extent that local conditions permitted, they introduced the plants, animals, and tools that they took for granted at home. Tragically they also brought a variety of epidemic diseases to which the Amerindians had no immunity. Those Iberians who returned to the peninsula carried with them New World plants, animals, an occasional native, and often venereal disease. Over time this "Columbian exchange" indelibly altered the demographic and economic landscapes of both the Old World and the New.

Ecological Changes

Millennia of native American life altered the landscape of the New World long before the arrival of Europeans. The presence of cities, villages, fortifications, raised fields, terraces, agricultural plots, roads, irrigation systems, deforestation, and substantial erosion in regions with dense native populations demonstrated that Europeans had not reached a pristine Garden of Eden.

The demographic catastrophe that native populations suffered profoundly affected the physical environment. With the total population in 1650 reduced perhaps 90 percent since 1492, human exploitation and pressure on the American environment and its flora and fauna lessened considerably. Raised fields in Yucatan and Peru were abandoned, as were many terraced lands used for agriculture in Mexico and Peru. Turtle pens in the Amazon disappeared, along with flood farming on its banks. Birds previously killed for their feathers enjoyed a reprieve. The abandonment of dams on rivers reduced pressure on spawning fish. Although humans and livestock placed pressure on some regions and at times ruined prosperous agricultural land through overuse and lack of fertilization, overall, Latin American forests in 1800 were more extensive than when the Iberians arrived.

Nonetheless, the Spanish and Portuguese conquests and settlement further modified the environment of the Americas. The creation of cities and towns, for example, Puebla, Potosí, and Salvador (Bahia), where none had existed before transformed not only the land where buildings were constructed but also nearby lands utilized to graze animals and to grow vegetables, fruit, grains, and other plants. Silver mining scarred the land's surface with pits, tunnels, processing plants, and tailings while promoting deforestation by using wood for fuel in smelting. The introduction of European plants altered land use as they replaced indigenous crops and previously uncultivated landscapes. The introduction of oxen and the European plow enabled unprecedented extensive agriculture, but also facilitated the spread of Old World weeds and promoted erosion. The greatest changes, however, arose from a combination of depopulation and the introduction of Old World domesticated animals.

Goats, pigs, donkeys, horses, mules, and especially sheep and cattle inaugurated significant environmental changes in the colonies. With few predators and abundant grazing land, these domestic animals expanded their populations rapidly until, in some regions, they exceeded the carrying capacity of their food supply. Where this occurred, their populations then plummeted before rising to a level that the overgrazed and impoverished plant base could sustain. This thirty-five- to forty-year process transformed the affected landscape as plants unable to survive overgrazing disappeared and others that were capable of sustaining browsing or were distasteful or inedible to the animals replaced them.

The availability of land and a corresponding low density of human habitation influenced where animals grazed. Spaniards as well as indigenous communities that adapted to new circumstances selected areas for pastoralism and sought to improve profits by altering the environment through plowing, burning, damming streams, and deforestation. The catastrophic decline in the native population accelerated these changes and made additional land available for grazing.

Some of the most consequential changes occurred when grazing animals moved onto land previously devoted to agriculture. The case of the Valley of Mezquital north of the Valley of Mexico exemplifies the extent to which the introduction of sheep in particular could alter the physical landscape in less than a century. When the Spaniards arrived, a dense native population grew corn, beans, squash, and other plants

The indigenous peoples of the Western Hemisphere found ways to benefit from the plants and animals introduced by Europeans. Here an Indian in traditional dress uses a plow pulled by oxen to prepare his field, while in the background other villagers use horses to thresh wheat. Oxen, horses, and wheat brought changes, but traditional culture persisted as well.

in spring-fed, irrigated fields in the southern portion of the Valley and maguey, mesquite, nopal cactus, and other plants in the dry portion. Trees covered the hills and wild animals were plentiful. Coupled with a 90 percent decline in the native population, the introduction of sheep and their meteoric growth from 34,000 in 1539 to almost 4.4 million in 1589 transformed the Valley. By the latter date sheep had displaced the native population; mesquite and other desert plants covered the formerly fertile flatlands; deforestation had denuded the hills; many springs had dried out; the irrigation system was in ruins; and erosion scarred the piedmont. Overgrazing and resultant environmental ruin brought a sudden drop in the number of sheep by 1599 to 2.9 million. The poverty of the natives of this once fertile region became renowned and by the end of the seventeenth century the name Valley of Mezquital, or "place where mesquite grows," was attached to the once flourishing agricultural region.

European livestock also affected the environment of the Andes. Here, too, grazing flocks of sheep trampled and in some cases destroyed once productive fields and harmed hillside terraces constructed to facilitate agricultural production and retard erosion. Rope bridges common in the Inca period could not withstand the weight and hooves of livestock and fell into disrepair. Flocks damaged sloped surfaces that then suffered erosion during periods of heavy rainfall. Expanding pastures also contributed to the destruction of scarce woodlands, already depleted before the arrival of the Spaniards.

The Spaniards' view of stagnant water as found in the lakes of the Valley of Mexico initiated perhaps the greatest change in the American landscape. Where the Mexica found rich sustenance in the fish, birds, and other edibles in the lakes and used their waters for a highly effective transportation network with some 200,000 canoes, the Spaniards hated the lakes and their salty waters, considering them the source of various illnesses, including fevers, constipation, and dysentery. Above all, the lakes represented floods that repeatedly damaged Mexico City starting in 1555. After a major flood in 1607 that dissolved adobe houses at their base, the government initiated a drainage project that gained momentum following a terrible flood in 1629. Work continued for the remainder of the colonial era and for most of the nineteenth century before completion. Its impact on the native population of the Valley was enormous, because of both the forced labor drafts employed and the loss of important resources for food and trade.

In contrast to the effort to eliminate the lakes of the Valley of Mexico, Spaniards in mining areas sought to harness water. This was particularly apparent at Potosí in Upper Peru. Primarily in the 1570s and 1580s, Spaniards oversaw the construction of a number of dams to provide hydraulic power for operating refining mills. By the early seventeenth century some thirty dams powered over seventy mills that were able to operate throughout the year, provided rainfall was normal. Smelting, used initially to separate silver from ore, made ravenous use of wood from Andean forests east of the mines. The introduction of the amalgamation process that used mercury reduced the pressure on forests but still required some wood. And, of course, mercury poisoned the environment, as well as causing high mortality among workers that used it.

Mining permanently changed the limited environments in which it took place. Sugar plantations also adversely affected the land. Portuguese planters in Brazil employed slash-and-burn techniques and were able to use lands for some ten to fifteen years before yields lost profitability. They then sent slaves to clear more land and began the cycle anew. In processing sugar, they used large quantities of firewood; transportation rather than a shortage of wood drove up their costs. The relatively few Portuguese enjoyed enormous resources of land and wood and showed little interest in conserving either.

In Latin America as a whole, nature made a comeback during the colonial era. Recognizing that the introduction of Old World plants and animals, expanded mining, new technologies like the plow, and the creation of new cities and towns significantly altered the Western Hemisphere, it is worth remembering that the most important single change in that environment was the rapid reduction of the native population in the sixteenth century. This dramatically reduced pressure upon the land and led, in some cases, for example, in parts of Central America and New Granada, to two centuries or more of new plant growth and reforestation. With the total population of Latin America at the close of the colonial era at perhaps only a third of the population existing at the time of the first encounters, the hemisphere's landscape was possibly under less pressure from human population after three centuries of European rule than when the Spanish and Portuguese arrived.

Notes

1. Hernán Cortés, *Hernan Cortés: Letters from Mexico*, trans. and ed. A. R. Pagden (New York: Orion Press, 1971), pp. 85–86.

2. Bernal Díaz, *The Conquest of New Spain*, trans. J. M. Cohen (New York: Penguin Books, 1963), pp. 148–49.

3. Cortés, *Letters*, p. 67.

4. Díaz, *The Conquest*, p. 214.

5. Miguel León-Portilla (ed.), *The Broken Spears: The Aztec Account of the Conquest of Mexico*, trans. Lysander Kemp (Boston: Beacon Press, 1961), p. 93.

6. Díaz, *The Conquest*, p. 406.

7. Agustín de Zárate, *The Discovery and Conquest of Peru*, trans. J. M. Cohen (Baltimore: Penguin Books, 1968), p. 236.

8. The Garrido quotes are from Matthew Restall, "Black Conquistadors: Armed Africans in Early Spanish America," *The Americas*, 57:2 (2000), 171.

9. John H. Parry and Robert G. Keith (eds.), *New Iberian World*, 5 vols. (New York: Times Books, 1984), V, p. 10.

10. John Hemming, *Red Gold: The Conquest of the Brazilian Indians* (Cambridge, Mass.: Harvard University Press, 1978), p. 142.

Suggested for Further Reading

Andrien, Kenneth J. and Rolena Adorno, editors. *Transatlantic Encounters: Europeans and Andeans in the Sixteenth Century.* Berkeley and Los Angeles: University of California Press, 1991.

Annals of the Association of American Geographers, 82:3 (September 1992).

Avellaneda, José Ignacio. *The Conquerors of the New Kingdom of Granada.* Albuquerque: University of New Mexico Press, 1995.

Cieza de León, Pedro de. *The Discovery and Conquest of Peru: Chronicles of the New World Encounter.* Edited and translated by Alexandra Parma Cook and David Noble Cook. Durham: Duke University Press, 1998.

Clendinnen, Inga. *Ambivalent Conquests: Maya and Spaniard in Yucatan, 1517–1570.* 2nd edition. Cambridge, England and New York, 2003.

Coe, Sophie D. *America's First Cuisines.* Austin: University of Texas Press, 1994.

Cortés, Hernán. *Hernán Cortés: Letters from Mexico.* Translated and edited by A. R. Pagden, with an introduction by J. H. Elliott. New York: Orion Press, 1971.

Crosby, Alfred W. *The Columbian Exchange: Biological and Cultural Consequences of 1492.* 30th Anniversary Edition. Westport, Conn.: Praeger, 2003.

Díaz del Castillo, Bernal. *The True History of the Conquest of New Spain, 1517–1521.* Translated by A. P. Maudslay. New York: Farrar, Straus & Giroux, 1966.

Hassig, Ross. *Mexico and the Spanish Conquest.* London and New York: Longman, 1994.

Hemming, John. *Red Gold: The Conquest of the Brazilian Indians.* Cambridge, Mass.: Harvard University Press, 1978.

Hemming, John. *The Conquest of the Incas.* New York: Harcourt Brace Jovanovich, 1970.

Hemming, John. *The Search for El Dorado.* London: Michael Joseph, 1978.

Himmerich y Valencia, Robert. *The Encomenderos of New Spain, 1521–1555.* Austin: University of Texas Press, 1991.

Jones, Grant D. *The Conquest of the Last Maya Kingdom.* Stanford: Stanford University Press, 1998.

Lamana, Gonzalo, *Domination Without Dominance: Inca-Spanish Encounters in Early Colonial Peru.* Durham: Duke University Press, 2008.

Léon-Portilla, Miguel, editor. *The Broken Spears: The Aztec Account of the Conquest of Mexico.* Translated by Lysander Kemp. Boston: Beacon Press, 1992.

Lopez de Gomara, Francisco. *Cortes: The Life of the Conqueror by His Secretary.* Translated and edited by Lesley B. Simpson. Berkeley and Los Angeles: University of California Press, 1964.

Melville, Elinor G. K. *A Plague of Sheep: Environmental Consequences of the Conquest of Mexico.* Cambridge, England: Cambridge University Press, 1994.

Metcalf, Alida C. *Go-Betweens and the Colonization of Brazil: 1500–1600.* Austin: University of Texas Press, 2006.

Miller, Shawn William. *An Environmental History of Latin America.* Cambridge, England: Cambridge University Press, 2007.

Muldoon, James. *The Americas in the Spanish World Order: The Justification for Conquest in the Seventeenth Century.* Philadelphia: University of Pennsylvania Press, 1994.

Restall, Matthew. *Maya Conquistador.* Boston: Beacon Press, 1998.

Restall, Matthew. *Seven Myths of the Spanish Conquest.* New York: Oxford University Press, 2003.

Super, John D. *Food, Conquest and Colonization in Sixteenth-Century Spanish America.* Albuquerque: University of New Mexico Press, 1988.

Thomas, Hugh. *Conquest: Montezuma, Cortés, and the Fall of Old Mexico.* New York: Simon & Schuster, 1993.

Thomas, Hugh. *Who's Who of the Conquistadors.* London: Cassell, 2000.

Townsend, Camilla. *Malintzin's Choices: An Indian Woman in the Conquest of Mexico.* Albuquerque: University of New Mexico Press, 2006.

Varón Gabai, Rafael. *Francisco Pizarro and His Brothers: The Illusion of Power in Sixteenth-Century Peru.* Translated by Javier Flores Espinoza. Norman: University of Oklahoma Press, 1997.

Yupanqui, Titu Cusi. *An Inca Account of the Conquest of Peru.* Trans. Ralph Bauer. Boulder, Colo.: University Press of Colorado, 2005.

THREE

RULING NEW WORLD EMPIRES

Chronology

1501–8	Papal bulls formalizing *patronato real* in the Indies for Spanish Crown
1503	House of Trade established in Seville
1511	First *audiencia* created for Indies in Santo Domingo
1524	Council of the Indies founded; twelve Franciscans inaugurate "spiritual conquest" in New Spain
1530s	Hereditary captaincies created in Brazil
1535	Viceroyalty of New Spain created
1542	Viceroyalty of Peru created
1549	Portuguese Crown purchases captaincy of Bahia and names royal governor-general; first Jesuits arrive in Brazil
1557	Sale of municipal offices extended from Castile to the Indies
1569	Authorization of Tribunals of the Inquisition in Mexico City and Lima
1609	First high court of appeals (*relaçao*) established for Brazil
1610	Authorization of Tribunal of the Inquisition in Cartagena, New Granada
1633	Spanish Crown begins systematic sale of appointments to treasury positions
1677	Spanish Crown inaugurates systematic sale of appointments to provincial positions
1687	Spanish Crown begins systematic sale of appointments to *audiencias*

Imperial Organization and Administration

The New World's huge size and distance from Iberia formed an immutable background against which the Castilian and Portuguese crowns sought to establish and maintain their authority. Ambitious conquistadors in the Spanish colonies and early settlers there and in Brazil sought to become genuine aristocrats with all the seigneurial rights such status implied. Spanish and Portuguese rulers, in turn, opposed the emergence of a powerful, hereditary nobility located beyond their direct control. In addition, they expected the colonies to contribute to royal revenue. To address these problems, the Crowns relied on bureaucrats located both on the peninsula and in the Americas. The expansion of New World settlement invariably brought a complement of officials to the capital of each new colonial territory. For nearly three centuries the presence of royal bureaucrats contributed significantly to the colonies' overall political stability.

Problems of Time and Distance

The distance and resulting length of time for communication between the New World and Iberia affected both the offices established in the Americas and the authority their incumbents enjoyed. Winds and currents normally made the trip from Iberia to the Indies shorter than the return voyage. The following table indicates approximate convoy sailing times in the sixteenth and early seventeenth centuries to and from Cádiz, Sanlúcar, or Seville and selected ports. Many voyages, however, were shorter or longer, sometimes by several weeks. Sailing from Lisbon to Bahia took seventy to nearly one hundred days; voyages to Recife were a little shorter and to Rio de Janeiro slightly longer. The combination of winds and currents made the travel from Belém, near the mouth of the Amazon, and other northern Brazilian ports to Lisbon easier than to Bahia, thus making communication with officials in the metropolis more convenient than with those in the colonial capital. Slave ships from Angola could reach any Brazilian port in the comparatively brief time of thirty-five to sixty days.

A fleet sent from Spain to the Indies usually returned fourteen to fifteen months later. Annual fleets in the late sixteenth and early seventeenth centuries helped maintain orderly commerce and communication by reducing the time between departures. Small mail boats provided supplemental service, but their sailings were intermittent in the sixteenth century and often only two to four times a year in the seventeenth century, despite the growing irregularity of the fleet's sailings.

The coastal location of all of Brazil's major cities until the establishment of São Paulo facilitated their communication with Lisbon. The inland location of Mexico City and Bogotá, in contrast, added the extra time of land travel. Maintaining speedy communication with cities on the Pacific coast side of the Andes was even more difficult. Travel time from

Days from Andalusian port to		*Days to Andalusian port from*	
Canary Islands	13	Azores	31
Española	51	Florida	65
Havana	64	Havana	67
Cartagena	51	Cartagena	110
Vera Cruz	75	Vera Cruz	128
Isthmus of Panama	75	Isthmus of Panama	137

the mining center of Potosí to the Panamanian port of Portobelo, for example, was often seven weeks or more.

The constraints on the speed of communication between any location in the New World and Lisbon or Madrid gave officials resident in the New World greater authority than their counterparts on the peninsula had. At the same time, the distance separating the colonies from their metropolises exacerbated the problem of overseeing the officials themselves. The consequence was substantial flexibility when officials far from the source of their authority responded to local pressures.

Overview of Administration for the Spanish Colonies

The immense physical extent, the presence of densely populated and advanced sedentary civilizations, and scattered rich mineral deposits in the New World led the Crown of Castile to move quickly to gain control over conquistadors, settlers, and natives as successive regions were added to its domain. Most of the major administrative offices used to oversee its political and financial interests, provide justice to colonists and natives, and supervise the allocation of resources—primarily land, native labor, and offices—in the Indies were operating by 1535, although their number increased with later settlement. Fully developed by 1570, the administrative organization underwent little structural modification until the eighteenth century.

The Castilian Crown transplanted a number of institutions proven in Spain and the Canary Islands. General oversight of the colonies and administration of their largest territorial divisions followed the Aragonese model, in which a council resident at court provided the overall supervision and viceroys administered the largest territorial units—Aragon, Catalonia, and Valencia. Below the office of viceroy, the Crown turned to Castilian precedents and introduced regional courts, provincial administrators, and treasury officials. It also allowed the municipality and its local officials to exercise a variety of responsibilities. The one institution the Crown refused to introduce into the colonies was the *cortes*, an assembly attended by representatives from major towns and a potential brake on its authority.

The size of the New World possessions made imperative their division into more manageable administrative units. Accordingly, in 1535 Charles I created the Viceroyalty of New Spain for land running from Panama's northern border into the present United States as well as the Caribbean islands and part of Venezuela. The Philippine Islands also were included in this viceroyalty after their settlement in the 1570s. In the early 1540s, Charles created the Viceroyalty of Peru, which included Panama and all Spanish possessions in the Southern Hemisphere except for a strip of Venezuela. Not until the eighteenth century were additional viceroyalties created.

Soon recognizing that the viceroyalties were too large for many administrative purposes, the Crown divided them into units called *audiencias*. These territories increased in number as the lands and non-Indian population of the empire expanded. The *audiencias* were themselves subdivided into districts variously called *corregimientos, alcaldías mayores,* and *gobernaciones.* The smallest territorial unit, the municipality, included a city or town and its adjoining hinterland.

Listing the territorial units from smaller to larger—municipalities, provinces, *audiencias,* viceroyalties, and empire—suggests a pyramidal structure culminating in centralized authority held by the king and his advisers in Spain. A more accurate image, however, is that of a group of wheels with their hubs in the *audiencia* capitals and their spokes extending to the provinces. The Spanish court, in turn, formed the hub of a wheel whose spokes were each *audiencia.* From this perspective, the imperial administration was characterized by decentralization.

The Council of the Indies

The Council of the Indies was responsible for overseeing colonial affairs from its foundation in 1524 as a "royal and supreme council" until the early eighteenth century. It ranked below the Council of Castile or Royal Council but above all other councils in Spain. Like the older Royal Council for Castile, the Council of the Indies oversaw every kind of government activity in the colonies. Legislative, judicial, financial, commercial, military, and ecclesiastical matters fell under its purview in the blending of authority characteristic of Spanish administrative offices. The council issued laws, made recommendations to the monarch, approved major expenditures in the colonies, and heard cases appealed from the American *audiencias* and the House of Trade. It also made arrangements for *residencias,* the judicial reviews conducted at the conclusion of officials' terms of office, and occasional general inspections, or *visitas.* In addition, it exercised royal patronage over the Church in the American realms and recommended candidates for most of the high-ranking positions in the New World.

The council employed a variety of senior officials and support staff, with councilors assisted by crown attorneys forming its core. The first councilors were men with university training in civil or canon law, or *ministros togados* (robed ministers), who had previously served on a lower court. In 1604, however, Philip III began naming men with neither credentials in jurisprudence nor a common professional experience. The absence of professional criteria for the appointment of these ministers *de capa y espada* (cape and sword) opened the door to favoritism and abuse.

Only a dozen *ministros togados* named before 1700 had prior New World experience. Moreover, those who were familiar with American affairs usually advanced to the Council of Castile. The Crown's failure to come to grips with basic personnel issues thus weakened the Council of the Indies' ability to provide high-quality oversight and administration. The delays inherent in administration by committee, coupled with the ongoing

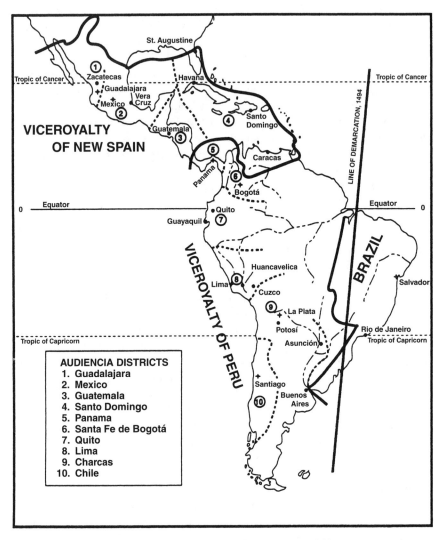

Map 5   Major Territorial Divisions in 1650.

problem of slow communication with officials in the New World, also
reduced the tribunal's effectiveness.

   Illustrative of the *togados'* careers during the Habsburg rule was that of
Asturian Alonso de Llano y Valdés. After study at the University of Salamanca, Llano entered the prestigious senior residential college at the University of Valladolid. He earned a baccalaureate in civil law in 1645 and
soon held chairs in law. After service in the Chancellory of Granada that
began in 1653, he briefly was regent of the Council of Navarre. Named a
minister *togado* of the Council of the Indies in 1664, he advanced to the
Council of Castile in less than four years. Although his well-established

bureaucratic family origins undoubtedly hastened Llano's progress, the kinds of positions he received before advancing to the Council of the Indies were typical, as was the absence of service in the New World.

Viceroys

When Charles I sent Antonio de Mendoza to New Spain as its first viceroy, he was acknowledging that despite having taken political power from Cortés, his earlier efforts to establish order and stability in the region had failed. Mendoza, the scion of one of Castile's most illustrious noble families, introduced the requisite aura of proximity to the monarch and display of authority. As Charles's personal representative, he lived in a palace with sixty Indians in constant attendance and a personal escort of gentlemen.

As the foremost executives in the colonies, the viceroys were responsible for general administration; the imposition, collection, and disbursement of taxes and the remittance of surplus revenue to Spain; the construction and maintenance of public works; the maintenance of public order; defense against both internal rebellions and foreign enemies; support of the Church; protection of the Indians; and the exercise of patronage. At the same time, other high-ranking officials, ecclesiastical hierarchies, *audiencias*, treasury officials, and corporate bodies constrained the viceroys' ability to act independently. The Council of the Indies received from these political rivals correspondence regarding the viceroy's activities and issued an endless stream of orders for implementation. Although the viceroy could delay them and contribute to a revision of directives through the formula *obedezco pero no cumplo* ("I obey but I do not execute"), repeated failure to carry out royal mandates invited conflict and judicial scrutiny after the *residencia*.

Mendoza was the first of ninety-two viceroys in the Indies. Although he and several other viceroys in the sixteenth century served for a decade or more, the average tenure in office for viceroys in the seventeenth and eighteenth centuries was between six and seven years. With few exceptions, viceroys were born and reared in Spain; for them the New World was a place to serve but not their home. Especially with its earliest appointments, the Crown exercised special care to name men of impeccable social standing and demonstrated ability. Most bore titles of nobility. Viceroys expected and, despite legal prohibitions, often sought to use their office to benefit both themselves and the large retinues of family, friends, and retainers who accompanied them to their post. By naming retainers to lucrative commissions and positions and smiling beneficently when their minions married well-placed local women or their wives' ladies-in-waiting made favorable matches, the viceroys set an example that other bureaucrats tried to emulate.

Each *audiencia* district had an executive head. The viceroys themselves exercised direct authority over the *audiencia* in which their capital was located. By the late sixteenth century in the subordinate *audiencia* districts, each court had a president-governor who held executive authority. In most cases this official also was in charge of defense for the district and held the title captain-general. Raids by corsairs, Sir Francis Drake, and other English sea captains led the Crown to replace university-trained jurists with experienced military officers as presidents and captains-general of most *audiencias*. Like viceroys, these men were political appointees, served term appointments, and often considered the Americas a place for a tour of duty rather than a permanent residence. Although some entered into illegal commercial activities with local entrepreneurs for private financial gain, their usual intention was to return to Spain with their earnings rather than to invest permanently in local production. This sentiment helps distinguish these term appointees from those men named to lifetime positions: *audiencia* ministers, treasury officials, and numerous municipal officeholders.

Native Sons, Radicados, *and Outsiders*

Most officials became enmeshed in the local society of the city to which they were posted. Some were "native sons," men with positions in the region of their birth. Others were *radicados*, men born elsewhere who had become "rooted" in local society. Although "outsiders," or newcomers to the region of service, regularly received bureaucratic positions, those with lifetime appointments tended to become *radicados* within a few years. Thus most officeholders were fully integrated into local society and were joined to nonofficeholders in a myriad of social and economic ways. Keenly sensitive to local needs, on occasion they could frustrate the implementation of unpopular royal legislation.

For high-ranking positions in the colonies, the Castilian Crown preferred to name outsiders. The sale of appointments in the seventeenth and early eighteenth centuries, however, compromised this principle. Native sons and *radicados* increased in number and prominence while royal control over colonial government fell to its nadir around 1750. Conversely, local elites enjoyed an unprecedented access to power, both directly through securing offices and indirectly through family and economic ties to officeholders.

The Sale of Offices and Appointments in Spanish America

Following the Crown's bankruptcy in 1557, Philip II extended the practice of selling offices from Castile to the Indies. Municipal offices were among the first to be affected, as the Crown not only put them up for sale but also increased their number in its search for additional revenue. By 1606 the list of posts for sale included the full range of fee-collecting, honorific, and municipal offices. A decree in that year provided that present and future purchasers could hold their posts in full propriety and could pass them on to heirs upon payment of specified taxes. The solid entrenchment of local families in local office for generations, in short, was blessed by law.

The municipality was the cornerstone of Spanish rule and settlement. Wherever colonists settled, they created a town council (*cabildo*) to oversee the development and administration of the new community. Originally they elected aldermen to administer town affairs and magistrates to provide local justice. Additional officials included a clerk, a sheriff, a standard bearer, and an inspector of weights and measures. The *cabildo* distributed town lots and nearby garden plots, supervised the construction and maintenance of roads and public works, provided protection against fraud in the markets and against criminal activities in general, regulated holidays and processions, and performed a variety of other duties essential to a settled, civilized existence. For revenue the *cabildos* relied on the rent or lease of town property, local judicial fines, and other modest sources.

An examination of Lima's city council illustrates the expansion of locally born aldermen after three *limeños* purchased their offices in 1561. By 1575 native sons began to outnumber their peninsular counterparts. With rare exceptions, *limeños* henceforth enjoyed numerical preponderance. Similar extensive local representation was present in the elected office of magistrate. Native sons also dominated in Mexico City and numerous other locations. Although the power of the Spanish American city councils declined in the seventeenth and eighteenth centuries, municipal office positions still enhanced the social status of incumbents.

Excluded from the category of salable offices were positions that the Crown correctly considered most central to its maintenance of authority, revenue, and security—those held by the political administrators and professional bureaucrats. Under unrelenting financial pressure, however, the Crown gradually turned appointments to these offices as well into a source of revenue, although never alienating the posts in perpetuity.

When Spain's repeated involvement in European wars exhausted the Crown's finances, it started selling appointments to treasury posts and the tribunals of accounts in 1633. Provincial administrative positions went on the block in 1677. A decade later the systematic sale of *audiencia* appointments began, and by 1700 a desperate Crown had even sold appointments to the office of viceroy.

The importance of the sale of offices and appointments to the composition of the bureaucracy and its activities cannot be overestimated. First, sales altered the character of bureaucratic recruitment. Service at home, if an appropriate position were available, was far more attractive for both peninsulars and creoles than was service in another district on either side of the Atlantic. Thus an immediate result of such sales was to raise the proportion of native sons and *radicados* in bureaucratic offices. The necessary corollary to this changed recruitment was diminished royal authority over colonial officeholders. In addition, the purchase of an office increased the pressure on the incumbent to secure not only a reliable income but also a profit on his investment. Given the modest salaries associated with most non-fee-earning positions, the temptation to resort to extralegal sources of income was irresistible for many bureaucrats. This, too, worked against the Crown's interest.

Treasury officials throughout the Indies and auditors of the tribunals of accounts established in Lima, Mexico City, and Santa Fe de Bogotá in 1605 received lifetime appointments. Even though these officials usually earned substantially lower salaries than did the *audiencia* ministers, their compensation was well above that earned by the average government employee. Because of the salary, rank, security, and, in somes cases at least, financial opportunities available for a person with access to government funds, there was considerable demand for appointments.

When in 1633 the Crown finally turned to systematically selling appointments to treasury positions, it found that the purchasers were often young and inexperienced. Their youth ensured both limited maturity and knowledge and, barring premature death, decades of service. In addition, as money replaced merit as the primary criterion for appointment, would-be purchasers sought the most coveted posts, those in the viceregal capitals. Native sons were especially anxious to secure these offices and, once in place, showed no desire to leave. This limited the potential for advancement from regional subtreasuries and undoubtedly intensified the social, political, and economic ties that the officials shared with the leading local families.

The *audiencias* also had little turnover. The tribunals were the supreme courts of their districts and subject to appeal to the Council of the Indies only in cases involving very large sums of money. In addition, they had administrative and legislative responsibilities. Named for life or the pleasure of the king, *audiencia* ministers commonly resided many years in a single location. Once in Mexico City or Lima, ministers most commonly left the court only by death. The combination of major responsibilities and protracted service by their ministers made the *audiencias* the most important single civil institution in the Spanish colonies.

Before 1687, few men began their *audiencia* careers in their home district. Nonetheless, the Crown named Americans in every decade from the 1580s onward: Nearly a quarter of all *audiencia* appointees from 1610 to 1687 were creoles. The initiation of systematic sales of *audiencia* appointments in late 1687 not only enabled more Americans to reach the courts but also increased the number of native sons. By resorting to the sale of supernumerary or extra appointments, moreover, the Crown clogged the normal chain of advancement from the smaller regional courts to the viceregal courts and greatly expanded the number of *radicados* throughout the system. The sales, which continued during each time of war until 1750, brought unprecedented local direct and indirect access to the tribunals, thus enabling local elite families to influence judicial and political decisions.

Unlike purchased municipal, treasury, and *audiencia* positions, the post of provincial administrator—variously called *alcalde mayor, corregidor,* and *gobernador*—was for a term appointment. In the sixteenth century the Crown had introduced provincial administrators both to provide sustenance for non-*encomenderos* and poor *encomenderos* and to expand the royal authority from the urban areas into the countryside and over the indigenous population. The posts were numerous—eighty-eight in Peru and about two hundred in New Spain in the early seventeenth century. Most provincial administrators held only a single appointment, and service of five years or less was common. Unlike in Castile, where lawyers were named to many *corregimientos*, in the New World the Crown preferred men with military or at least militia backgrounds.

During the century after the stabilization of these provincial positions between 1570 and 1580, the notorious system of *repartimiento* took root. Although located varying distances from the viceregal capitals, the provincial administrators were regularly closely linked to them economically. Using goods provided on credit by merchants in Mexico City and Lima, the officials participated in the profitable *repartimiento* of merchandise by which Indians purchased mules, clothing, food, and other items on credit. In some regions at least, avaricious officials subjected their production to monopolistic control as well.

By 1677 an ever more financially desperate Crown began to sell appointments to provincial positions. Soon nearly all of these positions had passed from viceregal to royal provision. As with treasury posts, the Crown sold appointments of *corregidor* and *alcalde mayor* on an individual basis, with the amount and terms of the agreements varying. Unlike the situation for municipal, treasury, and *audiencia* posts, however, creoles seem to have secured fewer, rather than more, provincial offices after the sales began. This may have been because wealthy and well-educated creoles, especially those who went to Spain, devoted their attention to securing either the more prestigious *audiencia* and treasury positions or hereditary offices. In addition, the close link between the *repartimiento* of merchandise and the provincial officials made it particularly advantageous for monopolistic merchants in Spain to lend the purchase price and travel expenses to men whom they knew personally and whom they could trust to distribute their goods, that is, usually men born in Spain. Ties with merchants in Lima and Mexico City persisted as well, however, and provincial officials, whether native sons, *radicados*, or outsiders, formed an important part of the colonial economic world.

The anticipated expenses for a five-year term of the *corregidor* of the Peruvian province of Chancay in the mid-eighteenth century offer a glimpse of the financial requirements of provincial administration: Manuel de Elcorrobarrutia paid 16,000 pesos for his appointment plus an additional 4,000 pesos for fees and taxes. Paying an assistant and an agent and a lawyer in Lima consumed another 7,000 pesos. Personal living expenses he estimated at 15,000 pesos. Gratuities to officials in Lima, entertainment for the viceroy when he visited Chancay, and expenses for the *residencia* and audit cost 9,000 pesos. Interest on this total was 8,700 pesos. To distribute through *repartimiento* 1,900 mules, the *corregidor* anticipated paying 67,004 pesos. This amount purchased the mules and paid for their feed and distribution, tax, salary for collection agents, and interest. But he expected to receive only 80,000 pesos from selling the mules and thus had to sell other items for 46,724 pesos to cover his investment. With only 1,125 able-bodied adult males in the province in 1754, each household had to contribute an average of 112 pesos for this *corregidor* to break even. In the final analysis, the money paid to the Crown to secure this office, the commercial profits of the merchant speculator who advanced the funds to purchase the appointment, and the "profits" earned by the *corregidor* himself all were paid out of the collective earnings of this Indian community.

One unplanned result of the sale of appointments and offices and the evolution of a bureaucracy drawn largely from the native born and *radicados* was an increasing compatibility between colonial administration and the requirements of local elites. Bureaucrats who borrowed money from merchants and other affluent colonials were not likely to enforce vigorously laws that harmed them. Although the venal antecedents for this sensitivity to local interests are clear, the practical result was to reduce the potential for dangerous conflicts between powerful interest groups in the New World and the distant metropolis.

Brazilian Counterpoint

Portuguese administration in Brazil developed more slowly and modestly in scale than did its Spanish American counterpart. The early concentration of the small colonial population in several coastal locations, the difficulty of intracolonial communication between northern and southern settlements, and the absence of a powerful and ambitious group of conquistadors contributed to a more regionally decentralized and smaller administrative system than that found in the Spanish colonies.

Administrative responsibility for Brazil was divided among various agencies and offices in Portugal. There was no Portuguese equivalent to Spain's Council of the Indies until a decade-long experiment in the early seventeenth century. Then in 1642 the Braganza dynasty created the Overseas Council which exercised many functions for Portugal's empire similar to those of the Council of the Indies. The Desembargo do Paço located in Lisbon oversaw judicial matters for Portugal and the empire, appointing, promoting, and reviewing the conduct of royal magistrates.

Initially the Portuguese Crown sought to treat Brazil as part of the royal factory system used in Africa and Asia. When French merchants began trading for dyewood directly with the natives, however, John III (1521–57) decided that a permanent colony was necessary. In the 1530s he granted to twelve men with good court connections hereditary captaincies extending inland from the Atlantic coast to the Line of Tordesillas. These "donatary captains" received rights similar to those granted in Portugal and the Atlantic islands earlier. Each recipient was to colonize and defend his captaincy in return for a number of revenues, the right to grant land and name numerous officials, and jurisdiction in most criminal and civil matters. The Crown retained several royal taxes and its monopoly over the dyewood trade. But with the exception of São Vicente and Pernambuco, the private enterprise donatary system was not successful. Continued French pressure, moreover, convinced John III to regain some of the authority bestowed in a manner analogous to that employed by the Castilian Crown.

In 1549 John purchased the captaincy of Bahia from its owners and named a governor-general to administer it. Following this political reorganization, exploration, Indian campaigns, and colonization proceeded in the north, beginning in the 1570s. The Portuguese settled Paraíba in the 1580s, Rio Grande do Norte in 1598, Ceara in 1610, Maranhão beginning in late 1615 with the arrival of an expedition to expel the French from a short-lived settlement, and Belém and the lower Amazon from 1616 to 1630.

As the chief executive in Brazil, the governor-general had responsibilities and restrictions similar to those of the Spanish American viceroys. He exercised general oversight of administration, defense, Luso-Indian relations, the treasury, the secular clergy, trade, and land grants. Legislation circumscribed his activities in many ways, however. The governor-general was prohibited from investing in trade or agriculture and could travel outside Bahia only with royal permission. He was subject, moreover, to a special investigation (*devassa*) during his term in office and a review (*residencia*) at its conclusion, checks similar to the Spanish *visita* and *residencia*. Named to a three-year term, many governors-general served longer, some more than two decades. Most came from Portugal's upper nobility and had been professional soldiers; none had been high-ranking clerics. Usually they reached Brazil accompanied by kin and retainers eager to benefit from their patron's largesse.

Governors served as the commanders in chief of their captaincies and were responsible for overseeing treasury and judicial offices and protecting the natives. Like the governor-generals, they were to act under standing instructions and directives sent from Lisbon and were subject to the *devassa* and *residencia*. The importance of military security on the exposed Atlantic coast led the Crown to name seasoned military veterans with administrative experience as governors. In the seventeenth century the governors of Pernambuco, Maranhão, and Rio de Janeiro were *fidalgos* and/or in a military order, but rarely titled nobles. Professional soldiers of commoner origins sometimes held the governorship of a less important captaincy. Nearly every governor was born in Portugal; among the few Brazilians named, almost none served in their native province. In striking contrast with Spanish America, there is no evidence that governorships were sold.

In 1621 the northern captaincies of Ceara, Maranhão, and Pará were united as the state of Maranhão, whose separate administration continued until 1772. The remaining captaincies were included in a single unit called the state of Brazil. In subsequent territorial reorganizations, the Crown generally added jurisdiction to the governors in Pernambuco and Rio de Janeiro at the expense of the governor-general. It also enhanced the governors' titles; by 1715 both were "governor and captain-general." By 1772 Brazil had nine captaincies-general. Although the office of viceroy replaced that of governor-general in 1720, this change in title was window dressing for a post whose effective authority had been reduced in favor of the governors and captains-general who communicated directly with the authorities in Lisbon.

Although since the late Middle Ages the Portuguese monarchs had relied on royal magistrates to extend their authority at home, they gave the donataries the right to name magistrates in their captaincies if they did not personally oversee the administration of justice. With the decision to assert royal control in 1549, however, John III superimposed a superior royal magistrate to handle appeals from municipal and donatary-named judges and to serve as the royal judge for the captancy of Bahia. Not until 1609, nearly a century after the first Spanish American *audiencia* was created, did the Portuguese Crown establish a high court of appeals (*relaçao*) for Brazil in the city of Salvador. Suppressed in 1626 after the Dutch seized Salvador, the court was reestablished in 1652 and remained the sole high court in Brazil until the creation of another in Rio de Janeiro in 1751. As in Spanish America, the judges had administrative and advisory responsibility in addition to judicial service. Their frequent use in assignments outside the court adversely affected its administration of justice and led to repeated complaints about its dilatory conduct.

The most professional bureaucrats in Brazil, members of the high court of Bahia came primarily from modest families neither peasant nor noble. All had a university degree in law, almost invariably earned at the University of Coimbra in Portugal, the only university in the Portuguese world empowered to confer degrees in civil and canon law. Magistrates received appointments for a term of six years, but some stayed longer, occasionally over two decades. Their protracted service routinely brought closer ties to the region they served. Frequent promotions to a court in Portugal, usually the High Court of Oporto, and the paucity of Brazilians named to the Bahia tribunal, however, meant that the judges' social and economic bonds to the region were less common and intense than those of their counterparts in Spanish America. Corruption, nonetheless, was typical, and magistrates in Brazil repeatedly engaged in commercial affairs and often sought to become landowners. Because most magistrates reached Brazil in middle age, few married locally. The ten native-son magistrates, not surprisingly, were most involved in the local society and economy.

Except for the high executive and judicial posts and municipal council positions, virtually every office in Brazil could be obtained by purchase or royal concession. The key fiscal offices, for example, were proprietary, and the problems of graft and embezzlement noted in Spanish America were present in Brazil as well. The practice of farming out to private tax collectors the tithe, customs duties, and other imposts compounded the - financial mismanagement.

As in Spanish America, the municipal council was the fundamental institution for the administration of the towns and their surrounding jurisdictions. The councils were important, among other reasons, because they distributed and leased municipal and common land, fixed the prices on numerous commodities, maintained roads and other public works, helped control slaves, policed the town, and oversaw public health and sanitation. Councils collected taxes and fines, licensed vendors, and leased municipal property for their income. In Salvador the council had three aldermen, two local magistrates, and a municipal attorney selected annually from a list of eligible candidates in a complicated indirect electoral process. Although after 1696 a royal magistrate presided over the council and the governors named the aldermen from eligible citizens, the councils remained important spokesmen for local concerns. The fact that the aldermen were elected prevented the councils from becoming the closed and self-perpetuating corporations that emerged from the sale of the position of *regidor* in Spanish America. But in both Brazil and Spanish America, citizens valued council seats for their prestige as well as for the personal economic benefits available through participation in government.

Although the Portuguese Crown employed *corregedores* as royal agents in the districts in Portugal, it did not extend this middle level of administration to Brazil. Instead, it relied on governors and city councils to administer the reasonably compact zones of settlement along the coast and sent circuit magistrates into less populous regions. Not until the economic boom that began with the discovery of gold in Minas Gerais in the 1690s did the Crown devote much attention to providing administration in the vast Brazilian interior.

The single most impressive feature of bureaucrats in the Iberian empires was the extent to which they were rooted to the region in which they served. Time after time the Crowns turned to newly appointed outsiders when they wanted to effect changes. Thus they employed visitors to investigate abuses or the failure to implement specific legislation. The extent of innovation, however, was often modest. Deeply rooted local elites, of which high-ranked officials formed a part, proved resilient to challenge. When examined closely, so-called change and reform often turned out to be the old politics with a few new players. Yet it was precisely the flexibility and resilience produced by the fusion of individual bureaucrats' interests and those of other members of the elite in their district that reduced pressure within a system of bureaucratic rule.

The Colonial Church

The Church joined the colonial bureaucracy as a major institutional buttress of European power in the New World. Nurtured by the Crown financially and legislatively, the Church in Spanish America prospered under a degree of royal control greater than that exercised in Spain itself. Conversion of the Indians, the theoretical justification for the Iberian presence in the Indies, was the Church's initial priority.

The primary vehicle of acculturation, conversion drew the indigenous peoples into the cultural orbit of the Spanish and Portuguese settlers. The missionaries simultaneously tried to shield the Indians from the corruption and immorality of the European settlers and the labor demands of an encroaching colonial economy. In addition, they imposed Christian beliefs, social practices such as monogamy, and political organization through a mission system that undermined the Indians' potential for resistance and rebellion. These changes helped prepare the indigenous communities for integration into the emerging colonial order.

The Church in Spanish America also ministered to the Spaniards there, dominated their education, and provided social services for which the Crown was unwilling to assume direct responsibility. By the 1570s, the initial evangelical commitment was noticeably diminished. A royal policy favoring the secular clergy over the orders contributed to the malaise. In subsequent years, the Church consolidated its gains, participated in nearly every dimension of colonial life, and accumulated and displayed its wealth. Spiritual enthusiasm and utopian vision declined, and an era of ecclesiastical routine began, although individual examples of clerical activism remained. The composition of the clergy, moreover, began to change noticeably. By the early seventeenth century, creoles far surpassed peninsulars numerically and firmly anchored the Church in the fabric of colonial society.

Royal Patronage

The Spanish kings' control over the Church rested on their *patronato real,* or royal patronage. Papal bulls in 1501 and 1508 formalized a degree of oversight implicit in the papal donation of 1493, and subsequent legislation spelled out the extent of supervision exercised by the Council of the Indies. Through their royal patronage Spanish monarchs assumed responsibility to promote the conversion of the Amerindians and to support the colonial Church. The Crown received control of tithe income, the tax levied on agricultural production and livestock, to sustain the ecclesiastical hierarchy, its physical facilities, and its activities. It also controlled the founding of churches, convents, and hospitals and the appointment of and payment to ecclesiastics. Clerics needed royal licenses to sail to the Indies, and their movement upon arrival was inhibited. The Council of the Indies examined all papal documents for statements that infringed on the Crown's patronage. Only after the council's approval could these materials be sent to the New World.

The Portuguese Crown also exercised a supervisory control over the Church. The *padroado,* patronage, derived from a series of papal bulls issued between 1456 and 1514. The king controlled the creation of colonial bishoprics, the appointment of bishops, the movement of missionaries, and the evangelical efforts among the Indians. The Portuguese Church, however, lacked the wealth and political power of the Spanish Church. The end of Muslim rule in Portugal in the thirteenth century gave the Church a history different from that of its Spanish counterpart. Still, Portugal's later expansion into North Africa and especially India gave the Portuguese Church some of the crusading zeal and material rewards gained in Spain during the long Reconquest.

The Evangelical Effort

The conquests of Mexico and Peru opened the most populous regions of the American mainlands to clerics anxious to convert the natives to Christianity. Although clerics accompanied Cortés on his march to Tenochtitlan, systematic efforts to convert the indigenous population awaited the arrival of the regulars, as members of the religious orders were known. Cortés repeatedly urged Charles I to send friars, preferring them to the more worldly secular clergy. Twelve Franciscans arrived in May 1524, the first contingent of an order that would lead conversion efforts in New Spain. In the following decade Dominicans, already active in the Caribbean colonies, and Augustinians joined in the "spiritual conquest." Although all of the orders emphasized conversion, the Franciscans approached the effort with a millenarian hope that their evangelization and the creation of a primitive apostolic church would be followed by the second coming of Christ.

The friars faced numerous obstacles to their conversion campaign. The many native languages posed a special problem, and the dispersed residential patterns of natives outside the urban centers hindered rapid evangelization. Superficial resemblances between native and Christian religious practices increased the difficulty of presenting Christianity as new and distinct. Yet the friars enjoyed some advantages as well.

The conquest transferred political power to the Spanish and gave great prestige to the Christian religion, for the gods of the Aztec and Inca had been undermined. Unlike the native conquerors in central Mexico, the Spaniards refused to respect the gods of the vanquished; the Christian God was to stand alone. The destruction of indigenous religion was systematic and persistent. Priests in particular were singled out for persecution; prudence thus dictated that the natives, whatever their private beliefs, publicly comply with their conquerors' religion.

About eight hundred friars were residing in Mexico by 1559. At first they directed much of their attention to converting the native chieftains (*caciques*) and nobles who, they anticipated correctly, would bring their peoples with them into the Church. Although the Crown wanted the natives to learn Spanish, many religious quickly began to study and preach in the languages of the peoples they were evangelizing. One prodigiously learned cleric, Andrés de Olmos, preached and wrote in more than ten Indian languages. The Aztec language, Nahuatl, received the most attention, for many native peoples were able to comprehend instruction in that tongue in addition to their own. Friars also taught Nahuatl where it had not previously been used, in order to establish a common language in New Spain, while keeping the natives separated from other Europeans who, they feared, would corrupt them. In Peru the friars promoted Quechua and Aymara over the other indigenous languages.

To segregate the natives from Europeans and to streamline their own activities, the friars founded villages to bring together Indians scattered throughout a region. The Indians' declining population further stimulated this process. The Augustinians were particularly effective at founding new villages. In Michoacán, for example, they gathered together natives who had been dispersed around Tiripitío and built, using Indian labor, a town complete with plaza, convent, hospital, water supply, and well-constructed houses. In towns such as this the friars oversaw political and economic activities as well as religious affairs.

By baptizing the natives, the friars obliged the Church to provide the sacraments of marriage, confession, communion, and confirmation that would enable the new converts to live as Christians. Christian insistence on monogamous marriage immediately ran up against the polygyny common among the Indian elite, especially in Mexico. Even after two generations of natives baptized during their youth and educated in Christian precepts, some Indians still married one wife in the Church and kept other women as concubines, although this custom faded away over time.

Many Indians responded enthusiastically to evangelization. Religion was a central feature of native life before the conquest, and the vanquished could not imagine existence without belief in the supernatural. In addition, they at once recognized the Spaniards' veneration of images of the Virgin, the Cross, and clerics. The customary Spanish practice of building churches or at least placing crosses on preexisting religious sites reaffirmed the sacredness of the locations and promoted syncretism, the fusion of Christian and indigenous beliefs. The natives' veneration of Our Lady of Guadalupe, the most celebrated image of the Virgin Mary in New Spain, was associated with the persistence of their earlier devotion to the native goddess Tonantzin. The Indians perceived Guadalupe-Tonantzin as "God," much to the dismay of the Franciscans, who opposed the syncretic religious beliefs and practices that came to characterize "Christianity" among the natives. Crediting Our Lady of Guadalupe with miraculous healings, Indians flocked throughout the colonial era to her sanctuary on a hill just north of Mexico City.

In 1526 the Franciscans opened the College of Santiago Tlatelolco near Mexico City to train for the priesthood the sons of the native nobility. The students were taught reading, writing, music, Latin, and philosophy, among other subjects. Some mastered Latin and could translate it into Spanish and Nahuatl. Yet the college and the effort to train a native clergy ultimately failed. Antinative sentiment among many non-Franciscan clergy fueled opposition to the ordination of natives. No alumni entered the clergy, and with its principal reason for existence negated, the Tlatelolco experiment ended. From 1555 to 1591, Indians were formally prohibited from receiving ordination. Subsequent unofficial discrimination ensured perpetual inferiority for Indians in the Mexican Church.

Vasco de Quiroga entered the Franciscan order after serving as *oidor* on the second Audiencia of Mexico. In Michoacán he invested most of his own wealth in the creation of mission communities modeled on Sir Thomas More's *Utopia*. All land was held communally. New skills based on European technology were taught, but labor was closely regulated so as to prevent abuse. In addition to a church, the settlements provided hospitals and a wide array of social welfare benefits. After his appointment as bishop of Michoacán in 1537, Vasco de Quiroga continued to promote the use of mission settlements, a strategy later used successfully by the Jesuits and other regulars as the Christian frontier was pushed north to Texas and California and south to the Río de la Plata region.

The Dominican Vicente de Valverde and several other clerics accompanied Pizarro to Cajamarca. Franciscans and Mercedarians had arrived before Atahualpa's execution, and Augustinians appeared in 1551. However, the intensive evangelization of New Spain's "spiritual conquest" was not duplicated in Peru. Although the disruption of civil war undoubtedly hindered efforts at conversion, it appears that the quality of the early clerics in Peru was inferior to that of the friars in Mexico. Not until the first Conciliar Council of Lima in 1551 did the Church launch a full-scale attack on surviving Incan religious activities. Declaring all Andean people who had died before the conquest to be in Hell, the council vigorously attacked the worship of *huacas* and ancestors. Priests and government officials henceforth destroyed *huacas* and burned mummies whenever possible. The response in the central Andes was a millenarian movement in the 1560s that believed that the *huacas*, angry at being deserted for Catholicism, had brought epidemics, from which the only escape was a return to traditional religious beliefs. Considering the movement heretical and thus treasonous, the state was able to eliminate the threat by the 1570s.

Religious orders spread throughout the Spanish empire, often advancing its boundary of effective settlement. Nearly twenty years after reaching Brazil, the Society of Jesus arrived in Peru in 1568 and New Spain in 1572. Quickly the Jesuits came to dominate elite education in the cities. In addition, the Society soon began to establish missions in numerous locations, from the northern frontier of Mexico to Paraguay. The first of the famous Guaraní mission villages in Paraguay was founded in 1610. By 1707 there were thirty villages with nearly 100,000 Indians.

The Society of Jesus dominated the evangelical effort in Brazil after the arrival in 1549 of Manoel da Nobrega and five other Jesuits in Salvador; the few Franciscans who had been living in Brazil had shown little interest in converting the Indians. Defeated Indians near Salvador provided the Jesuits' first converts. As in New Spain and Peru, European military successes enhanced the prestige of the new religion and enabled superficial conversion. The Jesuits concentrated the Indians in villages (*aldeias*) in order to maximize the evangelical potential of their small numbers. After 1557, when voluntary concentration failed, the Jesuits supported Governor Mem de Sá in crushing

Portrait of San Ignacio Loyola, founder of the Society of Jesus (Jesuits).

the remaining armed resistance. By 1560 more than forty thousand Indians were in the Jesuit *aldeias* of Bahia alone, and by the end of the century the colony's 169 Jesuits controlled nearly the entire pacified Indian population.

In Brazil the missionaries promoted the use of Tupí as a common language. In the *aldeias* they taught crafts, introduced new crops, and enforced European work habits and social practices—monogamy and an abhorrence of nudity, in particular. They also fostered European culture, especially music.

After the early achievements—mass baptisms and the creation of the first *aldeias*—the Jesuits realized the shallowness of the conversion experience. Old beliefs persisted, intermingled with Christian doctrine. By the 1560s this frustration was clearly revealed in their reports and letters. As they recognized the difficulty of converting adults, the Jesuits began to emphasize more the close supervision and education of young males. When some of these young converts denounced their own elders for continuing ancient customs, the missionaries happily noted their achievement.

The development of mission settlements as a conversion tool led necessarily to a conflict between the Church and the settlers. The colonial economies of Latin America depended on Indian labor. Miners, planters, and *obraje* owners coveted control over converted Indians already accustomed to the discipline and organization of the missionaries and familiar with rudimentary European technology. Because the missionaries, especially the Dominicans and the Jesuits, tried to defend the Indians from what they saw as exploitation and abuse, they continually found themselves in political and judicial conflict with the settlers. When epidemics drastically reduced the Indian population, these pressures grew. In Brazil, for example, the Jesuit Antônio Vieira's efforts to protect the Indians led to a revolt and the temporary expulsion of the Society from Maranhão and Pará in 1661. Earlier, Jesuits working with the Guaraní in disputed borderlands that separated Brazil and Paraguay had armed their Indians against slave raiders from São Paulo. Forced to choose between the claims of the missionaries and those of the wealthy colonial elites, the monarchs of both Spain and Portugal moved to restrict the Church's control over pacified Indian communities.

The Mature Church

The secular clergy made up the ecclesiastical hierarchy that extended from parish priests upward to cathedral chapters, bishops, and archbishops. Unlike the regulars—many of whom took vows of poverty and whose subsistence was provided by their orders—secular priests were primarily responsible for their own financial security, which led them into a variety of economic activities. Although they were supposed to refrain from wholesale or retail trade, crafts, and direct employment outside the Church, not all seculars observed these restrictions.

Secular clergy were present in Brazil from the first decades but had little influence. Indeed the Jesuit Nobrega characterized the secular priests of Bahia as "irregular, apostates and excommunicates." When the first bishop of Bahia arrived in 1552, he had little interest in converting the natives. In 1676 the bishop of Bahia was elevated to archbishop, and by the late eighteenth century six bishoprics were subject to Bahia. Although the development of the episcopal structure coincided with an expansion in the secular clergy, approximately half of the bishops appointed before 1800 were regulars.

The establishment of bishoprics and then archbishoprics in Spanish America and an increase in the number of secular clergy led to conflict with the regulars. At issue was the control of the native population and its labor and income. The regulars, moreover, were justly proud of their accomplishments and loath to share the benefits with seculars whom they considered inferior in ability and commitment. Their antagonism was not limited to words. On one occasion in 1559, seculars raided the Dominican convent in Puebla, Mexico, sacked it, broke the prior's teeth, and departed with every item of value. In a similarly uncharitable spirit, on another occasion Franciscans armed six hundred Indians from the Toluca region of Mexico with bows and arrows and shields and then led them in the destruction of a church under the care of secular clergy.

In 1568 Philip II named a committee to investigate the relations between seculars and regulars. The resulting Ordenanza del Patronazgo of 1574 increased the power of the secular clergy and limited the regulars' activities. Eventually, secular priests took over many Indian parishes, or *doctrinas*. Henceforth the regulars' mission activities, when they took place, were in isolated frontier areas.

By 1600 the Church was beginning the financial ascent that would make its economic base second to none in the colonies. The growth of commercial agriculture in New Spain, Peru, Central America, and Brazil brought unprecedented revenues from the tithe in the 1590s. With the Jesuits leading the way, the regular orders—save perhaps the Franciscans—became active and successful landowners. In New Spain and Peru, the expansion of mining and commerce after the conquest era also created excess capital that its owners used, in part, to endow pious works.

Pious works included chantries, the foundation of convents and colleges, and the provision of dowries and burial funds. Frequently an individual established a chantry to celebrate in perpetuity privately administered memorial masses for his soul. The founder and his heir typically designated a family member as chaplain. This strategy had the great advantage of retaining in the family the income of the endowment, whether it had been established with cash, a gift of property, or through encumbering real property as though it were mortgaged by pledging specified annual payments.

The Church was the most important source of mortgages, normally receiving a return of about 5 or 6 percent in the sixteenth century. The conditions of the loan, however, had to be such that the recipient was buying capital rather than simply borrowing money at interest, a transaction that canon law forbade as the sin of usury. Not only was the Church the major source of investment capital, it also became the major colonial property owner.

As time went on, tithes; fees that clerics received for marriages, burials, and other services; gifts; and pious works enabled the church and individual clerics to become extremely wealthy. The Church acquired both urban and rural property. The Jesuits, other regular orders, and individual secular priests actively operated in the colonial marketplace, producing sugar, wine, textiles, pottery, and other products. In Mexico City and other large cities, the Church was the largest landlord, renting its property to both residential and commercial users. By employing part of its wealth and income to sustain cultural activities and welfare functions for the poor, the Church added substantially to the well-being of colonial society.

Some orders routinely opened schools in conjunction with their convents in order to educate later generations to enter the orders or assume other responsibilities in society. The Jesuits in Lima began organizing schools from the time they reached the City of Kings in 1568. The Jesuit college in Bahia had 215 students by 1589 and offered a curriculum that extended from the elementary grades to the study of theology. Together with the Dominicans, the Jesuits dominated education until expelled from Portugal, Spain, and their colonies after 1750. The Dominicans were influential in the founding of Lima's University of San Marcos which was established in 1551 but functioned as a convent school until the 1570s. The University of Mexico, also established in 1551, held its first classes in 1553, in part as a result of efforts by Archbishop Juan de Zumárraga. Eventually universities were created in nearly every major city in Spanish America.

The immediate result of establishing universities in Spanish America was a greater number of educated creoles for vocations in the Church and the royal bureaucracy. In consequence, the composition of the clergy began to change noticeably. By the early seventeenth century, creoles had gained prominence in both the secular clergy and at least several of the regular orders. Although a few well-placed *castas* and Indians initially enjoyed limited educational opportunities, they were later excluded from the universities, colleges, and even primary schools. This restriction was imposed in Lima in the 1640s, despite the Jesuits' resistance. Brazilians also entered the Church, although the absence of a university during the colonial period retarded this development.

The presence of Europeans and American-born clerics in both the secular and regular clergy added a further rift to the already divided Church. Conflict focused on the highest positions, especially in the orders, save for the Jesuits whose provincials and supervisors were named in Europe. Europeans believed themselves superior to their American rivals by virtue of their birth in the Old World. This became a grave problem in Spanish America, for the growing creole majority threatened the peninsulars' dominance in provincial elections. The peninsulars responded by obtaining decrees that authorized the mandatory alternation of offices between themselves and creoles. In mid-seventeenth-century Peru, only the Franciscans and Jesuits were not bound by this forced rotation in office. Beginning in the 1660s the peninsular Franciscans sought, and in 1683 received, final approval for rotation in office. Eventually the Franciscans in Brazil also instituted alternation in office.

There was less conflict among the secular clergy of Spanish America. The American-born religious repeatedly sought and at times secured high ecclesiastical offices. By 1640 five men born in the Viceroyalty of Peru had been named archbishops, and another twenty-three had been named bishops in the New World. Nonetheless, peninsulars secured most of the appointments at these levels. The five high-ranking positions that constituted the cathedral chapters, in contrast, routinely had heavy creole representation from at least the early seventeenth century. Creoles also predominated at the parish level, although by 1700 there were visible numbers of *mestizo* priests and even a few Indians. European immigrants were noticeable in some of the wealthiest parishes.

The increase in number of American-born clerics in the seventeenth century and the Church's growing economic influence bound it to American soil in a way that the early focus on missionary activity had not. Nearly every colonial family of the middle and upper sectors had relatives in one or more of the Church's branches. Leaving aside the pervasiveness of religion in colonial society, the clergy themselves were pervasive in creole society at its most fundamental level, that of the family.

The León Garavito y Illescas family illustrates this pattern. Francisco de León Garavito emigrated to Lima where he prospered as a merchant, property owner, law professor, government attorney, and alderman. About 1574 he married Isabel de Illescas. The wealthy couple's sons included an *oidor* of the Audiencia of Panama, three Dominicans, a Jesuit, and a priest in Lima. Isabel's four sisters entered Lima's prestigous convent of La Encarnación early in the seventeenth century, and three of her daughters followed them. All became nuns of the black veil, that is, full voting members of the house, and one was elected abbess.

The seven nuns of the Illescas and León Garavito families underscore the presence of women in ecclesiastical vocations. Convents enabled women to pursue a religious life, control their own affairs, obtain and provide education, and, in many cases, live a very comfortable existence. Protected from the demands of husbands and families, many nuns cultivated the arts and literature, providing a venue for the transfer of European culture. The majority of convents date after 1570 and reached their numerical apogee in the seventeenth century. At their height, the thirteen convents in Lima housed more than 20 percent of the city's women. Far fewer were founded after 1700 than earlier, and in Peru, at least, the number of nuns fell sharply beginning in the early eighteenth century.

The first convent in Brazil was founded in Salvador in 1677. Before then, small numbers of Brazilian women seeking this contemplative life entered convents in Portugal or the Azores. By the end of the eighteenth century three more convents were added. But Mexico City still had proportionately twice as many nuns as did the capital of colonial Brazil.

The many religious orders for women in the colonies were founded locally and maintained only loose ties to metropolitan establishments. Franciscan, Carmelite, Augustinian, and all other orders before the 1750s were devoted to contemplative routines and played no substantial educational or charitable roles. The elite within these orders were nuns of the black veil, the most educated group of women in the colonies. Almost exclusively colonial born, they brought with them sizable dowries, and they alone could vote and serve in offices in the convent and sing the canonical hours in the choir. The Convent of N. S. da Mercedes was founded in 1735 in Bahia by the wealthy heiress Ursula Luisa de Monserrat, who also became its first abbess. Rich families commonly purchased or built the quarters or cells for their daughters and made specified donations to the houses. Although convents

San Martín de Porres was the illegitimate son of a Spanish nobleman and his black servant. He entered the Dominican order in Lima, Peru, where he became famous for his visions and an ability to heal the sick.

occasionally waived the required dowry—most frequently for women of unusual musical ability—they did enforce the social prerequisites. In the convents in Lima, for example, nuns of the black veil were daughters of socially prominent families and accordingly were addressed as "Doña."

Other women in colonial convents lacked family ties to the local social and economic elite. Nuns of the white veil served as housekeepers and in other activities considered inappropriate for the nuns of the black veil with whom they lived. Born into modest white and mixed-race families, their limited opportunities in the convents reflected their social and economic inferiority. Still lower were the poor, mixed-race women who served the nuns of the white veil and were allowed to wear nuns' habits. With servants and black slaves present as well, the convent in many ways mirrored the society outside their walls.

The convents participated actively in the colonies' economic life. Not only did their residences, some occupying several city blocks, require constant attention, but the nuns and their servants, who totaled nearly a thousand persons in some of Lima's larger convents in the seventeenth century, were important consumers as well. In addition, the convents owned urban property both for their own residences and schools and as sources of income. As did other bodies within the Church, the wealthy convents earned capital by providing mortgages, mainly on urban properties. Unlike many male orders, however, the female orders normally did not engage in agricultural production.

The early presence and importance of the convents, the vigor of the male religious orders, the size of the secular clergy, and the continued support of both the colonists and the Crown combined to make the Church in Latin America a powerful, wealthy institution whose influence permeated colonial life. Although examples of individual clerics failing to observe their vows and conniving with colonists to exploit the Indians certainly can be found, their number pales in comparison with the many clergymen who sought to establish and maintain Christianity among the native peoples. A bastion of European culture and civilization, the Church in Latin America retained its strength throughout the colonial era.

The Inquisition

In 1569 the Spanish Crown replaced the earlier and unsatisfactory episcopal inquisitions in its colonies by authorizing the establishment of tribunals of the Inquisition in Mexico City and Lima. A third tribunal was approved for Cartagena in 1610. Unlike the fear of converted Jews (*conversos*) that had prompted the tribunal's creation in Spain in 1480, the tribunals in the New World were founded out of the Crown's desire to maintain the purity of the Catholic faith against the spread of heretical Protestant beliefs brought to the Indies by foreign interlopers. Once created in the colonies, the Inquisitions of Peru and New Spain periodically persecuted "New Christians"—converted Jews and their descendants—who persisted in the faith of their ancestors. Within their districts the tribunals held jurisdiction over all non-Indians who had received Christian baptism. Protestants, by virtue of their baptism, were subject to the Inquisition.

The colonial tribunals were similar to their peninsular predecessors in organization and procedure. Normally a tribunal had two inquisitors, an expert who examined evidence for heresy, a prosecutor, a constable, and a notary. Other officials were added as necessary. In addition, tribunals had in each province of their jurisdiction investigators or commissaries, who could be lay or clerics, and lay police, or *familiares*, to arrest suspects and enforce the bodies' decrees. Although the first inquisitors were born and educated in Spain, by 1640 the tribunals in Mexico City and Lima had each received at least one creole inquisitor. A sprinkling of Americans continued to secure appointments as long as the Holy Office existed.

Because it was a powerful body independent of civil and ecclesiastical hierarchies, the Inquisition unavoidably conflicted with both. Its authority, moreover, made it an attractive ally for persons who found the other hierarchies unable or unwilling to support their ambitions. The judicial privileges enjoyed by the tribunal's agents further enhanced the advantages of cooperation and encouraged the participation of wealthy citizens. The tribunal also sought *familiares* who were well placed in local society, an approach that guaranteed prominent support.

The Inquisition initiated a case only after receiving a denunciation. Although self-denunciation was possible, usually by an individual who anticipated lighter penance as a result, generally a third party levied the charge. The accepted procedure was for the inquisitors to gather corroborating evidence before taking further action, a process that could drag on for years. When the evidence seemed conclusive, the tribunal's agents arrested and jailed the accused and sequestered his or her property for later auction as necessary to pay the costs of imprisonment.

The most important feature that distinguished the Inquisition's procedure from that of other tribunals was secrecy. The accused was totally cut off from the outside world while the case proceeded; in some cases this isolation lasted years and terminated only with death. Moreover, the victim was ordered to confess an offense so that he or she could receive absolution from and reconciliation with the Church. The victim, however, was not informed of the charge or the accuser. In a majority of cases, probably most, these omissions were not a major problem, for the accused was indeed guilty. For an innocent party, however, the problems of demonstrating innocence through such means as naming personal enemies were formidable.

The Inquisition prescribed punishment or penance at an *auto de fé* or, literally, an "act of faith." An *auto de fé* could be private or public. Here the condemned revealed remorse for their sins and professed their hatred of heresy. Public *autos* were great spectacles that public officials, clerics, nobles, and the general populace attended. Throughout its existence in Spanish America, the Inquisition ordered death, a penalty given only to heretics who would not recant, in no more than a hundred cases, perhaps 1 percent of the total considered. Bigamy, blasphemy, and other offenses against public morality were the Inquisition's primary concerns. For such offenses, fines, flogging, confiscation of property, gagging, exile, and service on the galleys were the principal punishments. Punishments were more severe in the early years of the Holy Office than later. After the middle of the seventeeth century the largest *autos de fé* had taken place, and the importance of the tribunals had begun to dwindle.

A major part of the Inquisition's efforts to protect the colonists from heresy and unorthodox ideas involved censorship. This included both searching ships that arrived at colonial ports for prohibited literature, works listed on the Spanish *Index* of forbidden publications, and censoring manuscripts before they were published in the New World. Although these activities certainly limited the amount of protest literature that entered the colonies and slowed the publication of locally written works, the censors were most interested in ecclesiastical materials.

The Spanish population as a whole supported the Inquisition in the colonies. Most Spaniards did not feel personally threatened by the tribunal. They considered protection from heresy a worthy objective and actively participated in prosecuting those persons who strayed too far from the accepted morality. In an era in which formal political representation was absent, moreover, the Inquisition provided, during its first century of existence in particular, an alternative institution from which the colonists could seek support for their own purposes. The political dimension of the Inquisition gave added importance to the repeated conflicts, often over seemingly trivial matters, that the inquisitors had with civil and ecclesiastical authorities.

Portugal established an effective Inquisition only in 1547. Although there were several tribunals in Portugal and one in Goa, a separate tribunal for Brazil was not created. Bishops, familiars, or other agents that the Portuguese Holy Office employed in the colony investigated persons accused of heresy or other offenses. Those persons considered guilty were shipped to Portugal for trial. The procedures employed were similar to those in Spain and Spanish America except that the Portuguese Inquisition may have been even more harsh in its early years.

On three occasions the Portuguese Inquisition sent special agents to Brazil. The first reached Bahia in 1591 and spent four years investigating the numerous New Christians residing in the colony. Two other inquisitorial visits took place in 1618 and 1763–69. As in the Spanish colonies, local agents rather than special investigators usually filed charges of bigamy, blasphemy, reading of prohibited literature, and other infractions. Such offenses led to investigations far more often than did allegations of heresy.

The Church provided for the spiritual life of a diverse and complex population and was one of the principal buttresses of social stability and public order in both Spanish America and Brazil. It organized much of colonial society's communal life through public celebrations associated with the religious calendar. By converting Indians and blacks to Christianity, it extended European cultural values; and its role in education and public charity further emphasized its centrality in the lives of rich and poor alike.

Suggested for Further Reading

Alvarez de Toledo, Cayetana. *Politics and Reform in Spain and Viceregal Mexico: The Life and Thought of Juan de Palafox, 1600–1659.* Oxford: Clarendon Press; New York: Oxford University Press, 2004.

Andrien, Kenneth J. *Crisis and Decline: The Viceroyalty of Peru in the Seventeenth Century.* Albuquerque: University of New Mexico Press, 1985.

Bradley, Peter T. *Society, Economy, and Defence in Seventeenth-Century Peru: The Administration of the Count of Alba de Liste (1655–61).* Liverpool, United Kingdom: Institute of Latin American Studies, University of Liverpool, 1992.

Burns, Kathryn. *Colonial Habits: Convents and the Spiritual Economy of Cuzco, Peru.* Durham: Duke University Press, 1999.

Cañeque, Alejandro. *The King's Living Image: The Culture and Politics of Viceregal Power in Colonial Mexico.* New York and London: Routledge, 2004.

Cervantes, Fernando. *The Devil in the New World: The Impact of Diabolism in New Spain.* New Haven and London: Yale University Press, 1994.

Cook, Alexandra Parma, and Noble David Cook. *Good Faith and Truthful Ignorance: A Case of Transatlantic Bigamy.* Durham: Duke University Press, 1991.

Cutter, Charles R. *The Legal Culture of Northern New Spain, 1700–1810.* Albuquerque: University of New Mexico Press, 1995.

Garza, Federico. *Butterflies Will Burn: Prosecuting Sodomites in Early Modern Spain and Mexico.* Austin: University of Texas Press, 2003.

Giles, Mary E., editor. *Women in the Inquisition: Spain and the New World.* Baltimore: Johns Hopkins University Press, 1999.

Green, Toby. *Inquisition: The Reign of Fear.* New York: St. Martin's Press, 2007.

Griffiths, Nicholas. *The Cross and the Serpent: Religious Repression and Resurgence in Colonial Peru.* Norman: University of Oklahoma Press, 1996.

Haring, C. H. *The Spanish Empire in America.* New York: Oxford University Press, 1947.

Hyland, Sabine. *The Jesuit and the Incas: The Extraordinary Life of Padre Blas Valera, S.J.* Ann Arbor: University of Michigan Press, 2003.

Kamen, Henry. *The Spanish Inquisition: A Historical Revision.* New Haven and London: Yale University Press, 1998.

Las Casas, Bartolomé de. *Short Account of the Destruction of the Indies.* Trans. Nigel Griffin. Baltimore: Penguin, 1999.

Mello e Souza, Laura de. *The Devil and the Land of the Holy Cross: Witchcraft, Slavery, and Popular Religion in Colonial Brazil.* Trans. By Diane Grosklaus Whitty. Austin: University of Texas Press, 2004.

Myers, Kathleen Ann. *Neither Saints Nor Sinners: Writing the Lives of Women in Spanish America.* New York: Oxford University Press, 2003.

Nader, Helen. *Liberty in Absolutist Spain: The Habsburg Sale of Towns, 1516–1700.* Baltimore: Johns Hopkins University Press, 1990.

Nesvig, Martin Austin, editor. *Local Religion in Colonial Mexico.* Albuquerque: University of New Mexico Press, 2006.

Owensby, Brian. *Empire of Law and Indian Justice in Colonial Mexico.* Stanford: Stanford University Press, 2008.

Perry, Elizabeth Mary, and Anne J. Cruz, editors. *Cultural Encounters: The Impact of the Inquisition in Spain and the New World.* Berkeley and Los Angeles: University of California Press, 1991.

Poole, Stafford. *Juan de Ovando: Governing the Spanish Empire in the Reign of Phillip II.*
   Norman: University of Oklahoma Press, 2004.

Saeger, James Schofield. *The Chaco Mission Frontier: The Guaycuruan Experience.*
   Tucson: University of Arizona Press, 2000.

Schroeder, Susan and Stafford C. M. Poole, editors. *Religion in New Spain.*
   Albuquerque: University of New Mexico Press, 2007.

Schwartz, Stuart B. *All Can Be Saved: Religious Tolerance and Salvation in the Iberian
   Atlantic World.* New Haven and London: Yale University Press, 2008.

Schwartz, Stuart B. *Sovereignty and Society in Colonial Brazil: The High Court of Bahia
   and Its Judges, 1609–1751.* Berkeley and Los Angeles: University of California
   Press, 1981.

Silverblatt, Irene. *Modern Inquisitions: Peru and the Colonial Origins of the Civilized
   World.* Durham: Duke University Press, 2005.

Van Oss, A.C. *Church and Society in Spanish America.* Amsterdam: Aksant, 2003.

FOUR

POPULATION AND LABOR

Chronology

1518	Crown authorizes importation of slaves from Africa
1520	Smallpox reaches New Spain
1520s	Smallpox reaches Peru; first *encomiendas* distributed in New Spain
1530s	Measles appears in New Spain and Central America; first *encomiendas* distributed in Peru
1542	New Laws threaten *encomenderos* and order abolition of Indian slavery
mid-1540s	Major pestilence strikes New Spain and Central America
1550s	"Congregations" and labor drafts (*repartimiento*) introduced in central Mexico
1560s	Jesuits in Brazil resettle natives
1562	First smallpox epidemic in Brazil
1570s	"Reductions" and forced labor drafts (*mita*) imposed in Peru by Viceroy Francisco de Toledo
1590s	Labor drafts introduced in eastern highlands of Colombia
c. 1625–50	Nadir of native population in New Spain; free wage labor largely supplants *repartimiento* in New Spain
1718–20	Epidemic reduces population of Peru to low point of colonial era

Changes in the Colonial Population

The arrival of the Spanish and Portuguese initiated major population changes in the Americas. For the indigenous peoples, European conquest and settlement triggered a demographic disaster. In contrast, the small numbers of Iberians who had conquered and then settled the New World expanded as immigration and, within a few years, natural reproduction swelled their ranks. The African slave trade added a third racial group to the colonial gene pool, and, in some geographic areas, African slaves and their descendents became a majority of the population. Finally, free and forced sexual unions among Europeans, Indians, and blacks resulted in the creation of new ethnic and cultural identities. These groups would increase in number and importance throughout the colonial era.

The relative importance of the decline of the native population, European immigration, the African slave trade, and the development of new mixed identities varied by region. Urban and rural areas typically exhibited substantially different racial compositions, rates of population growth or decline, and even definitions of ethnic identities. Within specific geographic areas, the effects of an epidemic or new economic opportunities, for example, the discovery of gold or silver, could dramatically influence internal resettlement and migration.

The Indian Population

The size of the Americas' indigenous population at the time of the Iberians' arrival is unknown. Scholarly estimates range from about 8 million to over 100 million. Substantial differences also appear in the population estimates for each major region. Did central Mexico have fewer than 5 million inhabitants or over 25 million? Did the Andean region have 3 million or 30 million or more? Did Central America have fewer than 1 million or over 10 million? Did Brazil have 1 million or more than 6 million? There is no consensus among the experts. However, a total indigenous population of between 35 million and 50 million seems plausible. The fact that the indigenous population plummeted soon after the Iberians arrived is not disputed.

Efforts to estimate the size of indigenous populations begin with a limited number of imperfect sources. Among the most reliable are archaeological studies that examine precontact housing, burial sites, land use and settlement patterns, social structure, and native technologies, but these are available for only a very limited number of locations. Written sources produced by Europeans include contemporary estimates by participants in the conquests and early settlements, records of Spanish and Portuguese authorities who counted native populations to assess labor and tribute obligations, early censuses, and church records of baptisms and burials. Notably absent are comprehensive population counts.

Some scholars begin with a source such as an early list of tributaries or an estimate of Christian converts and then multiply the original number by some estimate of family or household size to approximate total preconquest population. Others assume the mortality rates of known epidemics in a region and then extrapolate backward from a later figure. Either approach yields numbers that are inherently unreliable. Using the improved documentation available after the Spanish Crown began reforming tax collection in the mid-sixteenth century, however, results in a much narrower and more reliable range of estimates than those produced for preceding years.

Disease

Multiple reasons explain the sharp reduction in the Americas' indigenous populations. The loss of life, physical devastation, and disruptions of native agriculture and trade that accompanied the conquest took a terrible toll. The mistreatment and abuse of Indians by Spanish and Portuguese settlers increased mortality rates by undermining long-established systems of social welfare and mutual assistance. Forced labor obligations imposed by colonial governments weakened family and kinship structures, leading in many cases to lower fertility rates and higher infant mortality rates because of malnutrition. The combined effects of these assaults on indigenous society were multiplied by the cultural crises and psychological traumas associated with conquest and forced conversion. Buffeted by this complex of threats, Indian peoples had limited ability to resist the deadly epidemic diseases unintentionally introduced by Europeans and Africans.

More than any other single reason, epidemic diseases to which the native populations had no immunity led to astronomical mortality rates. Smallpox reached Mexico before the defeat of the Mexica, devastating the population of Tenochtitlan during the Spanish siege. The deadly trajectory of the disease then moved through southern Mexico into Central America, reaching the northern fringes of the Inca Empire by the mid-1520s. Measles first appeared in New Spain and Central America in the early 1530s. In the mid-1540s, a virulent pestilence accompanied by bleeding of the nose and eyes produced high mortality rates in central Mexico and Central America. One Spanish settler in Guatemala wrote to the king saying, "God sent down such sickness upon the Indians that three out of every four of them perished."[1] Thirty years later, another outbreak, perhaps typhus or plague, afflicted the same areas, again killing tens of thousands if not more. Five other pandemics struck Central America by 1750.

After 1540, the Andean region suffered repeated epidemics. Either typhus or pneumonic plague carried off about 20 percent of the population in 1546. This was followed in the 1550s by measles, smallpox, and influenza outbreaks. Smallpox would later repeatedly assault the indigenous population. With the epidemic of 1718–20, the population of the Andean area fell to its lowest level. Smallpox raged throughout Brazil from 1562 to 1565. This first infection was brought to Salvador, Bahia, by a ship from Lisbon. Within three or four months, thirty thousand Indians had died in nearby Jesuit missions, and eventually the disease spread from Pernambuco to São Vicente. The later African slave trade touched off a succession of epidemics in the seventeenth and eighteenth centuries.

These examples document important differences in the magnitude and timing of native population declines across the New World. In many regions the downward trend eventually gave way to recovery as native populations gained increased immunity to the new diseases. In other areas, the Caribbean islands for example, indigenous peoples were essentially eliminated by the effects of conquest and disease.

Regional Population Changes

The most extensive demographic research has focused on central Mexico, the region from the isthmus of Tehuantepec to the northern limits of the Aztec Empire. Woodrow W. Borah provided the following estimates of its population:

Year	Native Population
1518	25.2 million
1532	16.8
1548	6.3
1568	2.65
1585	1.9
1595	1.375
1605	1.075
1622	0.75

Source: Woodrow W. Borah, *Justice by Insurance: The General Indian Court of Colonial Mexico and the Legal Aides of the Half-Real* (Berkeley and Los Angeles: University of California Press, 1983), p. 26.

The figures in this table are estimates, not exact counts, and those for the period before 1568 have provoked substantial dispute. Many scholars are more comfortable with an estimated population of 10 million to 13 million for 1518 rather than 25.2 million. However, most historical demographers agree that the native population decreased rapidly after the arrival of Cortés and reached its lowest point in the second quarter of the seventeenth century. By 1650 the indigenous population began a period of sustained growth that, except for periods of cyclical decline caused by epidemics and famine, continued throughout the remainder of the colonial era.

The century-long decline of the native population in Mexico cannot be generalized to every region and locale. Population losses were greatest in tropical coastal regions where contacts with arriving Spaniards were most frequent and the hot and wet climate proved hospitable to the more rapid transmission of the new diseases. Native populations never recovered in these regions, unlike at the higher elevations of the more temperate interior. There recovery began by the mid-seventeenth century and slow growth followed. In the Valley of Mexico, an estimated preconquest population of between 2.9 and 1.5 million fell to about 325,000 by 1570. One of the Spaniards with Cortés, Bernardino Vázquez de Tapia, stated that more than a quarter of the population of Tenochtitlan died of smallpox during the siege. The Valley's population reached a low of about 70,000 in 1650 before rising to about 120,000 in the 1740s and 275,000 by 1800. New Spain as a whole followed in rough outline the demographic experience of the Valley of Mexico with the Indian population increasing from its low point early in the seventeenth century to 3.7 million by the late eighteenth century.

The chronology experienced in the Yucatan was different from central Mexico. The native population of Yucatan had probably reached its apogee a century or more before the Spaniards arrived when a collapse of urban centers, wars, and various other calamities led to a decline in population. This decline accelerated as a result of the devastation of the Spanish conquest and the appearance of new diseases. The region's estimated population fell from perhaps 800,000 in 1528 to 240,000 by 1550 and 185,000 by 1605. A period of recovery ended about 1645 with another wave of diseases that reduced the population to a new low in 1740. After this date the region experienced strong population growth for the remainder of the colonial era.

Even before the first Spaniards entered Central America, plague and smallpox had been introduced along native trade routes, reducing the highland population by as much as a third. Scholars of this region estimate the original population at between 2.25 and 5 million in 1520. By 1570 the population had fallen to 500,000. Writing in 1532, one Spaniard noted that measles had "swept the land, leaving it totally empty [of Indians]."[2] Subsequent pandemics reduced the population further.

Peru also lost much of its indigenous population after the Europeans reached the New World. The first smallpox epidemic probably struck between 1524 and 1527. Estimating a population of about 9 million in 1520, Noble David Cook argued that the indigenous population fell to 1.3 million natives by 1570 and declined further to only 600,000 by 1630. The earliest demographic collapse occurred in the densely settled narrow coastal valleys. The lower-lying regions of the northern highlands also experienced extensive population losses. Dispersed pop-ulations of the mountain valleys proved more resistant to epidemics of typhus, smallpox, and measles sweeping through the region, although they suffered heavy losses as well. In contrast with the chronology for central Mexico, the native population of Peru did not reach its low point until the early eighteenth century. Recovery after 1720 raised the population by the mid-eighteenth century to around 610,000, roughly equal to what it had been a century earlier, and to about 700,000 in 1800.

Colombia's population followed a similar pattern. The proportion of natives in the province of Tunja in the eastern Andes fell about 80 percent from the mid-1530s to the mid-1630s. To the east, Venezuela dropped 50 to 75 percent. Ecuador's early population decline was precipitous, but recovery began by the end of the sixteenth century. Several lesser epidemics in the seventeenth century caused only temporary setbacks in the recovery. Modern scholars estimate that Brazil's Indian population in 1500 ranged from lows of from 1 million to 1.5 million to highs of from 5 million to 6 million. After developing population estimates for each identifiable group, John Hemming suggested a total population of about 2.4 million. As in Spanish America, a decline in the native population in Brazil followed the appearance of Europeans.

Flight and Forced Migration

The appalling drop in the native population is only one part of this complex story of cultural and social change. The flight and forced migrations of Indians from their lands also altered Latin America's demographic map during the colonial era. To escape the military depredations of the conquest, tens of thousands relocated to safer regions. This migration continued, and even accelerated in some places, with the establishment of Spanish and Portuguese settlements and the arrival of thousands of additional Europeans. As natives dispersed into the countryside, moving away from long-established indigenous centers that attracted the largest number of Europeans, religious conversion efforts and supplies of forced labor for the settlements were affected. Facing organizational and economic difficulties associated with epidemics and migration, clerics and colonial officials sought to gather together the Indians in new or expanded and reorganized communities under more direct European supervision.

Spanish efforts to concentrate surviving Indian populations, called congregation or reduction, occurred in Central America in the 1540s, in Yucatan in the 1550s, and in central Mexico in two stages, first in the 1550s and later from 1593 to 1605. The process in each area followed similar patterns: Smaller outlying towns were combined with larger native communities, or separate towns or villages were joined in entirely new communities with the original settlements then razed. Sometimes large Indian communities were moved to a nearby location with the buildings constructed in imitation of the characteristic Spanish grid pattern. These forced relocations made additional lands available to Spaniards, even if there was no immediate rush to secure it.

In the 1560s initial efforts to concentrate indigenous populations that had survived the first waves of epidemic failed in Peru. Under the firm administration of Viceroy Francisco de Toledo, however, the resettlement or "reduction" of as many as 1.5 million Indians was imposed on southern Peru. Toledo sought to group the Indians into as few Spanish-style towns as possible. For example, over two hundred existing villages in one region were consolidated into only thirty-nine towns. In some cases as many as eighteen villages were telescoped into one. Repeated efforts were made to resettle the indigenous people of Huarochirí who struggled to maintain their traditional lands. In the end the Spanish combined over one hundred small settlements into seventeen villages each with about 1,000 to 1,700 residents. Nevertheless, within twenty years the people of this region had successfully reasserted their traditional residential patterns.

The Portuguese pursued similar policies in Brazil. The Jesuits actively promoted the resettlement of pacified Indian populations from small villages to larger mission communities, called *aldeias*, believing that this would facilitate Christian conversion and eliminate cultural practices such as cannibalism and polygyny. Under Portuguese Governor-General Mem de Sá the number of *aldeias* went from two in 1557 to eleven with a population of about 34,000 in 1562. The inadvertent effect of these forced relocations was to increase the Indians' vulnerability to epidemic diseases. After 1560 both bubonic plague and smallpox devastated Brazil. As a Jesuit leader put it, "The number of people who have died here in Bahia in the past twenty years seems unbelievable."[3] Portuguese laws and colonial custom exacerbated the losses from disease by permitting colonial governors to assign Indians from villages supervised by clerics to settlers as forced laborers. In the end the *aldeias* proved unattractive to the Indians. One observer noted, "The Jesuits once governed more than fifty *aldeias* of these Christian Indians, but there are now no more than three."[4]

In response to these pressures and to the epidemics many natives moved voluntarily. Initiated by individuals, families, or sometimes larger groups, even villages, these migrations varied regionally in scale. In Yucatan, for example, these population movements seem to have been much larger than in central Mexico, suggesting that the relative success of congregation in central Mexico resulted largely from the greater potential for coercion enjoyed by Spanish authorities near the colonial capital. Where Spanish power was weaker, as in Yucatan, Indians were able to maintain traditional elements of their social and economic structures. For example, over a third of the native population in Yucatan resided outside the congregated towns imposed by the Spanish. Many had, in fact, fled into unpacified areas to escape colonial controls. Some left the congregated towns for new, outlying settlements in the same region, putting distance between themselves and colonial authorities. Others moved away from their communities of birth to escape burdens imposed by traditional ethnic authorities. These strategies were all designed to provide a release, however temporary, from multiplying taxation and labor obligations exacerbated by declining population.

Before the arrival of the Spanish in Peru the Inca had a hereditary class of laborers, *yanaconas*, who were exempt from traditional labor service. *Yanaconas* were not tied to a specific *kuraka*, community, or *ayllu* but had a special service relationship to the state. In colonial times Andean Indians who were allies of the Spanish or worked on their estates were identified as *yanas*, or *yanaconas*. More quickly Hispanized than Indians who remained in traditional *ayllus*, *yanaconas* were tied to the emerging Spanish colonial economy, often finding employers far from their birthplace. The growth of this population accompanied Spanish impositions of tax and labor obligations that reduced the benefits associated with *ayllu* membership.

The *mita* was the most onerous obligation imposed on native peoples in the Andean region. The indigenous peoples had developed a reciprocal labor system, called the *mita*, long before the conquest. The Spanish forced Indian communities to provide labor on a rotational basis in mines, agriculture, textile factories, and other activities. The most infamous *mita* was designed to ensure a reliable annual labor pool of over thirteen thousand Indian men to work in the mines of Potosí alone. Drawing on the Indian communities closest to the mines, it required one-seventh of the adult male population to work at Potosí for one year out of seven. The work was dangerous and injuries and loss of life were common. Despite these dangers, some Indians who performed *mita* service at Potosí chose to remain at the mines as wage laborers, rather than returning to their homes. By its nature the *mita* led to substantial population dislocations in the southern highlands, since wives and children accompanied *mita* laborers to the mines. Anxious to avoid *mita* service thousands fled their homes, thereby surrendering traditional rights provided by membership in an *ayllu*. The number of *yanaconas* surged as a result.

A second category of voluntary migrants, the *forasteros*, expanded quickly at the same time. Spanish officials classified Indians who had moved away from their traditional *ayllus* to reside in other indigenous communities as *forasteros* (strangers or foreigners). Although these migrants lost their hereditary rights to farm *ayllu* land, they paid lower tribute payments and were exempted, like *yanaconas*, from forced labor service in the *mita*. The growth in *yanacona* and *forastero* populations, coupled with recurrent epidemics, increased the pressure on those who remained in the *ayllus*, forcing many men to return to Potosí more often than every seven years. The costs were devastating. By the early 1680s the Indian population of Upper Peru had been reduced to roughly half of its level in 1570. Among those who survived, residency patterns and kinship ties had been transformed. In the sixteen provinces subject to the Potosí *mita*, half of the Indian population was classified as *yanacona* or *forastero*. In the fourteen neighboring provinces that were exempt from *mita* obligations, approximately three-quarters of the population were classified as *forasteros*. The scale of this movement away from traditional *ayllu* membership suggests the terrible pressures of Spanish *mita* duties and tribute payments.

The Iberian Population

Population growth characterized demographic change in the Iberian population. Immigration accounted for the initial expansion. Soon, however, increased numbers of Iberian women in the colonies led to the natural growth of the population.

The number of emigrants from Spain to the Indies is unknown. Given the smaller number of ships sailing to the Indies beginning in the second quarter of the seventeenth century, it is probable that emigration decreased steadily from then until at least 1720. The number of European Spaniards arriving then rose again, although never to the level reached between 1550 and 1650.

The following table is based on information regarding ships sailing from Spain between 1506 and 1699:

	Passengers	Sailors Remaining in America	Total	Average per Year
1506–60	56,935	28,736	85,671	1,558
1561–1600	104,910	52,272	157,182	3,930
1601–25	74,400	35,912	111,312	4,452
1626–50	54,640	28,864	88,504	3,340
1651–99	29,348	10,853	40,201	820
Totals	320,233	156,637	476,870	

Sources: Magnus Mörner, "Spanish Migration to the New World Prior to 1810: A Report on the State of Research," in Fredi Chiapelli, editor, *First Images of America* (Berkeley and Los Angeles: University of California Press, 1976), vol. 2, pp. 766–67; and Lutgardo García Fuentes, *El Comercio Español con America (1650–1700)* (Seville: Escuela de Estudios Hispano-Americanos de Sevilla, 1980), chap. 4.

Although a few foreigners, mainly Portuguese, entered the Spanish colonies, the Crown always tried to regulate immigration and limit access to its own subjects. Protestants, descendants of Jews, *moriscos*, and gypsies were excluded by law from the Spanish Indies, but small numbers entered anyway.

Emigration

Little is known about the history of Portuguese emigration because the Lisbon earthquake of 1755 destroyed many records. In 1584, the pacified coastal region of Brazil had an estimated population of 57,000, of which whites, a group that must have been largely immigrant, numbered 25,000. By 1600, the total population is believed to have been 150,000, of which 30,000 were white. A century later an estimated 100,000 whites made up a third of the population of Brazil's settled areas. These estimates of the white population included substantial numbers of American-born whites and white and Indian mixtures, who because of their high status were considered white. Since fewer women left Portugal for Brazil than Spain for Spanish America, the natural increase of whites was also lower.

The Portuguese emigrated to Brazil to take advantage of the sugar and mining booms. Both events caused an increase in the total number of arrivals and in the number of emigrants from the middle and upper classes. In the early eighteenth century, perhaps three thousand to four thousand people left Portugal each year, primarily from the populous northern provinces, for the new mining regions of Brazil. Worried by the size of the exodus, in 1720 the Portuguese Crown tried, with some success, to restrict emigration.

Most of the first emigrants to the Spanish colonies were young men who joined the early expeditions of exploration, conquest, and settlement. By the middle of the sixteenth century, however, such adventure-hungry and unskilled young men were not encouraged to go west. Instead, artisans and professional men, civil officials, clerics, servants and retainers, and women and children now swelled the ranks of emigrants. For the rest of the century the percentage of women almost doubled, with officials, clerics, their retinues, and skilled craftsmen also rising in number. Most of the emigrants came from Andalusia and Extremadura; by 1600 roughly one of every five males, two of every five females, and one of every two merchants hailed from the city of Seville alone.

Mexico attracted the largest number of settlers in the sixteenth century, over a third of the total. Peru and Upper Peru (Bolivia) together received about a quarter. The Antilles, New Granada, and Tierra Firme were destinations for another quarter of the emigrants, and the Río de la Plata and Central America accounted for just under a tenth. The remaining emigrants were spread throughout the other regions of the empire—Chile, Florida, Venezuela, and Ecuador.

The emigrants left Spain for a variety of reasons: Those who departed in the years of Columbus, Cortés, and Pizarro sought glory and fortune, but later emigrants had more mundane goals. Most hoped to escape the growing economic problems in Spain and Portugal. Many had relatives established in prosperous regions who wrote glowing accounts of life in the New World. Ties to family, in fact, were the main reason for emigration.

By 1600 the number of Spaniards born in the New World exceeded the number of recent arrivals. Between 1570 and 1620 the Spanish population roughly trebled, from perhaps 125,000–150,000 to around 400,000. About half of the growth is attributed to natural increase. With every generation the creole population's proportion of the Spanish population in the Americas grew. The decline in Spanish emigration after 1625 meant that the number and proportion of peninsulars within the white population continued to fall.

Spanish and creole populations were distributed across the colonies unevenly with the largest concentrations found in Mexico and Peru. By the mid-seventeenth century, there were 200,000 Spaniards and creoles in Mexico and another 350,000 in the rest of the colonies. These were not fixed populations. Many Spanish immigrants and poorer creoles moved from colony to colony, chasing brighter prospects. The discovery of rich mineral deposits in Mexico and Upper Peru in the sixteenth century attracted thousands of Spaniards from the Antilles, for example. The white population of Potosí in Upper Peru exploded after the discovery of silver, reaching 3,000 Spaniards and 35,000 creoles by 1610. As silver production fell in the late seventeenth century, however, the white population was reduced to a small minority in a city of only 8,000.

The Spanish population was most numerous in and near the urban centers: Mexico City had 2,000 *vecinos* in the mid-sixteenth century and 3,000 by 1570, a number that continued to rise until the end of the colonial era, at which time about 70,000 Spaniards resided in the city. It is estimated that by the late eighteenth century just over half of the Spanish population of the Indies lived in urban areas.

Starting from a negligible number at the time of conquest, the population of Spanish descent had grown to almost a quarter of the total population by the 1790s. By that time as well, the number of racially mixed people had become increasingly visible.

The African Population

Blacks were present in large numbers in the Americas during the era of conquest and settlement. Thousands participated in the military campaigns against indigenous peoples. The majority of the earliest residents were the descendants of African slaves imported into Portugal and Spain during the fifteenth century. Most were slaves, although many managed to gain their freedom. The development of colonial economies coincided with the decline in native population because of epidemics. The demand for labor could not be met from free immigration or from the small population of slaves in Iberia. As a result, Spain and Portugal began to send slaves to the Americas directly from Africa. Because Portugal controlled areas along Africa's Atlantic coast, the slave trade to Brazil quickly dwarfed imports to the Spanish colonies. Spurred by the early development of the sugar industry in the late sixteenth century and by a mining boom after 1695, Africans and their American-born descendents came to constitute the single largest component of the Brazilian population. During the sugar industry's expansion in the seventeenth century, the number of slaves imported to Brazil averaged about 5,600 per year. By 1810 more than 2.5 million African captives had arrived in Brazil. Despite the rising tide of slave imports, the growth of the black population of colonial Latin America was slowed by both the sexual imbalance in the slave trade and by high mortality rates. Because the purchasers of slaves preferred males to females, approximately two males to one female were imported in the course of the trade. Moreover, extremely high mortality rates were found in the deadly disease environments of the tropical lowlands of the Caribbean Basin and Brazil where the richest sugar plantations were located. As a result, the plantation areas depended on a steady flow of new African slaves, rather than natural increase, for labor.

New Ethnic Groups

By the end of the eighteenth century, people of mixed descent were an extremely important population group in colonial Latin America, having grown more rapidly than any other sector of the population. In 1580 when the permanent settlement of Buenos Aires established Spain's control of the Río de la Plata region, men of mixed descent, the sons of European fathers and Indian mothers, were the majority of this "Spanish" settler population. Sexual relations between European men and Indian women were common from the early era of exploration. Indeed, according to R. C. Padden, the Spanish "commonly left more pregnancies in their camps than they did casualties on the field of battle."[5] These relationships were seldom formal or long lasting. Rape and the use of other forms of coercion were common. But the prestige and military successes of European men in the New World led some indigenous families to seek relationships. Both Cortés and Pizarro had numerous relationships with

Indian women and fathered mixed children, *mestizos.* Doña Marina, the famous Malinche, had a succession of Spanish partners.

Although some European men married Indian women, particularly in the early years when European women were very scarce in the colonies, few mixed children were legitimate according to the understandings of the time. Most were regarded as either "natural children" or illegitimates. In each case the child was born out of wedlock, but the birth status of illegitimates could never be improved because the marriage of the parents was prevented by close blood ties or because one or both were already married. Illegitimacy was a difficult stigma to overcome, but the status and behavior of the European father commonly determined the child's prospects. If a son or daughter had an ongoing relationship with a rich or powerful father, the mixed child was commonly included in European society, enjoying the father's social status. Indian mothers raised mixed children not acknowledged by their fathers in traditional culture. The status of the mixed population in the early decades of the colonies was complex and unpredictable. Some experienced discrimination while others were able to obtain positions of responsibility and leadership. As this population grew and as the number of Spanish women in the colonies increased, the status of the *mestizo* population fell and became generally associated with illegitimacy. In Portuguese America this mixed population was called *mamelucos, mestiços,* or *caboclos.* In the late sixteenth and seventeenth centuries the mixed population increased dramatically, playing a crucial role in enforcing Portuguese authority in the frontier zones and in protecting Brazil from French, and later Dutch, military interventions.

The arrival of Africans introduced a third ethnic group into the Americas. African slaves and their American-born descendents, both slave and free, contributed to the growing complexity of New World identities. Very few Spanish or Portuguese residents of the colonies married black women. Less formal contacts, especially in the plantation zones where the slave population was concentrated, were common. Children born to slave mothers and white fathers, called mulattoes or *pardos,* inherited the mother's legal condition, bondage, unless freed by the father. Africans and their descendents also established relationships with Indians. Most commonly these were between black men and Indian women. Offspring of these relationships were termed *zambo* in some regions but mulatto in others.

The consequence of relationships across ethnic boundaries was the rapid growth of a nonwhite, non-Indian population. Approximately 45 percent of the Spanish Empire's population of 14.1 million around 1800 was non-Indian and over 20 percent of it was *mestizo* or *pardo.* The term *casta* became the most common umbrella term in the Spanish colonies for any nonwhite who was not clearly an Indian.

The establishment of colonies by Spain and Portugal transformed the Americas demographically. Throughout the region Indian populations declined by up to 90 percent. In temperate climates, especially at higher altitudes, indigenous peoples experienced a modest recovery after the six-teenth cen-tury, but nowhere was the indigenous population as large in 1800 as it had been before the Europeans reached the New World. Euro-pean populations increased as a result of both natural reproduction and, at least until the mid-seventeenth century, immigration. In the Caribbean islands and adjacent lowlands and in the lowlands of the Pacific slope, African slaves largely replaced the native populations that had been dev-astated by disease. Finally, these new populations of Europeans and Africans mixed with indigenous peoples and with each other, producing new Amer-ican peoples and cultures. This mixed population expanded rapidly in the late sixteenth century and continued to increase its proportion of the total population of Latin America as the colonial era progressed.

Indian Labor

The domestic and export economies of colonial Latin America rested largely on forced labor. Although supplemented over time by African slaves and a growing *casta* population, Indians provided the labor power that over-came Spain's limited capital resources and technology in developing min-ing and agriculture for the export market and agriculture, grazing, and textiles for the domestic market. Brazil's sugar plantations were well estab-lished by the mid-sixteenth century with the labor of Indian slaves. With the development of the African slave trade, they became less dependent on Indians, and by the early seventeenth century, the sugar plantations of Penambuco and Bahia were worked mainly by African slaves.

Because the Indians rarely volunteered to work for the Iberian settlers, colonial officials evolved various forms of compulsory labor and fiscal demands to mobilize them. Depopulation, the separation of labor from goods as tribute, the conversion of goods into cash as tribute, and the compulsory purchase of goods from Spanish officials all forced changes in the organization of labor. Indians were compelled to participate in the monetized colonial economy, an economy that overlapped but did not totally replace the indigenous one. The methods used to secure labor varied by region and over time. *Encomienda, repartimiento/mita,* free wage labor, *yanaconaje,* and slavery were the principal means employed in Spanish America. In Brazil, Indian slavery provided much of the agricultural labor initially, but from the 1570s planters increasingly relied on African slaves.

Encomienda

Both the Spanish Crown and individual Spaniards wanted to profit from their presence in the New World. With the exception of the Incan treasure, plunder produced only modest riches. But in Mesoamerica and the Andean region, urbanized, economically advanced societies were accustomed to providing agricultural surplus and labor as tribute to native overlords even before the conquest. The problem for the Crown and the conquistadors was how best to harness this labor power.

In the Caribbean, Spaniards employed an early form of *encomienda* as well as slavery to appropriate Indian labor. *Encomienda* Indians on Española were forcibly moved to the gold fields; subjected to outrageous demands for labor, food, and, in the case of women, sexual favors; and even sold. They were scarcely distinguishable from the enslaved natives imported from other islands and Tierra Firme. Faced with incontrovertible evidence of this excessive exploitation, Ferdinand issued the Laws of Burgos in 1512, the first systematic attempt to regulate the Spaniards' treatment of the Indians. Better work conditions, adequate food and living standards, and restrictions on punishment were among its many, though unenforced, provisions.

By the time the Spaniards reached Mexico, the allocation of Indians through *encomienda* was fixed in conquistadors' minds as an appropriate, if not indispensable, reward for their actions. Cortés, despite fearing a repetition of the demographic disaster he had witnessed in the islands, yielded to his followers' clamor and assigned them Indian *caciques* and their peoples. Grants of *encomienda*, often the most valuable spoil available, subsequently accompanied conquest in each region the Spaniards occupied.

The conquistadors and early settlers who received *encomiendas* constituted the colonial aristocracy for several decades. Their large households dominated city centers, and their rural enterprises tied the Indian communities to the marketplace. The *encomiendas* themselves varied enormously in size and value. The Crown confirmed Cortés in *encomiendas* totaling 115,000 natives, a statutory number probably far below those he actually held. Pizarro assigned himself 20,000 tributaries for his services in Peru. Thirty *encomiendas* in the Valley of Mexico in 1535 averaged 6,000 Indians each, far above the legal maximum of 300. More common than large awards, however, was the grant of a single *cacique* and his people.

Even in central New Spain and Peru, the number of *encomenderos* was never large. Only 506 *encomenderos* have been identified for New Spain from 1521 to 1555, by which time a number of *encomiendas* had reverted to the Crown. Peru never had more than about 500 *encomenderos*, and by 1555 only 5 percent of an estimated Spanish population of 8,000 held Indians in *encomienda*.

Initially the mainland *encomienda* supported essential elements of indigenous culture and economy. Except where precious metals were found, the *encomenderos*' demands were similar to those of the preconquest indigenous elites. The well-established patterns and the settled nature of the indigenous agricultural economies of central Mexico and Peru altered the labor practices of the Caribbean *encomienda*. In Española and Cuba, *encomenderos* routinely moved Indians to the gold mines, thus breaking the natives' ties to their lands. But even though Cortés, Pedro de Alvarado, and others forcibly enlisted Indians as military auxiliaries and porters, the *encomenderos* usually tried to profit from the existing indigenous economy. In comparison with the Caribbean experience, the *encomienda* in Mexico and Peru had a more settled character.

The small number of conquistadors and the administrative problems inherent in the tribute system forced reliance on indigenous leaders to serve as middlemen. The *kurakas* in Peru organized and supervised the delivery of labor and goods for sale and exchange in the urban centers where the *encomenderos* resided. The *kurakas* also acted as intermediaries for the *encomenderos* in efforts to limit or transform the tribute requirement. Indeed, the Andean tradition of mutual service may have mitigated the abuses that marked the behavior of the first generation of *encomenderos* in New Spain.

In central Mexico, the early *encomenderos* appeared to have learned nothing from their predecessors in the Antilles. They overworked the Indians, forcing them to construct buildings, provide labor for farms and mines, and transport goods. They seized the Indians' property and women and beat, jailed, and killed those that resisted. Some *encomenderos* sold the Indians' labor, whereas others pushed them off their land in order to introduce cash crops and grazing animals. The *caciques* and Indian nobles who required taxes on top of the *encomenderos'* demands added to the commoners' burden.

The *encomenderos'* central concern was income, and they made every effort to extract tribute goods that could be sold at a profit. Tribute payments varied, depending on local resources and skills. They were paid in cash or in foodstuffs, raw materials, and finished goods. One Mexican *encomienda* in the 1540s provided daily two chickens, fodder for horses,

Two *encomienda* laborers are forced to work in a primitive textile *obraje*. Both the loom and the spinning wheel represent European technology transfers to the colonies.

wood, maize, and, every eighty days, shirts, petticoats, and blankets. Depending on the region, *encomiendas* supplied cotton mantles, cacao, cochineal, llamas, wheat, and coca. Regardless of the monetary benefits of selling tribute goods, most *encomenderos* also demanded labor for service in their homes, on their rural properties, or in their workshops.

When the *encomenderos* could use the Indians' labor to enter the profitable export business, they altered the traditional economy. Hence, the *encomenderos* in Central America demanded cacao as tribute and became, in effect, cacao wholesalers for the large Mexican market. The *encomenderos* in Tucumán and Córdoba organized Indian men, women, and children to produce textiles for the growing market at Potosí after the discovery of silver there in 1545.

The New Laws

The catastrophic native depopulation, the growing Spanish emigration, and the denunciation of the *encomenderos'* abuses came to a head in the 1540s. Correctly suspicious that the *encomenderos* wanted to become a New World version of the Castilian aristocracy, the Crown listened to colonists excluded from grants of *encomienda* and to a small, articulate group of clerics who condemned the *encomienda* as a major source of the ills suffered by the natives. The most effective lobbyist was the Dominican Bartolomé de las Casas, whose efforts led to the New Laws of 1542.

The New Laws authorized a viceroy for Peru and *audiencias* in Lima and Guatemala as part of their provisions to create a more effective administration and to improve the judicial system. But they are best known for prohibiting Indian slavery, attacking the *encomenderos* in general, and ordering in particular that individuals responsible for the civil war in Peru be stripped of their *encomiendas*. This last provision and one prohibiting new assignments of *encomiendas* and ordering the reversion of existing ones to the Crown upon the death of their incumbents angered the *encomenderos* and their supporters. The ensuing rebellion in Peru brought the death of the region's first viceroy, and in New Spain, a wiser viceroy, Antonio de Mendoza, refrained from the laws' enforcement rather than provoke rebellion.

Faced with the unexpectedly violent reaction, the Crown relented, and by allowing succession for a second "life," it enabled the *encomenderos* to pass on their grants for another generation. But ironically, as a result of the civil wars and the frequent lack of heirs, many of the *encomiendas* had already become part of the royal patrimony and provided tribute to the royal treasury, tribute whose collection was overseen by royally appointed *corregidores*, who were named for a short term rather than for life. The slow transfer of *encomiendas* from private to royal domain meant a shift in power away from the original colonial aristocracy in central Mexico and Peru. Before 1570 about three-quarters of the *encomienda* income in the Valley of Mexico had reverted to the Crown, and so extensions of *encomiendas* for third and fourth lives had little significance. *Encomiendas* and other types of labor services and tribute in kind did survive in Paraguay, Yucatan, remote areas of Central America, New Granada, Chile, and northwestern Argentina until the late eighteenth century. Although essential to these areas' economies, their size and value were not important enough to the Crown to make their complete suppression necessary.

Repartimiento/Mita

As direct control of the *encomiendas* passed into the hands of colonial officials, the Indian communities increasingly were required to substitute cash tributes for the earlier payments in kind, although this transition was never completed. For tributaries to meet annual payments of up to eight pesos, they had to produce goods for the market and work for wages. In the areas near the major Spanish towns and the mining camps of New Spain and Peru, wage labor and market agriculture thus became a fixture of the Indians' lives. Elsewhere, however, the natives participated less in the money economy. But by 1600, Indian communities throughout much of the empire had reorganized to meet the monetary requirements of the colonial state and the Church as well as to satisfy new needs associated with the assimilation of the European material culture.

Neither cash tribute nor the desire to work for wages to subsidize the purchase of nonsubsistence goods drew enough Indians away from their traditional production to provide the amount of cheap labor demanded by Spanish landowners, miners, and textile manufacturers. In addition, the diminished Indian population that survived the early epidemics often lived far from the new economic centers, particularly the mining regions of Mexico and Peru. Thus large numbers of Indian laborers had to be relocated.

The solution to this problem was a system of rotational labor drafts, called *repartimiento* in New Spain and *mita* in Peru. Compulsory labor service had been common in both the Aztec and Inca empires, and Spaniards had used it from the beginning of the colonial period for the construction of roads, aqueducts, fortifications, churches and public buildings, and for some agricultural purposes. Formal *repartimiento/mita* drafts were established in New Spain in the 1550s, the central Andes in the 1570s, and the eastern highlands of Colombia in the 1590s. Under this system the Indian communities filled a quota of laborers for a prescribed time, usually two to four months of the year. The workers then could apply the minimal wages they received to their tribute and other required payments.

This labor system differed according to region. In New Spain the *repartimiento* supplied labor mainly for agriculture, although silver miners also used it in central Mexico. The *mita* was the labor base for the early Peruvian mining industry, on coastal plantations, and for road repair and maintenance projects. In Quito and Tucumán, labor in textile factories (*obrajes*) was a common form of *repartimiento* service. In Central America, *repartimientos* provided labor for wheat farming and indigo production.

Their use in the latter activity was illegal, but both the producers and royal administrators came to regard the small fines as part of the labor cost. In Oaxaca, where Indians were assigned primarily to Spanish wheat farmers, the *repartimiento* made up only about 4 percent of all tributaries.

The most important manifestation of this system of forced labor was imposed on the indigenous peoples of the Southern Andes. The discovery of rich silver deposits at Potosí created an enormous need for labor, and Indians were compelled to work from the beginning in the 1540s. However, the initial system had been undermined by competition among Spanish miners and by various strategies of resistance evolved by indigenous communities. In 1572 Viceroy Toledo transformed the *mita* to provide an annual labor draft of roughly thirteen thousand Indians for the mines of Potosí. In the sixteenth and seventeenth centuries it was common for Indians assigned to the Potosí *mita* to purchase an exemption by paying the equivalent cash payment of a wage laborer. As the silver played out miners increasingly took the cash as income. The historical labor burden of Andean communities, a system that began as reciprocal obligations within the *ayllu*, had become the forced transfer of wealth from poor Indians to rich Spaniards.

In some regions the *repartimiento/mita* remained an important mechanism for mobilizing Indian labor until the end of the colonial era. The mining *mitas* in Peru, the *repartimiento* for textile *obraje* labor in Ecuador, and the agricultural *repartimiento* in Central America survived into the nineteenth century. In central New Spain, the *repartimiento* was important to agriculture for less than a century, but in the north, in New Galicia, this system continued to supplement free labor until the early eighteenth century.

Free Wage Labor

The continuing decline of the native population and the growth of the Spanish population rendered the *repartimiento* an inadequate source of labor for agricultural and mining production. Large estate owners (*hacendados*) and miners in central New Spain solved the need for a regular supply of labor by contracting directly with Indians and *castas*, often paying wages slightly higher than those paid for *repartimiento* labor. Originally a supplement to *repartimiento* labor, in time free wage labor replaced it. Indians who lost their lands through sale or usurpation and those who found the financial demands of their village unbearable formed a pool of labor available for hire and, in some cases, for permanent residence on the *haciendas*.

By 1630 free wage labor had largely supplanted *repartimiento* in New Spain, and the number of *hacienda* residents, often *castas*, was expanding. The forced labor draft remained in use in the Valley of Mexico only for the interminable project of draining Lake Texcoco. By the late sixteenth century in Peru and Upper Peru, free wage labor was more prevalent than *mita* labor in the mining districts. In Chilean agriculture, free wage labor became important in the mid-seventeenth century, and a century later it was widespread in Ecuador and the eastern highlands of Colombia. Throughout Spanish America, powerful landowners and mine owners were able to control the cost of labor and keep wages at artificially low levels. Wage earners may have been free, but a true labor market seldom existed.

An outgrowth of free wage labor was debt peonage. *Hacendados*, miners, and owners of *obrajes* sought to hold workers in debt in order to prevent them from moving to another job. For their part, the laborers sometimes demanded credit before accepting employment. In many cases, neither creditor nor debtor expected to ever settle the account.

Debt peonage associated with free wage labor varied greatly by region. It was common throughout New Spain, where the amount of debt ranged from averages of fewer than three weeks to eleven months of work. The extent of debt peonage varied over time as well, remaining generally constant in Morelos in the eighteenth century but eroding in Guadalajara owing to the workers' weakened bargaining power as a result of demographic expansion. Debt peonage seems to have been more widespread in Ecuador than in Mexico, less prevalent on the coastal estates of Peru, but on the Jesuit estates in Tucumán, its use to tie down workers was routine. In Chile, peonage eventually took the form of *inquilinaje*, or land loans.

Indian Slavery

The progression from *encomienda* to *repartimiento/mita* to free wage labor and at times debt peonage—the classic pattern of labor institutions in Spanish America—appeared first and was achieved most fully in New Spain, but one or more stages could be found across the colonies. During times of economic transition distinct labor systems coexisted or competed in close proximity. For example, in early New Spain, African slaves who served as foremen on rural estates supervised some *encomienda* laborers. And, in the early eighteenth century, *mita* laborers in the silver mines of Potosí worked alongside free wage laborers and slaves. Two other Indian labor systems, Indian slavery and *yanaconaje*, were significant to the early development of colonial economies.

Chattel slavery was the most repressive form of Indian labor in the early colonial period. Where mineral wealth and surplus agricultural production were absent, enslaving the natives rather than assigning them to *encomienda* proved more attractive to Spaniards eager for immediate profit. Thousands of Indians in the Caribbean had been enslaved by the first generation of settlers. Despite reservations, the Crown accepted the enslavement of Indians, notably those who refused to acknowledge its authority and submit peacefully. Under pressure from the Spanish colonists, some native *caciques* enslaved free Indians. As the Indian population declined on Española, Spanish adventurers sought captives on neighboring islands. Once defined as slaves, Indian captives were bought and sold as chattel.

Forms of forced labor viewed by the Spaniards as slavery were common in Mesoamerica before the conquest. Informants told the Spanish that natives fought to capture slaves for labor or sacrifice. In addition, thieves, rapists, and poachers, among others, could be sentenced to enslavement for crimes. This tradition provided a convenient justification for the expansion of even harsher forms of slavery by the Spaniards. During the conquest of Central America captives were commonly branded and divided among Spaniards as booty. A lively trade in Indian slaves expanded across the region because of the demand for native labor elsewhere. Nicaragua's principal economic activity in the 1530s was enslaving Indians who were then sent to Panama and Peru. There is no agreement on the number of slaves shipped out of Central America, but estimates range from fifty thousand to hundreds of thousands forcibly exported between 1524 and 1549. Depopulation and the Crown's attack on the mistreatment of Indians in the New Laws brought slavery to an end by 1550 in Central America, however. Alonso López de Cerrato, named to preside over the recently established *audiencia* for much of Central America (Los Confines), reached the region in 1548 and implemented the new prohibitions on holding native slaves, much to the dismay of numerous colonists and traders. Spanish slave raids continued on the Venezuelan coast until the early seventeenth century, and native enslavement persisted on the northern New Spain frontiers until the early eighteenth century. In Chile and northern Argentina the enslavement of Indians was an ongoing part of frontier warfare well into the eighteenth century.

The enlarged Portuguese presence after 1530 worsened the labor problem in colonial Brazil. Despite Jesuit protests, slaving expeditions became commonplace as the expanding sugar industry required more laborers. The theory behind the expansion of slavery in Brazil was similar to that in Spanish America. "Just war," cannibalism, and the ransom of Indians captured by other natives in intertribal war in return for lifetime servitude were acceptable justifications for enslavement. With the demonstrated profitability of sugar the numbers of Indian slaves rose, reaching approximately nine thousand on the sugar plantations of Bahia alone.

The coastal Indian population fell as a result of enslavement, increased warfare, and, beginning in 1562, the spread of disease. The slave traders then moved into Brazil's immense interior. By 1600, formal slaving expeditions (*bandeiras*) were becoming more frequent. Slavers from São Paulo, the famous *bandeirantes*, scoured much of south and central Brazil in the seventeenth century looking for Indians to capture and enslave. Jesuit missions, even in the Spanish colony of Paraguay, were particularly attractive targets, and the *bandeirantes* seized thousands of Indians from them in the early decades of the century. Although slaving expeditions continued in the interior until the mid-eighteenth century, the captured Indians were sent mainly to Rio de Janeiro, São Vicente, and São Paulo. On the sugar plantations of Pernambuco and Bahia in the northeast, African slaves had begun to replace Indian slaves in the 1570s, and by the 1620s the transition was nearly complete. However, Indian slavery persisted on Brazil's frontiers until the 1750s and illegally thereafter in a few areas. But by that time African slavery had long been the most important source of labor on Brazil's plantations.

Yanaconaje

In the Inca Empire individuals unattached to *ayllus* were called *yanaconas*. Growing in number even before Atahualpa's capture, the disruption of the Spanish conquest and the demands of the mining *mita* increased the number of uprooted natives. Spanish landowners willingly allowed them to settle on their estates in return for specified amounts of labor and produce. Among the benefits of this relationship, *yanaconas* were exempt from the *mita* and paid tribute at a lower rate. By 1600 the number of *yanaconas* was nearly equal to that of Indians who remained in traditional *ayllus* in Peru and Upper Peru. As the system matured it was known as *yanaconaje*.

Most *yanaconas* were tied to Spanish agricultural estates where they received some land for their own use in return for labor. Over time these *yanaconas* became rooted on a particular Spanish estate, a type of bound labor. Colonial bills of sale suggest that this dependent condition was enduring. Although *yanaconas* were not legal chattel, like slaves who could be bought and sold, they were often included with the estate on which they resided when it changed hands. Thus labor, as well as land, passed from owner to owner. One Indian complained to a Spanish bishop, "my employer has held me in his power and in servitude since my birth, more than twelve years ago, simply because my parents were his *yanaconas* and I was born on his *hacienda.*"[6] During this same period, silver miners also attracted *yanaconas* to Potosí. The rapid growth in the number of *yanaconas* in Peru led Viceroy Toledo to remove their exemption from tribute and to order them to remain in their current residence. This decision reinforced the *yanaconas*' status as a workforce tied to specific locations or estates. This relative lack of mobility distinguished *yanaconaje* from other "free" labor systems. By 1600 the number of *yanaconas* was almost equal to that of Indians retaining traditional land rights in Peru and Upper Peru. Versions of the institutions were retained in northwestern Argentina into the seventeenth century and, under the name *originarios*, in Paraguay into the 1790s. In some places *yanaconaje* persisted after independence.

Repartimiento de Bienes *and Indian Resistance*

Although the Spanish employed different forms of native labor, their purpose was always to convert labor into cash profit. Many Indians participated reluctantly in an inadequately integrated colonial economy with limited opportunities to earn the cash often necessary to meet tribute demands, pay religious fees, and purchase raw materials and finished goods. Over time the Spaniards devised a system of credit that enabled Indians to obtain needed items and even to obtain cash loans on the one hand while it provided substantial profit for participating officials and their merchant backers on the other. The *repartimiento* or *reparto de bienes* or *mercancías* reached maturity in the late seventeenth century and continued even after outlawed in the 1780s. Under this system, *corregidores* and *alcaldes mayores* effectively monopolized commerce between the Indians in their juris-diction and the outside by providing raw materials on credit and then purchasing the finished goods—cochineal in Oaxaca, coca in the *yungas* of Upper Peru, textiles in Quito—at low fixed prices that included the interest on the advances. Similarly, the officials made available on credit a variety of animals and consumer goods—mules and textiles were the most common in the Andes—at elevated prices that again reflected built-in high rates of interest and profit. The *corregidores'* judicial authority to collect debts gave them the security to sell on credit, although their abuse of this power provoked resistance that, in its extreme form, became rebellion. The ultimate effect of the *repartimiento de bienes* system was to create a permanent trade imbalance in the Indian communities that only native wage labor could make up.

Indians resisted labor demands in any way they could. Some fled their homes, surrendering their traditional right to land but retaining control over their lives. Sometimes indigenous chieftains refused to cooperate and were imprisoned or lost their positions as a consequence. Local rebellions were common, notably in the Andes. Spanish authorities routinely responded to such challenges with force, beating, imprisoning, and occasionally even execution. Rarely able to improve conditions through force, the Indian communities quickly learned to use the colonial legal system, which included courts designated for their cases. For example, they could hire lawyers and initiate suits to win a smaller *mita* quota or the payment of their statutory wages. Although these victories were often costly and seldom lasted, the Indians' resourcefulness and persistence were remarkable.

Spanish demands for labor and the commercial requirements of the colonial economy often severed the close relationship between the natives and their land. The need to meet tribute payments, serve in labor drafts, and pay for goods made available and, at times, imposed upon them by the *repartimiento de bienes,* forced Indians from their villages and into the Hispanic culture. The transformation of Indian culture, however, was never complete. The Indians continued to resist the commercialization of their labor and production long after the Spanish Empire had collapsed.

Slavery and the Slave Trade

Before the Portuguese voyages of discovery in the early fifteenth cen-tury, slavery in Western Europe had declined from its prominence in the latter stages of the Roman Empire to a marginal place in European social and economic life. But the Portuguese traders' explorations of Africa's Atlantic coast introduced them to the continent's indigenous slave trade, and by 1450 hundreds of African slaves were entering Europe each year. This flow seems to have peaked at about five hundred per year in the 1480s and then remained constant into the next century. Thus by the time that Columbus sailed, African slavery was well established in Iberia.

Slavery moved much closer to the legal and structural form it took in America when Portugal and Spain began to develop the Atlantic islands. The introduction of sugar cultivation from the eastern Mediterranean to Madeira and the Canary Islands hastened the adaptation of Iberian institutions and social forms to the special requirements of a colonial economic environment. Because these islands lacked an adequate labor force, sugar cultivation was linked to the African slave trade almost immediately. This stage in the development of slavery culminated in the Portuguese settlement of São Tomé. Located close to the African coast, it became the prototype of the plantation colony relying on heavy capital investment, monoculture, and a work force of African slaves.

Early African Slavery

Epidemic disease and a growing preference for black workers among Spanish and Portuguese settlers produced a ready market for African slaves. Indeed, investing in slaves proved to be a sound financial decision for many colonial miners and sugar planters. The owners of Brazilian sugar plantations, for example, found African slaves more profitable than Indian slaves who were less expensive, healthy, and productive. Nonetheless, it was primarily native labor that supported colonial enterprise in many parts of Latin America. *Encomienda, repartimiento,* and *mita* required little capital investment and had the added benefit of compelling native communities to provide the subsistence and maintenance of the workers. African slavery therefore prospered where diminished Indian populations could no longer sustain these alternative forms of forced labor. In the wake of staggeringly high indigenous mortality rates, the use of African slaves in agriculture spread from the Caribbean to the tropical lowlands of the Caribbean Basin and Brazil, sustaining the production of tobacco, cacao, indigo, and, of course, sugar.

Sugar cultivation was introduced in Española in the early sixteenth century. But the product's full potential in the New World was first realized in Brazil when the plantation model developed in the Atlantic islands took hold in the second half of the sixteenth century. In the early Spanish period Genoese merchants provided much of the capital and black slaves most of the labor. After the conquests of the Aztec and Inca empires, large numbers of Spaniards abandoned the older settlements of the Caribbean to seek their fortunes in Mexico and Peru. Shorn of investment capital and manpower, the islands could not compete successfully with the well-established Portuguese sugar estates of the Atlantic islands or the emerging production of Brazil.

Slavery was used successfully in the early mining industry in the mainland colonies. Placer mining with Indian labor had produced much of the mineral wealth extracted from Española before 1520, and many early settlers in Central America had prior experience in this industry. Initially, the *encomienda* and enslaved Indians formed the labor gangs in the gold-mining industry in Honduras and Guatemala. But high levels of mortality among native laborers drove the miners to import expensive black slaves. Several major gold strikes provided the necessary capital, and by the 1540s slaves were arriving in substantial numbers, eventually reaching three thousand. When profits fell, however, Central America's miners sold their African slaves to settlers in wealthier regions, like Peru, returning to the use of cheaper Indian labor. Although approximately five thousand slaves worked in the silver mines in Potosí around 1600, African slaves were much more important to the gold mining industry. Officials in Ecuador repeatedly asked to import slaves to work the region's gold mines, disingenuously suggesting this was good for the Africans. "The blacks would not be harmed; in fact it would be a service to them to be taken from Guinea, from una fire and tyranny and barbarity and brutality where without law and without God they live as savage brutes."[7]

The African Slave Trade

Spain had surrendered its right to establish outposts in Africa by the Treaty of Alcaçovas in 1479. Consequently it developed a system of monopoly contracts, *asientos*, with foreign merchants, usually Portuguese, to supply its American colonies with slaves. To secure the maximum fiscal benefit for itself and to prevent contraband trade, beginning in 1518 the Crown sold exclusive licenses to private enterprises, individuals, or monopoly companies to import into the colonies a set number of *piezas de Indias*, young adult males or their labor equivalent, within a limited number of years. Since women, children, and older or disabled men counted as fractions, a ship delivering one hundred *piezas de Indias* could actually unload two hundred or more slaves. Because the *asientista* usually earned greater profits from the introduction of contraband goods, few fulfilled their obligation to import a full quota of African slaves. The *asiento* bid up the cost of slaves, and the fleet system impeded efforts to market in Europe Spanish colonial plantation goods produced by slave labor.

Between the early sixteenth century and 1810, Spanish America received nearly one million African slaves. The following table reveals that the late eighteenth century—a time of dramatic expansion in sugar and other tropical products—was also the time of greatest volume in the slave trade:

Estimated Slave Imports to Latin America, 1551–1810

	Total Imports		Average per Year	
Years	Spanish America	Brazil	Spanish America	Brazil
1551–1600	62,500	50,000	1,250	1,000
1601–1700	292,500	560,000	2,925	5,600
1701–1810	578,600	1,891,400	5,786	18,914

Source: Philip D. Curtin, *The Atlantic Slave Trade: A Census* (Madison: University of Wisconsin Press, 1969), pp. 116, 119.

The booming sugar plantations of Cuba absorbed more than half of the slaves entering Spanish America after 1770, although Venezuela and the Río de la Plata region also increased imports. Overall, however, the Spanish colonies received only about 13 percent of all the slaves imported into the Western Hemisphere before 1820. Brazil and the Caribbean sugar colonies of France and Great Britain were the preeminent destinations. British North America, in comparison, imported slightly fewer than 350,000 slaves, or one-third the number that entered Spanish America.

An overwhelming majority of the slaves taken to America were from West Africa. On small islands off the coast and in fortified trading posts, the Portuguese, Dutch, French, and English maintained trading stations and exchanged manufactured goods, rum, and tobacco for the slaves offered by African middlemen. European merchants preferred young adult males because women, children, and older men cost the same to ship but sold at lower prices. In addition, African sellers were more reluctant to sell women, for they were vital in African agriculture and highly valued in the Saharan slave trade with the Muslims. The resulting permanent sex imbalance of two males to one female in the trade undermined the slaves' potential for family life and retarded the natural increase of the New World slave population. Colonial planters sometimes expressed preferences for slaves from a specific African region because certain cultures had reputations for hard work or docility—the two characteristics the owners valued most. Yet problems in organizing the African side of the trade prevented a systematic effort to meet these demands. Traders took slaves from wherever they were plentiful and cheap, and planters bought those that were available.

Brazil was the first American colony to introduce sugar agriculture on a large scale. After a succession of epidemics devastated the supply of forced Indian labor, the planters of the northeast coastal zone turned to black slavery as an alternative labor source, and by the 1620s they relied on it almost entirely. Portuguese traders who dominated the African slave trade to Europe responded quickly to the growing Brazilian market. Also, the proximity of Africa reduced transportation costs and the number of slave deaths in transit. The consequence of these advantages can best be seen in a comparative context.

During the seventeenth century, almost as many slaves entered Brazil alone as entered Spanish America and the French and British sugar colonies combined. Even in the eighteenth century, when the Caribbean's sugar production grew most rapidly, the Portuguese colony continued its dominance in the Atlantic slave trade. Although the total imports of the French and British Caribbean colonies were greater, no other nation's colonies imported as many slaves as did Brazil. By 1810 more than 2.5 million slaves had entered Brazilian ports.

Estimates of slave imports to the Americas tend to disguise the trade's effects on Africa and obscure its dreadful nature. Tens of thousands of Africans died even before arriving in Africa's slave ports. Thousands perished in the wars and civil unrest that the slave trade helped promote. Travel in crowded and pestilential ships claimed the lives of tens of thousands more Africans. The Caribbean sugar boom in the eighteenth century created a heavy new demand for slaves, and inhuman conditions and the resulting high mortality became even more common in the slave ships plying the Atlantic. In an extreme case, only 98 of the 594 slaves embarked on the *George* in West Africa in 1717 reached Buenos Aires alive. Overall, between one million and two million men, women, and children—more than 10 percent of all slaves leaving Africa—died in transit. Probably almost half as many blacks died violently in Africa as a result of the trade or on board ships as reached Brazil and Spanish America alive.

How profitable was the Atlantic slave trade? Some historians have argued that the profits from the trade and slave-based agriculture in the Americas played a central role in the development of modern capitalism. Others have claimed that the overall profit level of the trade was generally low and that many investors lost money. Common sense suggests that the trade would not have persisted for several centuries unless profits were fairly secure. The best estimates currently available indicate that profits averaged between 5 and 6 percent of invested capital during most of the time that the trade was legal. Nevertheless, many participants in the trade lost money, and some went bankrupt, including some of the most heavily capitalized monopoly companies. High profit levels were not uncommon, but the terrible mortality experienced on some slave ships and the unpredictability of slave prices in the New World limited profit levels over the long term.

The trade to Brazil was less limited by bureaucratic restrictions and, apparently, was more dependably profitable. Brazilians themselves participated in the trade throughout the sugar boom. Though profitable in the long run, the slave trade's earnings were more modest than some early commentators alleged, and individual voyages often brought losses. In the broad context of the expanding Atlantic commercial network, however, the slave trade unquestionably promoted the growth of European economic activity and the development of specialized export economies.

Plantation Slavery

The scale and periodization of the African slave trade were tied to the development of plantation agriculture. The sugar plantation more than any other part of the colonial economy rested on slave labor. Regional cycles of growth and decline in the production of sugar caused by soil exhaustion, new technologies, or political events elevated or depressed the demand for African slaves across the Americas. From the sixteenth century to the early nineteenth century Portuguese Brazil, French Saint Domingue (Haiti), and Spanish Cuba each dominated sugar production and served as the primary destination of the slave trade. Despite the central importance of sugar to the institution of slavery, large numbers, perhaps a majority of slaves, worked in occupations other than those in the cane fields. Black slaves worked on estates that grew indigo, tobacco, and cacao; in urban crafts such as tailoring, shoemaking, carpentry, blacksmithing, and bricklaying; and as stevedores, cowboys, and street vendors. In seventeenth-century Lima, for example, documents identify the African slaves Antón Mina as a journeyman bricklayer and Lázaro Criollo as a cobbler.

Plantations varied greatly in size and number of slaves. Most plantations of the Brazilian sugar zone had between sixty and one hundred slaves in the early seventeenth century, a number similar to that on an average plantation in the Old South of the United States during the cotton boom in the nineteenth century. In contrast, the sugar plantations of the French and British Caribbean in the eighteenth century typically had hundreds of slaves, and holdings of five hundred to one thousand were not unknown. During the Cuban sugar boom after 1795, planters often imitated the slave holdings found earlier in the French and English islands. In the Brazilian case, the smaller slave holdings are explained by the limited capital resources available to Portuguese planters, relative to the French, for example, and by the slowdown of Portuguese commercial activity after 1650.

Slaves in Brazil lived in very difficult conditions. Most commonly slave quarters consisted of small mud-walled or thatched huts or, in the largest estates, single-story barracklike buildings. When possible, slaves sought to erect dividers to provide some privacy for family life. Interiors were nearly bare, with the exception of rough mattresses or hammocks. Slave owners kept their expenditures for slave clothing to a minimum. Some seventeenth-century visitors to the sugar region referred to the nakedness of the slaves. Owners distributed clothing, or more commonly cloth for the slaves to make their own clothing, once a year. Men usually worked dressed only in a pair of pants that came to just below the knee. Slave women dressed modestly in skirt, blouse, and bodice. Children, especially young children, received the barest minimum of clothing. Few rural slaves had shoes, although rough, homemade sandals were common.

Many slaves suffered the health effects of poor diet. The comments of foreign visitors to Brazil as well as those made by royal officials and priests suggest that many, if not a majority, of plantation slaves went hungry. Portuguese colonial authorities even attempted to force plantation owners to raise enough food crops to feed their slaves. As the slave system matured, most slave owners provided garden plots that allowed slaves to supplement their rations. However, many slaves could tend their plots only on Sundays or after long days laboring in their masters' fields. Slaves also supplemented their ration by theft from plantation fields or the nearby farms of free farmers.

Despite these harsh material conditions and the demanding work schedule of the plantations, slaves formed families and raised children. Colonial Brazil recorded the highest number of legal marriages among the slave regions of Latin America, and less formal, long-term stable relations were even more common. The sex ratio imbalance in the slave trade and the conditions experienced on the plantations may have slowed family formation and lowered birthrates in the sixteenth century, but by the eighteenth century the birthrate among slaves born in Brazil was normal and the majority of Afro-Brazilians were native born. Portuguese law provided some protection for slave marriages. The marriage rate for slaves was lower than that of the free population and the highest rates were found on larger plantations. The ability of owners to separate husbands and wives through sales was very limited. Similar protection was not provided to parents, and it was not uncommon for children to be sold away from parents, especially when an owner died and sales were required to divide an estate among heirs.

Given the oppression of their captivity and the grim nature of their living conditions, it is not surprising that slaves struggled to gain some control over their lives. Most commonly slaves tried to limit their masters' claims on their labor by feigning illness, breaking machinery and tools, killing livestock, or simply refusing to work efficiently. Thousands ran away. In many cases runaways stayed near the plantation and sought through intermediaries to gain some advantage, such as better food or a better job. Fear that runaways were a threat to public order led Spanish authorities to impose harsh punishments. The law in Upper Peru stated, "The absence of a slave from his master's house for more than 4 days will result in a punishment of 50 lashes, after which the captive will be placed in stocks for public exhibit. . . . [I]f absent for more than 8 days he will receive 100 lashes and wear a 12 lb. leg iron."[8] Very often the fact that a slave was a chronic runaway was acknowledged in a bill of sale, stating for example that the slave was a "thief and runaway" or "ill disciplined and missing."

A smaller number of slaves escaped completely, forming free communities, or *quilombos* (called *palenques* in Spanish colonies), in remote areas, and often forming informal alliances with local Indians. By the 1670s there were as many as twenty thousand runaways in Brazil, perhaps half of them living in organized groups. Palmares in Alagoas was the largest Brazilian *quilombo*, holding out against punitive expeditions for decades before being destroyed in 1697. Runaway communities were also common in the Spanish colonies. Mexico, New Granada, Ecuador, and Venezuela all had large and long-lived *palenques*. In some cases, the Spanish authorities were forced to negotiate treaties that recognized the escaped slaves' freedom. One common condition negotiated with these communities was their agreement to pursue and return other slave runaways.

Masters often arranged with civil authorities to punish slaves in public places. These brutal punishments were intended to intimidate the slave population and emphasize the power of masters. This scene is from Rio de Janeiro, Brazil. As the whip is applied to a slave tied to the pillory, we can see another slave being forced forward for his punishment. In the right foreground a slave recently cut down from the pillory is supported in the arms of his friend.

In contrast with Brazil, the mature plantation complex did not develop in the Spanish colonies until the late eighteenth century when Cuba emerged as a major sugar producer. Spanish settlers used slaves in agriculture on the mainland from an early date—principally along the Caribbean coast in the production of cacao, indigo, and sugar. In Central America the expansion of indigo production in the eighteenth century was closely tied to the importation of slave labor. Although sugar estates in Mexico and Peru used slaves as the primary agricultural labor force, slavery was less common in these mainland colonies than in Brazil for two reasons. First, silver and gold mines drained risk capital, and slave labor, away from tropical export agriculture. Second, Spanish commercial regulations, including trade monopolies and the cumbersome fleet system, limited access to European consumers and thus potential profit.

Urban Slavery

Slavery had a more urban character in Spanish America than in Brazil. As a result of the slower development of plantation crops, a higher percentage of African slaves delivered to Spanish colonial ports spent their lives in urban settings. There they worked as manual laborers, household servants, skilled artisans, street vendors, and in a multitude of other occupations. Slaves constituted between 10 and 25 percent of the populations of Caracas, Buenos Aires, Havana, Lima, Quito, and Bogotá by the mid-eighteenth century. The free descendents of slaves, often of mixed parentage, were in many places the largest population group, pushing the African-descended population in tropical cities in particular to well over 50 percent. Although agricultural slavery predominated in Brazil, the colony's cities had large slave populations as well. In 1775, for example, the city of Salvador, Bahia, had more slaves than free whites in its population.

Some wealthy households maintained fifteen or more slaves as domestics. But most slaves lived in households of middling wealth where masters seldom had more than one or two slaves. The small scale of slave holdings and the intimacy imposed by urban architecture produced a slave society necessarily more fluid and humane than that found in plantation regions of Brazil or elsewhere. Few urban slaves experienced labor demands as brutal as those of the sugar harvest. Better fed and clothed than their rural counterparts, urban slaves lived longer and had higher birthrates. Urban slave populations had marriage and fertility rates closer to those of the free population than did rural counterparts. Not only were urban slaves more likely to marry than rural slaves, but these marriages were also more likely to be stable and lasting.

In urban settings most owners and slaves knew one another well. This was particularly true in the case of household slaves who commonly lived under the same roof as their masters. Slaves who worked as artisans and even some lesser skilled laborers also routinely shared housing with owners. One of the most important results of this familiarity was that manumission (the freeing of slaves by their masters) was much more common in cities than in rural settings. Yet even here only a small fraction of the slave population, often the American-born offspring of slave women and Spanish or Portuguese men, gained emancipation.

Slaves in Latin America were permitted to purchase their freedom, a right that benefited urban slaves in particular. If a slave and master were unable to agree on a price for freedom, Spanish and Portuguese law allowed slaves to have a judge set the price of manumission. Economic opportunities in cities enabled slaves to earn cash wages or gain income as small-scale retailers. Male slaves often earned wages as artisans or laborers; female slaves washed clothing, sewed, and sold goods in city markets. All of these groups were able to save some of their earnings, and the most fortunate were able to purchase freedom, swelling the size of the free black population. But even those who remained slaves had some discretionary income and autonomy. As a result, it was in urban centers that various voluntary associations appeared first among blacks.

Whether in cities or in rural areas dominated by plantations, slaves were ultimately at the mercy of their owners. As was true on plantations, some urban owners treated slaves badly, depriving them of adequate food and clothing or abusing them with whippings and other cruel punishments. Urban slaves, however, did receive limited protection from their proximity to courts and ecclesiastical authorities.

Colonial documents indicate clearly that slaves sought and often found help from the courts. Every *audiencia* assigned an attorney to protect the poor, slave and free, without charge. In many cases the courts forced owners to allow a slave to purchase his or her freedom or prevented owners from breaking up a marriage by selling one of the spouses. On occasion judges even ordered particularly cruel owners to sell their slaves. But in most cases, slaves' complaints of physical abuse, inadequate medical care, and even sexual assaults failed to secure the punishment of the abusive master or a transfer to a new master. Nevertheless, in contrast with judicial practice in the United States before the Civil War, the courts of colonial Latin America regularly presumed that a black man or woman was free unless an owner had clear proof of slave status.

More common than resort to the courts, aggrieved slaves took their fates in their own hands and ran away from difficult masters or harsh punishments. Runaways were common in cities like Rio de Janeiro, Salvador, Lima, Quito, and Mexico City, and in some cases, runaways congregated in small *quilombos* or *palenques* within sight of the city itself. Many claimed to be free when seeking work. Because large numbers of black freedmen were present in most colonial cities, it was difficult for the authorities, or potential employers, to identify runaways. Since slaves and free blacks in the same cities were commonly tied together by kinship, occupational training, employment, and the experience of racism that touched every person of color, many runaways found free blacks willing to shield them from the authorities and facilitate integration in the economy.

The Catholic Church owned more slaves than any other institution, business, or family in the Americas. Convents and individual priests owned slaves. By the eighteenth century the Society of Jesus was the single largest owner of slaves in the Americas. The Jesuits' vast economic presence in the Americas included urban rental properties as well as farms, ranches, and plantations. They produced wine, brandy, sugar, yerba, and other products that they transported and sold in distant markets. These enterprises, essential to funding the Society's educational and humanitarian activities, often rested on the labor of slaves. While some evidence suggests that slaves owned by the Church enjoyed marginally better material conditions and more frequent marriage than those on plantations owned by laymen, clerics also applied corporal punishment and solitary confinement to slaves. The Catholic Church also provided some protections for slave marriages and taught that slaves were capable of salvation. In small ways the Church limited the power of owners, but it never opposed the institution of slavery itself.

The African slave trade provided the labor power that permitted the development of plantation economies in Brazil, Venezuela, and the Caribbean. In other areas, including coastal Peru and Ecuador, Argentina, and parts of Central America, slave labor was an important supplement to Indian labor drafts and wage labor. By the eighteenth century, black slavery was essential to the largest agricultural export sectors in both Portuguese and Spanish America, and so these regions became the major centers of

Afro Latin American culture. The importation of black slaves also added to the genetic pool of Latin America and to the multiracial and culturally complex societies that characterized the colonial era.

Notes

1. Quoted in Noble David Cook, *Born to Die: Disease and New World Conquest, 1492–1650* (Cambridge: Cambridge University Press, 1998), p. 103.

2. Quoted in W. George Lovell, "Disease and Depopulation in Early Colonial Guatemala," *Secret Judgments of God: Old World Disease in Colonial Spanish America.* Edited by Noble David Cook and W. George Lovell (Norman: University of Oklahoma Press, 1991), p. 70.

3. John Hemming, *Red Gold: The Conquest of the Brazilian Indians* (Cambridge, Mass.: Harvard University Press, 1978), p. 144.

4. Ibid., p. 108.

5. R. C. Padden, *The Hummingbird and the Hawk: Conquest and Sovereignty in the Valley of Mexico, 1503–1541* (Columbus: The Ohio State University Press, 1967), p. 230.

6. Quoted in Ann M. Wightman, *Indigenous Migration and Social Change: The Foresteros of Cuzco, 1570–1720* (Durham, N.C.: Duke University Press, 1990), p. 83.

7. Quoted in Kris Lane, "Captivity and Redemption: Aspects of Slave Life in Early Colonial Quito and Popayán," *The Americas*, 57:2 (2000), p. 241.

8. Lolita Gutiérrez Brockington, "The African Diaspora in the Eastern Andes: Adaptation, Agency, and Fugitive Action, 1573–1677," *The Americas*, 57:2 (2000), pp. 216–217.

Suggested for Further Reading

Alchon, Suzanne Austin. *A Pest in the Land: New World Epidemics in a Global Perspective.* Albuquerque: University of New Mexico Press, 2003.

Alchon, Suzanne Austin. *Native Society and Disease in Colonial Ecuador.* Cambridge, England: Cambridge University Press, 1991.

Altman, Ida. *Transatlantic Ties in the Spanish Empire: Brihuega, Spain, and Puebla, Mexico, 1560–1620.* Stanford: Stanford University Press, 2000.

Andrien, Kenneth J. *Andean Worlds: Indigenous History, Culture, and Consciousness Under Spanish Rule, 1532–1825.* Albuquerque: University of New Mexico Press, 2001.

Bennett, Herman L. *Africans in Colonial Mexico: Absolutism, Christianity, and Afro-Creole Consciousness, 1570–1640.* Bloomington: Indiana University Press, 2003.

Bowser, Frederick P. *The African Slave in Colonial Peru, 1524–1650.* Stanford: Stanford University Press, 1973.

Carroll, Patrick J. *Blacks in Colonial Veracruz: Race, Ethnicity, and Regional Development.* Austin: University of Texas Press, 1991.

Coates, Timothy J. *Convicts and Orphans: Forced and State-Sponsored Colonization in the Portuguese Empire, 1550–1755.* Stanford: Stanford University Press, 2002.

Cook, Noble David. *Born to Die: Disease and New World Conquest, 1492–1650.* Cambridge, England, and New York: Cambridge University Press, 1998.

Deeds, Susan M. *Defiance and Deference in Mexico's Colonial North: Indians Under Spanish Rule in Nueva Vizcaya.* Austin: University of Texas Press, 2003.

Denevan, William M., editor. *The Native Population of the Americas in 1492.* 2nd edition. Madison: University of Wisconsin Press, 1992.

Díaz, María Elena. *The Virgin, the King, and the Royal Slaves of El Cobre: Negotiating Freedom in Colonial Cuba, 1670–1780.* Stanford: Stanford University Press, 2000.

Gibson, Charles. *The Aztecs Under Spanish Rule: A History of the Indians of the Valley of Mexico.* Stanford: Stanford University Press, 1964.

Henige, David. *Numbers from Nowhere: The American Indian Contact Population Debate.* Norman: University of Oklahoma Press, 1998.

Klein, Herbert S. and Ben Vinson. *African Slavery in Latin America and the Caribbean.* 2nd edition. New York: Oxford University Press, 2007.

Landers, Jane G. and Barry M. Robinson, editors. *Slaves, Subjects, and Subversives: Blacks in Colonial Latin America.* Albuquerque: University of New Mexico Press, 2006.

Lutz, Christopher H. *Santiago de Guatemala, 1541–1773: City, Caste, and the Colonial Experience.* Norman: University of Oklahoma Press, 1994.

Mattoso, Katia M. de Queirós. *To Be a Slave in Brazil, 1550–1888.* Translated by Arthur Goldhammer. New Brunswick, N.J.: Rutgers University Press, 1986.

McCreery, David. *The Sweat of Their Brow: A History of Work in Latin America.* Armonk, N.Y.: M. E. Sharpe, 2000.

Newson, Linda A. *Life and Death in Early Colonial Ecuador.* Norman: University of Oklahoma Press, 1995.

Pescador, Juan Javier. *The New World Inside a Basque Village: The Oiartzun Valley and Its Atlantic Emigrants, 1550–1800.* Reno: University of Nevada Press, 2003.

Powers, Karen Vieira. *Andean Journeys: Migration, Ethnogenesis, and the State in Colonial Quito.* Albuquerque: University of New Mexico Press, 1995.

Robinson, David J., editor. *Migration in Colonial Spanish America.* Cambridge, England: Cambridge University Press, 1990.

Russell-Wood, A.J. *Slavery and Freedom in Colonial Brazil.* 2nd edition. Oneworld Publications, 2002.

Whitmore, Thomas M. *Disease and Death in Early Colonial Mexico: Simulating Amerindian Depopulation.* Boulder, Colo.: Westview Press, 1992.

Wightman, Ann M. *Indigenous Migration and Social Change: The Forasteros of Cuzco, 1570–1720.* Durham: Duke University Press, 1990.

Zulawski, Ann. *They Eat from Their Labor: Work and Social Change in Colonial Bolivia.* Pittsburgh: University of Pittsburgh Press, 1995

FIVE

PRODUCTION, EXCHANGE, AND DEFENSE

Chronology

c. 1530	First large-scale silver strikes in New Spain
1543	Merchant guild (*consulado*) of Sevilla receives monopoly over legal trade with Indies
1545	Silver strike at Potosí
1546	Silver strike at Zacatecas
1550	Silver strike at Guanajuato
1550s	Introduction of amalgamation (*patio*) process for silver refining in New Spain; fleet system well established
1555	French capture and temporarily occupy Havana
1560s	Discovery of major mercury deposit in Huancavelica, Peru
1571	Introduction of amalgamation process in Peru
1572	Francis Drake's successful raid on Panama
Late 1570s	Regular trade between Peru, Mexico, and Manila
1580–1640	Crowns of Spain and Portugal held by same monarch
1592	*Consulado* approved for Mexico City
1604	Treaty of London ends conflict between Spain and England and establishes "effective occupation" as principle for colonial settlement
1613	*Consulado* approved for Lima
1620s	Decline of legal Atlantic trade between Spain and Indies begins; non-Spanish settlements in Caribbean and North America
1624–25	Dutch invasion of Bahia
1628	Dutch capture Spanish silver fleet off Cuba
1630–54	Dutch occupation of Pernambuco
1631	Spanish Crown prohibits trade between New Spain and Peru
1655	English seize Jamaica
Mid-1660s–1671	High point of age of buccaneers
1670s	Mexican mining production surpasses that of Peru
1680s	Portuguese found Colônia do Sacramento as center for contraband
1687	Major earthquake hits Lima and environs; results in grain imports from Chile
1690s	Discovery of major gold deposits in Brazil

The Mining and Sugar Industries

Colonies existed to increase the economic well-being and political strength of their mother countries. Their production and markets were intended to benefit solely their metropolises which regulated trade and imposed taxes to transfer colonial wealth to themselves. The Portuguese Crown heavily depended on revenue derived from its factories and colonies, first from those in Africa and Asia and later from those in Brazil. The Castilian Crown, too, came to rely on New World income. American bullion enhanced royal coffers and added muscle to Spain's ambitions and expensive foreign policies. Controlling transatlantic trade to prevent gold and silver from reaching foreign hands and safely transporting bullion to the peninsula preoccupied royal advisers from the early sixteenth century onward.

Most of the conquistadors in Mexico, Peru, and New Granada quickly squandered the enormous booty they had won. Few invested much in economically productive activities, and with the windfall gone, Spaniards in many settlements began to slip toward an impoverished life of subsistence farming and barter. Gold strikes in Mexico, Central America, and later New Granada slowed this decline briefly, but few deposits could be worked profitably for long. Gold mining, therefore, seldom could support the development of settled agriculture or the growth of Spanish towns. Silver mining, on the other hand, required large sustained expenditures of capital and labor and thus had a much greater impact on long-term settlement patterns. The discovery of rich silver deposits in Mexico and Peru stalled the process of economic contraction and initiated a period of unprecedented prosperity in Spain's American empire.

Starting with Columbus's avid pursuit of gold, Spain's experience in much of the New World largely revolved around precious metals. The gold and silver taken as booty in New Spain, Peru, and New Granada fed the search for their sources. By 1550 a number of major deposits had been found, and extensive mining was under way. Networks of urban centers and their rural dependencies were formed in response to the industry's special requirements. Even regions far away from the major mining centers of northern Mexico and upper Peru were organized to produce the food, fuel, livestock, and textiles that mines and miners needed. The production of silver and, to a lesser extent, gold also promoted the development of large-scale transatlantic trade and helped pay for Europe's growing trade with Asia.

Gold

The first American mining boom occurred in the Caribbean. Following the conquests on the mainland, goldfields were discovered in Mexico, Central America, New Granada, central Chile, and Peru. For the empire as a whole, the value of gold production exceeded that of silver in the years before 1540. Although gold remained paramount in New Granada and, briefly, Chile, silver production in New Spain, Bolivia, and Peru far out-stripped it in quantity and value.

Gold mining required little investment in machinery or plant. Miners used simple and inexpensive technologies to refine the gold flakes and nuggets. Most of the gold produced was panned or washed from the soil or riverbeds, although later there was some deep-shaft gold mining in Chile and New Granada.

Because miners could easily hide from royal officials the flakes and nuggets extracted from placer mines, no reliable estimate of colonial gold production is possible. Before 1550 more than 5 million pesos in gold was legally exported from Mexico, and another 10 million from Peru alone. By 1560 New Granada had produced over 7 million pesos worth of bullion, much of it in gold. Perhaps half of these totals was plunder taken from the Indians. Later gold exports reflect actual Spanish production. During the last half of the sixteenth century, somewhat less than 3.5 million pesos in refined gold was exported from Peru; Mexico produced another million pesos. Registered gold production reached its nadir in the 1660s and 1670s when a significant contraband trade existed, but an expansion was under way by the early eighteenth century.

In the 1690s the first major gold deposits were discovered in Brazil. The strikes in Minas Gerais were among the richest found during the colonial period, and Brazilian gold production nearly quintupled between 1700 and 1720. Production grew more modestly until 1735. It then expanded sub-stantially, peaking at nearly sixteen thousand kilograms between 1750 and 1754.

Silver

Large-scale silver strikes began about 1530 when Sultepec and Zumpango were discovered near Mexico City. Strikes in nearby Taxco and Tlalpuja-hua followed quickly. Major discoveries in the northern frontier zone—Zacatecas in 1546, Guanajuato in 1550, and Sombrerete in 1558—greatly expanded production in New Spain. In Upper Peru, the richest silver strike in America was at Potosí in 1545; a significant discovery at Castrovirreina in Peru followed about a decade later.

Silver always required more processing and hence more capital invest-ment and labor than did gold. At first the miners relied on smelting, a refining technique that used simple and inexpensive technology. The ore was broken up using heavy iron hammers and stamping mills, packed in a furnace with charcoal or some other fuel, and fired.

Because smelting was labor intensive and required an abundant supply of fuel, it was ill suited for mines in regions with small populations or with-out forests. Potosí's elevation, for example, was above fifteen thousand feet, well beyond the timberline. Even well-forested areas were quickly exhausted by the mining industry. Located north of the preconquest agricultural frontier, Zacatecas was far from the dense Indian populations needed for a disciplined labor supply. Such disadvantages increased the cost of fuel and labor and often restricted the use of the smelting process to only the richest ores. This, in turn, placed a cap on total silver production.

The amalgamation process, though more costly, greatly improved the profitability of silver mining and spurred production. It first was used in Mexico in the 1550s and in Peru in 1571. The *patio* process, as it was known in New Spain, involved mixing finely ground ore—which had been transported by wagon from the stamping mill—with catalysts (either salt or copper pyrite) and mercury. Workers spread the resulting paste on the stone floor of a large patio, and animals or bare-legged Indian laborers mixed it. After the mixture had "cooked" for six to eight weeks, workers washed it, removed the silver amalgam, and saved the leftover mercury for the next batch. The process employed in Peru was similar except that the mixture was cooked in large tanks rather than on a patio.

The need for mercury, or quicksilver, in the amalgamation process made its supply and cost crucial determinants of production levels. When supplies were abundant, miners and their financial backers were willing to invest in expensive new machinery and drainage shafts and to mine and process relatively poor-quality ores taken from older mines. High prices and short supplies tended to dry up credit and restrict exploitation to the richest surface ores.

Crown policy was more important than the free play of supply and demand in determining mercury's availability and price. The royal mine at Almadén in southern Spain at first supplied all the mercury used in the colonies. The discovery of a large mercury deposit in the early 1560s at Huancavelica, 220 kilometers southeast of Lima, expanded its availability. Quickly made a crown monopoly, Huancavelica's mercury mine supplied all of Peru's needs and exported a surplus to New Spain until the early seventeenth century. When its declining production proved unable to meet Peru's demand, particularly after 1620, the Crown, which had been sending Almadén's output to New Spain, assigned part of it to Peru and supplemented this supply between 1620 and 1645 with mercury from Idrija, Slovenia.

The Crown determined the price of mercury, although it auctioned to merchants the right to distribute it in the colonies. Responding to royal fiscal exigencies and not market conditions, the government demanded high prices and rarely considered the miners' economic plight. From 1617 to 1767 the price of mercury in New Spain remained constant, but at Potosí in 1645 it dropped from 104.25 pesos to 97 pesos a hundredweight (compared with 82.5 in New Spain) and remained at this level until 1779. In the seventeenth century, because miners were forced to invest heavily to drain the older mines and then often found lower-quality ores, the marketing and pricing of mercury worked to depress silver production. Then when the government experimented with lower mercury prices in the late eighteenth century, silver production rose.

Labor

Spaniards owned and supervised silver mines. Indians—supplemented in many mines by black slaves and some *castas*—performed the arduous physical labor. The major Mexican mines were located a great distance from the sedentary native population of the central plateau, whereas the Bolivian and Peruvian mines were relatively close to the Andean population. This resulted in important differences in the labor systems of the two viceroyalties.

After the initial use of *encomienda* and enslaved Indians, miners in central and southern New Spain benefited from *repartimiento* labor until the early seventeenth century. After this period it was no longer a crucial source of workers. In the northern mining districts, Indian and black slaves were numerous, but Indians hired as free wage laborers, sometimes bound by debt peonage, quickly became predominant. By 1600 free wage laborers constituted over two-thirds of a mining workforce that at that time numbered just over nine thousand for all of New Spain.

Reliance on free labor meant that Mexican mine owners had to adjust wages and working conditions to market conditions, paying high wages and offering other inducements during periods when high profits increased the competition for labor. Among the most common and highly regarded benefits was the right of workers to work on their own account on Sundays or to keep some portion of their production, often a specified amount of ore. When mines were worked out or mercury was scarce, however, workers had little protection. Wages fell, and even skilled miners were forced to seek other employment.

Because the colonial treasury derived substantial revenue from mining-related taxes and monopolies, officials consciously diverted scarce economic resources to support the vital mining industry. Thus faced with a declining Indian population in Peru, the state used its authority to ensure adequate labor to meet the needs of the mine owners. Such aid increased labor costs and reduced profit levels in competing sectors of the economy, but added to capital, technology, and skilled overseers, this government policy guaranteed the mining sector's long-term primacy in the economy.

In Peru the *mitas* in the 1570s supplied 13,500 workers for Potosí and over 2,000 for Huancavelica. Although these forced labor drafts continued at lower levels into the nineteenth century, Indians hired for wages also became important participants, particularly in the jobs requiring skilled labor. Of the 9,900 workers in Potosí in the early seventeenth century, just over half were free wage laborers. Black slaves made up 14 percent of the mining labor force in New Spain but were almost totally absent from Peruvian mining.

Wage laborers, increasing numbers of whom were *castas,* handled most of the skilled tasks below ground at Potosí. These *barreteros* used pry bars and hammers to break loose ore that the Indian laborers, often *mitayos,* then hauled to the surface in straw baskets or cloth or leather bags. Typically they carried loads of over a hundred pounds up steep ladders and through narrow tunnels with only a single candle for light. The heavy

Slave resistance took many forms. Running away was the most common. In Brazil and other plantation colonies slave owners paid bounties to men who hunted down runaways. Here a mounted slave catcher returns a bound captive.

burdens, the darkness, the long hours worked, the dangerous ladders, the blasting that became commonplace in the eighteenth century, and a host of respiratory ailments contributed to high levels of injury and death.

Production of Silver

The following graph shows silver production in Peru and Mexico from 1581 to 1810. Production rose until the early decades of the seventeenth century. Then a long period of decline followed in Peru. A similar contraction began and ended earlier in Mexico, which by 1700 was mining more registered silver than it had a century earlier. Incredible growth followed in the

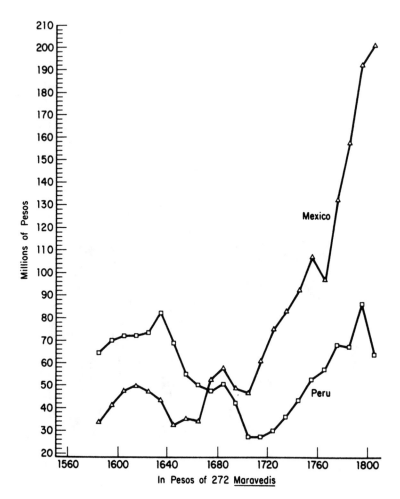

Registered silver production in Peru and Mexico, 1581–1810.

eighteenth century. Mexican industry experienced a boom in the first quarter of the century that was followed by successive spurts of growth that propelled registered output between 1801 and 1810 to over 200 million pesos, more than four times the amount for 1701–10. Although Peru's production more than tripled in the eighteenth century and even surpassed its seventeenth-century apogee, Mexico's production was well over twice as large as Peru's for most of the 1700s.

Sugar

The importance of sugar as an export in late-sixteenth and seventeenth-century Brazil rivaled that of silver for Mexico and Peru. Although gold and diamonds challenged its lead in the first half of the eighteenth century and tobacco, too, rose in prominence, sugar remained Brazil's most important export until supplanted by coffee in the 1830s.

The profitability of sugar production in Iberia and the Atlantic islands—Madeira, the Azores, the Cape Verdes, the Canaries, and São Tomé—led Portuguese settlers to introduce sugarcane into Brazil soon after Cabral's landfall. During the donatary period it became firmly established in São Vicente (on the coast of the present-day state of São Paulo) and Pernambuco. The extension of royal authority to Bahia in 1549 was accompanied by official efforts to foster a sugar industry. By the 1580s, the combined output of the northeastern captaincies of Pernambuco—the most important sugar region until the 1630s—and Bahia dominated the colony's production.

Sugar plantations (*engenhos*) required substantial capital to construct mills and purchase labor. Portuguese investors, including the original donataries, supplied much of the initial capital, but early profits enabled mill owners in Brazil to expand their operations. Typically an *engenho* had a mill that processed not only the owner's cane but also, for a charge of often 50 percent of the cane processed, that of a number of *lavradores,* cane farmers who were tenants, sharecroppers, renters, or independent landowners. This practice, unique at this time in the Americas, enabled men with little capital to plant cane and, in good years, to profit handsomely. At the same time it gave the mill owner some protection against falling prices or a bad harvest, by spreading the risks and costs of planting. Because the planters relied on credit—primarily supplied by religious institutions and merchants—to build mills, purchase slaves, cover expenses, and enlarge their operations, limiting their potential losses through processing *lavradores'* cane was a sound business practice. In addition, this relationship with the *lavradores* allowed the planters to benefit financially from economies of scale, by investing in more efficient, large-scale crushing and refining capacity.

Engenhos varied in value according to the amount and quality of land, the number of slaves, the condition of the mill and processing equipment, livestock, transportation equipment, and residential facilities. Land and slaves were the most expensive components of an *engenho*. Because most planters had over 20 percent of their capital tied up in slaves, fluctuations in slave prices could greatly affect their profit.

Unlike gold or silver, sugar had no intrinsic value. It was a bulky, perishable commodity that required rapid handling when harvested and timely transport to market and sale, to reduce storage costs that could drain profits quickly. These requirements limited the location of sugar plantations to coastal regions or along rivers where sugar could be transported inexpensively. The Bahian Recôncavo, the area surrounding the Bay of All Saints, enjoyed particularly good water transportation, a natural advantage that contributed substantially to its great success as a sugar-producing region.

Slave laborers performed a myriad of tasks associated with Brazil's sugar cultivation and processing. The slaves' supervisors might be whites,

Early-seventeenth-century view of Salvador, Bahia.

freed-men, or slaves themselves. Few *engenhos* had fewer than forty slaves; sixty to eighty was most common in Bahian mills. Field hands invariably outnumbered all other slaves combined, although individually they were less valuable than were house slaves, artisans, or skilled workers, to say nothing of labor foremen.

There was no technological breakthrough in sugar production to compare with the introduction of the amalgamation process in silver mining. Production rose principally from increased employment of land and labor. The most important technological improvement was the introduction by 1613 of a three-roller vertical mill to replace the older two-roller horizontal mill. Planters quickly adopted the new mill, for it was smaller, faster, easier, and less expensive to construct and more energy efficient than its predecessor. The new mill's advantages enabled some *lavradores* to open small mills and certainly contributed to a near doubling of mills from 192 in 1612 to about 350 in 1629.

Sugar production grew rapidly in the sixteenth century as rising prices stimulated investment. On Brazilian sugar plantations, Indian slaves continued to be the most important labor source until the end of the sixteenth century. Planters increased their importation of African slaves after 1570 and, during the remainder of the colonial period, this labor source sustained the growth of the sugar industry. Annual production increased from 6,000 metric tons in 1580 to 10,000 in 1610, and to between 15,000 and 22,000 in the 1620s.

With production remaining at 15,000 to 22,000 metric tons for over a century, the market price for sugar on the one hand and the cost of slave labor on the other largely determined the planters' profits. Sugar prices rose in the sixteenth century, declined in the 1610s, and increased again in the 1620s and early 1630s. Until mid-century, prices remained reasonably high, but general inflation reduced the planters' profit. Nonetheless, prices were strong enough for several more decades for planters to purchase slaves, whose prices had declined slightly since mid-century. A crisis for planters began in the 1680s when competition from foreign plantations in the Caribbean islands lowered sugar prices and drove up the cost of slaves. Although there were some good years subsequently, the overall position of the Brazilian planters was declining. The discovery of gold in Minas Gerais strengthened the competition for slaves. By 1710 a planter had to sell twice as much sugar to purchase a slave than had been necessary in 1635, a condition that persisted until 1750. Sugar's vulnerability to international competition meant that over the long term, planters had little control over their economic fortunes.

Bullion and sugar were the most important exports of colonial Latin America. Revenue from taxes, governmental monopolies, and other fiscal measures associated with these products were crucial supports for the Spanish and Portuguese Crowns. Consequently, colonial authorities directly encouraged and promoted mining and the sugar industry and sought to ensure the safe shipment of silver, gold, and sugar to Iberia. When necessary, these governments intervened to ensure a steady, cheap supply of labor. Thus officials in Peru maintained the *mita* for Potosí and Huancavelica. And, in the case of Brazil, Portuguese authorities promoted the African slave trade and, during the economic crisis of the seventeenth century, limited the financial liability of plantation owners. Mining and the sugar industry tended to determine the cyclical behavior of the colonial economies' market-oriented sector. That is, when profits expanded, other areas of the economies grew. When profits fell, all of the economies tended to contract, as there was also less capital for investment and consumption. It was precisely the centrality of mining and sugar in the imperial economies that separated them from other colonial exports.

Although each region of the New World tried to produce goods that would command a market outside its boundaries, no other products affected such large geographic areas or contributed so much to imperial finance as did silver and sugar. The fortunes of cacao in Venezuela, cochineal in Oaxaca, indigo in Central America, and hides in the Río de la Plata, to cite four examples, were important to local and regional economies, but their value to the Spanish Crown in terms of revenue or their impact on other areas of the colonial economies was modest in comparison with silver. Not until the eighteenth century would such regional exports emerge from the long shadow of mining and assume a significant place in the imperial economy.

International Trade and Taxation

Trade and taxation transferred to Europe much of the wealth from American mines and plantations. By the end of the sixteenth century, Europe benefited from, but did not yet control, a network of exchange that included America, parts of Asia, and the African coast. High profits generated by American exports subsidized a more diversified, less valuable mix of European imports, which included wheat, rice, olive oil, cod, wine, and textiles. The wealth produced by Spanish America and Brazil promoted the growth of European industry and subsidized the consolidation of European commercial and military power in Asia and Africa.

Transatlantic trade in general operated under several constraints. Time and distance, two sides of the same coin, limited the range of tradable goods. Days at sea, not absolute mileage, determined what could be transported profitably. Peninsular merchants could send perishable goods like wheat to Brazil but not to Peru and have it arrive in salable condition. Textiles and other manufactured goods, in contrast, could be sent anywhere. The limited availability and high cost of cargo space also affected what was transported across the Atlantic. On the American side, gold and precious stones, of course, were ideal, but silver was acceptable as well. Although both Iberian nations were only secondary actors by the eighteenth century, their New World colonies continued as important participants in European commercial expansion. Increasing the size of ships expanded the range of products that could be carried, but the cost of getting goods by sea from Lima to Panama and then by mule train across the isthmus for loading for export to Spain added substantially to their cost. In contrast, coastal Brazil and the Caribbean regions enjoyed lower freight costs and shorter transportation times to European markets. Thus products of less intrinsic value than gold and silver, even animal hides, could be exported profitably.

The Spanish Trading System

Legal trade between Spain and the colonies generally rose from 1504 to 1610 and then fell until well into the eighteenth century. Expansion coincided with conquest, settlement, the development of the mining industry, and the early growth of markets for European goods that resulted from immigration and the natural increase of the white and Hispanized nonwhite population. The decline was related to Spain's growing inability to supply colonial markets, to contraband trade, to foreign threats, and to the growing capacity of the colonies to produce many items previously imported. Falling registered silver production accelerated this downward trend for much of the seventeenth century. By the time mining production began its spectacular rise in about 1720, the trading system developed in the sixteenth century had long been in shambles.

At first transatlantic trade was only an adjunct to the transportation of men and supplies from Spain to the Indies. Settlers wanted wheat for bread, wine, olive oil, traditional sweets, horses and other livestock, weapons, and textiles but at first had little besides gold to exchange. As a result, many Spanish ships and sailors remained in the New World. Over half of the seventy-one ships arriving in 1520, for example, were purchased for use in inter-island trade or voyages of exploration.

The conquest, plunder, and settlement of the mainland and subsequent development of silver mining in Mexico and Peru transformed the size and character of Atlantic trade. Thousands of Spaniards eager to duplicate the conquistadors' achievements arrived in the years after 1530. Added to a growing creole and Hispanized *casta* population, they dramatically increased the market for European products. From 1506 to 1550, the volume of trade increased nearly tenfold. Dyes, medicinal plants, sugar, tobacco, and chocolate produced in the circum-Caribbean colonies were added to the more valuable gold and silver of Mexico, Peru, and New Granada on a lengthening list of New World exports.

A serious downturn lasted from 1550 to 1562 because the Spaniards had taken over most of the Indians' treasure, but silver production had not yet expanded sufficiently to maintain a high level of imports. With goods shipped to the Indies selling slowly and profits declining, investors and merchants withdrew from the trade. The Crown went bankrupt in 1557 and then seized private stocks of bullion in Spain. This deepened the depression as investors looked for ways to keep their money in the Indies.

The rising silver production in the 1560s, credited to the amalgamation process, brought renewed expansion in trade until 1592 when thirty years of high levels of transatlantic trade began. The initial dependence on imported agricultural products dwindled rapidly as the colonies' production of wheat, wine, and olive oil increased. Textiles and other manufactured goods replaced comestibles as favored imports. Regular trade with Manila, which began in the late 1570s, expanded so much that beginning in 1582 the Crown took steps to restrict it. Nonetheless, by the 1590s Mexican merchants were intermediaries in a dynamic trade between Peru and Asia. Chinese silks, porcelains, and lacquered wares were exchanged for silver. By the early seventeenth century the value of the Manila trade actually exceeded that of the Atlantic trade. One measure of the extent of this trade was the use of the silver peso in much of Asia. The Crown finally responded by limiting the number and size of ships sailing from Acapulco to Manila and banning all trade between New Spain and Peru in 1631, a ban that remained until the late eighteenth century. Although designed to stem the hemorrhage of silver across the Pacific, this commercial prohibition had a chilling effect on intercolonial trade in dyes, cacao, and other products as well.

After 1622 the Atlantic trade declined in both volume and value. The total shipments of goods outbound and inbound from Spain and the Indies fell 60 percent between 1606–10 and 1646–50. The several decades of decline in New Spain's silver exports after 1635 were particularly notable. After 1650 the value of goods legally exported to Spain continued to drop with New Spain's legal exports falling 75 percent from 1650 to 1699, and

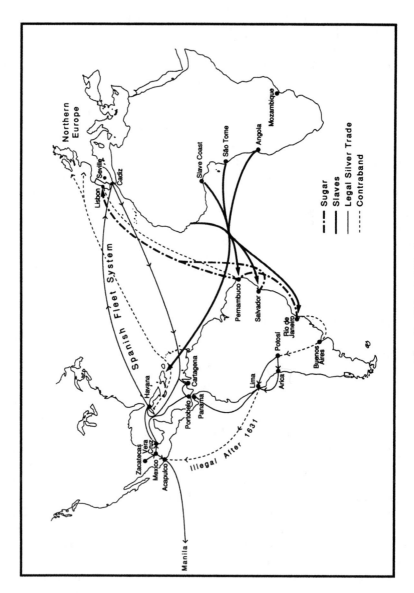

Map 6 Colonial Trade.

the value of Peru's exports plummeting even further. Contraband trade, on the other hand, flourished, and the amount of American bullion that reached Europe between 1660 and 1710 may have exceeded that for any earlier comparable period of time. The turnaround for increased legal trade with Spain awaited the 1720s.

Before the wealth of America was known, the Castilian Crown resolved to control the colonial trade for its own financial and political benefit. In 1503 it required trading ships to load and unload at the Andalusian port of Seville. Commerce with the colonies was placed under the supervision of the Casa de Contratación, or House of Trade, created in the same year. Some seventy miles up the Guadalquivir River, Seville was safe from foreign attack and was an established commercial, financial, and administrative center close to the supplies of grain, wine, and olive oil sought by colonial settlers. These advantages outweighed the city's inadequate facilities for docking, shipbuilding, and repair.

The first body created specifically to handle American affairs, the Casa authorized sailings, supervised the loading and unloading of ships, licensed emigrants, collected duties, kept track of American revenues, and handled judicial cases arising from the Indies trade until its abolition in 1790. The Casa was moved to Cádiz in 1717 because neither the Guadalquivir River nor Seville could handle the immense ships of the later years. Earlier, in 1668, the Crown had authorized the loading and unloading of transatlantic vessels in Sanlúcar de Barrameda. Cádiz became the major port in the trade after 1679, nearly four decades before the Casa was transferred.

The Casa worked closely with the wholesale merchants' guild, or *consulado,* of Seville after the Crown granted it in 1543 a monopoly over the Indies trade. Through the *consulado,* the wholesale merchants initially controlled colonial commercial activities by using agents they sent to the New World. In 1592 and 1613, however, the Crown authorized *consulados* for the wholesale merchants of Mexico City and Lima. Because these merchants had a monopoly over trade in their respective viceroyalties, they were largely able to determine the exchange value of silver and other colonial products. Consequently, commerce was generally more profitable than mining, and over time, wealth in the colonies often accumulated in the hands of merchants rather than miners or other producers. This reduced investment in production and restricted the colonial economy's ability to grow.

The depredations of pirates and foreign rivals forced Spain to protect its Atlantic trade. The Crown's solution was to create a fleet system for conveying goods and to limit transatlantic commerce to three major American ports: Vera Cruz for New Spain, Cartagena for New Granada, and Nombre de Dios (later Portobelo) for Peru and the remainder of Spanish South America. By 1550 the system of regular convoys to and from the Indies was well established. In the mature system, one fleet (the *flota*) sailed in May for Vera Cruz where its merchants traded European goods for Mexican silver and sometimes dyes, hides, and other products. A second fleet (the *galeones*) left Seville in August for Cartagena and then proceeded to the isthmus of Panama. At Nombre de Dios (or Portobelo), merchants traded goods for silver brought by sea from Lima and transported by mule train from Panama City. Once loaded with bullion and other exports of lesser value, the two fleets joined in Havana to sail in the spring for Spain.

Vera Cruz and the isthmian ports were steamy, pestilential, unhealthy sites nearly abandoned except when a fleet arrived. Word that the ships were offshore brought thousands of persons—including merchants, porters, muleteers, and prostitutes—to the ports to participate in the ensuing trade fairs. The inhospitable environment and pent-up demand promoted a feverish pace for these exchanges. *Consulado* merchants from Lima and Mexico City purchased European goods, principally textiles, in large lots and transported them to their warehouses in the capital cities. There they marketed the goods directly through their own outlets, through retailers and petty vendors, and through *corregidores* and *alcaldes mayores* who employed the *repartimiento de bienes* to sell to Indian communities.

Taxes on trade paid the cost of defending the fleets. The additional profit to be made through tax evasion, however, proved irresistible to many merchants. Bribing customs officials and sailors, mislabeling the contents of crates, and shipping more goods than were declared were three ways in which merchants cheated the Crown. Tax cheating reduced revenues, but the cost of effective protection for a fleet could not sink below a minimum level. Faced with inadequate revenues, the Crown responded by increasing taxes on trade, a step that in turn made tax avoidance even more attractive. The result was a trading system laden with fraud that mocked the Crown's efforts to maintain a commercial monopoly.

The Atlantic fleet system reinforced Seville's commercial monopoly and imposed a cycle of scarcity and glut on the colonial economy. Concentrating wholesale trade at one Spanish and three American ports, it favored heavily capitalized commercial houses. They were able to buy and sell in large quantities and anxious to limit the volume of colonial imports in order to secure high prices and handsome profits.

In a free market, the arrival of the fleet would have dramatically lowered the price of European goods in the major colonial cities. The monopoly power of the *consulado* merchants, however, prevented this market adjustment and kept the price of imports artificially high. Unsatisfied colonial demand caused by the inefficient fleet system also created high prices for European goods. At the same time, limited competition among Seville's merchants and their American agents forced down the exchange value of American silver, dye stuffs, hides, pearls, and other exports.

In Castile, the Seville monopoly and the fleet system also transferred profits from producers to merchants and speculators, thus eliminating incentives to invest in new technology or to hire additional labor. Because the origin of goods shipped to the colonies hardly affected the merchants' profits, Seville's *consulado* comfortably accommodated itself to the decline of Spanish industry after the mid-sixteenth century and the substitution of foreign goods in the American trade. By the 1620s, foreign merchants used *consulado* members as front men, shipped foreign goods, and controlled most of Spain's

Atlantic trade. French merchants in particular became increasingly prominent as the seventeenth century progressed. By 1700 perhaps no more than
one-eighth of the goods shipped to the Indies was produced in Spain.

The fleet system gradually failed to provide predictable and regular service.
The system occasionally faltered after 1580, and by the 1620s a complete
breakdown was clearly under way. Sailings became less regular; interruptions
of several years were common. From 1650 to 1699, twenty-five fleets sailed to
New Spain but only sixteen to the isthmus of Panama. By the end of the seventeenth century, the fleet system was nearly defunct; only four fleets sailed
to the isthmus from 1680 to 1699. Both the Spanish economic decline and
the growth of Dutch and English naval power had undermined the system.
Nonetheless, in meeting its primary responsibility—getting American bullion
safely to Spain—the fleet system was remarkably effective. Only in 1628 and
1656 did foreign rivals capture the bullion the fleet was carrying.

Contraband trade offered attractive possibilities for extra profits to colonial producers and serious fiscal problems for Spain because the traders
paid no taxes. In addition, it sometimes undercut the prices of Spanish
goods when the fleets did arrive. Portuguese merchants in Brazil gained
limited illegal access to the silver of Potosí through an active contraband
trade with Buenos Aires and Paraguay. British and Dutch competitors of
Spanish merchant monopolies used their Caribbean colonies to penetrate
overpriced, inefficient Spanish markets. Yet these exchanges were too
irregular and unpredictable to create significant new colonial investment
in export-oriented production. Perishable agricultural products, in particular, presented special problems for contraband trade. Nevertheless, in
Venezuela, coastal Central America, and Argentina, contraband grew in
importance during the seventeenth century and well into the eighteenth.

As long as the crippled fleet system and Seville's commercial monopoly
remained, contraband trade conducted within the fleet system and by foreigners dealing directly with colonists absorbed large quantities of American bullion. Only when a reforming Spanish government in the eighteenth
century encouraged production through tax reductions and a liberalized
commercial policy did legal colonial exports again thrive.

Brazil

Because Portugal focused its limited resources on developing the riches of
the East Indies during the sixteenth century, it exercised little control over
Brazil's early economic development. Until the mid-seventeenth century,
the Portuguese Crown allowed almost unrestricted trade between metropolitan and colonial ports. In addition to Oporto and Lisbon, small ports
like Caminha, Viana, and Aveiro regularly sent caravels to Brazil. Although
each Brazilian captaincy had a port, the sugar ports of Recife, Salvador,
and Rio de Janeiro were the most important. The ships transporting sugar
were generally small, 80 to 150 tons, and lightly armed. Although convoys
sailed in the 1590s in response to English privateering, their use was

irregular. Portuguese participated in the trade, but English and especially Dutch shippers operating under Portuguese licenses were the most important carriers in the sixteenth and early seventeenth centuries.

Since Holland's rebellion against Philip II in 1568, Spain had sought to regain control over its former possession. As part of this broader objective, in 1605 Philip III excluded the Dutch from trading with the Portuguese world, joined to the Spanish realms since 1580. The Dutch retaliated by raiding ships carrying Brazilian sugar. During the Twelve-Years' Truce (1609–21) between the Dutch and united Spanish and Portuguese crowns (1580–1640), Dutch commerce with Brazil boomed. Almost two-thirds of the ships in the trade were Dutch. They conveyed sugar to a number of European markets, including Amsterdam, where forty sugar refineries were operating in 1650. The end of the truce brought a renewal of hostilities and a Dutch invasion of Salvador in 1624–25 and the occupation of Pernambuco from 1630 to 1654. At last awakened to the threat posed by this unrelenting pressure, the Crown turned to protected convoys. It chartered the Brazil Company in 1649 to provide a fleet of warships to protect Atlantic routes in return for a monopoly of Brazil's most common imports—flour, olive oil, wine, and codfish—and the right to tax the colony's exports. New Christian investors resented by other important elite groups provided much of the leadership and capital. Undermined by religious bigotry and undercapitalized from the outset, the company never met its obligations, and the Crown took it over in 1664. Nonetheless, the fleet system survived this collapse and lived on for another century. Fleets of a hundred vessels were not uncommon, although one English observer remembered one early fleet as "the pitifullest vessels that ever I saw."[1]

A separate trade with Africa supplied slaves for the sugar industry. Although the Crown experimented with granting monopoly contracts like the Spanish *asientos,* the Brazilian slave trade was, in practice, hardly regulated and merchants resident in the colony organized and directed much of the trade with Africa. This relatively lax oversight of Brazil's trade with both Europe and Africa distinguishes the Portuguese commercial system from that of Spain and its colonies. Brazilian merchants, moreover, participated more in offshore commerce than did their Spanish counterparts.

British trade with Portugal and Brazil remained insignificant for several decades after sugar from English plantations in the Caribbean replaced Brazilian sugar in the mid-seventeenth century. Beginning in the 1690s, however, the mining boom in Brazil brought back prosperity. By failing to protect its own production of manufactured goods and by outlawing colonial production, Portugal encouraged the capture of the Brazilian market by British factories working through Portuguese commercial intermediaries. By 1750 British exports to Portugal valued at little more than 1.1 million pounds were producing a favorable balance of trade of nearly 800,000 pounds. Although some historians attribute this commercial ascendency to the Methuen Treaty of 1703 and its antecedents, shifting European political rivalries and Britain's early development of cotton textiles suitable for wear in the tropics were more important.

Taxation

The Spanish Crown taxed its American colonies enough that the empire as a whole not only paid the costs of its administration and defense but also produced a fiscal surplus for remission to the peninsula. New World revenues shipped to Spain became important about 1550 and expanded substantially during the reign of Philip II (1556–98). They totaled 20 to 25 percent of the Crown's revenue toward the end of Philip's rule, a substantial sum that helped finance his expensive foreign policy in Europe. Remittances generally declined in the seventeenth century, especially after 1640 for New Spain and after 1660 for Peru. In the 1590s half of the revenue collected in New Spain was spent in the Indies; this amount increased to nearly 80 percent a century later. Indeed, the amount of public revenue sent from Mexico to the Philippines in some decades of the seventeenth century was over half the amount remitted to Spain. For Peru, only 36 percent of the revenue collected in the 1590s remained there, but the amount leapt to 55 percent the following decade and to 95 percent in the 1680s, a consequence more of declining tax income than rising expenditures.

The Crown levied a variety of taxes in the New World. It raised rates and introduced new impositions when possible. The treasury in seventeenth-century Peru received income from over forty separate sources. Although the colonists paid less in taxes than did the Castilian peasantry, the colonial population bore a substantial burden relative to its resources. The importance of different taxes for royal revenue varied by district. Mining taxes and profits from the sale of mercury were paramount in the mining districts. Imposts on commercial transactions were central in the ports and administrative centers. And the importance of Indian tribute varied by region and with changes in the size of the Indian population.

With the exception of Indian tribute, the Crown normally farmed out tax collection until the second half of the eighteenth century. Tax farmers paid an agreed-upon sum to collect a tax for a specified length of time, with their profit coming from collecting a sum larger than that owed. Both private entrepreneurs and corporations farmed taxes. During most of the seventeenth century, for example, the Lima *consulado* collected the *alcabala* and the port taxes.

As Brazil's major source of wealth, the sugar industry was taxed accordingly. These taxes, however, reduced the price competitiveness of Brazilian sugar in the international market and restricted the capital available for investment in land, labor, and technology. Until the gold boom, tithes levied after 1551 on agricultural products contributed most among the New World revenues. Although sugar was only one of many items subjected to the tithe, the value of its production made its yield extremely important. In the 1590s, an import tax of 20 percent and a sales tax of 10 percent were imposed on goods entering Portugal from Brazil. With rising imports and sales of Brazilian sugar, again the industry paid a heavy price for its success. Colonial municipalities also taxed sugar, their responsibility to provide "voluntary" extra support on occasion adding to the burden. Slaves, too, were taxed intermittently after 1699, thus hitting the planters once more. Tax farmers routinely collected these and numerous other impositions until the late eighteenth century.

In both Brazil and Spanish America, the efforts of metropolitan merchants and colonial bureaucrats to control and limit commercial relationships failed. Neither Iberian state had the human and material resources necessary to realize its colonial vision. Their efforts, however, greatly influenced the direction of subsequent economic growth in the colonies.

Defense

The papal donation as modified by the Treaty of Tordesillas in 1494 gave Spain and Portugal dominion over the Indies. As exploration and conquest proceeded, exaggerated accounts of New World wealth circulated in the Old, arousing the cupidity of European monarchs and common adventurers. The flow of wealth from the American colonies was seen by Spain's European rivals as the basis for its aggressive military and political policies. Individual ship captains, merchants, and adventurers simply resented being excluded from exploiting the wealth of the New World. Nearly incessant conflict in Europe provided an excuse for French and English attacks on Spanish and Portuguese shipping and colonial towns.

In the early seventeenth century, the newly independent Dutch became the most aggressive rival of the Iberian powers. Their unprecedented pressure opened the way for the first successful non-Iberian colonies in the Caribbean and North America as well as the temporary occupation of northeast Brazil. The subsequent age of buccaneers left a swath of destruction that lasted until the late seventeenth century. In the ensuing worldwide colonial conflicts of the eighteenth century, the Americas became a regular theater of combat.

For the Spanish Crown, protecting the transatlantic trade and the remission of bullion, defending New World towns and territory, and controlling the entry of foreigners into the empire all were parts of the same problem. Deep involvement in European conflicts precluded focusing on New World defense, but the need for American revenue to sustain these commitments forced Spain to invest resources in colonial defense. The result was the ad hoc evolution of a defensive policy remarkably successful in protecting the shipment of bullion to Spain and the territorial integrity of the colonies. It was far less effective in keeping unwanted foreigners out of the empire and, by the 1620s, progressively less able to control trade.

Defense of the Indies originally meant protecting treasure dispatched to Spain from Caribbean and Tierra Firme ports. Thus early military planning focused on both naval protection for ships carrying bullion and the defense of the circum-Caribbean ports. In the mid-1570s, however, the need to defend the Pacific coast and especially the movement of silver from Peru to Panama became apparent. The later development of the Manila trade extended the defensive perimeter as Acapulco emerged as New Spain's premier Pacific port.

As the area subject to attack expanded, the cost of defending it increased as well. Always penurious, the Crown's willingness to spend money on New World defense fluctuated with the severity of specific threats, the availability of revenue, and the financial demands created by its European conflicts. Throughout the sixteenth century, the Crown was generally able to defend the Indies and its trading system. Pressure from the Dutch in the Atlantic and Pacific during the early decades of the seventeenth century, however, nearly overwhelmed Spain's capacities. Coming all at once, the declining silver production and government revenue, the tremendous expenditures and losses incurred during the Thirty Years' War (1618–48), the revolts of Catalonia and Portugal that began in 1640, and the growth of piracy prevented Spain from regaining control of the Caribbean.

The absence of significant bullion production until the close of the seventeenth century made Brazil less attractive than Spanish America was to foreign predators. Foreign threats were real, however, and French interest in the region persuaded the Portuguese to settle it. The greatest foreign threat to colonial Brazil came in the seventeenth century when the Dutch invaded and occupied northeastern Brazil in 1630. Their expulsion in 1654 did not end foreign incursions. Defending the vulnerable coastal ports remained a major preoccupation of colonial government, but Portugal's close ties with England and isolation from most European wars saved Brazil from becoming a major theater for conflict.

The Defense of the Americas in the Sixteenth Century

Spain's chronic immersion in European conflict began when Ferdinand intervened in Italian affairs in the 1490s. The accession of Charles I to the crowns of Castile and Aragon in 1516, his Habsburg inheritance of Burgundy and lands in central Europe, and his election as Holy Roman Emperor in 1519 intensified Spain's European involvement. Recurrent wars with France and, as the Reformation meshed with politics, Protestant territories continued until the Treaty of Câteau-Cambrésis in 1559. Charles's goal of a European empire, however, eluded him, and he abdicated in 1556. Philip II refocused Spain, turning it from central Europe toward the Atlantic, but he, too, spent his reign at war. Different enemies—Calvinist rebels in the Netherlands and, by the 1580s, England—brought the same financial consequence: bankruptcy.

Foreign threats to the Indies and its trade in the sixteenth century came from corsairs rather than national navies. Initially the corsairs inflicted their greatest damage on ships in the Atlantic triangle formed by the Strait of Gibraltar, the Canaries, and the Azores. Their focus shifted to the Antilles about mid-century, and their seizures increased. In addition, they raided coastal towns over one hundred times before 1585. The French capture, sack, and temporary occupation of Havana in 1555 was the most dramatic of these incursions. Stunned, Spain initiated a massive fortifications project that helped secure this key port until the British captured it in 1762.

In response to the corsairs' attacks, Spain first relied on armed convoys to transport merchandise and bullion across the Atlantic, on a patrol fleet in the Atlantic triangle, and on forts, artillery, and militia in the New World. As the corsairs increased their pressure in the Caribbean at mid-century, the coastal patrol squadrons became important. A French Huguenot settlement on Florida's east coast prompted the Crown to add military support to the expedition that was undertaking a long-planned colonization there. Pedro Menéndez de Avilés expelled the intruders and placed a garrison at St. Augustine. When the corsairs turned to the Spanish Main and Central America, Spain was forced to shift its defensive strategy. Spain had general success against the thirty to forty small foreign ships, about half traders and half raiders, that operated in the Caribbean in the 1570s. By the eve of Francis Drake's celebrated invasion in 1585, it had a balanced defensive system in place that included forts with garrisons, coastal patrols, and armed convoys and intelligence collection. Although the system did have weaknesses—badly deteriorated coastal galleys, defectively designed fortifications that were inadequately armed and manned, and small and poorly equipped militias—the cost of improving it substantially without greater provocation would probably have exceeded any resulting benefits.

Because the wealth of Brazil was revealed more slowly, Portugal faced a much smaller military threat from European rivals. Much of the first brazilwood exported from Brazil was ultimately consumed in France. As a result, merchants and mariners from Normandy and Rouen began to frequent Brazil's coast. They both traded directly with the Indians for dyewood and raided Portuguese ships. By the 1530s both the Portuguese and French were allied with traditional Indian rivals. This French threat led King John III to encourage active settlement. A dramatic rise in immigrants followed. Nearly forty years of frontier warfare and Indian attacks resulted from this rivalry. Yet France was unwilling to invest significant military assets in this struggle, at least in part because it regarded Portugal as a potential ally against Spain. Finally, in 1560 France's major Brazilian settlement at Rio de Janeiro fell.

The Portuguese and French were the first to breach Spain's trade monopoly. The English followed in 1562 when John Hawkins sought to introduce slaves and merchandise into the Indies. Denied permission to trade legally, he turned to contraband. Early success gave way to disaster, however, when the incoming Spanish fleet trapped his fleet off Vera

Cruz. This experience demonstrated that Spain would deal harshly with any foreigner in American waters and tended to promote piracy rather than contraband.

As Francis Drake's career illustrated, piracy could be both profitable and respectable. The most celebrated sixteenth-century interloper, Drake's exploits eventually won him wealth and a knighthood from a grateful Queen Elizabeth I. Originally an illicit trader, "El Draque" turned to privateering after Hawkins's fleet was captured. In 1572 he reached the Caribbean with some 70 men and two ships. Supported by runaway slaves, he seized three mule trains laden with Peruvian silver as they neared Nombre de Dios. Emboldened and enriched by his success, Drake circumnavigated the globe in 1577–80, terrorizing the Pacific settlements on his way. He returned to the Caribbean in 1585 with an invasion force of more than twenty ships and over 2,500 men. His plan to attack Santo Domingo, Cartagena, Nombre de Dios, Panama, and Havana and to secure Cartagena and Havana with permanent garrisons, however, failed. Santo Domingo's capture produced only modest plunder and ransom. Cartagena fell too, but casualties and loss of manpower from disease aborted Drake's ambitious plan. He abandoned the city but later destroyed the fortifications under construction at St. Augustine. He returned to England where in 1588 he participated in the English victory over the Spanish Armada.

Drake's unprecedented invasion exposed the vulnerability of the Spanish Indies. Although failing to disrupt permanently the communication and trading system, it partially achieved its general objective of weakening Spain's ability to wage war by forcing Philip II to spend a greater proportion of American revenue on defense. He ordered military engineers to develop a comprehensive plan for fortifying the Caribbean ports, always the most likely targets for enemy attacks. Construction followed in fits and starts, depending on the intensity of the military threats, but eventually the most important ports of the Caribbean and Spanish Main were fortified.

The Treaty of London in 1604 ended the conflict between Spain and England and brought to a close the age of Drake, whose own death had occurred in 1596 off the coast of Veragua during a final expedition stymied by the revitalized Spanish defenses. Although French and English efforts to break Spain's hold on trade and territory in the Indies had been generally unsuccessful, the treaty embodied a principle that would underpin changes in the new century. A weakened and financially troubled Spain acquiesced to abridgment of its claims as set forth in the Treaty of Tordesillas. Henceforth, "effective occupation" would provide legal justification for non-Iberian countries that planted colonies in the New World.

Dutch Threats in the Caribbean and Brazil

The Dutch largely determined the course of events in the Americas between the Treaty of London and the glory days of the buccaneers. Their belligerence had deep historical roots. A part of Charles I's Burgundian inheritance, the Netherlands rebelled starting in the 1560s. This costly conflict continued, save for the Twelve-Years' Truce (1609–21) until the Treaty of Munster in 1648 when Spain recognized the country's independence. In the New World, Dutch interlopers appeared before 1600 and occupied part of Guiana in 1616. Founded in 1621, the Dutch West Indies Company increased the threat to Spain, as it sought territory as well as booty. A major Dutch expedition on the Pacific coast caused near panic in Peru in 1624. In 1628 Piet Heyn seized an entire Spanish treasure fleet off Cuba in a spectacular and unprecedented exploit that brought agony to the Spaniards and an extraordinary dividend to company stockholders. The Portuguese Empire, however, suffered most from the company's attacks.

King Sebastian of Portugal died on a disastrous and misguided invasion of Morocco in 1578, without leaving a direct heir. Philip II of Spain successfully claimed the throne in 1580 and his heirs retained it until 1640. Even though Philip treated Portugal as a separate kingdom and employed only Portuguese advisers and officials, Spain's enemies moved quickly to include these new territories within the orbit of their ambition. Portugal's far-flung possessions in Africa, the Far East, and the Americas soon felt Dutch military pressure.

The Dutch West Indies Company attacked Brazil for its sugar production and also because it was perceived to be a weak link among Spain's possessions. After briefly holding Salvador in 1624–25, the Dutch later returned to Brazil in force. They took Pernambuco in 1630 and expanded their control over much of the rich sugar-producing region. Occupation by Protestant heretics and a declining yield from sugar, however, were more than the Catholic natives could bear. In 1645 Brazilians of all races and classes rose against the intruders in a revolt that did not end until January 1654, with the surrender of Recife and the remaining Dutch possessions.

While establishing their colony at Essequibo and meddling in Brazil, the Dutch took the Caribbean islands of Curaçao, St. Martin, and St. Eustatius. Dutch pressure on Spanish shipping and defenses also facilitated the establishment of foreign settlements on other islands Spain had left unoccupied. Already in 1605 Spain had forced its settlers in northwestern Española to abandon the region. In the 1620s and 1630s, the English occupied parts of Nevis, St. Kitts; and Barbados, Antigua, and Montserrat. The French seized Martinique and Guadeloupe and the remainder of St. Kitts. In the early seventeenth century as well, the Dutch, English, and French founded settlements in Virginia, New York, Massachusetts, and Canada in North America. Taken in 1655 as a consolation prize following an unsuccessful formal military invasion in the Caribbean sent by Oliver Cromwell, Jamaica became an important English possession in the West Indies. The island soon produced sugar for export, and its capital, Port Royal, became a major center for contraband and for several decades served as a base for English buccaneers.

The Age of Buccaneers

The Spanish abandonment of northwestern Española left a vacuum filled by growing numbers of cattle and swine. A few renegades, escaped slaves, and smugglers remained to collect the meat and hides. Their successors found attacking Spanish shipping and coastal towns more profitable. Originally called "cow killers" by the English and *flibustiers* (filibusters) by the French, these men are best known as "buccaneers" because of their use of a *boucan* or grill, for roasting meat over a fire. A contemporary described them as

> dressed in a pair of drawers and a shirt at the most, shod with the skin of a hog's leg fastened on the top, and behind the foot with strips of the same skin, girded round the middle of their body with a sack which served them to sleep in. . . . When they returned from the chase to the *boucan,* you would say that these are the butcher's vilest servants who had been eight days in the slaughter-house without washing themselves. I have seen some who had lived this miserable life for twenty years without seeing a priest and without eating bread.[2]

By 1630, similar groups had formed on nearby Tortuga. Spain's repeated efforts to end attacks on shipping by the buccaneers were never more than temporarily successful.

Major Spanish naval losses encouraged the buccaneers' exploits. The defeat of the Spanish fleet carrying reinforcements for troops in Flanders at the Downs in 1639 and a later disastrous loss of a combined Spanish and Portuguese fleet to the Dutch at Itamaracá off Pernambuco in early 1640 nearly destroyed Spain's once-great navy. Spain's inability to clear buccaneers and contraband traders from the Caribbean coincided with the reduction in the size and frequency of its trading fleets. Even coastal settlements were raided repeatedly by buccaneers seeking treasure and demanding ransom. By the early 1660s, there were some fifteen hundred to two thousand buccaneers, with Port Royal, Jamaica, serving as their primary base. Among them was the Welshman Henry Morgan, one of the most successful, notorious, and cruel of these pirates.

Morgan's profitable attack on the unsuspecting interior town of Granada, Nicaragua, in 1665 served as a rehearsal for his bold attack on Portobelo in 1668. With some four hundred Englishmen, he struck the port city from the undefended interior side. After capturing the defensive fortifications, the force began two weeks of looting that yielded over 250,000 pesos, silks, linen, other European merchandise, and the finest guns the Spaniards had mounted in the forts. The following year Morgan raided the Gulf of Maracaibo, Venezuela, but because French filibusters had pillaged the region thoroughly in 1667, the pickings were slim. A surprise attack on three Spanish warships sent to trap him as he left the Gulf, however, augmented his coffers. The imaginative corsair's greatest victory occurred in January 1671.

With a combined force of nearly fifteen hundred English and French buccaneers, he led a nine-day trek across the isthmus of Panama to attack its capital. Victorious once more, the assailants subjected the inhabitants to four weeks of pillage, rapine, and torture unprecedented in length and viciousness. By the time they left, Panama City had been totally destroyed by fire; when rebuilt, it was located on a new site. Morgan returned to Port Royal with loot and honor. He received commendation from the Council of Jamaica and ultimately knighthood and employment as lieutenant-governor of the island.

Morgan's sack of Panama was the last great English buccaneer raid. In the 1670 Treaty of Madrid, Spain officially recognized the English presence in the Caribbean, and both parties agreed to revoke letters of marque and reprisal so as to reduce piracy. Enforcement was initially sporadic, but England's recognition that profits from trade ultimately were more valuable than the buccaneers' booty led to more peaceful relations. The French buccaneers continued raiding from their base in Tortuga and gradually moved into part of Española. This led to the effective Spanish cession of the western half of the island to France, by the Treaty of Ryswick in 1697. With this treaty the era of the buccaneers at last drew to a close, and the economic development of the Greater Antilles could proceed.

The Defense of the Pacific Coast

In addition to the Caribbean, Spanish Main, and Atlantic coast of South America, the Pacific coast had to be defended. From the first expedition by the English pirate John Oxenham in 1575 until the mid-eighteenth century, English, Dutch, and French interlopers bedeviled Pacific coastal towns and shipping. By 1742 armed foreign contraband traders, privateers, and pirates had appeared on the Pacific coast of Central America or Mexico at least twenty-five times. Many of these expeditions also landed on the Pacific coast of South America. Above all else, these interlopers were drawn by the fabulous wealth carried by the Peruvian silver fleet to Panama and the Manila galleon from Acapulco to the Philippines.

Drake captured several ships off South America in 1578–79, including one with fourteen chests of silver pesos, 80 pounds of gold, 26 tons of silver bars, pearls, and jewels. To prevent a repetition, Viceroy Toledo initiated a convoy system to escort the silver from Lima to Panama. The raids of Thomas Cavendish in 1587, although yielding little booty from Peru, reemphasized the threat from the sea and prompted expanded protection of the silver fleet.

The Dutch sent major expeditions to the Pacific coast in the 1610s and 1620s. One in 1615 defeated the Spanish Pacific fleet off Cañete, Peru, and razed Paita. It failed, however, to capture either the Peruvian silver fleet or the Manila galleon. A large expedition that reached the Peruvian coast in 1624 intended not only to trade and raid but also to establish a colony. Although it destroyed Guayaquil, it too failed in its primary objectives. In response to these threats, the Spanish began to fortify Acapulco in 1616 and to strengthen the Pacific fleet.

Less frequent trade fairs at Portobelo meant fewer sailings to Panama and fewer naval vessels for the Pacific fleet. But even these reduced needs were hard to fulfill, despite greatly decreased remittances to Spain, because of declining revenue in Peru. Coastal defense needs, however, had increased, owing to attacks by buccaneers who, following Morgan's example, crossed the isthmus of Panama in pursuit of booty. From 1680 to 1690, English buccaneers caused enormous havoc from Panama to Chile. By the end of 1686, they had captured almost two-thirds of the Pacific merchant fleet. Faced with immense losses should the raiding continue, the Lima merchant guild funded the arming of merchant ships to protect the coast. This continued into the more peaceful decades of the early eighteenth century. Only after the terrible earthquake of 1746 destroyed Callao and severely damaged the ships at port did the Crown send warships to Peru. They were removed in 1748 following the peace with England.

On the Pacific coast of New Spain, buccaneer depredations provoked the use of a small permanent defense fleet beginning in 1690. The major concern, however, remained the protection of the Manila galleon. In 1710 an expedition by Captain Woodes Rogers captured the smaller of two galleons. The final noteworthy attack on the Pacific coast occurred in 1741 when Commodore George Anson led an English naval squadron into the Pacific and seized eleven Spanish vessels off the South American coast. He then crossed the Pacific to the Philippines, where he captured the west-bound galleon carrying a million and a half pesos. Only in 1762, during the Seven Years' War, would Spain lose another galleon to the English.

Soldiers, Militias, and the Cost of Defense

Few full-time soldiers served in the Spanish colonies before the British capture of Havana in 1762. Small forces served as viceregal guards. Troops were stationed in garrisons at fortified coastal ports and towns and in *presidios,* or frontier military outposts, in northern New Spain, southern Chile, and the frontier zones of the Río de la Plata where they fought against unconquered and rebellious Indians. Taken together, the regulars totaled only several thousand men.

The Crown relied on militia, rather than regular troops, when threatened by attack from the mid-sixteenth century onward. In 1540 the Crown required all able-bodied men to serve if called. At first the size of the white male population determined the number of available men, but eventually colonial authorities called on *mestizos,* free blacks, mulattoes, and even Indians for militia service. The colored militia in Lima performed so well during the Dutch threat in 1624 that its members won an exemption from tribute as a reward.

However many men were available for militia service, the Spanish government had a constant problem of supplying them with adequate weapons and ammunition. Royal strictures limited the importation of weapons by individuals and forced the Crown itself to supply most arms. Sixteenth-century corsairs in the Caribbean were regularly better armed than the militia, although the militiamen's preference for flight and preservation of life and property reduced the significance of their inferior weaponry and frequent shortage of powder. The viceroys of Peru in the seventeenth century repeatedly decried the shortage and poor quality and condition of their firearms.

Government expenditures for defense were modest until the mid-sixteenth century but then increased rapidly. By 1640 the Mexican treasuries were spending a third or more of their revenues on defense, as they provided heavy subsidies to the Caribbean and Philippines as well as for the defense of Mexico itself. By the late seventeenth century, military expenditures regularly exceeded the treasuries' remission of bullion to Spain. Spending far more on defense than they were remitting to Castile in the mid-seventeenth century, viceroys of Peru watched their defensive needs increase relentlessly in the 1670s and 1680s while regular revenues were declining. In the first full year of the War of Jenkins' Ear, regular defensive expenditures consumed 57 percent of the Lima treasury's income, and extraordinary expenditures pushed the total to 85 percent, or 1.2 million pesos. Defending the empire was expensive, but not defending it was unthinkable.

The empire in general and its trade and bullion shipments to Spain in particular were vital to the Spanish Crown. Judged by the retention of New World territory on the one hand and the rare loss of a treasure fleet on the other, royal defensive policy was generally successful. Yet Spain won innumerable individual battles at a cost of losing political hegemony in the Old World and commercial domination in the New. Its fronts were too many, its resources too thin to achieve victory. Every peso spent on defense in the Americas was one less available for expenditure in Europe; conversely, the court's constant demand for bullion forced New World officials to sacrifice military preparedness despite the constant expenditures. Ironically, even though Spain's power was waning on both sides of the Atlantic during much of the seventeenth and early eighteenth centuries, the greater retention and expenditure of royal revenue in the New World mitigated the government's financial demands and increased the colonies' self-reliance and self-sufficiency.

The Colonial Economy

The form and pace of economic development in colonial Latin America also helped determine both its social and political structures. Colonialism, of course, is a form of political subordination, but in the Latin American case the economy was often more important in forming a new social order from the remnants of indigenous culture and the migratory flows from Europe and Africa than were the institutions of empire. The geographic distribution of population, the class structure, and a legacy of state intervention in production and distribution all have roots in the colonial economy.

Conquest and the Indigenous Economy

European conquest and early settlement took a heavy toll on the indigenous economies of the Western Hemisphere. The destruction of Tenochtitlan, Cuzco, and other cities not only destroyed accumulated wealth in the form of public and private buildings but also disrupted traditional exchange relationships that encouraged specialized production and distribution. In addition, Iberians expropriated precious metals and other luxury goods. Because they invested very little in the colonial economy, Europe, not America, gained the economic benefits of this lost wealth. The conquest also wasted substantial human capital, the productive potential of skills and experience. The skilled sectors of Indian society— urban artisans, priests, and administrators—suffered the most in loss of life and forced migration in the aftermath of conquest, and the productivity of the Indian communities showed this. Epidemic disease, however, was what most affected the Indians' economic performance, and the collapse of the Indian population led to an equally large drop in their production and consumption.

Because the indigenous cultures of Brazil had not developed the levels of specialization and integration found in Mesoamerica and the Andean zone, the scale of postconquest contraction was reduced. Yet the near collapse of indigenous production that resulted from military action and disease contributed to the famines of the sixteenth century. Even without mineral wealth, European settlement remained confiscatory through the imposition of forced labor and slavery.

Despite the conquest's damage to the Indian population in Spanish America, important changes in the years before the major mining strikes of the 1540s set the stage for future growth. European technology and skills, new crops, new animal species that provided locomotion and food, and the flow of immigrants from Europe and Africa all contributed to Spanish America's ability to produce wealth. The new colonial system created larger, more unified trading systems that connected local producers to growing Atlantic and world markets, and the introduction of European monetary and credit mechanisms enabled some to reach these regional and international markets. It was mineral wealth, however, that defined the fundamental character of the Mexican and Peruvian economies in the same way that plantation agriculture did for Brazil and, later, the Spanish colonies of the circum-Caribbean.

The concentration of resources at the silver mining centers of Mexico and Peru and the sugar-producing regions of Brazil encouraged agricultural, grazing, and manufacturing production in adjacent areas. The founding of colonial cities and the development of transportation networks also reflected the special needs of these mining and plantation districts. On the periphery of these central economic zones, regionally significant economic activities like the production of cochineal in northern Oaxaca, cacao in Venezuela, and indigo in Central America helped guide the development of urban networks. The early development of these local export economies then influenced the distribution of colonial population and wealth.

The Greater Peruvian Region

The silver mines at Potosí profoundly affected the economy of much of South America. The introduction of the amalgamation process in 1572 led to silver production's quintupling between 1571 and 1575 and continuing to climb until the early 1590s. The population grew even faster. Potosí had 3,000 inhabitants in the 1540s, a reported 120,000 in 1580, and perhaps 160,000 in 1650. Its size and economic influence were unparalleled in the Americas and perhaps equal to those of contemporary London. The mining center gave form and direction to the economic potential of a region that included the Argentine *pampa,* the central valleys of Chile, coastal Peru, and Ecuador.

The region around Potosí could meet only a small fraction of the city's needs. As a result, a vast area entered Potosí's economic orbit in the boom years of the late sixteenth century. Tucumán in northwestern Argentina experienced two separate cycles of integration. In the 1580s it sent to the mines cotton textiles produced on native looms. After early profits, local *en-comenderos* bought European looms and built *obrajes* staffed by Indians. The region also produced woolen cloth after the introduction of sheep. This precocious manufacturing industry was faltering by the 1620s, however, when other regions with competitive advantages entered the Potosí market.

The grazing industry, nonetheless, kept the jurisdiction of Tucumán tied to Potosí. Through the annual livestock fair at Salta, the region sent thousands of mules, oxen, cattle, and horses to provide food and traction for the mines. This trade grew from 7,050 head in 1596–1600 to a peak of 69,027 in 1681–85. This distant region's economy depended almost completely on the performance of the Potosí mines.

Other regions and economic sectors also followed this pattern. The economy of Lima was closely tied to the meteoric growth and later slow decline of Potosí. When Potosí's production began to decline after 1592, increases in silver production for the viceroyalty as a whole muted the effects until the 1640s when a drop began that continued almost without respite until about 1720. Silver went overland from Potosí to the port of Arica and then by ship to Lima/Callao. Because after 1613 the Lima *consulado* exercised monopoly power in the import–export market, miners were at a disadvantage when they exchanged silver for European goods. The profits from this unequal exchange as well as the tax revenues sent to the capital from provincial treasuries gave life to Lima, fueling the opulent display of its elite and sustaining its commerce.

The growth of Lima, founded in 1535, to a population of some 25,000 in 1610 and perhaps 75,000 by the early 1680s stimulated market agriculture and manufacturing along the Peruvian coast and in Chile. *Limeños* in 1630 consumed more than 150,000 bushels of wheat, 75,000 pounds of sugar, 25,000 head of sheep and goats, 3,500 cattle, and over 200,000 jugs of wine. Olive oil, cheese, almonds, honey, and hundreds of other local and regional products also found a place in its markets. High-quality European textiles, iron goods, books, and other luxury items faced little competition in this market. Cheaper imported textiles, furniture, pottery, and agricultural products such as wine and olive oil, however, met increasing colonial competition.

Potosí and, especially after 1687, Lima, depended on distant food producers. A major earthquake in 1687 lowered grain production near Lima and gave Chile an essential place in the city's market. Ships built in Guayaquil and owned by Lima merchants tied Chile's wheat fields to Peru's urban consumers. Potosí received most of its food from Cochabamba, but wine, olive oil, and later brandy were carried across the mountains from Arequipa and the coastal plain. Potosí's populace also consumed large quantities of *yerba,* tea from Paraguay, and coca leaves from the Bolivian *yungas.*

Other distant manufacturers also benefited from the Potosí market. The mines' large population of permanent and temporary laborers created a profitable market for cotton and wool textiles. The *obrajes* of Tucumán, Cuzco, Trujillo, Cajamarca, and especially Quito produced cloth for this market throughout much of the colonial period.

During most of the seventeenth century more than ten thousand workers were employed in *obrajes* in Ecuador. Some slaves and convicts worked in these primitive mills, but Indian *mita* laborers supplied most of the labor. Although Spanish law classified these workers as free and required that they receive wages, *obraje* owners commonly used debt peonage and coercion to maintain a permanent, inexpensive work force. Responding to the dynamic growth of the textile industry, the surrounding region increasingly specialized in sheep raising and related tasks—shearing, cleaning, carding, and spinning. By the late seventeenth century, a textile industry dependent largely on the Potosí market dominated Quito's economy.

The economic history of Potosí's vast region of influence can best be understood by the cycle of its silver production. During the period of expansion, the high prices for goods at Potosí awakened the economic potential of an enormous area. Producers in distant regions could profit from supplying this market despite high transportation costs. The resulting competition among producers drove down prices and pushed less profitable participants toward other types of production, as in the case of Córdoba which moved from textiles and agriculture to grazing.

After 1592 silver production at Potosí began a long downward trend that worsened substantially after 1640 and continued into the eighteenth century. Although its production, even during its most disastrous years of the seventeenth century, compared favorably with the best yields of Zacatecas at the time, Potosí's decline rippled through the regional economy and exacerbated competition among its suppliers by reducing demand and depressing prices. Mule prices, for example, tumbled over 80 percent from the 1620s to the end of the century. Falling prices and declining profits affected all parts of society, but the weight fell disproportionately on the colonial workers, especially the Indian masses. The colonial elite, squeezed by the declining demand, used its economic and political power to maintain profits by transferring costs to the Indians. The most effective device developed to sustain their profits was the *repartimiento de bienes*. Not surprisingly, the most common goods in this trade were mules and colonial textiles, two products hit hard by the shrinking demand at Potosí.

Mexico and the Circum-Caribbean

The silver mines of Mexico played a similar role in its economic zone, but with several important differences. First, Mexico's silver production increased more gradually than did Peru's and therefore distorted the regional economy less. Mexico's silver production did not exceed Peru's until the 1670s, and only in the 1730s did it reach the 83 million pesos that Peru had produced a century earlier. Second, the location of the richest mines far from the dense population of central Mexico brought about the mine owners' earlier reliance on wage laborers. This difference in the labor market occasioned a relatively more equitable distribution of wealth and promoted a greater investment in production for the domestic market. Finally, Mexico's economy did not share Peru's isolation. Its producers were more successful in seeking European markets for exports other than silver.

After the conquest and following dissipation of much of its booty, Cortés and others sought means of making the new colony pay. The labor and commodity tributes of the *encomienda* allowed Spanish settlers to force Indian producers into new market relationships. Within two decades a colonial commercial system had appeared: Nearly without exception, the products were traditional, and the producers were Indians. New towns—particularly Puebla and the mining camps of the northern frontier—and the newly rebuilt Mexico City provided ready markets for both traditional and European food crops, livestock, and local artisan production. Because the Spaniards controlled marketing and could hold down labor costs, they were the major beneficiaries of the expanding markets.

By the early 1560s, exports from Mexico and Central America were in a period of dynamic expansion, and by the end of the century their cyclical behavior largely determined the rhythm of the regional economy. Silver mining led this growth and also aided the domestic economy by contributing to a dramatic increase in the money supply. This, in turn, encouraged investment in production and helped direct labor toward the most profitable areas of the economy.

Dyes were the nonmineral exports with the largest market. Some precious and semiprecious stones, medicinal plants, and other products also were exported in small amounts. Cochineal, a red dye made from insects cultivated on the nopal cactus, remained an important export until the end of the colonial period. *Encomenderos* required their Indians to supply cochineal as tribute, diverting it from domestic consumers and into the export market, although most production remained under the control of the Indian communities. Despite strong demands for cochineal, requirements of climate and limited labor skills slowed its growth. Epidemic disease and the spread of European livestock in the Valley of Mexico gave northern Oaxaca undisputed domination of this market by the seventeenth century.

Indigo, a blue vegetable dye, was the principal Central American export by 1600, although Yucatan was also an important producer. Indigo was a more "typical" colonial product than cochineal was; its producers faced stiff competition in the European market from similar products imported from other regions and rarely found prices stable. Forced Indian labor was common in indigo production, but *castas* and black slaves held many of the skilled jobs.

The presence of the largest white and Hispanized nonwhite population in Spanish America joined with a dynamic silver industry to create a diversified regional economy in Mexico. In the areas surrounding the silver mining centers of northern New Spain and the great urban center of Mexico City, market agriculture and grazing developed quickly. Wheat for the Spaniards and *castas,* maize for the lower classes, and a broad range of other rural products from the intoxicant *pulque* to olive oil found ready consumers. An enormous livestock industry also supplied the mules, oxen, and horses that tied together the major population centers, provided essential traction at the mines, and produced the hides used ubiquitously in an age without plastic. Although the domestic markets were somewhat less volatile than the export sector, the fortunes of rural producers generally rose and fell in response to changes in silver production and the size of the mining centers.

Manufacturing in colonial Mexico took two forms, the *obraje* and traditional artisan production. Textile *obrajes* were major employers in Querétaro, Oaxaca, and Puebla. Puebla's textile industry, in fact, remained competitive with imports even after independence. Mexican *obrajes* also produced pottery. Artisans provided consumer goods and industrial products ranging from luxury items to tools and implements for mines and farms. But both forms of colonial production found their markets limited, as wealthier private consumers generally preferred European goods, and by the eighteenth century, many European producers actually enjoyed a price advantage, owing to the development of the factory system. The *obrajes* survived, therefore, by targeting lower-class consumers and using the

Carpenters in colonial Brazil prepare lumber to be used in ship construction.

cheapest workers available—*repartimiento* laborers, convicts, and debt peons. Artisans compensated for their high production costs by providing individualized goods—jewelry, silverware, luxury clothing, coaches, and furniture—or specialized products for the mining and transportation industries.

Mexico was also the center of an important intercolonial commercial network. Wheat from the Puebla region found a market in Cuba. Central America relied on Mexican textiles, exporting livestock in return. However, cacao, or chocolate, a beverage once restricted to the Mesoamerican elite, was the preeminent product in this regional trading system. The conquest destroyed the indigenous elite's ability to enforce taboos against the lower class's consumption of cacao, and the Spanish *encomenderos* profited from this previously suppressed market. As consumption grew beyond the capacity of the traditional suppliers, new areas of production opened up.

Guatemala experienced an early cacao boom that peaked in the 1570s, owing to the decline in Central America's Indian population that helped create an opportunity for Guayaquil and Venezuela. But the Crown damaged Guayaquil's initial hold on the Mexican market when in 1631 it banned trade between Mexico and Peru in order to stop the flow of Peruvian silver to Asia. Although some Guayaquil cacao continued to enter Mexico by overland routes, from the 1630s into the eighteenth century, Venezuela controlled this profitable market. Exports rose from ninety bushels in 1622 to nearly fifteen thousand bushels forty years later and peaked in 1722 at forty thousand bushels. Although Mexico sent to Venezuela wheat and textiles in return, it maintained the balance of trade principally with silver.

Brazil and the Río de la Plata Region

After the desultory decades in which dyewood was Brazil's major export, sugar production took hold, and Brazil's economic history effectively began. Victory over the Indians of the northeastern coastal region gave planters a supply of cheap, if inefficient, slave labor. By the 1570s the planters had enough investment capital and labor to give Brazilian sugar an important share of the European market. Production grew rapidly until the Dutch seized Pernambuco, the major sugar-growing region, in 1630. During the quarter-century of occupation, Bahia emerged as the primary producer, a position it generally retained until the nineteenth century. After the expulsion of the Dutch in 1654, cyclical expansions and contractions resulted from disruptions in Atlantic trade and from new competition from Dutch, English, and French colonies in the Caribbean. Although there were interludes of prosperity after the mid-seventeenth century, sugar prices frequently were too low to match the generally rising price of African slaves. The discovery of gold in the 1690s and the subsequent mining boom exacerbated this serious problem for an industry already in economic trouble.

Even after the discovery of gold and diamonds, sugar remained the most important Brazilian export until the nineteenth century and continued to tie Brazil to Europe and less directly to Africa and Asia. It passed through Portugal to the Low Countries, England, and other European countries where it was exchanged for textiles and manufactured goods. Rum, tobacco, and other colonial products helped pay for slaves imported from Africa. Even an indirect Brazilian trade with Asia was sustained by Portuguese ships occasionally putting in at major ports to exchange spices and silks for sugar. As was true in the mining-dominated colonies of the Spanish Empire, merchants tied to Atlantic trade eventually gained ascendancy over producers. The planters' indebtedness to the merchants limited investment in production and, coupled with the heavy taxation of sugar, reduced Brazil's competitiveness as the production of Caribbean plantations both reduced markets in England and France and competed for sales elsewhere in Europe.

The sugar industry promoted the production and distribution of other goods and services. The costly refining equipment and slave labor of the sugar plantations required high production levels of cane in order to make a profit. As a result, few plantations were self-sufficient in food or livestock. Thus, the interior of the northeast and large areas of the southern coastal zone profitably produced manioc, maize, wheat, and livestock for plantation and urban consumption. As sugar exports rose, the regions economically tied to the northeastern plantation zone expanded. Eventually dried beef and other animal products from as far away as Buenos Aires entered this market. The concentrated nature and coastal location of the sugar industry further augmented this trade network. The plantation belt—indeed nearly all settlement in Brazil until the eighteenth century—was located along a narrow coastal strip that allowed distant producers to gain access to maritime shipping, thus avoiding the high overland transportation costs of the mining industries. It required the mining boom of the late seventeenth century to draw labor and capital into the Brazilian interior and create additional markets for regional producers.

Brazil was also linked to the Potosí mining complex through Buenos Aires. European goods and African slaves imported illegally via Brazil and Buenos Aires were cheaper at the mines than were those carried on the longer and more costly legal route via Panama. The rich profits of this trade were particularly important to Brazil, as it suffered a chronic shortage of specie until the discovery of gold. When Spain moved to cut off this hemorrhage of silver, by creating new interior customs barriers at Salta and Jujuy in the 1670s, Portugal founded, as a center for contraband, Colônia do Sacramento in 1680, across the Río de la Plata from Buenos Aires. Brazil also had commercial links to Venezuela and Paraguay, exchanging European goods for cacao and *yerba*. The collapse of the Spanish fleet system and a decline in registered silver exports from Spanish America in the seventeenth century helped contribute to a more integrated American commercial system, of which Brazil's ties to Potosí and the grazing frontiers of the Río de la Plata and Venezuela were a part.

Obstacles to Economic Development

The colonies of Latin America were dependent on economically weak European metropolises. During the sixteenth and seventeenth centuries, more dynamic economies in northern Europe eclipsed the economies of Spain and Portugal. As the colonies' needs for capital and technology grew after 1550, both Iberian nations began a long period of economic decline. Spanish authorities, in particular, attempted to compensate for the weakened home economy by increasing colonial taxes and legislating, often ineffectively, against American production of items that competed with Spanish exports; the colonial production of silk, olive oil, and wine, for example, was banned at various times. In addition, although some commentators in Iberia complained that emigration was damaging both Spain and Portugal, the colonies received too few skilled settlers to transfer the full range of European technology and skill.

A related problem was the development of a large public sector in both empires. Although the size and cost of the colonial bureaucracies were modest by modern standards, the costs of taxes and government intervention were substantial. Bureaucrats actively intervened in the colonial economies to drain capital from production and promote consumption; to the extent this consumption took place in Iberia, its effects damaged the New World economy. Import and export taxes, the tithe on rural production, and mining taxes all steered wealth away from mines, plantations, and farms to urban administrative centers, defensive installations, and naval forces protecting Atlantic shipping.

Other obstacles also hindered economic development. The colonies' chronic trade deficit with the metropolitan countries left them perpetually short of specie, despite the bullion production of Peru and Mexico. Inadequate monetary resources, particularly in Brazil before the discovery of gold and in colonies outside the silver-mining regions of Spanish America, inhibited growth in domestic and regional markets. A shortage of credit caused by the tardy development of banking and joint-stock companies worsened the problem. In the absence of banking services, wholesale merchants and religious institutions were the only sources of investment capital. The conservatism of these lenders pushed capital toward rural enterprises or real estate, for they provided land and buildings as collateral, and away from investment in new technology, especially in manufacturing. Finally, substantial amounts of capital were used to establish and maintain the colonial Church.

Geography also raised grave obstacles to economic development. Extremely rugged terrain separated the great mining centers of Mexico and Peru from populous commercial centers. Mountains, jungles, and deserts presented natural barriers to human enterprise. European goods unloaded in Buenos Aires had to travel more than a thousand miles on unimproved road before reaching Potosí, and this route was less difficult than the one from Arica. Freight carried from Quito to Guayaquil passed along a dangerous stretch of muddy road. In 1590 the engineer Juan Bautista Antoneli called the strategically important mule trail that connected Panama City with Nombre de Dios the "filthiest way in the world." Because few navigable rivers linked the major population centers, mules, humans, and, in flat terrain, ox carts moved the colonial produce. The resulting high transportation costs limited the profitability of both domestic and export production.

Despite the many obstacles, Latin America's colonial economies produced a wide variety of goods and distributed them, according to demand and competition, through local, regional, and international markets. The collective energy, initiative, and creativity of individuals were ultimately responsible for the region's achievements, and individuals as well suffered the consequences of economic failures.

Notes

1. C. R. Boxer, *The Portuguese Seaborne Empire, 1415–1825* (London: Hutchinson & Co., 1969), p. 224.

2. Arthur P. Newton, *The European Nations in the West Indies, 1493–1688* (London: A. & C. Black, 1933), p. 170.

Suggested for Further Reading

Bakewell, P. J. *Silver and Entrepreneurship in Seventeenth-Century Potosí: The Life and Times of Antonio López de Quiroga.* Albuquerque: University of New Mexico Press, 1988.

Bakewell, Peter J. *Silver Mining and Society in Colonial Mexico: Zacatecas, 1546–1700.* Cambridge, England: Cambridge University Press, 1971.

Baskes, Jeremy. *Indians, Merchants, and Markets: A Reinterpretation of the* Repartimiento *and Spanish Indian Economic Relations in Colonial Oaxaca, 1750–1821.* Stanford: Stanford University Press, 2000.

Bradley, Peter T. *Society, Economy, and Defence in Seventeenth-Century Peru: The Administration of the Count of Alba de Liste (1655–61).* Liverpool, United Kingdom: Institute of Latin American Studies, University of Liverpool, 1992.

Bradley, Peter T. *The Lure of Peru: Maritime Intrusion into the South Sea, 1598–1701.* New York: St. Martin's Press, 1989.

Chevalier, François. *Land and Society in Colonial Mexico: The Great Hacienda.* Translated by Alvin Eustis, edited by Lesley Byrd Simpson. Berkeley and Los Angeles: University of California Press, 1963.

Exquemelin, A. O. *The Buccaneers of America.* Translated by Alexis Brown. Baltimore: Penguin, 1969.

Farriss, Nancy M. *Maya Society Under Colonial Rule: The Collective Enterprise of Survival.* Princeton: Princeton University Press, 1984.

Fisher, John R. *The Economic Aspects of Spanish Imperialism in America, 1492–1810.* Liverpool, United Kingdom: Liverpool University Press, 1997.

Frank, Andre Gunder. *Mexican Agriculture 1521–1630: Transformation of the Mode of Production.* Cambridge, England: Cambridge University Press, 2008.

Fuente, Alejandro de la. *Havana and the Atlantic in the Sixteenth Century.* Chapel Hill: University of North Carolina Press, 2008.

Hoberman, Louisa Schell. *Mexico's Merchant Elite, 1590–1660: Silver, State, and Society.* Durham: Duke University Press, 1991.

Klein, Herbert S. *The American Finances of the Spanish Empire: Royal Income and Expenditures in Colonial Mexico, Peru, and Bolivia, 1680–1809.* Albuquerque: University of New Mexico Press, 1998.

Lane, Kris E. *Pillaging the Empire: Piracy in the Americas, 1500–1750.* Armonk, N.Y.: M. E. Sharpe, 1998.

Lane, Kris E. *Quito, 1599: City and Colony in Transition.* Albuquerque: University of New Mexico Press, 2002.

Lynch, John. *The Hispanic World in Crisis and Change, 1598–1700.* Oxford, England: Basil Blackwell, 1992.

MacLeod, Murdo J. *Spanish Central America: A Socioeconomic History, 1520–1720.* Revised Edition. Austin: University of Texas Press, 2007.

Miller, Shawn William. *Fruitless Trees: Portuguese Conservation and Brazil's Colonial Timber.* Stanford: Stanford University Press, 2000.

Pérez-Mallaína Bueno, Pablo Emilio. *Spain's Men of the Sea: Daily Life on the Indies Fleets in the Sixteenth Century.* Trans. Carla Rahn Phillips. Baltimore: Johns Hopkins University Press, 1998.

Phillips, Carla Rahn. *Six Galleons for the King of Spain: Imperial Defense in the Early Seventeenth Century.* Baltimore: Johns Hopkins University Press, 1986.

Schwartz, Stuart B. *Sugar Plantations in the Formation of Brazilian Society, Bahia, 1550–1835.* Cambridge, England: Cambridge University Press, 1985.

Spalding, Karen. *Huarochirí: An Andean Society Under Inca and Spanish Rule.* Stanford: Stanford University Press, 1984.

Stein, Stanley J., and Barbara H. Stein. *Silver, Trade, and War: Spain and America in the Making of Early Modern Europe.* Baltimore: Johns Hopkins University Press, 2000.

Vicente, Marta V. *Clothing the Spanish Empire: Families and the Calico Trade in the Early Modern World.* New York: Palgrave Macmillan, 2006.

SIX

THE SOCIAL ECONOMY: SOCIETIES OF CASTE AND CLASS

Chronology

1526–1600	16 Americans made knights in a military order
1549	Mulattos, mestizos, persons of illegitimate birth prohibited from holding encomiendas or royal offices
1552	Blacks in Peru prohibited from carrying swords, knives, or daggers
1554	Crown recognizes need to house and educate mestizos and mestizas
1555	Relatives of audiencia ministers forbidden appointment as corregidores
1568	Mestizos prohibited from receiving ordination
1574	Free blacks and mulattos to pay tribute
1575	Audiencia ministers and their children prohibited from marrying in district
1568	Blacks, mulattos, and mestizos prohibited from living with Indians
1587	Spaniards, blacks, mulattos, and mestizos forbidden to live in Indian villages
1588	Crown allows mestizos of legitimate birth to be ordained
1589	Blacks and mulattos may not have Indians serving them
1599	Mestizos prohibited from becoming notaries (*escribanos*)
1600	Spaniards prohibited from living in Indian villages
1602	First title of nobility in Peru other than that received by Francisco Pizarro in 1537
1609	First title of nobility in New Spain other than for Fernando Cortés (1529) and Miguel López de Legazpi (1569), founder of the Spanish colony in the Philippines
1627	Title Conde de Moctezuma granted to great-grandson of Aztec Emperor Moctezuma II
1627	Audiencia ministers forbidden to be godfathers of anyone whose case might come before them.
1631	Imposition of *media anata* on royal office holders
1676	Indians to reside in their designated districts in cities
1690s	Triumph of *paulistas* over fugitive slave community (*quilombo*) of Palmares, Brazil
1767	Segregation of natives to apply only in mission districts

Evolution of Colonial Societies

The formation and evolution of colonial society occurred within a context of rapid and profound demographic and economic change. The initial simplicity of a social order created by conquest could not be sustained, despite the efforts of the conquerors, early colonial administrators, and churchmen. As time passed, social distinctions proliferated. The dramatic decline and forced relocation of indigenous populations, the contemporary immigration of thousands of Europeans whose claims to high status could not be justified by participation in the conquest, the development of the African slave trade, and the rapid growth of a racially mixed population combined to overwhelm the social categories and economic arrangements established in the first decades of colonial rule.

Social organization on the Iberian Peninsula strongly influenced colonial societies in the Americas. Both Castilian and Portuguese societies were divided into three estates—nobles, clerics, and commoners. The first two estates enjoyed special privileges called *fueros,* such as tax exemptions and judicial rights, which separated them from the commoners who comprised over 90 percent of the population. Corporate bodies, like the military and universities, had special *fueros* as well. In specified circumstances, these organizations exercised judicial authority over their members, as did the Church, an authority that could be defended against the competing claims of other powerful institutions. Artisan guilds, for example, exercised substantial control over their members and enjoyed significant independence from the influence of noblemen and royal bureaucrats. To sixteenth-century Iberians, a properly ordered society was hierarchical, with power, wealth, and status all concentrated at the top. They neither believed in human equality nor had any enthusiasm for promoting social mobility.

In the American colonies of Spain and Portugal these beliefs and institutional arrangements were acknowledged and at times enforced. But distance from Europe; the mixture of races, ethnicities, and cultures; and the sometimes tumultuous performance of the colonial economies created more fluid and complex "societies of caste." In these societies Indians, Africans and their American-born descendents, and racial mixtures, *castas,* were defined as inferiors by law and discriminated against in practice. But these were also societies where men and women with substantial property were commonly presumed to be white even if their color or appearance might suggest otherwise. In the first decades of settlement, the mixed children and grandchildren of conquistadors and Indian women moved in elite circles and married Europeans. Race was defined largely by wealth, lineage, and power or, alternatively, by poverty and tributary status, rather than by biology. Yet culture, the mastery of Spanish or Portuguese, Christianity, mode of dress, and diet also contributed to contemporary attribution of race and ethnic identity.

In the male-dominated Iberian world, law and custom narrowly circumscribed the acceptable roles of women. Through often-violent relationships with native women, conquistadors and the men who followed them imposed domination from the start. Male clerics and bureaucrats articulated the patriarchal ideologies of Church and state. The lives of elite women and women of the middle groups were restricted by fathers in their youth and by husbands after marriage. Priests monitored the lives of women who chose the convent. No woman from what colonials considered a "decent" or propertied family could walk unescorted in the street, go to the market, have a job, or visit with a man alone without causing a scandal. Although a handful of wealthy and urban middle-class women were educated privately, only as widows did elite women gain some control over their wealth and act as their own economic agents. Women who rebelled, fled their homes, defied sexual customs, or resisted the demands of fathers and husbands suffered virtual incarceration in convents, hospitals, or houses of refuge or seclusion (*recogimientos*). There were differences in experience across the class structure, however.

Poor free and slave women lived difficult but active lives engaging in numerous social and economic activities. In cities and towns they dominated the daily markets and ran small businesses; in rural areas they were sometimes farmers and ranchers. The male ideal of familial control sustained by Church teaching and law obscures the important contributions of such women. Their capital investments, labor, and entrepreneurial skills were often significant, particularly for both the rural and urban working classes where many families were headed by women and where few married couples could survive on the income earned by the male head of household.

The colonial economy served as an arena where individuals and groups defined social status, race, and ethnicity as well as material needs. Both culture and economic opportunities helped determine these definitions. That is, European immigrants sought goals different from those of creoles, Indians, or *castas*. Securing an adequate income necessarily meant satisfying class and ethnic cultural norms and realizing individual ambitions for social status. Among privileged groups, income levels allowed men and women to purchase distinctive discretionary items such as costly European or Asian textiles. The middle groups imitated these styles and fashions as best they could, always finding ways to distinguish themselves from the poor. The poor struggled to satisfy the most fundamental material needs, notably food, clothing, and shelter. But even the poorest families usually had a religious image or two in their homes.

The colonial character of the Latin American economies, particularly the structural instability of the export sector, increased the vulnerability of all social classes. The profits of a merchant who imported European textiles, the income of a muleteer, the wages of a colonial weaver, and the ability of a sheep rancher to repay a loan all were tied to the volume of trade carried by Spanish fleets, the productivity of the colonial silver mines, and demographic changes. Alterations in any of these could redistribute income and opportunities among the colonial society's classes.

The Elites

The great distances separating the major centers of wealth in Spanish America and Brazil precluded the emergence of a single colonial elite in either empire. Rather, a local elite of men and women dominated the political, economic, social, and cultural life of each urban core and its surrounding rural area. Despite differences arising from location and the presence or absence of certain economic activities, for example, silver mining, it is possible to generalize about local elites.

Colonial elites were heterogeneous and often interlocking mixes of ranchers, planters, miners, merchants, high-ranking churchmen, and bureaucrats constantly renewed through intermarriage and the incorporation of successive generations of newly successful entrepreneurs and royal appointees sent from the Old World. Most members of the elites pursued activities that crossed economic boundaries rather than limiting themselves to a single career or area of investment. For example, some churchmen and royal officials used kinsmen and friends as front men for commercial undertakings and many merchants invested in large-scale mining and agricultural activities. Except for high-ranking bureaucrats and churchmen, wealth, influence, family, and social connections were more important than occupation in determining elite membership. For all members of the elites, wealth was power. Military victory over indigenous peoples placed European-born Spaniards (peninsulars) and Portuguese (*reinóis*) at the top of the colonial social hierarchy. Their American-born descendants called creoles in Spanish America and *mazombos* in Brazil also assumed this rank.

Yet very few of the conquistadors and early settlers came from distinguished families or could legitimately boast the Spanish title of *don* or the Portuguese *dom*. They often assumed, however, that participation in military campaigns had elevated their social status to levels similar to Iberia's lower nobility. Starting with the second and third generations born in the New World, their heirs displayed no reticence in using these terms of honor, claiming that their ancestors had been ennobled through participation in the conquest and settlement of the New World. This assumption of a de facto noble status (*hidalgo* in Spanish or *fidalgo* in Portuguese) reflected the harsh colonial realities where Europeans saw themselves as superior to Indians, African slaves, and racially mixed persons of illegitimate birth. Nevertheless, use of the title *don* came into general use among members of the Indian nobility as well, as colonial authorities came to rely on this class to collect taxes and organize labor drafts.

The wealthiest and most powerful colonists in Spanish America and Brazil imitated the culture of the Iberian nobility, demanding deference from inferiors, living in great houses surrounded by retainers, and, whenever possible, following the fashions and styles of Europe. Very few of these local magnates, however, sought or received titles of nobility. The Spanish Crown bestowed the title of marquis on both Cortés and Pizarro as a reward for the conquests of Mexico and Peru but subsequently created few titles in the colonies. By 1750 it had granted fewer than ninety titles in Peru and only twenty-seven in Mexico. Most of these rewarded prominent bureaucrats, organizers of militia units, and wealthy individuals who had donated large sums to the royal treasury in times of financial need. But although peninsulars often received the original titles, creoles routinely inherited them. Thus over time the titled nobility of Spanish America became increasingly creole. Although the wealthiest sugar planters in Brazil imitated the style of the Portuguese aristocracy, few sought formal titles of nobility. A knighthood in the Spanish military orders of Santiago, Calatrava, or Alcántara or the Portuguese orders of Christ, Avis, or Santiago confirmed an individual's nobility at a lower cost but could not be transmitted to one's heirs.

In the Iberian world, *limpieza de sangre* or *limpeça de sangue*, the concept of blood purity, was central to Christian identity in general and elite identity in particular. Limited in Europe to the absence of any Jewish or Muslim antecedents, this racial concept expanded in the colonies to include lineage unconnected to African or Indian blood lines. In Brazil the terms "infected blood" or "defect of blood" were used to identify someone with Jewish or African antecedents and served as the basis for exclusion from elite organizations or marriages into elite families. Clearly the offspring of two Spanish or Portuguese parents entered life with advantages denied other children.

Long-term, large-scale changes in the performance of the economy altered the relations of wealth and power within and among the colonial elites. For example, the sixteenth-century decline in the Indian population undermined the wealth and social power of the *encomendero* class and elevated that of Spanish officials and merchants. In the seventeenth century a decrease in silver production transferred economic power from miners to merchant creditors at Potosí. And in the case of the Brazilian gold boom after 1695, mining profits increased the competition for labor and forced up the cost of slaves needed for the colony's faltering sugar industry. In these and numerous other examples, economic forces, some local and others international in nature, transformed social structures.

Colonial elites developed strategies to meet these crises. With few exceptions, elite families diversified their holdings to limit damage caused by failure in any one sector of the economy. João Peixoto Viegas, the illegitimate son of a Portuguese cleric who immigrated to Brazil around 1640, provides an example. He built a traditional commercial career exporting Brazilian sugar and importing wine and slaves. As pressures developed in the sugar trade, he moved capital to large rural estates based on livestock and market agriculture. The successful Zacatecan silver miner Joseph de Quesada provides another example. By the time of his death in 1686, he had transferred much of his wealth to an extensive rural estate with thirty thousand head of sheep while maintaining his mining property. And finally, Lima merchant Juan de Quesada y Sotomayor attempted to secure his status in the 1630s by purchasing a bureaucratic appointment in Lima's royal treasury.

Elite residence in Lima, Peru.

The Bureaucracies of Church and State

The men recruited in Spain and Portugal to run the bureaucracies of Church and state rarely were men of great independent wealth. In the colonies, however, their salaries and other material benefits placed high-level bureaucrats near the apex of society. To equal the annual salary of nearly 5,000 pesos received by an *oidor* of the Audiencia of Lima normally required investing capital of 100,000 pesos, an amount of money held by very few. Yet the wealth of the most prosperous miners, merchants, and planters far overshadowed the resources of this administrative class. As a result, most bureaucrats and even high churchmen believed they were materially deprived and undercompensated, a perception that led many to enrich themselves through abusing institutional power and employing government revenues for personal gain.

Because the colonies lacked adequate credit mechanisms, access to institutional funds often gave officials a competitive advantage in the marketplace. In 1630 an official of the Tribunal de Cuentas of Lima alleged that the viceroyalty's *corregidores* owed the treasury 1,654,057 pesos. Similarly, a *visita* conducted by the president of the Audiencia of Guatemala in 1717 found that the *contador* of the local treasury owed the Crown 30,000 pesos and that his predecessor still owed 4,000. In all of these cases, officeholders had invested public funds in private-sector enterprises or lent them to kinsmen or business associates.

Spanish and Portuguese administrative practice clearly contributed to this problem. Officials at every level were relatively underpaid. In addition to the expenses of travel to the colonies and setting up new households, European appointees often arrived with substantial debts incurred in securing office. Particularly in the seventeenth and early eighteenth centuries, many purchased their appointments outright, and others spent large sums to gain a favorable hearing for their applications. In the Spanish case, appointees after 1631 had to pay one-half of their first year's salary as a tax (*media anata*). These and other burdens encouraged corruption.

Many bureaucratic appointments in Spanish America were sold to the highest bidder. Among them, the office of provincial administrator offered the greatest potential for private gain through commerce. Because the salaries of these offices were nearly the same, the different prices paid from region to region suggest the range of extralegal income. For instance, in the late seventeenth century, a term as *corregidor* in the cotton- and cochineal-producing area of Oaxaca cost more than seven thousand pesos, whereas a similar post in the much poorer and less populated district of Chihuahua brought only seven hundred pesos. High officials also participated illegally in commerce. In 1629 the bishop of Popayán charged that the governor, Captain Juan Bermúdez de Castro, so monopolized the local textile trade that other merchants avoided the town.

Although less venal and corrupt as a group, churchmen also sought material advantage for themselves and their families. Archbishops and bishops commonly advanced the careers of nephews and other relatives. Archbishop Alonso de Montúfar of Mexico City, for example, appointed his nephew to the post of *maestrescuela* in 1555 over the opposition of the cathedral chapter. Others operated openly in the economy. In the 1620s Archbishop Juan Pérez de la Serna of New Spain was found to be operating a butcher shop in his palace. More often bishops and archbishops used their control of the agricultural tithe and fees charged for the administration of the sacraments for private gain. Clearly the churchmen's greed often hurt the society's poorest members. In one notorious case, efforts by Bishop Alvarez de Toledo of Chiapas in 1712 to increase the tithe collection touched off a bitter Indian rebellion.

The ornate exterior of the church of La Merced in Antigua, Guatemala. The richness and dominating presence of church architecture signaled the power and authority of the ecclesiastical establishment in colonial Latin America.

Merchants

No group more actively pursued ties with other elite groups than did the merchants. Spanish wholesale merchants, in particular the members of the merchant guilds (*consulados*) of Mexico City and Lima, were among the richest, most powerful residents of the New World. The monopoly trade system created by the Spanish government in the early sixteenth century was the basis for their position.

Because competition among these privileged merchants was limited, they were generally able to influence, if not control, the exchange values of American exports. In the mining regions of Peru and New Spain, merchants gained the upper hand through their control of credit and the supply of mercury and other essential imports. In the absence of other credit sources, they provided the capital needed for digging new shafts or buying new equipment. Some merchants bought semirefined silver at a discount or received commissions for exchanging minted coins for refined silver. Alonso de Peralta Sidonia summarized their behavior in 1603: "The merchant gives clothes or money for forty or sixty days, to be paid for in silver; . . . on each mark [worth sixty-five *reales*] he takes six *reales*, and in many places, eight [this would be between 9 and 12 percent profit]; and this is an established business."[1]

Although the great merchants benefited from the monopolistic commercial policy of the Spanish Crown, there was a natural tension between their pursuit of private gain and this inflexible system. Consequently, wealthy merchants frequently engaged in illegal trading. In 1646, authorities in Mexico discovered a number of merchants, including the former head of the *consulado*, shipping enormous quantities of illegal silver to the Philippines. Mexican merchants repeatedly violated laws prohibiting the shipment of European goods to Lima via the port of Acapulco.

Wholesale merchants also controlled the retail sale of imported goods. Many owned retail shops or had family ties to retailers in provincial centers, and through these connections they maintained profitable prices despite market fluctuations. On the export side, merchants advanced credit to *corregidores* and other officials and in return received special consideration in the purchase of Indian production. Cotton mantles, cochineal, coca, and, to a lesser extent, cacao flowed through this network of mercantile and administrative interests.

In Brazil and in peripheral regions of the Spanish Empire like Venezuela, the Río de la Plata region, and the Caribbean islands where no *consulados* existed, merchants faced more direct competition from legal rivals and from contraband. Nevertheless, in time these merchants also gained substantial advantages over colonial agricultural and grazing interests. In seventeenth-century Brazil and eighteenth-century Venezuela, the creation of state-sanctioned trading companies promoted this process. However, the merchants' ascendancy in these regions was rooted in the largest merchants' ability to set exchange values by working in concert through short-term partnerships or price-fixing agreements and in the absence of adequate credit.

Throughout the Atlantic region, Jews and New Christians (Jews forced to convert to Christianity by the governments of Spain and Portugal) were active participants in long-distance trade. In Spanish America, in particular, New Christians faced prejudice, discrimination, and sometimes persecution by the Inquisition. Brazil had a larger population of New Christians than did Spanish America. These New Christians were able to gain positions of influence and power denied them in Portugal. In the period before the Dutch occupation of Pernambuco (1630–54), they dominated Brazilian commerce, playing a crucial role in contraband trade through Buenos Aires to the silver mines of Upper Peru. Because some collaborated during the Dutch occupation, at times reasserting their Jewish faith, the entire New Christian community suffered a decline following the Portuguese triumph.

The Rural Elites

Elite families frequently invested in both urban and rural enterprises. In the mature colonies, many of these families derived much of their wealth and status from estates devoted to agriculture or grazing. More than any other class, the greatest colonial planters and ranchers lived a traditional seignorial life, enjoying great wealth and commanding large numbers of slaves and free dependents. Yet despite their considerable economic and social power, planters and estate owners often found their interests subordinated to those of the commercial elite.

The very nature of large-scale rural enterprise created a need for credit. Because income from agriculture was concentrated in the period following the harvest, landowners were forced to borrow to cover their expenses during the remainder of the year. In addition to these expected needs, the unpredictable effects of droughts, pests, and changes in market conditions generated extraordinary debts that endangered the very survival of a rural enterprise. Most rural elites, therefore, found it necessary to forge strong ties with the Church and the merchant community, the two major sources of credit during the colonial period. A small minority of the landed elite sought to perpetuate their family's wealth and prestige through the legal device of entail called *mayorazgo* (Spanish) or *morgado* (Portuguese). An entail prevented heirs from selling or dividing the property it included and thus enabled estates to remain intact from generation to generation. It is, perhaps, an indication of the market orientation and materialism of colonial society that very few wealthy families, only about one hundred in colonial Mexico, sought to establish *mayorazgos*. Numbers were also retarded by the Spanish Crown's hesitancy in supporting the expansion of this institution to the colonies.

The owners of rural estates used their wealth and political connections to manipulate the market for foodstuffs and thus maximize profit at the expense of the very large subsistence sector. In years of abundant harvests Indian communities and *casta* farmers were able to sell their surplus corn, potatoes, and other staples in the market. Good harvests, therefore, lowered prices and reduced profits for heavily capitalized, large-scale producers. As a result, they attempted to control the flow of goods to urban consumers in order to create artificial scarcity. Unlike smaller producers compelled to sell as soon as the harvest was complete, the *hacendados* sold most of their production later in the year when prices peaked. The largest producers actually held wheat and corn in their warehouses until famine years when their sale could earn enormous profits. Municipal councils attempted, often unsuccessfully, to limit the devastating consequences of these market strategies by buying grain and holding it in municipal warehouses and by setting retail prices. However, price gouging during famines was common.

Plantations serviced the export market. Primarily located in tropical regions and dependent on slave labor, they required larger capital investments than any sector other than silver mining. The richest plantations of the sixteenth and seventeenth centuries were in Brazil, but in tropical areas where Indian population losses were most dramatic, like the Caribbean Basin and coastal Peru, they also dominated local economies. Dependent on costly slave labor, sugar planters competing in the international market also needed to invest in expensive refining machinery. Sugar production offered substantial economies of scale, lowered costs, and increased profits from the development of larger refineries and the planting of additional land. As a result, average plantation size and the numbers of slaves increased with the passage of time. This gave the advantage to rich planters who typically enjoyed the best access to credit. Similar changes affected cacao and tobacco planters, although they required less capital.

Among the wealthiest colonial groups in Brazil, planters were often plagued by indebtedness. While rivalry and competition existed between native-born planters and Portuguese merchants, the volatile nature of the sugar industry, with high rates of turnover in plantation ownership and the constant need for new capital, promoted business dealings and marriage alliances.

Although the European demand for New World plantation products increased steadily throughout the colonial era, production tended to grow faster still. Tobacco production spread from the Caribbean to Paraguay. Cacao plantations were found in Brazil, Mexico, Central America, Ecuador, and Venezuela. In the late seventeenth and eighteenth centuries, heavily capitalized sugar plantations brought into production on the French, Dutch, and English islands of the Caribbean forced down the profits traditionally earned by Brazilian planters. Faced with intense international competition, the planters struggled to remain profitable.

Unlike the *hacienda* owners who tried to dominate local markets, planters who competed internationally were unable to influence prices by withholding their production from market. Indeed, debt service and the possibility of spoilage made it impossible to wait for favorable prices. These conditions led planters to seek government intervention to guarantee markets and stable prices. In the late seventeenth century, Venezuelan cacao planters gained steady profit in the Mexican market only because Spanish imperial commercial policies kept Guayaquil's cheaper cacao from competing legally. Tobacco and sugar planters in both Portuguese and Spanish colonies sought similar monopolies to eliminate competition and protect profits.

Urban and Rural Middle Groups

Colonial society was dominated by interconnected families of powerful bureaucrats, clergymen, miners, merchants, and landowners, most of them of European descent. But the endurance of the Iberian empires also depended on the loyalty and energy of the more numerous population of the colonial middle groups. Viewed as clients or dismissed as rustics by the elite, these groups provided the muscles and sinews of the imperial structures. As merchants and peddlers they connected the flows of goods across the Atlantic with local consumers. As priests, teachers, and intellectuals they extended the reach of the Catholic faith and the languages of Spain and Portugal. And, in times of foreign threat or local rebellion, they provided fiscal resources and the leadership of the colonial police and military forces that held the empires together.

Although immigrants from Iberia were influential in Spanish America and Brazil throughout the colonial period, the impact of immigration was greatest in the sixteenth and eighteenth centuries. The majority filled occupations of the middle ranks. They engaged in almost every economic activity. Some owned modest rural property or an urban store. Others filled ecclesiastical positions, practiced law or served as notaries, held minor offices, clerked in retail shops, owned or managed a tavern, supervised urban or rural laborers or mine workers, plied a trade, or even performed unskilled manual labor. Although neither wealthy nor socially prominent, the immigrants' pride in birth and racial identity along with the accompanying privileges separated them from the remainder of the population. Most retained strong loyalty to their home region in Iberia and many used these ties to family and friends in Seville, Lisbon, or other cities and towns to facilitate business contacts, loans, or arranged marriages. Regardless of their birthplace, almost all immigrants considered themselves superior to their New World cousins.

The Urban Middle Groups

The top of the urban middle sector was comprised of manufacturers, master artisans, retail merchants, middle-ranking officials of the colonial government, and priests. Priests and bureaucrats were the most secure, as their status depended on institutional prestige and predictable, if modest, incomes. The other groups depended on unpredictable market conditions to maintain their status. Members of the urban middle sector routinely imitated elite practice and attempted to protect their status and income by creating institutional guarantees.

Master craftsmen in skilled trades were organized collectively to set quality control standards, work rules, recruitment criteria for apprentices, and training procedures, as well as to limit product lines. Their intent was self-consciously conservative. To prevent levels of competition that would endanger the group's status, they sought to limit individual freedom in the market. This system of self-regulating craft monopolies was beginning to weaken in Europe before the settlement of America, and the nature of colonial society undermined it further. Guilds were most powerful in the largest cities of the Spanish colonies, Mexico City and Lima in particular, but in smaller cities and in Brazil guilds were seldom established and, when

Textile production was an important component of the economy of colonial Spanish America. Here wool yarn is prepared for weaving into cloth.

present, were weak. The use of slaves and, in the sixteenth century, forced Indian labor undermined guild ideals and traditional artisan values.

The slow trickle of European immigrants willing to enter artisan crafts led Spanish and Portuguese masters to train Indian, *casta*, and slave apprentices. As a consequence, the racially and culturally heterogeneous artisan community of the New World was freed in custom, if not statute, from many of the traditional restraints found in Europe. Master artisans often attempted to reduce labor costs by using slaves or by ignoring the apprenticeship system and hiring lesser-skilled temporary labor. The most successful of these masters were, in effect, manufacturers. Some owned *obrajes* dependent on Indian and *casta* labor. But more often, the masters depended on the help of one or more journeymen and apprentices to satisfy the needs of neighborhood customers. Nearly all artisan producers owned their tools and carried a small inventory, but only a few owned their shops and homes. Almost every master artisan purchased raw materials on credit and then found it necessary to offer credit to clients. Although essential to business, these relationships of debt and credit dramatically increased the vulnerability of artisans and small manufacturers during periods of economic recession. One result was the fairly common practice of fleeing creditors by moving to another city.

Retail merchants operated across a broad scale of enterprise. The most successful sometimes rivaled *consulado* members in wealth. The poorest operated small neighborhood shops or participated in the open-air markets that ringed the central plaza. Many were little more than agents for wealthy wholesalers, their income deriving from their ability to anticipate supply and demand. Profits were associated with risks: Would a fleet arrive next year? Would contraband undercut the prices of goods purchased on credit from a wholesale merchant? Could inventory be protected against theft? Were their customers good credit risks? Credit helped sustain retail sales. Even at the level of the neighborhood grocery, shopkeepers carried large numbers of small debts, and the retailer himself was commonly indebted to the wholesale merchant and to family and other kin.

Most retail merchants operated in a geographically restricted market. Many, in fact, served a single urban neighborhood. Because increasing the volume of trade by entering new markets or expanding credit to customers was very risky, retail merchants were more likely to seek additional profits through diversification. Most typically, they invested in real estate, particularly urban rental property, but investments in the retail sale of alcoholic beverages and the maintenance of gaming establishments were also common.

Petty bureaucrats, secular priests, and other religious had uniformly modest incomes but a relatively secure status. Many middle-level officials owed their positions to patronage. Once in office, these men sought to solidify and improve their association with their powerful patrons and local elite families. They sought marriages with the daughters of landowners or merchants, marriages that would bring dowries and potential inheritances. Most members of this group supplemented their salaries with tips and bribes. Others sought opportunities to enter commerce as investors.

By the end of the sixteenth century urban areas of Spanish America were home to numerous secular priests, priests who were not members of orders such as the Franciscans or Dominicans. Those who acquired parishes through patronage or competitive searches received a small salary augmented by fees paid by parishioners; poor Indians and other commoners often complained that fees for baptisms, marriages, and funerals were exorbitant. Some parishes were so rich that the priest could, in effect, subcontract his sacramental duties to vicars in order to pursue other interests. Through a chantry or *capellanía*, other priests obtained the income from an endowment, often established by a deceased relative, for saying a specified number of prayers annually on behalf of the founder. Many priests and nuns were also involved in business, and their personal ownership of urban and rural property was not uncommon. One nun, Catarina de Telles Barretto of the Desterro convent of Salvador, Bahia, owned rental property, lent money, and owned twelve slaves who prepared and sold sweets. Her private estate at her death was worth half the annual income of her convent.

Rural Middle Groups

Some regions hosted significant rural middle groups. On the northern frontier of the Viceroyalty of New Spain, in the Bajío, and in the south in Oaxaca, for example, there were numerous small holdings, ranches and farms that produced food and livestock for local markets. Some were little more than subsistence producers who in good years sold surplus to nearby consumers. Others, however, were substantial properties that employed seasonal laborers and concentrated on cash crops. The use of seasonal workers kept labor costs low, but the scale of enterprise and limitations in local demand commonly restricted profits. As a result, very few members of this group acquired the land and resources necessary to enter the elite.

This social type was, perhaps, best exemplified by the *lavradores de cana* of the Brazilian sugar zone. Although dependent on nearby plantations for refining and processing, in many cases these cane producers were wealthy individuals who owned slaves and land. In other cases they were little more than sharecroppers who were dependent on the owners of refining establishments. The high cost of land, slaves, equipment, and plants for refining limited their advancement. Although their place in the production process curtailed their profits during boom times, the *lavradores* had lower fixed costs and lower levels of indebtedness than planters and therefore had less risk of catastrophe during periods of falling prices. The labor of family members, wives and daughters as well as sons, was crucial to *lavradores de cana* throughout the productive cycle, but especially during the harvest.

Small independent farmers and ranchers in Spanish America also relied on the labor of wives and daughters, as few produced enough income to hire temporary workers. This was very evident in the Río de la Plata region, especially in what is now Uruguay, where women worked alongside husbands and fathers on the wheat farms and smaller ranches. Contemporary censuses, in fact, suggest that widows and single women ran many of these rural establishments.

The Broad Base of Colonial Society

Discriminatory laws, prejudice, racially targeted taxes like Indian tribute, and labor obligations like the *mita* constrained the lives of indigenous peoples, black slaves and freemen, and *castas*. Indeed the urban and rural poor that comprised the broad social base and vast majority of the population of colonial Latin America lived lives bounded by material deprivation and violence. Their labor harvested crops, cared for livestock, mined and refined silver and gold, manufactured textiles, and moved goods from place to place. They were the market women, stevedores, soldiers, day laborers, beggars, prostitutes, and vagrants who established themselves in the public spaces of cities and towns. They were also the most common inhabitants of jails, the most likely to be forced into military service, and the only groups that experienced the harshest corporal punishments like brandings and whippings.

It is difficult to generalize about the income levels, material conditions, legal constraints, and opportunities for social mobility experienced by these groups. There was no set pattern. Some hereditary Indian leaders owned land and livestock and enjoyed substantial income, some slaves gained their freedom through manumission, and a small number of peddlers or laborers saved some money and purchased a building lot or house. There were also important regional differences. At a time when the *mita* still disrupted indigenous lives in the southern Andes, most Indians in central Mexico had escaped from forced labor obligations. Opportunities and challenges were always different for men and women as suggested by the higher rates of manumission for female slaves. Nevertheless, the harsh conditions generally imposed on these groups by colonial political and economic structures defined in essential ways the nature of colonial societies.

Poverty and the routines of forced labor developed different characters in urban and rural areas. In the countryside the use of labor compulsion was widespread. The labor demands of the *repartimiento/mita*, the requirement that Indians pay tribute in cash, and the forced sale of goods to Indian communities in the Spanish colonies were heavy burdens. In effect, indigenous peoples were being required to subsidize the farms, ranches, mines, and *obrajes* of the elite with their labor, earning in return wages that seldom met subsistence needs. In Brazil the plantation economy depended on the forced labor of African slaves. Even where compulsion was less visible, few free agricultural laborers, whether Indians, free blacks, or *castas*, were able to buy land or, if landowners, avoid domination by powerful owners of ranches and plantations.

The greater complexity of urban economies meant that cities in Spanish America and Brazil offered additional opportunities to their large and diverse underclasses. At the top were skilled journeymen, market people, peddlers, servants, soldiers, and sailors. At the bottom were beggars, thieves, prostitutes, and the impoverished victims of accidents or diseases like leprosy. All these groups lived in difficult conditions, with many sleeping in the streets or in back rooms and struggling each day to find the money to buy food. Unemployment or illness could force even relatively skilled members of this class to seek charity by begging.

Some urban slaves lived in material circumstances superior to those of the great mass of the free working class. While all slaves suffered from racial prejudice and the other consequences of bondage, slaves in elite households often lived much better than did the multitude of free *castas* who sought employment each day. Some slaves, particularly those owned by men and women of modest means, lived outside their owners' households and pursued employment on their own. In a minority of

The central market of colonial Buenos Aires (top) and a woman from the country delivering water to the city (bottom).

cases they were able to acquire small amounts of property and purchase their freedom. Many female slaves participated in market activities; in colonial Brazil, in particular, enterprising slave women dominated the urban markets.

Urban wage laborers and some free agricultural laborers and artisans in rural areas generally worked from sunrise to sunset, as did slaves in the countryside. The workweek ran from Monday through Saturday, but numerous religious and secular holidays interrupted this routine. Urban workers customarily received breaks for lunch and refreshment and in some artisan shops employers provided meals. Apprentices and some journeymen slept in their employers' back rooms. For many workers, these forms of compensation in kind were essential to their struggle for survival.

Both the changing market demands for labor and wage custom determined the workers' pay. Wage custom was the association of a certain daily wage, *jornal*, with a specific job, and as a result, the wages of the unskilled changed very little over long periods. Only sustained high labor demands could break this pattern. A similar wage structure existed in the skilled crafts, in which all masters were likely to pay the same wage to their journeymen. Few men worked fifty-two six-day weeks. Rather, many endured periods of unemployment each year. Because few skilled or unskilled wage laborers had any savings or investments, extended unemployment or illness often led to destitution. Some guilds offered medical assistance to their members, but most workers turned to the Church for assistance. Although women were barred by statute or custom from most skilled and unskilled manual labor, the evidence is overwhelming that they did work. Most often they were found away from the jealous scrutiny of guilds and magistrates, producing and selling goods made in the home or, particularly in regard to textiles, providing much of the *obraje* labor force.

Most colonial populations included some soldiers, government lackeys, and, in the ports, sailors. Uniformly underpaid, these men were often compelled by necessity to seek part-time employment. Their participation in the urban labor market accordingly depressed urban wages and often stirred resentment by the local population. Some Spanish soldiers actually had to beg when their wages were not paid.

Peddlers and market vendors, whether male or female, shared the low incomes and vulnerability of the wage laborers. Often in debt, their meager inventories were subject to theft and spoilage. And unlike artisans and other skilled workers, these petty retailers could not rely on wage custom and institutionally established labor recruitment mechanisms. They thus lived on guile and pluck, and only a handful ever achieved material security. For many the eventual fall from peddler to thief or beggar was all too predictable.

Every colonial city also was home to prostitutes, thieves, and beggars. Propertied men and women demanded protection from their blandishments and attacks in the crowded streets, but little protection was offered. Most of the underclass lived lives of incredible deprivation, although fashionable prostitutes or skillful thieves might have fleeting moments of high income. For example, four *casta* women set up a house of prostitution in Lima in 1631 and enjoyed a brief period of good business: "These men come and go, in and out of the house day and night," complained the authorities.[2] But public

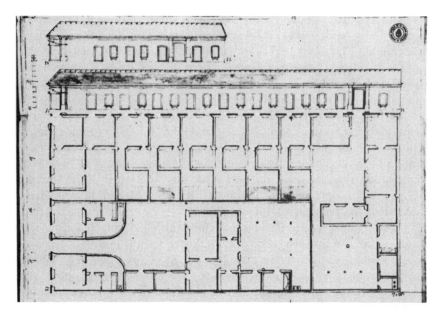

Architect's design for an apartment block.

outrage led to the dispatch of Pascuala de Cabeza and the others to a shelter for "lost women."

Latin Catholic culture was tolerant of beggars and poverty. The Church viewed the indigent poor as part of the God-given social landscape, not as a social aberration, and urged Catholics to remember them as fellow Christians and to give alms for their sustenance. Members of mendicant orders, in seeking to imitate Christ's poverty, begged for their daily bread. *Cofradías* and other religious sodalities that shared these sentiments regularly offered alms to beggars following the funerals of members and during special feast days. As a result, swarms of beggars congregated around the churches and public buildings in every colonial city. The very poor also sustained themselves on offal from municipal slaughterhouses, on spoiled and stale bread from bakeries, and on the limited generosity of wealthy households willing to give them alms.

Indians

As colonial society matured, pre-Columbian distinctions of culture and class among the highly urbanized and socially stratified indigenous societies of Mesoamerica and the Andes were often compressed and at times virtually eradicated. In Brazil, Chile, the Río de la Plata region, and the Caribbean region of South America, Portuguese and Spanish settlers found village cultures or dispersed semisedentary populations. In these colonial regions, settlers and colonial officials viewed indigenous groups as potential military rivals or as potential laborers.

The process of compressing the great diversity of indigenous cultures and social organizations began with the creation of a new identity, that of "Indian," that had not existed before the conquest. Although originally employed as a racial description, "Indian" also became a cultural term and, for the Spanish Crown, a fiscal category that defined obligations for the native population. The development and implementation of Indian policy by agents of the Spanish and Portuguese crowns gave this artifact of colonial rule political and economic meaning. Policies intended to ameliorate injustice, as in the New Laws of the Spanish colonies, or to enrich the exchequer, as in the imposition of tribute, had the effect of blurring distinctions of culture and class. In Mexico, for example, the application of tribute eliminated a traditional distinction between commoners with and without access to communal land. In Peru *yanaconas* improved their status relative to *ayllu* members, who retained traditional land rights, by seeking employment among Spanish settlers.

Chastened by the demographic tragedy of the Caribbean colonies and committed to the conversion of the Indians, the Spanish Crown initially promoted the development of a racially segregated society on the mainland. Legislation barred Spaniards, other than missionaries, and *castas* from Indian settlements. Eventually, even *encomenderos* were restricted from visiting their tribute populations. But this attempt at social engineering soon collapsed. The effects of epidemic disease, resettlement efforts, and the growth of the market economy overwhelmed the statutory isolation of the indigenous peoples as the increasing pace of contacts with Europeans irrevocably altered native culture.

The conquistadors and the Crown initially recognized the legitimacy of the native elites. Both Cortés and Pizarro tried to advance the process of pacification by using captive rulers drawn from the traditional ruling families, but the experiment quickly ended in Mexico. The last Inca pretender died in Spain in 1627, a completely Hispanized seeker of royal patronage. Some Spaniards married Indian women of the highest rank in order to lay claim to traditional tribute and other privileges. As a result, within two generations the upper ranks of the Indian nobility of central Mexico and Peru became racially mixed and culturally Spanish. The political organization and economic structures of Brazil's indigenous populations were less compatible with the hierarchies imposed by the new colonial order than were those of Mesoamerica and Peru. As a result, few Portuguese settlers married Indian women. There were no Brazilian social equivalents of the sisters and daughters of Moctezuma or Atahualpa.

Despite initially favoring some Indian lineages, the general pattern was for indigenous royal families and great territorial nobles to lose ground or be pushed aside. The progressive deterioration of the chiefdom of Tepaneca in the Valley of Mexico illustrates this phenomenon. Juan de Guzmán Itzollinqui became the native ruler in 1526. His inheritance included substantial property and the services of some four hundred retainers. He received an annual tribute of corn, wheat, chilies, tomatoes, salt, wood, and fodder in addition to labor services. His heir proved less fortunate. In the 1560s the Marqués del Valle, a son of Cortés, seized some of the *cacique*'s inherited traditional lands. Changes in colonial labor law then forced him to pay for labor he had previously received in tribute. By 1575 the patrimony of the grandson of the original colonial era *cacique* was reduced to fifty-one retainers and a tribute of twenty-three pesos. In the late eighteenth century, the incumbent *cacique* financed a costly personal appeal at the Spanish court by working as a carpenter. After his direct request for assistance was rejected, this descendant of the once-powerful Mesoamerican ruling class died in poverty in a Spanish prison.

However, local indigenous authorities survived where they were essential to the functioning of colonial labor and fiscal systems. The *caciques* of Mexico, the *batabs* of Yucatan, and the *kurakas* of the Andes, for example, oversaw the collection of tribute payments and labor for the *repartimiento/mita*. The men who held these positions usually came from traditional noble families, but there were numerous cases in which ambitious commoners who proved useful to the Spanish or were tied to them by shared economic interests pushed aside rightful leaders. Although materially poor relative to much of the Spanish population, these Indian leaders often owned private land and livestock and were exempted from tribute and labor service. In Brazil no hereditary native leadership class survived the conquest and evolved to assume an intermediary role in the colonial order such as collecting taxes and organizing forced labor drafts.

As the colonial order matured, this class of cross-cultural intermediaries became increasingly Hispanized. Fernando Uz, a hereditary *batab* in Yucatan in the early seventeenth century, was granted the position of Indian governor and later served as translator and senior aide to the Spanish governor. Other members of this class used the Spanish legal system to further their own interests or the interests of their communities against *encomenderos*, landowners, *corregidores*, and priests. In Peru, ethnic descendants of the Incas went to court to protect their exemption from the *mita*. Use of the courts to gain and retain the office of *kuraka* was also common. The proliferation of new secular and religious offices within the Indian communities provided additional opportunities for traditional families. Indian *alcaldes* and *regidores* were generally related to local rulers. Offices in Church-affiliated institutions like *cofradías* and secular positions in the local parish like choirmaster, teacher, and lay assistant were also filled from the traditional ruling families.

Crucial to the survival of Indian communities was maintenance of traditional land rights. Indians quickly learned to use the colonial legal system for redress of grievances, especially in administrative centers and towns close to agents of the Spanish judicial system. Nowhere was this more evident than in central Mexico. Nahuatl-speaking Indians employed evolving strategies that altered in response to changing colonial realities in their efforts to win property disputes. Initially these communities often appealed to the precedent of preconquest land tenure arrangements or to an unbroken succession of inheritance. During this same period some members of the indigenous nobility based private claims on Spanish land grants given after the conquest or on land purchases. In the seventeenth century Indian litigants relied on written documentation, notably bills of sale and wills, to demonstrate the legitimacy of their claims. Changes in the Indians' approaches in working within the Spanish legal system in regard to property issues was but one consequence of their forced adaptation to colonial rule.

Another change involved the relationship between Indian men and women. Spanish judicial practice and social expectations combined to strengthen the authority of fathers and husbands. In central Mexico and the Andean region, preconquest practice had provided men and women with what some scholars call parallel and complementary roles that gave somewhat greater independence to women. In the colonial period, a more rigid and hierarchical relationship developed with women more clearly subordinated to men. Here as elsewhere, family relationships were transformed as well with the native population gradually accepting the Spanish emphasis on the nuclear family headed by the father.

Accommodation and adaptation rather than conflict or rebellion thus characterized native responses to Spanish rule in areas where large indigenous populations had depended on agriculture. At the same time, however, it is important to recognize that rebellions and other forms of resistance such as migration away from Spanish settlements did occur. In the Andes and Maya regions as well as along the northern frontier of New Spain rebellions provided strong challenges to Spanish authority from the sixteenth to the late eighteenth century.

One important measure of the native population's ability both to retain preconquest cultural characteristics and to adapt to the cultural and economic impositions of the colonial regime can be found in language. The well-studied Nahuatl-speaking population of central Mexico most clearly reveals both the continuities with the indigenous past and alterations after conquest. Documents written in Nahuatl reveal almost no change in the language until the 1540s. During the following hundred years, the language incorporated large numbers of Spanish nouns. After 1650, Spanish linguistic influence continued to increase as bilingualism became more common.

In some places, indigenous languages survived even as Indian peoples declined in number under the onslaught of disease and conquest. In Yucatan the Maya language survived to the end of the colonial period as the region's primary language. As one official put it, "The language generally spoken in this province by Indians, mestizos and pardos is the Maya language."[3] The Guaraní language of Paraguay also became the common regional language. And, in São Paulo, Brazil, mixed-race frontiersmen who pushed the borders of Portuguese settlement west, exploring the interior, raiding Indian communities in Paraguay for slaves and discovering gold at the end of the seventeenth century, spoke a related indigenous language, Tupí.

Indigenous peoples found ways to survive by forging relationships with the dominant market-based economies of the Europeans. Here two Pampas Indians sell animal pelts and feathers in front of a European shop in Buenos Aires.

The great mass of Indians found the weight of the colonial order a nearly intolerable burden. In the decades immediately following the conquest, the goods they produced and the labor they provided sustained the combined weight of growing Spanish and Portuguese populations and the surviving vestiges of the traditional ruling class. Once the Indian population began to decline, the demands for labor and tribute undermined communal bonds and led large numbers of individuals, and sometimes entire families, to migrate. They headed for the bush beyond the control of colonial officials and settlers or, more often, sought work on Spanish farms and ranches or in other Indian communities. Once located on the farms and ranches of settlers, they were commonly exempted from forced labor.

The response of the *caciques* of the *audiencia* district of Quito to Spanish pressure is instructive. In the latter sixteenth century, *caciques* in the center of the district successfully hid from Spanish census takers a substantial number of migrants who had entered their jurisdictions from

Indian porter carrying a Spaniard on his back.

poor outlying regions. It was only in the latter seventeenth century that the Spaniards were able to identify these *forasteros* and force them to pay tribute. A change had taken place, however. Sixteenth-century migrants who had fled primarily because they had lost their land to Spaniards still retained strong ties to their home community. By the end of the seventeenth century, migrants were much more likely to have broken these connections. Drawn to textile *obrajes* and *haciendas*, they permanently entered the Hispanic sector of the colonial world. By 1700, over half of the native population of the *audiencia* district lived away from their original native community.

Throughout the colonial period the population continuously flowed away from Indian communities and toward Spanish cities and towns. These migrants were pushed by the harsh realities of tribute and labor service and pulled by the possibilities of greater independence and opportunity. Most lived the hand-to-mouth existence of day laborers or *obraje* workers, but a small minority learned trades and entered the class of propertied workers. Whether successful or not, these migrants were the primary contributors to a process of assimilation and cultural change that helped produce the colonial working class.

After the initial enslavement of natives in the coastal regions of colonial Brazil, subsequent slave raids in the interior of the colony pushed surviving Indian populations away from Portuguese settlements. The absence of a Brazilian equivalent of the *repartimiento/mita* that exercised such a powerful influence in natives' decisions to relocate in the Spanish colonies also reduced the presence of natives in urban centers.

Indian communities survived the colonial experience, but only after being substantially altered. Communal landholding practices in particular proved remarkably resilient, despite the effects of population loss and the advent of market forces. The Indians' oversight of numerous local affairs also continued in many regions, especially those distant from colonial urban centers. Yet the vitality and relative abundance of the precontact agricultural community were lost because of external demands for labor and land. In its place developed the impoverished peasant village still visible in Latin America.

Blacks

Men and women of African descent arrived in colonial Latin America during the period of conquest and initial settlement. After a brief period when participation in military campaigns against indigenous groups allowed some black slaves to gain their freedom and, in limited cases, to become landowners, a system of oppressive racial discrimination was developed in the colonies. Within decades of the first settlements blacks were allocated to an inferior position in society that was imposed both by law and by informal mechanisms of discrimination.

The low status of African slaves had been established in Portugal and Spain before 1492. With few exceptions, Africans and their descendents first entered Iberia as slaves, the lowest social rank. Legally defined as chattel, goods that could be bought and sold, slaves enjoyed few opportunities or protections, despite a limited body of law and religious teaching that recognized their humanity and religious potential. The social burdens associated with slavery were then carried to the colonies and reinforced by the African slave trade.

In the first decades of the colonial period blacks were temporarily invested with an intermediary social position superior to that imposed on the defeated Indian peoples. The crushing military defeat suffered by the Aztecs, Incas, and other indigenous peoples led conquistadors and settlers to devalue Indian culture and achievements. Because there were few Europeans in the Americas relative to the indigenous population, black men, especially in the Spanish colonies, became in effect representatives of the emerging colonial order. As allies of the conquerors, blacks served militarily in the pacification of frontier zones, managed and supervised Indian laborers, and directed the urban household staffs of the wealthiest and most powerful Spaniards. During this fluid transitional period before colonial social structure became fixed, many slaves gained their freedom. The effects of this movement from slavery to freedom were multiplied because all children born to black fathers whether slave or free and Indian mothers were free. One Spaniard's will noted: "The Five children of María Yndia shepherdess, wife of the Negro Manuel, shepherd of this [estate], although they are the children of said black slave they are not slaves."[4]

The exercise of unprecedented power by Spaniards and their black auxiliaries over defeated Indians led to accusations of abuse. The Spanish Crown responded by promulgating a series of unenforceable laws that prohibited most contacts between blacks and Indians. Blacks were barred from living in Indian villages. Marriages between blacks and Indians were prohibited and blacks who had sexual relations with Indian women were to be sentenced to one hundred lashes for the first offense and to having their ears cut off for the second. In general, however, these draconian laws limiting interactions between blacks and Indians were seldom enforced. Moreover, no evidence confirms that blacks were more likely to abuse Indians than Europeans. Rather, distant Spanish authorities responded to reports of aggressive actions by blacks and acted on their prejudices because they failed to understand the new status slaves experienced as agents of Spanish power in a world of defeated and demoralized indigenous societies.

The punitive nature of these early laws foreshadowed the later efforts by Spanish and Portuguese colonial authorities to control and discipline a growing black population. Throughout the colonial period, mutilations, whippings, and brutal executions were the all-too-predictable responses to transgressions by slaves and black freemen. Slaves who resisted their masters violently or who participated in slave rebellions were routinely executed. Chronic runaways were punished by the loss of ears, feet, or hands. A law written to punish runaways in Cartagena made clear the brutal nature of the slave regime. One hundred lashes were given to a slave who returned to his master after a week as a runaway. For a slave who was captured after a month, "he should have his genital organ cut off . . . [and he should be] placed in the pillary [*sic*] of this city, so that the blacks might learn from this example; which sentence should be done publicly, where everyone may see."[5]

Owners were seldom shy in using corporal punishments. Whippings were very common in agricultural zones, especially on the largest plantations where masters and overseers directed scores of slaves. But whippings were frequent even in urban settings where slaves and masters lived in close proximity. Owners unwilling to wield the whip themselves could take slaves to police authorities for punishment or incarceration. Ironically, free blacks were often punished more severely than slaves whose owners had a stake in protecting their value as property. In 1793, for example, the slave Pedro and his free friend Juan Carlos were arrested for stealing a pair of shoes. The slave was sentenced to twenty-five strokes of the whip. His free mulatto friend was sentenced to death, a sentence commuted to a ten-year term in the garrison of a frontier fort. Regardless of whatever material or political advantages blacks had gained relative to Indians, the colonial legal system always punished their insubordinations and crimes harshly.

As the African slave trade to Latin America expanded in the seventeenth and eighteenth centuries, slaves became available in greater numbers and at lower prices. This permitted the widespread use of slaves in agriculture and mining, especially in the gold mines of Brazil and in the Chocó region in New Granada. It also enabled members of new social groups, including many of modest means, to purchase slaves. By the end of the seventeenth century nearly every elite or middle-class household, including those of shopkeepers, low-level colonial officials, and artisans, had one or more slaves. Some members of the Indian elite also owned black slaves.

The Catholic Church was the largest single owner of slaves in colonial Latin America. However, the Church also helped to restrain the ill treatment of slaves, particularly in Latin American cities, and to protect slave marriages. Christian rituals, processions, and celebrations of saints' days provided relief from the drudgery of daily life for the slave community. Although the Church limited in small ways the power of owners, it never opposed the institution of slavery itself. Perhaps more importantly, the Church never justified slavery based on the presumed inferiority of Africans and their American-born descendents, a justification that became common among Protestant denominations in the United States. Racial discrimination was an institutionalized part of both civic and religious life in colonial Latin America, but the Catholic Church recognized the essential humanity, the soul, of black slaves in Latin America.

The most important organizations of the black community were based on European models. Within the Church slaves found ways to create collective organizations and establish rituals and practices that helped to humanize their captivity. Lay brotherhoods, *cofradías*, gave slaves an opportunity to participate actively in the communities' civic and religious life. Some brotherhoods collected funds to help purchase their members' freedom, provide minimal health care, or pay for decent burials. *Cofradías* also played a crucial role in the religious life of the black community, organizing black participation in the secular and religious celebrations that gave expression to communal civic consciousness. In areas with large African-born populations, there were also social organizations based on African identities—Congos, Benguelas, or Yorubas, for example. Besides uniting individuals from distinct cultural and language groups, these associations helped keep alive elements of African tradition and also provided an organized means for adapting to the harsh realities of the colonial slave system. At the same time the size of the African population and African cultural distinctiveness helped to foster a separate identity among American-born slaves and freemen.

The development of the slave trade had important consequences for the evolving colonial social structure. Direct trade with Africa broke the close association between the black population and the dominant culture of the European conquerors. Between 1580 and 1700 approximately 385,000 slaves entered Brazil while 430,000 more arrived in the ports of Spanish America. The cultural distinctiveness of an increasingly African slave population and the social effects of harsh labor and brutal discipline promoted negative racial stereotypes and reinforced the effects of discriminatory legislation and racial prejudice brought from Portugal and Spain.

Because European immigrants never met the colonial demand for skilled labor, slaves and freemen in urban areas gained access to most manual trades, despite discriminatory laws issued to prevent slaves from competing with whites. Male slaves worked in nearly every artisan trade, in lesser-skilled jobs in transportation, and in domestic service. In many larger cities, black artisans even created their own guilds. Many skilled slaves hired their own time and provided their owners with a monthly income. Female slaves dominated most of the urban markets. They also produced and sold sweets, did laundry, and, of course, provided the domestic labor in many households.

Some slaves in Iberia and many more in the colonies gained their freedom. Acculturated slaves who had been born in the colonies were much more likely than slaves brought from Africa to gain liberation. Owners manumitted slaves as an act of religious piety, or for some exemplary service, or in return for a cash payment made by the slave. In the urban economy many slaves had the opportunity to earn and accumulate money. This facilitated manumissions and led to the growth of a large free black community. Portuguese and Spanish law actually provided a framework for determining a slave's fair market value and the supervision of his or her self-purchase. As a result, purchased manumissions became the most common road to freedom in both Spanish America and Brazil. Masters also freed other slaves without payment, particularly children and the elderly. It was common for freed slaves to then save so that they could purchase the freedom of family members who remained in bondage. Indeed, the commitment and enterprise of black families were as responsible for the rapid growth in the free black population as were imperial laws and Catholic beliefs. By the end of the eighteenth century, free blacks accounted for 40 percent of the population of Salvador, Bahia, and 20 percent of the population of Rio de Janeiro. During this same period in Spanish Buenos Aires about 1 percent of the slave population gained freedom each year. But although manumission was far more common in Latin America than in the British colonies, the majority of African slaves and their American-born descendants lived and died in bondage. And free blacks continued to carry the stigma associated with slavery. There is no doubt that the lives of all free blacks were constrained by a broad array of discriminatory legislation and prejudice, regardless of their achievements.

The racially mixed population filled interstices in both rural and urban society in Brazil. Mixtures of the three original racial groups proliferated in the violent and unsettled early years of the colony. Indian-white and black-Indian mixtures were important in the early decades, particularly in frontier zones, but it was the black-white mixtures, the *pardos*, that came to hold the central place in the work force. Free *pardos* and blacks provided the majority of the skilled urban work force. Even in the largest cities with the largest populations of Portuguese immigrants, free blacks made up more than 50 percent of this skilled work force. Mixed-race persons often were supervisors in the sugar industry. Indeed, the *pardos* were essential to the peace and stability of the colony, filling the enlisted ranks of the military and the constabulary. Transportation, construction, and nearly all occupations associated with Atlantic shipping depended on the mixed groups, especially the *pardos*.

Of particular note was the importance of Brazil's black and *pardo* population in the arts, especially music, painting, and sculpture. The best-known Brazilian artist was Antonio Lisboa, the son of a Portuguese immigrant and a slave woman. Afflicted with leprosy in middle age, he was known as Aleijadinho, the "little cripple." He designed both the interiors and the exteriors of many of Minas Gerais's finest churches, and he was also an accomplished sculptor, best known for his depiction of the Twelve Prophets at Nosso Senhor de Mattosinhos.

As the New World colonial societies matured, a complex mix of racial, cultural, and economic influences determined relations of wealth and power. Although all these societies were hierarchical, sharing an archaic European ideal of a static precapitalist social order, the colonial social realities were, in fact, more fluid and unpredictable than contemporary bureaucratic formulations suggest. The distinction between Indian and European, conquered and conqueror, proved to be remarkably durable. However, as time passed and racially and culturally intermediate groups appeared, the boundary between these two categories lost much of its early precision.

Differences in wealth and power, class differences, were also present from early times. As racial and cultural boundaries blurred, these distinctions increased in importance. A strong correlation between the system of racial stratification and the class structure can be found throughout the colonial period. This correlation was weakest in urban areas during the periods of economic expansion and strongest in rural areas remote from market forces. There were obvious exceptions; some traditional Indian noblemen enjoyed relative material abundance, and some immigrants survived only as beggars. Color prejudice and discrimination were, however, mechanisms for distributing wealth and organizing labor: Race relations in colonial Latin America always also had a class character.

Notes

1. P. J. Bakewell, *Silver Mining and Society in Colonial Zacatecas, 1546–1700* (Cambridge, England: Cambridge University Press, 1971), p. 211, n. 3.

2. Quoted in Luis Martín, *Daughters of the Conquistadors: Women of the Viceroyalty of Peru* (Albuquerque: University of New Mexico Press, 1983), p. 165.

3. Quoted in Wolfgang Gabbert, "Social Categories, Ethnicity and the State in Yucatán, Mexico," *Journal of Latin American Studies*, 33 (2001), p. 468.

4. Lolita Gutiérrez Brockington, "The African Diaspora in the Eastern Andes: Adaptation, Agency, and Fugitive Action, 1573–1677," *The Americas*, 57:2 (2000), p. 213.

5. Quoted by Peter Wade, *Blackness and Race Mixture: The Dynamics of Racial Identity in Colombia* (Baltimore: Johns Hopkins University Press, 1993), p. 79.

Suggested for Further Reading

Andrien, Kenneth J., editor. *The Human Tradition in Colonial Latin America.* Wilmington, Del.: Scholarly Resources, 2002.

Bristol, Joan Cameron. *Christians, Blasphemers, and Witches: Afro-Mexican Ritual Practice in the Seventeenth Century.* Albuquerque: University of New Mexico Press, 2007.

Chambers, Sarah C. *From Subjects to Citizens: Honor, Gender, and Politics in Arequipa, Peru, 1780–1854.* University Park: Pennsylvania State University Press, 1999.

Charney, Paul. *Indian Society in the Valley of Lima, Peru, 1532–1824.* Blue Ridge Summit, Pa.: University Press of America, 2001.

Cohen, David W., and Jack P. Greene, editors. *Neither Slave Nor Free: The Freedmen of African Descent in the Slave Societies of the New World.* Baltimore: Johns Hopkins University Press, 1972.

Cope, R. Douglas. *The Limits of Racial Domination: Plebeian Society in Colonial Mexico City, 1660–1720.* Madison: University of Wisconsin Press, 1994.

Diffie, Bailey W. *A History of Colonial Brazil, 1500–1792.* Edited by Edwin J. Perkins. Melbourne, Fla.: Krieger, 1987.

Ferry, Robert J. *The Colonial Elite of Early Caracas: Formation and Crisis, 1567–1767.* Berkeley and Los Angeles: University of California Press, 1989.

Francois, Marie Eileen. *A Culture of Everyday Credit: Housekeeping, Pawnbroking, and Governance in Mexico City, 1750–1920.* Lincoln: University of Nebraska Press, 2006.

Garrett, David T. *Shadows of Empire: The Indian Nobility of Cusco, 1750–1825.* Cambridge, England: Cambridge University Press, 2005.

Gosner, Kevin. *Soldiers of the Virgin: The Moral Economy of a Colonial Maya Rebellion.* Tucson: University of Arizona Press, 1992.

Haskett, Robert. *Indigenous Rulers: An Ethnohistory of Town Government in Colonial Cuernavaca.* Albuquerque: University of New Mexico Press, 1991.

Haskett, Robert. *Visions of Paradise: Primordial Titles and Mesoamerican History in Cuernavaca.* Norman: University of Oklahoma Press, 2005.

Jackson, Robert H. *Race, Caste, and Status: Indians in Colonial Spanish America.* Albuquerque: University of New Mexico Press, 1999.

Katzew, Ilona. *Casta Painting: Images of Race in Eighteenth-Century Mexico.* New Haven and London: Yale University Press, 2005.

Kellogg, Susan. *Law and the Transformation of Aztec Culture, 1500–1700.* Norman: University of Oklahoma Press, 1995.

Lewis, Laura A. *Hall of Mirrors: Power, Witchcraft and Caste in Colonial Mexico.* Durham: Duke University Press, 2003.

Liss, Peggy K. *Mexico Under Spain, 1521–1556: Society and the Origins of Nationality.* Chicago: University of Chicago Press, 1975.

Lockhart, James. *Spanish Peru, 1532–1560: A Colonial Society.* 2nd edition. Madison: University of Wisconsin Press, 1994.

Mills, Kenneth. *Idolatry and Its Enemies: Colonial Andean Religion and Extirpation, 1640–1750.* Princeton, N.J.: Princeton University Press, 1997.

Ramírez, Susan Elizabeth. *The World Upside Down: Cross-Cultural Contact and Conflict in Sixteenth-Century Peru.* Stanford, Calif: Stanford University Press, 1996.

Restall, Matthew. *The Maya World: Yucatec Culture and Society, 1550–1850.* Stanford: Stanford University Press, 1997.

Schroeder, Susan, editor. *Native Resistance and the Pax Colonial in New Spain.* Lincoln: University of Nebraska Press, 1998.

Serulnikov, Sergio. *Subverting Colonial Authority: Challenges to Spanish Rule in Eighteenth-Century Southern Andes.* Durham: Duke University Press, 2003.

Stavig, Ward. *The World of Tupac Amaru: Conflict, Community, and Identity in Colonial Peru.* Lincoln: University of Nebraska Press, 1999.

Teja, Jesús F. de la and Ross Frank (editors). *Choice, Persuasion, and Coercion: Social Control on Spain's North American Frontier.* Albuquerque: University of New Mexico Press, 2005.

Terraciano, Kevin. *The Mixtecs of Colonial Oaxaca: Ñudzahui History, Sixteenth through Eighteenth Centuries.* Stanford: Stanford University Press, 2001.

Weber, David J. *Bárbaros: Spaniards and Their Savages in the Age of Enlightenment.* New Haven and London: Yale University Press, 2005.

Williams, Caroline A. *Between Resistance and Adaptation: Indigenous Peoples and the Colonisation of the Chocó, 1510–1753.* Liverpool, United Kingdom: Liverpool University Press, 2004.

Wood, Stephanie. *Transcending Conquest: Nahua View of Spanish Colonial Mexico.* Norman: University of Oklahoma Press, 2003.

Yannakakis, Yanna. *The Art of Being In-between: Native Intermediaries, Indian Identity, and Local Rule in Colonial Oaxaca.* Durham: Duke University Press, 2008.

Zeitlin, Judith Francis. *Cultural Politics in Colonial Tehuantepec: Community And State Among The Isthmus Zapotec, 1500–1750.* Stanford: Stanford University Press, 2005.

SEVEN

THE FAMILY AND SOCIETY

Chronology

1514	Indians allowed to marry freely with Indians and Spaniards
1530	Indians with more than one spouse are to live with first spouse or be punished
1539	Prohibition of unmarried women traveling to the Indies without a license from the king
1540	First female convent in Mexico City
1561	First female convent in Lima
1563	Officials to encourage blacks to marry blacks
1568	First female convent in Puebla, New Spain
1572	Legitimate offspring of free or slave blacks and Indian women declared tributaries
1572	Caciques and their eldest sons declared exempt from tribute and *mita* service
1578	Men in Spain with wives in the Indies are to return there and live with them
1605	Final authorization of a foundling home in Lima
1618	Men married in Indies must obtain a license to go to Spain and post bond that they will return to their wives
1677	First female convent in Brazil
1718	King provides financial assistance to foundling home in Havana
1774	Mexico City poor house opens
1776	Royal Pragmatic to prevent marriage between unequal parties under the age of majority without parental consent
1794	Abandoned children are to be considered legitimate and white

Family: The Foundation of Colonial Society

The family was the basic social unit in colonial Latin America. While race, wealth, occupation, and gender all helped to identify an individual's position in the social structure, these attributes were usually evaluated in the framework of a broadly defined family. "Family" in this context meant not only the biological family, but also the larger set of family relations created by marriage and by forging alliances through the selection of godparents, the arrangement called *compadrazgo* in Spanish and *compadrio* in Portuguese. Appreciating the totality of a family's economic and political activities thus provides a better understanding of the colonial world over time than chronicling an individual's successes and failures.

Collective family objectives influenced and colored the opportunities and goals of its individual members. The family's power to mold individual choices grew out of its ability to grant or withhold scarce assets such as credit, land, and political influence. Education, marriage, occupation, and even travel were familial concerns that framed and limited individual choice. To ignore these claims commonly meant losing access to family support in the realization of individual ambitions.

The advantages, or burdens, of familial associations had a longitudinal character, for status was achieved and asserted across successive generations. A family's lineage, services to the Crown, and privileges all helped place its individual members within the social order. As a result, ambitious men and women worked to elevate the reputations of their families as platforms for their own ambitions as well as the aspirations of their kin and heirs. This was most common among the elite, but ambitious government officials and other propertied groups, like urban professionals, also took care to protect and enhance family reputation.

Although early censuses suggest that nuclear families and single-parent households were the most common residential units, the extended family was the effective social and economic unit for both Iberians and Indians throughout much of the colonial world. Members of the Indian nobility prided themselves on their lineages just as much as did members of the settler elites and were equally capable of exploiting the benefits of familial connections and resources. Long after the conquest, *caciques, kurakas, batabs,* and other hereditary indigenous elites normally married within their own rank and thus maintained their social distance from Indian commoners. But indigenous commoners as well perceived the family as a basic social unit and also exercised control over marriage decisions that were often crucial to the maintenance of land rights or to assistance during droughts and other difficult economic times. The continuing importance of indigenous kinship groups in Peru and central Mexico testifies to the strength of family ties. One example is found in colonial Yucatan where patrilineal extended families of up to five related males, their wives, and unmarried daughters formed the basic rural economic unit. But this was not unique. Nearly everywhere in the colonies, it was the strength of these familial associations that allowed Indian communities to survive despite the heavy demands for tribute and labor by colonial authorities.

The experiences of the mixed population, the *castas,* are more difficult to generalize. In the early decades that followed the military phase of European occupation, some Spanish and Portuguese settlers married Indian women. Many more lived in less formal arrangements. In both Peru and New Spain, for example, nearly all the early *encomendero* households included women from the indigenous nobilities.

An important number of the mixed children from these relationships were raised within the households of their European fathers and shared their desire to advance familial ambitions. These indigenous women and their children were important cultural intermediaries who transmitted language, customs, technologies, and folkways back and forth between the two communities.

As the number of European women in the colonies grew and as elite males increasingly saw advantages in asserting the purity of their bloodlines, the pattern of raising *mestizo* children in the homes of their European fathers weakened. When not recognized by their fathers and separated from the communities of their mothers, and thus from traditional rights associated with their mothers' lineages, these orphaned or abandoned children often sought to survive in colonial cities and towns. These population centers increasingly became the focus of an emerging *casta* culture that mixed elements of indigenous, European, and African cultures.

By the seventeenth century Church officials and colonial authorities widely assumed that nearly all *castas* were illegitimate. Indeed, the vast majority of the mixed population struggled for their daily bread as rural or urban laborers or as artisans and petty retailers with few connections to either European or Indian kinship groups. For these men and women there was little opportunity to pursue systematically the ideal of elevating family reputation in imitation of the elite. Nevertheless, family reputation or individual reputation for honesty, hard work, or courage could be turned to advantage in the neighborhood or village.

Marriage

In the eyes of the Spanish and Portuguese crowns and the Catholic Church, the sacrament of marriage alone was the basis for a legitimate family. Although many Iberians engaged in relationships with women of varied backgrounds, their marriages rarely crossed ethnic boundaries, even in the early decades of settlement when few European women were available. The richest and most powerful men in the colonies, of course, sought marriage with women of their own culture and class. Children of these legitimate families benefited most from their fathers' social position and fortune. While formal dissolution or divorce terminated a few marriages, union for life, if not love, was the general rule that underlay Spanish and Portuguese matrimonial practices and the accompanying elaboration of the extended family.

Although marriages most commonly united couples from the same or adjoining ethnicities and social classes, it was not uncommon for Iberian males in the colonies to have less formal relations with Indian, black, and *casta* women. These relationships might include the couple visiting openly or even living in the same household. Such unions had a publicly known sexual character and children frequently resulted. In some of these cases the woman, although denied the status of wife, had broad supervisory responsibility for the shared household. It was in these more enduring relationships that mixed-race children born outside wedlock might be legally recognized by their Spanish or Portuguese fathers. Deeply held prejudices associated with differences in color or culture therefore limited the likelihood of marriage across ethnic boundaries for the wealthiest groups, but did little to slow the development of less formal unions and the rate of miscegenation.

Elite marriages were in large measure economic and political alliances forged to further family ambitions; wealthy men and women thus routinely chose marriage partners after evaluating the potential impact of these decisions on their kinsfolk's ambitions. Similar considerations affected other groups as well. In areas with large indigenous populations and traditional economic and cultural practices, Indians normally married Indians, although some unions with blacks and with persons of mixed ancestry took place as well.

In racially diverse cities and mining camps, ethnic boundaries seldom constrained the selection of marriage partners or the formation of less formal arrangements. The marriage practices among mixed-race groups varied. In general it was common for *castas* to marry within their own group, a *mestizo* with a *mestiza*, for example. Marriages with members of other mixed groups or with blacks or Indians were not unusual, however. In urban settings, residency (neighbors marrying neighbors) or occupation (shoemakers marrying the daughters of shoemakers) was often more important than ethnicity to marriage choices.

In Spanish America, the marriage rates for Spaniards and Indians were higher than those for *castas*. The *casta* pattern differed, in part, because this group was largely denied access to both traditional Indian landholding rights and to full participation in the Spanish economy. These men and women were therefore less constrained by family preferences, seeking mates, establishing families, and marrying in response to their own needs and resources.

Marriages were less frequent among black slaves than among the free population. The sexual imbalance in the slave trade, impediments inherent in the legal position of slaves, and often the active opposition of masters worked to inhibit slave marriages. Slave marriages were more common in urban areas than on plantations or farms. Urban slaves were more likely to have income, as artisans or market women, for example, that enabled them to absorb the costs of marriage. Nevertheless, the obstacles were very real. In Peru before 1650, less than 8 percent of slaves ages twenty to twenty-five and less than 15 percent of slaves ages twenty-six to thirty-five married. Women in both age groups married more frequently than men. As a result of these obstacles to marriage, many slave families were forged in less formal long-term relationships unsanctified by the Church. Given the obstacles faced by this oppressed population, the creation and maintenance of family structures were therefore remarkable. In one exceptional example, over 60 percent of the adult slaves on the sugar Engenho Santana in Ilhéus, Brazil, were married or lived in consensual unions in 1731.

Regardless of ethnicity or class, men in colonial Latin America generally married younger women. The average ages of both husbands and wives at marriage, however, varied significantly from one social sector to another. Elite families in both Brazil and Spanish America routinely incorporated older, successful immigrants through marriage. Few immigrant males who married in the Indies were minors; many were in their mid-thirties and a substantial number were forty or older. Among immigrant merchants and bureaucrats, marriage was commonly deferred until the individual was well established and able to arrange an alliance with a woman who could provide a dowry, an advance on a woman's inheritance granted prior to her marriage. Colonial-born males of wealthy families, in contrast, tended to marry earlier, for they could depend on their relatives' position in local society.

Portrait from eighteenth-century Mexico City of the young daughter of a free black woman and a Spaniard. Free black women were often targeted by discriminatory sumptuary laws that barred them from wearing rich garments and expensive jewelry. The intention was to install a clear boundary between white women and *castas*.

Contemporaries considered girls of fourteen years to be old enough for an initial marriage, although some married even younger. Elite parents often encouraged daughters to marry at a young age, as youthful marriage helped ensure premarital virginity and thus the maintenance of family honor as well as a high reproductive capability. In Spanish America, European and creole men were normally about four years older than their wives. Among the elite, males were often older and their wives younger at the time of marriage than was the case for other groups. For example, when Pedro Jiménez de los Cobos, a native-born alderman of Mexico City, married Clara Leonor del Sen in 1684, he was twenty-seven and she was just fourteen. Peninsular Juan Martínez de Lejarzar married a creole woman in Querétaro when he was forty-nine and she was twenty-three. Similarly, in Brazil a large number of Portuguese high court judges married much younger Brazilian women.

There were also notable variations by ethnicity, region, and time period. The limited evidence available suggests that a higher proportion of Indians married than did Spaniards and that Indian males married at an earlier age than did their Spanish counterparts. As did Spaniards, Indian males usually married younger women, but generally the age difference was smaller. *Casta* males commonly married even earlier than did Indians and, unlike whites or Indians, often married women older than themselves. *Casta* brides averaged about twenty-four years of age; the grooms, about twenty-three. Three regional cases suggest the variety of experience. Among the largely *casta* population of Parral in northern New Spain in the eighteenth century, men were on average seven years older than their brides. At about the same time in Ouro Prêto, Brazil, white males married at about thirty years of age. Their wives were about twenty-two, the typical age in the Spanish colonies. In Buenos Aires by 1800 the age difference of husbands and wives had reached nearly ten years.

Indian women generally married earlier than other women. In northern New Spain Indian women married at between 16 and 18 years, about two years younger than white and mixed-race women in the same region. Again there were also regional differences, with women in cities deferring marriage two to three years longer than those in villages and smaller towns. While the average age of all women at first marriage in eighteenth-century Parral was 19.2 years, the average was higher, nearly 23 years, in the larger Mexican cities of Guadalajara and Mexico City. Scholars believe that the average age of women at first marriage may have increased in the eighteenth century.

Women of the white elite and middle groups were more closely controlled than were poorer women. Visitors to Brazil commonly noted the jealous constraints imposed on women. For example, women of both rural and urban elite families seldom ventured from home without a chaperon except for mass or a closely supervised religious festival or public occasion. Their reputations protected by restricted contacts with men outside the family, custom even banned these elite women from participating in dinner conversation.

Male concern for daughters' chastity and wives' honor at times led to violence. Indeed, courts in colonial Spanish America and Brazil could send a woman suspected of infidelity to a convent or house of seclusion merely on the testimony of her husband or father. The sometimes draconian efforts to control and isolate wives and daughters from temptation were not foolproof. Amorous men could elaborate complex assaults on the virtue of even married women. In one notorious case, the son of a judge in Potosí seduced the wife of a wealthy rival, convincing her to help arrange her husband's murder. When discovered, the powerful families of the two lovers sent the woman to a convent and paid off the victim's family.[1]

There is also convincing evidence that these houses of seclusion, or *casas de recogimiento*, were used by women of all classes and ethnicities to escape abusive or unhappy marriages. Given that husbands had few checks on their authority and, in the worst cases, could "correct" their wives physically, this institution provided some protection to a battered or bullied wife. In most cases this was only a short-term solution. But by involving religious and legal authorities in her case the wife did gain leverage in negotiating for changes in behavior or time to pursue annulment or divorce with the ecclesiastical authorities.

A significant minority of free adults of all races and social classes remained single. Limited evidence suggests that this was even true among the Spanish population, in which it appears that a quarter or more of the men and women over the age of twenty-five never married. This high rate probably reflected the effects of racial prejudice that made Europeans and their American-born descendents reluctant to marry outside their ethnic group or below their class status and thus left them with a small pool of acceptable spouses. Some Spanish and Portuguese males withdrew from this process by becoming priests or by entering convents. Women also entered religious communities as nuns voluntarily or sometimes under pressure from their families who were desperate to avoid providing dowries beyond what a convent required. Other groups—*castas*, Indians, and blacks—were routinely denied these alternatives to marriage.

Convents were established in the sixteenth century in Spanish America. As part of complex family strategies designed to select desirable marriage partners, many young girls were placed in convents prior to their marriages in order to insulate them from the temptations of the secular world. Although women with strong religious vocations entered the convent to realize their ambitions for a life of prayer and contemplation, others found themselves there so that their families could reduce the number of potential heirs or protect against the depletion of resources by the payment of dowries. Diego de Zárate of La Plata, Upper Peru, for example, placed three of his six daughters in a local convent and arranged for a fourth to enter upon the death of one of three nuns.

Before the establishment of convents in Brazil, elite families sent unmarried daughters to convents in Portugal and the Azores, thus restricting the pool of potential brides for elite males. Although the Crown did not ban this practice until 1732, the foundation of the first nunnery in Salvador, Bahia, in 1677 had already given these families a colonial alternative that expanded with the creation of additional convents.

Practical concerns as well as romance determined the selection of marriage partners, especially among elite families. Cash and property were often more alluring than physical charms in selecting marriage partners, as marriage linked not just bride and groom but also their families. Marriage offered the opportunity for two prominent families to join and expand their economic and political activities or for a wealthy male immigrant or sometimes for a rising but not yet socially prominent family to unite with a family richer in status than in worldly possessions. A woman did not need a

Two examples from the Spanish colonies of portraits representing ethnic mixing.

dowry to marry, and a declining proportion of women in Brazil and Mexico were receiving them by the mid-eighteenth century. Nevertheless, a substantial dowry clearly enhanced the likelihood that the woman would contract an advantageous marriage. A dowry provided a bride with some financial security as well as underwriting some of the new couple's expenses. The husband administered the dowry but was responsible for maintaining its value, for it remained the property of his wife and the potential inheritance of her children, or, if she died childless, her family. In a small number of cases, women were forced to protect their interests in court. In 1693, for example, Phelipa Tello de Guzmán sued to remove her property from the control of her spendthrift husband.[2]

Dowries were powerful tools used to accomplish a family's claim to elite status. The more prosperous a bride's family, the more apt it was to dower her. The size of the dowry varied with the family's wealth and number of daughters. In Mexico City, Lima, and Salvador brides from rich families often received dowries of cash, jewels, slaves, clothing, art objects, and furniture worth over 10,000 pesos. Some dowries included a house, *hacienda*, or mine, but normally these properties went to male siblings.

Grooms could also enhance their attractiveness through the provision of *arras*, a groom's gift to his bride. This was often a sum equal to 10 percent of the groom's assets at the time of the marriage. The *arras* became part of the bride's personal estate, improving her financial future. Just as the dowry boldly stated the wealth and power of the wife's family, the *arras* reflected the husband's financial resources. The wording of the gift often testified to the bride's honor, virginity, and social position. The scale of these marital arrangements can be seen clearly in the marriage of María Antonia de la Redonda y Bolívar and Francisco Delgadillo de Sotomayor in Lima in 1668. She brought to the marriage a dowry worth 61,500 pesos, while her husband, the future city councilman, provided her with *arras* of 20,000 pesos.

Few provincial families provided dowries of more than several thousand pesos. Even among artisans and petty merchants, however, a small dowry of a few hundred pesos or a slave could provide the opportunity to expand a commercial undertaking or escape from debt. The importance of a dowry was such that, in both Brazil and Spanish America, charitable organizations provided modest dowries for fortunate orphaned young women.

Family Size

Family size in the colonial world was largely determined by the wife's age at marriage and by the era's high infant, childhood, and childbirth mortality rates. A family's economic and social standing influenced fertility and mortality rates and therefore family size. The urban and rural poor suffered from nutritional deprivation; lived in smaller, poorly ventilated homes; had limited access to potable water; and worked in more dangerous and arduous jobs.

These conditions affected both fertility and mortality rates relative to elite and middle groups. Fertility and mortality rates also had an ethnic character. Indian women, for example, had both higher fertility and a shorter life expectancy than did European and *casta* women. Despite these differences of class and ethnicity, high infant and childhood mortality rates commonly claimed the lives of half of all children born in the colonies before adulthood. Moreover, it was very likely that potential fertility would be interrupted by the death of either the wife or her husband before the end of a woman's fertile years. For the women of all classes, the complications associated with pregnancy and childbirth were the most common causes of early death. Custom kept most widows and widowers from remarrying for at least one year after a spouse's death. Nevertheless, remarriage was common, particularly among men and women with some property. A brief period as a widow did reduce a woman's fertility, however, even in cases of remarriage.

Given the limited strategies of family planning available, the age of women at marriage was the most important determinant of family size. In early modern Spain a relatively late marriage age (twenty-five years on average) limited a woman's reproductive period to approximately fifteen years. During this period she was likely to have five or six children. By way of comparison, evidence suggests that colonial women married about three years earlier on average than did women in Spain and that their longer average reproductive span led to additional births.

Many women in the colonies also had children outside marriage. Trial marriages were common among young indigenous men and women before the imposition of colonial rule. The Catholic Church attempted to eradicate this practice because it directly challenged the sacrament of marriage. Called *sirvinacuy* in the Peruvian Andes, these trial marriages were intended to test the compatibility of the couple and therefore promise the likelihood of an enduring marriage. In the 1570s Viceroy Toledo noted that Indians believed that the practice was necessary for the "peace, contentment, and friendship" of a marriage.[3]

Elite and other propertied families saw premarital sex and the possibility of illegitimate birth as threatening to their status, and, of course, sex outside of the sacrament of marriage was, according to Catholic doctrine, a sin. Despite these constraints, scholars who have examined age at first birth, rather than age at marriage, suggest that in many cases women had begun having children before they married. The Church and public opinion tended to be more permissive with premarital sexual relations when the woman had received the "promise of marriage" prior to engaging in sexual behavior. Children born in these relationships could be legitimized even if the parents never married. Sexual relations initiated without these ritual commitments were more common. In both Brazil and Mexico in the eighteenth century, evidence suggests that perhaps 20–40 percent of children were born outside of marriage.[4]

This pattern was most visible in rural regions and among the urban poor, two groups for whom the cost of the marriage was often prohibitive. There were very high rates of illegitimacy among all groups, especially among the *castas*. In the majority of cases where illegitimate children were born to *casta*, black, or Indian mothers, these children were raised by their mothers in single-parent households. Among whites, however, only a small minority of illegitimate children were acknowledged by their mothers. For elite families in particular, fears of a damaged reputation provoked efforts to keep the pregnancies of unmarried daughters or the birth of illegitimate children secret. Many of these children suffered a cruel fate, left at the door of an orphanage, given to servants or poor relations to raise as their own, or simply abandoned. Some priests were willing to connive with a powerful family to create a disguising fiction that would protect the woman's reputation and allow the child to be raised by the mother. Typically this involved the claim that the mother had adopted a foundling.

Indigenous populations never completely recovered from the devastating pandemics of the sixteenth century; in some regions, like the Caribbean islands, they had nearly disappeared. With the passage of time, however, mortality rates from new epidemics declined and indigenous populations began to recover in Mesoamerica and the Andean region. By the end of the seventeenth century indigenous families in the colonies were about the same size as those of Castilian peasant families, approximately four or five individuals. However, given the much earlier age at marriage of Indian women compared with their Spanish contemporaries, a difference of more than four years, this similarity in family size actually indicates the higher mortality rates suffered by indigenous peoples.

The largest families were often found at the top of the colonial social order. Elite families in the Spanish colonies and Brazil were often very large, imitating the family patterns of the European nobility. The early age of marriage of many elite women and frequent remarriage of elite widows who were still in childbearing years and had substantial inherited property resulted in many years of reproductive capacity within the married state. The children of elite families also had a better chance of reaching adulthood than did the children of the poor because of better diet, hygiene, and housing. The higher survival rate of these advantaged children necessarily translated into larger families in the colonial elites.

Fertility could be affected by the workings of the colonial economy. Many occupations required men and women to live apart for months and, in some cases, even years. Merchants often traveled long distances to find favorable market conditions. But the likelihood of separation was commonly greater at the bottom of the social order. Employment in the merchant fleets that crossed the Atlantic or as muleteers and wagon drivers involved in long-distance trade that connected Buenos Aires and Potosí, for example, divided husbands and wives for long periods. Military service in distant garrisons or on naval vessels demanded similar sacrifices. The *mita* labor rotations could divide Andean indigenous households, although it was not uncommon for wives and children to follow men to the mines.

Some evidence suggests that colonial families tried to manage fertility and control family size. The absence of reliable means of contraception other than sexual abstinence meant this was difficult at best. The teachings of the Catholic Church and prevailing custom were unambiguously pronatalist. The Church taught that efforts to avoid pregnancy such as coitus interruptus were sinful. The numerous potions provided to women by curers, midwives, and *brujas* (witches) had little practical efficacy as agents of birth control or abortion. Nevertheless, the Inquisition predictably detained and prosecuted anyone known to have offered these services to a woman desperate to avoid pregnancy.

Many women prolonged breast-feeding to lower the chances of pregnancies. One colonial woman from a large family recalled her mother's plight: "I remember quite well that when I had reached the age of five, my mother still nursed me at her breast . . . to avoid childbirth yet again. After I was born she began to entreat the Lord to send her no more children, for she was quite worn out with the number she already had. But the Lord, who knows full well what is best for us, did not grant her wish; and yet again, to test her patience, after I turned five He sent her twice more into childbirth."[5] Some modern scholars have pointed out that the reliance of elite women on wet nurses to breast feed their children may have increased their fertility and average family size. The family size of slaves who served as wet nurses in elite and middle group households, on the other hand, may have been smaller because of the extended lactation of these women.

The Family as an Economic Unit

Elite families in both Spanish America and Brazil commonly emphasized their Iberian origins to distinguish themselves from persons they considered social inferiors. Elite officeholders clearly depended on their connections in Iberia and worked hard to maintain and enhance these ties. But most elite families in the colonies in the sixteenth century could trace their social ascendancy to a single participant in the early period of conquest and settlement or sometimes to the efforts of several close relatives, like the Pizarro brothers, for example, rather than to European connections. For the founders of elite families in Spanish America, the windfalls of the age of conquest, early mining discoveries, political offices, *encomiendas,* and the accumulation of urban and rural real estate often combined to form the foundations of family prestige. The Brazilian pattern was similar, but the smaller indigenous population, the absence of an early mining boom, and the comparatively few colonial administrative positions slowed the growth of elite family wealth. In both cases, however, elite families strongly influenced the marriage decisions of heirs. Their intention was to perpetuate family status while diversifying their holdings through investment in agricultural and pastoral activities, trade, and other activities appropriate to the region of residence. These economic underpinnings were often fragile, however, and in the seventeenth century many elite families faced a series of challenges.

Few descendants of the first *encomenderos* in Spanish America passed on to their heirs resources equal to those of their own inheritance. The growth in international trade and the decline in Indian populations transformed colonial social and economic structures. Mining also proved unreliable, since a rich vein of silver could unexpectedly play out, leading to a contraction in elite wealth. As a result of this turmoil, few prominent families in the seventeenth century traced their origins to conquerors, *encomenderos,* or early miners.

After about 1640, the pace of territorial expansion slowed in many areas of Spanish America and subsequent periods of economic depression and stagnation slowed access to the upper levels of the social order by new families. At the same time fiscal constraints limited the growth in royal offices; only inheritable municipal offices could readily be passed on to family members. Castilian inheritance laws also undermined elite continuity by forcing the division of family wealth among heirs, except in the small number of cases where elite families had received permission to create an entail, *mayorazgo.* Even in these cases the heir to an entail was often required to support brothers and sisters in the parent's will. Although heirs were generally poorer than their parents, the decline in status was seldom precipitous and the privileges and social eminence of a prominent family could be shored up through marriage alliances with other elite families.

In seventeenth-century Brazil, in contrast, expansion into the interior, the growth in the sugar industry, and, at the end of the century, the discovery of gold and other precious minerals provided more opportunities to accumulate wealth and improve social status than were then available in the Spanish colonies. Huge cattle ranches spread throughout the Brazilian northeast. The Dias d'Avila and Guedes de Brito families established de facto sovereignty over the region, waging war against the Indians and in 1696 even evicting the Jesuits from a nearby mission. In São Paulo, in the south, the wealth of the elite expanded rapidly as a result of growing exports of both Indian slaves taken in raids in the interior and agricultural products, like wheat, rum, and sailcloth, produced by the Indian slaves retained by the settlers. Here, as in the Spanish colonies, economic diversification and control of political offices helped protect elite family positions against the effects of inheritance and economic volatility. Despite these time-tested strategies, some elite families declined or disappeared completely. Some died out after two or three generations because of infant or child mortality or because heirs chose not to marry or failed to produce children. Others were absorbed into the nonelite white population as a result of financial reverses or a surfeit of heirs.

A notable exception to these general patterns was the Gómez de Cervantes family. Resident in central Mexico since the conquest, it remained prominent beyond independence. But even though its longevity was extraordinary, the means by which it preserved its elite status were not. The Gómez de Cervantes family survived as an elite family not only because generation after generation of male heirs carried on the family name. Strategic marriages initially linked the Gómez de Cervantes family to other families of conquistadors and *encomenderos* and later united heirs with families that could provide substantial cash dowries. Establishing an entailed estate that included both urban and rural properties maintained an economic base for successive generations. However, the entail also meant that many potential heirs received smaller material legacies and, as a result, entered the Church or created independent economic bases. Some members of each generation sought positions in the colonial bureaucracy, often as provincial administrators, and their service created a record that heirs could emphasize as they, in turn, solicited positions. In addition, the practice of sending younger sons and daughters into ecclesiastical careers and convents enabled the family to maintain its estate. A willingness to reduce expenses by retiring to the family *hacienda* during difficult financial times also helped prevent the kind of economic disaster that overcame many elite families who, by the third generation, were dependent on *encomiendas*, mines, or commerce. None of these actions alone was adequate to maintain the family's economic position or social status, but together they were able to prolong its elite status for more than three centuries.

Spanish law required an equal division of assets among children; if an adult child had already died but left behind children of his or her own, that person's share went to those grandchildren. Nevertheless, elite families developed many strategies to distribute their wealth among potential heirs unequally, surrendering the prospects of some children to advance those of others. This improved the chances that at least one or two branches of the family would maintain elite status. In seventeenth-century Brazil women were more commonly beneficiaries of this strategy than males. The decision to give daughters rich dowries that reduced the future inheritances of their brothers forced sons to make their fortunes through slave raids on frontier Indian communities or in agriculture. Large dowries enabled daughters to contract successful marriages. When Maria Gonçalves married in 1623, for example, her dowry was more than triple the value of her brother's inheritance eighteen years later. More than a hundred years later Bento Pais de Oliveira clearly expressed the logic for favoring daughters: "I have seven children . . . and as my sons have the natural ability to care of themselves and even though the love I have for all my children is the same, piety and compassion dictate that I think more of my daughters."[6] Ultimately such discrimination against sons led the Portuguese Crown to place upper limits on the size of dowries to protect the interests of other potential heirs.

Parents in humble circumstances also attempted to provide their children with the skills and resources necessary to maintain if not improve their circumstances. For the sons of lower level colonial officials, military men, and professionals like lawyers and surgeons this meant at least some primary schooling or, in some cases, a university education. For artisans and small retailers it meant placement as an apprentice in a craft or shop. While some of these families provided daughters with a basic education, few young women had this opportunity. More commonly, care was taken to facilitate a suitable marriage by providing a small dowry. In other cases parents helped secure admission to a convent where literacy was promoted, as was education in needlework and other skills thought suitable for women.

Small inheritances from the estates of parents could also prove influential in the lives of men and women with few resources. Juana Carvajal of Buenos

Husbands and wives commonly worked together to earn their living. In this illustration a husband and wife produce rough pottery to be sold in their village.

Aires received a single male slave from the estate of her widowed father. Over the course of the next fifteen years, she sold this slave and purchased two young slaves who were then trained as carpenters. She then used their earnings to purchase a small rural property. When she died in 1746, her two sons and husband enjoyed a more secure position because of Juana's careful management of her small inheritance.

The Effects of Inheritance Law

Without careful planning and some good luck, the inheritance laws of Spain and Portugal could undermine the ability of colonial elites to accumulate wealth and invest in production. These laws severely limited discretionary authority over the disposition of an estate. In Spanish America all wealth acquired by a husband and wife during a marriage was divided among surviving heirs according to a formula that provided only limited flexibility. A widow regained control of her dowry, if she had one, as well as any *arras* her husband had provided. She also inherited one-half of all wealth generated during the marriage. At the time her husband died, of course, the widow was often already a mother or grandmother who would eventually pass on the value of the dowry and *arras* to her children or grandchildren. While inheritance law mandated certain dispositions, it did allow parents to further family ambitions by favoring one or more children over others. It also allowed those who had suffered long illnesses, for example, to recognize and reward their caretakers. For example, Rosario Salas of Chile used this discretionary power to provide a dowry that would allow her daughter Ana Josefa to enter a convent thus recognizing the loving care provided during her final illness.

The remaining estate was divided so that one half went to the surviving spouse, and the other half was divided among surviving children or other heirs. Unless the family could agree to shared management, it was likely that agricultural or mining enterprises would be sold and divided to meet the law's requirements. This formula often proved disruptive in commerce and manufacturing where the need for division undermined all forms of business partnership. For this reason, a few of the wealthiest Spanish-American families petitioned for the right to create an entail, *mayorazgo*, the legal device that reserved in perpetuity the largest portion of an estate for a single heir, to circumvent the forced division of properties. It was more common for heirs or executors to manipulate the management of estates by overvaluing some properties relative to others and allowing wealth-producing property to reach the hands of favored heirs. Thus, some heirs might receive their shares in the form of clothing, household goods, and jewelry while others gained control of ranches, mines, and slaves.

Portuguese inheritance law was broadly similar to the Spanish model, but provided for complete community. This meant that the dowry and any other property owned by husband or wife at the time of marriage would be divided among heirs. In both Iberian traditions, through a written will a decedent could make a differential bequest of a third of the estate to a favored heir. Even when the Portuguese reformed inheritance law in the eighteenth century, parents retained the right to prefer one heir within the new restrictions.

Women in Colonial Societies and Economies

Within the parameters established by race and social standing, gender played the most important role in determining an individual's place in colonial Latin America. Colonial society was patriarchal, and the activities of men and women, and thus husbands and wives, reflected a differentiation of roles that, while it varied by region, could be traced back to both the Iberian and indigenous heritages. In accord with established gender roles, men held all civil offices, made political decisions, and dominated the most lucrative economic activities. Men most commonly performed the heavy manual labor of fields and mines, constructed buildings and ships, worked on roads, and transported goods as carriers, muleteers, and seamen. They performed military service and held all ecclesiastical posts, except those in the convents. And only males could secure a higher education or enter a *consulado* or, in most cases, an artisan guild.

The social and economic reality of colonial life was far more complex than is suggested by this description of a largely male dominated society. Any general summary would obscure the full range of women's important contributions. Elite women, notably widows, managed vast and complex holdings of mines, agricultural properties, and real estate. When husbands were absent or when women headed households as single parents, they often filled traditional male positions in the economy as artisans, landlords, farmers, and ranchers. Moreover, women dominated most public markets as buyers and sellers. They also held marginal, and sometimes dangerous, positions in medicine and religion as curers, potion makers, fortunetellers, and spirit mediums. The capital investments, labor, and entrepreneurial skills of women were particularly significant in less privileged groups. Among the rural and urban working classes, few families were able to survive on only the income earned by the male head of household, as the cost of basic necessities almost invariably exceeded the income of any single worker, whether peon, cowboy, weaver, cobbler, blacksmith, or carpenter.

Many women worked outside the home. Brazil's sugar estates and smaller cane farms depended on the labor of women both slave and free throughout the production cycle, but especially during the harvest. Small independent farmers and ranchers also relied on the labor of wives and daughters, as few produced enough income to hire temporary workers. Recent studies of rural Uruguay, for example, suggest that women and their children owned and worked a substantial number of farms. Retail sales in many urban and rural markets were largely dependent on women, who sold thread, brooms, and other handicrafts as well as producing and selling sweets, bread, and pastries. Women also held an important place in colonial manufacturing: Some skilled textile manufacture was completely in their hands, and in Mexico City as early as the sixteenth century there were female guilds with female officers. Women also worked in textile and ceramic factories or *obrajes*. In Guadalajara in 1769, women owned one-third of the bakeries. Even in artisan trades, in which female participation was strictly forbidden, women commonly contributed labor. Poorer masters who could not afford the set wages of journeymen or the expense of an apprentice relied heavily on the labor of their wives and children to prepare raw materials and maintain tools. Typically a master shoemaker sewed the finished shoes and boots, but relied on his wife to prepare and cut the leather. Despite guild regulations that required a widow to remarry from among eligible guild members in order

Childhood was viewed as an anticipation of adult life. In this eighteenth-century portrait of Joaquín Sánchez Pareja Navarez, a young boy, he is posed in a military uniform with a rifle.

to keep her husband's shop open, widows commonly ignored this requirement, becoming in effect independent master artisans without formal license. Often the women of this class supplemented family income by taking in washing, renting rooms, or working as domestics.

All elite households required female domestics to cook, clean, and serve as wet nurses. Few of these women were free. Early in the colonial era nearly all female servants were Indians compelled to serve a Spanish master. Compulsion survived in some regions until the end of the colonial era. On frontiers, continuing warfare with indigenous peoples provided a steady flow of female captives forced into domestic service. The African slave contributed a second stream of women compelled to serve others.

Nearly every elite household in Spanish America and Brazil had black slaves, the majority of whom were often women. They cleaned, cooked, made clothes, and provided nearly all the essential household services. Female slaves were often given as part of a dowry, suggesting the belief that they were a required part of what was called a "decent" household. A smaller number of poor free women were employed as servants, and their everyday lives were almost indistinguishable in drudgery and material poverty from those of Indian and slave servants. But free women, no matter how poor, could seek alternative employment, had greater volition in the selection of partners, and less often suffered corporal punishment. Female slaves were more likely than males to gain their freedom through manumission. Among these women, the largest number purchased freedom by earning the money to pay their owners the equivalent of their market value. This demonstrates that even enslaved women operated in the economy, producing and selling goods or providing labor for compensation. This broad engagement in the economy, especially in cities, made slave women primary agents of cultural change for the slave community. They were also more vulnerable to sexual exploitation, as were the indigenous women who served in Spanish and Portuguese households. As a result, they were coerced participants in the emergence of mixed populations and the forging of new cultural identities that blended the traditions of America and Africa with those of Europe.

The primary responsibilities of wives in elite and mid-level families were associated with the home. They were to bear and rear children, manage domestic affairs, and instill cultural values. Although the Spanish and Portuguese ideal called for married women to devote themselves to being mothers and wives, even elite women often took an active role in ensuring the family's economic well-being. Particularly in families in which the husband traveled to maintain distant investments in agriculture or mining or to undertake commercial ventures, wives often had the day-to-day responsibility for managing rental properties or shops. Recent research has documented a very large number of female-headed households in which widows and single women with children made their own way in the world. In late colonial Buenos Aires, women headed 38 percent of the city's households; in contemporary Ouro Prêto, Brazil, the percentage rose to 45. Many colonial families were fluid in structure and flexible in function. Patriarchal ideals were commonly subverted by necessity or by choice.

Widows from the propertied sectors of colonial society enjoyed the greatest freedom of action and participated most extensively in the colonial economy. In Spanish America, a widow enjoyed full control over her dowry and the *arras,* if provided by the husband; in addition, she received half of all wealth acquired during the marriage. As a widow she usually also administered her children's inheritances while they were minors. One of the most remarkable of these women was Doña Jerónima de Peñalosa, widow of a wealthy and powerful lawyer who in the sixteenth century served as a judge and adviser to the viceroy of Peru. Once widowed, Doña Jerónima managed the family's vast economic holdings that included real estate, orchards, farms, mines, and a sugar mill in addition to property in Spain. She never remarried, choosing to manage, even expand, the family's wealth. When she died her eldest son inherited an entailed estate and her other children were provided for, with three sons sent to Spain for a university education and another put in the Church; her daughter was provided with a rich dowry of 35,000 pesos.[7]

Although some obstacles existed to a woman serving as executor of a deceased husband's estate when the widow Doña Jerónima assumed this role, the practice became much more common at all levels of society by the eighteenth century. In Chile, Salvador de Turcio named his wife, María Josefa Salas, as executor. She used this power to manage his inheritance so that their daughters were well provided for. In short, women owned and operated, at times with the aid of male relatives, rural and urban properties, mines, *obrajes*, and other economic investments. As widows they were often able to pass on these assets to their daughters. For example, Izabel Maria Guedes de Brito, a daughter of one of the largest landowners in northeastern Brazil, took full control of her family's business affairs following the death of her husband in the late seventeenth century. Thus widows in particular and women in general had substantial economic power, sometimes multiplying their economic power by controlling credit.

A sketch of the Baquíjano y Carrillo de Córdoba family illustrates the importance of marriage and kinship ties, diversified investments, varied occupations, and a widow's continuation of her late husband's business activities in an extended elite colonial family: Juan Bautista Baquíjano emigrated to Lima from Vizcaya in the early eighteenth century, joined a prominent compatriot merchant, worked hard, and prospered. At the age of forty-four he married the twenty-year-old *limeña* María Ignacia Carrillo de Córdoba, the daughter of a distinguished family that could trace its ancestry to conquistadors and early settlers in Chile and Peru. The marriage was a classic match between a wealthy, older peninsular and an established creole elite family with extensive familial ties in the region.

After marriage, Juan Bautista continued to prosper. One of Lima's wealthiest residents, he had investments in shipping, commerce, and agriculture. In 1755 he purchased the title Conde de Vistaflorida. His death in 1759 left his wife with seven minor children. María Ignacia continued her late husband's business ventures with the assistance of her brother Luis, a chaplain at the viceregal palace. Her affairs prospered, and the estate she left her heirs exceeded Juan Bautista's.

The surviving Baquíjano y Carrillo children extended the family's influence and power. The elder son and second Conde de Vistaflorida settled in Madrid where he invested in commerce, lent money, bought government bonds, and provided his relatives with a convenient voice at court. The younger son, José, became a minister on Lima's *audiencia*. Given the family's wealth, it is surprising that neither son married. Through marriage, however, the five Baquíjano daughters further strengthened the family's eminence in Lima. Their husbands brought expanded ties to the city council, the *consulado*, the militia, the *audiencia*, and even the viceroy. The diversification of political ties, incorporation of successful peninsulars, and continuing investment in shipping, agriculture, and trade typified an elite family's strategy to maintain and enhance its position.

The Culture of Honor

Along with other elements of Iberian culture, Spanish and Portuguese immigrants brought to the Americas a fundamental concern for honor. Honor meant the recognition and defense of individual and family position in the social hierarchy. It was a way of sorting out the colonial world's incredibly complex relationships of class, gender, race, wealth, and culture. As defined by a modern scholar, "Honor is above all the keen sensitivity to the experience of humiliation and shame, a sensitivity manifested by the desire to be envied by others and the propensity to envy the success of others."[8]

Honor preoccupied elite families. They paid close attention to every interaction, from the competition for offices and rewards, to business dealings of all kinds, the marriages of children, the selection of godparents, and even seating arrangements at public dinners. Honor defined one's equals and inferiors. As such it controlled who was invited into a home, who stood and who sat, who kept a hat on and who removed it. Disagreements over the order in which administrative groups, clerics, or colonial officials marched through the streets during feast days or celebrations of the coronation of kings produced lawsuits that lasted years. If individuals or groups allowed themselves to be treated as inferiors without protest or revenge, if they failed to react appropriately to challenges to their honor, they lost status. The competing claims to honor and precedence both arranged society hierarchically and potentially destabilized it.

Wealthy and powerful families worked together to improve their reputations, creating the material basis for their claims to honor. This meant the careful management of marriage alliances, inheritances, and the cultivation of friendships with other powerful and ambitious families. In particular, families used dowries to solidify marriage alliances with, for example, a man of noble blood or an immigrant from Iberia with unambiguous lineage. One observer of marriage practices in São Paulo, Brazil, noted: "The Paulistas could give their daughters extensive land, Indians, and slaves in their dowries. . . . [W]hen they selected husbands for them, they were more concerned with the birth [ethnicity and noble descent] rather than the property of their future sons-in-law."[9]

Families also sought to secure offices in the bureaucracy, militia commands, or offices in religious brotherhoods. This pursuit of reputation was often very expensive and wasteful. It required large gifts to endow churches or convents or support for civic projects or local celebrations. It led to the maintenance of a lavish household with numerous servants, generous feasts, and entertainments for guests. And it also led to the careful cultivation of public image. The act of going from home to church or to an audience with the viceroy required the mobilization of family resources, clothes, jewels, elegant transportation, and the escort of servants and dependents. Many who had gained their wealth through commerce also found it necessary to buy landed estates to meet better the expectations of those they sought to impress.

These concerns explain in large measure the willingness of wealthy creoles to provide large dowries to cement marriage alliances with European immigrants. They also explain the commonly expressed disdain for the mixed population and for the poor, groups presumed to have no claims to honor. These ambitious families understood gender in relationship to honor. Males sought to exercise close control over wives and daughters, since their sexual reputations put the honor of males at risk. Women in elite families were restricted to the home or church except when closely supervised by male relatives. Poor women enjoyed none of these protections against the advances of men in the street or market. They were, however, much less dependent on males generally.

But honor was not a rigid template that fixed all social relationships in predictable ways. Elite men and women found their way around this close supervision. Priests sometimes connived with the pregnant daughters of elite families to disguise their condition. Their illegitimate children might be identified as orphans and be "adopted" by the mother. Or, with a generous dowry, the daughter might still find a potential husband. Although the illegitimacy of a man or his immediate ancestors was supposed to bar him from high colonial office, many rich and connected men found ways around the prohibition. Some were inconvenienced by evidence that an ancestor was a Jew or Muslim or black. Among the most common resort in these cases was an appeal to the king asking that he declare the obstacle removed; these requests were commonly lubricated with a substantial gift. By the eighteenth century this process of appeal for the removal of what were viewed as stains on reputation was regularized as *cédulas de gracias al sacar*.

Elite families saw honor as a unique characteristic of their class, but it is clear that concern for honor spread across the social order. Members of the urban middle sector, physicians, lawyers, even master artisans came eventually to assert their honor in legal proceedings and, on occasion, in violent confrontations with those who presumed to insult them. Men of humble circumstances, journeymen and day laborers, explained violent assaults in terms of the need to answer an insult or as an effort to avoid being shamed. Even among the society's most vulnerable group, slaves, there was a clear regard for reputation and, when offended, a willingness to find remedy in violence or sometimes in the courts.

The basic social unit in the colonial world, the extended family was most effective at its upper reaches. As each region in the Indies achieved economic and social maturity, its most prominent families intermarried as well as incorporated through marriage successful newcomers, normally peninsular males, into their midst. Although the timing varied, this establishment and consolidation of extended families took place in settings as diverse as Recife, Salvador, Santiago, Lima, Popayán, Guatemala, and Puebla. Indian societies also maintained families, although epidemics, forced relocation, and voluntary migration worked against their perpetuation. The centrality of family in the colonial world was hardest on the free mixed-race population. The prevalence of illegitimacy among the early generations in particular made impossible the kind of familial ties and support common to the majority of society. But as the number of persons of mixed ancestry increased, their families conformed to the colonial ideal of the extended family.

Notes

1. Ana María Presta, "Portraits of Four Women: Traditional Female Roles and Transgressions in Colonial Elite Families in Charcas, 1550–1600," *Colonial Latin American Review*, 9:2 (2000), pp. 245–246.

2. Edith Couturier, "Women and the Family in Eighteenth-Century Mexico: Law and Practice," *Journal of Family History* (Fall 1985), p. 297.

3. Quote in Ward Stavig, *The World of Tupac Amaru: Conflict, Community, and Identity in Colonial Peru* (Lincoln: University of Nebraska Press, 1999), p. 41.

4. Robert McCaa, "Gustos de los padres, inclinaciones de los novios y reglas de una feria nupcial colonial: Parral, 1770–1814," *Historia Mexicana*, XL:4 (1991), p. 583.

5. Quote from Kathleen Myers, "A Glimpse of Family Life in Colonial Mexico: A Nun's Account," *Latin American Research Review*, 28:2 (1993), p. 75.

6. Quote in Alida C. Metcalf, "Fathers and Sons: The Politics of Inheritance in a Colonial Brazilian Township," *Hispanic American Historical Review*, 66:3 (1986), p. 480.

7. Ana María Presta, "Portraits of Four Women," pp. 242–244.

8. William Ian Miller, *Humiliation and Other Essays on Honor, Social Discomfort, and Violence* (Ithaca, N.Y.: Cornell University Press, 1993), p. 84.

9. Quote in Alida C. Metcalf, "Fathers and Sons: The Politics of Inheritance in a Colonial Brazilian Township," *Hispanic American Historical Review*, 66:3 (1986), p. 467.

Suggested for Further Reading

Boyer, Richard. *Lives of the Bigamists: Marriage, Family, and Community in Colonial Mexico.* Albuquerque: University of New Mexico Press, 1995.

Gauderman, Kimberly. *Women's Lives in Colonial Quito: Gender, Law, and Economy in Spanish America.* Austin: University of Texas Press, 2003.

González, Ondina E., and Bianca Premo, editors. *Raising an Empire: Children in Early Modern Iberia and Colonial Latin America.* Albuquerque: University of New Mexico Press, 2007.

Gutiérrez, Ramón A. *When Jesus Came, the Corn Mothers Went Away: Marriage, Sexuality, and Power in New Mexico, 1500–1846.* Stanford: Stanford University Press, 1991.

Johnson, Lyman L., and Sonya Lipsett-Rivera, editors. *The Faces of Honor: Sex, Shame, and Violence in Colonial Latin America.* Albuquerque: University of New Mexico Press, 1998.

Metcalf, Alida C. *Family and Frontier in Colonial Brazil: Santana de Parnaíba, 1580–1822.* Berkeley and Los Angeles: University of California Press, 1992.

Nazzari, Muriel. *Disappearance of the Dowry: Women, Families, and Social Change in São Paulo, Brazil, 1600–1900.* Stanford, Calif.: Stanford University Press, 1991.

Powers, Karen Vieira. *Women in the Crucible of Conquest: The Gendered Genesis of Spanish American Society, 1500–1600.* Albuquerque: University of New Mexico Press, 2005.

Premo, Bianca. *Children of the Father King: Youth, Authority, and Legal Minority in Colonial Lima.* Chapel Hill: The University of North Carolina Press, 2005.

Schroeder, Susan, Stephanie Wood, and Robert Haskett, editors. *Indian Women of Early Mexico.* Norman: University of Oklahoma Press, 1997.

Socolow, Susan Migden. *The Women of Colonial Latin America.* Cambridge, England, and New York: Cambridge University Press, 2000.

Stern, Steve J. *The Secret History of Gender: Women, Men, and Power in Late Colonial Mexico.* Chapel Hill: University of North Carolina Press, 1995.

Twinam, Ann. *Public Lives, Private Secrets: Gender, Honor, Sexuality, and Illegitimacy in Colonial Spanish America.* Stanford: Stanford University Press, 1999.

Van Deusen, Nancy E. *Between the Sacred and the Worldly: The Institutional and Cultural Practice of* Recogimiento *in Colonial Lima.* Stanford: Stanford University Press, 2001.

EIGHT

LIVING IN AN EMPIRE

Chronology

1521	Mexico City founded
1535	Lima founded; first book published in Mexico
1537	First royal *protomédico* reaches Lima
1553	University of Mexico opens
1570s	University San Marcos opens in Lima
1580	Permanent settlement in Buenos Aires
1604	Theater (*Corral de las Comedias*) opens in Lima
1629	Worst flood in Mexico City's history
1641	First printing press in Guatemala
1687	Earthquake devastates Lima
1695	Death of Sister Juana Inés de la Cruz in Mexico
1746	Earthquake devastates Callao and Lima
1773	Earthquake prompts relocation of Guatemala City

Colonial Settings

European conquest and settlement altered the New World's architectural environment as well as its political, economic, and social structures. In a remarkably short time, the conquerors' cathedrals, convents, administrative buildings, and private residences replaced the pyramids, elevated plazas, ball courts, and palaces of the indigenous elites. In important ways, both the surviving indigenous traditions and the imported European architectural forms helped create the context for the evolution of Latin America's colonial societies.

The architectural progression from indigenous to mature colonial was clearest in central Mexico and Peru where large urban centers existed before contact. When the Spaniards settled in regions outside the great Andean and Mesoamerican civilizations, they established new towns unencumbered by the architectural legacies and city plans of the Indian past. Eventually, however, common features of a colonial style in construction and town planning appeared throughout Spanish America. Because the indigenous

Brazilian people had not constructed urban centers, Brazil's colonial experience was similar to that of Spain's peripheral colonies.

The Conquest Period

The most important native cities suffered severe damage during the conquest: The battle for Tenochtitlan completely destroyed the city, and much of Cuzco was reduced to rubble as well during Manco Inca's rebellion of 1536. In both cases colonial authorities decided, for political reasons, to rebuild the cities as Spanish centers. Despite the capitals' distance from the sea, Pizarro and Cortés understood that rebuilding them symbolically legitimized the authority of the new colonial order.

Many Indian cities, for example, Jauja in Peru and Tlaxcala in Mexico, survived the conquest period nearly unscathed. Their concentrated population and nearby agricultural resources attracted Spanish settlers, who asserted political authority and then moved quickly to impose a new urban landscape. As a result, they destroyed many of the Indian structures to make room for churches, government buildings, and Spanish residences.

In regions without previous settled agriculture and urbanization, the Spaniards founded towns to organize and control the indigenous population. Missionaries and civil authorities encouraged and, if necessary, forced the concentration of the Indian population to facilitate Christianization and compel participation in the colonial economy. In each case, Spanish and Portuguese settlers imposed their own concepts of urban social organization, architecture, and city planning. Yet even in this new environment, elements of indigenous experience survived in construction techniques, decorative motifs, and residential patterns.

The Early Colonial Period

The conquistadors and early settlers defined their colonization of the New World by founding cities, which they saw as their link with European civilization and culture. On his second voyage, Columbus founded the first Spanish colonial town, Isabela, on Española. Its precipitous failure foreshadowed the later collapse and abandonment of many early settlements, most frequently because their sites were unhealthy or the nearby Indian population declined. Yet Santo Domingo, the present capital of the Dominican Republic, and many smaller towns survived. By 1525 the historian Gonzalo Fernández de Oviedo compared Santo Domingo favorably with Barcelona, one of Spain's larger and more prosperous cities.

Spaniards founded over 190 towns and cities in the Americas by 1620, at least half of them before 1550. But Indian attacks, an unhealthy climate, and earthquakes, among other reasons, caused many of these early settlements to move to more favorable locations. For example, Vera Cruz, founded hastily by Cortés, was relocated to a more protected harbor. Nevertheless, by 1600 most of the major urban centers of modern Spanish

America were in place. In Brazil, by comparison, fewer than forty cities and towns, almost all within a few miles of the coast, had been founded before 1650.

The City Plan

From the outset of colonization, the Spanish Crown actively promoted urban planning. It urged royal administrators and conquistadors to avoid swampy or insect-ridden terrain and admonished them to ensure the availability of adequate water and arable land before settlement. In 1573 Philip II promulgated ordinances that codified the Crown's conception of how Spanish cities in the New World should be built. The basic pattern was a grid: A large plaza at the center of the city served as a marketplace, hosted religious and secular ceremonies, and displayed a pillory, gallows, or other symbol of royal justice. The plaza was not to be smaller than two hundred by three hundred feet or larger than three hundred by eight hundred feet. In major administrative centers like Lima, Mexico City, Bogotá, and Guatemala, the cathedral, governor or viceroy's palace, and city council building bounded the plaza. Lesser cities had fewer and smaller public buildings, but the central plaza always served as the political and religious focus of community life.

When geography restricted this form of orderly development, the grid pattern was found only at the city center. Uneven terrain imposed irregular street patterns on Potosí and other mining towns located in mountainous areas. In the very few fortified cities found in the Spanish colonies, the walls tended to deform the grid, as Lima and Cartagena demonstrate. On the frontier, where secular authority was often weak, the Church imposed similar requirements on the missions. Resettled Indian populations, congregations, and mission settlements—for example, the famous Jesuit reductions of Paraguay—followed a grid pattern, with the church and other public buildings located on a central plaza. Their walled courtyards provided a defense against hostile attacks and offered a sheltered place for instructing crowds of Indian converts.

The Portuguese Crown was less directly involved in city planning than was the Spanish Crown, and so Brazilian colonial cities generally developed more spontaneously. Nevertheless, most of the important cities did have a grid pattern in the city center and, like towns and villages, a central plaza complete with pillory as a symbol of royal justice. Because Brazil's major commercial and administrative cities were located on the coast, they were vulnerable to attack. Defensive walls and other fortifications, consequently, often influenced the direction of urban growth.

A System of Cities

Within a century of the initial rush to establish towns in Spanish America, a durable rank order could be found among the region's larger cities and towns. The viceregal capitals of Mexico City and Lima quickly became dominant. By 1630, 58 percent of the Spanish population of the Audiencia of Mexico lived in Mexico City, and 55 percent of the Spanish population of the Audiencia of Lima lived in Lima. The two capitals were followed in importance by Puebla, Bogotá, Guatemala, and Santo Domingo. The third rank included Panama, Quito, Cuzco, Guadalajara, La Plata (now Sucre), and Santiago de Chile.

Spanish immigrants initially settled near Indian population centers. The *encomienda* system reinforced this early attraction. Later the discovery and exploitation of rich mineral deposits brought rapid population growth in mining centers like Potosí and Zacatecas. The profitable commercial activity of port cities like Cartagena, Havana, and, to a lesser extent, Portobelo and Vera Cruz drew a civilian population as well as military garrisons. In each case, increased numbers of Spanish residents and the developing market economy brought imperial recognition in the form of fiscal and administrative structures. Once in place, the public sector's ability to collect and disburse funds reinforced the order established initially by demography, physical resources, and commercial activity.

This rapid proliferation of towns did not, however, result in strong economic ties among the major cities of Spanish America. The cities of British North America, by comparison, were significantly more integrated. Geography, cumbersome regulations, or, in some cases, statutory prohibitions inhibited regional and intercolonial trade in the Spanish colonies. Generally, colonial cities were tied more closely to Seville and Cádiz by their economic and political structures than they were to one another. Because the exportation of sugar so completely dominated the Brazilian economy from the mid-sixteenth to the early eighteenth centuries, this pattern of colonial isolation and dependence on the metropolis was even more sharply defined.

The Colonial City

The rectilinear core of the colonial city, the *traza*, was overwhelmingly European in culture and architecture. Around the central plaza crowded the most impressive secular and religious buildings. Nearby were the residences of the elite. Most Spaniards, both immigrants from Europe and their American-born descendants, lived with their servants and slaves in large homes in this central district. The most affluent *mestizos* and other *castas* emulated them in residences located as close to the plaza as possible.

Urban churches and convents were immense bastions towering over their surroundings and laden with ornate decoration. The finest ecclesiastical buildings demonstrated the centrality of religious sentiment in colonial culture as well as the Church's great wealth. Although architecturally derivative, the cathedral in Mexico City was the largest and most splendid in America. Other capital cities, too, boasted magnificent churches. In general, Brazil's churches also followed European models, although on a smaller scale. Yet the best of these churches is still able to impress a viewer. Visitors to Lima noted:

> [T]he cathedral, the churches of St. Dominic, St. Francis, St. Augustin, the fathers of Mercy, and the Jesuits, are so splendidly decorated, as to surpass description. . . . The altars, from their very bases to the borders of the paintings, are covered with massive silver. . . . The walls . . . are hung with velvet or tapestry. . . . The whole church is covered with plate, or something equal to it in value; so that divine service is performed with a magnificence scarce to be imagined.[1]

Even in the richest mining centers and administrative capitals of Brazil and Spanish America, no secular construction rivaled the cathedrals and the richest convents. In Brazil, government policy prohibited governors and other officials from constructing unnecessarily expensive residences and office buildings. The viceregal palaces of Lima and Mexico City were large, well-constructed buildings that lacked the architectural interest of the great palaces of Europe. Few secular buildings, other than perhaps the palace of Cortés, compared favorably with European ones.

Typically, the buildings of Church and state as well as the residences of the wealthiest and most powerful royal officials, prelates, and elite families fronted on central plazas where the city's primary markets were held. Many buildings in colonial city centers had exterior arcades to shelter buyers and sellers from the elements. In some cities the municipal government provided separate market stalls.

The City as Arena

The central plaza served as an arena for a variety of public spectacles. During the year, numerous secular and religious processions concluded with a mass at the cathedral. The order in the processions reflected the colonial social hierarchy, with prelates, high-level secular officials, and knights of the military orders enjoying places of honor. Deviation from this expected system of preferment provoked protests and even litigation. Commercial and artisan corporations maintained a similar hierarchy. Bullfights, *autos de fé*, and public executions also drew enormous crowds to the plaza.

The ostentatious display of the colonial elite impressed European visitors. Thomas Gage, an English-born Catholic priest resident in Mexico and Central America in the early seventeenth century, wrote admiringly about the richly decorated coaches that filled the streets of Mexico City. In the later afternoon fashionable men and women paraded around the tree-lined park in the center of the city. Young men dressed in their finest clothes rode horses, and older men and women rode in coaches driven by black slaves in bright liveries. Even the viceroy often appeared with members of his court. Venders sold cool drinks and sweets to those who stopped to watch this elaborate ritual. Courting and flirtation were also part of the elite's life. Gage wrote of swordfights and other violent confrontations caused by overly direct attention to women by ardent admirers. Some contemporary accounts noted the scandal created by the visible presence of prostitutes or the mistresses of prominent citizens. By the eighteenth century, even lesser cities like Buenos Aires provided parks or shaded straight routes where their elites could amuse themselves.

The elite's houses were distinguished by their scale and construction. Most were two-story dwellings built of cut stone or brick, often with interior patios and attached carriage houses and stables. The exteriors were seldom decorated. Heavy shutters protected windows, but second-story balconies, their privacy protected by carved blinds, provided a view of the street below. An abundance of sitting rooms and bedrooms offered more privacy.

A contract signed in 1631 for the construction of a house in Popayán illustrates: The master carpenter, Francisco González Leuro, built a two-story house facing the central plaza for the wealthy merchant Diego Daza. The first floor held four two-room shops and some storage space. The second floor contained four bedrooms and a sitting room with a balcony and large shuttered windows. Servants probably slept downstairs. Almost certainly the kitchen was a separate building behind the residence.

This type of floor plan was common. Even the wealthiest colonial merchants used the first-floor rooms of multistory homes and the corner rooms of single-story homes for retail activities. The floor plan of a merchant's home in Córdoba, Argentina, for example, shows the front left-hand corner room to be used for commerce. Many homeowners not directly involved in trade or manufacture also rented space to small shopkeepers and artisans. The result was a nearly universal intermixing of commerce, manufacture, and housing throughout the cities of colonial Brazil and Spanish America.

The homes of high-ranking officials, mine owners, wealthy merchants, and other members of the colonial elite were richly decorated. Their wills often specified in detail chairs and tables imported from Spain; china, carpets, and silk curtains carried by the Asian trade; and settings of silver produced by skilled colonial artisans. Some households contained musical instruments, and a few had libraries, mostly filled with religious and moral tracts. Paintings, statuary, and other decorative objects were also typically religious in nature, but by the eighteenth century, secular art, particularly portraits, was increasingly popular.

Away from the central plaza lived the majority of the poor, mostly Indians, *castas*, and free blacks, in sprawling impoverished *barrios* that generally lacked the orderliness of the central city's grid. Streets were narrower and unpaved. During rainy seasons the heavy carts and mule trains that connected colonial cities to agricultural and mining communities turned the streets into seas of mud where pedestrians passed at some peril. During dry seasons, winds coated passersby with the dust from the unpaved, often dung-covered, thoroughfares. The small, mud-colored adobe houses of the urban poor fronted directly on the street. Only parish churches and poorer convents afforded architectural relief from the monotonous and squalid landscape of these humble suburbs.

Yet significant differences in status and material conditions could be found in the *barrios* as well. Some poor Spaniards, usually recent immigrants, lived among the *castas*. Skilled Indian artisans and a small number of traditional Indian political authorities represented the upper end of the neighborhood social pyramid. Below them were market gardeners, laborers, porters, and petty merchants. At the very bottom were Indians temporarily drawn to the city as *repartimiento* workers or engaged in voluntary, unskilled day labor.

Housing conditions in the poor *barrios* differed dramatically from those in the central *traza*. Most desirable were the large apartment blocks owned by wealthy investors or the Church and privately owned single-family dwellings. Very few urban wage earners, however, could afford to rent or own such housing. The majority of colonial urban working-class families lived in single rooms or rooms divided by blankets and shared with other families. Single men and women often lived in the back rooms of the commercial and manufacturing establishments where they worked. The less fortunate found shelter in hallways, storerooms, or patios for a few *reales* a month. For the totally destitute, life on the street was a last resort.

The relatively high cost of housing, particularly housing adequate for family life, forced many young men and women to defer marriage and childbearing. It also meant that working-class women and children were much more vulnerable to intimidation, sexual assaults, and common insults. In this environment, husbands and fathers commonly found themselves defending their family's honor with knives or fists.

Members of the working class owned few material possessions. Probate records suggest that the homes of unskilled workers, journeymen, and street peddlers contained little more than a few straight-backed chairs, a rough table, a chest, straw-filled mattresses, and one or more religious icons. Food was eaten with one's hands or with a knife or spoon from wooden or cheap ceramic plates. The entire wardrobes of most men and women were on their backs, although many did own an extra shirt or a poncho that could double as a blanket at night.

Most of the unsanitary, dangerous, and noisy urban businesses were located in suburban *barrios*. Bakeries and the kilns of brickmakers that posed fire threats, slaughterhouses and tanneries that exuded noxious odors, and the corrals that serviced local and long-distance freight businesses were scattered among the homes of the poor. Numerous gaming and drinking establishments provided some pleasure and diversion for the lower classes. Mexico City, Lima, and other large cities had dozens of regulated dispensaries, but unlicensed bars were common throughout colonial Latin America. The beverages of choice changed from one region to another, but the urban poor consumed enormous amounts of *pulque, chicha,* rum, wine, and other alcoholic beverages. Drunkenness and related acts of violence, like the endemic poverty and political powerlessness that supported them, were familiar features of the urban landscape.

Rural Settlement

Two settlement patterns predominated in the countryside. Both Iberians and the indigenous high civilizations emphasized the village over dispersed rural settlement. Where these heritages overlapped, mainly in Mesoamerica and the Andean zone, rural life centered on the village. On the periphery of these areas, where grazing was more important than agriculture—for example, in Brazil, the Río de la Plata region, and the *llanos* of Venezuela—dispersed residential patterns were more common, if not always predominant. Villages were not miniature cities. Few had a grid pattern or large-scale religious or secular buildings. The social focus was as likely to be the general store as the church. Smaller villages commonly had a church, but rarely a resident priest. In these agricultural communities, farmers lived near one another and walked to their fields. This pattern was particularly strong where Indian populations maintained their preconquest communal landholding system.

Residential construction depended on adobe and local timber. Houses typically had a single room and a separate kitchen constructed of less substantial material. More prosperous families added additional rooms to the original structure as their needs changed and resources grew. In some places, corrals were attached directly to residences, but in other regions they were located on the fringe of the village. Thomas Gage left a vivid portrait of rural housing in the Indian and *casta* villages of Guatemala:

> Their houses are but poor thatched cottages, without any upper rooms, but commonly only one or two rooms below. They dress their meat in the middle of one, and they make a compass for fire with two or three stones, without any chimney to convey the smoke away. This spreadth itself about the room and fillth the thatch and the rafters so with soot that all the room seemed to be a chimney. The next room, where sometimes are four or five beds according to the family, is also not free from smoke and blackness. The poorer sort have but one room where they eat, dress their meat, and sleep. . . . Neither have they in their houses much to lose, earthen pots, and pans, and dishes, and cups to drink their chocolate being the chief commodities in their house. There is scarce any house which hath not also in the yard a stew [sweat house], which is their chief physic when they feel themselves distempered.[2]

Large Estates

Large estates, many painstakingly amassed over years through numerous small grants, purchases, bequests, and usurpations of native lands, dominated much of the most valuable countryside in many parts of Latin America by the early seventeenth century. The lay and ecclesiastical owners of these estates earned profits by selling agricultural and pastoral products. Location, climate, and access to labor, however, affected both what they could produce and whether the market would be primarily local, regional, intercolonial, or international. The most heavily capitalized large estates

were plantations focused on the international market. The sugar plantations (*engenhos*) developed in Brazil after the mid-sixteenth century served
as a model for the later Spanish plantations (*ingenios*) in the Caribbean.
Tobacco, indigo, and cacao also were frequently produced on plantations.
Less capitalized estates often devoted to growing wheat or other grains or
raising livestock were variously termed *haciendas* or *estancias* in Spanish
America and *fazendas* in Brazil. Location frequently precluded their productions being sold beyond nearby markets. Northern New Spain was a
classic example of colonial *haciendas* established to serve a regional market, in this case Zacatecas and other mining centers.

The Brazilian *engenho* shared two characteristics with the *hacienda*: extensive landholding and physical isolation. Important differences were
manifested in the architecture, however. First, sugar cultivation required
a much larger and more expensive labor force than did livestock raising
and agriculture on *haciendas*. The presence of more workers compelled
planters to build larger residential compounds. Second, sugar refining was
a complex, multistage procedure, and plantations thus required large
investments in separate buildings for crushing the cane, boiling and skim-
ming the juice, and storing the final product.

Because enormous profits were earned during boom periods, prosperous plantation owners had surplus capital with which to construct impressive residences. The *casa grande* was commonly built in a Portuguese style.
Its more prominent characteristics included a tower, roofs that inclined on
all four sides, external stairs, and a long veranda. Most were two-story structures. Family life was largely confined to the second story, and the servants
used the first floor for food preparation, laundry, and other household
tasks. During the heady boom years of the early seventeenth century, successful planters were able to fill their homes with furniture imported from
Europe and carpets and ceramics from Asia.

Most slaves lived in barracks, although some plantations had single-family
housing. Barracks helped to prevent runaways but severely hampered the
development of family life among slaves. Their impoverished material conditions limited slaves' cultural life. Forced isolation limited their access to
religious and secular instruction, and collective forms of expression, such
as the lay brotherhoods found in the towns, could not be regularly sustained in the harsh work environment of the plantation.

In regions where the population density was very low, *haciendas, estancias,*
and *fazendas* provided the physical focus for both social life and production. The owner's large house dominated the *hacienda*'s residential core,
which might include a blacksmith's shop and often a pottery and carpentry shop as well. Some of the wealthiest *haciendas* maintained a chapel,
although resident priests were seldom present. The largest estates covered
many square miles and had outlying corrals, line shacks, and some
dispersed housing for tenants. Single male employees, particularly those
without family in the region, lived in dormitories. Married employees
resided in small adobe homes near the owner's house.

Isolated Rural Dwellings

The small ranches and farms of freeholders and tenants shared the rural landscape with the *haciendas,* plantations, and, at times, Indian villages and missions. Isolated family housing was scattered along the northern frontier of New Spain, in the southern *pampa* of the Río de la Plata, and in the interior grazing area, the *llanos,* of Venezuela. The inhabitants were very poor. They used adobe or woven sticks covered with mud to construct their houses. Doors and window coverings, if there were any, were fashioned from animal skins. Furniture was almost unknown. Cattle skulls served as chairs, and packed-earth platforms covered with straw or skins, as beds. The physical isolation of these dwellings diminished the material and emotional supports of the traditional Iberian and indigenous social networks. Other forms of cultural support—literacy and access to religious consolation among them— also were directly dependent on population density.

The architectural environment of colonial Latin America helped shape and control a diverse mix of competing social groups. As in the advanced preconquest indigenous societies, colonial city planning and urban architecture contained a political message: The colonial cities asserted and sustained the authority of the colonial white elites. The monumental architecture of the city center—the labor and wealth frozen in the walls and decorations of the cathedrals, convents, governmental offices, and palaces—served to awe and intimidate the masses. When used as an arena for *autos de fé,* bullfights, and executions, the central plazas helped direct the energies and anger of the masses toward safe symbolic targets.

At another level, the physical settings provided by houses, gaming establishments, taverns, shops, and small manufacturers operated more subtly to help fashion the values of family and class. This context was more directly the result of the inequalities imposed by the colonial economy and Iberian social attitudes. The physical environment sometimes shaped and sometimes reinforced colonial perceptions of race and gender, decisions about marriage and child rearing, and feelings of solidarity with or alienation from coworkers. More than a place to reside and work, the urban and rural living environments reflected both the highest aspirations and the deepest despair present in the colonial world.

Colonial Settlement and Natural Disasters

Devastating natural and made-made disasters periodically struck these colonial societies, afflicting particularly the poorest and most vulnerable sectors of society. Earthquakes, hurricanes, and flooding brought tragedy to individuals, families, and at times cities and entire regions.

Earthquakes, a continuing scourge in Latin America, repeatedly brought terror. Accompanied by earthquakes, the eruption in 1600 of Huainaputina, a volcano southeast of Arequipa, Peru, buried a sizable region with more than a foot of ash in places. With pastures blanketed in ash, livestock losses in the area exceeded 75 percent. Where wine production the previous year had been 200,000 large jugs, in 1601 it was 10,000 jugs of almost undrinkable alcohol. More quakes in 1604 damaged buildings and irrigation canals and caused flooding.

The eighteenth-century travelers Jorge Juan and Antonio de Ulloa listed thirteen violent quakes that struck Lima, Peru, and its environs between 1582 and 1746. The most devastating occurred in 1687 and 1746. Earthquakes of October 20 and December 2, 1687, hit Peru's central coast. Besides damaging numerous buildings in Lima and leaving thousands homeless, the quakes seriously disrupted and in some cases almost destroyed irrigation systems in coastal agricultural valleys. Crop yields fell and merchants turned to Chilean wheat producers to meet demand, creating a reliance that continued throughout the eighteenth century. Disease followed hunger, and by the early 1690s Lima's population had declined by about 50 percent, falling to under forty thousand.

In the 1746 earthquake, "the greatest part, if not all the buildings, great and small, in the whole city, were destroyed, burying under their ruins those inhabitants who had made sufficient haste into the streets and squares."[3] Worse, a tsunami struck Lima's port of Callao, sinking nineteen ships in the harbor and carrying four inland. About thirteen hundred persons died in Lima, and only some two hundred of a population of roughly four thousand survived in Callao. The catastrophe was unparalleled in colonial Peru. Major earthquakes also struck Quito and other Ecuadoran sites repeatedly. Nearly twenty major earthquakes hit Chile between 1570 and 1800; those of 1647 and 1730 severely damaged the capital of Santiago.

Earthquakes also afflicted Mesoamerica. Mexico City and Jalisco were struck in 1611, and Oaxaca suffered a quake in 1701. Among the most devastating was the earthquake of 1773 that hit the capital city of Santiago, Guatemala. Tremors of 1717 and 1765 had prompted consideration of moving the city (now known as Antigua, Guatemala), and some families had actually departed to locations perceived as safer. The quake of 1773 led to permanently moving the capital with its administrative offices twenty-eight miles to the valley of La Hermita, although thousands of inhabitants refused to abandon the old city.

Europeans knew about the destructive power of hurricanes in the Caribbean from the time of Columbus, who witnessed one in 1494. Indeed, in 1502 the admiral warned the newly arrived governor of Española, Nicolás de Ovando, to detain a fleet of thirty sail poised for the return voyage to Spain because of the threat of hurricanes. The governor persisted, and some five hundred men and all but one ship perished. In the same year, the hastily constructed town of Santo Domingo was severely damaged when winds ripped its wooden buildings. Although some stone was used in rebuilding, hurricanes of 1508 and 1509 again devastated the city. Nor was Cuba spared. Ferocious hurricanes in 1519, 1525, 1527, 1557, and 1558 caused damage across the island. A hurricane in October 1768 killed over a thousand people, almost leveled the city of Havana, and destroyed more than fifty ships in the bay.

The most notorious flooding of the colonial era occurred in central Mexico. Although protracted raining often brought flooding in low-lying regions surrounding the lakes in the Valley of Mexico, colonial officials focused on flooding in Mexico City. Built on the ruins of Tenochtitlan as a symbol of Spanish rule, the city's location on an island crossed by canals was inevitably at odds with a Castilian culture dependent on animal transportation. Constructing streets and plazas above the houses meant that the dwellings suffered first from rising water. The initial solution to flooding was to emulate the earlier native solution by building a new dike. The idea of draining the lakes by means of a long canal, however, was current by the mid-1550s. As the lakes silted from erosion that followed deforestation, the water problem in Mexico City worsened. After damaging floods in 1604 and 1607, the viceregal government initiated the famed Desagüe project to drain the lakes. The drainage tunnel opened in late 1608 but quickly proved inadequate. The worst flood in the history of New Spain occurred in 1629, leaving the city under water for four years and provoking a temporary exodus of perhaps three-quarters of its population. So bad was the crisis that Philip IV proposed rebuilding the city on the mainland. Instead the tunnel was turned into an open trench, and native labor drafts were used to maintain and expand it until the end of the colonial era. Crises still recurred, however, with flooding in 1692 followed by food shortages and then food riots. Not until the late nineteenth century was the drainage of the lakes completed, leaving salt flats and a city that has been literally sinking into the muck of the centuries ever since.

Daily Life in the Colonies

Daily life in the colonies reflected the extremes of social position and wealth, on the one hand, and the great disparity between urban and rural environments, on the other. For the rural majority, tedium broken only by religious activities and occasional secular celebrations was the rule. Generally, the richer and more complex life of ritual and social interaction of the precontact indigenous cultures subsided as the effects of epidemic disease, miscegenation, and the penetration of the market economy forged the colonial rural culture. Urban dwellers enjoyed more frequent and varied entertainment than did rural residents, but most of them, too, lived a precarious existence marked by a long working day, minimal diet, and poor health. Crime and violence threatened urban and rural residents alike. Although elites alone had access to all of the pleasures present in the colonial world, the less advantaged groups could enjoy religious celebrations, drinking, music, games, and other diversions.

Labor

From the time they were children, most members of colonial society spent their daylight hours working. Whether engaged in agriculture, ranching, domestic service, mining, or other occupations requiring manual labor, the hours were long and the compensation modest. The struggle for survival consumed most of their energies.

Sundays and religious holidays offered the only respite for manual laborers, and the special requirements of planting and harvesting could cancel even these unpaid breaks. Indians and other free rural laborers routinely toiled from ten to twelve hours a day for up to three hundred or more days a year. Slaves, particularly on sugar plantations, often worked longer. On Jesuit sugar estates in Peru, for example, the day began at 4:30 A.M. in the winter and 5:15 A.M. in the summer. Slaves and other workers labored after morning mass and breakfast until sundown except in the grinding mills where, during harvest, the workday extended beyond midnight. Indian employees in the textile *obrajes* of Ecuador worked from 6:00 A.M. to 6:00 P.M. six days a week except for seven weeks per year when they were permitted to sow, weed, and harvest their fields. In the early seventeenth century, *mita* laborers had their workweek reduced from six to five days, with Sundays and Mondays off. Their shifts, whether day or night, were theoretically twelve hours, but an oppressive quota system requiring them to deliver a specified amount of ore often extended the hours of toil.

As in Europe at the same time, wages paid to the majority of free workers in the colonial era seldom exceeded the subsistence level. In the case of *mita* laborers and some *obraje* workers, wages were substantially less than the cost of subsistence, and as a result, those family members who remained in the villages had to provide a portion of the workers' food needs. Such minimal payment reinforced the social order. Spaniards and Portuguese considered nonwhites their social inferiors and believed that wages that would keep them mired in poverty were both just and appropriate. They thought, moreover, that low compensation encouraged productivity and discouraged idleness.

Despite extreme fluctuations in the prices of basic foodstuffs, principally maize, wages generally remained stable in each category of employment after the mid-seventeenth century. Unskilled rural workers in Ecuador received fifteen to twenty pesos a year plus housing and food allotments, the total compensation being roughly equivalent to that received by an urban day laborer in Quito. Because Spanish employers deducted the tribute of eight pesos from the wages paid to Indian laborers, the workers' net pay was reduced substantially. Most *hacienda* peons in the Valley of Mexico were receiving two *reales* a day by 1650, a rate that remained standard 150 years later. The cash value of the total compensation—money, food, housing, and clothing—varied by region and date, but its worth was often too small to provide the necessities for survival. In Brazil, free rural laborers, in both grazing and agriculture, usually received some of their compensation in the form of permission to graze a few animals or plant a small garden. Only among the more skilled artisans of Brazilian cities did earning potential exceed subsistence costs. *Hacendados* and owners of mines and *obrajes* often advanced wages to workers to make up this shortfall, not out of kindness but to maintain a stable and dependent labor force. By

A poor woman who earns her living doing laundry carries clothes to the river in Buenos Aires. This work was commonly done by slaves. Use of tobacco of all kinds was common among men and women of all classes.

combining their meager income with a frugal diet, minimal shelter, and a set of homespun or inexpensive clothing, laborers clung to life precariously.

Urban manual laborers earned higher cash wages than did their rural counterparts, but they usually had correspondingly higher living expenses because they had to buy housing, food, and clothing. Cities, however, offered more opportunities for employment as artisans, retailers, or workers in a variety of services that offered higher compensation. Church and government positions, as well, were concentrated in urban areas. Combined and often intertwined with wholesale merchants and successful landowners, clerics and officials received and expended incomes that provided the cities with a rich and colorful social life.

Clothing

Clothing revealed status in the colonial world just as it did in Europe. Early commentators noted the contrast between the finely woven and decorated cotton garments worn by indigenous nobles in central Mexico and commoners' attire made of coarser henequen fabric. Inca nobles donnedhigh-quality,

By the eighteenth century, members of the colonial elite sought opportunites to display their wealth. This Mexican woman's dress is made from costly imported cloth, and she is posed next to a harpsichord for her portrait. The false beauty mark near her right eye was another common affectation.

multicolored cotton clothing that distinguished them from commoners in plain dress. Despite varied styles, colors, and weaves, however, native clothing typically was simple in design and shape. Native weavers produced rectangular fabrics that were most easily wrapped into wearable garb or turned into straight-sided garments such as tunics, skirts, loincloths, ponchos, and capes. Shaped and closely fitted clothes were rare.

The early importation of steel shears from Europe led to a transformation of Amerindian clothing. Shears enabled tailors to produce trousers, shirts, and other items favored by Iberian males. The rapid expansion of bands of sheep made wool widely available, while imported cloth from Europe and later from East Asia added variety and fineness to the array of fabrics available.

Clerical attitudes reinforced the use of European-style clothing. Spaniards initially thought nakedness a sign of poverty rather than scandalous behavior. This attitude soon gave way to demands that natives dress modestly, and Spanish clerics quickly set about altering their clothing practices. Before long, Indian males were wearing long pants, shirts, and jackets or vests, sometimes under a native tunic. Native women's wear changed less, although skirt length increased. Dress codes, of course, affected appearance only in public. To their dismay, clerics could not prevent, for example, Maya women from wearing "indecent and scandalous"—that is to say, "topless"— garb at home or Maya men from donning only a loincloth.[4]

Not content with altering native dress, the Spanish issued legislation to freeze the imposed styles in time. Fashions changed for Spaniards, typically behind European trends, and local and regional styles emerged as well. Natives, however, were to continue wearing the same style generation after generation. Indeed, distinctive local garb—for example, hats with unique color or decoration—came to identify the wearer's village in the same way that today's baseball caps identify Cardinals' or Yankees' fans.

Although a majority of the colonial population wore homespun clothing or items made from cheap textiles manufactured in *obrajes*, the well-to-do provided a market for European and East Asian textiles turned into more stylish clothing by thousands of tailors and seamstresses. The craft guilds in Mexico City in 1788 testified to the importance of the production of clothing and provision of accessories and cosmetic services in the bustling viceregal capital. Weavers of different kinds of cloth and workers in the textile sweat shops (*obrajes*) totaled well over three thousand. The tailors' guild numbered over twelve hundred members, nearly two-thirds of them masters and journeymen. Seamstresses, who made women's clothes, were undoubtedly at least as numerous. Buttonhole makers numbered eighty-nine. Nearly two hundred hatmakers and even more shoemakers were present, while over eight hundred barbers and two hundred hairdressers plied their trades.

Many visitors to colonial Latin American commented on the luxuriousness of dress exhibited by all classes. A British officer in Lima in the 1720s reported, "Of all the parts of the world, the people here are the most expensive in their habit." This was reiterated by a French visitor who stated that Lima's women had "an insatiable appetite for pearls and jewels, for bracelets, earrings and other paraphenalia, which saps the wealth of husbands and lovers." The demand for rich imported textiles was sufficiently strong that they remained the most important single import throughout the colonial era.

This passion for luxurious dress influenced what *castas* and even slaves purchased. Some observers saw women's clothing as an embellishment of colonial cities. "The beauty of [Mexico City] is in its inhabitants, because of their elegance and cleanliness. . . . The poorest woman has her pearls and jewels, and considers herself unhappy if she does not have her gold jewellery to wear on holidays."[5] Powerful families advertised their wealth by dressing their slaves and servants in rich clothes. In Rio de Janeiro it was customary for rich women to be accompanied in their outings by "four or five extremely well-dressed black women . . . ornamented with many necklaces and earrings of gold."[6] Such display of luxury attracted criticism from some wealthy families as well, for they recognized that it tended to blur class lines. In response, colonial officials imposed sumptuary laws that regulated clothing and jewelry worn by race and class.

The Crown had allowed native leaders and nobles to differentiate themselves from commoners by wearing different fabrics and styles, but sought to prevent them from imitating Spanish fashions. Colonial authorities were more ambitious in their efforts to restrict the clothing for *castas* and blacks. In the mid-seventeenth century, the Viceroy of Peru and Audiencia of Lima issued an order that "no mulatto woman, nor Negro woman, free or slave, wear woolen cloth, nor any cloth of silk, nor lace of gold, silver, black or white" under pain of confiscation of the offensive clothing, 100 lashes, or exile.[7] Such sumptuary legislation proved ineffective. Travelers in mid-eighteenth-century Lima noted that "the lower classes of women, even to the very Negroes . . . [seek] to imitate their betters, not only in the fashion of their dress, but also in the richness of it."[8]

Diet

Culture, taste, habit, availability, and price determined the composition of diet. European plants and animals quickly came to supplement indigenous staples such as maize, beans, squash, and chilies in Mesoamerica; potatoes and quinoa in the Andes; and manioc in the Caribbean zone and Brazil. Europeans, Indians, and Africans altered their diets and tastes to incorporate previously unknown or expensive foods and obtained more variety and protein as a result. Regional products, moreover, gave Latin American meals a flavor distinct from the fare found on Iberian tables.

Maize remained the dietary staple of the indigenous population of Middle America after the conquest and was prominent in other regions as well. High in carbohydrates, maize kernels were often finely ground and cooked as tortillas, prepared in gruel, or steamed. Whether served in these forms

Food was commonly sold in the streets and open-air public markets of colonial cities. The figure on the left carries sausages while the figure on the right carries intestines cleaned and ready to be stuffed with pork.

or others, maize provided as much as 90 percent of the calories in an Indian's diet in the seventeenth century and still accounted for some three-quarters in the mid-twentieth century. The rural *casta* population was similarly dependent on maize. Beans in their numerous forms also were a major source of protein throughout the colonial era, as they had been before. Squash, pumpkins, and gourds provided both calories and protein. Whether consumed raw or in sauces, chili peppers and tomatoes added both vitamins and flavor to the colonial diet.

Domesticated European animals were the most notable postconquest supplements to a diet that remained based on preconquest plants. Chickens, pigs, sheep, and cattle thrived in the New World and offered an unprecedented amount of protein. Indians prized eggs, and chickens soon became intrusive residents in most villages. Pork and mutton also won favor. Beef, in contrast, gained comparable popularity more slowly, initially perhaps because the Indians associated cattle with the destruction of their crops. By the eighteenth century, however, beef was a common dietary item in northern New Spain and in most of Brazil and the Río de la Plata.

Africa also contributed to the New World diet. Bananas, kidney beans, and okra followed in the wake of the slave trade. Although the slaves' diet was generally inadequate in calories and nutrition, Africans sought to imitate the cuisine of their homelands whenever possible. The legacy of these traditions survives in the recipes of modern Cuba and especially Brazil.

Europeans and individuals emulating their taste in food ate very differently than did the majority of the population. Not only did they normally consume their meals at tables, absent in native houses and in the homes of many *castas,* but they tried to eat the kinds of food that were standard in Europe. This loyalty explains the continued significance of wine, olive oil, and even wheat in colonial imports for decades after settlement. Urban markets and retailers generally offered a variety of foodstuffs that included local and regional products and imports. As income increased, family diets diversified and improved.

Wheat baked into bread was the principal ingredient of Europeans' and their creole cousins' diet. In fact, there was a distinct class identification associated with white and dark breads: The more affluent households consumed only white bread and considered dark bread to be a poor person's food. A prosperous male from the upper class consumed at least two pounds of bread, four ounces of meat, some vegetables, and oil or fat each day. Even country stores in the Mexican mining towns in the first half of the seventeenth century stocked a diverse mix of foods for those who could afford them. Shrimp, oysters, honey, lentils, spices, bananas, vinegar, salt, sugar, chocolate, beans, cheese, garlic, molasses, lard, and figs appeared on shelves far from Mexico City.

Unlike the indigenous population, Europeans and other advantaged groups acquired most of their protein from meat. Mutton was a favorite in the Spanish colonies. Despite a population of about fifty thousand, Lima in the mid-eighteenth century required just two or three head of cattle a week for the small number of peninsulars who alone ate it regularly. Pork was more popular, although the celebrated Spanish travelers Jorge Juan and Antonio de Ulloa considered it inferior to that served in Cartagena de Indias. Lard was used extensively in cooking, a custom begun before domestic olive oil was available. Proximity to the Pacific Ocean enabled residents in Lima to have fresh fish in their diet instead of the salted cod common in Europe. Not only were the corbina and king's fish superior to those in Spain, but anchovies were plentiful as well. Crayfish from the River Rimac added another source of protein.

In Brazil, the Río de la Plata region, Chile, and Venezuela, the proliferation of European livestock, particularly cattle, made beef a fairly common part of the diet. By the early eighteenth century, slaves in Brazil were given small amounts of dried beef from the *pampas* region and *sertão,* or fresh beef, from the nearby ranches of the interior. Most Brazilian planters reduced the cost of feeding their slaves by allowing them to cultivate garden plots. Some slaves produced enough to sell the surplus to other slaves or in the local market. The very poor, beggars and prisoners, seldom consumed protein and relied almost entirely on the nutrients provided in bread. Prisoners in the Salvador, Bahia, jail received bread rations twice a week and a supplement of soup and a piece of meat on Sundays. This chronic undernourishment caused seventy prisoners to die of starvation between 1733 and 1736. Most prisoners throughout the colonies depended on charity for their survival.

Fruit and vegetables supplemented the bread and meat in the European diet. Both Spaniards and Portuguese planted gardens and fruit trees wherever they settled and the climate and terrain allowed. Travelers marveled at the variety and quantity of items available: Figs, grapes, pomegranates, oranges, lemons, bananas, other fruits, and green salads graced the tables in Mexico City. A seventeenth-century traveler to Lima was so struck by the abundance and excellence of its fruit and vegetables that he declared it to have "the richest Lent . . . in the world."[9] Even in inhospitable Potosí, high in the Andes, fruits of many kinds imported from lower valleys were available year-round in the markets.

As a dessert or a snack between meals, sweetmeats were extremely popular throughout the colonies. A traveler in Mexico City in 1625 noted their abundance with astonishment. In Cartagena they were not only plentiful, but residents considered eating some a necessary preliminary to drinking a glass of water. Juan and Ulloa noted much more restraint in Lima where, despite the quantity available, the inhabitants ate sweetmeats only as a dessert, and then but rarely. Slave and free black women produced and sold sugared sweets and pastries in all of Brazil's major cities.

The consumption of beverages accompanied and at times supplanted that of food. By the eighteenth century the most popular nonalcoholic beverage in much of Spanish America was cacao, or chocolate. Before the Spaniards arrived, nobles and warriors in Middle America had been its primary consumers. They drank it as a cold or tepid beverage made from ground cacao, water, maize flour, and chili. The consumption of cacao spread to the region's general Indian population after the conquest, and by the late sixteenth century the number of Spaniards in New Spain who drank the cacao beverage was growing. The Europeans changed the Indians' recipes, however, sweetening the beverage with vanilla, cinnamon, and sugar. With Guayaquil and Venezuela joining Central America as major centers of cacao production in the early seventeenth century, the market continued to expand. Cacao became the favorite beverage in colonial Mexico: Its consumption among the elite was high, and it was also a common drink in hospitals and convents. In South America, *yerba mate*, or Paraguayan tea, was also extremely popular, particularly among the creoles. In Quito, Lima, the south of Brazil, and numerous other locations, many drank *yerba* in both the morning and the evening.

Alcoholic beverages were a frequent complement to meals and were drunk liberally at other times as well. Spaniards brought a taste for wine from Iberia and imported the drink in large quantities. Domestic production followed settlement quickly where the climate and soil were appropriate. By the late sixteenth century, substantial supplies of potable and sometimes fine-quality wine were available in major markets of South America. Arequipa emerged early as a major producer, but by 1600 landowners in Ica, Pisco, and Nazca had ended its original dominance. At mid-eighteenth century, Lima was importing an inferior white wine from Nazca and red and dark red wine from Pisco, Lucumba, and Chile. The latter's vintages included muscatel and held the highest reputation among connoisseurs in the city. Wine was produced in Mendoza by the late seventeenth century, and despite transportation difficulties the region helped supply the needs of Upper Peru and Buenos Aires. Imports from Spain and Peru supplied the markets in Mexico and Central America in the absence of a significant regional viti-culture and despite prohibitions against interregional trade.

Brandy, the distilled, high-alcohol-content cousin of wine, emerged as the beverage of choice in the late seventeenth century because of both its greater potency and its better traveling characteristics. Originally used for medici-nal purposes, the drink's popularity burgeoned, and imports from Seville, Cádiz, and, especially after 1679, the Canary Islands increased accordingly. New Spain, Cuba, and Venezuela were the major markets; production in Peru became important about 1700. By 1717 the Spanish miners there drank it in preference to wine, which they left to the lower classes. In Cartagena, Juan and Ulloa reported, even the "most regular and sober persons" invariably drank a glass of brandy daily at 11:00 A.M. to strengthen the stom-ach and whet the appetite. Among the less abstemious, however, *hacer las once,* as the custom was called, degenerated into a daylong activity. Brandy soon became the poor man's luxury among urban laborers, cowboys, and even slaves. In Quito, Peruvian brandy was a special favorite of peninsulars.

Whereas well-to-do Spaniards drank quality wine or brandy, most of society imbibed less pretentious beverages. These included *chicha,* a beer made from corn, drunk in the Andes; *pulque,* an intoxicant derived from the maguey or century plant, enjoyed in Mexico; and *aguardiente de caña,* a potent distilled drink derived from sugarcane and produced in Brazil, Paraguay, the Caribbean Islands, New Granada, and other locations where cane grew. On some Brazilian sugar estates slaves were given a rum ration before heading to the fields in the morning. In central Mexico during Aztec rule, commoners drank *pulque* on ritual occasions, but the nobility drank it more frequently. After the conquest, alcohol consumption increased as commoners escaped traditional taboos regarding *pulque* and obtained access to imported Spanish wines as well. Indians considered drinking to stupefaction acceptable behavior in ritual situations. Among the Andean peoples, drinking was an expected part of ritual observance. The Mamaq of the Rimac River valley, for example, celebrated the matu-ration of their crops with the feast of Chaupinamca, at which men and women danced and drank for five consecutive nights. Such behavior drew the condemnation of Spanish authorities, although some Spaniards prof-ited from the sale of alcohol to natives.

A heavy consumption of alcohol, in short, was a common feature of colo-nial society, as it was in the preindustrial societies of Europe. Owners of vine-yards, canefields, and land devoted to maguey cultivation pushed to expand production and profit. Despite recognizing the social consequences of alco-hol abuse, the Spanish government proved unable to limit its growth, at least in part because it benefited directly from taxes on its production. In Brazil, rum production and consumption were encouraged by a tithe exemption.

Rum also became a significant export in the growing direct African slave trade. The masses, in particular, consumed alcohol in great quantity as they sought temporary relief from the misery always present in their daily lives.

Tobacco and Coca

An appetite suppressant, tobacco complemented both diet and the consumption of alcohol. Smoked and snuffed by natives long before Columbus's first voyage, tobacco caught the attention of Europeans starting in 1492. A 1565 pamphlet by a physician in Sevilla extolled its virtues as a cure for virtually all ailments suffered by humans and animals alike. By the late sixteenth century clerics smoked and snuffed tobacco with such frequency that an ecclesiastical decree prohibited them from doing so before the mass. Over time the practice of smoking rolled tobacco became commonplace. Eighteenth-century observers commented that men and women of all races and economic status smoked cigarettes and cigars and went out with a bag containing flint, tinder, and steel to light them. Smokers who refused an offered cigarette or declined to allow the host to light it committed a serious social faux pas. A 1764 proposal for a poorhouse in Mexico City called for distributing two packs of cigarettes weekly to inmates who smoked. Consumption of legally produced cigarettes in New Spain in 1806 averaged more than two daily per inhabitant; the actual number smokers consumed per day is unknown. Far fewer cigars were smoked and snuff enjoyed even less popularity. The habit of chewing tobacco, however, was widespread among the poor. In Lima, at least, women used slender rolls of tobacco to clean their teeth, a process that involved chewing the end of the roll and then rubbing the teeth with the masticated leaves.

The coca shrub cultivated in the Andes for centuries prior to the Spanish conquest provided leaves that served as another appetite suppressant. While the Inca nobility had enjoyed the privilege of chewing the leaves accompanied by a little ash, the Spanish conquest enabled the broader populace to participate. Chronicler Pedro de Cieza de León reported in the 1540s that natives kept a coca chew in their mouths throughout their wakeful hours because "it makes them feel little hunger, and [at the same time] strong and vigorous."[10] Later observers confirm that the use of coca continued to be widespread. In 1678 Potosí's leading merchant purchased roughly 300,000 pounds of leaves. In the late eighteenth century, coca was a close second to brandy as the most valuable South American merchandise sold in the mining center and major market of Potosí. The popularity of chewing coca in the Andes has continued to the present day, while its high intensity cousin cocaine has a world market.

Illness and Medicine

Epidemic diseases introduced from Europe and Africa repeatedly swept through Latin America, beginning before the fall of Tenochtitlan. Smallpox, measles, typhus, influenza, pneumonic plague, and pestilential fevers were the most prominent killers. Poor sanitation practices, inadequate water supplies, and a general absence of sound hygiene promoted disease and poor health. The streets of large cities were running sewers filled with human and animal excrement. Slaughterhouses discarded their waste where dogs and other scavengers could carry it near the houses. The city councils of Buenos Aires and other towns regularly repeated prohibitions against leaving the bodies of slaves and carcasses of livestock in the street. Few colonial residents had access to safe wells. Although aqueducts were constructed in some of the larger cities, most residents bought water from peddlers or used sometimes-contaminated rainwater that was collected in ceramic or wooden tubs. The dangers inherent in these conditions were compounded by poor personal hygiene. Few people bathed regularly; soap and clean clothes were luxuries limited to the more affluent groups in colonial society.

Against these grave health threats, contemporary medical practices offered little hope. Nor were medical practitioners very effective in curing the host of other ailments, notably rheumatic and other fevers, stomach ailments, catarrh, syphilis, abscesses, and tumors that weakened the population and frequently brought premature death. Treating injuries successfully was also usually impossible with the techniques and medicines at hand. As a result of these inadequacies, most of the people in the colonial world spent much of their lives ill or in pain.

Spanish physicians began arriving in the New World on Columbus's second voyage. The mainland conquests drew them in their train as wounded, diseased, or simply ill conquistadors sought and paid for medical assistance. Within a decade after their founding, the city councils of Mexico City and Lima were already trying to eliminate charlatans, by requiring licenses to practice, licenses for which only university-trained and -certified physicians were eligible. The Crown soon named royal medical examiners to continue this worthy objective. Despite such efforts, charlatans with fraudulent credentials were a common feature of colonial life throughout the Spanish colonies and Brazil.

Licensed physicians were the elite of the medical profession, but before the late eighteenth century, the profession itself had little to recommend it in either the New World or Europe. From the sixteenth to the nineteenth centuries, a baccalaureate in medicine entitled a man to begin practice. University instruction in medicine drew heavily on Hippocrates and Galen. Modernization of the curriculum began in the late eighteenth century, but very few students matriculated in this unattractive career.

Surgeons held a status far below that of physicians. Often associated with barbering and bloodletting, surgeons seldom bothered to get official approval to practice. Most had no university training; rather, they apprenticed with an "approved" surgeon for four or five years. Tightened standards and more formalized instruction awaited the late eighteenth century.

Phlebotomists, or bleeders, ranked below even surgeons among medical practitioners. Apprenticeship of three or four years replaced any

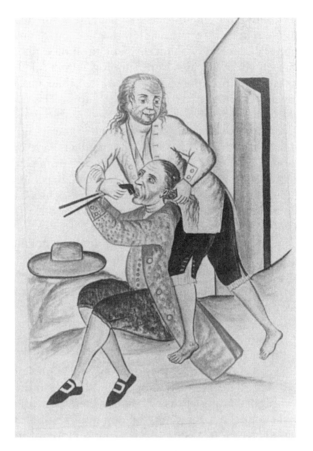

An itinerant tooth-puller practices his trade in the street.

academic work. Oral examinations, moreover, meant that phlebotomists did not need to be literate. Examiners expected them to know only about veins and arteries and how to put on leeches and cupping glasses, to open ulcers and boils, and to extract teeth. Outside the major colonial cities, barbers usually provided these services. Barbering, a traditional artisan occupation, mixed medical and dental work with hair cutting and shaving. In small towns without guilds, there were few effective controls on the training and practice of these men, with malpractice and abuse the predictable results.

Unlike all other aspects of medical practice, delivering babies was almost exclusively a female profession, although wealthy women in larger cities often sought assistance from a licensed surgeon as well. Few midwives were formally trained or licensed, and most relied more on superstition than anatomical knowledge. The deadly combination of frequent pregnancies and poor medical practice made complications in childbirth one of the most common causes of death for colonial women. As in Europe at the same time, even physicians regularly recommended treatments that endangered both mother and child. The respected Mexican doctor Juan Manuel Venegas, for example, advised the following procedure for expelling a dead infant from the womb: application of an enema made from "'a chicken cut open down the back,' a mule's sweatpad cooked in urine, and infusions of feathergrass and leaves of senna," followed by a "drink of horse manure dissolved in wine."[11]

Inadequate opportunities for formal medicine instruction and the low status of medical practitioners in general combined to produce few physicians. The University of Mexico conferred only 438 baccalaureates in the faculty from 1607 to 1738, and the University of San Marcos in Lima probably conferred even fewer. In Guatemala the University of San Carlos graduated only 30 bachelors of medicine from 1700 to 1821. Graduates, moreover, established their practices in urban centers where the Spanish populations were eager for their services. Rural villages rarely if ever had a physician. Because Brazil lacked a university, all of the colony's Portuguese physicians were immigrants or colonials trained in Europe.

The small number of legally qualified physicians opened the way for quacks and healers who diagnosed illnesses, bled victims, and prescribed remedies for the majority of the colonial population. Sometimes foreigners, sometimes friars, often mixed-race males and females with a private stock of remedies or access to a local apothecary, these persons lacked any formal medical training, although some had observed physicians while working as hospital attendants. In regions with large populations of African slaves, native remedies that combined the bark, roots, and leaves of plants with spiritualist practices were frequently employed, even by the more affluent members of society.

Apothecaries stocked the items that physicians and other medical practitioners prescribed. The inventories contained oddities drawn from centuries of folk medicine and Galenism in Spain as well as items unique to the Indies. As in Europe, druggists sold products whose efficacy frequently rested more in the mind than the body: Tapir's hoof, human cranium, llama fetuses, lizard excrement, spiderwebs, dried and powdered earthworms, gander droppings, pearls, amber, and garnet sat on the druggists' shelves along with rose-colored oil and honey, several varieties of animal grease, mercury, and bezoar stones secured from the stomachs of llama, vicuna, and other ruminant animals. Purgatives included balsam, snakeskin, corn meal, and tobacco.

Although the Spanish population lamented the persistent shortage of physicians, as in Europe, there was nonetheless a healthy skepticism about the efficacy of medical treatment. The Peruvian poet Juan del Valle Caviedes voiced disdain for physicians individually and as a group:

> And wherever the book says *doctor,*
> Be attentive, because you should read there
> *Executioner,* although the latter
> Is a little weaker.

> Wherever it says *prescription*
> You will say *sword*
> Because sword and executioner
> End up being the same.
> Wherever it says *bloodletting*
> You should read *throatcutting*
> And you will read *scalpel*
> Wherever it says *medication.*
> Wherever it says *laxative*
> Read he finished off the patient.
> And where it says *remedy*
> You will read *certain death.*[12]

Poverty and disease go hand in hand, for the conditions creating the first produce an environment conducive to the second. Widespread poverty, an inadequate diet, hard labor, and unsanitary conditions at work and home combined to produce both high mortality and lower labor productivity. For most inhabitants in the colonial world, life offered few pleasures and fewer rewards.

Crime and Punishment

Crime and violence accompanied the settlement of the New World and remained permanent features of colonial daily life thereafter. Colonial authorities regularly dealt with cases of robbery, assault, and homicide, but many paid less attention to violations of legislation intended to protect Indians and slaves from physical and financial abuse. Consumer fraud, particularly by bakers and other food vendors, was also an ongoing preoccupation. Colonists, moreover, proved adept at conniving with underpaid officials to defraud the government; evading taxes and customs duties was only one of many ways in which they did so. Ironically, although both hardened criminals and more genteel malefactors threatened society, their punishment at times provided grisly entertainment, particularly in the capital cities.

Because the law enforcement bureaucracy was very small, most crime went undetected by the royal authorities. Within rural Indian villages, local leaders dealt with cases of robbery, adultery, and rape. On the plantations and large ranches of Brazil and the Spanish colonies, landowners or their agents exercised de facto judicial authority, usually administering corporal punishment. The death penalty, however, remained a prerogative of the state. Homicide, sedition, and aggravated assault required the intervention of the colonial judiciary, but these cases accounted for comparatively few violations of the law. Local and royal officials in cities, in contrast, dealt with the full spectrum of crime.

Thieves found irresistible the urban centers with their unlit streets and few night patrols. The concentration of cash, jewels, and other movable property within their bounds and the desperate living conditions of the urban poor meant that neither the wealthy nor the impoverished were immune from theft. In August 1629, for example, robbers took more than ten thousand pesos from the downtown store of Lima merchant Christóbal Lario. An almost daily occurrence, such robbery prompted the *consulado* to hire three night watchmen to patrol the shopping district. Not even this action, however, was effective. The following year, burglars entered the residence of another merchant, Benito de Orozco, while he and his wife were sleeping. The intruders threatened him with sword and dagger and stole his jewels and clothing. Robberies of a small grocery store and a mulatto silversmith's shop were reminders that thieves attacked persons of modest means as well.

Assault with a deadly weapon, often a butcher or household knife, was commonplace in both rural and urban areas. Armed assaults were so frequent in rural areas of Argentina and Uruguay that shopkeepers protected themselves and their merchandise with iron or sturdy wooden bars. The offenders were almost always male and usually young. The victims also were usually young males. Only rarely were assailants and victims strangers, and many times they were family members, neighbors, or fellow workers. Primitive medical practices, furthermore, increased the likelihood that a wounded victim would die. Juan Antonio Suardo, a clerical diarist, recorded from 1630 to 1635 nearly sixty murders and deaths resulting from assault in Lima. On one of many occasions involving passion, an irate husband stabbed both his wife and a priest after discovering them in *flagrante delicto*. During a particularly violent night in 1634, within an hour and a half a Spaniard, a mulatto, and a black lost their lives in assaults in different parts of the city.

Civil authorities regularly administered punishments in public to remind the populace that robbery, violent acts, and other crimes could bring severe retribution. Judges routinely ordered terms of hard labor in *obrajes,* port facilities, the galleys, or military service. In the sixteenth and seventeenth centuries, numerous offenders held in the royal jail in Lima were sent to Chile to fight against the Indians. Whippings were another common sentence, even for minor offenses. In the Mixteca Alta region of New Spain, six to fifty lashes were the usual punishment for peasants in the seventeenth century. One day in 1634, eleven Indians were whipped in Lima as *ladrones famosos,* or "renowned thieves." On occasion, judges combined whippings with a sentence of forced servitude. One slave was lashed and sent to the galleys for attacking a Spaniard with a sword and then resisting arrest. The use of lashings was discriminatory, for unlike the rest of society, Spaniards were spared corporal punishment.

Executions were less frequent in the Spanish colonies and Brazil than in the English colonies. This difference arose both from the Iberian legal systems' receptivity to pleas of extenuating circumstances and an appreciation that dead offenders could provide no labor. It is possible, moreover, that except for a concerted effort to clear central Mexico's main roads of highwaymen in the eighteenth century that led to numerous hangings, executions became less common after 1700. Rarely ordered even for homicide in late eighteenth-century central Mexico, executions were frequent in early seventeenth-century Peru. Judges were most likely to order execution in cases of murder, attempted murder, robbery, and sodomy. From 1630 to 1635 alone, Suardo recorded over forty executions in Lima.

Executions, especially those for sodomy and bestiality, attracted sizable crowds of people. The burning in Callao of a *mestizo* and a mulatto convicted of sodomy drew numerous spectators from Lima. Even more spectacular was the execution of the Aragonese merchant Thomas Buesso, convicted of sodomy and bestiality. An "infinite number of persons on foot, on horseback, and in coaches" gathered at 4:00 P.M. on November 13, 1630, to watch the authorities whip Buesso's black male lover and burn both the merchant and the unfortunate dog he had molested.

Entertainment

Daily life in colonial cities offered variety and excitement far removed from the routine of the countryside. Bells in churches and convents marked the hours. Processions honoring religious holidays mixed with civic celebrations to add color, sound, and festivity to urban life. The concentrations of wealth in the largest colonial cities enabled expenditures for public display rarely possible in other cities and beyond the imagination of villages. Even the funerals of wealthy residents became public celebrations.

Urban life focused on the plazas and streets. In Spanish America, bullfights were staged in a plaza whose entrances were closed for the event. Plazas were also the sites for jousting on horseback with cane spears, military parades, public *autos de fé*, executions, religious and civil processions, and fiestas of all sorts. Vendors of fruit, sweetmeats, beverages, ices, and other tasty tidbits hawked their goods there. On crowded, dirty streets passed mules laden with goods, horse- and mule-drawn coaches and chaises, ambulatory vendors selling their wares, wives and servants on their daily shopping trips, persons going to and from work, and children playing or going to school.

Public festivals provided entertainment for rich and poor alike. While every municipality, parish, guild, and brotherhood honored the day of its patron saint, large cities offered the most frequent and lavish festivities. Of the ninety or more festivals celebrated annually in late seventeenth-century Mexico City, those associated with a new viceroy's entrance into the city, the oath to a new monarch, and Corpus Christi were the most elaborate. The capital's city council lavished special attention on viceregal entrances, spending sums that substantially exceeded its normal annual budget and a total that surpassed everything it spent on all other city-sponsored festivals combined. The expenditures provided observers with parades featuring elaborately decorated floats depicting historic events, native dancers and musicians, bullfights, fireworks that went on for hours, a huge triumphal arch nearly four stories high, mock jousts, and military demonstrations. A viceregal reception in Lima in 1648 featured nearly 300 bars of silver paving the area encompassed by the triumphal arch; another reception in 1667 included two arches and over 550 silver bars. In 1621 the oath to the king festival in Mexico City offered not only elaborate fireworks that included monsters, snakes, dragons, and castles, but also silver coins that members of the city council threw to the crowd following each pledge. Following their accession in 1700, the Bourbons, Spain's new ruling dynasty, deemphasized the viceregal entrance while simultaneously enhancing the importance of the ceremony surrounding the oath to the monarch. Thus in Mexico City's lengthy celebration of Ferdinand VI's coronation in 1747, some twenty thousand spectators enjoyed watching more than ninety-five bullfights over ten days.

Viceregal entrances and oaths to the monarch were magnificent spectacles, but sometimes many years passed without an opportunity to celebrate either event. The eight-day Corpus Christi celebration, in contrast, was an annual event established in Mexico City within two decades of the fall of Tenochtitlan. The Mexico City festival featured plays performed outdoors to accommodate crowds of spectators as well as a procession that accompanied the Eucharist through the streets. In the late seventeenth century, government officials, clerics, religious brotherhoods, professors, students, civic groups, and artisan guilds in the procession paraded with carefully constructed giants, big heads, little devils, a dragon, costumed dancers, special altars of silver, decorated carts, and floats. Corpus Christi thus brought together the populace of Mexico City as it emphasized that all persons, regardless of birth, social position, or economic means, shared a common religion. These immensely expensive and popular celebrations not only attracted huge audiences from the urban population but also pulled in large numbers of people from surrounding villages and towns. Each celebration was organized as a script that expressed the official ideologies of Church and state. The events' organizers thus took enormous care to arrange participating groups hierarchically and to use rituals to confirm traditional authority.

In Mexico City, Lima, and Salvador, Bahia, the presence of viceregal courts, archbishops, and other prominent and powerful civil and ecclesiastical authorities as well as wealthy merchants and landowners sustained an intense calendar of social activities. Several examples of social life in Lima illustrate the types of entertainment available: On New Year's Eve 1629, Viceroy Conde de Chinchón staged a dramatic presentation in the palace at 3:00 P.M. for the *audiencia* ministers and their wives. Five days later he invited them to celebrate his son's birthday amid general rejoicing and fiestas. On January 12, 1630, a private citizen, Don Francisco Flores, sponsored a bullfight and party for a large number of male and female friends at a town near Lima. When an Augustinian secured a chair at the University of San Marcos later in the month, his friends informed the populace by awakening them with trumpets and drums; great bell ringing and fireworks continued the celebration the following night. The arrival of a new archbishop in early February prompted another round of celebrations, bell ringing,

Native, African, and European traditions contributed to the development of music, dance, and games in the colonies.

and fireworks highlighted by a "splendid dinner" at which sixty-four different dishes were served. On occasion, the viceroy, his wife, and a large retinue joined in the daily stroll around the plaza mayor and nearby streets that enabled people to show off their finery, see friends, and be seen by the populace present.

The humble as well as the wealthy participated in fiestas. The day after an elaborate official celebration in honor of the birth of Prince Baltasar Carlos in 1629, petty retailers in Lima decorated their stalls with hangings and flowers and the central plaza with trees and fourteen large figurines. Persons of all walks of life filled the plaza in the afternoon to celebrate, and fireworks entertained the entire city in the evening. In the next several weeks, guilds of confectioners, grocers, hatmakers, tailors, shoemakers, silversmiths, and merchants each provided fiestas, many complete with bull-fights and fireworks. Smaller cities and towns offered similar celebrations on a reduced scale. Even Indian villages invested their scarce resources in the celebration of feast days and secular holidays.

The completion of a new parish church in a small town in the bishopric of Cuzco in 1672 attracted numerous participants and spectators for the three-day event. Featured were the usual fireworks, bullfighting, dancing, papier-mâché figures, food, and an acrobat. Even if not participants in the formal events, workers in all locales enjoyed the informal drinking, gam-bling, singing, and dancing that accompanied them. Bullfights held in blocked-off city plazas were extremely popular and cockfights could attract hundreds of spectators. When only brief periods separated holidays, for example, Christmas, New Years, and Epiphany or Twelfth Night, workers in Chihuahua simply took an extended two-week holiday rather than returning to work. On the weekends, too, mineworkers who worked a three-hour walk from the town often carried their Saturday and Sunday enter-tainment beyond the weekend and celebrated "Saint Monday," despite their employers' opposition.

Although the plazas and streets were the centers of city life, families also entertained at home. Residences of wealthy citizens contained silver uten-sils and serving pieces; numerous paintings, often religious; books; mirrors; gilded chairs; a large table; and an ornate desk. The principal residential amusement for the elite was card playing, accompanied by gambling, an activity popular among Iberians before settlement of the New World. Par-ticipants included nearly anyone with pesos to lose. Despite prohibitions to the contrary, Dr. Antonio de Morga, president of the Audiencia of Quito from 1615 to 1636, entertained prominent citizens nightly in an atmo-sphere reminiscent of a gambling parlor. During his tenure, his wife over-saw their illicit gains reach some 200,000 pesos. In Guatemala City at about the same time, *audiencia* President Gonzalo de Paz y Lorezana prohibited gambling at cards in private houses in order to monopolize it in his own. In Mexico City, Thomas Gage reported that gambling was so popular that women invited gentlemen to visit them for no purpose other than to bet at cards. Gambling was also a passion among the lower classes, and there were few cantinas or *pulperías* that did not offer the opportunity to play cards or dice or wager on games of skill. Here suspected cheating or unexpected losses often led to knife fights and brawls.

Cockfights provided a venue for diversion and public gambling for rich and poor alike throughout the Americas. Despite periodic royal and cler-ical efforts to ban it, the sport was extremely popular. Raising fighting cocks was widespread in Mexico, although birds imported from the Philip-pine Islands were considered superior. An itinerant friar in New Spain in the 1760s noted enthusiasts paying more than twenty pesos for a particu-larly promising rooster. With blades fastened to their left legs, the cocks fought to the death in small amphitheater-shaped settings surrounded by wagerers perched on boxes and benches. In Mexico City, merchants, judges, clerics, and "numerous riffraff of all kinds" attended cockfights and bets on some fights reached a thousand pesos.[13] Attendance at cockfights was so great that the entrepreneur of the Old Coliseum in Mexico City claimed they were responsible for his inability to present plays other than on Sundays.

Death and Dying

The mortality rate was high in colonial Latin America as in Iberia and elsewhere at the time. Childbirth took a heavy toll on women and infant death was frequent. Primitive sewage disposal resulted in human waste mixing with that of livestock and other animals on city streets. Epidemic diseases struck repeatedly, leaving countless victims in their wake. In an era before modern sanitation, workplace safety regulations, and antibiotics, early death was commonplace.

Whenever possible, clerics administered last rites to dying parishioners, regardless of gender, race, or class, and then conducted funeral services. Ubiquitous in cities, priests and friars were often scarce in rural areas and small villages, an absence that resulted in natives burying a body themselves or occasionally even hanging it from a tree or throwing it into a ravine for

The threat of early death was ever present in colonial society. Elite families sometimes memorialized the premature deaths of their children. In this painting by an unknown Mexican artist, the body of Don Tomás María Joaquín Villas is surrounded by symbols of religious faith.

the benefit of scavenging animals. The absence of ordained priests, moreover, enabled some preconquest burial practices to continue as cases in Yucatan illustrate.

Proper Christian burial included a procession to the grave made by a cleric, family, friends, and members of a confraternity if the departed belonged to one. Wealthy families might give clothes and food to the poor who attended the funeral or carried torches. Increasingly elaborate processions recognized higher family status or unusual sanctity of the deceased. The death of a countess in Mexico City in the mid-seventeenth century was followed by a procession including the viceroy and all of the city's nobility and clergy. Similarly, the death in 1671 of a beloved professor of law at Lima's University of San Marcos brought out the viceroy, *audiencia* ministers, city council members, members of the cathedral chapter, and the most distinguished people in the capital. When Mercedarian Fray Pedro Urraca, considered a holy man, died in Lima in 1657, the same luminaries attended with the entire populace of the city. Following the interment, the family of the deceased traditionally went into mourning for a period of up to a year.

The cost of a Christian funeral was, at least for many Indian families, the most onerous financial liability they faced, in part because of the charges assessed by the priest. The official fees in place in Mexico for most of the colonial era required Indians to pay a resident priest sums roughly equivalent to the wages received for two to three weeks of manual labor. Spaniards in Mexican villages paid more than twice the amount that natives paid for a funeral and over four times as much for a first-class funeral, including a gratuity for the grave digger and pay for the singers. Charges for some native burials in the bishoprics of La Paz and Cuzco could exceed twenty-five pesos, an amount greater than a manual laborer earned for fifty days of work. In Yucatan, the high cost of burial meant that many native families resorted to clerical assistants rather than priests to conduct funerals.

As in Iberia, elite families in colonial cities sought interment in chapels and the floors of cathedrals, parish churches, and convents. Burial sites near images of saints were considered most desirable for salvation as well as display of social status. An observant visitor could identify rankings among prominent families of the past and present in the mosaic of markers on church and convent floors. Such desirable locations were expensive. The Franciscans in Vera Cruz, for example, charged a sum greater than a laborer in Mexico City could earn in more than three months. The use of funeral shrouds was commonplace in Brazil as well as Spanish America, and the Franciscans, in particular, benefited from their sale. The volume of cadavers in populous cities meant that burial sites were constantly being reopened. In many years in the late eighteenth century, over 2,500 persons were buried in Lima's parish churches and hospitals alone. Scarcely a day passed without a burial in the cathedral, the city's most favored site. Most cadavers were simply deposited in common vaults, however, for individual burial was limited almost exclusively to the upper strata of the capital's society.

The practice of providing burials within the buildings and grounds of religious institutions and hospitals located in cities resulted in an identifiable stench associated with the bodies' decomposition that not even extensive use of incense could hide. The belief that bad-smelling air carried disease, the so-called miasma theory, convinced enlightened critics that burials should be moved outside of cities. Although in 1787 the Crown ordered the cessation of burials in churches and the creation of new suburban cemeteries, it took decades in some places for the innovation to bear fruit.

An adult with wealth and foresight frequently left a will. After an opening statement that invoked God or the Trinity, the document routinely embodied a number of formulaic sections. These included a profession of religious faith and declaration of sound mental health, designation of a burial site, a declaration of the testator's desire for eternal life, and a provision for one or more cycles of masses to be held in order to speed the soul's journey through purgatory. When financially possible, and on occasion even when doing so was financially inadvisable, the testator established endowments to provide for masses said in perpetuity, often by a male relative. The practice of leaving the Church part of one's estate, or even the totality in the absence of familial heirs, was sufficiently common that the Crown legislated conditions under which such a bequest could be made. Over time the resulting transfer of land and income to the Church was enormous. A wealthy parishioner's death could be a financial boon to the Church.

Work, inadequate compensation, tiresome meals, and illness were the lot of most persons in colonial society. For this vast majority of the population, life offered almost no possibility of significant improvement. Only occasional fiestas broke the routine. For the elite, on the other hand, daily life was markedly different. Their income allowed them to purchase luxury goods both imported from abroad and produced locally. Their diets were varied, their entertainments numerous. The divergence in daily life for nobles and commoners apparent in Aztec and Inca society as well as Spain and Portugal before the conquest continued in the colonial world, as the local elites enjoyed a material and social existence that bore little resemblance to that of most of society.

The Cultural Milieu

Colonialism subordinated the indigenous and later creole cultures to European cultural hegemony. Undergirded by Catholicism, cultural colonialism proved to be more durable and resistant to American efforts to establish an independent cultural identity than did the more visible political and economic structures it helped sustain.

The cultural milieu in colonial Latin America varied according to the intensity of a region's contact with Europe, its wealth, and the composition

of the local society. The elites in major administrative centers tried to repli-
cate Iberian cultural institutions and practices. The movement of officials,
churchmen, merchants, and others to and from the colony and metropolis resulted in an ongoing transfer of Iberian high culture—European books
and ideas, music, and art—to the major colonial cities, whether located on
the coast or inland. In poorer and geographically isolated colonial towns
and rural areas, the limited high culture available revolved around religious
instruction and celebrations. Wherever there were large indigenous populations or numerous African slaves, the inhabitants drew on non-European
traditions and modified Iberian cultural expression into a unique popular
culture.

Origins of a Colonial Culture

In any clash between literate and preliterate societies, historical understanding, the past itself, becomes the possession of the literate culture. In
the case of Latin America, the creation of colonial societies through conquest and settlement was seen through the lens of European chronicles
and histories. Written from the victors' perspective, these accounts
enshrined a concept of European cultural superiority that persisted long
after the colonies became politically independent.

The origins of this colonial culture began with the chronicles and
histories written soon after the discovery of the Americas. In letters, reports,
and logs filled with inaccurate European and biblical references, Columbus made the first attempt to recast American realities according to European intellectual categories. The creation of this mythical New World
coincided with the conquest and settlement of the real America. Bernal
Díaz del Castillo, for example, identified the great cities of Mesoamerica
with places mentioned in the popular romance *Amadis of Gaul.* Not only
the reports of Cabeza de Vaca but also the mythological flight of seven Portuguese bishops from the invading Muslims stimulated Coronado's search
for the "Seven Cities of Cíbola."

The conquistadors were rough and generally unlettered men who wrote
few works of lasting historical or literary value. A major exception was the
foot soldier Bernal Díaz. His *True History of the Conquest of Mexico,* a highly
personal and readable narrative of the epic event, has been translated into
English, German, French, and Hungarian and still finds many readers.
Cortés's *Letters from Mexico* demonstrates his high intelligence and curiosity and provides an unequaled glimpse into the great leader's mind. Nicolaus Federmann, one of the Welsers' captains in Venezuela, and Pedro de
Valdivia, the conqueror of Chile, also left similar, although lesser-known,
chronicles of their exploits. A number of the participants in the conquest
of Peru later also wrote about their experiences. The most important
early chroniclers of Brazil were Pêro de Magalhães de Gândavo, the Jesuit
Fernão Cardim, and Gabriel Soares de Sousa.

Missionaries were anxious to discover and understand the languages, customs, and histories of the indigenous peoples. Although the results of their findings were uneven in quality and even the most important of their works found an extremely limited contemporary audience, many scholars still consult them. The writings of the Jesuits Manoel de Nobrega and José de Anchieta remain particularly valuable sources for Brazilian history. By 1572, at least 109 books to aid evangelization had been written in New Spain alone, most of them by Franciscans. Far from being pedantic scholarship, these and many similar works were intended to facilitate the process of conversion and cultural change.

The early churchmen also wrote a number of historical and ethnographic works, which were often marked by a genuine sympathy for the indigenous peoples as well as thoroughness and intellectual rigor. The Dominican Bartolomé de las Casas, bishop of Chiapas, exemplified this close identification with the plight of the conquered peoples. In his numerous writings he portrayed the Indians as innocent victims of Spanish cruelty. The Franciscan Fray Toribio de Benavente, known as Motolinía, wrote an extremely informative *Historia de los Indios de la Nueva España*. Other Franciscans of the first generation—friars Andrés de Olmos, Martín de la Coruña, and Francisco de las Navas—also wrote important ethnographic writings that later writers used with or without appropriate attribution. Fellow Franciscan Fray Bernardino de Sahagún put the learning of a lifetime of missionary work and study in Mexico in his monumental *Historia General de las Cosas de Nueva España*. Unfortunately, Philip II ordered the manuscript confiscated in 1577 as part of a general prohibition against published descriptions of native customs and superstitions. This effort to prevent the subversive effect such knowledge might have on Christian doctrine meant that Sahagún's *Historia General*, Motolinía's earlier completed *Historia*, or numerous other valuable ethnographic works were not published until centuries later. Felipe Guaman Poma de Ayala's depiction of Inca and colonial life in Peru was not printed until the twentieth century.

Education

Iberian settlers naturally wanted to raise their children in the religious and intellectual traditions of Europe. To avoid the high cost and danger of transatlantic travel, colonists established schools, seminaries, and universities in the New World. After the conversion of the native peoples, the Church achieved its greatest success in founding institutions that protected and transmitted the intellectual authority of Europe through education. By the end of the sixteenth century, most of the orders had shifted their scarce educational resources from the native nobility to meeting the needs of boys and young men from the Spanish and creole elites. The Jesuits, in particular, were successful in attracting to their *colegios* the sons of well-placed colonial families. They founded the first of ten *colegios* and four seminaries in Brazil in 1556; their first *colegio*, San Pablo, in Lima in 1568; and *colegios* in Mexico beginning in 1574.

Colegios offered courses in humanities, philosophy, theology, and languages. The school day was long, as students started at 7:45 A.M. and took courses and participated in mandatory religious services until after 5:00 P.M. By the early seventeenth century, San Pablo had five hundred students, and from the 1660s to the 1760s, it had over a thousand students.

In the Spanish colonies, settlers, ecclesiastics, and civil authorities pushed from an early date for the creation of universities. In 1551 the Crown authorized the founding of universities in Mexico City and Lima. Both were modeled on Spain's great University of Salamanca. During the sixteenth and seventeenth centuries, universities proliferated in the Spanish colonies, and by the end of the colonial period, well over twenty institutions had conferred nearly 150,000 university degrees. Ten "major" universities offered doctorates in all the conventional faculties: arts, theology, law, canon law, and medicine. The remaining "minor" universities conferred degrees in only some faculties, usually arts and theology, and were frequently run by the Jesuit or Dominican orders. Until the late eighteenth century, Aristotelian logic, metaphysics, and physics dominated the three-year arts curriculum.

In contrast with Spanish America, no university was established in colonial Brazil. Portugal had a well-established educational system, and so Brazil's most important thinkers and writers graduated from its prestigious University of Coimbra. The seventeenth-century Brazilian poet Gregorio de Matos, for example, was educated by the Jesuits in Bahia before studying at Coimbra, where he received a doctorate in law. One reason for the absence of a university in Brazil was the relative weakness of the Church. With only three bishoprics established by 1700, the potential patronage for learning and the opportunities for university graduates were limited.

At first, professorial appointments were based on the results of open competitions judged by the university's governing body, students, and alumni on the faculty. Cronyism and aspirants catering to students' taste, however, soon corrupted the system. As a result, by the late seventeenth century, the students had lost their vote in the selection process. Salaries were usually quite low and remained unchanged throughout the colonial era. Holding an academic chair, however, was both prestigious and a useful stepping-stone for ecclesiastical and secular preferment that complemented and at times replaced university employment.

Student bodies were composed solely of males, most of whom came from ambitious middle-class and well-to-do creole families in the capitals and provincial cities. By law the Indians, particularly Indian nobles, were permitted entry into universities, but few attended. The racially mixed children of wealthy or well-connected Spaniards had little trouble overcoming the racial proscriptions designed to exclude all persons with "tainted blood." Blacks and mulattoes had the greatest difficulty entering universities. They repeatedly met prejudice and protest and found it difficult to receive degrees even after completing the required course work and examinations.

By the end of the seventeenth century, the general intellectual level in the colonial universities, as in Castile, was very low. Professors often did not attend class or, when they did lecture, did so perfunctorily. In some cases they actually knew nothing about the subjects they were supposed to be teaching. The worst abuses in Mexico were associated with the chairs in Indian languages. In part the corruption of colonial universities was the natural result of the selfish vocationalism that drove ambitious youths to seek degrees, particularly in civil and canon law, required for some of the most desirable and powerful positions in the Church and state.

Books and Printing

Books were carried by the Iberian explorers, conquistadors, and settlers from the earliest days of colonization. Light reading, for example, romances of chivalry, found room in at least a few conquerors' luggage as they trekked across the New World. Clerics imported religious works that included breviaries, Bibles, and missals. Despite routine examination by the inquisitors of Seville and the colonial Inquisitions, prohibited literature also could be found in many libraries.

Although the literate colonial population of Spanish America continued to import a wide variety of books from Spain, the introduction of printing presses in the colonies enabled the publication of New World editions of Old World classics and also offered local authors an opportunity to see their prose and verse set for posterity. The first press in Mexico began publishing in the mid-1530s; its oldest extant book, a catechism in Spanish and Nahuatl, dates from 1539. By 1600 three hundred books had been published in the viceregal capital; a century later the number exceeded twenty-three hundred. Printing presses began functioning in Lima in 1583, Puebla in 1640, and Guatemala during the following year, although the Guatemalan experiment had to be renewed in 1660. In the eighteenth century, another fourteen cities boasted presses. Never allowed to compete seriously with Spanish publishers, the New World presses initially focused on works for evangelization and subsequently published a broader range of works, which included books on history, geography, law, medicine, and other fields. Numerous, and at times short-lived, newspapers appeared in the late eighteenth century.

Colonial publications in Spanish America were overwhelmingly religious. Churchmen, the most avid devotees of literature, published numerous sermons, theological studies, and works to assist evangelization, as well as biographies of outstanding clerics. Sermons were usually printed through the largesse of a benefactor interested in advancing the career or satisfying the ego of a particular cleric. By the mid-seventeenth century some sermons contained a strong element of creole self-consciousness. In New Spain this was particularly evident in works devoted to the Virgin of Guadalupe.

The audience for both colonial publications and imported books was extremely small. Probably no more than 10 percent of the colonial population was ever functionally literate, that is, actually used reading and writing skills. The active intellectual community was much smaller, probably never more than a few thousand at any one time. In the late seventeenth century, only a few hundred individuals in Mexico City participated in its intellectual life and were aware of the major controversies and new ideas that were stimulating the European intellectual community.

In contrast with Spanish America, no printing press was available in Brazil until 1808. As a result, Brazilian authors sent their works to Lisbon for publication. Without a printing press, the dissemination of ideas and the essential connection of writer and audience were nearly impossible. Without universities and their libraries, the concentrated intellectual energies of faculty and students, and the fiscal resources that they brought together, Brazil lacked the critical mass necessary to promote creative activity at the level found in the great cities of Spanish America. Although literary production was limited, the major themes and styles noted in Spanish America were nonetheless present.

Colonial Intellectuals

Despite the problem of isolation, censorship, and limited audience, Spanish America produced a number of significant intellectuals, although few of the first rank. This failure—if failure it was—resulted from the heavy weight of the colonial situation itself. The work of colonial intellectuals was necessarily derivative, imitating European style and theme. Originality was instead found in the evocation of the American landscape or the celebration of American heroes.

A number of works celebrated the heroic era of colonial history, such as *La Araucana* (1569), the epic poem by Alonso de Ercilla, and *Comentarios Reales de Los Incas* (1609), by the Peruvian mestizo Garcilaso de la Vega. The American themes of *La Araucana* and *Comentarios* were representative of what became a general pattern of increased creole self-confidence and self-consciousness in the Spanish colonies.

The outstanding seventeenth-century literary figure in Brazil was the Jesuit Antonio Vieira. Born in Lisbon in 1608, Father Vieira migrated to Brazil at the age of six and was educated at the Jesuit *colegio* in Salvador, Bahia. There he fought hard in the order's effort to improve the condition of Brazil's native peoples, and when he returned to Portugal to pursue this battle, his prose became well known in Europe.

The Baroque period, roughly the seventeenth and early eighteenth centuries in Latin America, was marked by great technical skill, exuberance in decoration, and a concern for the fabulous and supernatural. Entries in poetry tournaments, popular from the late sixteenth century, frequently demonstrated a Baroque spirit. This period also was characterized by a growing interest in nature, an interest pursued increasingly through rational inquiry and measurement. In the next century, this marginal intellectual direction gained in prestige, through the reflected glories of the European Enlightenment. Yet the triumph of rationalism and scientific method was never complete in Latin America.

The inherent tension between the competing claims of reason and religion that was typical of the Baroque can be detected in the lives of two of colonial Spanish America's great intellectuals. Pedro de Peralta y Barnuevo, eventually the rector of the University of San Marcos in Lima, was an early eighteenth-century mathematician and cosmographer known to contemporaries as a "monster of erudition." He also devoted himself to practical projects, such as supervising the city's fortifications. Yet toward the end of his life Peralta expressed disillusion with learning and worldly concerns. His last great work, *Passion and Triumph of Christ,* was an archetypical Baroque expression of religious enthusiasm that alleged that knowledge of God is not subject to rational inquiry.

The Mexican creole Carlos de Sigüenza y Góngora was an even more remarkable individual. His father had been tutor to a son of Philip IV, and his mother, also a Spanish immigrant, was related to the poet Luis de Góngora. Sigüenza entered the Society of Jesus as a youth in 1662 but was expelled for a breach of discipline. Although he later became a priest, his efforts to gain readmission to the Society failed. Turning to an academic career, he secured the chair of mathematics and astrology at the University of Mexico in 1672 at the age of twenty-five.

Sigüenza's achievements can be grouped into two broad categories, archaeology and history and mathematics and applied sciences. He learned Indian languages and collected artifacts and manuscripts. Most of his research on the indigenous civilizations of Mesoamerica was either not published or failed to survive, but we know that he examined topics as diverse as the ancient calendar and the genealogy of the Aztec royal house. He also wrote histories of the University of Mexico and the city cathedral. Although not a theoretical mathematician, Sigüenza made a well-recognized contribution to engineering projects and to astronomy. He owned a telescope with four lenses and labored tirelessly to measure the movement of heavenly bodies.

Sigüenza's interest in comets led him into a heated debate with the noted Jesuit Eusebio Kino. In this dispute the creole scholar upheld the role of reason and science against the authority of the classical sources and the Church fathers. Like other Baroque intellectuals, he did not find it necessary to resolve apparent contradictions between faith and science. In his history of the Corpus Christi convent, he uncritically narrated a series of miracles associated with the institution's development.

Sigüenza's final testament, like his life, left unresolved the contest between reason and superstition. He requested that surgeons examine his mortal remains to discover the cause of his painful death, leaving explicit suggestions as to which organs might hold the key. At the same time, he noted that he owned a hat worn by Francisco de Aguiar y Seijas, a deceased friend and the former archbishop of Mexico. Because some sick people had experienced relief when they touched the hat, Sigüenza provided for it to be placed in a church where the sick could continue to seek its miraculous powers.

The most remarkable colonial intellectual of the Baroque was the Mexican nun Sister Juana Inés de la Cruz (1651–95). An illegitimate child from a modest provincial family, the precocious and beautiful young woman attracted the attention and patronage of the viceroy's wife. Despite these advantages, she entered a Carmelite convent at age fifteen. Unhappy with this order's strict discipline, she left it for a Jeronymite convent, where she remained until her death.

Unlike most of the colonial period's literature, Sister Juana's poetry still finds an audience. Its durability is largely the result of her mastery of the lyric form and the emotion and intelligence that it communicates. Unlike

Partrait of Sor Juna Jres de la Cruz used as fronttispice in a biography published in 17000.

many of her contemporaries, Sister Juana escaped the deadening habit of mere verbal cleverness and decoration. Her best verse illuminates the inherent tension and conflict between the claims of reason and emotion and the claims of science and revelation:

> My soul is confusedly divided into two parts,
> One a slave to passion, the other
> measured by reason.
> Inflamed civil war importunately
> afflicts my bosom. Each part
> strives to prevail, and amidst
> such varied storms, both contenders
> will perish, and neither one will triumph.[14]

Sister Juana was also aware of the unequal and unfair burdens she carried because of her sex. Indeed, some of her critics viewed her passion for knowledge and willingness to question as rebellious and unfeminine. Given her personal history, her questioning of society's double standard was particularly powerful:

> Which has the greater sin when burned
> by the same lawless fever:
> She who is amorously deceived,
> or he, the sly deceiver?[15]

As her fame increased and her work, much of it secular, won an audience in the Old World as well as the New, Sister Juana was criticized by some religious authorities: Members of her order, her confessor, and the hierarchy, including the bishop of Puebla, revealed their displeasure. In 1693, after going through a period of self-doubt and unhappiness, she finally gave up her unequal struggle with the representatives of conservative opinion in the Church. She renounced her worldly possessions, including her beloved library and mathematical and musical instruments, signing what was in effect a surrender in her own blood: "I, Sister Juana Inés de la Cruz, the worst in the world." Turning to a harsh discipline of fasting and mortification of the flesh, her health declined rapidly, and she died in 1695.

Popular Culture

Most of colonial society experienced cultural life in forms different from those enjoyed by the literate population. The statutory and material subordination of the colonial masses resulted naturally in the devaluation of the artistic and intellectual values that survived from the indigenous or African cultures or were created along with an evolving creole folk culture. Yet, despite the elite's prejudice and the limited resources, elements of these minority cultural traditions did contribute in important ways to the artistic and literary development of Latin America.

Because the masses were denied access to a formal education, the popular culture escaped some of the inhibitions found in the works of the great creole intellectuals. Illiteracy and, in many cases, cultural distinctiveness permitted a cultural independence and exuberance denied to the completely Hispanized and educated minority. As a result, dance, music, theater, and, to a lesser extent, literature in Latin America carry the thematic, rhythmic, and mythological imprint of the popular culture.

Because the culture of Christian Spain was officially that of the colonies, the popular culture developed by expropriating some of the forms of symbols sanctioned by Church and state. The people created a tradition that celebrated their values and needs by insinuation rather than conflict. The forms most susceptible to this process were dance, religious theater, music, and the *máscara* or *mascarada*. The *máscara* was a parade of costumed men and women, sometimes associated with a theme and sometimes not. Over time, these various forms of expression developed rules of style and theme, one being a tendency to lampoon the pretensions and conceits of the metropolitan culture.

One *máscara* in Puebla, New Spain's second city, included a float on which effigies of the viceroy and his wife were beaten. Lesser public officials and even religious leaders often shared this humiliation. It was also common for social conventions to be stood on their head. For example, dressing as a member of the opposite sex was a popular feature of *máscaras*. Even within the more constrained confines of religious processions and plays, the people found opportunities to express their cultural distinctiveness. One scholar has found strong evidence of rites associated with Huitzilopochtli in the celebrations devoted to the Virgin de la Soledad. Folk music and dance also helped perpetuate native American or African traditions and represented the struggle of the colonial masses for dignity and autonomy.

Popular dances and songs manifested sentiments and values that colonial officials, inquisitors, and clerics often found offensive and in bad taste. One document of the Mexican Inquisition characterized the dances and accompanying lyrics of the lower classes as "lewd and provocative of lasciviousness, causing grave ruin and scandal to the souls of Christendom and in prejudice to the conscience . . . and [were an] offence [*sic*] to edification and good customs."[16] In similar language, the Bishop of Oaxaca lamented that the dances "are not only occasions to sin, but also are sinful in and of themselves . . . because of the lasciviousness of the words, the gestures and movements, the nudity of the dancers, the reciprocal touching of men and women, by taking place in suspicious lower class houses, in the country, in poorly lit neighborhoods at night, and at times when the judges cannot discover them."[17]

Spanish and Portuguese authorities attempted to repress the musical tradition of Africa brought to the New World with the slave trade. Both colonial administrators and the clergy saw these African legacies as potentially subversive and sought to promote European musical traditions by recruiting musicians from the black community. As early as the 1560s the Lima city council was receiving repeated complaints about black slaves beating drums and dancing in the streets without inhibition. It responded by trying to limit dancing to two plazas, but these efforts were never very effective as blacks continued to sing, dance, swear, and gamble throughout the city. Music and public dances (the *candombes*) held by Afro-Argentines in Buenos Aires in the latter half of the eighteenth century also caught the attention of public authorities. The viceroy granted permission to allow the Congo and Cambundá ethnic fellowships to hold dances on Sundays and holidays despite repeated complaints that the dancers engaged in immoral movements. Some of these dances attracted as many as two thousand participants; one Easter blacks dancing outside a church were so loud that the priest could not conduct services. Drummers and other musicians using percussive instruments provided music that the white population usually disliked. One

A group of musicians and dancers in the streets of Trujillo, Peru.

traveler in the 1770s recorded that the sound was so "annoying and dis-agreeable as to provoke one to stop up his ears and to cause the mules to stampede, and they are the most stolid and least flighty of animals."[18]

Before the Conquest, Indian cultures employed singing and ritual danc-ing in feasts and ceremonies honoring their deities, and music and dance persisted as a part of native culture throughout the colonial period. Indigenous music in the Andes, for example, employed several varieties of handmade wooden flutes, a type of small guitar, a base drum, a tam-bourine, and a native harp. The seven-hole bamboo flute (*quena*) was par-ticularly popular with men tending flocks and accompanied sweet and melancholy chants (*yaravís*) that professional musicians later turned into songs performed at home by young women from elite families. It was from this conflicted process of cultural synthesis that Latin American popular music originated.

Like music, the theater provided entertainment enjoyed by every segment of society. Initially plays were performed in church courtyards as clerics sought to instruct through entertainment. Free-standing theaters followed, however, and in Lima one known as the "Corral de las Comedias" opened in 1604. Seventeenth-century productions included such plays as "Noah's Ark" and "Love in Lima Is Fortuitous." Other theaters followed, but the Col-iseo de Comedias reconstructed following the earthquake of 1746 was the most important. Small towns also enjoyed theater; in the Peruvian munici-pality of Pisco, for example, an amateur group of mulatto actors presented a play, "The Powerful Prince," in honor of the Feast of the Scapulary. The quality of productions varied, with one of the most scathing evaluations pro-vided by a French traveler who attended the theater in Caracas at the beginning of the nineteenth century. "All the pieces, in themselves most wretched, are, moreover, miserably performed. The declamation of this the-atre . . . is a species of monotonous stammering, very like the tone in which an infant of ten years old recites a badly studied lesson. No grace, no action, no inflection of voice, not a single natural gesture; in a word, nothing of that which constitutes the actor of a common theatre."[19]

Festivals, theater, music, and dance punctuated the lives of the colonial populace. The lubricant of everyday life, however, was gossip. Whether res-ident in a major city, small town, or mining camp, people talked. Their conversations often focused on people: themselves and their families, rel-atives, friends, and compatriots. Residents promptly queried any stranger arriving in town in an effort to find out a person's home region or *tierra*, occupation, and reasons for traveling. Once *tierra* was established, conver-sation turned to other persons from the same locale. Rumors and innu-endos grew with repeated telling, and no town was so out of the way that serious personal indiscretions could remain unknown. Muleteers, peddlers, migrant workers, and travelers of all sorts purveyed news of those they had seen elsewhere. One of the few known colonial diaries provides great detail that clearly passed from mouth to mouth. One revealing entry reported the death of one Don José Félix de Agüero as follows. "The first word to come from his house at dawn was that he had hanged himself from a water storage rack. Later, word circulated that he had choked from phlegm."[20] In short, curiosity and idle talk combined to fuel still more conversation in an incessant exchange of information, rumor, and potential scandal.

The high culture of colonial Latin America's largest cities was overwhelmingly derivative in nature. Intellectuals and artists looked to Europe for inspiration and hoped to win European acclaim for their work. Despite the continued European influence, however, colonial intellectual life developed a unique character. An inherent tension between the pride colonial intellectuals felt in the New World's unique environment and history and their deference to European canons of taste led some to defend angrily their native regions against European critics. This was manifested in the study of the great indigenous civilizations and in an enthusiasm for natural history.

The evolution of authentically Latin American cultural traditions depended more on popular forms of dance, music, theater, and humor that blended elements of indigenous, European, and African experience. These popular forms of cultural expression often met resistance or repression from colonial authorities. Commonly these clumsy forms of opposition stimulated new sources of creative energy as common men and women disguised or adapted cultural forms that had been banned. Eventually, in intellectual life and popular culture, as in the marketplace, men and women grew restive within the constraints of the colonial order.

Notes

1. Jorge Juan and Antonio de Ulloa, *A Voyage to South America* [abridged], The John Adams Translation (New York: Alfred A. Knopf, 1964), p. 181.

2. Thomas Gage, *Thomas Gage's Travels in the New World*. Edited by J. Eric Thompson (Norman: University of Oklahoma Press, 1958), p. 221.

3. Juan and de Ulloa, *Voyage to South America*, p. 206.

4. Nancy M. Farriss, *Maya Society Under Colonial Rule: The Collective Enterprise of Survival* (Princeton, N.J.: Princeton University Press, 1984), p. 94.

5. Quotation from Rebecca Earle, "Luxury, Clothing and Race in Colonial Latin America," in Maxine Berg and Elizabeth Eger, (eds.), *Luxury in the Eighteenth Century: Debates, Desires, and Delectable Goods* (Oxford: Macmillan, 2003), pp. 220–21.

6. Quotation from Rebecca Earle, "'Two Pairs of Pink Satin Shoes!!' Race, Clothing and Identity in the Americas (17th–19th Centuries)," *History Workshop Journal* 52 (2001), p. 183.

7. Robert Ryal Miller, translator and editor, *Chronicle of Colonial Lima: The Diary of Joseph and Francisco Mugaburu, 1640–1697* (Norman: University of Oklahoma Press, 1975), p. 92

8. Juan and Ulloa, *Voyage to South America*, p. 201.

9. Antonio Vázquez de Espinosa, *Compendium and Description of the West Indies,*

translated by Charles Upson Clark (Washington, D.C.: Smithsonian Institution, 1942), p. 428.

10. Cited in Peter Bakewell, *Silver and Entrepreneurship in Seventeenth-Century Potosí: The Life and Times of Antonio López de Quiroga* (Albuquerque: University of New Mexico Press, 1988), p. 145.

11. John Tate Lanning, *The Royal Protomedicato: The Regulation of the Medical Professions in the Spanish Empire*. Edited by John Jay TePaske (Durham, N.C.: Duke University Press, 1985), p. 309.

12. Ibid., pp. 226–27.

13. Ilarione da Bergamo, *Daily Life in Colonial Mexico: The Journey of Friar Ilarione da Bergamo, 1761–1768*. Edited by Robert Ryal Miller and William J. Orr. Translated by William J. Orr (Norman: University of Oklahoma Press, 2000), pp. 121–23.

14. Irving A. Leonard, *Baroque Times in Old Mexico* (Ann Arbor: University of Michigan Press, 1959), p. 178.

15. Ibid., p. 189.

16. Quoted in Sergio Rivera Ayala, "Lewd Songs and Dances from the Streets of Eighteenth-Century New Spain," in William H. Beezley, Cheryl English Martin, and William E. French (editors), *Rituals of Rule, Rituals of Resistance* (Wilmington, Del.: Scholarly Resources, 1994), p. 31.

17. Quoted in Ibid., p. 40.

18. Concolorcorvo quoted in George Reid Andrews, *The Afro-Argentines of Buenos Aires, 1800–1900* (Madison: University of Wisconsin Press, 1980), p. 167.

19. F. Depons, *Travels in South America, During the Years 1801, 1802, 1803, and 1804* (2 vols., London: 1807; reprinted by AMS Press, Inc., New York, 1970), II, p. 177.

20. Miller, *Chronicle of Colonial Lima*, p. 147.

Suggested for Further Reading

Bailey, Gauvin Alexander. *Art of Colonial Latin America*. London and New York: Phaidon, 2005.

Baker, Geoffrey. *Imposing Harmony: Music and Society in Colonial Cuzco*. Durham: Duke University Press, 2008.

Barickman, B. J. A. *Bahian Counterpoint: Sugar, Tobacco, Cassava, and Slavery in the Recôncavo, 1780–1860*. Stanford: Stanford University Press, 1998.

Baudot, Georges. *Utopia and History in Mexico: The First Chronicles of Mexican Civilization, 1520–1569*. Translated by Bernard R. Ortiz de Montellano and Thelma Ortiz de Montellano. Niwot: University Press of Colorado, 1995.

Bauer, Arnold J. *Goods, Power, History: Latin America's Material Culture*. Cambridge, England, and New York: Cambridge University Press, 2001.

Beezley, William H., Cheryl English Martin, and William E. French, editors. *Rituals of Rule, Rituals of Resistance: Public Celebrations and Popular Culture in Mexico*. Wilmington, Del.: Scholarly Resources, 1994.

Bergamo, Ilarione da. *Daily Life in Colonial Mexico: The Journey of Friar Ilarione da Bergamo, 1761–1768*. Edited by Robert Ryal Miller and William J. Orr; Translated by William J. Orr. Norman: University of Oklahoma Press, 2000.

Bleichmar, Daniela, Paula De Vos, Kristin Huffine, and Kevin Sheehan, *Science in the Spanish and Portuguese Empires, 1500–1800*. Stanford: Stanford University Press, 2008.

Boyer, Richard, and Geoffrey Spurling, editors. *Colonial Lives: Documents on Latin American History, 1550–1850*. New York: Oxford University Press, 2000.

Boyer, Richard. *Lives of the Bigamists: Marriage, Family, and Community in Colonial Mexico*. Albuquerque: University of New Mexico Press, 1995.

Brading, D. A. *The First America: The Spanish Monarchy, Creole Patriots, and the Liberal State, 1492–1867*. Cambridge, England: Cambridge University Press, 1991.

Cañizares-Esguerra, Jorge. *How to Write the History of the New World: Histories, Epistemologies, and Identities in the Eighteenth-Century Atlantic World*. Stanford Stanford University Press, 2001.

Carlyon, Jonathan E. *Andrés Gonzalez de Barcia and the Creation of the Colonial Spanish American Library*. Toronto: University of Toronto Press, 2005.

Carrera, Magali M. *Imagining Identity in New Spain: Race, Lineage, and the Colonial Body in Portraiture and Casta Paintings*. Austin: University of Texas Press, 2003.

Curcio-Nagy, Linda A. *The Great Festivals of Colonial Mexico City: Performing Power and Identity*. Albuquerque: University of New Mexico Press, 2004.

Dean, Carolyn. *Inka Bodies and the Body of Christ: Corpus Christi in Colonial Cuzco, Peru*. Durham: Duke University Press, 1999.

Donahue-Wallace, Kelly. *Art and Architecture of Viceregal Latin America, 1521–1821*. Albuquerque: University of New Mexico Press, 2008.

Ganson, Barbara Anne. *The Guaraní under Spanish Rule in the Río de la Plata*. Stanford: Stanford University Press, 2003.

Garrett, David. *Shadows of Empire: The Indian Nobility of Cusco, 1750–1825*. Cambridge, England: Cambridge University Press, 2005.

Haslip-Viera, Gabriel. *Crime and Punishment in Late Colonial Mexico City, 1692–1810*. Albuquerque: University of New Mexico Press, 1999.

Hoberman, Louisa Schell, and Susan Migden Socolow, editors. *Cities and Society in Colonial Latin America*. Albuquerque: University of New Mexico Press, 1986.

Hoberman, Louisa Schell, and Susan Migden Socolow, editors. *The Countryside in Colonial Latin America*. Albuquerque: University of New Mexico Press, 1996.

Juan, Jorge, and Antonio de Ulloa. *A Voyage to South America*. Tempe: Arizona State University Press, 1975.

Kagan, Richard L. *Urban Images of the Hispanic World, 1493–1793*. New Haven, and London: Yale University Press, 2000.

Katzew, Ilona. *Casta Painting: Images of Race in Eighteenth-Century Mexico*. New Haven, and London: Yale University Press, 2004.

Kinsbruner, Jay. *The Colonial Spanish-American City: Urban Life in the Age of Atlantic Capitalism*. Austin: University of Texas Press, 2005.

Lanning, John Tate. *The Royal Protomedicato: The Regulation of the Medical Profession in the Spanish Empire*. Edited by John Jay TePaske. Durham, N.C.: Duke University Press, 1985.

Lavrin, Asunción. *Brides of Christ: Conventual Life in Colonial Mexico*. Stanford, Calif.: Stanford University Press, 2008.

Lockhart, James. *The Nahuas After the Conquest: A Social and Cultural History of the Indians of Central Mexico, Sixteenth Through Eighteenth Centuries*. Stanford, Calif.: Stanford University Press, 1992.

Mangan, Jane E. *Trading Roles: Gender, Ethnicity, and the Urban Economy in Colonial Potosí*. Durham, N.C.: Duke University Press, 2005.

Martin, Cheryl English. *Governance and Society in Colonial Mexico: Chihuahua in the Eighteenth Century*. Stanford: Stanford University Press, 1996.

Miller, Robert Ryal, editor. *Chronicle of Colonial Lima: The Diary of Joseph and Francisco Mugaburu, 1640–1697*. Norman: University of Oklahoma Press, 1975.

Mundy, Barbara E. *The Mapping of New Spain: Indigenous Cartography and the Maps of the Relaciones Geográficas*. Chicago: University of Chicago Press, 1996.

Norton, Marcy. *Sacred Gifts, Profane Pleasures: A History of Tobacco and Chocolate in the Atlantic World*. Ithaca: Cornell University Press, 2008.

Núñez, Fernando, Carlos Arvizu and Ramón Abonce. *Space and Place in the Mexican Landscape: The Evolution of a Colonial City*. College Station: Texas A&M University Press, 2007.

Osorio, Alejandra B. *Inventing Lima: Baroque Modernity in Peru's South Sea Metropolis*. New York: Palgrave Macmillan, 2008.

Pagden, Anthony. *Spanish Imperialism and the Political Imagination: Studies in European and Spanish-American Social and Political Theory, 1513–1830*. New Haven and London Yale University Press, 1990.

Pierce, Donna, Rogelio Ruiz Gomar, and Clara Bargellini. *Painting a New World: Mexican Art and Life, 1521–1821*. Denver: Frederick and Jan Mayer Center for Pre-Columbian and Spanish Colonial Art, Denver Art Museum, 2004.

Poma de Ayala, Felipe Guaman. *The First New Chronicle and Good Government: On the History of the World and the Incas up to 1615*. Austin: University of Texas Press, 2009.

Querejazu, Pedro, and Elizabeth Ferrer, curators. *Potosí: Colonial Treasures and the Bolivian City of Silver*. New York: Americas Society Art Gallery in association with Fundación BHN, La Paz, 1997.

Trusted, Marjorie. *The Arts of Spain: Iberia and Latin America 1450–1700*. University Park: Pennsylvania State University Press, 2007.

Viqueira Albán, Juan Pedro. *Propriety and Permissiveness in Bourbon Mexico*. Translated by Sonya Lipsett-Rivera and Sergio Rivera Ayala. Wilmington, Del.: Scholarly Resources, 1999.

Voekel, Pamela. *Alone Before God: The Religious Origins of Modernity in Mexico*. Durham, Duke University Press, 2002.

Walker, Charles. *Shaky Colonialism: The 1746 Earthquake-Tsunami in Lima, Peru, and its Long Aftermath*. Durham: Duke University Press, 2008.

NINE

IMPERIAL EXPANSION

Chronology

The Spanish Colonies, 1680s to 1762

The death of Charles II in 1700 provoked the War of the Spanish Succession. Aided by his grandfather, Louis XIV of France, Philip V, the designated heir, was confirmed as monarch by the Treaty of Utrecht in 1713. The first Bourbon king confronted a deterioration of trade, revenue, and administrative control worsened by the conflict. Although the empire's population increased slowly, the consumption of legal imports remained at low levels. One important reason for this commercial stagnation was the aggressive intervention of foreign traders, especially the French. In addition, empirewide mining production reached its nadir during this period. Mexican silver output grew, but the increase failed to overcome a drop in Peruvian silver production.

Philip V faced familiar problems: how to increase American tax revenues, how to protect the empire, and how to expand Spain's commercial relationship with the colonies. More efficient administration, better revenue collection, an effective defense, and the elimination of contraband were related objectives. An improved defense required greater revenue which in turn required the reinvigoration of legal transatlantic trade. A more effective administrative system was a clear precondition in order for the Crown to gain the greatest benefit from efforts to increase revenue. Between 1713 and 1762, the Crown took a number of steps to realize these objectives. It generally pursued the conservative strategy of seeking to eliminate abuses, rather than attempting structural change. However, some new policies were dictated by the financial and defensive requirements arising from war or the threat of it.

War, Foreign Threats, and the Empire

French pressure during the War of the Spanish Succession forced the new Bourbon monarch Philip V to grant his ally commercial access to New World trade. This marked an important legal break in Spain's long-defended claim to monopolistic control over colonial trade. The Treaty of Utrecht gave the English, who had opposed Philip's succession, important economic concessions—the *asiento*, a monopoly contract to import slaves, and the annual ship. A quarter-century of recrimination between Spain and England over contraband trade associated with these privileges finally culminated in the War of Jenkins' Ear (1739–48).

A dispute between Spain and Portugal over colonial boundaries resulted in a conflict over the Portuguese Colônia do Sacramento on the Río de la Plata in the first half of the eighteenth century. The Treaty of Madrid in 1750 called for an exchange of territory, but the failure to implement the provisions fully led to nullification of the agreement and a renewed but inconclusive war. The issue was far from resolved when Charles III became king in 1759.

New Spain's northern boundary of occupied territory, although sparsely settled, expanded substantially in the late seventeenth and early eighteenth centuries. Threats from the Indians, the French, and the English underscored the need to provide additional defense in the borderlands. The Jesuits established missions in northwestern New Spain as far north as Arizona. After the loss to Indian forces in the disastrous Pueblo revolt of 1680, New Mexico was not resettled until the 1690s. In Texas a series of missions and garrisons were built in the early 1720s as a buffer against French threats to northern Mexico. The establishment of a fort on Pensacola Bay in 1698 and its return to Spain in 1722, after two and one-half years of French occupation, solidified the Spanish presence on the northern Gulf coast. However, French traders remained in Louisiana. In Florida the successful defense of St. Augustine against the English during the wars of the Spanish Succession and Jenkins' Ear emphasized the importance of this northern redoubt in New Spain's defensive perimeter.

Challenges to Spanish authority in the Viceroyalty of Peru led to a major administrative reorganization. The vulnerability to enemy attack of lands adjoining the Caribbean and the problem of contraband trade led the Crown to create a third viceroyalty, out of the northern portions of the Viceroyalty of Peru. The new Viceroyalty of New Granada combined the *audiencia* districts of Santa Fe de Bogotá and Quito and the coastal districts of Venezuela. Initially established in 1717 and suspended six years later, New Granada was permanently reestablished in 1739. In this final organization, New Granada also gained jurisdiction over Panama.

Administrative Reforms: An Uneven Course

After gaining international recognition of his rule in 1713, Philip then pursued military victory over Catalonia, which in 1705 had joined the rest of the Crown of Aragon in supporting the Habsburg claimant Archduke Charles. Peace enabled the monarch to consolidate his authority in Spain. He immediately indicated that the Habsburg's patrimonial approach to ruling would yield to a more unitary and centralized vision, by terminating the autonomy of the Crown of Aragon in 1716. Tighter control, more efficient administration, a reduction in special privileges that ran counter to royal financial and political interests, and the greater centralization of authority in Madrid were the order of the day for Spain. The same approach would be extended to the colonies in the succeeding decades.

Philip V appointed secretaries of state with specific responsibilities that cut deeply into those previously exercised by councils. In this administrative reform, the Council of the Indies lost a great deal of its authority after 1717. Although it remained unchallenged in its judicial powers and continued to enjoy patronage over judicial and ecclesiastical positions, the council lost power to the secretary of state for the Indies in financial, military, commercial, and general administrative matters. Henceforth one person—the secretary—rather than a committee was responsible for general oversight of the Indies.

Besides restructuring colonial administration at court, the Crown made several efforts to improve administration in the Indies. New Spain, the major source of American bullion since the 1660s and the most populous colony in the New World, received increased attention. Beginning in 1710 Philip sent a series of special investigators to examine the viceroyalty's administrative institutions and to secure additional revenues to support his wartime expenses. For more than two decades these agents found accounts in arrears, evidence of fraud, and numerous other abuses. These royal agents proved better at identifying than rectifying abuses, however.

From the late seventeenth century to the mid-eighteenth century, the fiscal demands of war repeatedly frustrated efforts at administrative reform in the colonies. The systematic sale of appointments to *audiencia* positions that began in 1687 continued until 1750. During this period, efforts to gain control over the courts by appointing meritorious outsiders floundered with each outbreak of war. Renewed sales brought a rush of purchasers who, particularly in Peru, erased the modest gains. Beginning in the 1750s, however, improved finances enabled the Crown to stop selling *audiencia* appointments and slowly to start regaining authority. Probably over 80 percent of the creoles but scarcely 10 percent of the peninsulars named from 1687 to 1750 purchased their initial *audiencia* appointments. Almost 40 percent of the Americans named, moreover, were native sons, men appointed to the tribunal located in their region of birth.

The termination of sales at mid-century began a decline in the number of native sons, and before 1763 the new direction of appointments was unmistakable. Of twenty new men named, only four were creoles. The simultaneous royal reluctance to permit additional ministers to establish local ties set the stage for a dramatic assault in the 1770s on the remaining native sons and *radicados,* or locally rooted ministers.

The continued sale of appointments to provincial administrative positions until the mid-eighteenth century undercut intermittent efforts to control exploitation of the natives by provincial administrators. Indeed, the cost of an appointment intensified the financial pressure on purchasers and undoubtedly resulted in even greater abuse of office, especially the forced sale of goods to Indian communities. In response to a situation that its own actions had exacerbated, the Crown attempted in 1751 to regulate the prices that officials could charge for forced sales to Indian communities. Its efforts to curb abuse failed, however, and the much resented exploitation continued unabated.

The Crown sought also to improve revenue collection. The Habsburgs had relied on tax farming for the collection of taxes. In contrast, the Bourbons gradually began to place tax collection directly in the hands of royal bureaucrats. Early moves in this direction affected the powerful *consulados* of Lima and Mexico City. In 1724 the Crown assumed direct control over the *alcabala* and other commercial taxes long administered by Lima's *consulado.* Thirty years later it extended this approach to Mexico.

Demographic Expansion

The population of the Spanish colonies as a whole increased during the first half of the eighteenth century. Precise data for the period are not available, but a number of regional examples point toward demographic expansion. The population of New Spain, for example, grew by nearly 50 percent between the mid-seventeenth and mid-eighteenth centuries. The growing Spanish and *casta* populations accounted for a disproportionately large share of this increase, although the Indian population was also growing. The native population of Peru fell briefly as a result of severe epidemics in the 1720s, but growth resumed by mid-century. Caracas grew slowly but steadily throughout the early eighteenth century and by mid-century had perhaps 30,000 people. Buenos Aires increased from a population of about 11,600 in 1744 to 26,125 in 1778. Chile increased from 95,000 people in 1700 to 184,000 in 1755. In Cuba, the population perhaps tripled between 1700 and 1760, numbering some 160,000 in the latter year. The only notable exception to this pattern of significant demographic expansion was the *audiencia* district of Quito. Its population scarcely grew during the century and its capital city, with a population of just over 20,000 at the close of the century, was perhaps only half as large as it had been during the latter half of the seventeenth century. With this exception, however, the growing availability of labor and a larger pool of consumers stimulated both greater economic production and increased trade.

Mining

The combined registered silver production of New Spain and Peru reached a very low level in the 1690s and did not improve until the 1720s. Conditions were different, however, in the two viceroyalties. After 1670 New Spain emerged as the premier silver producer. Buoyed by increased mercury supplies from Spain and rising silver production at Zacatecas, Mexico's output climbed in the 1670s and 1680s before falling until the 1710s. Registered production then reached new highs in each subsequent decade and averaged over 10 million pesos a year in the 1750s. A shortage of mercury in the early 1760s brought a temporary decline, but new production records were set in each following decade to 1810.

Registered silver production in Peru hit bottom between 1701 and 1720 but then began to improve. Accelerated by the 1736 reduction in the tax rate from a fifth to a tenth, registered production rose in each subsequent decade to the end of the century. Despite the recovery, Peru's production never came close to that of New Spain. The northern viceroyalty was producing roughly twice as much silver as Peru was at mid-century, and this margin had increased by 1800.

Estimated gold production based on official sources in seventeenth-century Colombia was worth only a small fraction, well under 10 percent, of Peru's registered silver production, although actual production was probably much more than that amount. In the eighteenth century, gold production set new records each decade and may well have been triple the amount for the previous century. Elsewhere, gold mining regained ground in Chile in the 1690s and increased throughout most of the eighteenth century. Gold production also grew in Mexico and Peru, although their combined total was always less than that of New Granada.

Remission of Bullion and Imperial Profit

Mexico's replacement of Peru as the foremost silver-producing viceroyalty after 1670 was reflected in the amount of public revenues sent to Castile. Between 1651 and 1660, Peru sent 8.6 million pesos to the metropolis, and New Spain sent 4.3 million. In the 1660s, New Spain's remissions exceeded Peru's. By the decade from 1741 to 1750, Peruvian remissions had fallen to 500,000 pesos, whereas those from New Spain had increased to 6.4 million. In the following decade, New Spain's contribution rose to over 16 million pesos, while Peru sent nothing.

Bullion remitted to Spain was only one source of revenue that the Crown derived from the Indies. Comparing the remission of bullion from New Spain and Peru with figures from Cádiz's treasury office records for the Indies reveals that the bullion regularly provided less than 40 percent of the funds collected. Peninsular taxes on the Indies' trade and various fees, fines, and loans collected on the peninsula contributed, from 1731 to 1770, up to three-quarters of the revenues. The highest average revenues were collected during the reign of Ferdinand VI (1746–59) and thus coincided closely with the higher level of silver production in New Spain.

Although the significance of American bullion for both the Spanish Crown and the expansion of European trade around the world was immense, its glitter has unfairly overshadowed an even more important source of royal revenue for much of the eighteenth century. The Crown created a royal monopoly over Cuban tobacco in 1717. Although the contraband sale of Cuban tobacco was often triple the amount of tobacco sent legally to Spain in the 1720s and 1730s, the monopoly made enormous profits from processing and selling the Cuban leaf. From 1740 to 1760 about 85 percent of the tobacco processed by the royal factory in Seville came from Cuba. This monopoly produced annual profits that grew from nearly 4 million pesos in the early 1740s to over 5 million by the late 1750s. Profits from the tobacco monopoly in the 1740s, in other words, exceeded the revenues remitted from New Spain and Peru by more than 400 percent. In the 1750s, the royal income from the tobacco monopoly was still more than twice as large as the extraordinarily high remissions of bullion.

Commerce

The transfer of the House of Trade from Seville to Cádiz in 1717 once again brought together administrators, merchants, and ships in a single port. José Patiño, for example, was an administrative official in the navy and president of the House of Trade in the same year, thereby demonstrating the Crown's recognition that seapower and commerce went together. Later secretary of state for the Indies, navy, and treasury, Patiño tried to strengthen Spain through greater commercial exploitation of the empire.

Under Patiño's leadership, Spain pursued a mercantilist economic policy. Spain had traditionally sought to exclude European rivals from colonial trade in order to ensure its monopoly of bullion. After the 1730s this policy was tied to an effort to promote American production outside the mining sector. Because importing goods from sources outside the empire upset the balance of trade, mercantilist policies encouraged, for example, sugar production in Cuba and cacao production in Venezuela.

Although the Crown had allowed two small ships to sail each year from Seville to Buenos Aires beginning in 1618 and had always permitted a modest number of single ships to transport goods to the Indies, it refrained until the eighteenth century from authorizing major changes in the fleet system. Beginning in 1701, French ships were allowed to stop at Indies ports for repairs and provisions, which opened the door to illicit trade with Peruvian and Chilean ports. The value of French ships for defense against England and the impossibility of providing regular fleet service during the War of the Spanish Succession prevented the suppression of this contraband. By 1724, 150 French ships had sailed for Spain's Pacific coast colonies. On occasion colonial officials blatantly skimmed off a percentage of the profit. The quantity of merchandise lowered prices and spelled ruin for the long-decadent fleet system going through Portobelo and the isthmus of Panama. It also weakened the Lima merchant class, and, since European cloth was the major item imported, added to the woes of the declining textile industry in Ecuador. The Treaty of Utrecht granted the *asiento* to the South Sea Company which established a commercial post in Buenos Aires. From 1715 to 1738, over sixty English ships entered this port carrying slaves and an unknown quantity of merchandise. In addition, illicit goods funneled to Buenos Aires through Portuguese Colônia further diminished the markets for legal goods shipped through Lima.

The annual ship authorized by the *asiento* for the Portobelo fair also caused difficulty for Spanish merchants. The English sent a larger ship than authorized and sold their less expensive textiles tax free. Because English goods sold for 30 percent less than did goods imported by Spanish merchants, the appearance of an English ship at the fairs of 1722, 1726, 1729, and 1731 disrupted the market. Competition from French and English goods dramatically altered traditional commercial ties between Peru and Spain.

In 1720 the Crown stated its desire to reestablish an effective fleet system. This effort to reinstate regular fleet sailings also expanded the use of single, licensed ships sailing directly from Cádiz to designated Atlantic ports. Ironically, this provision undercut the larger objective of maintaining a fleet system, for it challenged the high transportation costs and monopoly prices of the trade fairs at Portobelo and Vera Cruz. Buenos Aires, in particular, benefited from the greater use of register ships. Through it flowed goods to Upper Peru and Chile, although such transfers required special permission. As a consequence, Peru was less well stocked than Chile was. Faced with a shrunken market, the *consulado* merchants in Lima, some of whom engaged in contraband trade, opposed holding new fairs.

Although seven fleets sailed to Vera Cruz and four to Portobelo between 1717 and 1738, single ships sailing with purchased licenses transported over 20 percent of the total transatlantic tonnage. The outbreak of the War of Jenkins' Ear, however, marked the true transition from the fleet system to reliance on register ships. With Portobelo destroyed and the fleet system for South America moribund, the Crown in 1740 extended the use of register ships to the Pacific. The change arose from the sensible belief that fast single ships could more easily escape English naval squadrons than could convoys.

The length of the war also demonstrated that register ships provided faster and more dependable transportation. Purchased permits authorized register ships to sail from any Spanish port to any South American port between Concepción and Callao. Nearly twenty ships reached Callao by 1748, and over thirty-five more by 1761. The quantity of merchandise reaching Chile and Peru was so great that only by lowering prices and raising the pressure on the Indians through forced purchases could the merchants sell their wares. One contemporary in Lima reported that "the convents are filled with merchants who have closed their doors and declared themselves bankrupt."[1] Merchants who were no longer protected from competition by means of monopoly sought a return to the fleet system. The new ties created through register ship trading, however, could not be overturned. Despite the merchants' complaints, both consumers and the Crown benefited from an increased volume of trade. As the postwar years demonstrated, between 1717 and 1738, register ships carried a greater average volume of goods than had the fleet system. Between 1739 and 1756, register ships handled nearly all the trade between Spain and the Indies. Although six more fleets sailed to New Spain in the following two decades, register ships accounted for 80 percent of the ships sailing from Spain to the viceroyalty.

Comparing the average annual shipments to Spain of selected colonial exports from South America (excluding Venezuela) reveals substantial growth in the legal trade. In the 1720s and 1730s, an average of five ships a year carried approximately 2 million pesos of silver and 850,000 pesos of gold, 210,000 pounds of cacao, 50,000 pounds of cascarilla, and 7,500 hides. After the War of Jenkins' Ear, between 1749 and 1755 an average of ten ships a year transported 3.2 million pesos of silver, 2.75 million pesos of gold, 995,000 pounds of cacao, 160,000 pounds of cascarilla, and 42,000 hides. Figures for ship sailings demonstrate the dramatic expansion of trade from 1700 to 1761. There was an average of 195 sailings in each of the first two decades, a number that increased to an average of 370 in the following two decades before jumping to 447 in the 1740s and 582 in the 1750s. In 1760 and 1761 alone, the number of sailings, 189, was equal to the total between 1700 and 1709.

The estimated tonnage (*toneladas*) transported between Spain and the Indies rose substantially as well. Between 1681 and 1709, the annual average was 6,041 *toneladas*, which increased between 1710 and 1740 almost 50 percent, to an average of 8,696 a year. In the first twenty years in which register ships were used extensively, the amount of goods carried averaged 17,636 *toneladas*, nearly triple the average for the first period.

The introduction of monopoly trading companies charged with handling trade and eradicating contraband from a specified region was another innovation of the first half of the eighteenth century. The most successful company was the Caracas Company, established in 1728. This group of primarily Basque merchants received a monopoly over trade with Venezuela. There was constant friction between Venezuelan cacao planters and company officials, especially over the prices imposed in Venezuela and the curtailment of the planters' participation in the more profitable contraband trade. Nonetheless, cacao production and legal exportation increased substantially under the company's administration. Before the company's establishment, cacao exports totaled approximately 2.5 million pounds annually, which rose to 5.25 million pounds annually between 1730 and 1748 and to 6.4 million between 1749 and 1765. Under company rule, moreover, Venezuela for the first time became fiscally self-supporting. Instead of draining Mexican resources for subsidies, the region actually returned a profit to the Crown starting in the early 1730s.

In Cuba, trade and population expanded in the first half of the eighteenth century. Largely as a result of natural increase, the population grew from perhaps 50,000 in 1700 to about 160,000—about a quarter of which were slaves—in the late 1750s. The shortage of regular shipping between Cádiz and Havana, however, had long hindered the development of a legal tobacco trade, although contraband flourished. After earlier experiments proved unsuccessful, the Crown awarded a contract in 1740 to a group of Havana merchants, who formed the Havana Company. The company tried to cut tobacco production so as to eliminate a surplus sold illegally and to increase the production of sugar. It gained a monopoly over the purchase and export of 3 million pounds of high-quality Cuban tobacco to Spain for manufacture at the royal factory in Seville. It also received special tax treatment for exported sugar and hides. Under the company, Cuban trade expanded to a higher level. In the mid-1730s, for example, there were only twenty sailings in five years, a number that grew to fifty-nine between 1758 and 1762. Havana's trade with other American ports, particularly Vera Cruz and Portobelo, also rose, although the total volume was far less than that of the Spanish trade.

The expanding trade reflected increased colonial production. At the same time, the greater regularity of shipping induced producers of agricultural and pastoral products to raise their output even further. An important consequence of this was the economic growth of regions distant from the commercial centers of the old fleet system, and previously able to import only a limited quantity of expensive goods. The Río de la Plata, Chile, Venezuela, and Central America, areas previously on the periphery of imperial trade, had already grown economically before the elimination of further barriers to trade in the second half of the eighteenth century. Each region also had a growing population and rising exports of agricultural or pastoral products. The Río de la Plata benefited, too, from exporting bullion obtained by sending imported goods—textiles, slaves, iron, and other items—into the mining areas of Upper Peru and from trade with Chile. Chile's renewal of gold production in the 1690s further strengthened an economy already expanding as a result of substantial wheat shipments to Peru.

Despite the widening colonial trade, Spanish exports remained limited primarily to agricultural products—wine, brandy, olive oil, and spices—and iron and iron tools not manufactured in the Indies. Indeed, until the late colonial period, most textiles sent to the Indies continued to be reexports of foreign goods. In addition, Spanish exporters in Cádiz remained mainly front men for foreign merchants.

Economic expansion was the most important development in the Indies between the late seventeenth century and the British capture of Havana in 1762. The more efficient exploitation of colonial exports and the expansion of colonial markets were mandatory for Spain in order to participate again as a great power in European affairs. Its conservative approach to trade, however, meant that government initiatives focused on reestablishing and making more efficient the old fleet system. European affairs outside colonial concerns, moreover, occupied most of the Crown's attention during the early decades of the century. Consequently, the greater use of register ships after 1740—the most important alteration in Spain's transatlantic trading system since the development of the convoy system in the sixteenth century—largely took place as a result of individual initiatives to supply American markets through direct trade and as a necessary defensive response to English naval superiority. The results demonstrated the superiority of register ships over the fleet system and prepared the way for its final elimination in 1789. By that date, however, the Crown had long ceased relying on halfway measures and ad hoc defensive responses to make the empire stronger economically and militarily. Building on the stronger economic base developed during the first half of the century, the Crown was following a conscious and persistent policy of increasing royal authority and colonial revenues instead of the earlier piecemeal and inconsistent efforts.

Map 7   Colonial Latin America: Political Organization.

Brazil in the Age of Expansion

The discovery of substantial gold deposits beginning in the mid-1690s inaugurated a boom in previously unsettled areas in the Brazilian interior. The rapid growth of population and the attraction of mineral wealth in Minas Gerais and other mining regions led the Portuguese Crown to enlarge the colonial bureaucracy. New transportation networks and commercial relations were developed to supply the mining camps. The prosperity of the mining region placed pressure on the established sugar-producing regions of the northeast by introducing price inflation and greater competition for labor and capital. By the mid-eighteenth century, Brazil's economic center had moved south, although the value of sugar exports continued to exceed that of gold. The transfer of the viceregal capital from Salvador to Rio de Janeiro in 1763 culminated a series of administrative changes that reflected the south's greater economic and political importance as well as heightened tension with Spain along Brazil's border.

But boom became depression as gold production descended steadily after peaking in the early 1750s. The interior's days of glory passed quickly, but by the early 1780s the coastal provinces enjoyed a renewed prosperity. Bolstered by the importation of unprecedented numbers of slaves and improved market conditions, sugar production expanded rapidly in the 1790s. The greater demand for tobacco, cotton, rice, coffee, indigo, and cacao also contributed to coastal Brazil's renewed economic vitality. New government policies helped stimulate this recovery and channel benefits to Portugal.

Administration

The growth of mining centers far from established settlements forced the Portuguese Crown to create new administrative, judicial, and treasury districts. Subdividing the immense territory previously under the jurisdiction of the

Charcoal delivered to city of Rio de Janeiro.

governor and captain-general of Rio de Janeiro into smaller territorial units was the first step. In 1709 a new captaincy-general, São Paulo e Minas do Ouro, was separated from Rio's jurisdiction. This was later divided, in 1720, into the separate captaincies-general of São Paulo and Minas Gerais. In 1748 two additional captaincies, Goiás and Mato Grosso, were created. After further reorganization in the early 1770s, Brazil had nine captaincies-general and nine subordinate captaincies.

In 1752, a second colonial high court, the new *Relaçao* of Rio de Janeiro, was established. The great distance separating the frontier mining camps from the old administrative centers led to the subdivision of captaincies into judicial districts (*comarcas*). Both Minas Gerais and Bahia, for example, were divided into four districts. Judicial committees made up of the governor and the senior treasury official of the captaincy and the senior judge of the *comarca* provided justice in the new districts.

The administration in Brazil was centered on the towns. By formally elevating mining camps to townships, the Crown committed itself to providing at least skeletal royal administration. The simultaneous extension of land grants and other privileges to these new towns and their officials encouraged further settlement of the interior. Beginning in 1693 a number of new towns were created to improve law and order and to streamline the collection of royal revenue. Although the establishment of towns and the introduction of administrative institutions definitely strengthened royal control in Minas Gerais, there still was little effective control in the sparsely inhabited captaincies of Mato Grosso and Goiás.

A central feature of these administrative reforms was the creation of new treasury offices. Mints were built in each major mining area, to which miners brought their gold for weighing, extraction of the royal fifth, and casting into bars. In addition, the Crown tried to limit access to the mining areas so that taxes could be collected on imports. Colonists in mining areas were also subject to the usual crown monopolies of salt, wine, and olive oil. Taken together, these taxes, the tithe, and local taxes contributed both to the rising royal revenues and the exorbitant cost of living in the mining regions.

During the second half of the eighteenth century in particular, the Crown sought to tighten its grip on Brazil. Sebastião José de Carvalho e Melo was the powerful royal minister who dominated affairs of state from 1750 to 1777. Titled the Marquis of Pombal after 1770, he correctly perceived that Portugal's fortunes rested on the prosperity of its huge American colony. Expanding the Brazilian economy and trade with the metropolis, collecting and expending its tax revenues, and securing its defenses, particularly in the lands adjoining Spanish America, were central to his goal of strengthening Portugal.

Under Pombal the Ministry of the Navy and Overseas Territories, established in 1736, gained control over colonial affairs. It oversaw general policy implementation and proposed high-ranking civil, military, and ecclesiastical appointments to the king. Pombal expanded the authority of the Board of Trade created in 1755 to develop Portuguese industry and reduce the kingdom's reliance on British imports. Its enlarged scope was recognized in 1788 when it became the Royal Committee for Trade, Agriculture, Factories, and Navigation for Portugal and the Colonies.

The establishment of a new royal treasury in 1761 centralized accounting for Portugal and the empire. Headed by Pombal himself as inspector-general, this agency centralized the supervision of revenue collection and expenditure. The next step in the Crown's fiscal reorganization was the creation during the 1760s and 1770s of treasury boards in each captaincy-general. Within their jurisdictions, the boards oversaw the activities of all departments of the royal exchequer. Double-entry bookkeeping was introduced in Brazil in 1764, but the shortage of trained personnel limited its effectiveness.

The Church

The stronger and more centralized Portuguese monarchy of the eighteenth century took numerous actions that reduced the power of the Church, its foremost institutional rival. Under Pombal the government broke the long-standing tradition of equal and complementary authority exercised by church and state.

The rapid economic and demographic expansion of the interior gold-mining regions was not accompanied by a parallel expansion of clerical influence and authority. The first friars on the scene were deeply involved in gold smuggling, and consequently the Crown banned all religious orders from Minas Gerais in 1711. This ban was not, however, accompanied by an effort to attract secular clergy to the region. Efforts to eliminate the extortionate practices of greedy priests, by paying clerics from the royal treasury and limiting the fees charged for the sacraments, proved ineffective. In fact, these policies kept the Church from establishing itself as securely in the mining zone as it had in northeastern Brazil during the first stages of settlement.

The expulsion of the Society of Jesus from Brazil in 1759–60 demonstrated the Crown's ability to destroy its opponents. The Society was solidly entrenched in Brazil when the Crown signed the Treaty of Madrid in 1750. Jesuit opposition to this treaty, exaggerated rumors of the Society's wealth, and Pombal's outrage at the Jesuits' opposition to his creation of a joint-stock company to exploit the resources of the interior led to the expulsion of the Society from Portugal and the empire and the seizure of its properties. The Crown sold some rural estates but maintained others as royal domain. Jesuit churches passed to the secular clergy, and the Society's colleges were often converted into government or military facilities. Because of the Jesuits' central role in education, the expulsion had a chilling effect on Brazil's cultural life. The diversity and scale of Jesuit holdings meant that the government's action affected urban real estate, ranching, sugar production, and farming. And because the Society was also the colony's largest institutional slave owner and a source of investment credit,

Pombal's decision had unforeseen consequences for the labor and capital markets as well.

The Crown then turned its attention toward the assets of the other orders. It seized the rich cattle ranches and other property of the Mercedarians and forced other orders to lend it money in exchange for government bonds. Coupled with the state's lukewarm support for the secular clergy, these actions toward the Jesuits and other regular clergy represented a significant weakening of the Church in Brazil.

Demographic Expansion

The population of Brazil increased from perhaps a million in 1700 to about 1.5 million at mid-century and over 2 million in 1800. Although the mining boom shifted the population south and west, the traditional agricultural economies of the coastal regions maintained their larger, more densely settled populations. Nonetheless, the great gold rushes to the interior were clearly responsible for attracting new immigrants, expanding the slave trade, and stimulating internal migration. This process, in turn, led to the creation of a more diversified, more integrated colonial economy.

Immigrants from Portugal averaged perhaps three thousand to four thousand annually during the first twenty years of the century. The flow was sufficiently heavy that in 1720 the Crown strictly limited it through new licensing procedures. After that the annual total probably never reached two thousand. During the first half of the century most of these immigrants went to the mining zones.

In the mining camps Portuguese immigrants soon outnumbered the frontiersmen from São Paulo who discovered the mines. Mining camps also received an enormous influx of black slaves. In the eighteenth century, Brazil imported approximately 1.7 million slaves from Africa. Despite this large number, labor demands and capital resources of the mining districts drove up prices and created an internal trade that took slaves away from the plantations of northeastern Brazil. African slaves thus soon formed the backbone of the work force. In Minas Gerais the number of slaves had reached about thirty thousand by 1715, and in Minas Novas slaves were the majority of a population that reached about forty thousand within three years of the initial gold strike.

The drop in gold production that began in the 1750s reoriented the African slave trade toward the newly developed agricultural areas of the coast and, after 1791, to the sugar zone near Salvador. The imports of slaves during the second half of the eighteenth century almost certainly equaled those between 1700 and 1750. Between 1800 and 1810 another 200,000 slaves were imported. Because the African slave trade continued to carry a high proportion of males to females, there was a low rate of natural reproduction in this portion of the slave population. Among slaves born in Brazil, birth rates were similar to those of the free population. Nevertheless, a high mortality rate—the result of tropical diseases like yellow fever, poor nutrition and medical care, rudimentary housing, and harsh working conditions—continued to limit the growth of the slave population.

The racial composition of Brazil in the early nineteenth century naturally reflected the massive importation of slaves; nearly two-thirds of the population was African or of African descent. Slaves were the most numerous class, 38 percent of the population. Free blacks and mulattoes together made up 28 percent, an amount equal to that of the white population. Within the settled regions of Brazil, Indians represented only 6 percent of the population.

Brazil's population at the turn of the nineteenth century was densest on the northeastern coast. The captaincies-general of Pernambuco, Bahia, and Rio de Janeiro accounted for nearly 60 percent of the population. The mining region of Minas Gerais was the most populous single captaincy-general, with over 400,000 inhabitants, 20 percent of Brazil's population. Brazil's two largest cities were on the coast: the populations of Bahia and Rio de Janeiro, both major exporting cities, hovered around 50,000, and both increased by 50 percent or more after 1750. In contrast, the third largest city, São Paulo, grew little in this period. Although only thirty miles from the Atlantic, the city's transportation and communication with the coast were impeded by difficult terrain. Still, São Paulo had 24,000 inhabitants in 1803. The ports of Recife and Sâo Luis were the only other cities with populations in excess of 20,000 persons. Ouro Prêto, the most populous city of Minas Gerais, demonstrated the volatility of boomtown populations, falling from some 20,000 inhabitants in the 1740s to just 7,000 in 1804.

Society

Brazilian society in the eighteenth century remained hierarchical. Place of birth, wealth, occupation, race, and legal status were used to classify individuals and assign privileges and rights. The mining boom and later agricultural recovery altered the demographic components of this colonial society and extended the social apparatus of class and race across new territory. Although the society in 1808 shared important characteristics with that of 1700, it was more dynamic and fluid and also more violent and unpredictable.

The mining boom attracted a wave of immigration from Portugal. Only a tiny minority of these new arrivals made fortunes in gold and diamond mining, but their presence altered society significantly. As a result of this relatively large population of recent immigrants, the settlements of the mining district and southern coastal region confronted much more directly the cultural and political meaning of colonial status. The inherent tension between metropolitan assertiveness and the natural proprietary sense of the colonial natives eventually led to armed conflict in 1708–9. The War of the Emboabas (tenderfeet) pitted the Paulistas against the Portuguese and northern Brazilian migrants. Significantly, the interlopers prevailed.

Another important result of the century's economic dynamism was the creation of a large number of newly wealthy men. The mining elite of boom-towns like Ouro Prêto and Sabará were generally rough, uncultured men with little prior experience in the exercise of power or the enjoyment of social leadership. Their wealth gave them the ability to build and consume on a grand scale, but their combination of exuberance and limited cul-tural breadth produced as many excesses as works of art. As one contem-porary put it,

> Those who had amassed great wealth from their diggings were led thereby to behave with pride and arrogance. They went about accompanied by troops . . . ready to execute any violence and to take the greatest and most frightful revenge, without any fear of the law. The gold incited them to gamble lavishly, and heed-lessly to squander vast sums on vain luxuries. For instance, they would give one thousand *cruzados* for a Negro trumpeter; and double that price for a mulata prostitute, in order to indulge with her in continual and scandalous sins.[2]

The cotton, rice, and cacao booms produced their nouveau riches as well. The recovery of sugar prices and an expanded Atlantic trade reinvigorated these sectors of the landed elite, but in the late eighteenth century, social power in Brazil was more dispersed than before. The social and political consequences of this geographic dispersion were magnified by the new elite's predisposition to stay in the countryside. Governor Luís Antônio de Sousa complained in 1766 that São Paulo was a desolate place because plan-tation owners visited town only on the most important occasions.

These centrifugal forces were partly compensated by greater economic in-tegration. Merchants, government officials, and large-scale agriculturalists diversified their investments to protect themselves from changing market con-ditions. There was a reciprocal social integration as well. Increased physical mobility, the diversification of economic activity, and a set of social presump-tions that emphasized family-based associations all encouraged elite families to establish cross-sectoral linkages through marriage and godparents.

These patterns could also be found in the middle sectors, but an added racial dimension made them more complex. Skilled artisans, lower-level functionaries, junior officers, retail merchants, and other groups that made up the middle groups of the colony's cities were drawn from immigrant and native-born whites and from racially mixed populations, and none was likely to be deeply rooted in a region. Instead, they often sought marginal economic benefits by moving to new locations. The most successful acquired property, owned and employed slaves in their households and businesses, and were officers in the colonial militia. This diverse class also provided the social arena in which miscegenation played an important role. Unsure of their status and ambitious for upward social mobility, the mem-bers of this class were careful to measure the racial antecedents and economic prospects of their prospective mates.

In rural areas the middle sector included the *lavradores de cana*, the independent cane growers who helped supply larger refiners and a growing class of small-scale farmers who seldom relied on slave labor. Also common were tenants who traded labor or a portion of their crops for the right to farm or ranch on another's land and skilled rural workers, including overseers, artisans, skilled refining workers, and ranch foremen. With the exception of the *lavradores*, they were usually racially mixed persons. Both *lavradores de cana* and tenants were particularly vulnerable to fluctuations in the economy. Because they were often in debt and unprotected by diversification, falling prices, drought, and other natural disasters could ruin them.

The urban and rural underclass formed the base of Brazil's free black and mulatto population. Illegitimacy, family instability, and criminal behavior were common, but these problems were similarly present among poor whites as well. Because the colonial economy invested little in education or training, the underclasses of both city and countryside had few opportunities for upward social mobility. During boom periods most could secure steady employment and, as a result, adequate food and minimum housing. But when bust followed boom, the demand for labor fell, and many poor people were forced into begging, crime, or migration. Slaves, however, still remained the largest class of deprived colonial residents.

Gold Production

Efforts to estimate Brazil's gold production are limited by the unreliability of the surviving tax records. Whether based primarily on tax or foundry records, production estimates must be increased to include contraband. Sixteen times more valuable than silver per ounce, gold tempted miners to employ all manner of ruses to avoid the heavy taxes levied by the Portuguese Crown. Indeed, one contemporary estimated that over two-thirds of the gold mined in Brazil was never declared.

Recent estimates of gold production indicate a rapid expansion from 1700 to 1720, slower growth for the next fifteen years, and a second boom until mid-century. The overall peak was reached in 1750–54 when production in Goiás reached its apogee and that of Minas Gerais, consistently Brazil's largest producer, was still very high. Overall production then decreased steadily. The total between 1795 and 1799 was almost identical with that between 1706 and 1710. A conservative estimate of real production would double the production figures found in tax records. The result is an average annual gold output from 1735 to 1764 of over 27,000 kilograms. This amount was equal in value to the production of more than 14 million Spanish silver pesos, thus exceeding in value Peru's best comparable thirty-year period (1611–40). The value of Mexico's bullion production did not surpass that of Brazil's peak years until the 1780s.

Sometime after 1720, diamonds were discovered near the gold boom town of Vila do Principe. Miners and colonial officials initially tried to keep the discovery secret to avoid taxes and regulation. By 1730, however, the Crown moved aggressively to organize and control exploration

Closely supervised slaves mining diamonds in Brazil.

and development. The flow of Brazilian diamonds caused a crash in European prices and led the Crown to send military units to enforce an outright ban on production. Controlled production was then permitted by a system of monopoly arrangements, although smuggling remained common.

Brazil's gold production and the simultaneous boom in diamond mining in northern Minas Gerais increased the flow of funds to the royal treasury. At the same time, the development of these mining regions produced countervailing demands. Although never adequate to deal with the needs of the turbulent interior, the establishment and continued operation of administrative, judicial, military, and ecclesiastical organizations were nonetheless expensive. This cycle of taxation and expenditure worked to redistribute wealth away from the mining sector to other social groups and geographic regions, most importantly to the metropolitan economy. It may well be that the public sector's role in Brazil tended to limit investment in exploration, technology, and labor—thereby hindering the growth of production—but it also helped expand the colony's middle sectors, thus encouraging a more broad-based consumer class and stimulating domestic as well as transatlantic commerce.

Economy and Trade

As had occurred in the mining districts of Spanish America, rich mineral strikes in Brazil quickly brought together entrepreneurs, laborers, adventurers, freeloaders, clerics, and royal officials. All required food and drink, housing, and clothing. The more successful also sought luxury items whose consumption would reveal their good fortune.

There were numerous beneficiaries of the growth of the mining regions. The salted beef industry of southern Brazil, for example, profited by the demand for nonperishable food in Minas Gerais. An abundance of gold and a scarcity of nearly every article of basic consumption led to massive price inflation in the mining zone. This, in turn, promoted the rapid development of livestock raising, agriculture, and artisan manufacture. Cattle raising near the mines prospered as miners sought to reduce their dependence on beef imported from other regions. Royal land grants of several square leagues enabled cattlemen to settle near the mines or along transportation arteries. Land grants also enabled small farmers and stockmen to produce staples like pigs and chickens and manioc and other crops. Slaves cultivated a variety of crops for their own subsistence and in limited amounts for market. Thus prosperous agricultural and pastoral activities flourished with the rise in number of miners, slaves, and other residents.

The decline in the gold and diamond production that began in the late 1750s inaugurated a period of economic depression for Brazil. Economic recovery was not evident until the early 1780s and was largely confined to the agricultural belt along the coast. International conflicts, increased industrial demand in Europe, and the devastation of Haiti's sugar production after 1791 as a result of revolutionary violence combined to promote Brazilian agricultural exports. Total sugar exports roughly doubled between 1790 and 1807, reaching nearly 25,000 metric tons in the last year.

Grown commercially beginning only in 1760, cotton emerged as Brazil's second leading export by the close of the century. Production began in Maranhão, and for some forty years the captaincy held the lead among Brazilian regions. By the early nineteenth century, however, Pernambuco was exporting a greater amount of higher-quality cotton. The growth of French and especially English cotton textile industries during the early stages of the Industrial Revolution inflated prices and spurred production. Although dependent on expensive slave labor, cotton could be processed for less money than could sugar. In addition, because there was no cost equivalent to that of the necessary grinding and refining of sugar, cotton could be produced more quickly in response to escalating demand. In 1782 England imported about 9,000 pounds worth of Brazilian cotton. Within five years Brazil's cotton exports to England surpassed 150,000 pounds in value and occasionally surpassed 200,000 pounds in succeeding decades. Although Brazil supported an unfavorable balance of trade with Portugal and England at mid-century, by 1791 England was exporting silver to pay for Brazilian imports.

In the late eighteenth century, tobacco, produced primarily in Bahia, continued to be exported legally to Portugal and as contraband to Buenos Aires and Upper Peru. It was particularly important to sustaining the trade in slaves on the African coast. Far surpassed in value by both sugar and cotton as the century closed, tobacco nonetheless remained a vital export for Bahia, winning profitable markets in Africa and in the distant Canadian fur trade. Other exports included hides, rice, wheat, coffee, cacao, and a number of lesser products. Rio de Janeiro was the colony's export leader, followed by Pernambuco, Bahia, and Maranhão.

The continuation of a profitable trade in Brazilian agricultural exports, especially sugar, and the windfall profits of the gold and diamond booms led Portugal to abandon its efforts to promote manufacture begun in the late seventeenth century in the face of serious deficits and fiscal crisis. The Methuen Treaty of 1703, and the Brazilian bonanza tightened Portugal's commercial ties with England. In exchange for preferential treatment for its wine, Portugal increased imports of English cloth, ready-made garments, tools, hardware, and metals. Brazil's gold and diamonds were used to balance Portugal's chronic trade deficit. The unexpected and rapid decline in gold production after 1750 reduced the royal revenues substantially, at a time when Lisbon was still being rebuilt after the destructive earthquake of 1755 and Portugal was having to pay the costs of war with Spain.

Faced with declining trade and a revenue shortfall in the 1760s and 1770s, the Crown tried to improve the quality of Brazilian sugar and tobacco exports and develop more profitable marketing arrangements. In addition, it attempted to stimulate northern Brazil's economy and revive the long-suffering northeastern coastal zone. The Marquis of Pombal created local boards of inspection in Brazil's leading ports and established monopoly trading companies to stimulate agricultural production and promote exports. Inspection boards were set up in Salvador, Rio de Janeiro, São Luis do Maranhão, and Recife. They mediated disputes between producers and merchants and supervised weights and measures and quality control. More importantly, they set wholesale prices, theoretically at levels to maximize the market share of Brazilian exports. In practice, however, this strategy increased profits for the Portuguese shippers and merchants at the expense of the colonial growers and refiners. Colonial manufacturing, on the other hand, was actively discouraged. This approach culminated in 1785 when the Crown prohibited colonial manufacturers from producing textiles other than rough cloth used for slave clothing.

In 1755 the Crown established the Company of Grão Pará and Maranhão, granting it a twenty-year monopoly over shipping and the slave trade with the northern captaincies. This action was accompanied by a prohibition against itinerant Portuguese traders participating in colonial trade. A second Company of Pernambuco and Paraíba was founded in 1759 to handle trade with these two captaincies. Together these companies represented a conscious effort to rationalize the Luso-Brazilian trading system. Until their demise following the death of José I and Pombal's fall from power in 1777, the monopolistic companies increased slave imports and provided more reliable shipping for the regions they served. They also promoted the consumption of products produced in new Portuguese state-supported factories whose creation Pombal had encouraged. When local economic interests and the Jesuits protested against the creation of the first of these monopolies and a simultaneous change in Indian labor policy, Pombal reacted forcefully to silence the dissent.

British opposition to changes in the Luso-Brazilian trading system and the threat of renewed warfare on the border with Spanish settlements in the Río de La Plata prevented Pombal from extending the monopolistic trading companies to Rio de Janeiro and Bahia. Instead, he sought to expand trade by ending the fleet system in 1765. Henceforth, licensed individual ships carried most of the goods between Portugal and Brazil. In the following year, the prohibitions against coastal trade among Brazilian ports were removed.

Expanding Brazilian trade helped Portugal enjoy a favorable balance of trade with other European nations. Even its historic imbalance with England was reversed by 1791, largely as a result of the reexport of Brazilian products. However, these favorable trade statistics merely disguised Portugal's long-term structural disadvantage in commercial competition. Not only did Portuguese ships carry large amounts of British goods to Brazil, but from 1801 to 1807, metropolitan manufactures and legal reexports of English goods declined substantially as a result of increased British smuggling. In 1800 alone, thirty British ships reached Rio de Janeiro. As a consequence Portugal frequently had an unfavorable balance of payments with important Brazilian captaincies. Unable to compete with England's increasingly efficient manufactures, Portugal was also losing its profitable position as a transportation and commercial link between Brazil's plantations and England's factories.

Luso-Spanish Rivalry

Beginning in 1680 with the first foundation of Colônia do Sacramento across the estuary of the Río de la Plata from Buenos Aires, Portugal challenged Spain's control of a region that extended from the estuary north to the captaincy of São Paulo and from the Atlantic west to the Uruguay and Paraná rivers. Portugal was interested mainly in commercial access to the silver of Potosí. Spain, in turn, wanted to close down the contraband trading post of Colônia and gain a buffer zone between Buenos Aires and Brazil. These conflicting objectives led to repeated Spanish attacks on Colônia in the 1760s and 1770s.

By the Treaty of Madrid (1750), Portugal gave up its claims to Colônia and the lands adjoining the Río de la Plata. Spain relinquished the lands between the Uruguay and Ibicui rivers, where the Society of Jesus had seven missions and some thirty thousand neophytes and agreed that the Society and its charges would withdraw from the region. This compromise agreement failed, however, because of opposition by powerful interests in Portugal and Spain. Resistance by the Jesuits and mission Indians led to open warfare between 1754 and 1756 and convinced royal advisers in both

Iberian countries to push for the expulsion of the Society. The treaty's abrogation in 1761 left war as the final recourse.

In October 1762, Spanish troops led by Pedro de Cevallos, governor of Buenos Aires, took Colônia and then conquered coastal Rio Grande in Brazil. Under the terms of the Peace of Paris, Spain returned Colônia but continued to occupy coastal Rio Grande. Intermittent armed conflict and ineffective efforts to blockade Colônia led to decisive action in 1776. An expeditionary force of nearly twenty thousand men led by the first viceroy of the Río de la Plata, Pedro de Cevallos, took Santa Catarina Island and Colônia in 1777 but failed to recover Rio Grande. The Treaty of San Ildefonso signed in October 1777 finally settled the boundary conflict. Portugal regained Santa Catarina and coastal Rio Grande but lost Colônia. Spain retained the Seven Missions lands and the Banda Oriental. This boundary remained unchanged until the Portugueseseized the Seven Missions lands in 1801.

Luso-Spanish rivalry carried a heavy price. Both countries committed vast sums of colonial revenue to support soldiers, sailors, and ships. Falling mining revenues and depressed trade in the 1760s and 1770s left the Portuguese Crown particularly hard-pressed. Administrators in Brazil curtailed unnecessary expenses, borrowed money, and delayed paying bills whenever possible. The costs of maintaining a large army created a budget deficit and diverted funds from investment in infrastructure. From the mid-1770s onward, the viceregal treasury's debt increased substantially, despite reduced remittances to Portugal.

The Enlightenment

As the eighteenth century progressed, the writings of the French *philosophes* and other "enlightened" authors entered the intellectual cultures of Portugal and Spain. The Enlightenment's challenge to traditional authority, its emphasis on the use of reason, and reliance on observation, experience, and experimentation reached the colonies, but only a few colonial residents in urban centers actually read and discussed the new ideas. However, a larger number were initiated indirectly through sermons, informal discussions in academies and salons, and illegal pamphlets and graffiti.

With no university in the colony, young Brazilian men had to travel abroad for higher education and professional training. Portugal's University of Coimbra attracted the most Brazilian students, but others attended Montpellier in France and a few studied at other universities. Following the expulsion of the Jesuits, who had dominated education in Portugal as well as Brazil, Pombal reformed Coimbra's curriculum. After 1772 a reinvigorated faculty employed modern methods emphasizing experimentation, observation, and the critical use of reason. Students of this era returned to Brazil carrying exciting new ideas and recent publications that circulated in a wider circle.

One manifestation of the Enlightenment in Brazil was a new passion to examine the natural environment. Geography and biology gained a wider audience. The collection and classification of indigenous plants became popular among some intellectuals. And naturalists helped instill a growing pride in Brazil and an awareness of its uniqueness.

The Enlightenment's arsenal of ideas also contained revolutionary political and economic implications, many of which were manifested in the American and French revolutions. The ideals of independence, liberty, equality, and fraternity quickly found Brazilian partisans, although few people actively argued for a revolution against Portuguese authority. In Brazil, educated men and women generally worked to reform commercial and political structures rather than to instigate violent change. This moderation was rooted in the colony's dependence on slave labor and a racial caste system that inhibited the development of Brazilian nationalism. In the decades before 1808 there were only two major conspiracies against Portuguese rule, and both failed.

Conspiracies

The Mineiro conspiracy in Ouro Prêto in 1789 included intellectuals who admired the emerging United States and whose libraries contained works by Voltaire and other popular *philosophes*. More important than ideology as a spur to revolt, however, were the massive debts that some of the captaincy's richest men owed to the treasury. Fear that the Crown was about to collect these debts led these more powerful conspirators to view the end of Portuguese rule as the only answer to impending financial doom. Discovered before they could take action, the plot's leaders were arrested. Social eminence, economic resources, and the questionable actions of the captain-general saved almost all of the plotters and their silent partners from death. Only one participant, of modest means, was executed.

In Salvador nine years later, a group of conspirators, which included some slaves, several free mulattoes, and a few whites, issued a call to overthrow the colonial government and establish a republic that would provide "freedom, equality, and fraternity." The social and economic implications of mass emancipation and a definition of citizenship without racial requirements in a captaincy in which whites made up only one-fifth of the population stirred the authorities to action. Four leaders were executed, and the other participants were punished. Regardless of their birthplace and individual grievances, the white merchants, planters, and officials of Bahia believed that their self-interest required the maintenance of the slave system and racial discrimination.

In the opening years of the nineteenth century, Brazil was at a new peak of prosperity. Far more of the colony was settled and economically productive than in the 1690s before the mining boom. The colony's population had more than doubled, and vast areas of the interior had been brought within its economic and political spheres. Both the value and the diversity of exports had grown as well. More and more enlightened residents praised Brazil's progress and welcomed the promising future. Already the economic center of the Luso-Brazilian empire by the end of the eighteenth century, Brazil became its political center as well with the arrival of the Portuguese court in 1808.

New Spain, Peru, and the Reforms of Charles III

The British capture of Havana in 1762 compelled Charles III and his advisers to institute reforms that were more ambitious and costly than those of their predecessors. The preservation of the empire and the guarantee of its economic and fiscal benefits for the metropolis required a better military defense. Military preparedness, however, was costly. To obtain the necessary additional revenue, the Crown turned to the colonies, with reforms intended to integrate the colonies more effectively with Spain. The Crown improved tax collection and instituted new royal monopolies, took steps to raise the colonies' production of exportable primary goods and the importation of Spanish goods, and moved to tighten control over their administration. As was true in Portugal under Pombal, a greater centralization of authority and regalism characterized Spanish rule from the fall of Havana to the Napoleonic invasion of Spain in 1808.

The Peace of Paris in 1763 ended the military hostilities between Spain and Britain known as the Seven Years' War. Although Havana and Manila returned to Spanish rule after a brief British occupation, and France ceded Louisiana to Spain, the loss of Florida underlined the empire's continued vulnerability. In 1765 the Crown moved to increase revenues in New Spain which subsidized the defense of Cuba, the Philippines, and Louisiana, by dispatching a visitor general, José de Gálvez, to the empire's richest and most populous colony. When later named secretary of state for the Indies in 1776, Gálvez also sought improved fiscal benefits from South America. The reform effort in both viceroyalties succeeded in expanding revenue and improving defense. However, the pace of demographic growth during the half-century before the wars of independence was probably more important in determining the contours of daily life in these longtime cores of the empire.

Military Threats and Military Reforms

Faced with the threat of renewed British attacks, the Spanish Crown took the unprecedented step of creating colonial armies. Despite differences in the timing and nature of the reform in each viceroyalty, in both New Spain and Peru the number of authorized regular forces more than tripled between 1760 and 1800, reaching 6,150 in New Spain, excluding the frontier outposts in the north, and about 2,000 in Peru. Colonial militias were also expanded substantially after 1760, but these troops were seldom adequately armed or trained. In 1800 militiamen numbered almost 24,000 in New Spain and probably no more than 18,000 in Peru.

The creation of standing armies in the colonies brought unprecedented numbers of peninsular officers and soldiers to the New World. The consequent predominance of peninsular officers in the highest ranks aggravated the discrimination that creoles already felt in the civil and ecclesiastical hierarchies. In contrast with the regular officers' positions, creole representation was heavy in the militia, in which positions could be purchased. Suspicions about the reliability of creoles, however, led the Crown routinely to assign each unit a regular army officer from the peninsula to supervise training.

As inducements to enlistment, the Crown extended to the colonial armies a number of benefits, including the military *fuero*, the judicial right for officers, soldiers, and their dependents to be heard by a military rather than a civil court in a variety of civil and criminal cases. The benefits offered, however, were inadequate to lure many volunteers into colonial armies that featured low pay, harsh discipline, and poor prospects for advancement. Consequently, recruiting teams scoured taverns, gambling dens, and jails. The alcoholics, gamblers, and vagabonds they enlisted joined convicted criminals sentenced to serve their terms in the army. New recruits in New Spain and other colonies often received defective weapons and were sometimes charged for repairs. Provincial militia units received weapons that were scarcely usable. Because they often were not paid, some soldiers pawned or sold their weapons, uniforms, and shoes in order to survive or for drinking and gambling or, sometimes, to aid their desertion. Not surprisingly, contemporaries frequently considered soldiers more as scourges than defenders of the land, and as a result, the army failed to become an honored and prestigious institution in the colonies.

Despite the poor condition of both the regulars and militiamen, the defense of New Spain and Peru was expensive. In late eighteenth-century New Spain, often over 60 percent of the central treasury's expenditures went for defense. Although the total outlay was large throughout the period, it more than doubled between the early 1760s and the early 1780s. In Peru, Indian rebellions raised military costs even more.

Armed resistance rose in the eighteenth century among the exploited Indians of the Andean colonies. There were five uprisings in the 1740s, eleven in the 1750s, twenty in the 1760s, and twenty in the 1770s. The violent climax of Indian protest occurred in 1780 under the leadership of José Gabriel Condorcanqui, also known as Tupac Amaru II. This *kuraka* from the Cuzco region led a general insurrection that pulled together a mixed force of Indians and *castas*. This protest against a harsh existence sought the redress of long-standing abuses and the implementation of specific reforms. Tupac Amaru wanted the *repartimiento* of goods ended, the *corregidores* removed, better working conditions instituted in the mines and *obrajes*, the *mita* terminated, and an *audiencia* created in Cuzco. The rebels executed a hated *corregidor* in November 1780 and gathered supporters, particularly near Cuzco. An army sent from Lima soon was victorious, and in May 1781 the captured leader was executed. The death of Tupac Amaru, however, did not end the rebellion; leaders in neighboring regions kept up the struggle. Before peace was restored in 1783, the rebellions had cost 100,000 lives, making them the most violent and costly uprisings since the period of Manco Inca in the sixteenth century. Even though these protests failed militarily, they forced the termination of the *repartimiento* system and led to the establishment of the Audiencia of Cuzco. By raising the specter of race and class warfare, moreover, they strengthened the creoles' allegiance to Spanish rule and delayed Peru's independence.

The Expansion of Bureaucracy

The need for greater revenues to support defensive expenditures in the New World and to provide resources for its policies at home prompted the Crown to tighten its control over administrators, to assume direct responsibility over previously contracted activities, and to increase the number of crown monopolies. Although the origins of bureaucratic expansion predated the fall of Havana, the most dramatic efforts to reassert and increase royal control came afterwards. In both New Spain and Peru, the number of bureaucrats increased, and the cost of administration grew.

The Crown's loss of administrative power relative to that of the local elites was apparent in 1750. By selling appointments and positions, the Crown had created the kind of corrupt, inefficient bureaucracy it deplored. Lacking the funds to buy out the purchasers, often young native sons, the Crown embarked on a policy of attrition accompanied by a conscious policy of favoring peninsulars to fill vacancies as they appeared. By favoring the peninsulars for the most important new offices in the colonies, the Crown further diluted, although never eliminated, local influence in government.

The consequence of these changes in appointment policy and the termination of sales was visible in both viceroyalties. In 1750 only one of fifteen ministers on the Audiencia of Mexico had been there less than five years. Thirty years later, thirteen of eighteen ministers were newcomers. In Lima, thirteen of eighteen ministers in 1750 had been born in the colony, but by 1780 only five native sons remained. Later appointments clearly revealed the heightened and continued discrimination against native sons.

Complementing its conscious efforts to reduce local representation in established administrative institutions, the Crown also attempted to expand its authority through directly administering previously farmed or alienated activities. Doing so increased the number of bureaucrats. Overall, the number of government employees in Lima nearly doubled between the mid-1770s and 1790. In New Spain the number of well-paid posts probably quadrupled as a result of these reforms.

The best-known administrative innovation was the establishment of the intendant system, a direct response to the abuses of the *corregidores* and *alcaldes mayores*. As José de Gálvez, the most vigorous supporter of the system's introduction, noted on concluding his *visita* in New Spain, it will be

> more satisfactory and practicable for the chief executive of this kingdom to have under his immediate orders twelve *intendentes*, carefully chosen, whose character is above reproach, than to have to suffer and contend with two hundred wretches who, with their empty title of judges, have come to constitute an independent judicial sphere, wherein, driven by their own greed, they work out their own fortunes at the expense of the royal treasury and the ruin of the people.[3]

Adopted from French and Spanish precedents, the intendants represented a new layer of colonial administration linking district administrators to central authorities. The 7 intendants named for Peru in 1784 were directly in charge of 58 subdelegates who replaced the previous *corregidores*. In New Spain, the 12 intendants named in 1786 oversaw roughly 150 district administrators. By creating larger administrative units under officials with substantially greater authority than the previous *corregidores* and *alcaldes mayores* had, the Crown sought to make its power as effective in the countryside as in the cities and towns.

Intendants were responsible for public administration, finance, administration of justice, and military preparedness within their provinces. The improvement of the local governments, promotion of economic growth, encouragement of public works, and especially oversight of the collection of revenue were among their specific obligations. In contrast with the previous district administrators, intendants also exercised royal patronage over the ecclesiastical institutions within their provinces.

These powerful, prestigious, and well-paid new positions went almost exclusively to peninsulars. Many were professional soldiers, but some were lawyers and treasury officials. They secured their appointments by merit, not purchase, and—far more frequently than the *corregidores* whose authority they subsumed—intendants placed the royal interest above personal gain.

Despite Gálvez's great hopes, the intendant system did not yield the anticipated benefits. Although income rose substantially in Peru immediately after the system was introduced, it then fell. In New Spain, Crown revenues actually rose during the 1770s, before the introduction of the intendants. The intendant system also failed to provide good administration and justice in the countryside because it was flawed at the district level. The subdelegates who replaced the *corregidores* and *alcaldes mayores* were at first prohibited from using the *repartimiento* of merchandise; their legal compensation was limited to a small percentage of the tribute they collected. Protests against the prohibition of the merchandise *repartimiento* followed immediately in New Spain. When it became

Imperial reformers were concerned with improving public order and protecting property. In most large colonial cities, streets in the downtown areas were illuminated at night and patrolled by night watchmen.

clear within a decade that stringent enforcement was impossible, many subdelegates, particularly those in parts of southern and southeastern Mexico and in the highlands of Peru, returned to the old system of profiting from the sale of goods on credit and advances of raw materials and even cash.

The intendant system fared better in the provincial capitals than in the countryside. Typically, the intendant sought to revitalize a city council by enlarging its membership, often by recruiting prominent, long-resident peninsulars of the city, raising its revenues, and making a variety of improvements in public services. Improved roads and bridges, street lights, and better sanitation and water supplies increased civic pride. With the limitations placed on the employment of native sons in a number of other government institutions, the *cabildos* increasingly became the primary political arena for local grievances in many parts of the Spanish Empire.

Regalism and the Expulsion of the Jesuits

In the eighteenth century, the monarchs of Spain and Portugal followed a broad policy of expanding their authority at the expense of other institutions and interests. The expansion of monarchical power over the institutions of the Catholic Church is known as "regalism." The regular clergy who had grown powerful during the first hundred years of the colonial era became the primary target for those seeking to augment royal authority. In 1749 Ferdinand VI of Spain decreed that all parishes still ministered by mendicant orders should be transferred to the secular clergy. An early attempt at secularization failed in the sixteenth century, and many churches in indigenous areas remained in the hands of the regular orders two centuries later. This new effort proved more successful. In Mexico, for example, nearly every parish was in the hands of secular priests by the mid-1760s. A related directive that ordered the removal of parish priests who lacked skill in the native languages spoken by their parishioners was less successful.

Charles III built on his predecessor's actions and further moved to change the balance between the formerly interdependent and equal partners of Crown and Church. Believing the Church's jurisdiction should extend over lay persons only in matters of conscience, the Crown reduced ecclesiastical immunity, principally the privilege of asylum, and also the personal legal immunity that clerics enjoyed in many areas.

The Crown's willingness to challenge ecclesiastical institutions became evident in 1767 when Charles expelled the Society of Jesus from his realms. Although the immediate cause was a series of municipal riots in Spain in 1766—believed by some to have been instigated by the Jesuits—the roots of the expulsion lay elsewhere. The Jesuits' refusal to acknowledge monarchical authority as being above papal authority defied regalist doctrine. In addition, the Jesuits had obstructed in the past the implementation of royal policy. Their preeminence in education and close ties to wealthy and prominent lay persons also gave them extensive influence. Finally, the Society's wealth tempted a monarch whose resources were stretched.

The expulsion of 680 Jesuits from New Spain and over 500 from Peru, a majority of whom were native born, shocked colonial opinion. Rioting broke out in the mining region of New Spain and also in Valladolid and Pátzcuaro, where workers were already dismayed by the more stringent tax collection and the imposition of excise taxes on *pulque.* José de Gálvez himself led a ruthless expedition to restore peace. In Peru the expulsion provoked astonishment, but the Jesuits were deported without significant protest.

Following their expulsion, the Crown confiscated the Society's estates and other assets. In Peru the value of the 203 *haciendas* and over 5,200 slaves seized was approximately 6.5 million pesos. In less than a decade, over half of these had been sold. The Society's rural holdings in New Spain brought the Crown over 5 million pesos. This rapid transfer of property created a local vested interest opposed to the Society's return and thus acted to counter pressure from those families angered by the expulsion of sons, kinsmen, and teachers.

The Enlightenment

The expulsion of the Jesuits deprived New Spain and Peru of their most prominent educators and created a shortage of qualified teachers. At the same time, the expulsion removed the foremost advocates of scholastic thought and thus facilitated the widespread introduction of a more modern approach to knowledge. By the close of the eighteenth century, skepticism of authority, observation of nature, experimentation, and analysis based on inductive reasoning had transformed the intellectual milieu of the colonies.

Even before 1767, in both viceroyalties, there were glimmers of an unmistakable swing toward modern approaches to knowledge and an emphasis on science and useful knowledge. The most noted supporters of these changes were active in the 1780s and 1790s. Their intellectual heirs sustained their reform agenda and, after 1810, added the political enthusiasms of the American and French revolutions.

The most widespread expression of enlightened ideas in Peru appeared in the *Mercurio Peruano*, a biweekly paper published in Lima in the early 1790s by a local variant of the many economic societies founded in the Spanish world since 1763. Through the *Mercurio*, the supporters of progress tried to provide Peruvians with useful knowledge of their region and information relevant to their daily lives. Thus the *Mercurio* published articles that advocated burial outside churches for reasons of health, supported more efficient mining techniques, and analyzed the viceroyalty's commerce. Although its publication demonstrated the presence of a number of self-proclaimed adherents of modern ideas, the *Mercurio's* demise in 1795 reflected how small that number was. At no time did the number of subscribers reach four hundred.

As in Peru, periodicals reached a broader audience in New Spain than did *colegio* and university courses. The foremost Mexican publicist was the cleric José Antonio Alzate y Ramírez (1729–99), an advocate of scientific knowledge and its application to contemporary problems. His *Gaceta de Literatura* (1788–95) provided a stream of informative articles on medicine, applied science, agronomy, and a host of other scientific topics. As did the writers of the *Mercurio Peruano*, Alzate focused on the viceroyalty of his birth and wrote articles intended to improve it.

Accompanying and further accelerating the spread of modern ideas in the colonies were Crown-sponsored scientific expeditions and the creation of new, specialized institutions designed to encourage specific activities. The decade-long botanical expedition of Hipólito Ruiz and José Antonio Pavón reached Peru in 1778 to collect samples and make drawings of plants that would enhance the Royal Botanical Garden in Madrid or be of medicinal value. A similar expedition was undertaken in New Spain in 1787. In related initiatives, a chair of botany was created at the University of Mexico, and a botanical garden was established. The Royal Academy of San Carlos was established in the capital in 1784 to teach painting, sculpture, and architecture, and the Royal College of Mines followed in 1792.

Although efforts to establish a school of mines in Peru failed, in the late 1780s the viceroyalty hosted an expedition of European mining experts led by the Swedish baron Thaddeus von Nordenflicht. Part of a royal effort to introduce the latest European mining techniques into the viceroyalty, the experts labored without notable success until 1810. A similar expedition led by the Basque Fausto de Elhuyar, who was trained at Europe's finest mining centers, reached New Spain in the late 1780s. Both missions confirmed the Crown's willingness to encourage experimentation and the initiation of new methods for utilitarian ends.

Demographic Expansion

Populations grew throughout the Western World during the second half of the eighteenth century. New Spain and Peru shared in this general growth, although at substantially different rates and with significant regional variations. There was internal migration in both viceroyalties, but neither received large numbers of immigrants from Europe.

Between 1742 and 1810, the population of New Spain rose from about 3.3 million to 6.1 million inhabitants. This impressive upward trend occasionally suffered reverses, most notably in 1785–86 when an estimated 300,000 persons died as a result of a catastrophic harvest failure and attendant epidemics. Growth was particularly rapid in the regions north and west of Mexico City as a result of both migration and natural increase. Northern New Spain had 26 percent of the viceroyalty's population in 1742 and 38 percent by 1810. The city of Guadalajara more than tripled in population from 1750 to 1810, largely as a result of migration from the surrounding rural areas. Mexico City was also a magnet for migrants, growing from 113,000 in 1793 to 137,000 in 1803.

The population of Peru reached its low point in the early 1720s as a result of a series of devastating epidemics. Recovery was well under way by 1750, however, and except for a temporary loss after the Indian rebellion led by Tupac Amaru in 1780, the population grew for the remainder of the colonial era. The census of 1792 listed 1,076,122 inhabitants. By 1812, natural increase, particularly among the Indian population, and territorial reorganization brought the total to about 1.5 million.

Breaking down the population totals reveals the substantial increase in the mixed-race and white populations. In the mid-seventeenth century, *castas* comprised a little over 5 percent and Indians some 86 percent of the population of New Spain. Despite an actual increase in numbers, Indians had dropped to about 74 percent of the total population by the 1740s and to only about 60 percent by the close of the eighteenth century. The population considered white grew to 18 percent, and the *castas*, with 22 percent, emerged as the second largest socioracial group in the viceroyalty. The 1792 census indicated that Peru had a smaller proportion of Spaniards (13 percent) and Indians (56 percent) than New Spain did. *Castas* accounted for 27 percent. Although the slave population in New Spain was negligible, Peru had over forty thousand (4 percent) black and mulatto slaves, most of whom resided in the intendancy of Lima.

The population change in both New Spain and Peru in the second half of the eighteenth century was almost entirely dependent on natural increase. Unlike Brazil and Cuba, to cite extreme cases, neither viceroyalty was a major participant in the African slave trade. The immigration of whites was also numerically inconsequential. In the early 1790s, Mexico City had only 2,359 peninsulars, almost all males. The booming mining center of Guanajuato had only 314 adult male peninsulars, Querétaro just 190, and Antequera 274. The viceroyalty as a whole probably contained fewer than 15,000 peninsulars at the close of the century. Peninsular immigration to Peru was even smaller than to New Spain. With fewer opportunities in trade and in civil, military, and ecclesiastical positions, the attractions were limited. Although individual peninsulars sometimes secured wealth, power, and prestige, especially through commerce, they were not demographically important in these two viceroyalties.

The white population was concentrated in or near the cities and towns in both New Spain and Peru. According to contemporary accounts, 67,500 whites, almost half of the city's total population, lived in Mexico City in 1803. Guanajuato and Antequera both had over a third of their population classified as Spaniards, the census term for whites. In Peru, the provinces of Lima, Arequipa, and Cuzco together contained 42 percent of the viceroyalty's Spanish population in 1792, and the majority of these whites lived in cities.

Society

The hierarchical socioeconomic structure based on race, occupation and wealth, culture, corporate affiliation, and legal privileges that had developed in the sixteenth century persisted in the late eighteenth century. At both the top and bottom of this hierarchy, race and class correlated closely. Peninsulars and creoles dominated the upper class, which included owners of large estates and mines, wholesale merchants, high-ranking royal officials and clerics, professionals, and large-scale retailers. Indians made up the majority of the very large lower class of unskilled manual laborers and servants in the countryside. In a number of cities and larger towns, *castas* and slaves numerically dominated the lowest-paid, least-skilled positions. Between these extremes was a growing middle stratum. Character-ized by racial heterogeneity, this stratum was expanding in response to the increased complexity of the economy and new opportunities promoted by a growing population and the reforms of Charles III. In urban areas the majority of employed white males could be found in artisan, retail, and other middle-level occupations. Even more numerous were the *castas*, par-ticularly *mestizos* and mulattoes. A small number of Hispanized Indians were present as well. In rural areas, independent farmers with small or middle-sized holdings included creoles and, in some regions, *castas* and Indians.

An expanded population and the growth of mining production, trade, and commercial agriculture in New Spain after 1750 led to a growing gulf between rich and poor. Those families that owned estates that sold wheat, corn, meat, *pulque*, and other products to expanding urban markets, and those that owned productive silver mines or invested in wholesale trade achieved unprecedented

Because so many colonial residents were illiterate, every town or city had profes-sional letter writers. This is one of the many letter writers who worked in the cen-tral plaza of Mexico City.

prosperity. In the late eighteenth century, about one hundred, primarily creole, families in Mexico City, and perhaps ten elsewhere in the viceroyalty had assets of approximately one million pesos or more. Their immense fortunes, rather than titles or other honors, separated them from the other members of a larger elite of lesser landowners, mine owners, merchants, and high-ranking bureaucrats and ecclesiastics. Unable to enter their ranks through marriage or to compete with them economically, this lower elite was tied to their superiors by shared business interests and a common aversion to the lower orders. The great families owned numerous estates in different regions of New Spain, both as protection against natural disasters and as collateral in a society based heavily on credit. They integrated their agricultural investments by controlling the processing and marketing of goods produced on their estates, and they attempted to dominate the marketing of imported goods in regions in which they held properties. Lima had more titled nobles than Mexico City did, but only a handful of millionaires.

At the opposite end of the socioeconomic spectrum in New Spain was a growing underclass. Access to adequate land to sustain a family became more difficult as the villages' expanding populations exceeded their resources and as inheritance divided farmers' rural properties into parcels insufficient for subsistence. Consequently, a steady flow of migrants from the countryside sought a better life in the cities. As the largest city in the empire, Mexico City, not surprisingly, had the largest underclass. During periods of economic crisis or famine, the city's destitute may have constituted a third or more of its population. Unskilled workers found permanent employment difficult to obtain and usually were forced to look for work each day. With urban wages remaining nearly static during the eighteenth century and prices increasing after 1775, the plight of the poor worsened. Unfortunate Indians, *castas*, and some whites found themselves trapped in this broadening pool of poverty. But in 1796 a third of the persons arrested by Mexico City criminal authorities were whites; Spanish birth was no guarantee of prosperity.

With a much smaller base population and a slower rate of growth after 1720, Peru was spared the demographic pressure on land that caused such suffering in portions of Mexico. Lima's population experienced only modest change from the 1740s to the 1840s, hovering between fifty thousand and sixty thousand inhabitants. There was no equivalent of the stream of migrants responsible for Mexico City's rapidly rising population in the decades immediately before 1810. Although a gulf between a small, wealthy white elite and a large, poor working class had long been present, Peru did not experience the expansion of poverty or of a large underclass as had occurred in New Spain.

Few persons born in New Spain and Peru after 1750 enjoyed substantial upward social mobility. Downward social mobility, as defined by the society's racial prejudices, on the other hand, was commonplace. Examinations of marriages in Antequera, Querétaro, Guanajuato, and León, New Spain, in the 1790s reveal incomplete but suggestive information. Intermarriage between Spaniards and nonwhites was not uncommon. Even in cases in which mulatto or Indian women married Spaniards, the offspring suffered the general prejudice of the white population against *castas*. Because Spaniards in interethnic marriages were usually poor artisans or laborers, their children enjoyed none of the advantages that a well-to-do family could provide: education, capital, and influential friends and relatives. In the modest provincial town of Antequera in 1792, an elite of 327 contained only 4 nonwhites. Although there were another 17 nonwhites in the intermediate professional and shopkeeper group, this number was insignificant compared with 290 whites. The increasing size of the under-class in New Spain's cities, moreover, underscored the frequency of down-ward social mobility; the presence of members of every racial background emphasized its pervasiveness.

A major exception to this general pattern of downward social mobility was achieved by a small but highly visible number of peninsulars. The most successful arrived in the New World to work as business apprentices for peninsular uncles or other kinsmen who had sent for them. After years of training and forgoing marriage, the most promising married cousins or the daughters of business associates, joined their fathers-in-law's busi-nesses, and prospered. The wealthiest peninsulars used international trade as the basis for their fortunes but usually diversified as quickly as possible by investing in rural properties and other real estate. In New Spain, An-tonio de Bassoco, a Basque merchant and investor in mines, agriculture, and loans, parlayed his father-in-law's legacy of 250,000 pesos in 1763 into a fortune of 2.6 million pesos by the time of his own death in 1814. In Peru, the Navarrese millionaire Pedro de Abadia invested in international trade, agriculture, and mining. Peninsulars were also active merchants in the provinces. Creoles participated in trade as well, both in the provinces and in the viceregal capitals, but were seldom among the most successful.

The expansion of the bureaucracy also brought more peninsulars into the elite. The introduction of standing armies and efforts to revitalize the militias augmented the numbers of peninsular officers serving in the viceroyalties. Archbishops and bishops, too, were usually peninsulars dur-ing the late eighteenth century.

The economic, social, and political power and visibility of a few penin-sulars should not obscure the failure of many to improve their position. From the perspective of creole males, however, all peninsular males held jobs that might have gone to them. Moreover, the successful peninsulars who married almost invariably married creole women of good family, thus reducing the most attractive pool of potential wives for ambitious American-born males. Among the most prominent creole families, nev-ertheless, a wealthy or well-placed peninsular son-in-law was an asset. The peninsulars, in turn, benefited from incorporation into established fam-ilies whose political connections and economic resources could further their ambitions.

Silver Production

Silver continued to be the major export for both New Spain and Peru from the mid-eighteenth century until 1810. Although the creation of the Viceroyalty of the Río de la Plata in 1776 severed Potosí and the rest of Upper Peru from the Viceroyalty of Peru, registered silver production in Lower Peru ultimately exceeded that of the older mining region. Starting from a low base of about 2.3 million pesos produced during the decade between 1700 and 1709, Lower Peru's production rose to 16.2 million pesos in the 1760s. Silver continued to be produced at a faster rate in Peru than in New Spain, rising to a peak of 44 million pesos in the 1790s, although Peru's total production remained far lower than New Spain's.

Registered silver production in New Spain was lower between 1701 and 1710 than at any time since the 1670s. Then it began to grow rapidly and nearly doubled, to an annual average of over 9 million pesos, by the decade from 1741 to 1750. After expansion in the next decade pushed production to well over 100 million pesos, there was a brief decline owing to a shortage of mercury. Starting in 1769, output climbed again. Annual production reached 10 million to 15 million pesos a year in the 1770s and continued its ascent into the first decade of the new century. The most spectacular single year was 1804, when over 25 million pesos were produced.

The great growth in New Spain's silver production that began in 1776 was aided by large infusions of capital drawn from international commerce, expensive drainage projects, improved supplies of mercury, the use of gunpowder for blasting, and a variety of tax incentives. Approximately ten operations, each with over a thousand workers and a capital investment of more than a million pesos, dominated Mexican mining. The largest mine, the Valenciana, had more than three thousand workers. In some years its owners, the newly titled condes de Valenciana, received profits of over a million pesos.

In Peru, mercury supplies from Spain, necessary when the Huancavelica mine was exhausted, raised production at the older mines, and new strikes in the province of Trujillo led to a rising overall production that peaked in 1799. In contrast with New Spain, Peru's mining was characterized by numerous small-scale, undercapitalized enterprises averaging scarcely a dozen employees per mine.

The Rural Economy

The glitter of precious metals should not obscure the importance of agricultural and pastoral production in the two viceroyalties. The cultivation of maize, wheat, potatoes, and other staples occupied most of the viceroyalties' working populations. In the closing years of Charles IV's reign, livestock in New Spain provided about 30 percent of the viceroyalty's gross domestic product. This sector was dominated by large-scale producers, some with herds of cattle and sheep in excess of 100,000 head.

In contrast with the natives of New Spain, Indian commoners, chieftains, and communities in Peru more commonly raised livestock. In southern Peru, flocks of sheep and herds of cattle were small according to Mexican standards, but their ownership was more dispersed. Few estates had as many as thirty thousand sheep. As in New Spain, livestock production fell, beginning in the 1780s. The Tupac Amaru revolt and a depressed market for wool also led to a decline in Peru. Although Mexican producers sent cattle and sheep five hundred to six hundred miles from the northern pastures to Mexico City, Puebla, and other central Mexican markets, Peruvian producers rarely sent their animals more than sixty miles away, because of higher transportation costs and smaller markets.

The demands of a growing population and static or declining livestock herds increased beef prices in New Spain after mid-century, and inflated food prices emerged as a general problem in the viceroyalty about 1775. Workers were caught between higher prices for maize, wheat, beef, and other basic comestibles and stagnant wages. In Peru, prices for agricultural and manufactured goods apparently declined from 1755 to 1790. Sheep were far more important than cattle in Peru, and a collapse in the demand for wool in the 1780s, in large part because of the increased importation of European textiles, lowered prices. Although inflation appeared in Peru about 1790, it was less destructive than that in New Spain.

Trade

Beginning in 1765, the Spanish Crown slowly reduced its restrictions on colonial trade. After experimentally opening the Spanish Caribbean to trade with selected metropolitan ports, it expanded this "free trade within the empire" to Louisiana, Yucatan, and Campeche. In 1778 the new system was extended to the remainder of the mainland empire except New Spain and Venezuela. By 1789 these two colonies were also allowed to trade with sixteen Spanish ports. Reductions in duties and restrictions on intercolonial trade opened up trade further. The result was a remarkable tenfold expansion in the value of exports from the colonies to Spain from 1778 to 1796, when war with England initiated a permanent alteration in colonial trade.

Under the new trading system, a flood of European products, a growing proportion of which were of Spanish origin, reached Peru. Indeed, its higher silver production enabled Peru to remain Spain's most valuable trading partner in South America, and Peru's cities and mining centers were growing markets for imported goods: Between 1785 and 1796, Peru received 22 percent of all exports sent to America from Cádiz.

The influx of imported textiles and other goods reduced prices for consumers and led to more commercial activity. Numerous new retail stores opened, frequently under the ownership of peninsular immigrants. At the same time, lower-priced imported textiles manufactured in Spain and England weakened the market for the *obraje*-produced textiles already competing with inferior but cheaper cloth woven in small local establishments in the highlands.

The volume of Mexican trade depended heavily on the quantity of silver available for exportation. A jump in silver production beginning in 1776 was followed by a substantial expansion of trade. Between 1785 and 1795, imports from Spain averaged about 5.8 million pesos. Despite enormous variations in volume as a result of Spain's frequent involvement in wars, the average grew to about 8 million pesos between 1796 and 1810. Goods from other colonies and neutrals raised the total trade to over 11 million pesos. At the same time, private bullion exports averaged 8.3 million pesos. Overall, bullion accounted for nearly three-quarters of the value of Mexico's exports. Cochineal, sugar, and other products comprised the remainder.

Revenues

Royal revenues in New Spain rose dramatically from 1740 to 1775. Mining, increased trade, the first shifts from tax farming to direct collection by royal officials, and a growing population helped fuel this growth. In the 1770s, there was another spurt in revenue when the Crown imposed new taxes, increased some old ones, and took over the collection of the sales tax (*alcabala*).

The higher tax revenue based on trade reflected a general growth in commerce. Commercial taxes exceeded revenues from mining beginning in the 1780s, yielding an annual average of more than 4.8 million pesos for the years 1780 to 1809. The revenues from monopolies were even greater. Excluding tobacco, they nearly tripled in the 1780s and averaged 6 million pesos from 1780 to 1809. The establishment of a tobacco monopoly in 1765 initiated a new and highly lucrative source of revenue that produced net profits approaching 3 million pesos a year by the late 1770s and averaged over 3.5 million pesos two decades later. Mining revenues exceeded 4 million pesos annually in the 1780s and 1790s but dropped to under 3.4 million from 1800 to 1809. Tribute grew with the native population, rising above 1 million pesos annually in the 1770s and contributing over 1.6 million pesos each year from 1800 to 1809. After 1780, new taxes and loans related to the expenses of war became the most important sources of royal revenue, growing from 28 percent in the 1790s to 63 percent of the total from 1800 to 1809 as the viceregal government fell deeper and deeper into debt.

After 1775, inflation accounted for much of the nominal growth. Although the real value of revenues increased over 2.5 times from 1712 to 1793, there was no increase from 1793 to 1810. The revenues of Mexico's central treasury grew in nominal value from 69 million pesos in 1791–95 to 112 million in 1806–10, but at the same time real per-capita income dropped.

In Peru, revenues collected in the Lima treasury in the 1750s were slightly less than from 1701 to 1710. The first sign of real growth was in the 1760s when sales tax revenue more than doubled. Total revenues remained almost the same until the 1780s, when the growth of sales tax revenues and income from mining and from other treasuries in Peru pushed the totals to their highest level of the century. Despite the onset of inflation, revenues fell by over 10 percent in the 1790s and continued to decline in the following decade. As in Mexico, the government borrowed to bridge the gap between normal revenues and expenditures. Although Mexico's treasury remitted over 90 million pesos in public revenue to Spain from 1761 to 1800, Peru's treasury sent none.

In 1808 Mexico was by far the richest and most populous colony in the Hispanic world. Peru, in contrast, was struggling to retain its second rank against the emerging regions of the empire's periphery. In both viceroyalties, however, the population was larger, and mining production and trade were greater than a half-century earlier. Reforms had strengthened the royal authority and increased tax revenues. Yet all was not well. Mining production had peaked in the 1790s. Although government revenues continued to rise in the following decade in New Spain, extraordinary measures underlay the increase, and deficit spending had become the rule. In Peru, revenues dropped after reaching their apogee in the late 1780s. Both viceroyalties were experiencing inflation, which reduced the real value of taxes and, especially in New Spain, brought increasing misery to an expanding underclass. There had been economic growth in both viceroyalties after 1760, but its peak had passed by 1800. Moreover, this growth had not been accompanied by development. New Spain and Peru remained thoroughly colonial in their economies, societies, and institutions on the eve of independence.

The Emergence of the Periphery in Spanish America

During the late colonial period the population and economies of the once-stagnant peripheral colonies in Spanish America grew rapidly. At times famines and epidemics or short-term disruptions of both the Atlantic commercial system and regional trade interrupted this growth. Nevertheless, the economic expansion of the periphery during the last hundred years of the empire equaled the rapid growth experienced during the early stages of the mining boom in Peru and New Spain.

The emergence of Cuba, Venezuela, Chile, the Río de la Plata region, and New Granada added substantially to the empire's economic vitality. While Peru's and Bolivia's silver mines partially recovered from a lengthy depression and Mexico's economy grew substantially, the simultaneous expansion of European manufacturing and American agriculture transformed the character of the Atlantic economy. Within the peripheral colonies, merchants and landowners involved in the production and sale of agricultural exports— tobacco, cacao, *yerba*, wheat, coffee, sugar—and hides and processed animal products were the primary beneficiaries of this altered economy. Many small

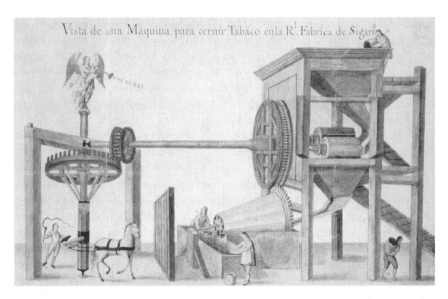

Vista de una Máquina, para cernir Tabaco enla R.¹ Fabrica de Sigarᵣˢ

In the eighteenth century the newly established tobacco monopoly produced an important new stream of revenue for the Spanish Crown. This massive machine was used by the Mexico City tobacco factory to produce snuff.

farmers supplying the food needs of growing colonial cities, retail merchants, and, in at least some cases, urban workers also earned more income, consumed more goods, and lived more comfortable lives.

It is difficult to determine precisely what promoted growth in the peripheral regions. The performance of their economies during this period reflected improved conditions in Europe generally and in Spain particularly. After over a century of metropolitan economic stagnation, there were clear signs of a renewed dynamism. By the end of the eighteenth century the greater consumer demand and the development of new markets in America and elsewhere stimulated Spanish manufacturers to introduce new and more efficient technologies in textiles and metallurgy. This led, in turn, to greater productivity and lower prices. To maximize these benefits, manufacturers needed new markets and new sources of raw materials. These opportunities and challenges stimulated investment and entrepreneurship in the long-dormant economies of the Caribbean and Southern Cone colonies.

Population growth and empirewide tax and commercial reforms enhanced the beneficial effects of the growing European demand for regional products. Changes in administrative structure also encouraged economic growth. The creation of two new viceroyalties, New Granada and Río de la Plata, pumped money and people into Bogotá and Buenos Aires and facilitated regional commercial integration. Finally, military expenditures tended to redistribute wealth from the older mining economies to the agricultural and grazing economies of the periphery.

Administration

Spain's effort to improve its colonial defenses, increase its revenue collection, and tighten its administration touched the peripheral colonies even more than it did the old viceregal centers. Defensive considerations had already led to the permanent establishment of the Viceroyalty of New Granada in 1739. Cuba became a captaincy-general in 1764 following the return of Havana to Spanish rule. Venezuela gained greater political and fiscal autonomy in 1777 when Caracas was made the capital of a captaincy-general. The creation of the Audiencia of Caracas in 1786 severed Venezuela's dependence in judicial matters on distant tribunals and confirmed the capital's dominance within the captaincy-general. Although long identified as a captaincy-general, in the late colonial era Guatemala also won additional regional autonomy.

The most significant change in colonial political organization occurred on the Viceroyalty of Peru's southeastern flank. This vast, sparsely populated region was vulnerable to both military attack and commercial penetration by Spain's rivals. Until finally evicted in 1776 by a large military force led by Pedro de Cevallos, the Portuguese maintained Colônia do Sacramento as a center for contraband trade on the east bank of the Río de la Plata. Cevallos's victory was followed by the creation of a new viceroyalty in 1777 that included Argentina, Uruguay, Paraguay, Bolivia, and part of Chile. The establishment of an *audiencia* in 1783 in the capital of Buenos Aires completed the reorganization.

In addition to major territorial reorganizations and the creation of new *audiencias*, the colonial administration was structurally altered through the introduction of the intendant system. First installed in Cuba in 1764, the system was extended to Venezuela in 1776 and to the Viceroyalty of Río de la Plata in 1782. By 1790 intendants were present throughout the American empire except in New Granada. Among their most important contributions was an enhanced ability to collect taxes. These officials and other tax initiatives led to increased revenue, much of which was expended locally for defense and internal improvements.

The Church

The Church was much weaker in the peripheral colonies than in the wealthier and more populous viceroyalties of Peru and New Spain. Nevertheless, it was a significant part of their cultural life and often important to their politics. Because the peripheral colonies were generally poor until late in the colonial period, the Church as a whole lacked the manpower and economic resources to match the rapidly expanding power of the secular bureaucracy after 1750. The Jesuits, however, were nowhere more powerful than in their famous reductions in Paraguay. To a regalist Crown, these reductions symbolized the Society's arrogance and, more importantly, the political danger of its geographically concentrated power.

A market scene from Rio de Janeiro. Slave and free black women dominated the food markets of the city.

When Charles III followed the Portuguese precedent by expelling the Jesuits from his realms in 1767, the action had enormous consequences in the Río de la Plata. The removal of the Society dramatically changed land and labor relations in Paraguay. Subsistence agriculture declined while *yerba* and tobacco production grew. After 1767 the Jesuits' ranches and plantations, powerful economic actors in the peripheral colonies, were sold to private individuals, given to rival orders, or run by local secular authorities. In the end this process of religious divestment seconded the general progress of market expansion in frontier zones and further reduced institutional constraints on the penetration of capitalist cultural values.

Population

Between 1750 and 1850, Latin America's population grew rapidly. Overall, the colonial population expanded at the rate of 0.8 percent per year, roughly twice the rate of contemporary Europe. As a group, the peripheral colonies grew faster than did the rest of the empire. In some cases, this expansion far exceeded even that of New Spain. Venezuela, for example, increased from an estimated 330,000 inhabitants in 1780 to 780,000 in 1800. Chile grew from 184,000 in 1775 to 583,000 in 1810.

Unlike in New Spain and Peru, immigration played a crucial role in population growth in the peripheral colonies. The most important sources for new migrants were Spain and Africa. The faster flow of free migrants from

Spain and slaves from Africa not only stimulated the peripheral economies but also profoundly altered their social structure and, in some cases, culture. Migrants from other European countries and from the older, more established colonies supplemented the two main migratory streams.

The drop in the mortality rate from that of the sixteenth and early seventeenth centuries also added to the population. Although in New Granada the number of natives kept falling until the end of the colonial period, in general the Indian population was recovering by the late seventeenth century. Nonetheless, Indians generally remained more vulnerable to epidemic disease than other groups were and also were more likely to be victims of violence. In the frontier zones of Chile, the Río de la Plata region, and along the Brazilian border, slave raids and conflicts with settlers disrupted Indian family life and depressed fertility. Where peace and a stable agricultural regime could be established, Indian populations grew steadily after 1750.

The rapid growth of the *casta* population was particularly important because of the social and economic changes that accompanied it. The *castas* operated in the money economy as producers and consumers, thus contributing to the general economic expansion. By 1800 they were the largest racial group in most of the peripheral colonies. In Cuba, on the other hand, the rapid expansion of the African slave trade after 1762 reduced the demographic and cultural significance of the racially mixed population.

There are no reliable estimates for Spanish migration to the colonies in the eighteenth century. A total net migration to the peripheral colonies of forty thousand to fifty thousand, however, seems plausible. More important than the actual number was the fact that most of these immigrants arrived after 1762, which magnified the migration's political and social effects.

The increased vitality of the colonial economies attracted immigrants from Spain. The larger civil administration and military forces also drew Spaniards to the colonies, although most immigrants found employment outside the public sector. Trade was a steady magnet. In Buenos Aires after 1780, for example, 85 percent of the wholesale merchants were peninsulars.

The scale of European immigration to Spanish America was dwarfed by the flow of enslaved Africans. Between 1761 and 1810, colonists imported over 300,000 African slaves, most of whom entered the labor force of peripheral colonies. The Cuban economy rested increasingly on sugar production, and as a result slavery expanded rapidly into the nineteenth century. In 1760 the island was home to approximately 35,000 slaves. The sugar estates in the region of Havana averaged 45 slaves each. Beginning with Britain's promotion of slave imports during its occupation of Havana in 1762, sugar production soared. After Spain reasserted control, colonial authorities found it necessary to remove most of the obstacles that had previously limited slave imports. As a result, 140,000 slaves entered the Cuban work force between 1764 and 1810.

In response to a bigger but more competitive international market for cacao and the profitable introduction of tobacco, coffee, and sugar cultivation, Venezuela also received significantly more slaves. Because the colony depended heavily on the contraband trade in slaves reexported by the British in Jamaica and the Dutch in Curaçao, the currently accepted import estimate of 30,000 slaves between 1774 and 1810 is suspect. In 1810 the bishopric of Caracas alone had 64,462 slaves and 197,738 free blacks, out of a total population of 427,203.

The remainder of the Viceroyalty of New Granada—the modern nations of Colombia, Ecuador, and Panama—received a similar level of imports. Because the labor-intensive gold-mining industry of Colombia depended on slaves, the fourfold increase in registered production from the early to late eighteenth century suggests a significant overall growth in the region's supply of slaves. In the Chocó region, however, the number of slaves actually dropped after 1780.

The Río de la Plata region did not prove hospitable to the development of plantation agriculture. Nonetheless, customs records indicate a dramatic rise in slave imports after the creation of the new viceroyalty. At least 45,000 slaves entered the port of Buenos Aires between 1750 and 1810. The majority labored on the farms and ranches of the *pampas* or entered the urban labor force. Many slaves were in domestic service, whereas others provided much of the artisan and transportation work force. Those slaves not absorbed into the growing economy of Buenos Aires and its hinterland were sold in the interior, especially to the miners of Potosí.

Society

The demographic changes after 1750 led naturally to alterations in the social structure. The loosening of commercial restrictions after 1765 and the more important administrative and territorial reforms attracted Spanish merchants to the peripheral ports and capital cities. Peninsulars dominated the merchant elites of Buenos Aires, Caracas, Santiago, and Havana. In Buenos Aires, Tomás Antonio Romero grew wealthy from the mercury trade to Potosí and the importation of slaves. His contemporary, Gaspar de Santa Coloma, imported European goods and exported silver as a commission agent for Spanish commercial houses and also independently on his own account. As was common among wholesale merchants, both men provided credit to local producers and retailers. In Caracas, men like Domingo Zulueta and Juan Bautista Echezuría extended large amounts of credit to planters. Although Spanish merchants provided market intelligence, transportation and warehouse services, and essential credit, their social position and economic power ultimately rested on the dependable functioning of Spain's Atlantic lifeline.

In Venezuela and Cuba in particular, immigrant merchants married into rural elites. Many also invested directly in plantations and ranches so that by the end of their careers they were indistinguishable from wealthy creoles. In

Chile and New Granada, merchants and civil administrators forged lasting business and social ties. By the 1790s, merchants' fortunes were among the largest in these colonies, and the relative liquidity of their wealth gave them disproportionate economic influence.

New opportunities created by the expanding markets provided a fertile environment for the development of new rural elites—cacao planters in Venezuela, cattlemen in the Río de la Plata, *yerba* growers in Paraguay, wheat farmers in Chile, and sugar planters in Cuba. Most of the members of these new elites were "new men" from modest provincial backgrounds. Their ranches, plantations, and farms were located away from the traditional urban centers of social power, and this geographic dispersal and fragmentation of wealth and social power had important consequences in the period after independence.

The dominant cities of the peripheral colonies attracted artisans and lesser-skilled immigrants as well as merchants and bureaucrats. But in this expansive era, immigrants sought to escape manual labor by purchasing and training slaves or recruiting free *casta* apprentices. Nevertheless, the arrival of assertive new immigrants often led to bitter conflicts with the native born. In Buenos Aires, for example, such conflicts led guilds of silversmiths and shoemakers to fail in the 1790s. In some cities underpaid soldiers from local garrisons sought jobs in the civilian economy, undercutting wages and competing for employment. Although their absolute number was limited, the immigrants' visibility and assertiveness helped promote creole nationalism among the urban masses.

The slave trade had an impact on evolving social relations in all of the peripheral colonies except Chile. This tragic commerce alleviated the chronic labor problems and helped unleash the economic potential previously held in check by the fleet system. Yet the influx of African slaves also led to racial and cultural conflicts and further reduced the prestige of manual labor. In every occupation in which slave labor became important, both income and status tended to decline significantly. As a result, interpersonal violence, attacks on property, and other antisocial behavior developed an implicitly racial as well as class character.

By the end of the eighteenth century the peripheral societies generally were more racially and culturally heterogeneous than they had been fifty years earlier. There also was more social and geographic mobility: Where the slave trade had expanded, there was greater racial consciousness, but there was also more miscegenation and a proliferation of ambiguously defined social types.

The Peripheral Economies, Public Expenditures, and Trade

Demographic growth was crucial to the economic expansion of the late eighteenth century. Given the labor-intensive nature of the colonial economy, an expanding population reduced labor costs and promoted the exploitation of formerly marginal mineral and agricultural resources. More farm workers and ranch hands meant more rural production. Mining, transportation, and construction also were stimulated by the greater availability of workers.

All of the major cities of the peripheral colonies mushroomed during this period. Buenos Aires, Caracas, Bogotá, and Santiago more than doubled in size between 1770 and 1810. By 1780 Havana became the second largest city in the empire, with more than eighty thousand inhabitants. This growth of the urban population stimulated the development of market agriculture, construction, and services. The demand for European goods also increased substantially.

Another characteristic of the late colonial economic surge was the expansion of the market economy relative to that of the subsistence sector. This resulted in part from expanded silver production and mintage in both Peru and Mexico. The colonial money supply at last overcame some of the chronic cash shortage that had previously held back economic growth. The advantages of this increased monetarization were particularly important to the economies of the peripheral colonies, where both production for market and wage labor lagged far behind the levels in New Spain and Peru.

The administrative and territorial reorganizations of the Bourbon period, particularly those implemented during the reign of Charles III, increased tax revenues, whose expenditure stimulated the peripheral economies. By the end of the colonial period, the public sector was the single largest employer in most colonial cities. For example, the creation of new viceregal courts in Bogotá and Buenos Aires and the enhanced administrative authority of Caracas resulted in the appointment of numerous new officials who spent their salaries locally. Consumption expanded accordingly, most often at the profitable upper end of the market for goods, services, and housing. The administrative reforms also led to major new investments in government buildings and other internal improvements.

Expenditures by the municipal authorities often matched in scale those by the royal administrators. New office buildings, customs warehouses, harbor improvements, and a range of investments in street paving, water supply, public hygiene, and other forms of civic improvement injected public money into the economy. Skilled and unskilled workers and the local suppliers of building materials benefited from these expenditures.

The creation of state-run tobacco monopolies had dramatic and unforeseen consequences in the peripheral colonies. Once imposed, the monopolies limited tobacco production, set prices, processed and manufactured tobacco products, and controlled retail sales. Even though consumer demand in the colonies and in Europe pushed upward, tobacco growers gained only limited benefits. Consumers also found these poor man's luxuries increasingly expensive. The Crown, however, earned heady profits. Because the monopoly paid cash, the tobacco-producing regions of Venezuela, New Granada, and especially Paraguay were able to develop new commercial relations with regional and even international markets.

As cash replaced barter, the largest urban centers established more effective domination over the countryside.

The period after 1760 was also a time of renewed and expanded military commitments. Spanish garrisons were increased in size and readiness, and colonial militias were enlarged and provided with better weapons and training. This greater military commitment placed a heavy burden on the colonial treasuries. Regular army units in Cuba alone absorbed 647,775 pesos per year in salaries, but the local treasury had only 178,000 in income. Governmental solvency depended on subsidies from the Mexican treasury. In the jurisdiction of Buenos Aires, military salaries cost the treasury more than 3 million pesos between 1796 and 1800. Two smaller interior cities of the viceroyalty, Córdoba and Santa Fe, devoted nearly 90 percent of their public expenditures to military salaries and subsistence.

The secondary economic consequences of military expenditures were often significant. Major fortifications projects at Havana and Cartagena affected local labor markets and pushed up wages for both skilled and unskilled workers. Even in regions where military construction was limited, enlistments in regular army units and part-time militia service tended to alter the labor supply. In the region around Buenos Aires, for example, the military buildup exacerbated the preexisting labor shortage, thus encouraging the expansion of the grazing industry which used less labor than did farming or manufacturing. The greater manpower of the Spanish garrisons and colonial militias also affected the economies of these regions in other ways. The increased demand for food, shelter, and clothing stimulated production and led to higher employment levels. The fact that the government paid cash was in itself helpful to the entire economy, as this promoted more complex commercial relations. The military in Cuba spent more than 30 million pesos during Spain's participation in the British colonies' struggle for independence. This infusion of capital, in turn, directly underwrote the local elite's ambitious plans to enlarge the sugar industry.

The already-evident growth of the transatlantic trade received further stimulation as the Crown slowly initiated "free trade within the empire" after 1765. By 1789 all major Spanish American ports were participating in the new system. When war with Britain began in 1796, Spanish exports were disrupted, and the Crown further compromised the limitations on colonial commerce by permitting trade with neutral nations. The major beneficiaries of this policy were United States merchants, who quickly moved into the Cuban market, in particular.

The most spectacular example of economic expansion after 1760 occurred in Cuba. During the brief British occupation, Havana and its surrounding agricultural region responded hastily to the influx of cheap slave labor, commercial credits, and a ready sugar market. Although Spanish sovereignty was soon reestablished, the liberalized trade laws and tax breaks stimulated sugar production. The now-dynamic sugar sector continued to grow, pushing aside tobacco and other agricultural rivals. Between 1759 and 1789, the number of sugar mills tripled, and overall production grew nearly eightfold. Then in

The residents of colonial Latin America enjoyed sports and games where betting was common. In this painting wagers are placed on a cockfight. The large figure at the top served as judge. Since an amateur painted this scene, there is a problem with perspective. The most important and powerful figures on the elevated stage are large while the adult bettors arrayed around the ring are painted as miniatures.

1791 the slave rebellion in Haiti drove up world sugar prices and further accelerated the growth of Cuban production.

Each year Cuba's plantation economy moved inexorably toward its mature form; the average plantation size grew, and the average number of slaves per plantation increased. This in turn caused a social revolution in the captaincy-general. The new sugar aristocracy became Cuba's first authentic creole elite, eclipsing in wealth and prestige the local representatives of the Spanish Crown. In the countryside, many rural small holders, tobacco producers and market gardeners, were pushed off their land. In Havana and other cities, *castas* and free blacks in artisan and lesser-skilled jobs lost status and income in competition with slaves. Although the sugar boom made Cuba wealthier in absolute terms, the masses of this society suffered a relative decline in status and material well-being.

Both New Granada and Venezuela saw a substantial increase in exports, as well as some general economic expansion, in the late colonial period, but neither matched the incredible performance of Cuba. In the district of Antioquia in New Granada, gold production increased from 27,150 gold pesos in 1750 to approximately 250,000 in 1800. Imports followed the same upward curve, increasing fivefold between 1760 and 1800. Trade with Spain and taxation, however, removed much of this bullion from the colony's economy. Gold contributed nearly 90 percent of New Granada's average of 2 million pesos in annual exports in the last decades of colonial rule. Instead of stimulating significant real growth, the increased gold production brought inflation and helped finance imports, especially textiles, that competed with local manufacture. New taxes and monopolies wrung additional consumer demand out of the economy.

Venezuela followed the Cuban model more closely. The creation of the Caracas Company in 1728 had provided the colony with both a commercial link to Spain and a source of capital. As cacao cultivation spread, slave imports increased. Competition from other cacao producers in the late eighteenth century led Venezuelan growers to diversify into other exportable products. Livestock raising became a major industry that sent thousands of mules to the sugar islands of the Caribbean in exchange for slaves. Tobacco production increased after the creation of the state monopoly, but government policy limited the potential for growth. Exports of coffee, indigo, and sugar all went up after 1780. Geographic advantages gave Venezuelan producers and consumers access to the British and Dutch markets.

Chile was less affected by imperial reform and the development of the Atlantic market than were the three colonies geographically located along the dynamic Caribbean Basin or the Río de la Plata region. Still, between mid-century and 1800 the value of Chile's mining production more than doubled, to approximately 1 million pesos a year, and silver, gold, and copper became important exports. Wheat exports to Peru, a mainstay of the economy, continued to grow after 1750, although more slowly than in the first decades of the century.

The Viceroyalty of Río de la Plata was a great success story. By opening Buenos Aires to direct trade with Spain and other Spanish colonies and by linking the mines of Potosí to this port, the Spanish government provided the fiscal and monetary resources necessary to energize the region's long-dormant agricultural and grazing potential. Although the area continued to suffer from a chronic labor shortage, the slave trade and internal migration provided some relief.

By 1810 the combined economic weight of Buenos Aires's expanding consumer base and the capital resources of its wholesale merchants made the city both the undisputed center of an integrated regional commercial system and an entrepôt for the Atlantic economy. The capital's emergence tended to diminish the vitality of provincial towns such as Santa Fe, Asunción, and Córdoba that had previously controlled the regional markets for *yerba*, local wines, and textiles. By the end of the colonial period, only two Spanish American ports, Vera Cruz and Callao-Lima, ranked ahead of Buenos Aires in volume and value of commerce.

After the commercial sector, the grazing industry was the major beneficiary of the creation of the viceroyalty. Hide exports rose from 150,000 at mid-century to a high of 1.5 million in 1786 and averaged 1 million until 1806. Typical of this form of dependent colonial development, however, Buenos Aires imported most of its tanned leather from Spain. Salted-beef exports to the plantations of Cuba and Brazil grew, but production was inhibited by high salt prices and limited labor supply. Dried beef and lard also found export markets. As livestock requirements at Potosí increased after 1730, traditional producers in the interior provinces largely met the demand. Pastoralists around Buenos Aires, too, sent thousands of mules to the mining district each year.

The region's agricultural sector also expanded during the final four decades of the colonial period. As the city of Buenos Aires grew, orchards and farms spread across the neighboring *pampas*, but labor was so short that Indians, convicts, and vagrants were forced to help with the harvests. In the interior, transportation difficulties often hindered development. The wines and brandies of San Juan and Mendoza found eager consumers in both the capital and in Potosí, but rugged cart roads and long trips hurt quality and raised prices. Nevertheless, the growth of Buenos Aires stimulated the interior's production of wine, *yerba*, wheat, and textiles.

The economy of Paraguay underwent complex changes during the eighteenth century. Throughout the late Habsburg period, *yerba* production dominated this isolated colony. A chronic currency shortage and the dominant role of the Society of Jesus in production and distribution, however, held back market expansion. In the early eighteenth century the Jesuits produced roughly 25 percent of the total volume and 40 percent of the value of *yerba*. The Jesuits' success was furthered by their interregional network of correspondents and warehouses that provided better market intelligence than that received by independent producers and also by their ability to wait out price swings. The Society's expulsion in 1767 enabled rival producers to reallocate Indian laborers, purchase improved lands, and attract new capital. As a result, production increased, and more markets were found in Chile, Peru, and Brazil. This commercial vigor did not, however, improve the lot of the Paraguayan masses, who were increasingly pushed into debt peonage and tenancy.

Despite the remarkable growth of the peripheral economies, fundamental structural weaknesses remained. Much of the new growth was in exports, particularly of agricultural and grazing products. Yet bullion continued to dominate the relationship between several colonies and the metropolis. Chile exported nearly 900,000 pesos in gold and silver annually. Despite the growth in hide exports from Buenos Aires after 1776, silver from Potosí still contributed 80 percent of the value of all exports from the region. In New Granada, bullion provided 90 percent of export value. This hemorrhage of bullion drew down the colonial capital stock, limited the spread of commercial exchange, and hindered investment. The tardy development of banking, credit, and insurance in these colonies exacerbated the negative effect of the bullion loss.

Responding to new commercial opportunities, the producers of Cuban sugar; Venezuelan cacao, hides, and *yerba* from the Río de la Plata; and Chilean wheat increased their investments, improving the land and buying slaves or hiring free labor. The prosperity of these largely creole producers depended heavily on the fragile and unpredictable geopolitical relationships of the European powers. After 1792 Spain's shifting military alliances with England and then France led to the breakdown of the reformed commercial system that had helped stimulate growth. Unlike the bullion-based commercial system of the Habsburg era, the agricultural export economies promoted by the Bourbon reforms in the peripheral colonies could not wait out the disruption of the Atlantic trade. As a result, colonial producers successfully sought and developed new markets outside the legal commercial system. The United States, Britain's Caribbean colonies, and Britain itself replaced the old partners and further promoted exports of tropical products as well as bullion. This process loosened ties with Spain, encouraged economic nationalism, and strengthened the social power of creole elites.

The Enlightenment

The ideas of the Enlightenment circulated among a small minority of the urban elites and educated members of the middle sectors of the peripheral colonies. Nearly all of the great works of philosophical speculation, political and economic inquiry, and natural science were known in these colonies. Usually Spain played an intermediary role in the transmission of these ideas, either through the education of well-to-do creoles in the metropolis or through the discussion of the French and English works in Spanish books exported to the colonies.

Despite the official hostility of Church and state to many of the most important Enlightenment authors, priests and royal administrators were among those persons most likely to own and lend forbidden works. European and American travelers, participants in scientific expeditions, and technological advisers also acted as intermediaries in this intellectual revolution. Even sailors and merchants from the newly independent United

States contributed to this process by distributing in port cities potentially subversive tracts on republicanism.

The penetration of new ideas was advanced by the creation of secular organizations devoted to the twin totems of the new age: reason and progress. By the 1790s, economic societies had been established in many of the largest cities of the empire's periphery: Buenos Aires, Havana, Quito, Caracas, Guatemala, and Bogotá. Committed to promoting economic progress, these bodies typically published weekly journals that supported education, technological innovation, and broadened commercial relations. As educated colonials examined economic questions, some came to consider the Spanish commercial system as an obstacle to progress. Monopolies, special privileges, and restrictions on foreign trade—the very economic structure of empire—were attacked publicly. In Buenos Aires in 1809 the creole lawyer Mariano Moreno marshaled the economic liberalism of Adam Smith on behalf of free trade. Freemasons were also active in many peripheral cities. More explicitly political than the economic societies and organized in secret groups that led naturally to the conspiratorial style, the Freemasons later provided many leaders of the independence movements. Often their members were drawn from local elites tied to the export sector.

Protest and Popular Insurrections

There were a number of violent popular uprisings during the late colonial period, but they were not consciously connected with the intellectual ferment of the Enlightenment, and most of their leaders used the language of traditional Spanish law and Catholic theology to justify their actions. Most historians also separate these events from the later struggles for independence.

Popular violence and mob actions provoked generally by administrative corruption, new taxes, and high prices were common in colonial political life from the early seventeenth century onward. Royal officials were often targets for public frustration. In fact, competition and disagreement among civil bureaucrats, clergy, and their supporters repeatedly ignited violence and defined the political objectives of these conflicts. In the eighteenth century, however, the scale and duration of violent uprisings increased, and the most important of them directly threatened the metropolitan authority.

This change in the political character of popular protest originated in the administrative and fiscal reforms of the Bourbon monarchs. New taxes or the more efficient collection of old taxes provoked bitter protest. This was especially true when higher tax rates or new taxes pushed up the price of common consumer goods. The creation of private- and public-sector monopolies—the tobacco monopoly and the Caracas Company, for example—also led to litigation, protest, and, in some cases, rebellion. This occurred because the Spanish fiscal reform transferred the colonial tax burden away from the mining sector and Atlantic trade to articles of common consumption that directly affected the popular classes.

In 1749 cacao producers in Venezuela rebelled against the Caracas Company's heavy-handed monopoly. Led by the Canary Islander Juan Francisco de León, cacao growers resented the company's imposition of below-market prices and its inefficient provisioning of essential imports. More specifically, efforts by the company to prevent English and Dutch contraband threatened a further decline in earnings. Although the rebels gained the initial advantage, they disbanded their military force when a new governor promised remediation. After nearly two years of tense stalemate, the arrival of military reinforcements permitted Spanish authorities to arrest and exile the most prominent rebel leaders and reestablish the company's monopoly in a limited form.

Against a background of protracted decline of the local textile industry that adversely affected the whole of society, members of Quito's elite and popular classes united in 1765 and forced the government to withdraw a tax reform program intended to increase taxes and collect them more effectively. The coalition soon split on class and ethnic lines, however, and in an atmosphere of fear and mistrust all sides welcomed the arrival of royal troops in 1766. Lingering plebian mistrust doomed an elite rebellion in 1809.

In 1780 a large rebellion in Peru led by Tupac Amaru II helped ignite an uprising by the Indian masses of Upper Peru that lasted nearly three years. Although this rebellion of Aymara speakers maintained a loose alliance with Tupac Amaru's forces in the Quechua-speaking region of Cuzco, real cooperation against the Spanish was hindered by ethnic rivalries that antedated the Spanish conquest. Victorious Spanish authorities treated some white sympathizers mercifully but brutally executed Tupac Catari and other Indian leaders.

Although clearly directed against the conquest's social and economic consequences, these rebellions by the Indian masses in the Andean colonies did not directly challenge the king's authority or the legitimacy of the colonial regime. Like the earlier, less violent uprisings by white and *mestizo* colonists in Paraguay and Venezuela, Indian leaders proclaimed their loyalty to the king and focused their demands on eliminating or reforming the most corrupt and abusive elements of the colonial system, especially the *mita*, the forced sales of goods, and the sales taxes.

Right after the onset of the Indian uprisings in Peru and Bolivia, the colonial authorities in New Granada confronted a popular political protest. In order to pay for the defense of the colony against possible English attack, Spanish authorities increased the *alcabala*, raised tobacco and brandy prices, and limited the area where tobacco cultivation was permitted. The imposition of these tax and price increases combined in 1781 with the effects of bad harvests and an epidemic to produce rebellion.

The participants in this *comunero* revolt were drawn from the middle and lower sectors of provincial society and included *castas* and even Indians. Eventually a rebel force that numbered in the thousands marched on the nearly defenseless capital of Bogotá. Representing the Bogotá elite, Archbishop Antonio Caballero y Góngora appeared to surrender to most of the rebel demands, but once the armed *comuneros* dispersed, loyal troops reestablished control. Only a small rebel force led by José Antonio Galán refused to accept the settlement. But he was soon defeated and later executed.

The Haitian Revolution

The French Revolution began in 1789. By early 1793 a radical government had written a constitution, arrested and then executed King Louis XVI, and stripped the Catholic Church of most of its power and property. The radical democratic ideals of this revolution shook the old order in Europe and led to warfare on a global scale. These powerful forces precipitated revolution in the Americas as well.

In 1789 the French colony of Saint Domingue (now Haiti), the eastern half of the island of Española, was among the richest European colonies. Its plantations produced sugar, cotton, indigo, and coffee, accounting for two-thirds of France's tropical imports and generating nearly one-third of all French foreign trade. This impressive wealth depended on a brutal slave regime notorious throughout the Caribbean for its harsh punishments and poor living conditions. The colony's high mortality and low fertility rates created an insatiable demand for African slaves. As a result, in 1790 the majority of the colony's 500,000 slaves were African-born.

When Louis XVI called France's Estates General in 1789, wealthy white planters sent a delegation to Paris charged with seeking more home rule and greater economic freedom. The free mixed-race population, the *gens de couleur*, also sent representatives who sought to end racial discrimination and political equality with whites. Since the most prosperous *gens de couleur* were slave owners, they did not advocate abolition.

Growing political turmoil in France weakened the ability of colonial administrators to maintain order and, in the vacuum that resulted, planters, poor whites, and the *gens de couleur* pursued their narrow interests, engendering an increasingly bitter struggle. Given the slaves' hatred of the brutal regime that oppressed them and the accumulated grievances of the free people of color, there was no way to limit violence once the control of colonial officials and slave owners slipped.

By 1791 whites, led by the planter elite, and the *gens de couleur*, were engaged in open warfare. This breach between the two groups of slave owners gave the slaves an opening. A slave rebellion began on the plantations of the north and spread throughout the colony, destroying many of the richest plantations and killing many masters and overseers. Eventually, the rebellious slaves gained the upper hand under the leadership of François Dominique Toussaint L'Ouverture, a former domestic slave, who created a disciplined military force. His position strengthened in 1794 when the radical National Convention in Paris abolished slavery in all French possessions. After overcoming his rivals in Saint Domingue, Toussaint led an invasion of the neighboring Spanish colony of Santo Domingo and freed its slaves.

Portrait of François Dominique Toussaint L'Ouverture

News of this revolution spread quickly throughout the hemisphere. In the plantation regions slave owners and colonial officials feared that the victories of slaves in Haiti would provoke rebellion. As a result, they did everything they could to identify potential rebels and suppress the transmission of revolutionary propaganda. As far away as Buenos Aires, alarmed authorities arrested scores of suspected conspirators as fear of slave rebellion took hold.

After Napoleon took power in a conservative reaction to the excesses of the revolution, he attempted to establish firmly French control of its Caribbean colonies, both Haiti and Guadeloupe, and reestablish slavery. He sent large military forces to both islands. Initially successful in Saint Domingue, the French captured and exiled Toussaint to France where he died in prison. Although the French succeeded in Guadeloupe, in Haiti they lost tens of thousands of soldiers to yellow fever and military resistance. In 1804 Toussaint's successors declared independence, and the free republic of Haiti joined the United States as the second independent nation in the Western Hemisphere.

Spain's peripheral colonies experienced dramatic changes in the late colonial period. Population grew at unprecedented rates, and the mix of races, classes, and cultures was altered as well. At the base of the social pyramid, the flood of imported slaves undermined the dignity and independence of free labor, introduced greater cultural diversity, and heightened racial tensions.

At the middle and upper levels of the social order, the arrival of Spanish immigrants helped heighten the creoles' sense of cultural distinctiveness and a nascent nationalism. The increased European demand for colonial products led to a territorial expansion of grazing and agriculture. This in turn meant the physical dispersal of those groups that wielded social and economic power. After independence the political consequences of this process were manifested in numerous rebellions against the political elites of the capital cities. The fact that the "new men" of the late colonial period often produced goods that carried little traditional prestige—hides, sugar, coffee, *yerba*—itself contradicted established assumptions about social rank.

The more fluid character of the recently formed elites of these colonies—New Granada is a significant exception—was little constrained by the recently reformed and expanded colonial state. Viceroys and governors appointed to the peripheral colonies were commonly military men or career civil servants with little independent wealth or prestige. Intendants and subdelegates did not intimidate or awe the newly rich of the frontier regions. Even the hastily constructed or poorly converted commercial buildings that housed the new representatives of the Bourbon monarchs in these regions lacked the intimidating scale of the architectural props for royal authority in New Spain and Peru. In many ways the Bourbon state was more irritating than awe inspiring.

The relations of production and exchange in place by the 1790s were profoundly different from those inherited from the Habsburg period. At the beginning of the eighteenth century, the peripheral colonies sustained only small-scale interregional and international exchange relations. But by the 1790s their economies were closely linked with Europe and the United States. As a result of this transformation, they were richer but also more dependent. Fluctuations in distant markets, foreign wars, and shifting European alliances all came to play crucial roles in determining local economic conditions. Although these changes were set in motion by Spain's administrative and commercial reforms and funded in part by the investments of Spanish merchants and joint-stock companies, the Spanish market could not absorb the productive potential of the increasingly dynamic peripheral colonies.

Notes

1. Sergio Villalobos R., *El comercio y la crisis colonial* (Santiago, Chile: Universidad de Chile, 1968), p. 77.

2. C. R. Boxer, *The Golden Age of Brazil, 1695–1750* (Berkeley and Los Angeles: University of California Press, 1962), p. 53.

3. C. E. Castañeda, "The Corregidor in Spanish Colonial Administration," *Hispanic American Historical Review* 9:4 (November 1929), p. 448.

Suggested for Further Reading

Andrien, Kenneth J. *The Kingdom of Quito, 1690–1830: The State and Regional Development.* Cambridge, England: Cambridge University Press, 1995.

Andrien, Kenneth J., and Lyman L. Johnson, editors. *The Political Economy of Spanish America in the Age of Revolution, 1750–1850.* Albuquerque: University of New Mexico Press, 1994.

Brading, D. A. *Church and State in Bourbon Mexico: The Diocese of Michoacán, 1749–1810.* Cambridge, England: Cambridge University Press, 1994.

Brading, D. A. *Miners and Merchants in Bourbon Mexico.* Cambridge, England: Cambridge University Press, 1970.

Brown, Richard F. *Juan Fermín de Aycinena, Central American Colonial Entrepreneur, 1729–1796.* Norman: University of Oklahoma Press, 1997.

Cahill, David. *From Rebellion to Independence in the Andes: Soundings from Southern Peru, 1750–1830.* Amsterdam: Aksant Academic Publishers, 2002.

Castleman, Bruce A. *Building the King's Highway: Labor, Society, and Family on Mexico's Caminos Reales, 1757–1804.* Tucson: University of Arizona Press, 2005.

Chandler, D. S. *Social Assistance and Bureaucratic Politics: The Montepíos of Colonial Mexico, 1767–1821.* Albuquerque: University of New Mexico Press, 1991.

Chowning, Margaret. *Wealth and Power in Provincial Mexico: Michoacán from the Late Colony to the Revolution.* Stanford: Stanford University Press, 1999.

Cornblit, Oscar. *Power and Violence in the Colonial City: Oruro from the Mining Renaissance to the Rebellion of Tupac Amaru (1740–1782).* Translated by Elizabeth Ladd Glick. Cambridge, England: Cambridge University Press, 1995.

Couturier, Edith Boorstein. *The Silver King: The Remarkable Life of the Count of Regla in Colonial Mexico.* Albuquerque: University of New Mexico Press, 2003.

Deans-Smith, Susan. *Bureaucrats, Planters, and Workers: The Making of the Tobacco Monopoly in Bourbon Mexico.* Austin: University of Texas Press, 1992.

Fisher, John R., Allan J. Kuethe, and Anthony McFarlane, editors. *Reform and Insurrection in Bourbon New Granada and Peru.* Baton Rouge: Louisiana State University Press, 1990.

Fisher, John Robert. *Bourbon Peru, 1750–1824.* Liverpool, United Kingdom: Liverpool University Press, 2003.

Garner, Richard L. with Spiro E. Stefanou. *Economic Growth and Change in Bourbon Mexico.* Gainesville: University Press of Florida, 1993.

Higgins, Kathleen J. *"Licentious Liberty" in a Brazilian Gold-Mining Region: Slavery, Gender, and Social Control in Eighteenth-Century Sabará, Minas Gerais.* University Park: Pennsylvania State University Press, 1999.

Hill, Ruth. *Hierarchy, Commerce, and Fraud in Bourbon Spanish America: A Postal Inspector's Expose.* Nashville, Tenn.: Vanderbilt University Press, 2006.

Johnson, Lyman L. and Enrique Tandeter, editors. *Essays on the Price History of Eighteenth-Century Latin America.* Albuquerque: University of New Mexico Press, 1990.

Kamen, Henry. *Philip V of Spain: The King Who Reigned Twice.* New Haven and London: Yale University Press, 2001.

Lanning, John Tate. *The Eighteenth-Century Enlightenment in the University of San Carlos de Guatemala.* Ithaca: Cornell University Press, 1956.

Lynch, John. *Bourbon Spain, 1700–1808.* Oxford, England: Basil Blackwell, 1989.

Lynch, John, editor. *Latin American Revolutions, 1808–1826: Old and New World Origins.* Norman: University of Oklahoma Press, 1994.

Marichal, Carlos. *Bankuptcy of Empire: Mexican Silver and the Wars between Spain, Britain and France, 1760–1810*. Cambridge, England: Cambridge University Press, 2007.

Maxwell, Kenneth R. *Pombal: Paradox of the Enlightenment*. Cambridge, England: Cambridge University Press, 1995.

McFarlane, Anthony. *Colombia Before Independence: Economy, Society, and Politics Under Bourbon Rule*. Cambridge, England: Cambridge University Press, 1993.

Minchom, Martin. *The People of Quito, 1690–1810: Change and Unrest in the Underclass*. Boulder, Colo.: Westview Press, 1994.

Offutt, Leslie S. *Saltillo, 1770–1810: Town and Region in the Mexican North*. Tucson: University of Arizona Press, 2001.

Ouweneel, Arij. *Shadows over Anáhuac: An Ecological Interpretation of Crisis and Development in Central Mexico, 1730–1800*. Albuquerque: University of New Mexico Press, 1996.

Paquette, Gabriel B. *Enlightenment, Governance, and Reform in Spain and its Empire, 1759–1808*. New York: Palgrave Macmillan, 2008.

Patch, Robert. *Maya Revolt and Revolution in the Eighteenth Century*. Armonk, N.Y.: M. E. Sharpe, 2002.

Patch, Robert W. *Maya and Spaniard in Yucatan, 1648–1812*. Stanford: Stanford University Press, 1993.

Pearce, Adrian. *British Trade with Spanish America, 1763 to 1808*. Liverpool, United Kingdom: Liverpool University Press, 2008.

Radding, Cynthia. *Wandering Peoples: Colonialism, Ethnic Spaces, and Ecological Frontiers in Northwestern Mexico, 1700–1850*. Durham: Duke University Press, 1997.

Robins, Nicholas A. *Priest-Indian Conflict in Upper Peru: The Generation of Rebellion, 1750–1780*. Syracuse: Syracuse University Press, 2007.

Rosenmüller, Christoph. *Patrons, Partisans, and Palace Intrigues: The Court Society of Colonial Mexico, 1702–1710*. Calgary: University of Calgary Press, 2008.

Safier, Neil. *Measuring the New World: Enlightenment Science and South America*. Chicago: University of Chicago Press, 2008.

Serulnikov, Sergio. *Subverting Colonial Authority:Challenges to Spanish Rule in Eighteenth-Century Southern Andes*. Durham: Duke University Press, 2003.

Stavig, Ward, and Ella Schmidt, Editors and translators. *The Tupac Amaru and Catarista Rebellions: An Anthology of Sources*. Indianapolis: Hackett Publishing co.: 2008.

Stein, Stanley J. and Barbara H. Stein, *Apogee of Empire: Spain and New Spain in the Age of Charles III, 1759–1789*. Baltimore: Johns Hopkins University Press, 2003.

Tandeter, Enrique. *Coercion and Market: Silver Mining in Colonial Potosí, 1692–1826*. Albuquerque: University of New Mexico Press, 1993.

Taylor, William B. *Magistrates of the Sacred: Priests and Parishioners in Eighteenth-Century Mexico*. Stanford: Stanford University Press, 1996.

TePaske, John J., translator and editor. *Discourse and Political Reflections on the Kingdom of Peru by Jorge Juan and Antonio de Ulloa*. Norman: University of Oklahoma Press, 1978.

Thomson, Sinclair. *We Alone Will Rule: Native Andean Politics in the Age of Insurgency*. Madison: University of Wisconsin Press, 2003.

Vinson III, Ben. *Bearing Arms for His Majesty: The Free Colored Militia in Colonial Mexico*. Stanford: Stanford University Press, 2001.

von Humboldt, Alexander. *Political Essay on the Kingdom of New Spain*. Edited by Mary Maples Dunn. New York: Knopf, 1973.

TEN

CRISIS AND POLITICAL REVOLUTION

Chronology

Date	Location	Event
1807	Iberia	French invasion
1807	Portugal	Court flees to Brazil
1808	Spain	Abdications of Charles IV, Ferdinand VII
1808	Spain	Madrid uprising against the French, May 2, 1808; juntas; Central Junta
1808	New Spain	Elite Spaniards overthrow viceroy
1809	Upper Peru	Juntas in La Paz, Chuquisaca
1809	America	Elections for representatives to Central Junta
1810	Spain	Regency; General and Extraordinary *Cortes*; French occupy Andalusia
1810	Caracas, Buenos Aires, Santiago, New Granada	Formation of juntas to rule in the name of Ferdinand VII
1810	New Spain	Hidalgo Revolt
1810	Buenos Aires	Sends first of three unsuccessful expeditions to Upper Peru
1810–11	America	Elections for deputies to General and Extraordinary *Cortes*
1811	New Spain	Hidalgo captured and executed; Morelos, insurgency
1811	Caracas	Independence, First Republic
1811	Banda Oriental	Artigas begins movement for independence
1811	Paraguay	Independence
1811	Cartagena, Quito	Declare independence
1812	Spain and Empire	Constitution of 1812

War and revolution dominated the Atlantic world for the half-century that followed the American Revolution. This conflict led to political independence for thirteen English colonies and the creation of a constitutional republic that implemented limited social reforms. The French Revolution, begun in 1789, had a more dramatic effect. It initiated a quarter-century of European warfare and furnished revolutionary rhetoric about popular sovereignty and individual rights. Many in Iberia and the colonies were excited by the discussion of liberty and freedom, but the execution of Louis XVI and attack on the Catholic Church convinced the majority that the French Revolution was an assault on civilization. The rise of Napoleon and the intensified cycle of war that followed increased popular anti-French sentiment. In Brazil and in Spanish colonies that depended on the labor of slaves, the Haitian Revolution added the specter of servile insurrection and racial conflict to the era's uncertainties. While large colonial majorities remained resolutely hostile to emerging democratic and egalitarian ideas, the language of natural rights, popular sovereignty, and equality slowly built momentum across the colonial world.

When Napoleon sent a French army into Portugal in 1807, he drove its royal family and court to Brazil. His fateful decision to use military power to place his brother Joseph on the throne of Spain unleashed a political revolution in the Hispanic world between 1808 and 1812. A popular, patriotic uprising against the French in Spain led the way, declaring the people sovereign and creating governments of resistance. Politically active citizens in municipalities in unoccupied Spain and the Americas were now drawn into a novel political process. This included indirect elections in Spain and its colonies, the articulation of local grievances, and, in some cities, the creation of juntas to rule until the French were defeated. The desire for greater political autonomy or home rule and full equality within an explicitly defined "Spanish Nation" that included both Spain and the dominions of its empire was widespread.

The political revolution between 1808 and 1812 entrenched the ideas of sovereignty of the people, a written constitution, representative government, the separation of legislative, judicial, and executive responsibilities, unprecedented equality before the law, and a broad definition of citizenship. During this same period the colonial population split among three tendencies. Loyalists believed that officials appointed by whatever government existed in Spain should govern the colonies. Autonomists remained loyal to Spain and committed to the empire but sought the creation of local governments enjoying broad authority over domestic policies within a reformed Spanish Empire. Separatists sought total independence from Spain. After 1814 separatists gained strength relative to autonomists and generally favored a republican form of government. To their loyalist and monarchist or royalist opponents, the separatists were rebels," "insurrectionists," "insurgents," or "revolutionaries." As supporters of independence, however, the separatists considered themselves "patriots" and, if they supported the creation of a republic, "republicans."

An Era of War and Crisis for Spain and Portugal

Charles III died in late 1788, leaving Spain and the empire peaceful and reasonably prosperous. The Crown's normal income was nearly adequate for routine expenditures, and the royal debt was modest. By early 1808, when his son Charles IV abdicated, however, the imperial panorama looked very different. Except for occasional interludes of peace, Spain had been at war since 1793. English fleets had destroyed its navy, built at enormous cost, and Napoleon determined Spain's foreign policy while exacting financial tribute. Spanish colonial trade increasingly benefited neutral shippers and British manufacturers rather than Spanish merchants and producers, and a rapidly growing debt burdened the royal treasuries in Spain and the colonies. In addition, the prominence of the powerful royal favorite Manuel Godoy, grandiloquently titled Duke of Alcudia, Prince of the Peace, and Admiral-General of Spain and the Indies, had discredited the royal family. The French occupied neighboring Portugal in the absence of the court, which fled the invaders in 1807 and sailed to safety in Brazil. Yet despite the numerous difficulties, almost no one in Spain, Portugal, or the colonies expected that in less than two decades the mainland empires in America would be independent.

The Cost of War

The execution of France's Bourbon monarch Louis XVI on January 21, 1793, led Spain into the coalition of countries fighting against the spread of revolution. The nation was united against regicide, and initially the war enjoyed popular support. Military defeats, however, cost Spain its remaining portion of the island of Española in the treaty signed in 1795.

Angered over Spain's ending hostilities with France unilaterally, England attacked Spanish shipping. These provocations, a belief that a land war with France was more dangerous than naval conflict with England, and varied dynastic ambitions influenced Spain to sign an alliance with the French republic. War with Britain began in October 1796. The defeat of the Spanish fleet off Cape St. Vincent in early 1797 opened the way for a British blockade of Cádiz until 1800. The Peace of Amiens in 1802 restored peace to Europe once more, and Spain, which already had ceded Louisiana to France, now lost Trinidad. Little more than a French satellite, Spain found itself in renewed conflict with England beginning in late 1804. Victory over the combined Spanish and French fleets at Trafalgar in 1805 gave Britain uncontested dominance over the seas.

Spain's nearly continuous involvement in war between 1793 and 1808 proved extremely costly in terms of both direct financial expenditures and the loss of trade and regular remittance of bullion from the colonies. An important consequence was that earlier policies to integrate Spain and the colonies economically gave way to short-term fiscal considerations. Reciprocity within the "colonial compact" succumbed to the Crown's desperate attempts to extract as much revenue as possible from the Indies, regardless of the consequences for the colonial economies.

An Overwhelming Debt

Spain's tax system proved unable to provide the funds needed to pay the extraordinary expenses of war. When initial borrowing proved inadequate, the Crown turned to Spain's own money market. In 1794–95 it issued treasury bills (*vales reales*) worth over 64 million *pesos de vellón*, a sum equal to nearly 75 percent of the total regular peninsular revenues in these years. Buoyed by the sale of these treasury bills and bonds, the treasury's income in 1795 was the largest of the era. Ominously, the nation's deficit was almost equal to total income in 1792, the last year of peace. Conflict with Britain in 1796 forced the Crown to issue additional bonds and treasury bills whose total value exceeded *all* normal treasury income from American colonies between 1792 and 1807. Napoleon's demand for financial subsidies beginning in 1803 and the renewal of hostilities with England late in 1804 quickly pushed the Crown to the brink of bankruptcy.

Neutral Trade

The rapid deterioration of Spain's finances after 1793 and the subsequent disruption of normal trading patterns profoundly affected Spain's commercial and political relations with its colonies. The strength of the Spanish fleet and the alliance with Britain during the French war enabled American treasure to continue to reach Spain. Protected convoys carrying bullion managed to maintain a reasonable level of trade with the colonies, although the number of sailings dropped. Conditions changed rapidly following the initiation of hostilities with Britain in late 1796.

The British blockade of Cádiz paralyzed Spain's transatlantic trade. Whereas 171 ships sailed from America to Cádiz in 1796, only 9 ships arrived in 1797. Spain's inability to maintain its trade with the colonies spurred colonial officials in Cuba and Venezuela to open their ports to neutral traders, a practice used previously during the American Revolutionary War. In Madrid, policymakers recognized that the colonies needed some trade outlets and that state services such as mail delivery and the provision of mercury and administrative supplies had to be continued. In addition, they wanted to maintain some portion of the traditional market share to prevent the colonies from establishing new industries and trade links that would ultimately undermine the entire colonial system. These goals underlay the Crown's decree of November 18, 1797, sanctioning neutral trade. Intended as a temporary wartime expedient to keep the imperial system afloat, the new policy facilitated the elaboration of non-Spanish commercial ties for colonial merchants and producers that could not be eliminated when peace returned.

The merchants of Cádiz fought tenaciously against neutral trade and secured a short suspension in April 1799. Widespread noncompliance in the colonies and the continued need for revenue, however, led the Crown again to allow neutral trade in January 1801. After a brief peace and an attempt to reestablish the prewar system, renewed conflict with England in 1804 forced the reauthorization of neutral trade as the Spanish crown sought to obtain bullion by any means in order to pay enormous financial commitments to France.

The commercial pressures experienced by the colonies varied. Regions that relied on the exportation of agricultural and pastoral products for their economic well-being—notably Cuba, Venezuela, and the Río de la Plata—had to sell them in a timely manner or watch them deteriorate. In contrast, New Spain and, to a lesser degree, Peru could store bullion until the return of peace and withstand two or three years of disrupted commerce by reducing consumption and promoting local manufactures and agriculture. The most immediate and persistent pressure for neutral trade thus came from the empire's emerging peripheral regions.

The United States' trade with Spanish America expanded immediately with the advent of neutral trade. Exports of American flour and substantial quantities of reexported British textiles flowed to numerous Spanish American ports; Havana and other West Indian ports were especially profitable markets. The United States' exports to the Spanish West Indies grew sixfold from 1795–96 to 1800–1, reaching nearly $11 million in the later period, and expanded fourfold for Spanish America as a whole.

Consolidation of Vales Reales

Cumulative deficits resulting from war and the French alliance forced Spain to take desperate financial measures. The massive issues of *vales reales*—essentially unbacked paper money—posed a particular difficulty because they had depreciated so much in value. In 1798 the Crown ordered the sale of property held by a variety of public and religious institutions in Spain. These institutions were to deliver the proceeds to the Crown in exchange for its promise to pay 3 percent interest a year. Although it had planned to retire the *vales reales* with these funds, the Crown used the money to meet current expenses. Frantically seeking additional resources to fight the second war with Britain, on December 26, 1804, Charles IV extended to the colonies the 1798 decree for the consolidation of *vales reales*.

In Spain, religious institutions affected by the consolidation held real property whose sale led to some land redistribution, increased commercialization of agriculture, and economic growth. In the New World most funds of religious institutions and pious works were invested in loans extended to *hacendados*, merchants, miners, and others. Consolidation, therefore, meant that debtors had to pay off their loans quickly, leading—especially in New Spain—to the loss of property or bankruptcy. Anger over the implementation of consolidation was widespread. Although the Crown collected more than 15 million pesos, over two-thirds in New Spain, it paid a heavy political price. Both creoles and peninsulars grew dissatisfied with a government that so cavalierly disrupted local economies and undermined personal finances.

Royal Family and Favorite

The prestige of the Spanish Crown diminished substantially during the reign of Charles IV (1788–1808). A well-meaning but lazy monarch, Charles took his wife's advice and devoted himself to hunting rather than affairs of state. By 1808 the Spanish people viewed him with pity and scorn. Hatred they reserved for Queen Luisa and Manuel Godoy, reputedly one of her lovers. Rising from a modest position in the palace guard, Godoy came to dominate the royal family. Some even claimed that he had fathered two children born to the queen in the 1790s. Whatever the truth, in 1792 the young favorite replaced the elderly and experienced Count of Aranda as prime minister. Save for a brief hiatus, Godoy remained the most powerful man in Spain until 1808. Thus, as the country endured the effects of war, fiscal crisis, and commercial decline, disgruntled opponents blamed Godoy for Spain's misfortunes. Despised by the aristocracy, distrusted by intellectuals and professionals, and widely hated by the populace, his sole supporters were the king and queen.

Portrait of Ferdinand VII painted by a colonial artist.

The hatred toward Godoy vented itself in a corresponding enthusiasm for Prince Ferdinand. As heir apparent, he embodied the hopes of everyone dismayed by Charles IV's virtual abdication of authority to a royal favorite. In March 1808, Ferdinand's supporters rioted in Aranjuez, where the royal family was then resident, and forced Charles IV to dismiss Godoy. On the following day, Charles abdicated in favor of Ferdinand. The Spanish populace greeted joyously the news of Godoy's fall and Charles's abdication, but the arrival of a French army of forty thousand men in Madrid dampened the festivities.

Napoleon and Iberia, 1807–1808

The French emperor, Napoleon I, made decisions in 1807 and 1808 that profoundly affected the Spanish and Portuguese empires. Having inaugurated in November 1806 the "continental system" prohibiting the European importation of British merchandise, in mid-1807 he tried to force Portugal to declare war on England and close its ports to British traders, a demand that Prince Regent John rejected. Angered, Napoleon secured passage across Spanish territory for a French army that captured Lisbon on November 30, 1807. Less than a week earlier, Prince John and the royal family; administrative, ecclesiastic, and military hierarchies; and numerous nobles—some ten to fifteen thousand people in all—had sailed to Brazil under British escort. As a result of this remarkable and unprecedented move, from 1808 to 1821 John ruled his empire from Rio de Janeiro rather than Lisbon.

Napoleon also decided to withhold recognition of Ferdinand VII as monarch and to rid Spain of the Bourbons. At Bayonne in May 1808, he obtained abdications from Ferdinand and Charles. Sending them into comfortable exile, the French emperor named his brother Joseph King José Napoleon I of "the Spains." A hastily assembled delegation of Spaniards at Bayonne then approved a constitution for "the dominions of Spain and the Indies" that gave Americans representation within a constitutional monarchy that would provide "political regeneration." Although Napoleon's designs failed, the rhetoric of reform and regeneration, a written constitution, representation in a legislature, equal rights for Spain and the overseas dominions, and constitutional protections for citizens echoed in patriot Spain and its overseas dominions.

Independence from France

The Napoleonic *golpe de estado*, or coup d'état, in Bayonne triggered mass resistance to French plans in Spain and, when news of this treachery reached them, throughout the American colonies. Even before the coup, on May 2, 1808, French troops had bloodily suppressed a mass uprising in Madrid. Hearing of the massacre, later in the day the city fathers of Móstoles, a small town near Madrid, declared war against the French.

The Junta Suprema of Sevilla then formally declared war against the French on June 6.

Rapidly formed provincial juntas in Spain framed their declarations in terms of loyalty to Ferdinand, defense of religion, and preservation of the territorial integrity of the deposed monarch's realms. They proclaimed their opposition to the French, their willingness to die rather than acquiesce in Napoleonic rule—in short, their independence. Whereas the British refer to the conflict that followed as the Peninsular War, for the Spaniards it was and remains the War of Independence.

In Caracas on November 22, 1808, the city fathers formally endorsed "the conservation of our Holy Religion, the restoration of our beloved King [Ferdinand], the perpetuation of an unalterable union of all Spanish Pueblos, and the [territorial] integrity of the Monarchy." Cities throughout Spanish America swore allegiance to Ferdinand—Havana, Mexico City, Vera Cruz, Campeche, Buenos Aires, Montevideo, Santa Fe de Bogotá, Santiago, Lima, and many more—and thereby independence from the rule of *El Rey Intruso*, or, less kindly, "Pepe Botellas" ("Joe Bottles"), as the Spaniards termed José I.

The French wanted to preserve the territorial integrity of the Spanish monarchy with its "rich prize" of the American dominions, as was clear in the title Napoleon gave his brother: "King of Spain and the Indies." French agents departed for America immediately. The representative of Napoleon seeking recognition for José I in Buenos Aires suffered arrest and the public burning of his official dispatches. Authorities also imprisoned the agent who landed in Puerto Rico on July 24 and seized the documents he was going to later distribute in Cuba. Although a *Gazeta Extraordinaria del Gobierno* of January 23, 1809, reported that all of the "agents of the tyrant Napoleon" had been arrested, more arrived later.

Authorities in Havana in February 1810 reported that the French had sent agents to Cuba via the United States, where they were to "stir the fire of discord and prepare our slavery and ruin." The captain-general reported in late July that "one of the perfidious Spaniards paid by France to disturb the peace" in the Indies would be executed the following day. Suspicion that the viceroy of Buenos Aires and the captain-general of Caracas favored the French led to their removal in spring 1810. Fear of French rule and the idea of a "loyal rebellion" to prevent it contributed to the Hidalgo Revolt in Mexico later in the year.

Governments of Resistance and Political Revolution, 1808–1812

The Napoleonic invasion of Iberia, the abdications of Charles IV and Ferdinand VII, the spontaneous creation of patriotic provincial juntas, and the imposition of King José Napoleon I initiated a political revolution. Beginning in 1808 it swept through Spain and the overseas dominions, permanently destroyed the unthinking and habitual acceptance of monarchy as embodied in the Habsburgs and Bourbons, and initiated representative, constitutional government. Political life in the colonies would never be the same.

Few Spaniards acknowledged the legitimacy of orders issued by Napoleon's representatives in Spain or the Spanish officials who worked with them (*afrancesados*). By the end of May 1808, newly formed provincial juntas in Seville, Oviedo, and many other locations claimed sovereignty until Ferdinand's return and led the initial resistance to the French. By late August they had agreed to create a single sovereign body—the Central Junta—to prosecute the war, maintain the British alliance and military support, and retain the colonies. Acting in the name of Ferdinand, the Central Junta's legitimacy was recognized throughout Spain and the Indies. Juntas created later in American colonies proved less able to cooperate, although they also claimed to represent Ferdinand.

The Central Junta convened in Aranjuez in September 1808, but military defeats drove it to Seville in December. In an effort to maintain the colonial financial assistance that Spain desperately needed, the Central Junta, on January 22, 1809, sought American representation. Subsequent French successes prompted the Central Junta, in the fall of 1809, to call "the General and Extraordinary *Cortes* of the Nation." Faced with some 350,000 French troops in Spain, the Junta evacuated Seville and turned over its authority to a five-member Council of Regency of Spain and the Indies in late January 1810. With the need to legitimize the government of resistance apparent, an unprecedented unicameral *cortes* began to meet on September 24, 1810, with an agenda that included writing a constitution. Elected deputies representing both Spain and the overseas kingdoms, as the colonies conceived themselves, crafted a constitution promulgated in March 1812. This remarkable document sealed a political revolution whose ideas persisted despite Ferdinand VII's efforts to restore the old regime following his return to Spain in 1814.

New World Juntas and the Pursuit of American Support

News of the shocking events in Spain prompted Americans who wanted formal political autonomy to argue for their equal right to establish juntas to govern on behalf of the captive Ferdinand. Conversely, persons who feared greater autonomy in the Americas, primarily peninsulars, argued for recognition of a patriotic junta in Spain, initially the Junta Suprema of Sevilla. In order to prevent the creation of a local junta, peninsulars in Mexico City deposed Viceroy José de Iturrigaray by a coup on September 15, 1808, an illegal action that destroyed the principle of legitimacy that had characterized Spanish rule for centuries. On September 21, a *cabildo abierto* in Montevideo created a peninsular junta, as its absolutist governor wanted. On May 25, 1809, the Audiencia of Charcas deposed its president, but his successor exiled the judges. In Quito on August 10, 1809, creoles overthrew the president of the Audiencia and established a junta as well. In Caracas the captain-general proposed the creation of a junta in July 1808 but quickly changed his mind and arrested the more than forty men who had petitioned for this action. Not until 1810 would proponents of juntas in the colonies be generally successful.

Various Spanish governments of resistance worked to retain the empire and its financial resources. The successive efforts of the Central Junta, the Council of Regency, and the *Cortes* of Cádiz also spread revolutionary doctrines and contributed to the politicization of the colonial population. The initial message was clear: Equality between Americans and Spaniards was forthcoming. In an unprecedented step, in October 1808, the Central Junta decided to add American representatives.

The language of the summons was remarkable. "Considering that the vast and precious dominions owned by Spain in the Indies are not properly colonies or factories. . .but an essential and integral part of the Spanish monarchy. . ." each of the four viceroyalties and six captaincies-general "must be represented" by a person selected by indirect elections. This promise of a new, inclusive relationship as part of a monarchy-wide government encouraged those wanting greater autonomy. Nearly one hundred colonial municipalities held elections, but only one American deputy actually reached the Junta Central before its dissolution. The importance of this experience lay in the Junta's declaration of the right of American representation and the municipalities' identification of grievances.

The widespread enthusiasm and allegiance pledged to Ferdinand VII by all governing bodies in the Americas in 1808 turned to pessimism as the French drove the Junta Central from Seville in late January 1810. Under siege on the Royal Isle of León near Cádiz, on February 14, 1810, the Regency called for American representation in the forthcoming monarchy-wide *cortes* in terms that rejected past Spanish behavior and implied that a new equality was at hand:

> From this moment, American Spaniards, you see yourselves raised to the dignity of free men; you are no longer. . .bent under a yoke [made] heavier the farther you were from the center of power, looked upon with indifference . . . destroyed by ignorance. Be aware that on pronouncing or writing the name of the person who will come to represent you in the national Congress, your destinies no longer depend on ministers, viceroys, or governors; they are in your hands.

The decree called for the election of a deputy by each district capital of jurisdictions identified in the earlier elections to the Junta Central and additional elections in Santo Domingo and the Interior Provincias of New Spain. On September 8, 1810, the Regency further specified that the Indies would have thirty substitute deputies (*suplentes*) in the *cortes*. For autonomists in the Americas, the *cortes* offered a potential way to pursue their goal of significant home rule within the context of the Spanish monarchy.

The explicit admission of Spanish oppression of Americans coupled with a declaration that they were now "free men" and thus equal to Spaniards both raised colonial expectations and reinforced the sense of grievance common among creoles. Americans interpreted the assertion that past oppression had ended as a promise that political and economic changes were near. Elections were held, and colonial municipal councils publicly discussed grievances as they prepared instructions for deputies.

News that the Central Junta had dissolved after appointing a Council of Regency gave new life to autonomists and encouraged the still small number of separatists in much of Spain's mainland empire. In Caracas on April 19, 1810, a *cabildo abierto* noted the Americas' status as "integral parts of the Crown of Spain," rather than colonies, and thus repositories of "interim sovereignty." Accordingly, it refused to recognize the legitimacy of the Regency established without "the vote of these faithful inhabitants." The new Junta of Caracas soon sent the captain-general of Venezuela and most members of the Audiencia of Caracas into exile.

In Buenos Aires, a *cabildo abierto* on May 25, 1810, created a Provisional Governing Junta of the Provinces of Río de la Plata in the name of Ferdinand VII and dispatched the viceroy and other leading officials to the Canary Islands. Although the composition and name of the ruling body in Buenos Aires would change numerous times in the following decade, this "May Revolution" initiated effective political autonomy under creole leadership.

In New Granada autonomists established juntas in Cartagena, Cali, Socorro, Santa Fe de Bogotá, and Santa Marta during July and August 1810. In an unusual action, the junta in Bogotá recognized the Council of Regency on July 21, but retracted this recognition five days later. Significant differences among the sixteen juntas created in New Granada precluded cooperation and the formation of a single government.

Elections for the Cortes

The Regency's call for a native-born representative from the capital of each district, a jurisdiction with precise meaning in Spain but not in the Indies, to the General and Extraordinary *Cortes* initiated a new round of elections in much of the empire. The number of deputies was based on political jurisdictions without reference to population, whereas deputies from Spain were to be elected on the basis of both jurisdiction and population. Recognition that most of Spain was under French occupation and that elections and travel from the Indies would be lengthy led the Regency to promulgate guidelines for selecting fifty-five substitute deputies, thirty for the Indies and twenty-five for Spain, from Americans and Spaniards resident in Cádiz.

Elections were held in American provinces not under insurgent control in late 1810 and early 1811. This meant that Paraguay, present Argentina, Chile, and parts of Venezuela and New Granada did not elect representatives.

As before, deputies brought instructions or lists of grievances with them, reinforcing the notion that deputies represented their regions and constituents.

The General and Extraordinary Cortes of Cádiz

The *cortes* opened in Royal Isle of León on September 24, 1810, with 102 deputies present: 27 from the Americas, 2 from the Philippines, and 73 from Spain. Fifty-six deputies had been elected by their constituents; 46 were substitutes (*suplentes*) selected locally. Not surprisingly, only one American deputy was not a substitute. By the time the *cortes* adjourned on September 20, 1813, a total of sixty-seven individuals had served as deputies representing the Americas and Philippines. As its first act of business, the *cortes* declared itself the legitimate, sovereign authority and the Spanish Nation's legislative body, distinct and separate from executive and judicial branches of government.

Creoles thought that the extent of American representation was the most important issue before the *cortes*. On the body's second day of deliberations, American deputies opened their campaign for the *cortes* to reaffirm explicitly the declarations of the Central Junta and the Regency concerning equal rights for the "overseas dominions" "as an integral part of the monarchy." After considerable discussion in secret sessions, on October 15, 1810, the *cortes* reaffirmed that Spain and the Indies formed a single monarchy and nation and declared that persons whose ancestors came from Europe and America, but not Africa, were equal in rights. Defeated in this effort to get the number of each hemisphere's deputies determined, American representatives reintroduced the issue when the *cortes* began to write the constitution.

The lengthy debate over American representation in the *cortes* focused on the definition of citizenship, for only citizens would be counted in apportioning deputies. The central issue was the status of free persons of African descent (*pardos*). Because the total population in the Americas was about 50 percent larger than that in Spain, counting *pardos* as citizens would give Americans a majority in the *cortes*. Again, however, the *cortes* refused to include all free residents in apportioning deputies. This defeat strongly suggested that the vaunted new equality was hollow.

This debate was also important because a number of American deputies emphasized the fundamental equality of all free men and made exaggerated claims for racial harmony in the Americas. Particularly in regions with a substantial *casta* population—for example, in Cartagena, New Granada—the American deputies' vocal support of equality for all free men took root. As a result, it stimulated *casta* support of home rule and ultimately independence.

Other issues, of course, were also important to the American deputies. With mixed success, they pressured their peninsular counterparts on free trade, an end to restrictions on agriculture and manufacturing in the colonies, the abolition of monopolies, a guaranteed percentage of bureaucratic appointments going to native sons, and the restoration of the Society of Jesus.

Numerous developments between 1808 and 1812 suggested that Spanish colonials could gain greater local and regional influence within the "Spanish Monarchy," as the *cortes* defined the whole of Spanish dominions in Europe and the Americas. At the same time, Spanish authorities permitted an unprecedented freedom of the press and the expression of political ideas.

The junta's authorization of constitutional municipal councils in all communities with one thousand or more inhabitants brought many thousands of new participants into the process of governance, as did the creation of provincial deputations. Although the failure to secure representation based on total population and the inability to obtain free trade frustrated many American deputies, their political gains were substantial.

Approved in March 1812, the Constitution of 1812 documented the political revolution that had transpired. The most liberal charter of its time, the constitution declared that sovereignty resided in the nation and that only the nation's representatives had the right to establish laws. Although retaining a hereditary monarch, it vested many of the powers formerly exercised by Spanish kings in the hands of an elected *cortes* that would write laws, determine public expenses, establish taxes, and approve treaties. Equality before the law, with few exceptions, replaced a myriad of exemptions and privileges, including those of the nobility. The mingling of legislative, administrative, and judicial powers that characterized old-regime institutions gave way to a clear separation of responsibilities. Audiencias were limited to judicial matters. *Jefes políticos superiores,* who replaced viceroys, exercised limited authority with an intendant and elected members of a provincial deputation. Initially advanced by a Mexican deputy, the new institution, called a *provincial deputation,* provided for significant provincial autonomy.

The collapse of traditional monarchical power, the political revolution that followed, and the growth in the number of separatists was apparent by the end of 1810. The transition from discussion to military conflict quickly followed. Contemporaries and later historians have identified both grievances and changes in the intellectual environment that served to justify the actions that followed.

Among the "causes of independence" are creole-peninsular hostility, a growing creole self-consciousness, trade restrictions, the Enlightenment, the precedent of the American Revolution, and the revolutionary ideology of the French Revolution. Although neither individually nor collectively were these "causes" responsible for the initiation of the insurgent movements, once open conflict was under way, they did affect the course of the war, justify actions that insurgents took, and influence new forms of political organization. Because the Portuguese royal family escaped from Napoleon in 1807 and established their court in Brazil, that colony necessarily experienced a fundamentally different trajectory toward independence than did the Spanish possessions.

The independence movements in both Spanish South America and Brazil lacked the coherence of ideology and leadership present in the

American Revolution. Because Spain's governments of resistance were fighting French armies until late 1813 and Ferdinand VII's resources were limited, the effort to retain the Spanish colonies depended primarily on the political will, economic resources, and military capacity of loyalists in the New World. Yet despite these grave limitations on royalist power, Spanish American insurgents won independence with great difficulty. In some regions the military campaigns and the resultant destruction of resources lasted more than a decade. Both the duration of these bitter contests and the equivocal political legacies inherited by the newly independent governments were linked historically to the colonial experience that had promoted class and race conflicts. Where these divisions were deepest, independence was achieved with difficulty, and democracy quickly failed.

Suggested for Further Reading

Archer, Christon I., editor. *The Wars of Independence in Spanish America.* Wilmington, Del.: Scholarly Resources, 2000.

Esdaile, Charles J. *Fighting Napoleon: Guerrillas, Bandits and Adventurers in Spain, 1808–1814.* New Haven, Conn.: Yale University Press, 2004.

Esdaile, Charles J. *The Peninsular War: A New History.* New York: Palgrave Macmillan, 2003.

Fraser, Ronald. *Napoleon's Cursed War: Popular Resistance in the Spanish Peninsular War, 1808–1814.* London and New York: Verso, 2008.

Graham, Richard. *Independence in Latin America: A Comparative Approach.* 2nd edition. New York: McGraw-Hill, 1994.

Kinsbruner, Jay. *Independence in Spanish America: Civil Wars, Revolutions, and Underdevelopment.* Albuquerque: University of New Mexico Press, 1994.

Langley, Lester B. *The Americas in the Age of Revolution, 1750–1850.* New Haven and London: Yale University Press, 1996.

Lynch, John. *The Spanish American Revolutions 1808–1826.* 2nd edition. New York: Norton, 1986.

Racine, Karen. *Francisco de Miranda: A Transatlantic Life in the Age of Revolution.* Wilmington, Del.: Scholarly Resources, 2003.

Rodríguez O., Jaime E. *The Independence of Spanish America.* Cambridge, England: Cambridge University Press, 1998.

Tone, John Lawrence. *The Fatal Knot: The Guerrilla War in Navarre and the Defeat of Napoleon in Spain.* Chapel Hill: University of North Carolina Press, 1994.

ELEVEN

FROM EMPIRE TO INDEPENDENCE

Chronology

1812	Spain and Empire	Constitution of 1812
1813	Spain and Empire	Elections for deputies to *cortes*
1814	Spain and Empire	Ferdinand VII returns, abrogates constitution
1814	Venezuela	End of Second Republic
1814	Chile	Royalist army defeats Chileans at Rancagua
1815	Venezuela	Morillo expedition from Spain arrives, reestablishes Spanish control
1815	New Spain	Morelos executed; insurgency and counterinsurgency continue
1816	United Provinces of Río de la Plata	Buenos Aires and provincial allies declare independence
1816	New Granada	Morillo expedition reestablishes Spanish rule
1817	Chile	San Martín's army defeats royalists
1818	Chile	Independence
1819	New Granada	Bolívar's victory at Boyacá; independence
1820	Spain	Riego Revolt; liberals in power; constitution restored; Ferdinand VII constitutional monarch
1820	Peru	San Martín's army arrives in Peru
1821	Venezuela	Independence follows victory at Carabobo
1821	Peru	Lima proclaims Peruvian independence
1821	New Spain	Plan of Iguala and Mexican independence
1821	Central American towns	Declare independence individually
1821	Panama	Declares independence from Spain
1822	Brazil	Independence

1822	Mexican Empire	Agustín I emperor
1822	Quito (Ecuador)	Sucre's victory at Pichincha means independence
1823	Mexico	Agustín I forced into exile
1823	Spain	French troops restore Ferdinand VII as absolute monarch
1824	Mexico	Iturbide executed; Federal Constitution
1824	Peru	Patriot victories at Junín and Ayacucho; Peru independent
1825	Upper Peru (Bolivia)	Independence
1826	Peru	Capitulation of Callao ends Spanish resistance

Ferdinand VII returned to his throne in 1814. Aided by British armies and Napoleon's withdrawal of troops after his disastrous Russian campaign, Spanish armies and guerrilla bands had defeated the French and forced his release. The monarch promptly abrogated the Constitution of 1812 and decided to use military force to resolve the political status of the colonies. His return removed the justification for juntas created in his absence. In fact, few remained, but the Buenos Aires junta and its successors exercised effective independence after 1810.

Well before Ferdinand's return, some autonomists in Spanish America had begun to shift from advocating self-governance within the Spanish Nation to accepting, when not actively supporting, full independence. Regional differences affected the timing of this shift in political objectives. Parts of the Constitution of 1812 and specific laws passed by the *cortes* galled numerous Americans. Some colonial officials, especially the *jefes políticos superiores,* the officials previously called viceroys, of New Spain and Peru, exacerbated these political problems by refusing to allow freedom of the press as decreed in 1810 and negating election results. Their selective enforcement of legislation undercut the legitimacy of the Spanish government. Nonetheless, in 1814 the elites in New Spain and Peru were still loyal to Ferdinand VII.

Ferdinand carefully ensured that Americans held seats on the Council of the Indies and in the American *audiencias* but quickly dispelled illusions of equality and refused to support a political solution to rebellions in the empire. Greeted on his return from France with widespread public enthusiasm and offers of military support, the monarch on May 4 nullified all acts of the *cortes,* including the Constitution of 1812. Additionally, he reestablished institutions and, insofar as possible, reinstated the officials in place at the time of his abdication. Although he promised to convene a *cortes* constituted as in the past, he never honored his pledge. Some leading liberals, including American deputies from New Spain, Peru, and Guatemala, were jailed before the monarch reached Madrid.

Ferdinand and the Failure of Absolutism

Ferdinand's resumption of absolute authority put in bold relief the political institutions and rights developed in Spain and the colonies after the French invasion. Before this event, the elites of Spain and the colonies, like the rest of society, were loyal to the Bourbons and their "absolute" monarchy. To defeat the French, liberals had fomented a political revolution that turned Spain and its empire into a constitutional monarchy, albeit without a resident king, thus dividing the supporters of monarchy into constitutionalists and absolutists. This division extended to the Indies, where many creoles had responded enthusiastically to elections and open political discussion while rejecting more radical republican ideas and independence.

Ferdinand's return to the throne and his suppression of the constitution recast politics in Spain's American colonies. Without the promise of representation, freedom of the press, and other political guarantees, public opinion in the Americas moved toward support for independence, a position popular in Caracas as early as 1811. Having rejected reform and compromise, Ferdinand then embarked on the dangerous course of using military force to impose order. This militarization of the conflict pushed colonial elites in "pacified" regions a step closer to independence. Property loss and harsh royalist reprisals in Venezuela, New Granada, Chile, and New Spain affected numerous elite families and undermined their earlier support of continued Spanish rule.

The failure of Ferdinand's policy was clear by the end of 1819. The cost of sending and maintaining troops in the New World was greater than normal Crown revenues could support. Already in debt in 1808, royal treasuries throughout the Indies were awash in accumulated deficits a decade later. Wartime destruction and the breakdown of regular commercial links between Spain and its colonies had taken their toll. Mines were flooded, commerce diminished, and colonial governments nearly bankrupt. Chile, the future Argentina, and Paraguay were effectively independent, and northern South America was on the cusp of independence.

Independence in Spanish America

Insurrections overlapped the political revolution that transformed the expectations of many active citizens in Spain and the Americas. The broader distribution of newspapers facilitated the spread of information and propaganda. Despite different chronologies, a number of similar characteristics were present in multiple theaters of the independence movements. These include an active press, localism and regionalism, economic crisis, a resort to arms, creole leadership, disease and desertion, insurgency and counterinsurgency, and borderless campaigns of conquest and liberation.

Spreading Revolutionary Ideas Through News and Propaganda

Despite efforts of the Spanish government to prevent the introduction of revolutionary ideas, they circulated in print and by word of mouth in Spanish America from the time of the successful revolt of the thirteen English colonies that formed the United States. Second-generation revolutions introduced more radical ideas from France and, more ominously, Haiti. Starting in 1808, new publications appeared in Spain, and the colonies and the press's importance expanded rapidly. Spain's alliance with England expedited the transfer of news, as numerous English ships carrying both English and Spanish publications arrived in colonial ports. Similarly, ships returning to Spain from Havana, Vera Cruz, Montevideo, and other ports carried accounts of revolutionary events in the Americas.

The Spanish *cortes* had approved freedom of the press on November 10, 1810, and included it in the Constitution of 1812. Fearing a free press would encourage subversion, some royal officials in the Americas suspended implementation. These repressive policies had limited effect because incendiary tracts published in rebel areas circulated widely. In addition, while colonial officials tried to limit access to news, publications from Spain reported political debates in detail, complete with the very language that inspired revolutionaries in the colonies: " popular sovereignty," "liberty," "equality," and "independence."

Localism and Regionalism

Tensions had long existed between colonial capital cities such as Lima, Mexico City, and Buenos Aires that had a strong peninsular presence and their distant, creole-dominated political dependencies. The creation of many rival juntas in Spain unintentionally served as precedent to justify claims of provincial autonomy by creole elites in smaller colonial cities and towns. The fate of the Viceroyalty of Río de la Plata after 1810 exemplifies the strength of autonomist sentiment, but similar conflicts occurred elsewhere as well.

Soon after news reached Buenos Aires that a Council of Regency claimed authority in Spain, many of the city's most prominent citizens met as a *cabildo abierto* on May 25, 1810. They created a Provisional Governing Junta of the Provinces of Río de la Plata in the name of Ferdinand VII and soon expelled the viceroy and other Spanish officials. Buenos Aires and most of the territory later encompassed in Argentina would never again be under Spanish control.

The new rulers in Buenos Aires struggled to retain control over the viceroyalty. Repeatedly unsuccessful military campaigns demonstrated that they could not. With Paraguay already independent and Upper Peru reattached to Lima, at last, in 1816, the Province of Buenos Aires and its remaining regional allies declared formal independence from Spain. Ultimately, the former viceroyalty became the separate nations of Paraguay, Bolivia, Uruguay, and Argentina.

Caracas was among the first colonial capitals to create a junta. After receiving news in April 1810 that the French occupied "almost all of the kingdoms and provinces of Spain," the city council established a junta to rule in the name of Ferdinand and ousted the local *audiencia* and the captain-general. The new government encouraged municipal councils elsewhere to create juntas as well. Once established, some of them resisted accepting the authority of Caracas. When the capital supported a declaration of independence on July 5, 1811, for example, the provinces of Coro and Maracaibo refused to do so. Venezuela would remain divided between separatists and loyalists into the 1820s.

The unity of colonial New Granada soon broke down as well. Between June 14 and August 10, 1810, Cartagena, Cali, Pamplona, el Socorro, Santa Fe de Bogotá, and Santa Marta formed juntas claiming to rule in the name of Ferdinand VII. Territories under the earliest juntas asserted autonomy, whereas others, like Cartagena, declared complete independence. Others remained royalist, a decision that often reflected long-standing antipathies toward neighboring cities. Because of New Granada's inability to coalesce into a stable political entity, the period 1810–1816 is known in Colombia as the "Patria Boba," or "Foolish Fatherland."

Crisis and Transformation of the Imperial Economy

Between 1808 and 1826 trade between Spanish America and the Atlantic world was transformed. Already disrupted by neutral trade because of war with England, traditional commerce between Spain and its colonies suffered further after the French invasion. Within five years Spanish American markets had few Spanish products but were full of British and other foreign goods, and foreign ships largely carried local exports. While the governments of resistance in Spain refused to allow their ally Britain to trade legally with the colonies, many officials in the Americas disregarded this policy in order to address serious fiscal needs, meet consumers' demands, and facilitate the export of cacao, cochineal, indigo, and other perishable products.

In 1809, for example, Viceroy Baltasar Hidalgo de Cisneros opened the Viceroyalty of Río de la Plata to British trade. Faced with the need to pay a militia of eight thousand men, he was desperate for the tax revenue available in cash through this commerce. The Buenos Aires junta and its successors followed this policy.

Despite such expedients, Spanish officials in the Americas never had adequate resources to meet military expenditures. Where the insurrectionists were in control, they similarly suffered fiscal shortfalls despite taxing trade as a major source of revenue. Viceroy of Peru Joaquín de la Pezuela (1816–1821) permitted foreign traders to enter the port of Callao and sell their wares in order to collect desperately needed customs revenues. In Chile, the patriot leader Bernardo O'Higgins opened the ports in 1817. Neither the volume of foreign trade nor the taxes collected enabled Spanish administrators or their revolutionary opponents to meet their fiscal obligations, but the damage done to local commercial interests was ruinous as traditional patterns of credit and exchange were destroyed. Exports from Spanish America during the years 1810–1826 suffered from the consequences of war, as well as from more mundane causes. Damage, flooding, and loss of workers in the mines of New Spain dramatically reduced silver mining. Peruvian silver exports also fell. In addition, rebellions reduced gold mining in New Granada, cochineal production in New Spain, and cacao exports from Venezuela.

Rightly worried about the safety of their investments, starting in 1810 Spaniards began moving their capital from the mainland colonies to Havana, Puerto Rico, and, after the expulsion of the French, back to Spain or France. Royalists leaving New Spain in 1814 allegedly took some 12 million pesos with them as they relocated to places still controlled by the king. Spain's imperial economy, based on trade restrictions, was failing in 1808 and was completely destroyed before the patriots in the New World achieved political independence.

Resort to Arms

The early military conflicts spreading across the colonies were between loyalists and insurrectionists, not narrowly between persons born in Spain or the colonies. In the initial conflicts, both sides asserted that they were fighting on behalf of Ferdinand VII. It became clear quickly, however, that armies were often fighting for local and regional control or for loot. Desertion rates were high, amnesties were frequent, and changing sides was common. Set-piece battles between armies were rare, and the armies themselves were very small in comparison with contemporary European standards. The royalists had 2,700 men at Boyacá, New Granada, in 1819 and the patriots, 2,800. At the largest battle of the wars at Ayacucho, Peru, in 1824, there were 6,000 republicans and 9,300 royalists.

Although insurgent armies often had strong local roots, both insurgents and royalists often depended on recruits from distant areas. The royalist forces stationed throughout the colonies numbered about 35,000 in 1800, but only some 5,500 were European Spaniards. The 41,000 troops sent from Spain between 1811 and 1818 had an immediate impact but were quickly diminished by battlefield casualties, desertions, and disease. The willingness of colonials to fight for the king would determine whether or not Spain's mainland empire survived.

Patriot armies also depended on a mix of local recruits and volunteers drawn from a wide area. In January 1817, José de San Martín led an army across the Andes from Mendoza to Chile, composed of political exiles from Chile, cowboys from the pampas, and units recruited in Buenos Aires that included large numbers of former slaves and freedmen. After winning the independence of Chile, San Martín sailed with his army, now reinforced by Chileans, to Peru in 1820. Similarly, Simón Bolívar led troops recruited in New Granada to combat Spanish forces in Venezuela. He later returned to New Granada to fight the Spanish loyalists with an army largely recruited in Venezuela. Along with his chief lieutenant Antonio José Sucre, Bolívar then led a mixed force of Venezuelans, New Granadans, and elements of San Martín's Argentine and Chilean army to liberate Peru, and Upper Peru.

For the poorest members of Spanish colonial society, service in patriot or loyalist military forces could be the means of upward social mobility. Slaves and former slaves were important to both royalists and rebels, especially in Venezuela, New Granada, and the Río de la Plata. In some cases wealthy patriots gave male slaves to the army, and in others patriotic governments compensated owners who enlisted their slaves. Royalist commanders sometimes followed suit. Many slaves simply ran away from their masters to enlist. In Peru, nonwhites made up about 85 percent of the manpower of the royalist forces by the 1820s. Similarly, in 1821, nonwhites made up at least 60 percent of the royalist army in Venezuela. Insurgents' armies at the same time were described as completely composed of "descendants from Africa"; although this observer probably overstated the African presence, free and enslaved blacks and *pardos* were numerically dominant in many regions. Whatever the exact number, nearly all slaves who served on either side of the conflict received their freedom.

Indigenous troops were crucial to both sides of the conflict in the Andes and parts of New Spain as well. Participation in these conflicts exposed indigenous forces to the large political ideas of the era and gave them exposure to regions far beyond their villages and towns. Some patriot leaders pressed for an end to many of the colonial obligations forced on Indians, but their old labor and tax burdens often survived in disguised form for decades.

Irish, English, and other foreign adventurers were also important. Nearly seven thousand of these foreign adventurers enlisted in Bolívar's army alone between 1816 and 1825. Far from a body of veterans of the Napoleonic Wars, probably more than two-thirds of them had no previous military experience; many went to Venezuela and New Granada for adventure; others intended to settle there after the fighting ended. Almost half, however, died of disease or while on campaign.

Disease and Desertion

Using soldiers far from their homes helped to reduce desertion rates, but it increased mortality due to change of climate, unsanitary temporary living arrangements, and disease. One of the worst locations was Vera Cruz, the port through which nearly all Spanish soldiers passed on their way to the interior of New Spain. Recurrent epidemics of yellow fever (*vómito negro*) at Vera Cruz proved deadly to many. Between 1815 and 1821, General Morillo and other royalist officers in Venezuela and on the coast of New Granada lost some 90 percent of their peninsular soldiers, most as a result of yellow fever, dysentery, smallpox, and other diseases and ailments. Foreign soldiers fighting under Bolívar's command experienced similar mortality rates. Of the

Argentine and Chilean army of 4,500 that accompanied José de San Martín to Peru in 1820, only 100 men were still around to fight at Ayacucho in 1824.

American Leaders

The best-known insurgent leaders came from a range of occupations and social backgrounds. Almost all were born in the Americas, and over half were born in the 1770s and 1780s; this group included Simón Bolívar, José de San Martín, Manuel Belgrano in Buenos Aires, Agustín de Iturbide in Mexico, and Bernardo O'Higgins in Chile. The oldest, born in the 1750s, included the professional advocate of independence Francisco de Miranda, parish priest Miguel Hidalgo in New Spain, and Cornelio de Saavedra, a militia officer and member of the first junta in Buenos Aires. The youngest, born in the 1790s, included students, notably Francisco Paula de Santander and Antonio José Sucre, and a cattle trader in the interior plains of Venezuela, José Antonio Páez, who became professional revolutionaries and, after independence, presidents of New Granada (Colombia), Bolivia, and Venezuela, respectively. The most aristocratic and wealthiest were Simón Bolívar of Venezuela and José Miguel Carrera of Chile. Although most leaders were creoles, their ranks included the mestizo cleric José María Morelos in New Spain, *pardo* Manuel Piar in Venezuela, and *casta* José Antonio Páez, also in Venezuela. Only a few, including Gervasio de Artigas in Banda Oriental and Agustín de Iturbide in Mexico, had signifi- cant military experience prior to 1810; the most notable of these veterans was José de San Martín, who had entered the royal army in Spain as a cadet at the age of eleven, fought against the French in the early 1790s and again from 1808 to 1811, and retired at the rank of lieutenant colonel.

The names of many men who headed small groups of insurgents have escaped the historical record. In some theaters these guerrilla leaders proved more important than the leaders of large armies. This was especially the case in New Spain from 1810 to 1821 but also was true at times in Upper Peru, New Granada, and Venezuela. Within weeks of the onset of the Hidalgo Revolt in New Spain in September 1810, guerrilla bands were disrupting commu- nication between Mexico City and Querétaro. Guerrillas also harassed traffic on the vital link between the capital and the port of Vera Cruz, forcing the royalists to use immense, slow, and expensive armed convoys.

Two leaders of insurrection were heroic on a grand scale. "The Liberator" Simón Bolívar was charismatic, persistent, and able to appreciate the need to defeat Spanish loyalists in all of South America. His weaknesses included his impatience with the day-to-day work of governing and administering and his sometimes unreliable military skills. "The Protector" San Martín also understood the big picture, had excellent organizational and tactical skills, and effectively instilled discipline. His largest failure was his inabil- ity to gain the independence of Peru with forces overwhelmingly drawn from Argentina and Chile.

A representation of the Mexican independence leader Father Miguel Hidalgo y Costilla.

Mexico had more martyrs than heroes. Hidalgo's Revolt lasted less than a year, although it initiated a decade of insurgency. José María Morelos, who inherited the insurrection in New Spain after Hidalgo's execution in 1811, effectively trained an army and began the drafting of a constitution, but he was captured and executed in 1815. Agustín de Iturbide, among the most effective officers in the Spanish forces in Mexico as they fought against Hidalgo and Morelos, achieved independence in 1821 through an alliance with patriots, but his attempt to create a Mexican empire failed in less than a year. When he returned from exile in 1824, he was captured and executed.

Portrait of Simón Bolívar at end of independence period.

Women in the Midst of War

Robbed and raped by soldiers, forced to watch the conscription of brothers and the execution of fathers and husbands, required to emigrate from their homes, and reduced to penury, many women suffered the consequences of civil war—often poverty and widowhood—without visible benefits. With large numbers of men enlisted in loyalist or patriot armies, women routinely bore the burden of overseeing businesses, farms, and ranches, in addition to their traditional obligations of managing households and children.

Some free and slave women took an active part in the conflicts as either royalists or insurgents. Although the First Republic turned down the offer of twenty-one women from Barinas, Venezuela, to join the republican army in 1811, it used the gesture as an example of patriotism to inspire others. Slave women embraced the opportunities presented by the political conflicts to provide services as cooks, servants, camp followers, and nurses, among other occupations, in the hope of gaining freedom. The mestiza Juana Azurduy of Chuquisaca, Upper Peru, worked with her husband to enlist men and weapons for the cause of independence. She also led troops in battle and cared for the wounded. Among the most celebrated women in the republican ranks was Manuela Sáenz, Bolívar's mistress. She participated as a soldier in the republican victories of Junín and Ayacucho in Peru, gaining promotion to the rank of captain after Junín. In New Spain, Josefa Ortiz de Domínguez, wife of the *corregidor* of Querétaro, contributed to the Hidalgo Revolt by informing conspirators that the government knew of the planned rebellion.

An educated minority of women participated in the lively debates that determined the future of their region. Others served as spies, attended meetings, raised and donated funds, delivered correspondence, aided recruitment and gathered information, accompanied husbands in military service, cared for the wounded, and, on one occasion, smuggled a printing press to the insurgents. All of these services involved substantial risk; in New Granada alone, royalists executed more than fifty women and imprisoned many more.

Insurgency and Counterinsurgency

Revolution, insurgency, civil war, and accompanying executions and atrocities touched nearly all of mainland Spanish America from northern Mexico to southern Chile. In Paraguay, armed conflict was brief. In Venezuela and New Granada, a generation came of age in the 1820s, having known little but conflict and violence. In Mexico, insurgency and counterinsurgency were unrelenting and forced much of the population to live in fear for a decade.

Both insurgents and royalist counterinsurgents relied on terror, summary justice and execution, "blood and fire," and atrocities to gain their ends. Insurgent atrocities against Spaniards in New Spain were under way on a large scale from the time Hidalgo's ill-disciplined forces murdered some six hundred of them at Guanajuato in 1810. The royalists responded in kind. After executing and decapitating Hidalgo and his chief associates in 1811, they sent the severed heads on tour throughout the region that had supported the rebellion and then displayed the skulls in iron cages located at the four corners of the city granary, site of the earlier massacre of Spaniards.

José María Morelos, the mestizo priest who succeeded Hidalgo as the principal insurgent leader, organized a disciplined military force that at its apogee controlled much of southern Mexico. Although Morelos oversaw the calling of a congress and the adoption of a constitution, his power was on the wane by late 1813 as a result of military losses. Morelos limited the use of gratuitous terror as an object lesson. Nonetheless, his forces often summarily executed captured royalist officers. On one occasion, a lieutenant tied two captured Spaniards to a tree and let them starve to death. Facing both Morelos's army and less restrained guerrilla forces in other parts of Mexico, royalist opponents continued to execute and decapitate rebels and to display their heads on pikes and to hang their bodies from trees. After capturing and trying Morelos, they executed him by firing squad. Spanish commander José de la Cruz articulated the extreme royalist position. "My system is to shoot hundreds by firing squads, to decimate the population of towns, and to make the name of the soldier as frightening as death itself."[1]

Because insurgents and bandit gangs, often composed of demobilized soldiers, easily dispersed and disappeared into the general population of a town or region, royalists in Mexico used "flying detachments" of some three hundred mounted troops. These swept through rebel territory to seize arms, horses, and livestock and to capture persons identified as rebels. Loyalist colonel Agustín de Iturbide also employed a scorched-earth policy and boasted of killing nearly one thousand rebels in two months. General and later Viceroy Félix de Calleja on occasion completely destroyed towns that supported the separatists.

The royalists often followed public executions with pardons or amnesties. Less than two months after the Hidalgo Revolt began, Calleja issued a pardon to rebels who would surrender, turn over their weapons, and identify their leaders. Not long after Hidalgo's defeat, Calleja declared that the insurrection was over, thus defining as criminals—"bandits, thieves, and delinquents"—and unworthy of pardon anyone who continued to struggle against Spanish forces. Nonetheless, royal pardons and even offers of general amnesty followed in succeeding years, a practice that allowed some insurgents to change sides repeatedly.

Although the execution of Morelos in 1815 ended the most organized and persistent rebellion, guerrilla bands and bandits kept the royalists focused on counterinsurgency throughout much of Mexico for the remainder of the decade.

Venezuela also suffered extensive terror as both sides executed civilians and soldiers. One insurgent leader promised his men promotions in return for the severed heads of Spaniards and even sent a head to Bolívar, who repudiated this policy. After royalists captured and executed the headhunters, however, Bolívar in 1813 declared "war to the death" against any peninsular who did not actively support the insurgency. Civil war was brutal, nasty, and relentless for over a decade.

Borderless Campaigns of Conquest and Liberation

A defining feature of the military conflict between loyalists and separatists in much of Spanish South America was its territorial expansion beyond a single colony. With the defeat of the rebel government in Venezuela, Bolívar fled in 1812 to Cartagena in the temporarily independent New Granada. From that base, he launched a particularly brutal campaign into Venezuela in 1813. With creole support, Bolívar was initially successful and entered Caracas, where he oversaw the creation of a centralized republic. But the royalist *caudillo* José Tomás Boves emerged victorious in 1814 with the support of *casta* cowboys from the plains of Venezuela.

The recently restored Ferdinand VII sent a large military expedition under General Pablo Morillo to Venezuela. His forces entered Caracas in May 1815 and by October had pacified most of New Granada. In order to pay for this costly military venture, General Morillo confiscated and sold the property of well-known republican leaders and their noncombatant supporters. This harsh policy proved counterproductive because it forced the creole elite to see independence as the best guarantee of their property.

Although Bolívar was unable to gain British aid, he did find valuable new allies. Alexandre Petión, the president of Haiti, provided significant assistance in return for a pledge to abolish slavery. Bolívar also won the support of two groups that had previously provided the Venezuelan royalists with their most effective troops, *casta* cowboys of the interior, now led by José Antonio Páez, and free blacks.

A congress meeting in Angostura in the interior of Venezuela in 1819 declared the union of Venezuela, New Granada, and the still unliberated Ecuador in the Republic of Colombia—often called Gran Colombia by historians—and named Bolívar president. Even as the congress met, however, an audacious military campaign was determining the future of Venezuela and New Granada. Bolívar crossed the Andes and defeated Spanish forces in New Granada at Boyacá, near the capital.

The southern prong of the wars of independence came through Chile, which San Martín had liberated with an army trained and recruited in present Argentina. In 1820 he sailed from independent Chile with an army and landed in Pisco, Peru. By this time, however, the political environment in Spain had changed, with important consequences for the separatists in America.

On January 1, 1820, Major Rafael Riego launched a military revolt in southern Spain among troops gathered for another large military expedition to the Americas. Bolstered by support in various cities of Spain, the revolt forced Ferdinand VII to accept constitutional government and triggered the final stage in the disintegration of Spain's mainland American empire. It was clear that Spain could not send another army to the Americas, and the new liberal government ordered commanders there to arrange cease-fires with the separatists.

In New Granada, Spanish General Morillo arranged a cease-fire with Bolívar and then departed for Spain, leaving the remaining royalist forces in northern South America under weak leaders. Although it took some time to defeat all pockets of resistance, the armies under Bolívar and his lieutenants Páez and Antonio José de Sucre were henceforth virtually unstoppable. Victory at Carabobo in 1821 meant the liberation of Venezuela. Sucre's success in present Ecuador the following year determined that that region would also join Colombia.

The final military campaigns in South America took place between 1819 and 1825. San Martín forced the leading citizens of Lima to declare independence from Spain in July 1821 without fighting a major battle in Peru, but he failed to extend his authority to the interior, to which an undefeated royalist army had moved. Now titled the "Protector," San Martín quickly found his new government in virtual bankruptcy and his army in no condition to confront the royalist forces. Recognizing his problems, he sailed to Guayaquil and met with Bolívar to seek support. Soon afterward, San Martín resigned as Protector and went into self-imposed exile, leaving Bolívar and Sucre to complete the independence of Peru and Upper Peru. Victories at Junín and Ayacucho in 1824 eliminated the royalist government and army in Peru. Sucre emerged victorious in Upper Peru the following year. In 1826 the last royalist bases in South America surrendered.

The End of Spain's Mainland Empire

After Ferdinand VII accepted the constitution, in New Spain the restoration of provincial deputations and hundreds of constitutional municipal governments took place with little delay. Two sets of elections for deputies to the *cortes* were held in New Spain by March 1821. This last opportunity for autonomy within the Spanish Nation proved fruitless and, in any case, was overtaken by the separatist solution.

In New Spain, a small group of the Mexico City elite worked with Agustín de Iturbide, a creole officer in the royalist army, to obtain complete independence. The resulting Plan of Iguala, agreed upon with surviving patriot leaders, was a masterful compromise that offered the throne of an independent Mexico to Ferdinand VII and protected peninsulars, the Church, and the army. Besides providing for independence, it continued the authority of the Spanish Constitution of 1812 until a constituent assembly could write one specific to Mexico. The success of Iturbide's agreement with the patriots was ensured by the refusal of Mexican municipalities to collect the hated tax that had supported the counterinsurgency on the grounds that it was unconstitutional. The arrival of the new *jefe político superior* Juan O'Donojú, a liberal who supported autonomy, sealed independence without a major battle as many royalist officers backed Iturbide and the Plan of Iguala.

Mexico created an empire in 1821, but, after Ferdinand refused the crown, it elevated the hero of independence, Iturbide, as Agustín I in July 1822. The Mexican Empire collapsed in less than a year, and, after a transition period, a federal republic replaced it in 1824.

In Central America, news of the Plan of Iguala led to the rapid loss of Chiapas to Mexico. After a brief association with Iturbide's empire, the remaining towns and provinces created a separate federal republic in 1824. Central America had achieved independence.

In Spanish South America between 1810 and the late 1820s, juntas, constituent assemblies, and congresses wrote foundational laws and constitutions to provide a framework for government; some twenty different codes were drafted in New Granada by the end of 1815, a majority for city-states such as Cartagena. Following explicit declarations of independence, constitutional republics quickly emerged as the governmental form favored by insurrectionists in New Granada and Venezuela. Although Manuel Belgrano advocated that the United Provinces of Río de la Plata become a constitutional monarchy with an Inca on the throne, and although San Martín also favored a constitutional monarchy for Peru headed initially by a European prince, these ideas had few partisans relative to those favoring some form of constitutional republics. Even Mexico, which created an empire in 1821, quickly adopted a federal republic.

Portugal and Brazil in an Era of Revolution

With the royal court safely in Brazil, the Portuguese began to accommodate to the new order until word of the popular uprisings in Spain sparked a popular revolt and the formation of patriotic juntas. Aided by substantial British military support, Portuguese volunteers cleared Napoleon's forces from most of the kingdom. New French invasions in 1809 and 1811 caused extensive property damage and perhaps nearly 250,000 Portuguese deaths. The nation's already weak transportation system was particularly hard hit, and as a result, commerce suffered. The cost of expelling the French encumbered the Portuguese treasury with debt and left the economy in crisis.

The decision of John VI, king after 1816, to remain in Brazil and elevate the former colony to the status of an equal kingdom created dissatisfaction in Portugal. As regent in the absence of John VI, British General William Carr Beresford's consistent sacrifice of Portuguese commercial interests prompted a rising tide of opposition. The decision to open Brazil to direct trade with friendly nations, especially Great Britain, and the revocation of prohibitions on colonial manufacturing further confirmed the arrival of a new era, formalized in a commercial treaty signed in 1810. Despite legislation designed to benefit Portuguese merchants and shippers, the old monopolistic system was gone, and trade between Brazil and Portugal plummeted between 1809 and 1813 to less than a third of its level between 1800 and 1804. As was the case with Spain, Portugal's empire as an economic unit had crumbled.

Political and economic subordination to Britain and anger over the monarch's decision to remain in Brazil stimulated a potent liberal opposition, particularly among merchants in port cities and urban intellectuals. With the spread of Masonic lodges, military officers, many influenced by British colleagues, joined the opposition. In some rural areas, elements within the aristocracy were also unhappy with administration during the regency, although this group had little sympathy for liberalism.

In 1817 Beresford was informed of a conspiracy that included General Gomes da Freire, a leader of the Portuguese Masonic movement. Beresford quickly moved to crush this threat, executing the popular military officer. When news of the 1820 military mutiny in Cádiz reached Portugal, a rebellion began in Oporto. As the movement spread, liberal political leaders in Lisbon and Oporto established juntas and sought the return of John VI from Brazil.

John resisted the pressure to return to Portugal, as he correctly recognized that once in Lisbon he would be reduced to a constitutional monarch subject to the whims of a popular government. Simultaneously, competing factions within the military struggled for control of the junta in Lisbon. Eventually the Spanish system of indirect suffrage was used to elect members of a constituent *cortes* in 1821. The first representative assembly held in Portugal since 1689, the *cortes* wrote a constitution that acknowledged popular sovereignty and established a unicameral legislature. The king's power was greatly limited, but the Church and aristocracy retained many of their privileges.

John VI finally returned to Portugal in 1821. Despite his earlier fears, he had to live with the liberal constitutional order only briefly. Important elements within the Church hierarchy and the aristocracy fought to return to the old regime, and an "absolutist" rebellion began in remote areas of the country. When a French army invaded Spain in April 1823 to restore Ferdinand VII to absolute power, a conservative military revolt began in Portugal. The constitutionalist government quickly fell, and John again ruled without formal political constraint.

Brazilian Independence

The arrival of the royal court in Brazil in 1808 dramatically changed the colony's political life and economy. Access to the court and the possibility of gaining a title of nobility drew the colonial elite into the monarch's orbit. Even though many Brazilians came to resent the arrogance and privileged status of the recent arrivals, this anti-Portuguese sentiment did not seriously undermine support for the king.

As prince regent and, after 1816, king, John VI moved quickly to address some long-standing grievances. He opened the colony's ports to free trade, removed the prohibition of colonial manufactures, and dropped some import duties. The court also helped stimulate colonial production by dramatically increasing the demand for goods and services. More than twenty thousand Portuguese and thousands of other European immigrants arrived in the city of Rio de Janeiro alone between 1808 and 1822. As the urban population of the capital rose toward 100,000, demand for housing, food, locally manufactured goods, and services expanded as well. Even the urban masses experienced small improvements in employment and wages.

The court was costly, and local producers largely paid its expenses through taxation. Portuguese émigrés who held the highest administrative and military offices often enjoyed high salaries and luxurious lifestyles provided by royal patronage. But even though this was a period of general prosperity, some members of the Brazilian elite came to resent this forced subsidy. Because John yielded to British pressure and agreed to restrictions on the slave trade, he lost support among sugar, cotton, and coffee producers. As slave prices rose and the price of agricultural exports fell following the return of peace to Europe in 1815, political unrest spread in Brazil's agricultural sector. Finally, the cost of committing military forces in Uruguay in 1811 and 1816 also proved unpopular.

Despite a growing undercurrent of dissatisfaction, there was only one significant Brazilian uprising against the monarchy. In Pernambuco in 1817, some planters, merchants, and churchmen joined what was basically a military rebellion. The leaders affected the customs of the French Revolution, addressing one another as "patriot" and offering the French constitution as a model for organizing government. This "republic" lasted less than three months. Once order was restored, additional troops from Portugal were brought in to garrison strategic points in Brazil.

Independence, however, did not result from the maturation of these colonial grievances or the spread of radical republicanism. Rather, events in Portugal destabilized Brazil. When Portuguese liberals summoned representatives to the *cortes* in 1820, Brazil was permitted to elect approximately seventy-five of the more than two hundred delegates. Although a liberal perspective dominated the reform agenda in Portugal itself, the economic agenda was traditional imperialism. The *cortes* leadership sought to subordinate Brazil's economic interests by reestablishing the commercial system that had existed before the French invasion.

John VI's position deteriorated when rebellious Portuguese soldiers in Belem created the first Brazilian junta in January 1821. In February the Portuguese garrison in Rio de Janeiro forced the king to reorganize his ministry and to accept the creation of juntas and the formulation of a liberal constitution. These events provoked a crisis among Brazilian political leaders. Although many supported the ideology of the Lisbon junta, they recognized that the loss of the court would mean a return to colonial status.

When John sailed for Portugal on July 26, 1821, he left his twenty-two-year-old son Pedro as regent in Brazil. These events made Brazilians more self-consciously nationalistic. The *cortes'* decision to reestablish limitations on Brazilian commerce and to reinforce Brazilian garrisons with Portuguese troops fed this sense of Brazilian distinctiveness. As Portugal reasserted its domination, seven Brazilian delegates to the *cortes* fled Lisbon rather than accept the new Portuguese constitution of 1822.

Events now moved quickly. In response to intense pressure, including a petition signed by eight thousand persons, Pedro refused the *cortes'* order to return to Portugal. The army in Brazil was purged of those soldiers and officers unwilling to swear allegiance to Dom Pedro, and troops sent from Portugal were denied permission to land. With the appointment of José Bonifácio de Andrada e Silva, a wealthy Brazilian with broad experience in Portugal, as head of a Brazilian cabinet, the break with the metropolis became inevitable. Although the other members of this advisory body were

Portuguese, all were committed to maintaining Pedro in Brazil in defiance of metropolitan authority.

Substantial disagreement remained over the institutional form and political content of the developing movement toward independence. José Bonifácio tried to prevent dramatic political or social change, believing that monarchy was the best insurance against the chaos that had engulfed the neighboring republics of Spanish America. Although more radical leaders forced the creation of a Constituent Assembly, the imposition of indirect elections and limited suffrage guaranteed that this body would be compatible with José Bonifácio's conservative vision. The jailing or expulsion of leading radicals further strengthened the conservative leadership.

After May 1822 it was decided that decrees of the Portuguese *cortes* would not be enforced without Pedro's permission. In the same month the prince was given the title of perpetual protector of Brazil. Then in June all appointees to the civil service were required to swear support for Brazilian independence. Finally, the provincial governments were ordered to prevent individuals appointed by the Portuguese *cortes* from taking office. Brazil was effectively independent.

While the prince was traveling in São Paulo, his wife met with the Council of State to inform them that the *cortes* was planning to send troops to Brazil, as it now regarded Dom Pedro and his advisers as traitors. Following the urging of José Bonifácio, Pedro declared Brazilian independence on September 7, 1822, and became Brazil's first emperor. The British government guaranteed the success of this bloodless movement by making clear to Portugal that it would not tolerate European military intervention in an independent Brazil.

Cuba: The "Ever Faithful Isle"

In 1826 Spain retained only Cuba, Puerto Rico, and the Philippine Islands as surviving outposts of empire. Cuba was economically and fiscally the most important possession and the beneficiary of a special relationship with Spain. Spared the turmoil of the 1810s and 1820s, Cuba's loyalty to the metropolis was strengthened by the arrival of Spanish exiles from former colonies.

Cuba's sugar industry grew after 1765. By 1790 planters had purchased over fifty thousand slaves. Sugar plantations rapidly increased from 10,000 acres in 1762 to over 150,000 acres three decades later. Further growth followed quickly after the slave revolution began in French Saint Domingue (Haiti) in 1791. The slaves' vengeance was Cuba's opportunity, and its planters did not hesitate. Bolstered by higher sugar prices resulting from Saint Domingue's plummeting production and thousands of French planters who arrived with slaves, capital, and expertise, Cuban sugar exports roughly tripled by 1815 and continued rising for decades. Coffee exports grew from about 175,000 pounds in 1792 to over 4.4 million pounds in 1826.

Ferdinand VII's policy toward the Cuban elites continued the favorable treatment begun earlier. In 1815 he yielded to planters who wanted to clear

Havana, Cuba, early in the nineteenth century.

previously protected forests in order to grow crops. He then abolished the long-lived tobacco monopoly and opened Cuban ports to world trade.

While the newly independent mainland countries struggled with economic devastation, fiscal insolvency, and political instability, the Cuban elites entered the second quarter of the nineteenth century expecting military and commercial benefits to continue. Their sensibilities were then offended when Cuba's colonial status was reaffirmed in 1836. Nonetheless, the Cuban elites continued to benefit from the island's direct relationship with Spain for much of the nineteenth century.

Spain After the Loss of the Mainland Empire

Spain emerged from French occupation confronting political and fiscal problems similar to those facing its former colonies after independence. Although in 1820 the Riego Revolt reestablished the Constitution of 1812, by the time the independence wars ended in the Western Hemisphere, Spain's second experiment with constitutional government was also over. Restored again to full monarchical authority in October 1823, Ferdinand VII exiled liberal politicians but was unable to send a major expeditionary force to the mainland colonies. The reality of fiscal bankruptcy forced him to listen to moderate schemes and rule more in the manner of an enlightened despot than a benighted reactionary. Indeed, he proved insufficiently conservative for some monarchists, who, among other things, deplored his failure to reestablish the Inquisition. The major political divisions that characterized Spain in the second quarter of the nineteenth century were within the monarchical tradition. This instability suggests that the Napoleonic invasion of 1808 had important long-term political effects on the mother country, as well as its empire.

Spain's loss of its mainland empire sealed the decline of the port of Cádiz initiated by the British blockade of 1797–1801. Loss of the colonies also reduced royal revenue in the short run by at least 40 percent, as remittances to the royal treasury and customs duties on trade with the mainland colonies ended. In terms of the Spanish economy as a whole, however, colonial independence had remarkably little impact.

The overall decline in Spain's national income resulting from colonial independence was probably no more than 2.5 percent. By the late 1820s, moreover, the temporary loss had been reversed by expanded Spanish exports that were 12 percent greater than during the heyday of "free trade within the empire." Thus European markets, supplemented by Spain's expanding trade with Cuba, Puerto Rico, and the Philippines, quickly replaced the former Spanish mainland colonial markets. Spanish ports, notably Barcelona and Santander, were able to pursue successfully new and expanded commercial opportunities for Spanish products.

Despite the limited economic consequences of the loss of the mainland empire, Spain stubbornly refused to accept the independent existence of its former colonies. Ferdinand died without having granted diplomatic recognition to any of his former American realms. Spanish liberals and conservatives alike opposed acknowledging independence, and Spain only slowly began granting diplomatic recognition to the new countries. Mexico was first in 1836, followed by Ecuador in 1840 and Chile in 1844; Honduras was the last. Its recognition in 1895 barely preceded the loss in 1898 of the remaining islands of empire: Cuba, Puerto Rico, and the Philippines.

Notes

1. José de la Cruz to Félix Calleja del Rey, Leon, Archivo General de la Nación, México, Sección de Operaciones de Guerra, 15 July, 1811, vol. 145.

Suggested for Further Reading

Anna, Timothy E. *The Mexican Empire of Iturbide.* Lincoln: University of Nebraska Press, 1990.

Barickman, B. J. *A Bahian Counterpoint: Sugar, Tobacco, Cassava, and Slavery in the Recôncavo, 1780–1860.* Stanford, Calif.: Stanford University Press, 1998.

Barman, Roderick J. *Brazil: The Forging of a Nation, 1798–1852.* Stanford, Calif.: Stanford University Press, 1988.

Benson, Nettie Lee. *The Provincial Deputation in Mexico: Harbinger of Provincial Autonomy, Independence, and Federalism.* Austin: University of Texas Press, 1992.

Blanchard, Peter. *Under the Flags of Freedom: Slave Soldiers and the Wars of Independence in Spanish South America.* Pittsburgh, Pa.: University of Pittsburgh Press, 2008.

Brown, Matthew. *Adventuring Through Spanish Colonies: Simón Bolívar, Foreign Mercenaries and the Birth of New Nations.* Liverpool, England: Liverpool University Press, 2006.

Bushnell, David. *Simón Bolívar: Liberation and Disillusion.* New York: Pearson Longman, 2004.

Bushnell, David, editor. *El Libertador: Writings of Simón Bolívar.* Translated by Frederick H. Fornoff. New York: Oxford University Press, 2003.

Bushnell, David and Lester D. Langley, editors. *Simón Bolívar: Essays on the Life and Legacy of the Liberator.* Rowan & Littlefield, 2008.

Cahill, David. *From Rebellion to Independence in the Andes: Soundings from Southern Peru, 1750–1830.* Amsterdam: Aksant, 2002.

Chasteen, John Charles. *Americanos: Latin America's Struggle for Independence.* New York: Oxford University Press, 2008.

Davies, Catherine, Claire Brewster, and Hilary Owen. *South American Independence: Gender, Politics, Text.* Liverpool, England: Liverpool University Press, 2007.

Dym, Jordana. *From Sovereign Villages to National States: City, State, and Federation in Central America, 1759–1839.* Albuquerque: University of New Mexico Press, 2006.

Earle, Rebecca A. *Spain and the Independence of Colombia 1810–1825.* Exeter, England: University of Exeter Press, 2000.

Hawkins, Timothy. *José de Bustamante and Central American Independence: Colonial Administration in an Age of Imperial Crisis.* Tuscaloosa: University of Alabama Press. 2004.

Helg, Aline. *Liberty and Equality in Caribbean Colombia, 1770–1835.* Chapel Hill: University of North Carolina Press, 2004.

Kraay, Hendrik. *Race, State, and Armed Forces in Independence Era Brazil: Bahia, 1790s–1840s.* Stanford, Calif.: Stanford University Press, 2001.

Lasso, Marixa. *Myths of Harmony: Race and Republicanism during the Age of Revolution, Colombia 1795–1831.* Pittsburgh, Pa.: University of Pittsburgh Press, 2007.

Lynch, John. *San Martín: Argentine Soldier, American Hero.* New Haven, Conn., and London: Yale University Press, 2009.

Lynch, John. *Simón Bolívar: A Life.* New Haven, Conn., and London: Yale University Press, 2006.

McFarlane, Anthony, and Eduardo Posada-Carbó. *Independence and Revolution in Spanish America: Perspectives and Problems.* London: Institute of Latin American Studies, University of London, 1999.

Marks, Patricia H. *Deconstructing Legitimacy: Viceroys, Merchants, and the Military in Late Colonial Peru.* University Park, Pa.: The Pennsylvania State University Press, 2007.

Vale, Brian. *Cochrane in the Pacific: Fortune and Freedom in Spanish America.* New York and London: Tauris, 2008.

Van Young, Eric. *The Other Rebellion: Popular Violence, Ideology, and the Mexican Struggle for Independence, 1810–1821.* Stanford, Calif.: Stanford University Press, 2001.

Walker, Charles F. *Smoldering Ashes: Cuzco and the Creation of Republican Peru, 1780–1840.* Durham, N.C.: Duke University Press, 1999.

Warren, Richard A. *Vagrants and Citizens: Politics and the Masses in Mexico City from Colony to Republic.* Wilmington, Del.: Scholarly Resources, 2001.

TWELVE

EPILOGUE

Chronology

Date	Location	Event
1811–1826	Americas	Independence of Spain's and Portugal's mainland colonies
1816–1840	Paraguay	Dr. José Gaspar Rodríguez de Francia *caudillo*
1824–1825	Americas	26 British mining associations formed to do business
1826–1828	Americas	Except for Brazil, all L.A. countries with foreign debt defaulted
1829	Mexico	Unsuccessful Spanish invasion
1829–1852	Buenos Aires	Juan Manuel de Rosas *caudillo* of Argentina
1830	Gran Colombia	Independent Venezuela, Colombia, and Ecuador replace Bolívar's Gran Colombia; death of Bolívar
1830–1837	Chile	Diego Portales *caudillo*
1830–1848	Venezuela	José Antonio Páez *caudillo*
1833–1855	Mexico	Age of Antonio López de Santa Anna
1836	Mexico	Secession of Texas
1836–1839	Peru & Bolivia	Short-lived confederation
1838	Central America	United Provinces of Central America dissolves into independent states of Guatemala, Honduras, Nicaragua, Costa Rica, and El Salvador
1846–1848	Mexico	War with U.S.; Mexico loses more than half of territory
1854	Peru	Abolition of tribute (*contribución indígena*)
1857	Ecuador	Abolition of Indian tribute

The former colonies of Latin America faced the difficult process of organizing new governments, establishing internal order, and promoting economic growth. Despite the magnitude of these tasks, the political and intellectual leaders of the early stages of the independence era were generally optimistic about the future. The native-born elite, like the conquistadors and early European settlers, believed that Latin America was richly endowed by nature, and many foreign visitors, particularly the British, shared this belief. According to these observers, Spanish and Portuguese rule had been the major impediment to material progress.

Much initial optimism had disappeared before the last royalist armies were defeated in Spanish America. Competing claims of regions, classes, colors, and

Map 8 Latin America in 1830.

ideologies had divided political life and promoted sectoral violence. These divisions and conflicts later appeared in Brazil in the 1830s, despite that nation's more peaceful transition to independence. The reduced authority and limited resources of newly independent governments, compared with those of the colonial period, led to an increase in banditry and other forms of civil disorder. In response, the propertied classes, hoping to protect their wealth, supported, or at least encouraged, various forms of authoritarian rule.

Early hopes for economic growth and prosperity faded quickly in the decades after independence. The wars for independence had been costly, and the loss of the established imperial commercial ties had often been economically disruptive. Even where trade had expanded and exports had increased, the benefits were not widely shared by the newly independent populations. The concentration of wealth was greater at the end of the nineteenth century than during the colonial period.

The Economy

The establishment of political independence in Spanish America exacted a heavy price. By 1830 nearly every region was poorer than it had been in 1800. These economic costs appear to have been greatest in the mining centers of Mexico and the Andean nations of Peru and Bolivia, where silver production fell by two-thirds. Plantation agriculture in Venezuela and Peru, the grazing industry of Argentina and Uruguay, manufacturing and cottage industries in Ecuador and Mexico, and internal trade throughout Spanish America suffered reverses. Brazil's unique path to independence enabled it to avoid most of the economic and social dislocations that proved so costly to its neighbors.

Many economic problems the new nations faced were rooted in geography and natural resources or were structural legacies of centuries of colonialism. The destructive effects of the political conflicts and military campaigns that led to independence only heightened these problems. Because the international context within which Latin America's new leaders attempted to remedy these difficulties after 1825 was more dynamic, expansive, and unpredictable than before, prior experiences, existing institutions, and established practice were of only limited usefulness.

The independence of Latin America coincided with the Industrial Revolution in Europe. As Europe and then the United States industrialized, Latin America became a specialized supplier of industrial raw materials, such as copper, tin, and hides, or agricultural products, such as sugar, coffee, and tobacco. This increasing dependence on one or two export products made these economies vulnerable to fluctuations in world market prices. Thus a decline in the price of a country's principal export had the potential to devastate a national economy and provoke political unrest.

Frontier militiamen in Argentina.

Manpower requirements during the wars for independence affected mining and export agriculture more than subsistence farming. The actual loss of life was relatively light in comparison with Europe's experience during the Napoleonic Wars. Nonetheless, the dispersal of soldiers caused by the long-distance campaigns of San Martín and Bolívar, the migration of those seeking to leave or avoid military service, and the depredations of invading armies multiplied the disruptive effects of enlistment and conscription.

Prior to independence, peninsulars had made up only a minuscule percentage of the total work force in colonial Latin America, but they were among the most experienced, best-trained sectors of the professional, commercial, and artisan classes. Through emigration, discrimination, expulsion, and loss of life, their productive energy was largely lost. Losses also occurred at the bottom of the labor force. Both egalitarian ideology and practical political necessity led to attacks on all forms of compulsory labor. Both San Martín and Bolívar abolished the *mita,* and nearly all the revolutionary governments in Spanish America outlawed the African slave trade soon after independence. Slavery itself had been weakened by gradualist emancipation laws and by manumissions granted as a result of military service. Once freed from compulsory labor obligations, few former slaves or *mita* laborers voluntarily accepted employment in the plantations or mines where they had been forced to work in the colonial period. As a result, cacao production in Venezuela and gold production in Colombia declined. Silver production in Peru and Bolivia also fell with the abolition of the *mita.* Only in Brazil did slavery emerge strengthened after independence. The widespread violation of agreements to end the slave trade in the 1830s and 1840s brought nearly 500,000 new African slaves to Brazil and facilitated the large-scale expansion of coffee production. Britain's use of both naval force and diplomacy forced an end to the slave trade in the 1850s. By this time, however, Brazil had established a market advantage in coffee.

Latin America also confronted the problem of depleted capital resources. In order to replace and restore production capacity damaged by the wars and to stimulate new growth, it was necessary to find large amounts of investment capital. The major sources of investment capital during the colonial era, the Church and the peninsular merchant community, were gravely weakened by

As competition increased from foreign manufactures, Latin American producers tried to find specialized local markets or used the labor of family members to stay competitive. Here a man and a women work together as blacksmiths.

expropriations, forced loans, and destruction in the wars. Many wealthy peninsulars had fled war-torn areas with their liquid capital, returning to Spain or sometimes settling in Cuba. During the era of civil wars and regional conflicts that followed independence, the Church remained under pressure because of its wealth. Although liberals and conservatives disagreed over the Church's role in education, intellectual life, and political discourse, both groups in the end forced it to subsidize government expenses. Numerous rebel leaders and, after independence, new governments relied on deficit spending. As a result, they commonly allocated customs duties and other revenues to debt service rather than to infrastructure improvements. Under pressure to stretch fiscal resources, governments debased their currencies and borrowed from foreign lenders. During the 1820s, Spanish American governments placed bonds with a nominal value of 18 million British pounds in Europe. After the cost of commissions and speculation, only about 10 million pounds reached the borrowers. By 1828 all Latin American countries except Brazil were in default and without access to European credit.

Other resources were also lost during the wars. Both royalist and rebel armies had routinely expropriated crops and livestock. One reason that Miguel Hidalgo was able to create and sustain an army of more than fifty thousand was the coincidence of his rebellion with the Mexican grain harvest. When the opportunity presented itself, marauding soldiers from both sides seized horses, mules, cattle, wagons, carts, and tools. Sea and river transportation were similarly devastated. Blockades, the spread of privateering, and the breakdown of customary tax and tariff laws led to the loss or diversion of much of Spanish America's shipping capacity. Mines deteriorated or were flooded. In Mexico it took half a century to regain the level of mineral production of 1800, and the mines of Peru and Bolivia never recovered.

Destroyed, deteriorated, and expropriated resources contributed to a decline in exports and generally low levels of investment. Sectors of the economy tied to the imperial commercial system, such as cacao and sugar production and silver mining, tended to suffer most. On the other hand, exports such as livestock products, coffee, and copper expanded after independence to meet the needs of an Atlantic market dominated by Great Britain. The high profits that resulted from the growing European passion for coffee led Venezuelan landowners to accept an interest rate of 15 percent to promote increased production in the 1830s. In contrast with much of Spanish America, Brazil suffered little in the transition to independence and therefore found few impediments to expanding its exports. Despite only limited mining in Chile during the colonial era, mining production boomed after independence. The greatest growth and most rapid recoveries occurred in the mineral and agricultural exporting regions that had natural linkages with the British or other European markets. Many of these new or expanded exports were subject to periodic, often violent, price changes as European tastes changed or as new producers entered the market. While prices were rising, Latin Americans invested heavily in expanding production, often borrowing funds at high interest rates. The inevitable collapse in prices that followed the appearance of new producers or a change in European demand usually had devastating economic and political consequences for the Latin American countries. This cycle of boom and bust remains characteristic of the region.

Although by 1850 new exports and new markets had overcome the economic costs of independence in most of Latin America, the new economic order was in some ways less advanced than the colonial system it replaced. In general the economies were less integrated and interdependent. Large-scale unified political and economic systems such as the Viceroyalty of Río de la Plata disappeared, and, as a result, formerly protected agriculture and industry disappeared, as well. Manufacturing and artisan production also fell throughout the region. One measure of these changes was the relative loss of the cities' economic importance. Only cities closely tied to the new exports—Buenos Aires, Caracas, Havana and Rio de Janeiro—escaped stagnation or decline.

The poor quality of transportation and communication also hindered Latin America's development. Neither Spain nor Portugal had invested significant resources in infrastructure, and the new governments were commonly poorer and less efficient. As a result, roads, bridges, and harbors often deteriorated after independence, and postal services were slow and unreliable. Only the largest cities regularly had newspapers and periodicals available. Consequently, goods moved slowly and at great cost, and merchants bought and sold with minimal market intelligence. Merchants in the capital cities of Buenos Aires, Caracas, and Rio de Janeiro commonly knew more about market conditions in Europe than about conditions in interior cities a few hundred miles away.

The shortage of local investment capital and the small size of domestic markets slowed the acquisition of new technologies. The steam engine, which had revolutionized manufacturing in much of Europe by 1830, entered Latin America very slowly, gaining importance only as an aid in draining mines before mid-century. For most of the nineteenth century, textile production and metallurgy in Latin America remained wedded to technologies that had been in place for more than two hundred years. Even such simple tools as the steel plow continued to be imported into the twentieth century.

Government and Political Life

Brazil's transition to independence was facilitated by the presence of a Portuguese prince in Rio de Janeiro. Independence came first without a change in constitution or law. Even the highest levels of the bureaucracy experienced little immediate change in personnel. In Spanish America, however, the transition was more dramatic and more complete. Virtually the entire edifice of the Spanish colonial order was scrapped, and few experienced high officials escaped dismissal within a few years after independence. Gone, too, was a monarchical system that had provided legitimacy and continuity over three hundred years. After 1811, region after region formally declared independence and began creating new constitutional and political practices.

Although monarchism found its supporters—San Martín and Iturbide being the most important—the revolutionary leadership in Spanish America was generally republican in principle. It was not, however, democratic in practice. O'Higgins, Bolívar, Páez, and Sucre, among others, accepted and exercised political authority and administrative power outside the limits established by constitutions. Representative institutions lost their importance as newly independent countries confronted centrifugal political threats. Local political loyalties destroyed Bolívar's vision of a Gran Colombia, subverted Central America's union with Mexico, and frustrated the re-creation of a United Provinces of the Río de la Plata. Real power was exercised by strong men, *caudillos,* who relied for their legitimacy on their clients and elite patronage rather than on election or formal institutions. Some *caudillos* called themselves liberals, others conservatives, but all used personal, not constitutional, authority. Among the many important *caudillos* were Juan Manuel de Rosas of Argentina, Diego Portales of Chile, José Antonio Páez of Venezuela, and Antonio López de Santa Anna of Mexico. Although all these leaders appeared as "great men" to admirers of their day, it is clear that their political importance resulted more from the relative diminution of centralized power and the reduction of state resources during the 1820s and 1830s than from their merits. All actors appear large on a small stage.

The state retained economic importance after independence, although limited resources reduced and constrained ambitions. Only the government of Brazil retained a colonial-era ability to influence the allocation of resources. Even in this case Great Britain's preponderant position as a trading partner limited the government's freedom of action. Politicians in London rather than Rio de Janeiro, for example, made the decision to end the slave trade. Virtually no independent government in Latin America was able to create and collect taxes as efficiently as its colonial predecessor. With the abolition of most colonial-era production and consumption taxes, Latin American governments by 1850 received nearly 80 percent of their revenue from customs duties and export taxes. These taxes inhibited regional trade, further disrupted colonial patterns, such as Chilean wheat exports to Peru, and advanced Spanish America's integration into the European market. In an extreme but not unique case, the provincial governments in Argentina imposed tariffs on one another's trade, effectively ending progress toward an integrated national market.

Nevertheless, the state remained the largest single employer and consumer. Thus it could expand or restrict consumption and production through budgetary decisions. In general, all Latin American nations lagged far behind Europe and the United States in providing an environment suitable for commercial and industrial investment. In some cases Latin American governments established central banks and promoted the creation of insurance companies in imitation of practices in Europe and the United States. But these efforts were nearly always limited in scope, and many were soon abandoned. New national monetary systems also proved less stable than the silver-based colonial system. In Argentina, for example, paper money quickly led to inflation; in Brazil the issuance of copper coins produced a similar result. Unpredictable government policies and fluctuating markets increased investment in property rather than in more risky enterprises.

After independence, the political importance of the military grew as civilian authority declined. Although current or former military officers often held executive power, political life was not militarized. In an era of civil war, regional secessionism, and ideological conflict, political peace could result only from the efforts of leaders capable of organizing and asserting military force. However, few successful military men of this period politicized or even professionalized the military. José Antonio Páez, the Venezuelan revolutionary era military hero and later president, actually reduced the regular army to eight hundred men in 1838. Juan Manuel de Rosas, the Argentine *caudillo* of the 1830s and 1840s, refused for fifteen years, despite inflation, to increase the nominal pay of officers and enlisted men. It was the increased importance of regional militias and other irregular military forces, not politicized regular armies, that changed political life in Latin America. This new military phase, often accompanied by violence, resulted from a breakdown in public order and central authority that tended to elevate the relative political weight of even small, poorly armed military forces. At root Latin American federalism was as much a military fact of life as it was an ideology.

The status of the Church became a bitterly divisive issue in the decades following independence. This conflict began with the Bourbon monarchs' efforts to subordinate the Church to secular authority. Clerical immunity from secular jurisdiction in criminal and civil cases, sanctuary, and control of patronage remained unresolved when colonial rule ended. New conflicts over secular education, religious freedom, and Church wealth effectively established the boundaries that separated conservatives and liberals. Finally, the papacy's efforts to reassert patronage rights in Latin America proved an incendiary issue, as new political elites sought to create a compliant and supportive episcopal structure. In many nations, Mexico and Colombia, for example, these struggles proved to be major obstacles to the development of stable national governments.

The political revolution of 1808–1812 altered the nature of political identity by transforming colonial subjects into national citizens; independence underscored this difference. In practice only male property owners enjoyed the full rights of citizenship. Even where the right to political participation was more broadly defined, rebellions and civil wars placed real power in the hands of charismatic leaders or generals, not voters. Yet political culture had changed dramatically. Through the political turmoil of the nineteenth century, men and women routinely asserted a new political dignity based on their citizenship.

Despite women's many important contributions during the struggles that led to independence, the first constitutions excluded them from active citizenship and the right to vote and hold office. The new civil codes went even further in strengthening male authority in public life and in the family. Even in poor families in which adult males were denied the right to vote, fathers and husbands were granted a legal authority over their wives and daughters that made the men, in effect, agents of the state. Legislation defined married women as minors and compelled them to accept their husbands' authority. Widows alone had some financial and legal independence, gaining the right to sign contracts and control their own property. Women's legal rights were expanded only slowly. Not until 1860, for example, did single mothers and widows in Mexico gain the right to direct their own families the way male family heads did.

Social Change

Independence brought about significant social change. Those born in the Americas now claimed the highest positions in the civil administration and eventually the Church, but these positions had lost much of their prestige and benefits by the 1840s as a result of inflation and depressed economies. As a result, members of the elite groups tied to new export economies that connected the region to Europe were less eager to place family members in these institutions than their colonial-era predecessors had been. Everywhere except Brazil, where a monarchical court survived, wealth became the primary denominator of status.

With the increased economic importance of export agriculture, rural social norms and manners and even the idealization of the large estate as a social entity gained wider acceptance. The owners of large estates felt less compelled to maintain urban households, and they were also less willing to acknowledge the cultural superiority of the urban groups. This process was counterbalanced, in part, by the presence of large numbers of Europeans, particularly British merchants, in the port cities and by the increased intellectual penetration of European ideas, styles, and tastes. Urban elites, especially commercial and professional groups, accepted these fashions and ideas and often asserted their superiority over indigenous customs and beliefs. They dressed in European styles, read European books and magazines, and ate foods prepared in imitation of European cuisine. Class differences quickly became cultural differences. These contradictory trends helped define the liberal/conservative or, alternatively, urban/rural conflicts of the middle decades of the nineteenth century.

Independence made little difference in the lives of the urban and rural masses. The *mita* was abolished officially, but in many countries governments forced compulsory labor on Indian communities into the twentieth century. Peru and Bolivia continued for decades to collect Indian tribute, their most important and reliable fiscal resource. In fact, this dependence on tribute led these same governments to provide minimal protection for the communal landholdings that helped the Indians pay the tax. The slave trade ended in most of Spanish America by 1830 and in Brazil in 1850, yet slavery persisted in many nations until mid-century and in Brazil until 1888.

Mixed-race officers of the revolutionary armies achieved a degree of upward social mobility. By 1850 a number of dark-skinned men had gained political and economic power, and a handful had become presidents. Yet color prejudice and active discrimination survived. Bolívar's characterization of the Mexican hero of independence Vicente Guerrero as the "vile abortion of a savage Indian and a fierce African"[1] suggests the limited racial enlightenment of this period. Despite persistent racism, every independent Latin American country experienced some social change: There was more physical and social mobility and greater ethnic and cultural diversity. A small flow of European immigrants was responsible for some societal changes. Brazil received nearly six thousand immigrants as early as 1842 and more than eighteen thousand immigrants in 1854. In Argentina, Welsh and Scottish sheepherders had an important impact. The Central American governments also promoted European immigration, although with little success. Nevertheless, the social order throughout Latin America remained rooted in the colonial past, and the persistence of white domination, particularly in rural areas, suggests that independence had brought little change to class relations.

Independence was an important watershed in the history of Latin America. In political and economic terms, the region was more dynamic and more vulnerable than before breaking with Spain and Portugal. Reduced legitimacy coupled with increased economic volatility fed the political instability of the region to 1850 and beyond. Underlying these changes were the vestigial social and economic structures inherited from the colonial era.

Note

1. Tulio Halperín-Donghi, *The Aftermath of Revolution in Latin America* (New York: Harper & Row, 1973), p. 34.

Suggested for Further Reading

Adelman, Jeremy, editor. *Colonial Legacies: The Problem of Persistence in Latin American History.* New York: Routledge, 1999.
Adelman, Jeremy. *Republic of Capital: Buenos Aires and the Legal Transformation of the Atlantic World.* Stanford, Calif.: Stanford University Press, 1999.

Adelman, Jeremy. *Sovereignty and Revolution in the Iberian Atlantic.* Princeton, N.J.: Princeton University Press, 2006.

Anna, Timothy E. *Forging Mexico 1821–1835.* Lincoln: University of Nebraska Press, 1998.

Arrom, Silvia Marina. *Containing the Poor: The Mexico City Poor House, 1774–1871.* Durham, N.C.: Duke University Press, 2000.

Blanchard, Peter. *Slavery and Abolition in Early Republican Peru.* Wilmington, Del.: Scholarly Resources, 1992.

Chambers, Sarah C. *From Subjects to Citizens: Honor, Gender, and Politics in Arequipa Peru, 1780–1854.* University Park: Pennsylvania State University Press, 1999.

Connaughton, Brian F. *Clerical Ideology in a Revolutionary Age: The Guadalajara Church and the Idea of the Mexican Nation, 1788–1853.* Translated by Mark Alan Healey. Calgary, Alberta: University of Calgary Press, 2003; Boulder: University Press of Colorado, 2003.

Ducey, Michael T. *A Nation of Villages: Riot and Rebellion in the Mexican Huasteca, 1750–1850.* Tucson: University of Arizona Press, 2004.

Earle, Rebecca. *The Return of the Native: Indians and Myth-Making in Spanish America, 1810–1930.* Durham, N.C.: Duke University Press, 2008.

Esherick, Joseph W., Hasan Kayah, and Eric Van Young. *Empire to Nation: Historical Perspectives on the Making of the Modern World.* New York: Rowan & Littlefield, 2006.

Guardino, Peter. *The Time of Liberty: Popular Political Culture in Oaxaca, 1750–1850.* Durham, N.C.: Duke University Press, 2005.

Haber, Stephen, editor. *How Latin America Fell Behind: Essays on the Economic History of Brazil and Mexico, 1800–1914.* Stanford, Calif.: Stanford University Press, 1997.

Hünefeldt, Christine. *Paying the Price of Freedom: Family and Labor Among Lima's Slaves, 1800–1854.* Translated by Alexandra Minna Stern. Berkeley and Los Angeles: University of California Press, 1994.

Jacobsen, Nils. *Mirages of Transition: The Peruvian Altiplano, 1780–1930.* Berkeley and Los Angeles: University of California Press, 1993.

Larson, Brooke. *Trials of Nation Making: Liberalism, Race, and Ethnicity in the Andes, 1810–1910.* Cambridge, England: Cambridge University Press, 2004.

Ringrose, David R. *Spain, Europe, and the "Spanish Miracle" 1700–1900.* Cambridge, England: Cambridge University Press, 1996.

Salvatore, Ricardo D., Carlos Aguirre, and Gilbert M. Joseph, editors. *Crime and Punishment in Latin America: Law and Society Since Late Colonial Times.* Durham, N.C.: Duke University Press, 2001.

Stevens, Donald Fithian. *Origins of Instability in Early Republican Mexico.* Durham, N.C.: Duke University Press, 1991.

Uribe-Uran, Victor M., editor. *State and Society in Spanish America during the Age of Revolution.* Wilmington, Del.: Scholarly Resources, 2001.

Walker, Charles F. *Smoldering Ashes: Cuzco and the Creation of Republican Peru, 1780–1840.* Durham, N.C.: Duke University Press, 1999.

A NOTE ON PERIODICAL LITERATURE AND SUGGESTED READINGS

A voluminous periodical literature continues to enrich the field and offers students and professionals important additions to other publications. The most useful English-language periodicals are *The Hispanic American Historical Review, The Americas, Journal of Latin American Studies,* the interdisciplinary *Colonial Latin American Historical Review,* and *Latin American Research Review.* Students who want to pursue ethnohistorical literature should check *Ethnohistory.* The *Handbook of Latin American Studies* provides a good annotated guide to current books and articles.

For this edition we have reduced the Suggested Readings almost exclusively to books published from 1990 to the present. We encourage students who want to pursue specific topics in greater depth by reviewing older literature to use the *American Historical Association's Guide to Historical Literature,* 3rd edition (Oxford University Press, 1995), volume II. Sections 36–38 provide references to both periodical and book literature related to native peoples of the Americas and Latin America before and after 1800. Charles C. Griffin (ed.), *Latin America: A Guide to the Historical Literature* (1971) is a landmark evaluation of materials published until the late 1960s.

The bicentennial of the beginning of Spain's War of Independence in 1808 has fostered substantial scholarly attention to both events in Spain and the political revolution and subsequent independence in the Spanish colonies. A recent historiographical review is Gabriel Paquette, "The Dissolution of the Spanish Atlantic Monarchy," *The Historical Journal* 52:1 (2009), pp. 175–212.

GLOSSARY

Aguardiente de caña. An alcoholic beverage distilled from sugarcane.

Alcabala. A sales tax.

Alcaldía mayor. An administrative province or district.

Aldeias. In Brazil, recongregated Indian communities associated with Christian conversion.

Alternativa. The rotation of clerical offices, especially in regular orders, between peninsulars and creoles.

Asiento. A monopoly contract to import slaves to the Spanish colonies.

Audiencia. A high-court and advisory body to a regional chief executive in the Spanish colonies; similar to a *relaçao* in Brazil. Also the territorial jurisdiction of such a court.

Auto de fé. An act of faith; a public or private event at which the Inquisition decreed punishment of transgressions.

Ayllu. The basic kin groups in the Andean region; family units claiming ties to a common ancestor.

Ayuntamiento. A municipal council, also known as a *cabildo.*

Bandeirante. A participant in slaving expeditions against Indians in Brazil. São Paulo was the most common origin.

Bandeira. A Brazilian expedition to capture Indian slaves.

Barrio. An urban neighborhood or district.

Batab. A term for a native chieftain in Yucatan.

Boucan. A grill for roasting meat over a fire.

Caballero (cavaleiro). A knight; the highest category of untitled nobles.

Cabildo. A municipal council, also known as an *ayuntamiento.*

Cabildo abierto. An extraordinary meeting of *cabildo* attended by representatives of the Church, other governmental institutions, and members of the economic elite.

Caboclos. In Brazil, a person of mixed Indian and white ancestry.

Cacique. An indian chieftain, usually hereditary. Known as a *kuraka* in the Andes and a *batab* in the Mayan region.

Calpulli. An Indian clan in Mesoamerica; the basic social and economic unit.

Capitulación. A contract between the Castilian Crown and a private citizen, usually outlining terms of exploration, conquest, and settlement.

Casa de Contratación. The House of Trade established in Seville in 1503, moved to Cádiz in 1717, and abolished in 1790. Oversaw Spanish trade with the colonies.

Casa grande. The "big house" or owner's residence on a Brazilian plantation.

Casta. A person of mixed racial background, which included African ancestry or the suspicion of it because of illegitimacy.

Chicha. An Andean alcoholic beverage often made from corn.

Cofradía. A lay religious brotherhood.

Colegio. A secondary school in the Spanish colonies and Brazil.

Comarca. A territorial jurisdiction in Brazil.

Compadrazgo. Godparentage.

Comunero. Supporters of a popular revolt. In Spanish America, rebels in Paraguay in 1720s and 1730s and in New Granada in 1780.

Congregación. Also known as a *reducción* or, in Brazil, an *aldeia*. A resettlement of Indians by Spaniards to aid in the Indians' conversion to Christianity.

Consulado. A merchant guild.

Converso. A convert to Christianity; usually applied to a converted Jew or a "New Christian."

Corregedor. A provincial administrator employed in Portugal.

Corregidor. A magistrate and chief administrative officer for a provincial jurisdiction. In much of Spanish America, the Spanish official charged with the administration of Indian communities.

Corregimiento. An administrative province or district.

Creole. A Spaniard born in the New World.

Cue. An Aztec temple.

De capa y espada. Here, a minister on the Council of the Indies who has not had university training in law.

Doctrina. An Indian parish.

Don, Doña. Lord; a title rare in the conquest but subsequently more commonly used.

Encomendero. The holder of an *encomienda* (q.v.).

Encomienda. A grant of authority over a group of Indians. It carried the obligation to Christianize and protect them in exchange for labor services and/or tribute.

Engenho (Sp. ingenio). The Portuguese term for sugar mill. Refers to the complete operation, including the physical plant, land, and slaves.

Español. A Spaniard born in the Old or New World; refers to both peninsulars and creoles.

Fazenda. The Brazilian term for *hacienda* (q.v.).

Flibustier. The French term for buccaneers.

Flota. The fleet that sailed from Spain to Vera Cruz.

Forastero. An outsider; a person residing in a region other than where born.

Fueros. Special judicial privileges enjoyed by a particular group, for example, ecclesiastical *fueros*.

Galeones. The fleet that sailed from Spain to Cartagena and Panama.

Gaucho. A cowboy, usually of mixed ancestry, in the Río de la Plata. Known as *llanero* in Venezuela and *vaqueiro* in the Brazilian backlands.

Gobernación. An administrative province or district.

Hacendado. The owner of a *hacienda* (q.v.).

Hacienda. A large estate devoted to livestock raising or agricultural activities. Known as a *fazenda* in Brazil.

Hermandad. The Holy Brotherhood; a league of law officers hired by municipalities in Spain.

Hidalgo (fidalgo). An untitled noble.

Hidalguía. A Castilian aristocratic ideal of nobility.

Huaca. A native Andean god; often thought of as an ancestor. Commonly represented as hills, stones, water, or mummies.

Ingenio. See *engenho.*

Inquilinaje. Peonage based on tenancy common in Chile.

Jefe político. The highest colonial administrative officer in reorganized system created in the Constitution of 1812, replacing the viceroy.

Jornal. A daily wage.

Khipus. Multicolored knotted strings that served as memory aids in preconquest Peru. Also known as *quipus.*

Kuraka. See *cacique.*

Labrador. The person who works the small property he owns or rents.

Ladino. The Central American term for *mestizo.*

Lavradores de cana. In Brazil, sugar cultivators who depended on an *engenho* for processing. Many were sharecroppers.

Limpieza de sangre. Blood purity; the absence of Jewish or Muslim ancestors.

Llanero. See *gaucho.*

Llanos. The southern plains of Venezuela.

Macehual. A Mexica commoner with access to land.

Mameluco. The offspring of Portuguese and Indian parents.

Máscara. A parade of costumed men and women.

Mayeque. A commoner in Aztec Mexico without access to land.

Mayorazgo. An entailed estate.

Mazombo. A Portuguese born in Brazil.

Media anata. Tax paid by officeholders, half of their first year's salary.

Mesta. The sheep owners' guild.

Mestizo. The offspring of Spanish and Indian parents.

Ministro togado. Here, a minister on the Council of the Indies with university training in law; so named because he wore the robe (*toga*) of the judiciary.

Mita. The colonial forced labor draft that provided Indian workers on a rotational basis. Most common in mining in Peru. Adapted from an Inca precedent.

Mitayo. An Indian forced to serve in *mita.*

Mitmaq. The Indian colonizers in Andean Peru sent to exploit an ecological zone or to help secure a conquered region.

Mulatto. Offspring of black and white or, in some regions, black and Indian parents.

Obraje. A primitive factory commonly used to produce textiles in Spanish colonies. Usually dependent on forced labor.

Palenque. A fortified hamlet of runaway slaves in Spanish America; called *quilombo* in Brazil.

Pampa. The plains of Río de la Plata.

Panaca. A deceased Inca's male descendants other than his chosen heir.

Pardo. A mulatto.

Patio process. A means of refining silver through its amalgamation with mercury.

Patronato real. Royal patronage over the Church. The right to nominate for Church offices and supervise Church administration.

Peninsular. A Spaniard born in Iberia.

Peso. A coin and monetary unit in Spanish America. The silver peso was valued at eight *reales* of silver.

Pieza de Indias. An accounting term in the Spanish slave trade. A male slave without physical defects between fifteen and forty years of age. Women and children were calculated as fractions of a *pieza.*

Pipiltin. Hereditary Mexica nobility.

Plata. Silver.

Pochteca. Long-distance merchants in Aztec Mexico.

Presidio. A frontier garrison.

Pulpería. A small retail shop.

Pulque. An alcoholic beverage made from maguey, popular in Mexico before and after the conquest.

Quilombo. See *palenque.*

Radicado. A Spaniard long resident in the colonies. The term suggests someone who is well connected with local interests through marriage, friendship, and business associations.

Recôncavo. The area surrounding Bahia's Bay of All Saints.

Repartimiento. The allocation of an Indian chieftain and his people to a Spaniard to provide labor; a forced labor draft (known as *mita* in Peru).

Repartimiento de bienes. The forced sale of merchandise to Indians by Spanish officials.

Requerimiento. The "requirement"; a statement read to Indians before battle urging them to accept Christianity and allegiance to the Castilian Crown; their failure to do so justified war on them.

Residencia. The judicial review of an official's conduct in office.

Sertão. The backland of Brazil.

Sirvinacuy. An Andean term for trial marriage.

Tlatoani. A "king" in preconquest central Mexico.

Traza. The rectilinear core of a colonial city.

Vaqueiro. See *gaucho.*

Vecino. A citizen of a municipality.

Visita. An official inspection into the conduct of bureaucrats, usually unscheduled and unexpected.

Yanacona. A native retainer or laborer bound to an overlord in the Andean region.

Yerba. An herbal tea indigenous to Paraguay.

Yunga. An Andean term for a warm, low-altitude zone.

Zambo. Offspring of black and Indian parents.

ILLUSTRATION SOURCES
AND CREDITS

pp. 2, 3, 5, 201: Photographs by Susan H. Johnson.

pp. 27, 54: Weinditz, Christoph, *Das Trachtenbach des C. Weinditz Reisen Noch Spanin*, edited by Theodor Hampe, Berlin: Verlag von Walter de Gruyter Co., 1927.

p. 37: Three-Figure Plaque, Benin Kingdom. Printed with the permission of the Cleveland Museum of Art.

p. 69: Guaman Poma de Ayala, Phelipe. *Nueva cronica y buen gobierno.*

pp. 89, 398: Baucke, Florian, *Iconografía colonial rioplatense, 1749–1769*. Buenos Aires: Viau y Zona, 1935.

p. 112: Pino (Mexican), *San Ignacio Loyola*. Printed with the permission of the Denver Art Museum, collection of Jan and Frederick Mayer.

pp. 117: Portrait of San Martín de Porres on tin. Printed with the permission of Ambassador and Mrs. Findley Burns.

p. 137: Peñafiel, Antonio. *Nombres geográficos de México*. Mexico: Oficina tip. De la Secretariade Fomento, 1885.

pp. 151, 161, 188, 226: Rugendas, João Mauricio, *Voyage Pittaresque dans le Brèsil*. Paris: Engelmann et Cie, 1835.

p. 162: Published with the permission of John J. TePaske and Herbert S. Klein.

p. 164: *View of Salvador, Bahía.* 1624 engraving published in Dordrecht, Netherlands. Printed with the permission of The John Carter Brown Library at Brown University.

p.199: Photograph by Asunción Lavrín.

pp. 206, 239, 272, 292, 346, 396: Martínez Compañón y Bujanda, Baltasar Jaime, *Trujillo del Perú a fines del siglo XVIII*. Madrid: s.n., 1936.

pp. 210 (top and bottom), 216: Vidal, Emeric Essex, *Picturesque Illustrations of Buenos Ayres and Monte Video, Consisting of Twenty-four Views*. London: R. Ackermann, 1820.

pp. 212, 262: Archivo General de la Nación, Buenos Aires, Argentina.

pp. 217: *"Modo de cargar a los indios a los que caminan."* Printed with the permission of the Museo de América, Madrid, Spain.

p. 229: Arellano (Mexican), *Diceño de mulata y ja de negra y espagño en la ciudad de Mexico. Cabeso de la America a 22 del mes de Agosto de 1711 Años*. Printed with the permission of the Denver Art Museum, collection of Jan and Frederick Mayer.

p. 232 (top): Attributed to Juan Rodriguez Juárez, *De Español y Mestiza produce Castizo*. Printed with the permission of Sir Edward Hulse, Breamore House, Hampshire, England.

p. 232 (bottom): Attributed to Juan Rodriguez Juárez, *De Español y Mulata produce Morisca*. Printed with the permission of Sir Edward Hulse, Breamore House, Hampshire, England.

p. 242: Unknown (Mexican), *Joaquín Sánchez Pareja Navarez*. Printed with the permission of the Denver Art Museum, collection of Jan and Frederick Mayer.

p. 263: Unknown (Mexican), *Lady with a Harpsichord*. Printed with the permission of the Denver Art Museum, collection of Jan and Frederick Mayer.

p. 278: Francisco Clapera, *De Barsino y Mulata, China*. Printed with the permission of the Denver Art Museum, collection of Jan and Frederick Mayer.

p. 280: Unknown (Mexican), *Don Tomás María Joaquín Villas*. Printed with the permission of the collection of Jan and Frederick Mayer.

p. 289: Print *Portrait of Sor Juana* by Joseph Caldevilla, frontispiece of biography published in Madrid in 1700. Printed with the permission of The John Carter Brown Library at Brown University.

p. 309: Debret, John Baptist, *Voyage pittoresque et historique au Brésil ...*, 3 vols. Paris: Firmin Didot Fères, 1834–39.

p. 316: Johann Baptist von Spix, *Reise in Brasilien*, 2 vols. Augsburg: G. Jaquet, 1846.

pp. 326, 331, 379: Linate, Claudio, *Costumes civiles, militaires et religieux de Mexique*. Bruxels: C. Sattanino, 1828.

p. 338: Printed with the permission of the Archivo General de Indias, Seville, Spain.

p. 340: Chamberlain, Sir Henry, *Views and Costumes of the City of Rio de Janeiro*. London: McLean, 1822.

p. 353: *Toussaint L'Ouverture*. Image from 1806 biography of J. J. Dessalines. Printed with the permission of The John Carter Brown Library at Brown University.

p. 362: Printed with the permission of the New Orleans Museum of Art.

p. 380: José Gil de Castro (1827). *Simón Bolívar*. Printed with the permission of The John Carter Brown Library at Brown University.

p. 389: Garnerey, Hippolite J. B., *Vues de la Havané et environs*. Paris: Bulla, 1836.

MONARCHS OF SPAIN AND PORTUGAL

Rulers of Spain, 1454–1833

Trastámara Dynasty	
Henry IV of Castile	1454–74
Isabel of Castile	1474–1504
Ferdinand of Aragon[1]	1479–1516
Philip I[2]	1504–06
Juana of Castile[3]	
Habsburg Dynasty	
Charles I	1516–56
Philip II	1556–98
Philip III	1598–1621
Philip IV	1621–65
Charles II[4]	1665–1700
Bourbon Dynasty	
Philip V	1700–24
Louis I[5]	1724
Philip V	1724–46
Ferdinand VI	1746–59
Charles III[6]	1759–88
Charles IV	1788–1808
Ferdinand VII[7]	1808–33

[1]Son of John II, king of Aragon, 1458–79; married Isabel of Castile in 1469.

[2]Son of the Habsburg ruler Maximilian I; husband of Juana of Castile; and father of Charles I, king of Castile and Aragon and Holy Roman emperor (1519–56).

[3]Daughter of Ferdinand and Isabel, her insanity allowed Ferdinand of Aragon to rule as regent of Castile until his death in 1516.

[4]Died without a natural heir. Named Philip of Anjou as his successor.

[5]Became monarch upon the abdication of father, Philip V. Louis's death brought Philip V back to the throne.

[6]Half-brother of Ferdinand VI.

[7]Assumed throne upon his father's abdication. Napoleon forced Ferdinand's abdication in 1808 and placed Joseph Bonaparte on the throne. Ferdinand returned as monarch in 1814.

Rulers of Portugal, 1438–1826

Avis Dynasty	
Alfonso V	1438–81
John II	1481–95
Emanuel I	1495–1521
John III	1521–57
Sebastian I	1557–78
Cardinal Henry	1578–80
Philip I[1]	1580–98
Philip II[2]	1598–1621
Philip III[3]	1621–40
Braganza Dynasty	
John IV	1640–56
Alfonso VI	1656–68
Peter II[4]	1668/1683–1706
John V	1706–50
Joseph I	1750–77
Mary I	1777–99
John VI[5]	1799/1816–26

[1]Also Philip II of Spain.

[2]Also Philip III of Spain.

[3]Also Philip IV of Spain.

[4]Regent, 1668 to 1683; king, 1683 to 1706.

[5]Regent as a result of Mary I's mental illness from 1799 to 1816; king, 1816 to 1826. Moved court to Brazil in 1808; elevated Brazil to rank of kingdom in 1815; and returned to Portugal in 1821.

INDEX